CHARLES R. LISTER

# The Syrian Jihad

*Al-Qaeda, the Islamic State and the*
*Evolution of an Insurgency*

HURST & COMPANY, LONDON

First published in the United Kingdom in 2015 by
C. Hurst & Co. (Publishers) Ltd.,
41 Great Russell Street, London, WC1B 3PL
© Charles R. Lister, 2015
All rights reserved.
Printed in the United Kingdom

A Cataloguing-in-Publication data record for this book
is available from the British Library.

ISBN: 9781849045902 (*paperback*)

This book is printed using paper from registered sustainable
and managed sources.

www.hurstpublishers.com

# CONTENTS

# CONTENTS

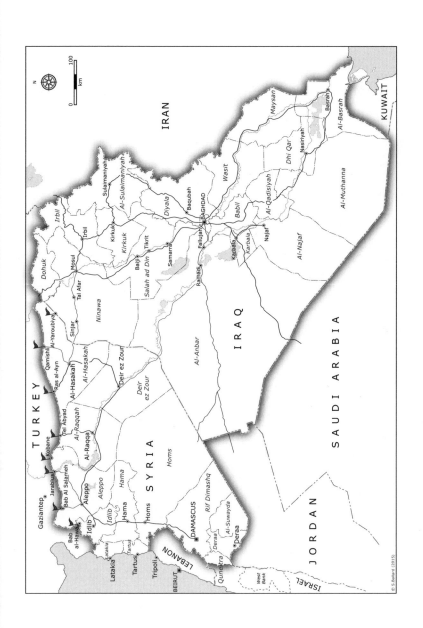

# ACKNOWLEDGEMENTS

This book is the result of over four years of research and personal experience of what must be one of the most tragic and deadly revolutions and civil conflicts in modern history. Knowing Syria personally, and having walked its streets, met and got to know its people, and fallen for its natural and architectural beauty and social vibrancy, the violence, hatred and destruction that has swept the country since 2011 is simply heartbreaking. The exponential growth of jihadist militancy is a major source of concern and will continue to be for many years to come. Its emergence, expansion and consolidation is therefore a subject that must be better understood.

Firstly, I'm grateful to the Brookings Doha Center for having hosted me as a roving Visiting Fellow since December 2013. A special thanks in this case must go to Salman Shaikh, for having taken me on and provided me with the intellectual space and scholarly independence that has allowed me to gain so much insight on Syria in recent years. The centre's broader research and administrative staff have also been a great support.

My position in the Brookings Doha Center also opened the door to my assuming a senior role within what has come to be a highly regarded Track II Syria process, funded by five Western governments. Within this endeavour, I'm particularly grateful for having had the chance to manage nearly two years of face-to-face engagement with the leaderships of over 100 of Syria's most powerful armed opposition groups around Syria's borders. The insight gleaned from this work and the experience of having got to know nearly all of the most pivotal actors involved in Syria's conflict has been invaluable in constructing the core content of this book. With this Track II process now under the tutelage of The Shaikh Group, this experience looks set to continue, and again, I'm thankful to Salman Shaikh for entrusting me with this.

# ACKNOWLEDGEMENTS

More broadly, I must also thank the hugely impressive network of Middle East, security, intelligence and terrorism scholars at The Brookings Institution, with whom I've shared many interesting engagements on Syria. These include William McCants, Shadi Hamid, Bruce Riedel, Kenneth Pollack, Tamara Wittes, Daniel Byman, Michael O'Hanlon and J.M. Berger. I'd also like to express my thanks to senior Brookings Institution staff like Martin Indyk and Bruce Jones for having supported my work and role within such an impressive organisation as Brookings.

This book has also inevitably been influenced by the excellent work and research done by other Middle East and Syria specialists, including Robert Ford, Noah Bonsey, Aron Lund, Emile Hokayem, Maxwell Martin, Thomas Pierret, Aaron Stein, Sam Heller, Hassan Hassan, Andrew Tabler, Faysal Itani, Aymenn Jawad al-Tamimi, Michael Weiss, Aaron Zelin, Charlie Winter, Thomas Hegghammer, Peter Neumann, Shiraz Maher, Raffaello Pantucci and Clint Watts. There are many more that could also be named, including countless eminently qualified journalists whose fearless and professional work over recent years continues to inform the general public of the Syrian situation. I'm also grateful to the many senior government officials involved in working on Syria who I have got to know personally—from those in the West, including from the United Kingdom, the United States, France, Norway, Sweden, Denmark, Switzerland, Germany, Italy, the Netherlands and Belgium; to those across the Middle East.

I also want to thank the academic peer reviewers responsible for taking the time to read through the manuscript and to have offered their valuable comments. Moreover, I am incredibly grateful to Hurst Publishers and Michael Dwyer for entrusting me with such a considerable piece of work. Despite the book focusing on such a dynamic and constantly changing subject, Hurst's staff and editor Mary Starkey were unfailingly quick, efficient and flexible in turning the manuscript into something publishable. I thank them all.

And finally, I must acknowledge how thankful I am to my whole extended family for their continued support, and especially to my extraordinary wife Jessica, for her love and patience throughout my endless periods of research and travel.

# PREFACE

In the future, historians will look back on 2011 as having been a truly remarkable year for the Middle East and North Africa. In what is still heralded as the Arab Spring, ordinary citizens of Tunisia, Libya, Egypt and Yemen took to the streets and confronted their corrupt and dictatorial leaders, sparking profound social and political change. Long-held institutional norms of keeping political dissent, and often frustration, within the confines of one's own home were shattered.

Although the Assad regime had clearly demonstrated in previous years its lack of interest in—or outright refusal to—reform in order to bring Syria into a new era, many still thought the country would escape the Arab Spring unscathed. However, when small protests began erupting in early 2011, Syrian security forces were unforgiving. Many ordinary Syrians who had taken to the streets in support of political freedom and self-representation, or in protest against the detention and torture of children in the southern city of Deraa, were threatened, arrested, and attacked with teargas and live ammunition. A total refusal by both local and national government to allow for open dissent directly encouraged the escalation of protest and the birth of a revolution.

In its early stages the Syrian revolution mobilised around issues of liberty, freedom, anti-corruption and democratic governance. The protests themselves were peaceful, with husbands, wives, children and grandparents all contributing towards a mass movement for positive change. However, a concerted security campaign aimed at suppressing this expanding revolution not only consolidated opposition to the Assad regime, but encouraged the mobilisation of local self-protection militias, which by the summer of 2011 had given rise to the Free Syrian Army (FSA) and a fledgling anti-government insurgency.

Well over four years later, Syria has become home to the largest, most complex and arguably the most powerful collection of Sunni jihadist movements in modern history. By September 2015, at least 30,000 foreign fighters, including as many as 6,000 from Europe,[1] had travelled into Syria to fight jihad—on a scale totally unprecedented for many decades. But it has not only been men who have travelled to join the Syrian Jihad. Several thousand women and children have also left for Syria, primarily to join what they perceive to be a fledgling 'Islamic state'.

Syria's unique status in Islamic prophecies relating to its central role as the source of battles that will precede the end of the world has been a major attraction for jihadist recruits from over 100 countries. The presence of well-established jihadist facilitation networks in Syria prior to the revolution, as well as the country's proximity to other jihadist hotspots in Iraq and Lebanon, have also contributed towards its newfound status as the centre of international jihad.

Several terrorist attacks and plots have since been both planned and inspired by Syria-based jihadists, whose hostility to the Western world was brought out into the open by US-led airstrikes in the country that began in late 2014. Those bombing raids had two principal targets: the so-called Islamic State (IS) and members of al-Qaeda affiliate Jabhat al-Nusra (the Support Front)—two jihadist movements which, despite once being organisationally linked, effectively declared war on each other in 2014. While IS had established a self-proclaimed caliphate stretching across parts of Syria and Iraq in mid-2014 and had called for and received pledges of allegiance from small jihadist groups and individuals around the world, the latter appeared to be evolving from being a pragmatic and widely popular Syrian jihadist movement into an organisation with a more overt desire to one day impose its Islamic rule in other parts of Syria, with or without the support of other factions.

This book is exclusively focused on one component of the Syria-based insurgency: the role played by Sunni jihadists and their Syrian Salafist allies. There are of course also Shia jihadists playing an equally significant role in the conflict, on the side of the regime and Bashar al-Assad. The interplay and interdependence of both these components will be scrutinised, as will the role of international state and sub-state actors on both sides of the conflict. However, the overarching focus of this book is to provide a detailed account of how the Syrian Jihad emerged, grew and has evolved throughout several years of brutal conflict. It will therefore follow a chronological format, beginning with early chapters detailing the initially peaceful stages of the revolution in early 2011; the socio-economic and socio-political underlying factors behind both the revolution and its susceptibility to jihadism; and an investigation of the Assad regime's dangerous flirtation with jihadist militancy that both directly and indirectly facilitated its emergence in the early days of the revolution.

This book is also driven and motivated by over four years of personal experience and engagement with hundreds of Syrian insurgents, from ordinary foot-soldiers to many of the most powerful group's leaders and senior political command structures, from secular nationalists to devout Salafists. Most of these men picked up weapons as a last resort to protect their communities, but they now find themselves embroiled in a vicious and seemingly intractable civil conflict. Many of these revolutionaries—from young men in their twenties to those in their fifties, all of whose lives have been thrown into turmoil since 2011—have become friends and acquaintances. It is hard not to take their stories personally, from a young IT graduate who lost seventeen members of his family in the horrific sarin gas attack outside Damascus in August 2013 to an older sheikh who spent three separate extended periods in prison living in inhumane conditions and being tortured merely for being an outspoken member of the political Islamist opposition. This is to name only two. None of these men particularly wanted to be carrying guns in their homeland, but the struggle for justice and freedom has become a very personal one.

The experiences, stories and comments of these men, all now insurgent fighters, are interwoven throughout this book. Many now reflect on the peaceful pre-revolution days and wonder: was all worth it? Why did the 'West' come to the aid of Libyans when they rose up against Gaddafi, but ignored the plight of Syrians when they were beaten, tortured, shot, blown up and gassed? This is a legitimate question worthy of more investigation.

Four years of concerted research and work on the Syrian conflict and its complex insurgency has also brought brought me into contact with jihadist militants, from al-Qaeda, IS and other independent and international groups. This access has been of immense value in acquiring greater familiarity with terrorist organisations that are otherwise off limits and closed to Western nationals. Maintaining contact and a sporadic dialogue with such individuals is a delicate task, but the insight gleaned proved time and again that it was worth the time invested. Nonetheless, the publication of an extensive policy-focused assessment of IS for the Brookings Doha Center in December 2014 incurred an aggressive reaction from Islamic State and its support communities online, thus placing this author on several official and unofficial IS 'lists'.

This experience served as a reminder of the intensity of jihadist self-awareness and self-protection amid international scrutiny and attack.

Knowing Syria as I do, with its extraordinary history, architectural and natural beauty and its superlatively welcoming people, the rise of jihadist militancy across the country is deeply concerning. That such groups, who hold such inherently violent and exclusionary ideologies, have become an integrated and fundamental component of the revolution and the anti-government insurgency is proof only of the failures of the international community to back a moderate Syrian nationalistic opposition that only wanted better things for their homeland.

Despite their broad ideological differences, most Syrians still involved in the revolution in 2015 want what they wanted in 2011, but the sheer power and intimidating dominance of jihadists has forced them to befriend their enemies. This book will tell the story of how this unfortunate state of affairs came to be. Where did the jihadists come from in the first place? How did they establish themselves, and what was their role in the revolution? What role did external actors play in facilitating the rise of jihadists and how might US-led and Russian intervention impact their status in Syria?

These questions and many more form the basis of *The Syrian Jihad*. Ultimately, we must also reflect on how a virtuous and well-meaning populist revolution, yearning only for the virtues of freedom, became transformed into an intractable civil war in which jihadists have found such a comfortable home.

Charles R. Lister, Doha, October 2015

# INTRODUCTION

Syria currently represents the centre of the world for jihadist militancy. Even the high-profile conflict in Iraq is a rung lower given the psychological pull of conflict zones for men seeking to attach an Islamist ideological fervour to a specific political–military cause. While September 2015 estimates suggested at least 30,000 non-Syrians have joined the jihad in Syria at some point since 2011, it seems likely that this number is probably higher. After all, intelligence officials from the UK alone revised that country's citizen flow into Syria from 600–700 in March 2015 to an extraordinarily higher estimate of 1,600 the following month, with an additional five citizens leaving for Syria every week.[1]

Such flows have significantly raised the profile and long-term sustainability of the jihad in Syria, but the domestic dynamics within Syria have played an equally significant role, if not one that is far more important.

Understandably, much has been written about the phenomenon that is the 'Islamic State.' Its slick media production, its brutal levels of violence, apocalyptic rhetoric, its effective fusion of fanatical Islamic extremism with ideals of Baathist Arab power, as well as its image as an international movement building a proto-state that spans across 100-year-old colonial borders, has seized the world's imagination. But although initially an Iraq-based organisation, IS benefited hugely from the conflict in Syria, and today the effective capital of its 'Islamic State' lies in the northern Syrian city of Raqqa. Moreover, much of the group's most valuable resources lie in Syria, where the immense complexity of the conflict offers it a sustainable long-term presence and territorial control.

The Syrian Jihad is about much more than IS, however. Countless other powerful jihadist groups have made Syria their base, many of which are led by and include within their ranks veteran jihadist figures with extensive experience in the upper echelons of al-Qaeda and other major jihadist organisations.

1

One of these groups is al-Qaeda's Jabhat al-Nusra, which has arguably established an even more sustainable presence in Syria than IS. Through an intricately stage-managed game of pragmatism and Machiavellian power politics, Jabhat al-Nusra has carved out a stake in Syria that over time has become both tacitly accepted and militarily powerful. Its sustained focus on recruiting heavily from within Syria's pro-opposition population has ensured it has, by and large, avoided the kind of isolation from popular opposition dynamics experienced by IS.

However, IS's dramatic advances in Iraq and its proclamation of a caliphate, not to mention its status as the primary focus of international airstrikes, has presented an existential challenge to Jabhat al-Nusra and its jihadist legitimacy. This has encouraged a shift within Jabhat al-Nusra's pragmatic posture, to the extent that it has begun to show signs of demonstrating the kind of belligerent and self-assertive behavior that got IS into trouble in 2013 and early 2014.

Syria's Jihad is therefore a complex story, involving a huge cast of jihadist actors operating within one of the most intense and multifarious civil wars in recent history. In establishing a base in Syria and by playing a role in its revolution, Sunni jihadists had a crucial part in internationalising the conflict.

One consistent theme throughout the Syrian civil war has been the sheer multitude of insurgent and jihadist protagonists involved. By early 2015 at least 150,000 insurgents within as many as 1,500 operationally distinct armed groups were involved in differing levels of fighting across Syria, some within broader umbrellas and fronts and others existing entirely independently. Although the emergence of the Free Syrian Army (FSA) in the summer of 2011 appeared at the time to herald the formation of an organised and moderate armed Syrian opposition, it quickly fell victim to the fact that its leadership was based outside Syria, in refugee camps in southern Turkey. Not only was its command-and-control potential thus hampered from the start, but its financial support was divided according to the respective interests of regional countries such as Saudi Arabia, Turkey and Qatar as well as governments in Europe and the United States.

In fact, the consistent failure of external states with interests in supporting the revolution to unify their provision of assistance explains not only the proliferation of insurgent factions, but also the opposition's incapacity to present a genuine threat to the Assad regime. The fact that groups found themselves having to compete with each other for funding and support, and in so doing were often moulding their image and ideological frames of reference towards those potential backers, meant that very few of them retained a consistent strength and long-term viability. Such inconsistencies ensured that external initiatives aimed at establishing a unified structure for the insurgency would almost certainly fail. Thus, separate attempts to establish and operationalise provincial military councils, the Supreme Military Council and a ministry of defence within the exiled interim government all fell far short of attaining anything like success on the ground inside Syria.

Moreover, although not immediately visible at the time, the FSA was only one of many armed insurgent movements to emerge in mid-2011. From June that year a number of more Islamist-minded factions were coming together and setting up bases outside Damascus, in Homs and in Syria's north. These were groups such as Kataib Ahrar al-Sham—which would go on to become the largest and arguably most powerful Syrian insurgent group—Suqor al-Sham and Liwa al-Islam, as well as the al-Qaeda affiliate Jabhat al-Nusra.

By mid-2011 a broad range of insurgent actors, which reflected the varied social backgrounds of Syrian society, had emerged. This did not augur well for a well-organised and unitary armed opposition. Moreover, as time passed, actors on the more Islamist end of the insurgent spectrum began demonstrating superior levels of internal organisation and insurgent coordination, and were thus enjoying sustained and reliable sources of support from outside sources. Qatar in particular played a key role in buttressing such groups in the conflict's first twelve months, while Turkey and Jordan had an influence on their borders with Syria which ensured that certain groups acquired more reliable channels of support than others.

It was within this context of insurgent proliferation, moderate failures to unify and escalating violence and brutality that jihadists found and established such solid foundations. Not only did Syria present an attractive proposition for prospective jihadists as a result of its prophesied place in Islamic tradition, but also its close proximity to Europe through Turkey undoubtedly facilitated the arrival of foreign fighters from a very early stage. Among the various early starters within the jihadist camp were several groups founded and led by Chechens. At first, these were not Chechens coming directly from Russia's North Caucasus, but rather individuals already residing within Turkey's well-established Chechen diaspora communities.

Jihadist groups also directly benefited from the failures of more moder: insurgents, which encouraged the perception that the jihadists were mc extensively and reliably funded, more professional, better armed and equi ped, and were therefore simply more successful in battle. As such, many Syri:

men involved in fighting for the revolution chose to join groups with a more extreme outlook than they were perhaps initially inclined to, but did so in order to be part of a 'winning team' and the better to fit in with what was an increasingly Islamist landscape, especially in northern Syria.

While revolutionary and of significant value to the outside world, the explosion in the use of social media to publish and promote battle updates, insurgent bulletins and other news arguably also discouraged broad opposition unity in Syria. Any group intending to be taken seriously in Syria maintained social media accounts on multiple different platforms, which by itself induced a dynamic of self-promotion that was often contrary to the presentation of a single unified opposition. Jihadists in particular proved especially adept at managing their use of social media and the production of qualitatively superior video and imagery output, which further demonstrated the reputation of professionalism that they were gaining on the battlefield.

Ultimately, however, while the Sunni jihadist component of Syria's insurgency fed off and benefited from others' indadequacies and failures, it also established and maintained its own unique internal dynamic. As the number of jihadist groups grew through 2013 and 2014, the two key nodes of al-Qaeda and IS (or its predecessor, the Islamic State in Iraq and al-Sham (ISIS)) emerged as defining influences around which other factions either aligned themselves or asserted continued independence. As 2015 began, both had effectively established their own unique modi operandi, and although they were pursuing the same objective, al-Qaeda (or Jabhat al-Nusra) had adopted an incremental approach towards establishing Islamic rule. These diverging strategies precipitated a significant debate within the broader jihadist community, which by extension split the world's jihadists into two camps.

However, while IS had manoeuvred itself into being an avowed enemy of the entire Syrian insurgency by late 2013 and early 2014, Jabhat al-Nusra had quite ingeniously redefined itself as a jihadist organisation enjoying a broad base of acceptance within Syria's opposition-supporting community. By pragmatically managing its relations with the broader insurgency, Jabhat al-Nusra was limiting the extent of its al-Qaeda-like objectives. However, at least within its senior leadership, the intent to one day establish Islamic emirates across Syria remained. Such objectives began to materialise more overtly in late 2014 until the rumblings of resistance induced a 're-moderation' in April 2015. Whether that would endure remained to be seen, but it is unlikely that the group's senior leadership and foreign fighter contingents will simply relinquish such goals, even amid rumours of an internal debate regarding its official relationship with al-Qaeda.[2]

All these developments relating to the jihadist insurgency, the broader Syrian opposition, external supporting states, the Syrian regime and its internal and external backers will form the spine of this book's narrative. The Syrian conflict and the jihadist insurgency evolved through a number of different phases. From the point at which the revolution began in early 2011 until mid-2012, the dominant theme was of a fledgling insurgency emerging amid an escalating regime crackdown on protest and opposition to its authority. The interplay between these two opposing dynamics ensured that the Syrian revolution turned into a bloody and complex civil conflict in which jihadist groups could establish a concrete foothold and integrate themselves within a broader cause widely seen as having legitimacy: fighting to protect Sunni civilians facing indiscriminate and brutal repression. Jabhat al-Nusra was the first such group to become active in Syria, announcing its emergence publicly in January 2012, six months after it had begun to form in the summer of 2011.

With nationwide conflict in Syria an established reality by mid-2012, the next phase was characterised by important insurgent victories that lasted until roughly mid-2013. While southern Syria was beginning to emerge as a key stronghold of moderate FSA factions with close links to neighbouring Jordan and also Saudi Arabia, the north was evolving into an environment more favourable to groups with an Islamic frame of reference, including jihadists. Through the winter of 2012–13 Islamists in northern Syria led a number of important strategic victories against the regime, thereby facilitating Jabhat al-Nusra's integration into the wider insurgency. That the US designation of the group as a terrorist organisation in December 2012 sparked nationwide protests in support of Jabhat al-Nusra illustrated how quickly the group had begun to win a degree of broad acceptance among Sunnis. Meanwhile, other jihadist groups were forming in northern Syria, several led by Chechens and others by experienced militants from North Africa and the Middle East.

Following a period of dramatic insurgent victories, the tide began flowing in the Assad regime's favour in mid-2013. After a concerted Hezbollah-led offensive succeeded in recapturing the town of al-Qusayr close to the Lebanese border in June 2013, the Syrian army—increasingly backed by Iran and foreign Shia militias—acquired a major morale boost, which led to a six-month period of opposition losses in Syria's strategically vital western border with Lebanon and around the country's largest city, Aleppo and the capital, Damascus. More than anything, this phase represented one of regime recovery rather than victory, and the long-term outcome was more of a strategic stalemate, in which neither the opposition, nor the jihadists, nor the regime and its supporting militias were in a position decisively to 'win' the conflict. This may have been a motivating factor behind the regime's otherwise hard to explain sarin gas attack on Damascus's East Ghouta suburbs in August 2013, which killed over 1,400 people.

Such horrific atrocities notwithstanding, the arrival of ISIS in Syria in April–May 2013 opened a rift within the jihadist component of the insurgency in Syria, whereby Jabhat al-Nusra ended up breaking away from ISIS—its mother organisation. Throughout the final months of 2013, ISIS operated as an increasingly self-assertive actor willing to attack and aggressively undermine other groups standing in its way. As inter-factional tensions rose across northern Syria, the regime became the only beneficiary.

This dynamic continued into early 2014, when Syrian opposition patience with ISIS's aggression ran out and a major offensive was launched against the group across northern and eastern Syria in January 2014. While the regime attempted to exploit the opening up of another front in the conflict, the major strategic shifts through mid-2014 were between ISIS and the remainder of the armed opposition, including Jabhat al-Nusra. ISIS sustained serious losses between January and March and withdrew altogether from three governorates, refocusing its forces around its power base in the northern city of Raqqa and in the eastern governorate of Deir ez Zour. Despite this, and perhaps in reaction to it, ISIS launched its own dramatic offensive in mid-2014 in Iraq, capturing the city of Mosul and marching south towards Baghdad, before proclaiming the establishment of a caliphate spanning parts of Iraq and Syria.

This dramatic series of events, and ISIS's renaming of itself simply as Islamic State sent shock waves around the world, but particularly across Syria. A new inter-jihadist competitive dynamic had emerged to challenge the jihadist credibility of al-Qaeda, and in particular of Jabhat al-Nusra. However, the most strategically consequential shift sparked by IS's successes was the initiation of US-led international military intervention—in the form of cruise missile and air strikes—against jihadist targets in Iraq (from August 2014) and Syria (from September 2014). This introduced a new and dangerous element of anti-Westernism into the conflict in Syria—especially within jihadist factions, but also across much of the wider opposition, which accused the West of willingly allowing over three years of civilian deaths at the Assad regime's hands, only later to intervene against the jihadists. The real danger was in the effect that the strikes had in definitively creating a new international enemy in the eyes of IS and Jabhat al-Nusra—both of which had previously been focused solely on the local conflicts in Syria and Iraq.

As 2015 began, therefore, the conflict in Syria had become a complex web of local, national, regional and international dynamics, involving many different actors. A very large number of battlefronts were active within Syria's borders, and jihadist militants continued to expand their influence. While the international community seemed more committed to countering IS in Iraq, it was becoming apparent that any anti-jihadist strategy in Syria remained limited more to counter-terrorism rather than a grand strategy aimed at eradicating these groups.

In March 2015 the broad scope of the insurgent 'opposition', including Jabhat al-Nusra, appeared to experience a significant boost, and by the end of the month a valuable Syria–Jordan border crossing had been captured and the city of Idlib had fallen into insurgent hands—only the second governorate capital to do so, after Raqqa. Insurgents inside Syria spoke at the time of increased levels of support being sent into Syria's south and north by regional states increasingly self-confident after militarily intervening against Houthi advances in Yemen. Opposition forces consequently continued to win significant back-to-back victories in Idlib governorate through the summer, raising a question mark over the Assad regime's potential to survive.

However, despite the rise in confidence and continued gains by the insurgency through the first months of 2015, the fact remained that both Jabhat al-Nusra and IS remained comfortably in place as major power-players in Syria. IS had spent several months preparing the ground for infiltrating areas around Damascus, further into Syria's interior governorates of Homs and Hama, as well as into the south, and looked far from being an organisation weakened by international attack. Meanwhile, Jabhat al-Nusra remained an integral part of the northern insurgency, and was still notably strong in southern Syria. Multiple other jihadist factions remained active and influential across Syria, and thus it was hard to see anything but a continued and significant jihadist militant presence in Syria in the months and years to come.

At the end of the day, the story of Syria's conflict and its evolution is extremely complex, but the trajectory of jihadist militancy within its ever-changing dynamics has steadily increased in scale and potential. A great many jihadist groups have emerged and established themselves on a local and sometimes national level in Syria, but generally, the pro-al-Qaeda, pro-IS and independent poles illustrate the entire jihadist landscape currently in existence. However, a crucial fourth pole is the expressly *Syrian* Salafist factions that largely retain similar conservative values as jihadists, but focus their existence solely within a Syrian operational perspective. Groups such as Harakat Ahrar al-Sham al-

Islamiyya (Ahrar al-Sham) and Jaish al-Islam, for example, have become invaluable links between jihadists and the broader insurgent opposition and, as long as these Salafists remain supportive and accepting of groups such as Jabhat al-Nusra, jihadists will reap the benefits of perceived legitimacy.

Simply put, and contrary to what many moderate FSA factions have said officially and on the record, a vast majority of Syria's insurgent opposition has fought alongside and coordinated closely with Jabhat al-Nusra since mid-to-late 2012. While such cooperation takes place despite vast ideological differences, it has continued because an effective military opposition to the Assad regime has been a more important priority. There is, however, a better potential alternative to such cooperation with jihadists: a closer and more beneficial relationship with the international community.

Despite this, the Western world has failed to sufficiently reach out to, engage with and support a broad enough section of the opposition inside Syria to persuade others to cease their support for jihadists. This remarkable lack of commitment to reinforce a *Syrian* insurgent opposition has directly provided the space for jihadists to emerge as the dominant players in Syria that they are today. Unless this level of commitment changes, Syria will continue to represent the centre of the world for jihadist militancy for many years to come, and the consequences for such policy shortsightedness will not only fall upon Syria and Syrians, but will affect the world at large.

# PART I

# SETTING THE SCENE

1

# BREAKING DOWN THE BARRIERS

## PROTEST

It took only twenty-eight days for the Tunisian people to overthrow their president, Zine El Abidine Ben Ali, from his twenty-three-year seat of near absolute power. That 'revolution'—and indeed what has become known as the Arab Spring—was sparked by a single tragic act of desperation and personal protest by twenty-six-year-old street vendor Tarek al-Tayeb Mohammed Bouazizi, who self-immolated outside the office of the governor of Sidi Bouzid on 17 December 2010. Forced through personal circumstances to become the main breadwinner for his family at the age of ten, Bouazizi, who was locally known as 'Basboosa', had been unjustly tormented by local officials for years. That he was again harassed early that fateful morning in December 2010 catalysed his transformation into an icon overnight. His story, and his subsequent death on 4 January 2011, struck a nerve for many throughout the region.

Thirty-eight days later protesters in Egypt overthrew President Hosni Mubarak, whose authoritarian rule in that country had lasted nearly three decades. At this point, the long-held but unspoken regional norm of avoiding demonstrations of public political opposition was well and truly destroyed. By late February protests had erupted in at least fourteen other countries across the Middle East and North Africa, including in Libya, where an armed revolution would end up co-opting the support of NATO and end in Muammar Gaddafi's death on 20 October 2011; and in Yemen, where sus-

11

tained political protest eventually forced President Ali Abdullah Saleh to resign on 27 February 2012.

\* \* \*

The common understanding of the Syrian revolution holds that it began on 15 March 2011, but this doesn't entirely tell the whole picture. In fact, the first notable incident of public protest against the government of President Bashar al-Assad took place in the north-eastern city of al-Hasakah on 26 January 2011, when a local man, Hasan Ali Akleh, poured a can of petrol over himself and set his body on fire. Although this act took place amid the tumult surrounding the proliferation in and escalation of various anti-government movements around the region, Akleh's apparent act of desperate protest did not precipitate immediate demonstrations across Syria.

While pre-existing Syrian opposition groups did call, via Facebook and Twitter, for a 'Day of Rage' across the country on Friday 4 February, nothing of note took place, with one relatively minor exception: On the morning of 5 February several hundred protesters took part in a demonstration in al-Hasakah, but with minimal fanfare or consequence.

Nonetheless, the significance of regional events was having its effect. A violent assault on a shopkeeper in Damascus'a famous Souq al-Hamadiyya by police on 17 February triggered an impromptu protest, where locals repeatedly exclaimed: 'Syria's people will not be humiliated!' Perhaps this represented the landmark moment, the modest turning-point in Syria's political consciousness, whereby an individual act of government thuggery catalysed a psychological rethink. Approximately 5,000 people ended up taking part in the unplanned protest in al-Hamadiyya, which, considering the centrality of its location, made the incident a telling one.

The key catalyst came in a series of developments in the southern city of Deraa, beginning on 6 March, when fifteen schoolboys, aged between ten and fifteen, were arrested and detained by members of the Idaraat al-Amn al-Siyasee (Political Security Directorate) for having painted the words *al-Shaab yureed eskaat al-nizaam* ('The people want to topple the regime') on a wall. The phrase had become well known as the slogan of the Arab Spring revolutions in Tunisia and Egypt, and although the children were clearly far too young to harbour genuinely threatening political motivations, they were nonetheless beaten and allegedly tortured in various ways, including by having their fingernails pulled out.[1] Meanwhile, as reports of their detention spread throughout the country, acts of sporadic and planned protest spread, although still on a comparatively small scale.

On 7 March thirteen prominent political activists serving prison terms in the infamous Adra prison in the north-east suburbs of Damascus released a joint letter declaring themselves 'prisoners of conscience' and announcing the start of a hunger strike. This strike, they said, was predicated on their demand for a complete cessation of 'political arrests' and for the government to remove 'injustices' and to restore 'rights that have been taken from civil and political life'.[2] Included in the list of thirteen signatories was Anwar al-Bunni, a human rights lawyer who had been sentenced to five years in prison for signing—along with nearly 300 other academics and political activists—the May 2006 Beirut–Damascus Declaration, which called on the Syrian government to respect Lebanon's independence and territorial integrity. Another hunger striker was eighty-year-old Haithem al-Maleh, a former judge and pro-democracy activist imprisoned in 2009 for 'affecting the morale of the nation' during a television interview on London-based opposition channel Barada TV.

The following day the government announced a presidential amnesty to political prisoners over the age of seventy—in honour of the fortieth anniversary of Hafez al-Assad's endorsement as president of Syria on 12 March 1971—thereby freeing Haithem al-Maleh. Later that day twelve Syrian human rights groups demanded that the government 'amend all laws that prevent human rights organisations from working openly and freely, and civil society from playing its role effectively'. The demands also focused on the rights of Syrian Kurds, who it said faced 'all forms of discrimination' and should immediately be 'entitled to enjoy their culture and use of their language in accordance with their civil, cultural, social, and economic rights'.[3]

On 10 March several dozen imprisoned Kurdish activists from the Partiya Yekîtî (Kurdish Democratic Unity Party) and Partiya Yekîtiya Demokrat (PYD, or Democratic Union Party) joined the hunger strike launched by prisoners in Adra, and two days later Kurdish protesters held demonstrations in the north-eastern cities of Qamishli and al-Hasakah.

As in other areas of the region, Kurds had long suffered from disproportionate levels of discrimination in Syria. Kurdish cultural gatherings, including for the annual New Year festival of Nowrūz, were effectively banned, and political gatherings were frequently met with violent repression. Such struggles had been an established reality for decades. In 1962, in a remarkable act of state-organised ethnic discrimination, a Syrian census stripped 20 per cent of the Kurdish population—approximately 100,000–120,000 people—of their Syrian citizenship, leaving them officially stateless and classified as *ajaanib* (foreigners). At the time, the government claimed that these Kurds were in fact refugees from Turkey who had illegally infiltrated al-Hasakah governorate in 1945. Subsequent evidence, including an investigation by Human Rights Watch, shows these government claims to have been largely false.[4] By 2011 this stateless Kurdish minority had multiplied to an estimated 300,000 people, all of whom had no right to hold government jobs; to vote in elections; to marry Syrian passport-holders; or to be awarded university degrees.

Tensions were rising in Syria, that much was clear; but the process of protest was still largely restrained and limited in scope. But on 15 March youth activists exploiting the new age of social media successfully organised protests in Damascus and Aleppo, collectively known as the 'Day of Rage'. The events, organised primarily through a Facebook page entitled 'The Syrian Revolution against Bashar al-Assad 2011', mustered several hundred people and, although security forces did not resort to force, six protesters were detained in Damascus's Old City. On the following day a similarly sized group of protesters demonstrated outside the Interior Ministry in Damascus's Marjeh Square, where families of political prisoners held aloft photos of their relatives whose release they were demanding. Thirty-five people were detained at that protest, including a ten-year-old boy, well-known philosophy professor Tayeb Tizini and prominent human rights activist Suheir al-Atassi. Similar protests erupted that day in Aleppo, Deir ez Zour, Hama, al-Hasakah and Deraa.

'The atmosphere was full of gas and only needed a spark to explode,' explained Amjad Farekh, a trainee dental surgeon from Damascus who ended up coordinating protests in the capital before helping found the small insurgent group Liwa Jaish al-Muslimeen in 2012. A member of Farekh's activist circle 'offered to set fire to himself' as an act of protest, but this was deemed to have been 'too much—we needed a more effective way'.[5]

If these initial indirectly coordinated protests failed to convince people that the ball was now rolling, events on Friday 18 March made it clear that Syria was entering a new and dangerous phase of instability. At this point the fifteen schoolboys in Deraa were still in detention, and relatives were making increasingly strident attempts to obtain more information and were demanding their release. The children happened to be members of many of Deraa's largest tribes and families, including the Zoubis, the Ghawabras, the Masalmas, and the Baiazids.[6] In a now infamous meeting several days earlier, senior representatives of the boys' families had met with the chief of Deraa's Political Security Directorate, General Atef Najib, who, although accounts still differ, was at the very least adamant that the boys' arrest and subsequent detention had been entirely justified.

Two accounts of this meeting have survived. One, propagated by supporters of the Assad regime, claims that Najib agreed to meet with senior family members in his private office, but proceeded to defend the legitimacy of their continued detention while admitting that several of the boys may potentially have been physically mistreated. The other, far more inflammatory, account is still widely shared amongst opponents of the government. This tells the story of a meeting in which Najib berated the boys' fathers for allowing their children's misbehaviour and effectively told them to forget their sons, go home and make more children with their wives—and, should they prove infertile, to deliver their wives to his office and he would ensure they gave birth to new sons. Whichever account is more accurate is now academic. Either would have been enough of an insult to ensure that further escalation was inevitable.

On 18 March the boys' families and hundreds of other local citizens marched through Deraa demanding the release of the children, a crackdown on corruption and the realisation of genuine democratic reform in Syria. The protest came to a standstill outside the residence of Deraa's governor, Faisel Kalthoum, where a gradually expanding conglomeration of security guards, riot police and Political Security Directorate personnel fired tear gas and water cannons, and then, for the first time, local security forces opened fire with small arms and four people were killed. In an instant, the Syrian revolution was born.

In the five days that followed President Assad deployed a government delegation, which included Deputy Foreign Minister Faisal Moqdad and senior military intelligence officer and Assad insider General Rostom Ghazali, to reassure locals that the central government was committed to ensuring justice. Although the children were finally released, multiple signs of torture on their bodies only added to the rising sense of fury within the local population. On 20 March protesters ransacked and set fire to the local Baath Party headquarters and several other municipal buildings, including the Palace of Justice. Reconciliation looked a very distant possibility, and became effectively impossible after security forces launched a two-day clearing operation aimed at defeating all areas of anti-government sentiment. This included an assault on the ancient al-Omari Mosque, which protesters had adopted as a central meeting point and makeshift hospital. At least five people were killed in the operation, which subsequent video footage showed had left blood lining the mosque's internal walls. Although Governor Kalthoum was sacked on 23 March and General Najib quietly removed from his post and placed under investigation in early April, this was too little too late.

Despite being the birthplace of the revolution, Deraa had long been seen as a base of government support. Hafez al-Assad had strategically elevated prominent Deraa-born men into senior positions of authority, such as tribal leader Mahmoud Zoubi as prime minister from 1987 to 2000; Sulayman al-Qaddah as head of the Baath Party between 1985 and 2005; and Farouq al-Sharaa as foreign minister between 1984 and 2006. But events in Deraa in early to mid-March 2011 under Bashar's tutelage put an abrupt end to that relationship of delicate and purchased trust.

\* \* \*

There were small protests across several other Syrian municipalities on 18 March, including at Damascus's ancient Umayyad Mosque, where Amjad Farekh and his brother were arrested and then imprisoned. According to Farekh, their arrest provided the 'spark in my home town of Qaboun', where more and more protests then followed.[7] By the time they were released a month later—after suffering torture—the revolution had been well and truly born. Notwithstanding these other protests, what happened in Deraa was the largest by some margin in terms of scale and, most importantly, would serve as the undisputed catalyst for the revolution and civil conflict that continues today. Deraa quickly became known as the Cradle of the Revolution, and much of the responsibility for that can be attributed to the actions of Atef Najib.

A cousin of Bashar al-Assad, Najib was one of five children born to an Alawite mother, Fatima Makhlouf—the sister of Anisa al-Assad, the wife of Bashar's father and former Syrian president Hafez al-Assad—and a Sunni father, Najib Alaah. As a young recruit to military school, Atef grew close to Bassel al-Assad, who as Hafez's eldest son, was at the time the favoured choice to succeed his father as president. However, Bassel's death in a car accident on 21 January 1994 left that duty to his less confident and somewhat geeky younger brother Bashar. Nonetheless, Atef quickly joined the intelligence apparatus, where his self-interested actions and aggressive behaviour saw him sacked some time in 1992. He remained out of service until the late 1990s, when his Assad family insider mother Fatima managed to acquire his re-employment in the *mukhabarat* (military intelligence) in Damascus's south-western suburb of al-Mezzeh. Growing increasingly wealthy through his management of a self-constructed and tightly controlled personal fiefdom—which he enforced by monitoring the police and local political figures—Atef had again begun to push his luck, and was steadily sidelined by officials above his pay-grade, including a distant relative and the former chief of Syrian intelligence in Lebanon, Ghazi Kanaan (aka Abu Yuroub). Having grown increasingly exasperated as a result of his declining level of influence, Atef grudgingly agreed to the post of chief of Deraa's Political Security Directorate some time in late 2008 or early 2009.[8]

While this may have seemed a demotion compared to his base in the centre of power that was Damascus, Atef soon set about constructing an intricate personal web of control around Deraa's extensive financial infrastructure, which was linked primarily to official and illicit cross-border trade with Jordan as well as the lucrative water rights industry. Power and money had become Atef's *raison d'être*, and he was in his self-righteous and self-serving element. Thus, with such power, Atef presided over the detention and probable torture of fifteen young boys, an act that almost overnight precipitated a revolution and civil conflict that changed Syria forever. While Atef was seen on occasions in Damascus's Four Seasons Hotel throughout the summer of 2011, his location today is unknown.

2

# UNDERLYING INSTABILITY

Despite proving itself as the 'Cradle of the Revolution', Deraa was by no means the only population centre to rise up so early against the authority of the Assad government. Protests quickly expanded in scale and geographical spread, not just encompassing governorate capitals but dozens of other towns and villages, including predominantly Sunni Muslim districts of the cities of Latakia and Tartous—both of which are key strongholds of Alawism, of which President Assad is a member. This was indeed partly a result of a conscious or unconscious (or both) element of 'group think', whereby the effect of protests across the region was intensely infectious, but it was also more than that. It was the result of something much deeper.

As a country, and particularly since the accession to power of Bashar al-Assad in 2000, Syria had developed a number of deeply damaging long-term structural weaknesses that in just such a time of potential instability had the capacity to accelerate localised sources of protest and instability into part of a nationwide movement. These pre-existing catalysts were particularly evident in the spheres of socio-economics; the relationship between the state and Sunni Islam; the continued prevalence of Syria's one-party state and endemic government-facilitated corruption; and the qualitative demise of the Syrian Arab Army (SAA).

The following pages will briefly cover these various aspects and their relative importance within pre-revolution Syria in relation to their role in encouraging the proliferation of anti-government protest and anger in early 2011. This is not intended to be an exhaustive assessment, nor is it meant to cover all the minutiae involved; there are many better sources dedicated to the subject. It is simply intended to provide some foundational context upon which to interpret the main subject of this book: the emergence, development and evolution of jihadist militancy within Syria's anti-government insurgency.

Socio-economically, Syria was balancing on a precipice. When Bashar al-Assad succeeded his father as president in mid-2000 he began putting into place the stepping-stones necessary for a new and, for Syria, revolutionary policy of Western-style neoliberalism and economic liberalisation. The comparatively modern Bashar—with roughly two years of experience under his belt working in ophthalmology at the Western Eye Hospital in London's affluent Marylebone—looked set to open Syria up to the wider world.

This initial promise helped spark the *rabia dimashq*, or Damascus Spring, whereby academics, intellectuals and others began a period of intensive discussion and debate over Syria's political and social future. This reformist culture led the establishment of so-called *mutadayaat*, or forums, where discussion groups would gather publicly to debate issues of perceived importance. As a sign of the times of hope, even members of the traditionally closed-minded Baath Party joined these forums, openly discussing the feasibility of political reform, the value of democracy and liberalism and other such populist topics. The rapid rise to prominence of the issue of political imprisonment—raised in this context in the famous Statement by 99 Syrian Intellectuals on 27 September 2000[1]—led to the release of several hundred detainees from Mezzeh prison in Damascus a little over a month later, in November.

All this apparent liberalising took place within a challenging political environment for Bashar, who, upon assuming office, was faced with his father's old guard, whose loyalty to the traditional Baath values of socialism and Arab nationalism did not go hand in hand with political liberalisation and a potential opening up to Western sources of investment. One of Hafez's most ardent supporters and head of the Military Intelligence Directorate, Ali Douba, was pushed aside quickly in February 2000, into a kind of forced retirement in the Douba family home town and ancient coastal fortress of al-Qurfays in Latakia's Jableh district. But others, including Bashar's brother Maher al-Assad—the commander-in-chief of the ultra-loyalist Republican Guard and the army's Fourth Armoured Division—remained in their seats, and as such, Bashar's policy of openness did not last long.

With such new and previously unknown political freedom, prominent members of the Damascus Spring perhaps began to push towards the invisible boundaries far too quickly. The red line was seemingly crossed in August 2001 when the secretary-general of the Syrian Communist Party and a key political activist, Riyad al-Turk, appeared to celebrate this newfound freedom in Syria by exclaiming on Al-Jazeera that 'the dictatorship has died'. Turk was promptly arrested in Damascus several days later on 1 September, and with that the Damascus Spring came to an abrupt end. Another prominent activist, Riyad Seif—who had teetered on the edge of establishing a new political party—was detained on 5 September; and prominent Syrian economics academic Aaref Dalila was taken in on 9 September. Many other activists met a similar fate that month, and were duly imprisoned for periods lasting throughout the 2000s.

While political reform and openness most certainly failed, Bashar's determination to introduce economic liberalism into state policy did not. On 10 October—around a month after the effective end of the Damascus Spring—the Syrian government submitted an official request to join the World Trade Organisation (WTO). Although this objective was only realised in May 2010, when the United States dropped its opposition as part of a wider initiative aimed at bringing Syria in from the cold, the sentiment coming from Assad's upper policy-making echelon was clear. But what was equally clear was that any process of at least partial integration into the international economic system was going to be a slow one. After all, Syria was widely regarded—rightfully so—as a thoroughly active member of the Iran-led axis; something that would become increasingly clear in the mid-2000s when senior elements within the Syrian government and security apparatus would actively facilitate the movement of jihadist recruits across the Syrian border into Iraq, where they contributed towards the escalating al-Qaeda-led insurgency against the US-led coalition.

Nonetheless, while clearly slow in the early 2000s, the momentum within Damascus to push liberal economic policies gained initiative upon the appointment of Abdullah Abd al-Razzaq Dardari to the post of deputy prime minister in charge of economic affairs in 2005. Dardari was a fluent English and French speaker with a thoroughly Western education: he gained his Bachelor's degree from the International Richmond University in the affluent London suburb of Richmond, and followed that up with a Master's degree from the University of Southern California and a post-graduate degree from the London School of Economics (LSE). After brief posts as a journalist for *al-Hayat* and as a representative of the United Nations Development Programme (UNDP), he joined the Syrian government, where he almost immediately became a key figure in the drafting of long-term economic policy. His background and liberal economic values made him a respected figure within the World Bank and the International Monetary Fund (IMF). His value within Bashar's economic strategy was clear.

From 2005 onwards privatisation of banking and business was actively encouraged on both state and municipal levels. On 7 May 2005 Dardari helped push through his Five Year Plan, which placed new emphasis on 'poverty mapping'; encouraging policy reform to integrate small and medium enterprises (SMEs) into the formal and state-administered sector; and withdrawing state control from areas of investment and other economic activities where 'market mechanisms are found to be worthy of playing an essential role'.[2] Dardari also began initiating a strident outreach to foreign banks and financial bodies in search of increased levels of foreign direct investment (FDI). He was seeking to add to the trend started in January 2004, when the Beirut-based Banque Bemo and the Riyadh-based Banque Saudi Fransi joined forces to establish Syria's first independent and privately owned bank, Banque Bemo Saudi Fransi. Contacts were soon made with a number of regional and international banks, including the Bank of Jordan (resulting in the establishment of Bank of Jordan Syria in late 2008); Fransabank (established in Syria in 2009); and Citigroup and HSBC.

By 2006 Syria's FDI levels had reached $600 million, which, when compared to a 1990–2000 average of $127 million, and only $180 million in 2003, represented a significant improvement. The numbers, however, were still far inferior to those of Syria's neighbours such as Lebanon, which in 2006 received $2.794 billion; Jordan, which received $3.121 billion; and Turkey, which received $20 billion.[3] But when including other sources of foreign investment, most of them less officially administered and recordable by UN bodies, Syria's received foreign investment level for 2006 reached a number around $1.6 billion.[4]

Unfortunately, although this push for economic liberalisation may have seemed a positively intended move by Syria's senior leadership, whether by direct orders from Bashar al-Assad or a consequence of long-established cronyism and elite-led corruption, the partial opening up of the Syrian economy served largely to benefit the pre-established ruling class. A lack of political reform explains much of this, as Syrian government policy continued to be implemented by Damascus-appointed officials at both provincial and municipal levels, almost all of whom tinkered with policy to suit their own financial ends.

As such, Syria did indeed experience increased wealth and improved and more competitive levels of capital accumulation, but the majority of this was placed in the laps of the ruling elite. And what wasn not, was more often than not taken in by the shadowy but immensely powerful *mukhabarat*. In some respects, enhanced levels of finance flowing towards private enterprise presented *mukhabarat* officials with an opportunity. Ironically, the localised power and social-level influence of these secret police officials increased as they sought to tighten their grip on the activities of local business owners.

Although Syria's gross domestic product (GDP) had risen to $59.15 billion (up from only $19.3 billion in 2000),[5] the gap between rich and poor had simply continued to widen. Salaries had continued to stagnate, and while economic liberalisation had opened Syria up to cheap foreign manufactured goods, this had had a dramatically damaging effect upon domestic manufacturing, which simply could not compete. Fuel prices had also risen notably, and access to water had both declined and become more costly. The middle class was particularly badly hit by this concurrent rise in the cost of living, while the rural working class, the majority of whom were reliant on income from the agricultural sector, struggled terribly.

The prospects for these rural farming communities were dealt a further blow by a series of deeply damaging droughts between 2006 and 2010. They struck the agriculturally vital north-east particularly badly, adding to the region's already existing struggles with rapidly diminishing groundwater levels—which were themselves a result of corrupt mismanagement and naively overambitious farming development projects. In fact, the management of water resources in Syria at the time was so complex—it involved elements within a total of twenty-two ministries, councils, commissions and directorates[6]—that simple-minded policy making was inevitable and opportunities for corruption would have been rife.

The 2007–8 crop season was hit the worst, with average levels of rainfall declining by 66 per cent from the normal annual average. As a result, crop yields declined by 32 per cent in state-irrigated areas, while other areas reliant on rainfall for watering plummeted by as much as 79 per cent—which combined meant that Syria's agricultural production declined to a level of 2.1 million tonnes, or less than half of the average of 4.7 million tonnes. For the first time in fifteen years Syria was forced to import wheat to feed its population.[7] And to add to the growing misery, the central government cancelled several key subsidies in 2008 and 2009, which resulted in dramatic increases in the prices of fuel (diesel increased from SYP7 ($0.14) to SYP25 ($0.53) in May 2008)[8] and agricultural fertiliser (increased from SYP450 ($9.60) to SYP900 ($19.15) in May 2009).[9]

The effects of drought, corruption and economic liberalisation, together with minimal political reform, meant that Syria experienced high levels of rural-to-urban migration in the 2000s. A great deal of this population movement was undertaken by agricultural workers, for whom farming had simply become no longer financially viable. Labour statistics show that an estimated 460,000 people stopped working in the agricultural sector between 2001 and 2007, representing a sector change of more than 10 per cent of Syria's total workforce and a 33 per cent decline in Syria's agricultural labour force.[10] The north-eastern governorates of al-Hasakah, al-Raqqa, and Deir ez Zour saw the most dramatic population shifts, with many people moving much further south, to suburbs around Damascus and also to the cities of Homs and Deraa. By 2009, for example, the UN estimated that between 60 and 70 per cent of villages in al-Hasakah and Deir ez Zour had become entirely deserted.[11]

The development of a number of sprawling, poverty-stricken suburbs comprising large numbers of financially frustrated and largely unemployed or underemployed citizens around Syria's urban centres was of significant consequence for the country's socio-political future. It was these people, the working citizens who felt cheated by a corrupt and often inept government apparatus, that started and led the country's first anti-government protests in early 2011.

All of this meant that by 2010, although economic growth and expansion was a reality, the pursuant failure of the government to distribute added income had caused considerable financial contradictions, putting the country's economy on a precipice of sorts. Socially, this economic policy mismanagement had further reinforced an already existing class divide in Syria, between the government-aligned political and economic elite.

In terms of religion, the presidency of Bashar al-Assad opened up more doors to Syria's Sunni majority than had been available during his father's time. Hafez al-Assad had sustained a complex relationship between his government in Damascus, the increasingly powerful mini-state that was the *mukhabarat*, and Sunni Islam. While his fundamental foundations within the secular and socialist Baath Party meant that religion played a minimal role within his political psyche, its central place within society could not simply be dismissed, and subtly institutionalised attempts were made to present Hafez as a pious man. In fact, immediately following the 1963 Baathist coup— known in Syria as the 8 March Revolution, and which would eventually propel Hafez to the presidency in 1971—the Baath Party, and by extension the Syrian government, maintained an often hostile relationship with portions of Syria's politicised Sunni community.

The Syrian branch of the Muslim Brotherhood represented an immediate barrier to the consolidation of Baath power following the 1963 coup. With political liberty and religious practice the first targets of the newly empowered Baath elite, supporters and members of the Brotherhood emerged in opposition. Alawites quickly came to dominate politics and the parliament, with the country's Sunni majority forced into subjugation. In such a context, Brotherhood militiamen clashed several times with Baath Party personnel in 1963, which prompted the swift and effective prohibition of the organisation in Syria in 1964. This, however, proved a deeply damaging decision, as portions of the Brotherhood soon came to represent armed opponents of Baath rule.

Beginning in 1964, the Brotherhood played a lead role in instigating a series of strikes, protests and riots across Syria. In the first incident of real significance, in April, Brotherhood supporters in the central city of Hama began taking control of key roadways and districts. Roadblocks were swiftly set up, stores selling alcohol were attacked and the imam of the city's Sultan Mosque, Sheikh Mahmoud al-Habib, emerged as a vocal supporter of what was widely perceived as a localised uprising.[12]

Several days into the localised revolt, the death of one pro-Baathist fighter during a riot near the Sultan Mosque proved the provocation necessary for then President Amin al-Hafez to approve an all-out assault by the National Guard on Brotherhood positions across the city. Focusing on the Sultan Mosque, the National Guard's tanks and field artillery took only two days to defeat what was the Syrian Muslim Brotherhood's first insurrection against Baath Party rule. At least seventy Brotherhood supporters were killed and their leader, Issam al-Attar, was forced into exile in Germany.[13]

With the Brotherhood thus banned in Syria and with the battle lines drawn, a prolonged period of tit-for-tat protests by the Brotherhood and unforgiving crackdowns by the Baathist security apparatus began. These tensions and hostilities continued both above and below the surface through the late 1960s and into the early 1970s, when Hafez al-Assad forced himself into the presidency (in 1970–1).

Two years later a newly proposed Syrian constitution was drafted, which included a clause specifying that the Syrian president did not have to be Muslim. This re-energised Brotherhood-led protests across the country, and by the late 1970s, following Syria's occupation of Lebanon in 1976, suspected Brotherhood-linked gunmen had begun carrying out sporadic assassinations and targeted small-arms attacks on key military, political and pro-Baath individuals, many of whom were Alawite.

All these years of rising tensions led eventually to an armed assault on the Aleppo Artillery School in the city's al-Roumseh district on 16 June 1979, which left as many as eighty-three training cadets dead. This was to be the first act of the so-called Fighting Vanguard (al-Talia al-Muqatila). Composed of followers of Brotherhood-affiliated Marwan Hadid—who had died in 1976, a year after his arrest for advocating armed jihad in Syria—and led by several individuals, including Adnan Uqla, Ayman al-Sharbaji, Husni Abu and Mohammed al-Zoubi, the Fighting Vanguard launched an armed insurgency against the Baath government and its Alawite leadership in what has commonly become known simply as the Islamist Uprising.

Following sustained violence, strikes, and protests that often brought entire cities and towns to a standstill, the government passed Law No. 49 on 7 July 1980, which made membership of the Muslim Brotherhood a crime punishable by death. Despite approximately a thousand Brotherhood members surrendering to authorities during an initial fifty-day amnesty, suspected Fighting Vanguard attacks continued across the country. While many attacks targeted Alawite officials and population centres, Sunni members of the state-sanctioned Muslim leadership (or *ulama*) were also targeted, including, most famously, Sheikh Mohammed al-Shami, who was shot dead in his mosque in Aleppo on 2 February 1980.

Following three large car bombings outside government-linked targets in Damascus in August, September and November 1981, the notorious insurrection in the city of Hama began. Fighting Vanguard and other Sunni gunmen seized control of the city, prompting a sustained three-week military bombardment campaign that killed somewhere between 10,000 and 40,000 people. This massive and largely indiscriminate use of military power, in what is now known as the Hama Massacre, brought the Muslim Brotherhood in Syria to its knees, and for many years the organisation essentially ceased to exist.

Syria subsequently suffered from what some have termed a 'turban drain',[14] as prominent Sunni scholars fled from Syria and settled in more accommodating countries elsewhere in the region. The 1980s represented an era of unrivalled political authoritarianism in Syria during which Sunni Islam and religion in general was kept tightly controlled by the state apparatus. Many mosques were open only at prayer time, and chose to shut their doors to the traditional hosting of religious lessons and discussions.

However, although Hafez al-Assad may have imposed a brutal defeat upon the Muslim Brotherhood in 1982, he could not escape the reality that Syria retained a majority Sunni population. The key to reasserting a peaceful equilibrium was acquiring and fostering relationships with Sunni leaders who would be willing to assume positions of public religious authority but simultaneously to be distinctly non-political and acquiescent to government expectations regarding the private practice of moderate Sunni Islam. As such, the government in Damascus presided over the establishment of the Hafez al-Assad Institutes for the Memorisation of the Quran (Ma'ahid Hafez al-Assad li'l Tahfiz al-Qur'an).[15] Unsurprisingly, the all-seeing *mukhabarat* kept a close eye on the institutes' activities.

Individual Sunni scholars deemed capable of providing popular depoliticised religious authority were also fostered and elevated into prominence, such as Sheikh Salih al-Farfour and Sheikh Ahmad Kaftaru. Others assumed prominent roles in the media, like Marwan Shaykhu, a senior officer in the Ministry of Awqaf (Religious Endowments), who held regular programmes on state radio and television[16] until the early 1990s.

A fascinating example of this state-facilitated and directed management of Sunni Islam is the case of the internationally respected Sunni scholar Sheikh Mohammad Said Ramadan al-Bouti. With an undergraduate degree and a Ph.D. from the famed al-Azhar University in Cairo, Bouti was by the age of thirty-six clearly a promising young mind within Sunni Islamic thought. Although more culturally motivated than political,[17] he wrote several times and in depth about the damaging consequences of the Western imported ideologies of Marxism and nationalism, claiming that the latter had been introduced into the Ottoman Empire by imperialists and Freemasons in order to undermine its structure.[18] But perhaps more important than any belief he held, Bouti's rejection of political Islam, and thus his opposition to the activities of the Muslim Brotherhood, stood him in good stead for acquiring the support of the Baath Party and, by extension, of Hafez al-Assad. Bouti took a public stand on state television against the 1979 Aleppo Artillery School attack and labelled those involved as bandits.[19]

Over time, as a senior staff member at the University of Damascus through the 1980s and 1990s (while holding several honorary and visiting professorships across the Arab world), Bouti achieved the remarkably rare and privileged position of having regular access to the president, with whom he could discuss—albeit often dismissively—subjects such as the Brotherhood and notable figures within conservative Sunni circles. This unrivalled seniority and acceptance within the beating heart of the Baath Party apparatus eventually saw Bouti appointed as the preacher of the Umayyad Mosque in Damascus's Old City during Bashar al-Assad's presidency in 2008. Ultimately, Bouti's perceived loyalty to the Assad family may have contributed towards his death in an apparent bomb attack in the al-Iman Mosque in Damascus on 21 March 2013, although some aspects of his death remain deeply mysterious.

The 1990s brought with them a number of coincidental domestic and international developments that contributed towards a partial revitalisation of Sunni Islam in Syria. Perhaps most interestingly, Hafez al-Assad's role in opposing the peace negotiations between the Palestinians and Israelis (particularly in Oslo in 1993) helped to facilitate the development of close relations between the government in Damascus and Sunni Palestinian resistance groups such as Hamas and Palestinian Islamic Jihad (PIJ). Despite appearing to fundamentally contradict the principle of total opposition to conservative and especially militant Islamism, this was part of an especially astute government strategy of adopting a foreign policy closely aligned with popular opinion (this would continue into Bashar al-Assad's presidency). At the same time, worsening levels of economic decline as well as continuing political frustrations helped encourage a revival of religious practice, particularly across the growing urban sprawl. But in terms of actual domestic policy, this shifting societal undercurrent was by no means understood by the state apparatus, and little was done to help incorporate this changing social dynamic.

In a sense, Sunni Islam was allowed to undergo a limited recovery within Syrian society, but only within the confines of what the government in Damascus deemed to be acceptable limits of practice. Public observation of Islam became somewhat more acceptable during the 1990s, and mosques gradually began providing the kind of social and public services that they had done in the past, and many previously exiled imams and scholars began returning to their homeland.

When Bashar al-Assad assumed the presidency in 2000, Hafez's minority complex gave way to Bashar's somewhat more self-confident posture. Almost immediately, Bashar presided over a partial revival of Sunni Islam within state-accepted circles and set about establishing friendly and eventually rather cosy relationships with moderate Sunni leaders, who were duly installed in positions of authority. In the political realm, Bashar appointed Sunnis into the positions of foreign minister (Walid Muallem, from February 2006), vice president (Najah al-Attar, from March 2006), deputy minister for economic affairs (Abdullah Abd al-Razzaq Dardari, from 2005) and ambassador to London (Sami Khiyami, from July 2004).

This gradual integration of Sunni Muslims into the spheres of officialdom and the loosening of the shackles binding religious communities continued throughout the 2000s. However, in 2008 the government began implementing various initiatives that brought back memories of the Hafez administration, such as dismissing female public-sector employees for wearing the *niqab* and allowing the *mukhabarat* to reassert their vigilance over mosque and religious studies activities.

While socio-economics were the key foundational factors behind the simmering popular resentment that erupted from March 2011 into a nationwide revolution, there were many long-term political frustrations in play too. Fundamentally, it was politics that was at the foundation of much of the revolution's causational factors. Most obviously, Syria was—despite the official government line—a one-party state ruled by a family and its loyalist clique. At times, since taking power in 2000, Bashar al-Assad and his perceived interest in opening up to the world appeared to herald a new era for Syria, beginning with long-desired political reform. But despite several apparent openings, particularly in 2000 and 2005, glimmers of hope were soon extinguished by the sheer weight of the all-seeing security apparatus.

The one apparent area of political policy that remained consistent with that of the administration of Hafez was Bashar's maintaining of a foreign policy that was by and large in keeping with popular opinion. In doing so, Bashar managed to sustain the line that he was qualitatively different from most of his peers elsewhere in the region, whose foreign policies often pandered to Western expectations. Considering Syria's complex geo-political location—wedged between the socially and politically intense state of Lebanon, the nearly NATO state of Turkey, the conflict-riddled Iraq and comparatively stable Jordan—this people-friendly foreign policy may well have been what kept Syria so stable during the years of relative instability that struck many of its neigbours throughout the 2000s.

Another often overlooked area of underlying instability was the state of Syria's military, particularly in terms of its level of funding and structural upkeep. As a result of an experience-driven realism, both Hafez and Bashar al-Assad fostered the development of a military apparatus that was, at its heart, commanded by an Alawite officer corps. The bulk of manpower was composed of young Sunni men, many of them conscripts. While in theory this sectarian division of labour would be perfectly effective in sustaining an inter-state war with, say, Israel, it has proven an inherently damaging structural disadvantage in fighting an internal civil war. As such, when the revolution began in March 2011, the SAA contained approximately 220,000 soldiers, but two years later, due to the possible unreliability and potential disloyalty of the

Sunni-dominant portions of the SAA, the military was forced to rely upon an Alawite-led core of roughly 65,000 personnel nationwide.[20]

Disregarding sectarian make-up, the SAA also suffered from a state of relative dissatisfaction and lack of investment. The military's withdrawal from Lebanon in 2005 had also served as a considerable blow to operational morale. While the SAA had benefited from strong levels of military investment during the presidency of Hafez al-Assad, particularly in the form of weapons purchased from the Soviet Union, Bashar spent comparatively little on expanding its capabilities, and much of the military's weaponry was deteriorating into disrepair.

As such, when the first signs of an armed insurgency began to appear in Syria in April and May 2011, the military was ill prepared to deal with what it faced.

To put it simply, several decades of mismanagement, corruption, violence and short-termist opportunism within the Assad family, the Baath Party and similarly invested spheres of political influence meant that when Mohammed Bouazizi set himself on fire in Tunisia on 17 December 2010, several key elements within Syrian society made a revolution a real prospect. And not only that, but it would serve to determine many of the defining characteristics of the revolution and the insurgency itself.

It is, however, worth emphasising at this point that despite the still-dominant role of Alawites and the Assad family within Syria's governing elite, the country was largely stable along its very varied ethnic and sectarian lines. Bashar al-Assad had in fact fostered a partial integration into officialdom of not only Sunnis, but also members of Syria's Christian, Druze and even Kurdish communities. As such, while sectarian undertones have today certainly ingrained themselves prominently as fundamental elements within the civil war in Syria, the revolution did not initially develop along strictly sectarian lines.

3

# SYRIA'S FLIRTATION WITH JIHADISM

While the eruption of the Arab Spring and pre-existing social, political, religious and economic structural issues in Syria may have made the country a ripe candidate for revolution, they did not necessarily indicate the potential for the dramatic growth in jihadist militancy that has been seen since 2011. Some of the reasons for it—and thus another underlying factor—may be found in Syria's recent past, during which the country's leadership established, exploited and attempted to manage extensive relationships with jihadist militants in order to export threats against its enemies, rather than face them at home.

In terms of the influence it has had upon the evolution of jihadist militancy within Syria's revolution, this 'flirtation' with jihadism could be said to date back to the first months and years after Bashar al-Assad's assumption of power in 2000.

Bashar took the mantle of power from his father Hafez at the beginning of a phase of more overt Islamic practice in Syria. This was at least partly the result of Hafez's opening up to Islam in the 1990s, when dozens of new mosques were constructed across the country and countless Islamic schools were established in which Qur'anic studies prevailed over traditional curriculums. An influx of foreign Islamic finance, particularly from Wahhabi Saudi Arabia in the late 1990s, meant that many of these institutions gradually took on a more conservative aspect, in a departure from their original roots, which were derived from more moderate Sufi Islamic practices.

Although Bashar initially sought to open up to Islamists in the hope of drawing them in and under his control, the already accelerating Islamic revival had become an independent phenomenon. Overt Sunni Islamist influence over society, particularly in large outlying towns and in urban centres, had begun to increase markedly. Jihadist militancy was growing roots in the southern city of Deraa and in the northern cities of Idlib and Aleppo, and one man in particular was emerging as a key player: Mahmoud Ouul al-Ghassi.

Based out of the al-Sahour Mosque in the north of Aleppo city, al-Ghassi, more popularly known as Abu al-Qaqaa, had begun adopting a more assertive posture in 1999, where he and his right-hand man Abu Ibrahim were building a close-knit following.[1] After arriving in the city in the late-1990s, Abu al-Qaqaa's first introduction to Aleppo came when he was brought to a local administrative building and introduced to the area's police chiefs. According to one of the chiefs in the room: A Military Intelligence officer brought this young man in.

> The man was dressed like a Pakistani and barely spoke a word. I don't know if he was shy or what, but the officer spoke on his behalf. We were instructed to produce a local ID card, a driving license and other documents for him, but without any registered address or other personal information. This was illegal in Syria, so we knew straight away, despite his youth and foreign appearance, that we were dealing with someone important. It was only years later that we realised who we had helped.[2]

At the time, escalating tensions in Palestine and continued conflict in southern Lebanon provided local sources of Islamist frustration in cities like Aleppo, while ongoing conflicts in Kosovo, Kashmir and Afghanistan contributed towards the transnational jihadist picture that Abu al-Qaqaa so keenly painted from the pulpit.

For this emerging Syrian jihadist core, the spectacular attacks of 11 September 2001 represented a tremendous victory against the 'great Satan', the United States of America. Within two weeks Abu al-Qaqaa and Abu Ibrahim held a celebratory festival in Aleppo, 'featuring video of hand-to-hand combat and training montages of guerillas leaping from high walls'.[3] This proved to be a test of the patience and willingness of the Syrian authorities to allow such an overt expression of support for an act that had dramatically changed the world overnight.

As it happened, Abu al-Qaqaa and a few of his followers were arrested by Syrian *mukhabarat* the following day, although they were released shortly thereafter. Since his public re-emergence in Aleppo in 1999, rumors had been floated across Syria and further afield that Abu al-Qaqaa was an agent of the Syrian intelligence apparatus, or that he was at least working with their tacit approval. His quick release did indeed look suspicious, and even more so when his Aleppo following, which had by now adopted the name Ghurabaa al-Sham (Strangers of the Levant), began holding public jihadist meetings and celebrations as regularly as once or twice a week by early 2002—all without any security suppression. In fact, some of these events were even attended by government officials, including one with the title 'The People of the Levant Will Now Defeat the Jews and Kill Them All'.[4]

There was no doubt that anti-American and anti-Israeli views had long found a place within Syrian society, at both official and unofficial levels. So it was not altogether surprising that isolated expressions of celebration developed after 9/11. Moreover, the all-powerful Syrian security apparatus built by the Baath Party and Hafez al-Assad was well known for infiltrating its substate adversaries as part of a strategy of covert control and intelligence collection. Commenting on this strategy in a 2010 meeting with a US delegation led by the then coordinator of counter-terrorism at the State Department, Daniel Benjamin, Syria's General Intelligence director Ali Mamlouk claimed that 'in principle, we don't attack or kill [jihadists] immediately. Instead, we embed ourselves in them and only at the opportune moment do we move.'[5]

Thus, while President Bashar al-Assad had proclaimed Syria's support for the USA amid the fallout of 9/11, his security apparatus continued to provide Islamists and jihadist circles the necessary space to operate, albeit under their constant surveillance. According to a detailed report by Ghaith Abdul-Ahad it was within this context that Abu al-Qaqaa's right-hand man Abu Ibrahim began to question how they were being afforded such freedom.

> We asked the Sheikh why we weren't being arrested,' said Abu Ibrahim. 'He would tell us it was because we weren't saying anything against the government, that we were focusing on the common enemy, America and Israel, that beards and epaulets were in one trench together.[6]

Despite questions behind the scenes, Abu al-Qaqaa's Ghurabaa al-Sham movement was growing in confidence, and seemed to have become a power in Aleppo that the government and its security forces were no longer able to restrain. Numbering over a thousand men, the movement's core began enforcing strict interpretations of *sharia* law on the streets of Aleppo's outlying districts and night-time patrols intimidated those who preferred Syria's traditionally liberal lifestyles.

It was perhaps fortunate then for Syria's security structures that the USA ended up launching an invasion of neighbouring Iraq in March 2003. With jihadists in Aleppo, Idlib, Deraa and elsewhere beginning to adopt an increasingly overt and public profile, the arrival of American and coalition armed forces and the eruption of conflict in Iraq provided a perfect opportunity for Syria to transform a potential internal threat into an exportable external one.

Abu al-Qaqaa, his followers in Ghurabaa al-Sham and many other less militant but nonetheless politically active Islamists began scouring urban centres across the country for recruits for the 'resistance' that Syrian state media was proclaiming on a daily basis. Meanwhile, Syria's Grand Mufti, Sheikh Ahmad Kaftaru, issued a *fatwa* making it *fardh ayn* (religiously obligatory) for all Muslims, both male and female, to resist the 'occupying forces' using any available means, including suicide bombings. The Grand Mufti's son, who by this time had become the more active component of his eighty-eight-year-old father's Damascus-based foundation, subsequently defended his father's ruling by claiming that 'every Muslim in the world is part of the same body. If you stick a needle in one part of the body, all the organs will respond.'[7]

Coming on the heels of the invasion and occupation of Afghanistan, the sheer 'shock and awe' of the initial stages of the US-led Operation Enduring (later Iraqi) Freedom aroused intense emotions across the Arab world. In Syria, where anti-American sentiment was already a widespread phenomenon, a desire to travel to Iraq and defend it against foreign invasion was rife—and Syrian authorities did little to prevent it. In fact, the Syrian Baath Party was widely accused of organising the recruitment of volunteers from across the country to join the 'resistance' in Iraq. The then Lebanese wing of Syria's Baath Party additionally contributed towards this mobilisation drive, reportedly collecting 200 recruits from around the border town of Arsal alone in late March 2003.[8]

As the initial invasion unfolded, busloads of Syrians were driven across Syria towards the eastern governorates of Hasakah and Deir ez Zour, where border guards willingly waved them through 'open gates'[9] into Iraq. Reports flooded in at the time detailing the arrival en masse of these foreign recruits. While then Iraqi foreign minister Naji Sabri claimed that 5,000 volunteers from across the Arab world had arrived within eleven days of the invasion,[10] 1,000 Palestinians from the Yarmouk refugee camp outside Damascus were reported to have signed up two days later.[11] Despite being in the midst of the Second Intifada, Palestinian Islamic Jihad also sent a 'wave' of willing suicide bombers to Iraq via Syria within ten days of the invasion to 'fulfill the holy duty of defending Arab and Muslim land'.[12]

Casualties from the first days of fighting also demonstrated the rapid internationalisation of the conflict, with a Palestinian Arab Liberation Front (ALF) fighter from Lebanon killed in a US airstrike on the first day of the war

(20 March) and another Palestinian volunteer killed when a bus he was travelling in was blown up by an American Apache helicopter on the main road between Syria and Baghdad.[13] British Special Air Service (SAS) commandos even detained four busloads of potential suicide bombers, all carrying Syrian passports, in Iraq's western Anbar province after their arrival from Syria.[14]

This was the start of a mass migration of Arabs towards Iraq—almost exclusively via Syria—that would come to define the development of a committed jihadist insurgency in that country. Crucially, it was something that elements within the Syrian security apparatus seemed determined to facilitate, despite President Assad's offer of unqualified assistance to the USA in its declared 'War on Terror'.

Notwithstanding their vast differences, this offer had been quickly accepted by the USA, which within weeks of the 9/11 attacks rendered Syrian national Mohammed Haydar Zammar from Morocco to Damascus's Far'Falastin prison in late October 2001. Zammar had been an active recruiter for al-Qaeda, including in Europe where he encouraged the coming together of chief 9/11 hijackers Mohammed Atta, Ramzi bin al-Shibh and Marwan al-Shehhi, as well as affiliated facilitators Said Behaji and Mounir El Motassadeq. After his covert transfer to Damascus—something not made public until the summer of 2002—US intelligence operatives were allowed to 'submit written questions to the Syrians, who relay Zammar's answers back'—an arrangement described in 2002 as one that 'insulates the US government from any torture the Syrians may be applying to Zammar'.[15] It is quite feasible that another equally significant al-Qaeda figure, Mustafa Setmariam Nasar (or Abu Musab al-Suri) found himself in a similar situation some years later. After he was detained by Pakistani security forces in Quetta in November 2005 Nasar's whereabouts were a total mystery until his lawyer, Clive Stafford-Smith, announced in June 2009 that his client was in Syria and may have been held there for 'some years'.[16]

The explosive start to the conflict in Iraq had therefore led to a rapid establishment of foreign-fighter recruitment and facilitation networks in Syria, for the express purpose of feeding a fledgling jihadist insurgency in Iraq. On one level, pre-existing Syrian Salafist figureheads took the reins of the recruitment networks themselves. People such as Abu al-Qaqaa used their pro-jihadist credentials to attract recruits both inside Syria and across the Middle East and North Africa. Another individual, Mohammed Majid (better known as Mullah Fuad), a Kurdish Islamist preacher based in Damascus, found himself on European authorities' radars as an apparent 'gatekeeper in Syria for volunteers intent on reaching Iraq'.[17] These initial networks fed many fighters into Ansar al-Islam and Jama'at al-Tawhid wa'l-Jihad (JTWJ), the latter being the antecedent movement of al-Qaeda in Iraq (AQI).

But on another level the establishment, expansion and consolidation of these networks throughout 2003 and into 2004 necessitated a strong element of government complicity—or a turning of two blind eyes, if one is being generous. A combination of established anti-Americanism in Syria, still-popular pan-Arabist unity and inter-Baathist loyalties between Assad's Syria and Saddam's Iraq meant that elements within the Syrian government and security apparatus used these networks and advanced their expansion. But as time wore on, the dominant actor in maintaining the durability of these foreign fighter networks—Syria's military intelligence, led by Assad's brother-in-law Assef Shawkat—had an express interest in ensuring that these hundreds and thousands of jihadists, many of whom definitively sought martyrdom, did not remain on Syrian territory for long.

Eastern Syria's 605-kilometre border with Iraq thus became a transit point for the region, and then the world's wannabe jihadists. Syria's tribally dominated and largely desert east had long been a region with 'extensive tribal smuggling networks ... much of which [had] traditionally received the explicit or tacit support from Syrian and Iraqi officials'.[18] Anything from livestock, electronics, cigarettes, foodstuffs and people had been smuggled through this region for decades. The border was porous anyway, with only two principal official crossings—at al-Yaroubiya in northern Hasakah and al-Bukamal in central Deir ez Zour—but these smuggling routes seemed tailor-made for foreign fighter recruiters in Iraq.

With things so decidedly loose on the Syrian side of the border, one would have thought the situation on the Iraqi side would have been tightened following the Saddam regime's overthrow. However, the catastrophically short-sighted decision by the chief administrator of the US-established Coalition Provisional Authority (CPA), Paul Bremer, to dissolve the entire Iraqi military, security and intelligence apparatus—known simply as CPA Order Number 2: Dissolution of Entities—meant that Iraq's 35,000-man border guard ceased to exist overnight.[19] With the exception of reconnaissance patrols by British and American special operations forces, foreign fighters were free to cross almost at will. While a US special operations taskforce did launch a cross-border raid 40 kilometres into Syrian territory in order to target a convoy of suspected senior Iraqi Baathists on 18 June 2003, this was very much the exception rather than the norm. In fact, it was the only publicly acknowledged cross-border operation by coalition forces until late October 2008.

Many independent and some interlinked foreign fighter recruitment and smuggling networks were established in Syria throughout 2003–5, all under the noses of the dominant military intelligence in eastern Syria. One individual who quickly assumed prominence was Badran Turki Hishan al-Mazidih, who was better known by his alias, Abu Ghadiya. A young Iraqi from Mosul in his mid-to-late twenties, Abu Ghadiya found himself appointed in early 2004 as chief of logistics for the fast-growing JTWJ militant faction of Ahmed Fadil al-Nazal al-Khalayleh (Abu Musab al-Zarqawi), which pledged allegiance to al-Qaeda and Osama Bin Laden in September 2004 and became AQI.

In this highly influential position, Abu Ghadiya controlled 'the flow of money, weapons, terrorists, and other resources through Syria into Iraq'. From his base in the town of Zabadani, north-west of Damascus, Abu Ghadiya and his cousin Ghazy Fezza Hisan al-Mazidih (Abu Faysal) 'obtained false passports for foreign terrorists, provided passports, weapons, guides, safe houses, and allowances to foreign terrorists in Syria'.[20] From Damascus, Abu Ghadiya's network of operatives and smugglers received recruits arriving by air at Damascus International Airport and by land from Jordan to the south, Lebanon to the west and Turkey to the north and managed their transport— ordinarily in groups of at least fifteen at a time—eastwards towards Iraq. The location of his base in Zabadani may well have been the venue for a number of meetings held between senior Syrian security officials, escaped Iraqi Baathists and AQI commanders throughout the 2000s, including two in 2009 (though by this point Abu Ghadiya was dead) that were attended by an individual working for Iraqi intelligence wearing a wire.[21]

This Syrian Baath–Iraqi Baath–al-Qaeda nexus was a relationship of convenience that established itself early on in the Iraqi conflict, sparked largely by the arrival of fleeing Iraqi officials in Damascus. The development of pragmatic associations between former Iraqi Baathists and AQI was made both inside Iraq on an operational level and in Syria on a command level, and is something that has survived into the current era of the Islamic State as a transnational organisation.

While the foreign fighter recruitment and smuggling networks continued to grow in 2004 and into 2005, the strategic calculus in Syria was subtly changing. Intense international diplomatic pressure was being exerted on the Assad regime to crack down on what was to all intents and purposes a freely operating terrorist recruitment operation on its soil. By late 2004 and early 2005 Syrian intelligence had discernibly shifted its posture, and had begun arresting mid-level AQI-linked facilitators in Aleppo, Damascus, Deir ez Zour and elsewhere. Included within those arrested early on, in January 2005, was Abu al-Qaqaa's right-hand man Abu Ibrahim, who was reportedly told by his interrogators that 'the smuggling of fighters had to stop'.[22] While a large proportion of these individuals were thought to have been released shortly thereafter, their subsequent activities in supporting the continued recruitment of foreign fighters for Iraq operations moved underground.

Earlier that month, perhaps in order to encourage the positive shift being detected in Iraq, then US deputy secretary of state Richard L. Armitage arrived in Damascus for a visit with Assad, after which he issued a statement proclaiming that 'Syria has made some real improvements in recent months on border security, but we all need to do more, particularly on the question of foreign regime elements participating in activities in Iraq, going back and forth from Syria'.

Much of the 'real improvements' Armitage was referring to were probably related to a process of significant expansion of Syria's border force and related security infrastructure on the Iraqi border. By the time Syrian forces had withdrawn from Lebanon in April 2005, Syria's total border force had been expanded to 10,000 personnel, a great deal of which was deployed along the Iraqi frontier. Although still small, this allowed Syria to deploy a far more numerically significant force than the 700 men it had previously stationed along the entire Iraqi border in 2003. Moreover, a total of 557 border posts—each between 1.0 and 2.4 kilometres apart, manned by between five and eight soldiers armed with personal weapons and one heavy machine gun—had been constructed along a new sand berm, which ranged from 6 to 12 feet tall along the entire frontier. Electricity poles were placed along known smuggler routes to flip vehicles driving at speed at night, a new 'integrated computer system' was introduced at all official border crossings and, in October 2005, all men between eighteen and thirty could be banned from crossing any Syrian border even when their documents should have allowed them to do so.[23]

Clearly, this was a dramatic improvement from the minimal security infrastructure that had been in place in 2003–4, but it didn't necessarily counter the potential for individual Syrian military and security commanders to gain financially from permitting continued smuggling. Moreover, the newly expanded border security force was composed primarily of poorly motivated conscripts who had no capacity to operate at night, when smugglers are most active. While the rate of foreign fighter influx from Syria into Iraq did decrease in 2005, it nevertheless continued throughout the year and began to re-expand considerably into 2006–7.

This coincided with, and perhaps reinforced, a very real qualitative growth in the scale and capability of the insurgency, led by AQI—which expanded into Majlis Shura al-Mujahideen (MSM) in January 2006 and then the Islamic State in Iraq (ISI) in June 2006. The establishment of the ISI, within which was a fully structured cabinet and provincial governor system, marked a rec-ognition within the MSM coalition that a new stage had been reached in the jihadist project in Iraq—that of practically building an Islamic state. While Iraqis continued to provide sufficient manpower to the ISI's escalating opera-tions in late 2006, it was the foreign fighters streaming in from Syria who brought with them cash and a willingness to carry out strategically invaluable suicide operations. According to the now famous 'Sinjar Records', at least 700 foreigners transited through Syria and into Iraq through just one single ISI crossing point at the northern town of Sinjar between August 2006 and August 2007. Of 576 who had recorded their nationality upon arrival in Iraq, this included at least 237 (41 per cent) from Saudi Arabia and 111 (19 per cent) from Libya. Speaking to the genuinely international nature of this single flow, 21 countries were represented by the 576 individuals whose records were seized and only 46 (8 per cent) of the fighters were recorded as Syrians.[24]

Diplomatic pressure, both in public and behind the scenes, therefore con-tinued throughout 2006–7. In his annual statement to the US Senate Select Committee on Intelligence, the director of national intelligence John Negroponte described Syria as a 'pivotal—but generally unhelpful—player in a troubled region'.[25] But highlighting its clear failures and complicity in facili-tating and allowing the export of terrorists into a war zone in which interna-tional coalition forces were the principal target did not seem to make a difference to Syrian behaviour. In fact, in a pointed reference, Syria's minister of information, Mohsen Bilal, reminded reporters during a diplomatic visit to London in September 2006 that his country did indeed have influence 'beyond its borders'.[26]

That same month, prominent Iraqi tribal leader Sheikh 'Abd al-Sattar al-Rishawi announced the formation of the Anbar Awakening Council, which would seek to combat the influence and territorial control of the ISI in west-ern Iraq. Although this bottom-up tribal movement, backed by US training, weaponry and finance, took some time to gain real power on the ground, its significant symbolism, combined with increasing social pushback against the

ISI's imposition of its extreme interpretation of *sharia* law—including banning women from purchasing 'sexually suggestive' cucumbers and prohibiting the production and sale of ice cream because it did not exist in the Prophet Muhammad's time—meant the foreign fighter flow began to slow, and many turned around and headed back into Syria.

The sudden arrival of such a 'returnee' flow into Syria posed a potential threat to the government in Damascus, whose Alawite elite represented an apostate enemy to ISI jihadists. As happened in March 2003, the decision was made to re-export these fighters to another zone of Syrian influence: this time west into Lebanon. Two primary destinations presented themselves to such fighters, namely the militant friendly Palestinian refugee camps in the southern town of Sidon (Ain al-Hilweh), home to the Asbat al-Ansar militant faction, and the northern city of Tripoli (Nahr al-Bared), where Fatah al-Islam was operating with increasing confidence.

Conveniently, Syrian military intelligence maintained extensive organisational links with both groups, and attempts were thus made to ramp up attacks in Lebanon targeting anti-Syrian individuals and interests. One such example came in early December 2006 when a fifty-man Fatah al-Islam cell whose members had previously been with the ISI in Iraq were accused by the United Nations of plotting attacks against thirty-six people with anti-Syrian agendas in Lebanon. Six members of the cell—four Lebanese, a Syrian and a Saudi—were subsequently detained during a gun battle in Nahr al-Bared while all the others escaped.[27]

Early the following year Fatah al-Islam's leader, Shaker al-Abssi, publicly proclaimed his organisation's intention to establish a small Islamic emirate in northern Lebanon, focused around Tripoli. On 13 February 2007, on the eve of the second anniversary of Lebanese prime minister Rafik Hariri's assassination (for which Syria is widely blamed) and less than a mile from the home of Pierre Gemayel—the son of former Lebanese prime minister Amin Gemayel and then a widely touted presidential candidate—two bombs detonated on passenger buses near Bikfaya in central Lebanon, killing three people. Fatah al-Islam and its Syrian links were immediately blamed for the attack, and four months later, on 21 June 2007, official charges were levelled against sixteen of the group's members for their role in the bombings.

Then followed the 2007 Lebanon conflict, in which the Lebanese Armed Forces (LAF) confronted Fatah al-Islam in its stronghold of Nahr al-Bared in what was the most intense fighting in Lebanon since the end of the civil war in 1990. This extraordinary three months of open warfare started quite ambiguously with a police operation on 19 May in search of suspects behind a recent bank robbery outside Tripoli. When their investigation took them to a Fatah al-Islam operated apartment in the city, a three day armed stand-off ensued, after which all three suspects were killed. In retaliation, Fatah al-Islam-affiliated gunmen throughout the Nahr al-Bared camp launched coordinated attacks on LAF positions on the camp's periphery, killing at least twenty-five soldiers. A tit-for-tat war then ensued through July and August, in which nearly four hundred people were killed before concluding with a victory for the LAF in early September.

This near-total defeat forced the surviving elements of Fatah al-Islam to flee to safety in Syria, where many ended up turning their guns on Syrian targets, on behalf of Fatah al-Islam splinter factions and the Syria-based group Jund al-Sham. Many of these attacks went largely unreported in both local and international media, but they appear to have sparked a renewed push within security circles to again expand networks for smuggling militants back into Iraq. By the end of 2007 US intelligence suggested, for example, that 85–90 per cent of foreign fighters in Iraq had come from Syria and that within that, 90 per cent of suicide bombers had entered Iraq from Syrian territory.[28] Well over a hundred foreign fighters were being smuggled from Syria into Iraq every month,[29] which represented a rate unprecedented since the start of the war in early to-mid 2003.

With the US-backed Sahwa steadily gaining ground against the ISI in Iraq and many jihadist militants now back in Syria after fleeing northern Lebanon, elements within Syria's intelligence apparatus set about yet again facilitating intensified flows of foreign fighters and supplies into western Iraq.

The year 2007 represented one of intense security dynamics on both sides of the Iraq–Syria border. In Iraq the ISI was under unprecedented pressure, with Iraqi security forces, Sahwa militiamen, the USA and coalition military troops and much of Iraq's Sunni society all acting to defeat its control over territory and resources. In Syria Abu Ghadiya and the ISI's border emir Abu Muthanna al-Ansari were working at a pace to ensure that their forces inside Iraq received the necessary reinforcements to sustain their fight.

While then US secretary of state Condoleeza Rice met with Syrian foreign minister Walid Muallem on the sidelines of an international conference on Iraq in Egypt's resort town of Sharm al-Shaykh in March 2007, the US military was seeking actionable insight into the ISI's cross-border recruitment networks so as to strike an existential blow to its capability. Established US operating procedures in Iraq made it practically impossible—without a presidential finding—to launch any operation into Syrian territory. This meant that Operation Daytona, launched by then commander of Multinational Force—Iraq (MNF-I), General David H. Petraeus, was structurally crippled in only being able to see one half of its mission picture at any one time.

One breakthrough did present itself, however. In early September 2007 intelligence indicated that Abu Muthanna al-Ansari was likely to be working out of a small village near the Iraqi town of Sinjar in northern Ninawa province, 55 kilometres east of the Syrian border. A specialist force, part of the 'hunter-killer' Task Force 88, was assembled and on 11 September, exactly six years after the 9/11 attacks in the USA, a team of commandos assaulted 'Objective Massey' and killed Abu Muthanna.

This was a big victory in the long-drawn-out battle with the ISI's vast recruitment network, but it perhaps paled in comparison with the 5 terabytes of data seized along with him. Now known as the Sinjar Documents, this captured data provided a detailed window into the bureaucratic and obsessively detail-oriented approach that the ISI had taken to its recruitment and reception of foreign fighters via Syria. Not only was a great deal learned about the inner workings of this immensely important element of ISI operation, but the documents also purportedly identified Syria's military intelligence chief Assef Shawkat as having been fully informed with regards to Abu Ghadiya's networks in Syria. Subsequent assessments by US intelligence, based on the Sinjar Documents, claimed that Syrian 'authorities quite likely infiltrated multiple networks, most notably the Abu Ghadiya network, to monitor threats to Syrian interests'.[30]

Diplomatic pressure was again rising against Syria, particularly also due to an air strike the Israel Air Force's 69th 'Hammers' Squadron had launched against a suspected covert Syrian nuclear reactor in al-Kibar only five days before Abu Muthanna's death.

For a number of reasons, September 2007 could be said to have been a turning point for Syria and its relationship with the ISI in Iraq. Abu Muthanna's death on 11 September brought to twenty-nine the number of senior ISI figures killed or captured by MNF-I forces that month, including Abu Osama al-Tunisi, Yaqoub al-Masri, Mohammed al-Afari, and Abu Taghrid—all of whom were killed. Ali Fayyad Abuyd Ali, the father-in-law of AQI leader Abu Ayyub al-Masri and reported senior ISI adviser, was among those captured.[31]

But the month was perhaps most significant for the killing of Abu al-Qaqaa in Aleppo on 28 September. Then based primarily out of the al-Tawabbin

Mosque in Aleppo—a facility known to have been intensively monitored and likely controlled by the Syrian government[32]—Abu al-Qaqaa had taken to travelling with an entourage of bodyguards, which many Syrians believed were employees of Syrian intelligence. Further feeding these suspicions, which had surrounded him for many years, Abu al-Qaqaa had also recently been appointed head of a government-funded Islamic school in the city. According to witnesses the perpetrator—who was captured shortly after the act—was a recently returned ISI militant from Iraq who had accused Qaqaa of being an American spy.[33]

It seems extremely unlikely that Qaqaa had been working for the USA, but his relationship with Syrian intelligence was almost certain—government officials attended his funeral, which was described at the time as having had 'all the trappings of a state occasion'.[34] Certainly, in the days and weeks following his death, commentary across the Middle East was obsessed with the issue of the ISI being a creation of hidden, mysterious and all-powerful intelligence bodies, including Syria's.[35]

Perhaps one of the clearest accounts of Syria's apparent role in backing and facilitating the expansion of AQI and the ISI in Iraq came in August 2009 when Mohammed Hassan al-Shammari, a twenty-nine-year-old Saudi Arabian ISI fighter who had been emir of operations in Diyala governorate until his arrest, provided a detailed account of the process he had undergone travelling to Iraq some years earlier. Shammari claimed that he flew into Syria from Saudi Arabia, and on arrival was met by an ISI-linked militant and driven to an al-Qaeda training camp somewhere in Syria, run by Abu al-Qaqaa, who he described as a Syrian intelligence agent. 'They taught us lessons in Islamic law and trained us to fight. The camp was well known to Syrian intelligence,' according to Shammari.[36]

In the following months, calls increased within Damascus for diplomatic contacts to be established with the USA, while in Iraq, General Petraeus was reportedly pushing President Bush for the same thing.[37] However, with the exception of a brief meeting on the sidelines of the Annapolis Conference on the Middle East in November 2007, Syrian–American contact remained largely cut off—the White House was still focused on destroying what remained of the ISI in Iraq and feared that reaching out to Syria could diminish or limit that effort. By this point the ISI was verging on facing full strategic defeat, with territorial control quickly vanishing and the leadership relocating north to the relative safe zone of Mosul. Despite this however, or perhaps as a result of it, Abu Ghadiya was running an operation to get his hands on 100

American military uniforms, presumably to launch a major attack somewhere in Iraq.[38]

With investigations into Abu Ghadiya's location and plans continuing apace, ISI militants launched a daring cross-border raid from Syria into the Iraqi border town of al-Qaim in Anbar governorate on 2 May 2008, and proceeded to capture and publicly behead eleven policemen. The attack was seen as a bold statement: the ISI could still operate freely across the Syria–Iraq border and as such, US interests in Iraq remained under threat. 'Compelling evidence suggests that Abu Ghadiya … was behind the murder of the Iraqi police officers', Petraeus would subsequently write after the attack, and 'the operation could not have been carried out without the acquiescence of Syrian officials at some level'.[39]

Syria was playing an increasingly dangerous game, attempting to balance external militant threats from both Lebanon and Iraq. Beginning in late 2007, various small splinter factions of Fatah al-Islam had begun inciting localised violence in areas of Syria, especially in Aleppo and Damascus. While much of this jihadist violence went unreported, seventeen people were killed when a suspected Saudi suicide bomber detonated a car bomb near a security building in Damascus on 27 September 2008—the deadliest such attack in Syria since 1996. Several fatal small-arms clashes also began erupting in the Palestinian Yarmouk refugee camp outside Damascus in October, but a true reminder of what Syria was harbouring within its borders came in July 2008 when Islamist prisoners in the infamous Sednayya prison in Damascus rioted and took staff hostage.

According to an account provided by Peter Neumann, this riot was closely linked to Syria's flirtation with jihadists and conflict dynamics in Iraq and Lebanon:

> After the Iraq invasion, Syrian intelligence officials offered Islamist inmates at this notorious facility … the chance to receive military training and fight against Coalition forces in Iraq. According to a leaked State Department cable, of those who accepted the offer and subsequently managed to return to Syria, 'some remained at large … others were sent to Lebanon, and a third group were re-arrested and remanded to Sednayya.' The ones who went back to prison felt 'cheated': they 'had expected better treatment, perhaps even freedom, and were upset over prison conditions.'[40]

A tense standoff continued in the prison for several months until January 2009, when Syrian special forces launched an unforgiving assault on the besieged areas of the facility, resulting in the deaths of over a hundred prisoners. Unsurprisingly, the entire series of events failed to make their way onto Syrian media, but what they did induce, for the first time in several years, was the beginnings of a more discernible crackdown by security forces upon existing jihadist networks inside Syria.

As if the situation could not have been getting any worse for Syria's control over events, US special operations forces also finally got the breakthrough they had been looking for for so long when intelligence emerged placing Abu Ghadiya on a farm 8 kilometres inside Syria opposite the Iraqi border town of al-Qaim. From this farm, in the village of al-Sukariyya, just north-west of al-Bukamal, Abu Ghadiya was running his foreign fighter recruitment network, which at the time was expanding into directing military operations in the border regions in coordination with members of the locally powerful al-Mashahda tribe.

As light was beginning to fade on 26 October, four Black Hawk helicopters carrying members of the CIA's Special Activities Division and US Army Special Operations Force personnel penetrated Syrian airspace. No more than twenty-four soldiers were dropped off at the site, and in a lightning raid Abu Ghadiya was killed, along with seven other people, whose identities remain disputed.

While some subsequent media reports claimed Syrian intelligence may have assisted US forces in coordinating the operation against Abu Ghadiya, the likelihood of that appeared reduced several months later when senior Syrian intelligence officials convened two high-level meetings in the spring of 2009 between Iraqi Baathists and ISI commanders in Abu Ghadiya's old safe haven of Zabadani north of Damascus. What those attending the meeting did not know, however, was that Iraqi intelligence had managed to turn one of their colleagues. He was sitting amongst them wearing a wire, recording every word.

In an in-depth report detailing these meetings for the first time, Major General Hussein Ali Kamal told Ghaith Abdul-Ahad the significance of the series of events:

'We had a source in the room wearing a wire,' at the meeting in Zabadani, General Kamal told me at the time. 'He is the most sensitive source we have ever had. As far as we know, this is the first time there has been a strategic level meeting between all of these groups. It marks a new point in history.'

The [Iraqi and Syrian] Baathists present led the meeting. Their aim, according to General Kamal's source, was to launch a series of spectacular attacks in Baghdad and thereby undermine Maliki's Shia-majority government, which had for the first time begun to assert some order in post-civil war Iraq.

By July 2009, the Interior Ministry had increased security at all checkpoints across the Tigris river into Baghdad, making a commute at any time of day even more insufferable than normal. And then General Kamal received a message from his source in Syria. The extra security at the bridges had been spotted by the attack plotters, he said. New targets were being chosen, but he didn't know what they were, or when they would be hit.[41]

On 19 August over 100 people were killed and 600 wounded when three explosive-laden trucks were detonated consecutively by ISI suicide bombers outside the Finance Ministry, the Foreign Ministry and near a police patrol in Baghdad. Back to General Kamal:

'I failed,' Kamal told me that day. 'We all failed.' Within hours, he was summoned to meet Maliki and his security chiefs. The prime minister was livid. 'He told me to present what I had to the Syrians,' Kamal later said. 'We arranged with Turkey to act as a mediator and I flew to Ankara to meet with them. I took this file'—he tapped a thick white folder on his desk—'and they could not argue with what we showed them. The case was completely solid and the Syrians knew it. Ali Mamlouk [the head of Syrian general security] was there. All he did was look at me smiling and say "I will not recognise any official from a country that is under US occupation." It was a waste of time.' Iraq recalled its ambassador to Damascus, and Syria ordered its envoy to Baghdad home in retaliation.[42]

Although the Baghdad attacks were a spectacular demonstration of the ISI's continued capacity to strike at the heart of the Baghdad government, its senior leadership had suffered considerable losses throughout 2009. In fact, by early 2010, thirty-four of the organisation's forty-two most senior officials had been killed or captured, with only a few adequately replaced. The ISI and Syria's capacity, and perhaps its will, to influence the jihadist project in Iraq was entering a period of decline, albeit perhaps a brief one.

It is therefore not entirely surprising that February 2010 saw a high-level meeting arranged between Syrian officials, including Syria's general intelligence director Ali Mamlouk, and a US delegation led by the US coordinator of counter-terrorism at the State Department, Daniel Benjamin. Potential security cooperation now appeared to to be in both sides' interests and, while almost certainly a coincidence, two-and-a-half weeks later Iraqi security forces detained Manaf Abd al-Rahim al-Rawi, the man widely blamed for running the ISI's suicide-bombing operations in Baghdad. The arrest gleaned vitally important intelligence, most importantly the locating of ISI leader Hamid Dawoud Mohammed Khalil al-Zawi (Abu Omar al-Baghdadi) and AQI commander Abu Ayyub al-Masri in a house near Tikrit, north of the Iraqi capital. To confirm, Iraqi intelligence had a flower box—concealing a listening device and GPS tracker—delivered to the house, where one month later, on 18 April 2010, both men were killed. Intriguingly, intelligence gained at the scene revealed the name of the leaders' courier, Ibrahim Awwad Ibrahim Ali al-Badri al-Samarra'iyy (Abu Bakr al-Baghdadi),[43] who would soon be named the new leader of the ISI and who would in the years to come expand his forces into Syria and proclaim the establishment of a caliphate.

Taken together, Bashar al-Assad's first ten years in power in Syria—2000–10—represented a continuation of his father's risky strategy of infiltrating and exporting internal threats so as to interfere in the affairs of Syria's neighbours. The war in Iraq undoubtedly provided Assad with an invaluable opportunity to divert increasingly confident Syrian and Lebanese jihadists into a war against 'Crusader' occupation forces, but equally, the scale of that conflict and the truly international nature of actors involved meant that the scope of jihadist militancy and its objectives could not have been controlled forever.

Moreover, the longer the ISI was operationally active in Iraq, the more blatantly obvious Syria's links to facilitating their sustainability would become. Genuinely intense diplomatic pressure combined with an international environment focused on bringing regional troublemakers 'in from the cold' made it increasingly likely that the USA and its allies in Europe would eventually seek to co-opt the Assad regime out of the 'Axis of Evil' and into a more responsible community of Midde Eastern states. With similar initiatives in Libya aimed at encouraging the moderation of Muammar Gaddafi, it was not surprising that such an approach was eventually made to Syria.

More importantly, elements within Syrian intelligence had helped create a true monster. While Fatah al-Islam, Jund al-Sham and Asbat al-Ansar all represented potential local threats to Syrian security and interests, the ISI was a globally connected organisation with a transnational goal—the establishment of a viable Islamic state and a caliphate.

As such, when the revolution's first protest began in al-Hasakah on 5 February 2011 the seeds were very much already in the soil not only for a militarisation of a protest-led revolution but for the emergence of a powerful jihadist dynamic within Syrian territory. Speaking in February 2012, Lieutenant Colonel Joel Rayburn, a former aide to General Petraeus, expressed this aptly:

> There is surely not in modern history a more perfect example of blowback than what is happening now in Syria, where Al Qaeda in Iraq's operatives have turned to bite the hands that once fed them ... Having terrorized the Iraqis for seven years, the Syrian regime now cynically seeks the world's sympathy as terrorism's victims.[44]

# PART II

# FIRST ON THE SCENE

# 4

# MARCH–DECEMBER 2011

## JABHAT AL-NUSRA FORMS

As government security forces violently cracked down on protests in the southern city of Deraa in late March 2011, a revolution was born. While President Assad signed off on limited and insufficient reforms, protests escalated across Syria, prompting the army to initiate concerted and coordinated military operations to subdue opposition. As violence thus escalated nationwide, Damascus released hundreds of political and Islamist prisoners through a series of presidential amnesties, before labelling the revolution as both extremist and a foreign conspiracy.

While the Syrian Muslim Brotherhood and al-Qaeda-linked ideologues had begun voicing support for a Syrian revolution, initial signs of armed resistance to government crackdowns began to emerge in May 2011. Two months later the Free Syrian Army had been formed and jihadists—many released from prison since March—had begun to coalesce and plan the formation of more Islamist-minded resistance factions.

By August 2011 several Islamist insurgent groups had been established in Damascus and in northern Syria, while the Islamic State in Iraq had dispatched a senior commander to establish a Syria-based wing. Between September and December, as violence across Syria reached particularly intense levels, the ISI branch came operationally into being and carried out its first attack—a double suicide bombing—outside Syrian military intelligence facilities in south-west Damascus on 23 December. Its official public emergence, however, was not to take place until January 2012.

\* \* \*

As has just been described, jihadist militancy had a well-established, though complex, history in Syria prior to the outbreak of protest in early 2011.

However, by the time people began taking to the streets in mid-March that year, what had been a quite extensive and well-oiled machine capable of simultaneously running operations of recruitment, logistics, financial transfer, gun running and military planning had been discernibly constrained since late 2008 and early 2009, when Syria's dangerous game of flirtation with jihadism had begun to backfire and an internal crackdown had been initiated.

That crackdown notwithstanding, a good number of jihadist individuals remained in place in Syria and were active, though on a lower and more covert scale than in previous years. Likewise, safe houses and affiliated cells endured across the country, especially in Homs, suburban Damascus, Aleppo, and naturally also in border areas in Syria's eastern governorates of al-Hasakah and Deir ez Zour, bordering with Iraq.

As with other sites of political protest against autocratic and dictatorial regimes across the Middle East and North Africa in late 2010 and early 2011, the global jihadist community paid immediate attention to events as they unfolded in Syria. For them, such uprisings in Tunisia, Yemen, Libya, Egypt and elsewhere did not just represent protest in favor of human rights, they constituted a natural outpouring of a desire for an alternative model of governance. Just as Islamist political parties saw this as an opportunity to present themselves as this viable alternative—as with the Muslim Brotherhood in Egypt and the Ennahda movement in Tunisia, for example—the very sudden explosion of popular revolution across the region presented itself to jihadists as an organic process of potentially existential value in their project of spreading the rule of Islam.

While the violent suppression by security forces of the 'Day of Dignity' protests in the southern city of Deraa on 18 March may have represented the birth of the revolution in Syria, events in the same city five days later on 23 March cemented the process of escalating violence. Early that morning, at around 1 a.m., security forces cut off electricity and communications links to the growing protest encampment at the city's Omari Mosque, before opening fire on protesters, killing at least six. As news of the incident spread that morning, more protests erupted across the city and several marches were launched from outlying towns towards the city. Almost all such protest groups were fired upon, and by the end of the day as many as thirty-seven people were reported dead by local activists and medical sources.[1] From this point on, protests acquired a notably more hostile character, particularly considering the now clearly established precedent of the regime's unforgiving suppression of dissent.

Three days later, on 26 March, a presidential amnesty was issued for the release of approximately 260 prisoners from Sednayya. Although claims continue to differ over the precise breakdown, it appears clear that the large majority of those released were Islamists of one kind or another, while others were members of political opposition bodies and Syria's Kurdish minority. This may have been an attempt to appease the growing anti-government sentiment across the country; but it is more likely that it was yet another devious attempt by the Assad regime to manipulate its adversary, this time by unleashing those it could safely label 'jihadist' or 'extremist' amongst its ranks. 'The regime wanted to play the cards of terrorism and militant gangs to scare Syrians and the international community at the same time,' according to Amjad Farekh, the trainee dental surgeon-turned-member of Liwa Jaish al-Muslimeen.[2] While some of those released had 'completed their prison terms … the regime's strategy was to distort and falsify the revolution—this is why many of those released had thoughts of extremism and militancy,' explained Abu Mustafa, a chief of external relations for conservative Islamist group Ahrar al-Sham and a senior member of its political bureau. Assad wanted to 'hire them indirectly in the direction of terrorism'.[3]

Whatever the motivation, the Syrian army began a rapid process of placing Deraa under near-total lockdown. Meanwhile, anti-government protests gained in confidence in Latakia, Tartous, Homs, Aleppo, Hama, Damascus and its countryside, Deir ez Zour, and Raqqa. As Assad labelled the protests a 'foreign conspiracy' on 30 March, his government—now lacking a cabinet, which had resigned on 29 March—legalised the wearing of the *niqab* by female school teachers on 6 April, only nine months after it had been banned in July 2010. The following day another presidential decree gave citizenship to 220,000 Kurds in the north-east, who had effectively been rendered stateless since the early 1960s. And on 21 April the president signed Decrees 161, 53 and 54, respectively lifting an official state of emergency, abolishing the restrictive Supreme State Security Court, and recognising the right to peaceful assembly. Nevertheless, these were merely cosmetic attempts at appeasement that translated into little practical change on the ground.

By this time protests had gained their own self-sustaining momentum, fuelled by the increasingly unrestrained security crackdown measures carried out by the army, the *mukhabarat*, the police, and the now-notorious *shabiha* thugs. On an entirely practical level, any genuine attempts at reconciliation by the central government were too little too late. Protester and other civilian casualties, as well as vast numbers of arrests and unexplained disappearances, were growing in number by the day. In recognition of its uncertain fate, in mid-April the Assad regime began definitively labelling the uprising in explicitly Islamist or extremist terms—'an armed insurrection under the motto of *jihad* to set up a *Salafist* state ... and spread terror across Syria',[4] for example.

By late April violence was reaching significant levels, with over a hundred people probably killed just on the 'Great Friday' of 22 April. Having been silent since the first protests, the Syrian Muslim Brotherhood lent its official support to the revolution on 28 April when, in a statement sent to Reuters, it called on people to 'Chant with one voice for freedom and dignity. Do not allow the tyrant to enslave you. God is Great!'[5] In what was perhaps unfortunate coincidental timing, the renowned Al-Qaeda-linked jihadist ideologue Abu Mohammed al-Maqdisi had released a statement in support of the Syrian protests that same day, providing the Syrian regime and its supporters with a perfect opportunity to label the Brotherhood and jihadists as working side by side—although this was of course not the case. Within days over 550 people had reportedly been killed in protests across the country, with several thousand others detained—all since 18 March. In addition to Deraa city, major military operations had been launched or were in the final stages of being prepared in at least ten other municipalities (al-Rastan, Homs, Baniyas, Douma, Saqba, Tafas, Jassem, Dael, Hama and Tel Kalakh).

As protests grew, and repression expanded and intensified, the first signs of a rudimentary fight-back began to emerge. Unverified reports of small ambushes, unsophisticated raids on checkpoints and sporadic incidences of small-arms fire targeting security-force patrols began in early May, especially in Homs, Deraa, Deir ez Zour and around Damascus. Meanwhile, the Syrian military and security apparatus also began to suffer from proliferating numbers of defections, and first- and second-hand accounts spread of soldiers refusing orders to fire on civilians and being executed, some of which were included in a July 2011 Human Rights Watch report.[6]

With attention inside and outside Syria focused on the protests and the emerging revolution, existing but disparate networks of jihadists across the country were beginning to communicate, aided especially by the initial releases from Sednayya on 26 March. These newly bolstered networks were further emboldened on 30 May when Assad signed Legislative Decree 61, which granted official amnesty to 'all members of the Muslim Brotherhood and other detainees belonging to political movements'.[7] Consequently, a further large number of Islamist and jihadist prisoners found themselves released from detention, mainly from Sednayya.

Many of these released individuals quickly assumed an active role in the revolution, including in forming some of the first armed groups to be established. For example, Hassan Abboud, a soft-spoken Salafist and former English teacher from Hama, led the establishment—along with at least half-a-dozen other Sednayya detainees—of Kataib Ahrar al-Sham in Idlib, which would by mid-to-late 2013 come to represent the largest and most powerful insurgent group in Syria, and one with links to al-Qaeda at that. Another example was Zahran Alloush, the son of a well-known Syrian sheikh based in Saudi Arabia, who had been detained outside Damascus in 2009 for his role in political Islamist activities. After his release Alloush went on to form the powerful Salafist group Liwa al-Islam, based in the Damascus suburb of Douma. Another former prisoner, Mohammed Adnan Zeitoun, better known as Abu Adnan al-Zabadani—who had joined the ISI in Iraq in 2008 but was detained after returning to Syria in 2009[8]—was responsible for launching an organised insurgency in his home town of Zabadani north-west of Damascus in mid-2011, and for eventually establishing Kataib Hamza bin 'Abd al-Mutallab. Many other similar stories can be recounted for the formation of other Syrian Islamist groups such as Harakat al-Fajr al-Islamiyya, Liwa al-Haq and Suqor al-Sham. Others, such as Rami al-Delati, an Islamist sheikh from Homs, emerged as influential coordinators of opposition activities, both civilian and armed.

However, while these groups largely retained a core Syrian foundation within their political objectives, many Sednayya detainees also went on to help lay the initial roots that led to the establishment of a covert ISI front in Syria, which had grander international intentions and links. Some of these were released in smaller numbers in June and July, after Bashar al-Assad's second speech failed to demonstrate a sufficient will to enact reforms and to de-escalate the security repression so as to placate his increasingly defiant citizens. 'As the Arab Spring started in other countries, I was sure it would reach Syria', said Mohammed Khadam, who would become the secretary of the Union of Syrians Abroad, 'but although I was deeply afraid of the brutal reaction the regime could reveal, I thought for some time that Assad would make some reforms and save the country. [However,] after his second speech (in June), I was certain this regime was never going to change its mentality—Assad was pushing the opposition into the battlefield.'[9]

These developments began to take shape in Homs, Aleppo and outside Damascus in July 2011, just as it had become clear that the regime had definitively adopted a security-focused solution to the revolution. Aware that events in Syria were escalating by the day, and keen not to miss an invaluable opportunity, the right-hand man of ISI leader Abu Bakr al-Baghdadi had a bold suggestion. A sharp-thinking former colonel in Iraq's air defence corps, Samir al-Khalifawi—better known simply as Haji Bakr[10]—implored his *emir al-mu'minin* (Commander of the Faithful) to make the necessary arrangements for the establishment of an ISI faction inside Syria. Khalifawi, whose intense focus on loyalty had been demonstrated in 2010 when he purportedly managed a concerted assassination campaign (using silenced weapons) against dozens of ISI commanders suspected of potential disloyalty after the coming to power of Abu Bakr al-Baghdadi in mid-2010, suggested sending a trusted Syrian ISI commander to lead this effort.

A month later, late at night, the ISI's *emir* in Iraq's Ninawa governorate, Abu Mohammed al-Jolani, crossed into al-Hasakah in Syria's north-east, along with six other ISI commanders,[11] a mixture of Syrians, Iraqis and Jordanians. Although still shrouded in much secrecy, Jolani's arrival in Syria in August, coming only four or five weeks after the formation of the largely moderate Free Syrian Army (FSA) by Syrian army defectors, would later prove to have been a defining moment in the course of the revolution.

In addition to instructing Jolani to establish an ISI front in Syria, Abu Bakr al-Baghdadi had also reportedly issued him and his fellow ISI comrades with two assassination missions against two Iraqi militant figures—Mohammed Hamdan of Jaish al-Mujahideen and Abdullah Yousuf (Abu Bakr al-Khatouni), who had former links to the ISI. Both of the orders were refused by Jolani, which perhaps was not so surpising in and of itself, considering his main mission of establishing a new militant organisation required a certain covert nature. But what was most interesting was that this was the second time in 18 months that Baghdadi had ordered men under his command to target Hamdan and Yousuf, both of whom were thought to be in Damascus at the time. After being injured in Iraq in early-2010, senior Iraqi ISI commander Maysar Ali Musa Abdallah al-Juburi, who went by the alias Abu Mariya al-Qahtani, was dispatched to Syria for surgery. Just prior to leaving, he received a direct order from Baghdadi to assassinate Hamdan and Yousuf, and also two other Iraqi militant commanders, Sa'adoun al-Qadi and Mohammed Hussein al-Juburi, both of Jaish Ansar al-Sunnah. Like Jolani in 2011, Abu Mariya also refused the orders.[12]

In the weeks after his arrival in Syria, Jolani travelled frequently, from al-Hasakah to Aleppo, Homs, Hama, Idlib and the Damascus countryside, establishing contact with small ISI-linked cells that had already begun to make initial arrangements for their activation.

Little can be said with certainty about Jolani. He is a Syrian, probably born in the late 1970s or early 1980s in the Golan region bordering Israel, and is thought to have been an Arabic teacher before travelling to Iraq to join AQI during the occupation.

One potential biography has been revealed for his life, which describes him as Osama al-Absi al-Wahidi, a relatively young man born in 1981 to a family originally hailing from Idlib, but residing in the desert town of Al-Shuhail in Syria's eastern Deir ez Zour governorate. He went through school in Deir ez Zour, before studying medicine at the University of Damascus. During this time in the early-2000s, the account claims, Jolani frequently travelled north to Aleppo to attend lectures given by Abu al-Qaqaa, where two years into his medicine degree, he was influenced to travel to Iraq to join Abu Musab al-Zarqawi's JTWJ in 2003.

According to the same account, Jolani quickly rose into a command position within the JTWJ and then AQI. Zarqawi's death in 2006, however, appeared to put a temporary end to Jolani's militancy in Iraq, sparking him to briefly return to Syria before crossing west into Lebanon, where he took up a role as military instructor within the Jund al-Sham group, which had loose ties to Al-Qaeda. Jolani's stint in Lebanon did not last long though, as he soon travelled back into Iraq, where he was promptly detained by American forces and incarcerated in the infamous prison at Camp Bucca, alongside dozens of other jihadist commanders and ideologues. He hid his Syrian identity by adopting another name, Awus al-Mosuli and was placed in the same cell as the leader of Iraqi armed group Jaish al-Mujahideen, Mohammed Hamdan. After his release from Camp Bucca in 2008, where he almost certainly met Abu Bakr al-Baghdadi, Jolani was purportedly promoted into the post of operational chief in Mosul, by then the area of Islamic State in Iraq's (ISI) most important investments.[13]

Whether such an account is truly accurate or not, Jolani clearly rose through the ranks of AQI's and the ISI's leadership ladder. His appointment into the ISI's most senior ranks in 2008 in Mosul was likely induced by the death of Swedish-Moroccan ISI commander Abu Qaswarah al-Maghribi in October 2008, who until that point had been the ISI's *wali* (governor) of Ninawa governorate, and thus protector of the most important centre of ISI power, in the city of Mosul. Jolani's appointment as Abu Qaswarah's successor, especially coming at a time when Abu Bakr al-Baghdadi and Haji Bakr were 'Iraqiising' the ISI senior leadership, spoke strongly to the respect Jolani must have enjoyed at the time. Certainly, his instruction to deploy to Syria in

August 2011 to establish a brand new ISI front underlined that eminent status yet further.

After his arrival in Syria Jolani married a Syrian woman, with whom he now has at least one son.[14] He has gained a reputation for maintaining intense secrecy regarding his identity, with his first television interview (aired on Al-Jazeera with presenter Tayseer Allouni in December 2013) and a second (filmed in two parts, again by Al-Jazeera, with presenter Ahmed Mansour in June 2015) only ever showing his back, shoulders and stomach. Even in internal meetings of Jabhat al-Nusra's senior leadership, Jolani is rumored to keep his face covered and go by his *kunya*, Abu Abdullah. 'He has a reputation for being a strategic thinker, not the kind of person to be showing off like some other leaders,' said another Abu Abdullah, a jihadist militant whose group is close to Jabhat al-Nusra.[15]

In October 2011, with violence continuing to escalate and tit-for-tat killings, reprisal attacks and criminally motivated kidnappings becoming a daily occurrence, several official Jabhat al-Nusra meetings were called in Homs and outside Damascus.[16] It was in these meetings that it was decided to establish Jabhat al-Nusra li-Ahl al-Sham min Mujahidi al-Sham fi Sahat al-Jihad—or simply Jabhat al-Nusra (the Support Front). Concurrently, while the Iraq-based ISI had agreed to provide approximately 50 per cent of its entire budget to its new Syrian front, additional support provided by pre-existing al-Qaeda financiers in the Gulf had begun to arrive via their own respective private networks. The fact that Jabhat al-Nusra was still a tightly guarded secret and the very idea of armed resistance in Syria was only weeks old meant that this private finance was unevenly and erratically distributed, based largely on personal relationships rather than along strict organisational lines. As such, early money ended up in the coffers of many different groups, including Ahrar al-Sham, which was specifically an early recipient of considerable support from private and potentially also government sources in Kuwait and Qatar.

In the formation meetings, Jolani and six others came to design the ideological foundations and religio-political objectives and strategy of Jabhat al-Nusra as an armed organisation. Within this initial Jabhat al-Nusra core were a number of prominent ISI figures, including the earlier named Abu Mariya al-Qahtani, who had travelled across the Iraq–Syria border with Jolani in August. An Iraqi born in Mosul, Abu Mariya had joined AQI at its birth in April 2004, and US intelligence links him specifically to an attack on an MNF-I checkpoint in Ninawa later in 2004. Also present in the formation meetings were two Palestinian Jordanians from Zarqa outside Amman,

Mustafa Abd al-Latif Saleh (Abu Anas al-Sahaba) and Iyad Tubasi (Abu Julaybib). Tubasi had been a close aide and brother-in-law to Abu Musab al-Zarqawi, having married his sister during the Iraqi occupation and fought alongside him in both Afghanistan in 1999–2000 and in Iraq. Latif had played a lead role as an ISI facilitator and recruiter of foreign fighters with Abu Ghadiya through the mid-to-late 2000s. In addition to Jolani himself, two other Syrians were in the meetings—one a Damascene Salafist, Anas Hasan Khattab, who played a key early role in coordinating with the ISI leadership in Iraq and with external financiers in the region and beyond and another being Saleh al-Hamawi, a Salafist who hailed from the town of Halfaya in Hama governorate. The seventh man in the room was a Palestinian, Abu Omar al-Filistini.[17]

Jabhat al-Nusra did not officially announce its establishment until 23 January 2012, when its media wing, al-Manara al-Bayda, released a video onto online jihadist forums known to be affiliated with al-Qaeda. The sixteen-minute video, entitled 'For the People of Syria from the Mujahidin of Syria in the Fields of Jihad', contained a long audio statement by Jolani in which he declared war on the Assad regime. He stressed, however, that this represented only half of the struggle ahead—Islamic law must also be established across *bilad al-Sham* (greater Syria, generally incorporating Syria, Lebanon, Israel, Palestine, western Iraq, and Lebanon), with all people united under Islamic rule. This was a clear expression of Jabhat al-Nusra's 'domestic' objectives, but Jolani also explained that his organisation had been formed by *mujahidin* (holy warriors) 'back from the various fronts', thereby immediately indicating an international and likely Iraq-heavy operational influence.[18]

This reference related directly to the very identity of Jabhat al-Nusra as being an organisation founded by *mujahidin* in (and from) the 'fields of jihad'—or *fi sahat al-jihad*, something explicitly contained within the group's full name. The fields of jihad is a term that had been frequently used by jihadists around the world, particularly those directly and indirectly affiliated with al-Qaeda, to refer to fighters operating in an active zone of military jihad, in Afghanistan, Pakistan, Algeria, Somalia, Iraq etc. So from the start Jabhat al-Nusra had identified itself using common al-Qaeda phraseology and as an organisation founded by individuals with previous fighting experience elsewhere.

While Jolani was undoubtedly keen to stress Jabhat al-Nusra's Syrian focus, his organisation's vision was global. The video had begun with an image of the Dome of the Rock in Jerusalem—a clear expression of ultimate intents in Israel and Palestine—and Jolani's speech had explicitly set out to condemn the

Western world and its assistance to the moderate opposition, thereby warning other factions to reject any such offers from abroad. He also rejected Turkey's role in backing the revolution due to its perceived will to bend to orders from the USA, while the Arab League was similarly denounced. Perhaps unsurprisingly, Iran was singled out for 'trying to revive the time of the Persian Empire'.[19]

Combining a Syrian focus with an international outlook, Jolani sought to present Syria—and *bilad al-Sham*—as a historical battleground between foreign imperialism and Islamic honour. By drawing on the examples of the Zoroastrian and Byzantine Empires, which he claimed 'Allah brought down', Jolani aimed to present the more recent establishments of the state of Israel (1948) and the (Shia) Islamic Republic of Iran (1979) as but part of 'an ongoing struggle against [Sunni] Islam'.[20]

The video also contained clips of Jabhat al-Nusra militants operating across Syria, including in the governorates of Idlib, Deraa, Damascus, Deir ez Zour and Hama. Perhaps most significantly, the video claimed responsibility for Jabhat al-Nusra's first major attack, a double suicide bombing outside Syrian military intelligence facilities in Damascus's south-western neighbourhood of Kfar Souseh on 23 December 2011, which had killed at least forty people. Although no other earlier attacks were claimed by Jabhat al-Nusra in this video or in later statements, several senior commanders subsequently insisted that the organisation had been operating militarily for several months before the December attack, though perhaps in a less official capacity. In fact, when the US Department of State came to designate Jabhat al-Nusra as an 'alias' of AQI (then generally used as shorthand for the ISI) on 11 December 2012, and thus as a terrorist organisation, it explicitly claimed that it had carried out attacks 'since November 2011'.[21]

Although Jabhat al-Nusra did not acknowledge its links to the ISI (until April 2013), the content of the 23 January video and other sources available shortly thereafter showed it to be an extreme jihadist organisation with likely international connections. Moreover, it received early statements of support from well-known jihadi ideologues, including Mauritanian sheikh Abu al-Mundhir al-Shinqiti, Lebanese sheikh Abu al-Zahra al-Zubaydi, Jordanian sheikh Abu Mohammed al-Tahawi, and Sheikh Abu Saad al-Amili.[22] Its public emergence also coincided with and met the desires of increasingly intense calls from within the online jihadist community for such an organisation to take up the path of jihad in *bilad al-Sham*.

\* \* \*

2011 was a year of significant change in Syria. Mass protest had begun to emerge in March and April, followed by increasingly intense military repression in May and June. By late July the first elements of organised armed resistance had been formed in the shape of the FSA (after its amalgamation with a loose umbrella known as the Free Officers' Movement), while several more Islamist-minded factions were coming together more covertly.

By late 2011 many areas of Syria had become open battlegrounds between resistance fighters and the Syrian military. The central city of Homs was under siege, with intensive artillery fire targeting opposition-held districts, while other surrounding towns such as al-Rastan and al-Qusayr were the scenes of sustained battle. In addition to Homs and some outlying suburbs of Damascus, Idlib in particular had emerged as the site of some of the most capable resistance fighters and factions, with significant guerrilla-style attacks in areas such as Jisr al-Shughour, Maraat al-Numaan and Binnish becoming a more frequent occurrence.

Although the revolution was still framed around demands for justice, freedom, equality and other such liberal mores, the regime in Damascus—dominated by members of the Alawite minority—was painting an increasingly sectarian picture, claiming that its opponents were Sunni extremists seeking the establishment of a Salafist Islamic state. Accusations were also beginning to emerge regarding Assad's exploitation of his strategic relationship with the Lebanon-based Shia militant organisation Hezbollah, particularly following an attack on UNIFIL peacekeepers in southern Lebanon on 11 December 2011, which was blamed on orders emanating from Damascus. At this stage, however, such suggestions of sectarian sentiment remained almost entirely on the regime's side, and still on a minimal level.

Thus, while Jabhat al-Nusra and many other Syrian Islamist factions were emerging on the ground in the latter months of the year, they remained representative only of peripheral objectives. Sectarianism was not the language of the revolution, and neither did Sunni Islamic demands feature within its founding platforms.

But this was a formative period, in which the various emerging actors were still finding their place within the chaos of revolution and emerging civil conflict. Despite being led primarily by defected army and police officers, the FSA was badly organised, insufficiently funded and poorly armed.

The year 2012 would therefore come to represent a significant make-or-break opportunity for the entire insurgency, but especially so for Jabhat al-Nusra and other emerging jihadist factions. Much of their senior leaderships had the potentially invaluable prior experience of having fought as insurgents in Iraq and elsewhere, which was something that only a minute portion of the FSA could have claimed at the time.

# 5

# JANUARY–AUGUST 2012

## JABHAT AL-NUSRA EMERGES

As 2012 began, Jabhat al-Nusra carried out its second attack, in Damascus on 6 January, and publicly announced its emergence in a video on 23 January. Its third attack, a double suicide truck bombing, targeted security facilities in Aleppo on 10 February. Through both its rhetoric and self-presentation, Jabhat al-Nusra placed an emphasis on limiting its operations to the Syrian theatre and to playing an assisting role within a broader revolution against oppression.

Despite attempting to portray its role in a positive light, Jabhat al-Nusra's media content was released exclusively to al-Qaeda-linked Internet forums, and it was a highly unpopular actor within the growing opposition movement in Syria. By the time al-Qaeda leader Ayman al-Zawahiri issued a statement on 12 February 2012 celebrating the resistance in Syria, the Western world appeared discouraged from showing the kind of support for moderate insurgency that it had done in Libya in 2011.

As reports began to emerge of massacres by Damascus-linked militiamen known as shabiha in March, small numbers of foreign fighters began arriving in Syria. Foreign finance also consolidated itself as a consistent dynamic in the Syrian revolution, much directed towards FSA factions, but some also to jihadists. The insurgency as a whole, meanwhile, was demonstrating increasingly professional tactics from early 2012, encouraged by considerable numbers of defecting soldiers.

As summer began and three of Syria's five northern border crossings with Turkey fell to the insurgency, several jihadist groups were formed in northern Syria, mainly led by Chechens. This coincided with the gradual acceptance and integration of Jabhat al-Nusra into the broader Syrian armed opposition, especially in Aleppo, where fighting erupted and intensified in July and August 2012.

* * *

The release of Jabhat al-Nusra's 'emergence' video on 23 January might have been a wake-up call for some involved in the revolution, but at the time it appeared to be a very small organisation, perhaps only capable of carrying out sporadic bomb attacks in urban centres.

Indeed, this is exactly what Jabhat al-Nusra represented in its first few months of publicly acknowledged existence. Its second attack—after the 23 December 2011 bombings in Kfar Souseh—came on 6 January, when a suicide bomber on foot detonated explosives near several buses carrying riot police in the al-Midan district of Damascus, killing twenty-six people. That this second attack went unclaimed in Jabhat al-Nusra's formation video released two-and-a-half weeks later underlined the fact that this was still very much a fledgling organisation getting to grips with connecting operational cells with the internal bureaucratic infrastructure of a terrorist organisation, such as those individuals responsible for producing and releasing media content and attack claims. What was clear from the beginning, however, were Jabhat al-Nusra's links to the broader al-Qaeda community, particularly through the fact that the Shumukh al-Islam online forum—also used then by the ISI—had become the primary distributor of its media material.

Jabhat al-Nusra's third attack came in Aleppo on 10 February, when two Syrian fighters detonated their explosive-laden vehicles outside security buildings in the al-Arkoub and New Aleppo districts of Aleppo city, killing a total of 28 people and wounding over 200 others. Both the 6 January and 10 February bombings were claimed in Jabhat al-Nusra's second video, again released by Shumukh al-Islam, on 26 February. The extensive forty-five-minute video explained that the attacks had been 'to avenge the people of Homs', who were currently under siege by the Syrian army. One of the two bombers, identified simply as Abu al-Baraa al-Shami, claimed that his attack was specifically in revenge for the rape of a woman by Syrian security forces. 'Brothers, hurry up and don't wait. Jihad is now in your country ... You don't need any fatwas,' Abu al-Baraa was recorded as saying. A portion of the video also contained an audio statement by Jolani, who repeated his declaration of jihad against the Assad regime and accused it of criminality in its reactions to the protests and developing revolution.

In these first few months, elite Syrian army units were being selectively deployed to launch major assaults on early strongholds of the FSA and other armed insurgent factions. This marked a strategic escalation by the regime, from an initial security solution to a wholehearted military one. In January, the Syrian army, and particularly its elite and specialist Fourth Mechanised

Division, commanded by Bashar al-Assad's brother Maher, focused its attention on targets around Damascus, particularly the north-western mountainside town of Zabadani (home to Mohammed Adnan Zeitoun and his Kataib Hamza bin 'Abd al-Mutallab) and Douma (stronghold of several Islamist factions, including Zahran Alloush's Liwa al-Islam). By late January and early February sufficient regime progress had been made in the Damascus region for the focus to be moved north towards the city of Homs and several of its outlying towns (such as Talbiseh, al-Rastan and al-Qusayr) where opposition confidence was on the rise. Other concerted operations were simultaneously launched to the south in the governorate of Deraa, the original birthplace of the revolution.

By the time regime forces had won a series of ferocious tactical victories in January and early February, Jabhat al-Nusra was still only minimally active in terms of armed operations. Nonetheless, this period in early 2012 represented a crucially important time for the group to present itself to its putative Syrian constituents and to the international jihadist community at large. Its mere arrival on the scene had an immediate and, at the time, perhaps overlooked impact—dissuading cautious officials in the USA and Europe from actively arming the FSA. While expressing some concern over exactly 'who the opposition movement in Syria is at this point', General Martin Dempsey, then chairman of the US Joint Chiefs of Staff, explained on 19 February that 'there are indications that al-Qaeda is involved [in Syria] and that they're interested in supporting the opposition ... until we're a lot clearer about ... who they are and what they are, I think it would be premature to talk about arming [the FSA].'[1]

Within the context of an emerging Syrian revolution, Jabhat al-Nusra principally saw itself as an Islamic movement extolling the virtues of 'real' Islam and the necessity of jihad as *fardh ayn*, or obligatory. While led by a Syrian, Jabhat al-Nusra's senior leadership was regional in nature, with leaders from Iraq, Saudi Arabia and Jordan all represented in its upper echelons of decision making. But this was not an image the organisation was keen to share. In fact, it was consistently keen to stress its Syrian foundations and Syrian objectives. Moazzam Begg, a former Guantanamo Bay detainee who is now the director of human rights organisation CAGE and has engaged extensively with the Islamist components of Syria's insurgency, claims that this 'Syria-first' policy was largely in place within Jabhat al-Nusra at the time: 'In the early days of [Jabhat al-Nusra] they ... did not accept foreigners, except possibly for suicide missions.'[2]

This emphasis on its 'Syrian-ness' was at the time tied into traditional Islamic prophecies that linked the merit and existential importance of jihad with the land and people of *bilad al-Sham*. According to Islamic tradition laid out in the *Sunna* and *Hadith*, the Prophet Muhammad prophesied that a saviour of Islam would one day appear in *bilad al-Sham* at the end of days in order to fight a final battle against the armies of the enemy of Islam. This Islamic saviour, or *Mahdi*, is the prophet Issa Ibn Maryam (or Jesus, Son of Mary), whose specific arrival on Earth, according to a *hadith*, would take place via *al-manara al-baydha*, the White Minaret, which many identified to be that named within Damascus's famed Umayyad Mosque. It is therefore no coincidence that Jabhat al-Nusra chose to name its media wing al-Manara al-Baydha.

> He (Dajjal, or anti-Christ) would then call (that young man) and he will come forward laughing with his face gleaming (with happiness) and it would at this very time that Allah would send Jesus, son of Mary, and he will descend at Al-Manara al-Bayda (the white lighthouse or minaret) in the eastern side of Damascus wearing two garments lightly dyed with saffron and placing his hands on the wings of two Angels. When he would lower his head, there would fall beads of perspiration from his head, and when he would raise it up, beads like pearls would scatter from it. Every non-believer who would smell the odour of his self would die and his breath would reach as far as he would be able to see.

> Sahih Muslim Book 041, Hadith 7015

Such millenarian thought retains popular acceptance within the international jihadist community, and the centrality of Syria within this tradition lent Jabhat al-Nusra a considerable advantage from the outset. Another well-known *hadith* had a similarly significant impact, as it claims that the Prophet Muhammad had told of three Islamic armies that would emerge in al-Sham, Yemen and Iraq prior to the apocalypse.

> You should go to Sham, for it is the best of Allah's lands, and the best of His slaves will be drawn there.

> And if you refuse, then you should go to Yemen and drink from its wells. For Allah has guaranteed me that He will look after Sham and its people!

> Imam Ahmad 4/110, Abu Dawud 2483

Perhaps the jihadi ideologue to have had the greatest influence on the strategy of Jabhat al-Nusra has been Syrian national Mustafa Setmariam Nasar (Abu Musab al-Suri). Although he was not altogether tied to such millenarian thought, Abu Musab al-Suri's famous 1,600-page tome, *The Call to Global Islamic Resistance*—written over a period of two years while on the run after the fall of the Taliban in Afghanistan in late 2001—did contain sporadic references to the promised return of the *Mahdi* prior to the 'advent of the Hour', when Islam's last adherents 'fight the anti-Christ'.[3]

Abu Musab's more strategically valuable contribution of jihadist thought, however, was his emphasis upon the value of 'individual jihad', whereby one's personal contribution towards the effort can avoid being tainted or wasted due to errors or losses caused by larger organisational decisions. On a more macro-level perspective, this means that jihadists should focus on acting in such a way as to ensure that society itself becomes more amenable to long-term jihad. In other words, 'the priority is to establish deep ties with local communities, even if that requires flexibility in some [Islamic] principles'.[4] Within Jabhat al-Nusra's context, that meant placing the focus on fighting the Assad regime (and not rival or non-Islamic factions), maintaining a pragmatic interpretation and implementation of the *sharia* (avoiding extremism), and acting as a social movement rather than solely a military force (being of service to society).

In fact, being of service to Syrian society and contributing positively towards the cause of the revolution at large was something specifically implied in Jabhat al-Nusra's name. Meaning to support or to provide assistance, the use of *nusra*, according to the reputed anonymous commentator on jihadist issues known as 'Mr Orange', suggested that the group's intent was to:

> support the uprising … [not] to lead it … They show themselves via their name as a group that is not excluding or imposing. They are not named Ansar al-Shariah (Supporters of Islamic Law)—a name that would exclude those who do not support Islamic Law. No, they are the supporters of the people.[5]

Jabhat al-Nusra therefore sought to present itself as a hyper-localised jihadist organisation that would implement a patient and long-term strategy focused on integrating into local dynamics and in shaping alliances, avoiding enemies and abstaining from an overly swift or extreme implementation of *sharia*. Interestingly, this was a line of thinking that was becoming increasingly popular within al-Qaeda's senior leadership in 2011–13. The *emir* of al-Qaeda in the Islamic Maghreb (AQIM), Abu Musab Abdul Wadud (or Abdelmalek Droukdel) stressed this in a letter to his forces in Mali in 2012, for example, using the image of AQIM as a parent and Mali as a child:

> The current baby is in its first days, crawling on its knees, and has not yet stood on its two legs … If we really want it to stand on its own two feet in this world full of enemies waiting to pounce, we must ease its burden, take it by the hand, help it and support it until it stands … One of the wrong policies that we think you carried out is the extreme speed with which you applied Sharia … our previous experience proved that applying Sharia this way … will lead to people rejecting the religion and engender hatred towards the mujahideen.[6]

Similarly, Jolani provided nearly indistinguishable advice to his fighters in 2012:

> Day after day, you are getting closer to the people after you conquered their hearts and became entrusted by them ... Beware of being hard on them, begin with the priorities and fundamentals of Islam and be flexible on the minor parts of the religion.[7]

Despite its conscious efforts to present itself as both authentically Syrian and less extreme than the recently comparable experience of al-Qaeda in Iraq, the general enthusiasm for the revolution in late 2011 and early 2012, with its populist nationalist ideals of freedom and human rights, meant that the emergence of a jihadist organisation such as Jabhat al-Nusra was initially a largely unpopular development. Although it had only carried out three claimed attacks by 1 March, at least 40 per cent of the fatalities had been civilian.[8] Moreover, the style and scale of the attacks had not been of the kind that strategically benefited the opposition; in fact, they only served to bolster the regime's claim that it was combating jihadist militancy. Moreover, the attacks themselves also attracted significant international media attention, much of which quickly drew parallels with the frequency of similar such bombings in neighbouring Iraq. Jabhat al-Nusra, therefore, was not winning the allies within the opposition that it so keenly sought.

This did not stop leaders in other Syrian Salafist factions such as Kataib Ahrar al-Sham, however, from seeking to learn from mistakes made in previous zones of jihad. 'All the [Islamist] leaders I spoke to were acutely aware of the disaster that had occurred next door in Iraq and wanted at all costs to avoid a repeat of the same in their country,' claimed Moazzam Begg.[9]

Meanwhile, the wider conflict was continuing to escalate, with particularly intense activity in Homs, where government forces were attacking opposition-controlled districts of the city. In particular, the world's attention had been caught by the fate of the Baba Amr district, where a brutal siege accompanied by concerted artillery fire had been initiated on 3 February, and turned the urban area into an apocalyptic scene of destruction. *Sunday Times* war correspondent Marie Colvin and photojournalist Rémi Ochlik notably lost their lives in one regime artillery blitz that appeared to target a makeshift opposition activist media centre in Baba Amr on 22 February. Such fierce and indiscriminate military assault had become a favoured tactic of regime forces and, at least in the immediate term, it was resulting in opposition defeats. Thus, Baba Amr fell on 1 March, when the last remaining 100 or so FSA fighters announced a 'tactical retreat'.[10] However, such ruthless violence and destruction fed into the kind of societal desperation and frustration that jihadists depend upon to find some measure of acceptance, if not support.

'We lost so many good men and of course many, many women, children and elderly in the city in those weeks, it was like Hell on earth. I don't blame the last fighters for giving up, anyone would have done the same, but the depression that came after made all of us welcome extremists. They were on our side, after all,'[11] said one former FSA fighter from rural Homs, who had watched as his city was taken in late February and early March. Indeed, both victories and defeats had potentially beneficial effects for jihadists such as Jabhat al-Nusra.

Within the escalation of the conflict as a whole came reports of 'massacres' seemingly committed by pro-regime militias and *shabiha* against civilians in known Sunni neighbourhoods. These also reinforced jihadists' self-perception as being protectors of a repressed people. One such early example came on the morning of 9 March, when regime ground forces and as many as thirty tanks broke into the Homs opposition stronghold and Sunni district of Karam Zeitoun.[12] While tank fire was directed indiscriminately at residential apartment buildings through the day, pro-regime gunmen launched a series of raids on 10 and 11 March, stealing and looting everything in their wake. By 11 March at least forty-seven women and children had been killed, many by having their throats slit and heads imploded with blunt objects.[13] Local activists also reported widespread stories of rape and indiscriminate murder.[14] This was the first such reported massacre—there were to be many more in the months to come.

Meanwhile, bolstered by a determination to protect its people and invigorated by ongoing regime officer defections, the FSA was continuing to expand in size and professionalism, with the sophistication of ambush tactics discernibly improving and the incidence of effective improvised explosive device (IED) use becoming a daily affair. But the conflict was also becoming steadily more international, which suited the grand scheme of jihadists such as Jabhat al-Nusra. Claims began to emerge in February 2012 that Iran was preparing to deploy as many as 15,000 military personnel into Syria to bolster its overstretched military,[15] while the FSA claimed on 27 January to have captured seven Iranians, including five members of the Revolutionary Guards.[16] The Iraqi Interior Ministry also began releasing statements claiming that foreign fighters were leaving its territory and crossing into Syria to join the fight, while jihadi forums online had begun to report the 'martyrdom' of foreign fighters, including a group of Kuwaitis in mid-February.[17] Moreover, the FSA was becoming increasingly vocal about their sourcing of light and heavy weaponry from abroad, with the help of foreign sources of finance in the Gulf.[18]

While the governments of both Saudi Arabia and Qatar were early supporters of the political and military opposition, it was the private financial networks, many of which were operated out of Kuwait but coordinated regionally, that played a key role in late 2011 and early 2012. As Elizabeth Dickinson has explained, it was the Syrian expatriate community in Kuwait that got the ball rolling, by persuading wealthy Kuwaiti individuals and charities to take up the cause of supporting the revolution. In late 2011 much of the assistance that resulted was channelled to humanitarian needs, but by early 2012 armed groups were being established and bolstered specifically by money being raised in Kuwait. The fundraising work of the Kuwaiti Salafist Revival of Islamic Heritage Society is one case in point. The Sheikh Fahad al-Ahmed Charity and individuals such as Dr Shafi al-Ajmi, Hajjaj al-Ajmi, former MP Jamaan Herbash and Salafists Waleed al-Tabtabae and Mohammed Hayef, as well as Nabil al-Awady and Ajeel al-Nashmi, all contributed towards a significant influx of foreign finance into the Syrian anti-government insurgency.[19]

Admittedly, at this point a large majority of this money was destined for armed groups affiliated to the FSA—a general trend that would continue throughout much of 2012. But that is not to say Jabhat al-Nusra did not have its own sources of external finance: it did. But that is not to say Jabhat al-Nusra did not have its own sources of external finance: it did. Since 2012, the US government has designated a considerable number of regionally based individuals as alleged financiers of the group's activities in Syria dating back to 2011, including two Jordanians it claimed were also linked to the terrorist organisation's broader international operations.[20]

Nonetheless, despite being channelled towards the moderate FSA, the majority of these early financial transactions set a dangerous precedent. Relationships of financial dependence were being established, whereby moderate FSA groups became tied to specific donors, whose political and religious expectations eventually proved to be debilitating to the ability of the FSA to coalesce within a single unified body. It was also dangerous because these relationships proved to last beyond the original groups that were created. Several of the Kuwaitis named above went on to exploit the contacts they gleaned in 2012 to begin financing more extremist organisations, including Jabhat al-Nusra, in 2013 and 2014.

Perhaps the most significant development within the early months of 2012, however, came on 12 February, when al-Qaeda leader Ayman al-Zawahiri issued his first statement on Syria since the outbreak of the revolution, in which he called on 'every Muslim and every honorable and free person in Turkey, Iraq, Jordan and Lebanon to go aid his brothers in Syria'.[21] Zawahiri's request for regionally based *mujahidin* to travel to Syria's 'fields of jihad' appeared perfectly designed to fit within Jabhat al-Nusra's self-identified mission to 'support' the revolution in Syria and spread Islam's rule.

Jabhat al-Nusra had announced its emergence in Syria three weeks earlier, and as such it was still a relatively unknown quantity. Pieced together with this statement from Zawahiri, levels of concern began to rise that al-Qaeda had found itself a new project.

In early March international pressure began to rise in support of a nation-wide ceasefire, as backed by the then United Nations and Arab League envoy to Syria, Kofi Annan. However, by the revolution's first anniversary peaceful protests had become increasingly rare, and instead the level of full-on conflict and horrific violence continued to escalate. It was within this context that Jabhat al-Nusra began to increase its operational tempo, with a suicide car bombing in Deraa on 3 March and a double car bombing outside a customs office and an air force intelligence facility in Damascus two weeks later on 17 March. In addition to such attacks, Jabhat al-Nusra was also now beginning to demonstrate signs of its potential to operate—albeit on a small scale—as a fledgling insurgent organisation, joining guerrilla-style ambushes, carrying out assassinations, planting and detonating IEDs in suburban Damascus and in rural areas of Idlib, Hama and Homs.

March also saw the emergence of a Lebanese former Fatah al-Islam member, Walid al-Boustani, and his short-lived 'Islamic Emirate of Homs'. Boustani had been a prominent commander in Fatah al-Islam's 2007 uprising and war with the Lebanese army in Nahr al-Bared, after which he was arrested, charged and imprisoned for his role in killing Lebanese soldiers. In 2010, however, Boustani and a fellow inmate—a Syrian, Mounjed al-Faham—escaped from their cells in Lebanon's infamous Roumieh prison by tying together bed sheets and blankets and abseiling down the prison walls late at night. Although Faham was caught not long afterwards, Boustani went into hiding in Ain al-Hilweh camp in southern Lebanon.[22] It was there, just south-east of the port city of Sidon, that Boustani and another fellow Lebanese former Fatah al-Islam commander, Abd al-Ghani Jawhar, agreed to travel into Syria and establish a new jihadist movement.

Shortly after crossing the Lebanese border into western Homs, Boustani teamed up with a small number of other Syrians and Lebanese Salafists to establish what they called the 'Islamic Emirate of Homs'. This proved a deeply unpopular move within the local anti-government communities. After a series of apparent assassinations of people who had publicly expressed their opposition to Boustani's emirate and widespread allegations that Boustani and Jawhar were looting FSA supplies and money, several local FSA units captured and executed him in mid-April. Around the same time Jawhar was killed in clashes with Syrian government forces, and as such, the 'Islamic Emirate of Homs' ceased to exist just as quickly as it had emerged.

Meanwhile, the UN had agreed to set 10 April as the date for all parties to the conflict to agree and put into place a Syria-wide ceasefire, as per Kofi Annan's plan. However, the brutal level of violence that had been reached by this point made such a proposition next to impossible to practically implement on the ground, not to mention the fact that groups such as Jabhat al-Nusra were certainly not interested in observing it. Nonetheless, that was not to matter. On 9 April the Assad regime announced that it would only observe a ceasefire on the condition that all opposition groups inside Syria and foreign governments supporting the revolution sign on paper a full renunciation of the use of violence in the Syrian crisis.[23] That proved to be the diplomatic nail in the coffin for Annan's already dying ceasefire plan.

Such a catastrophic failure by the international community to solve—or at least slow—the escalating violence in Syria represented fuel to the fire for jihadist movements, who had consistently denounced the diplomatic world for what it perceived as a refusal to protect (Sunni) Muslim civilians. From the very beginnings of the insurgency and the emergence within it of a jihadist component, a pivotal foundation of these groups' *raisons d'être* was the protection of innocents from oppression and violence. In fact, while *nusra* literally translates as 'support' or 'assistance', it is also a common Qur'anic term used to refer to a group of the Prophet Muhammad's seventy most staunch supporters who ensured his protection and support upon arrival in Medina.[24] *Jabha*, by extension, refers to a 'front' within a war or military campaign that necessarily requires the large-scale mobilisation of the people in order to muster up a defence against one's adversary. Taken together, therefore, the expression *jabhat al-nusra* represents something of particular importance for jihadists and Muslims loyal to the concept of the *umma*, or a collective and unified global Islamic community.

Sparked at least in part by the recognition of their defeat in Homs, the FSA began a coordinated shift of resources to Damascus throughout March and April in preparation for a planned escalation in the capital. Damascus was a seemingly impenetrable fortress for the regime, with its immensely valuable integrated series of military facilities atop Mount Qassioun over-looking the city and where Alawite loyalist districts such as Mezzeh 86, Ish al-Warwar and Haay al-Wurrud presented themselves as valuable islands of support. This FSA offensive began in earnest in late April, when targeted killings of regime officers became a daily occurrence, and IED, motorcycle and car bombings increased dramatically. Although it was still acting largely independently from these broader FSA operations, this Damascus offensive marked the first time that Jabhat al-Nusra contributed towards a multi-group opposition strategic offensive.

From the very early weeks of its coalescence in mid-to-late 2011, Damascus's northern suburbs had been a staging ground and base area for Jabhat al-Nusra's recruited fighters and senior leadership figures. As such, it sought to piggyback on the intensifying conflict dynamics in this area throughout April and May, by carrying out a flurry of IED attacks and tar-geted assassinations. Jabhat al-Nusra's claimed activities in Hama, Idlib, Deraa and Deir ez Zour, meanwhile, continued to grow at a similar rate. By June it had reached a rate of sixty attacks per month, up from only seven in March.[25]

In mid-2012 Syria was fast demonstrating the various characteristics of a civil war—something the International Committee of the Red Cross (ICRC) confirmed in July—and foreign fighters were beginning to flow into the coun-try on a more organised level. By July there were almost certainly at least 750 non-Syrians fighting in the ranks of the armed insurgency, many for Jabhat al-Nusra but some others also within the FSA.[26]

Many of these foreign fighters had arrived from Syria's neighbours, particu-larly Iraq and Lebanon, whose borders were notoriously porous and across which many jihadists had crossed over recent years. June 2012 marked the first public admission from Jordan that its own nationals were seeking to take part in Syria's conflict, when border police detained two Jordanians en route to Syrian territory.[27]

While remnants of Fatah al-Islam had made their mark, so too did the al-Qaeda-affiliated Kataib Abdullah Azzam, the leader of which, Majid bin Muhammed al-Majid, released a video statement on 19 June 2012 declaring his full support for the cause of the Syrian revolution, but cautioning against attacks that would anger the people.[28] Although a small organisation, Kataib Abdullah Azzam was a significant movement with multiple *kataib* (brigades) across the Middle East, specifically Katiba Yusuf al-Uyayri—named after the first leader of al-Qaeda in the Arabian Peninsula (AQAP)—which had been responsible for a boat-borne suicide bombing that targeted the Japanese-owned *MV M Star* oil tanker off the coast of the United Arab Emirates (UAE) on 27 July 2010; Katiba Ziad al-Jarrah—named after the Lebanese al-Qaeda hijacker and pilot of Flight 93 in the 9/11 attacks—which had by mid-2011 been responsible for a number of rocket attacks on northern Israel from southern Lebanon since 2009; and the lesser-known Katiba Marwan Haddad, which claimed responsibility for launching a Grad rocket and two mortar shells from Gaza towards the Israeli city of Ashkelon and the Zikim military base on 10 April 2011.

Despite not having played a recognised role in the Syrian conflict up to this point, a senior Kataib Abdullah Azzam commander, Tawfiq Taha, was reported to have fled his base in Ain al-Hilweh in May 2012 along with four Fatah al-Islam militants: three Palestinians, Haitham Shaabi, Ziad Abu Naaj and Mohammed Doukhi, and a Lebanese national, Abd al-Rahman Arefi.[29] Considering their organisations' links with the ISI in Iraq and its networks in Syria, they were almost certainly planning to join Jabhat al-Nusra.

As such, the 19 June statement by Kataib Abdullah Azzam was significant in and of itself. All three of its identified leaders were Saudi Arabian nationals on Saudi's list of eighty-five most-wanted terrorists, and had substantial histories within al-Qaeda and AQI. In addition to Majid, they were Ibrahim Suleiman Hamad al-Hablain (Abu Jabal) and Saleh al-Qaraawi, both of whom had also been designated international terrorists by the US government, in November and December 2011 respectively. It was therefore an organisation whose influence meant it was capable of 'punching above its weight' and whose statement of support for a conflict within its immediate vicinity aroused considerable attention at the time.

In addition to statements of support for the Syrian revolution, this development also coincided with the emergence of Syria's second notable jihadist group, Kataib al-Muhajireen. Formed in Syria's north-western governorate of Latakia, and based there and in western parts of Aleppo, Kataib al-Muhajireen was initially dominated by Libyans who had travelled to Syria after the fall of the Muammar Gaddafi regime. However, a growing contingent of Russian speakers from Chechnya and Dagestan quickly established a strong role within the group, and shortly thereafter its leadership was assumed by Tarkhan Tayumurazovich Batirashvili, an ethnic Chechen from Georgia's Pankisi Gorge. Commonly referred to as Omar al-Shishani (or Omar the Chechen), this tall, ginger-bearded man was set to play a major role in the evolution of Syria's jihadist insurgency in the months and years to come.

Born to an Orthodox Christian father and a Muslim Kist mother in the small Pankisi village of Birkiani on 11 January 1986, Omar al-Shishani grew up working as a shepherd in hills often used by militants crossing into Chechnya during the Second War of 1999–2000. It is likely that then, aged thirteen or fourteen, he had his first contact with Islamic insurgent fighters. His life took a different turn, however, when after graduating from high school, he joined the Georgian army, within which he was called up into a special reconnaissance group and then promoted to sergeant within an intelligence unit. When Georgian troops marched into Russian-defended South Ossetia in late 2008, Omar al-Shishani was deployed across enemy lines to conduct covert reconnaissance of Russian armoured columns, but a diagnosis of tuberculosis after the war in 2010 saw him discharged from the Georgian military on medical grounds. His mother died shortly thereafter, which his father later told the *Wall Street Journal* had left him 'very disillusioned'. He appears at this point to have begun engaging again with and potentially facilitating logistics for Chechen militants across the Georgian border, and in September 2010 Georgian authorities detained him and sentenced him to three years in prison for 'illegally harbouring weapons'.

After serving nearly half of his prison sentence, which he subsequently described as a life-changing experience that persuaded him to 'fight jihad for the sake of Allah', he found himself released. Within weeks he had flown to Istanbul en route to northern Syria, where elements of a well-established Turkey-based Chechen diaspora were already beginning to play an active role in humanitarian and military activities on behalf of the Syrian revolution.[30]

Another Russian speaker to arrive in Syria in mid-2012 was Muslim Margoshvili (better known as Muslim Shishani). Having fought alongside the famed Saudi jihadist Ibn al-Khattab in Chechnya in the mid-1990s and later with Abu Jafar al-Yemeni and Abu al-Walid al-Ghamdi, Margoshvili's extensive jihadist credentials in Russia's North Caucasus, and his previous experience as an officer in the Soviet Union's air defence force in Mongolia, gained him immediate respect in Latakia, when he arrived in the summer of 2012. Shortly thereafter he led the establishment of his own largely Chechen faction, Junud al-Sham.[31]

It was thus the summer of 2012 that marked the initial arrival phase of Russian speakers, largely from the North Caucasus region—commonly though simplistically referred to as 'Chechens'—into Syria. Some like Omar al-Shishani and Muslim al-Shishani had travelled to Syria from their home regions, while many others had come smaller distances, from within Turkey's extensive Chechen diaspora communities. However, it wasn't only 'Chechens' who began arriving in northern Syria in mid-2012. Another contingent that played an early influential role were Libyans.

One such individual was Libyan-born Irish citizen Mahdi al-Harati, who from April to August 2011 had founded and led the well-known Tripoli Brigade from Benghazi into Libya's capital Tripoli during the revolution that successfully toppled Gaddafi. Shortly after the fall of Tripoli to the revolutionary forces (including his powerful brigade), Harati was appointed as deputy commander of the Tripoli Military Council (TMC), which at the time was headed by Abd al-Hakim Belhaj, the former leader of the Libyan Islamic Fighting Group (LIFG), who had spent seven years in the infamous Abu Salim prison in Tripoli after being detained in Bangkok and rendered to Libya by the CIA.

Harati resigned from his post on the TMC in September or October 2011 and, after a proposition from several influential Syrians, began humanitarian work in northern Syria using connections he had established during the Libyan revolution with the Qatari government and other private Gulf-based financiers in Kuwait and Saudi Arabia. His first Syria-related visit took place in November 2011, when he accompanied Belhaj on a 'covert operation' to Istanbul and the Syria–Turkey border to meet with the FSA leadership.[32] After several months of travel in and out of northern Syria and southern Turkey, Harati and his brother-in-law Houssam Najjair led the establishment in April 2012 of his own armed faction, Liwa al-Ummah, based in Maraat al-Numaan in north-west Idlib governorate.[33]

Although not extremist by any means, but perhaps more ideologically aligned with the thinking of the Muslim Brotherhood, the role played by Harati and Liwa al-Ummah in Syria in 2012 was demonstrative of a process whereby the revolution and the anti-government insurgency was becoming steadily more international. Harati brought recent and successful revolutionary experience, and with it he demonstrated the value of organisation, reliable sources of finance and the role that non-Syrians could play in forming an influential armed faction on the ground. It was also an early example of an insurgent organisation with a strong Islamic frame of reference that represented an inherently political organisation with long-term objectives. In an interview with Mary Fitzgerald, for example, a twenty-eight-year-old Syrian Liwa al-Ummah fighter from Homs claimed that Harati's group 'is different from the other brigades in that it is not just fighting the regime, but it is also preparing for after the war. I think it will play a pivotal role now and in the future.'[34] This synthesis of Islam with the virtue of armed jihad in defence against oppression and the intrinsic need for a political vision was of course something that more extremist organisations such as Jabhat al-Nusra represented concretely, but with far more hardline intentions.

By August 2012 Liwa al-Ummah commanded approximately 5,000–6,000 fighters, most of whom were Syrian, but there were many others from Libya, and some from Turkey, Lebanon, Jordan, Iraq and the Gulf.[35] Another similarly sized group at the time was Kataib Ahrar al-Sham, a Syrian Salafist organisation formed in 'the second quarter of 2011'[36] by a core of six Syrians— Hassan Abboud (Abu Abdullah al-Hamawi), Abu Talha al-Ghab, Talal al-Ahmed Tammam, Khaled Abu Anas, Abu Saleh Tahhan and Khubayb al-Shami—that, from the time of its formation perceived itself as not just an armed resistance faction, but rather as an Islamic movement with a concern for social, religious, political, humanitarian and military affairs. It was, however, a quick developer, thanks to its earlier-mentioned funding relationships in Qatar and Kuwait. While clearly founded on conservative Salafist credentials—and containing a number of senior commanders with previous experience in Iraq and in al-Qaeda—it presented itself as a Syrian organisation concerned only with Syrian objectives. This was, however, a matter that would evolve over time.

That the opposition took control of three of Syria's five major border crossings with Turkey (at Bab al-Hawa, Bab al-Salameh and Jarablus) and one of two with Iraq (at al-Bukamal) in mid-July 2012 meant that foreign fighters could now cross into Syria with remarkable ease.

The capture of Bab al-Hawa on 19 July revealed clearly—perhaps for the first time—the strategic impact that jihadists were beginning to exert in battles across parts of northern Syria. A number of insurgent groups played a role in the successful assault. While the lead force was a comparatively moderate faction, Liwa Daraa al-Thowra, Jabhat al-Nusra and two shadowy affiliated units, Majlis Shura al-Mujahideen (MSM) and an unnamed group of Chechens, were prominently involved. Their hardline jihadist influence was visible in several YouTube videos released after the capture of the crossing in which fighters carrying black flags similar to that of the ISI called for the establishment of a caliphate in Syria. On the same day, after crossing the Turkish border near Bab al-Hawa, British journalist John Cantlie and Dutch photographer Jeroen Oerlemans were kidnapped by British fighters probably linked to Majlis Shura al-Mujahideen. During their captivity they were placed in the custody of a foreign fighter cell containing as many as fifteen British nationals.[37] They escaped a week later, and were rescued by a local FSA faction.

While the visible role of Jabhat al-Nusra and other jihadists was most prominent at Bab al-Hawa, they were also present, though on a more peripheral level, at Bab al-Salameh (then controlled by Liwa Asifat al-Shamal),

Jarablus (controlled by Liwa al-Tawhid) and al-Bukamal (controlled by a coalition of tribal forces).

The FSA had long established its senior leadership in refugee camps on the Turkish side of the border, with the full cooperation of Turkish intelligence, while the extensive networks of old smuggling routes had been used to cross into and out of Syria throughout late 2011 and early-to-mid-2012. But with the regime's loss of control over the official crossings from July 2012 onwards, the Syria–Turkey border truly became an open one, and this was leading to increasingly public concern within the opposition's senior leadership over the potential for jihadists to expand their role in Syria yet further. For example, the then chief of the FSA's Supreme Military Council, Brigadier General Mustafa al-Sheikh, told journalist Mike Giglio that 'they [al-Qaeda] are getting bigger and bigger, and day by day, they have more powerful positions inside the country.'[38]

With the Syrian military now employing both helicopter gunships and fighter-jet aircraft and the opposition controlling swaths of territory, including multiple towns and portions of cities which were under siege and daily government artillery fire, the Syrian revolution had transformed into an open civil conflict. The FSA had so far failed to represent more than a signifier of political identity for the many dozens of armed units now operating across the country. In fact, countless groups had begun identifying themselves specifically as independent and not aligned to the FSA, some for ideological reasons and others simply in recognition of the fact that the FSA appeared to be a fatally flawed 'organisation'. Nevertheless, the wider Syrian political opposition—represented broadly at the time by the exiled Syrian National Council—had received general recognition by the 'Friends of Syria' group of nations, but was also struggling to retain a sense of representation inside an increasingly violent Syria.

The fundamental dynamics of the Syrian revolution were therefore evolving significantly in mid-2012. Momentum was growing in favour of the opposition, with increasingly frequent forays being made into central Damascus. The Aleppo insurgency was gaining ground, border crossings were falling away from government control, and the Syrian army was being forced to redeploy forces out of predominantly Kurdish areas of Syria's north-east towards more active frontlines to the west and south—thus introducing the Syrian Kurdish Partiya Yekîtiya Demokrat (PYD) and its armed wing, the Yekîneyên Parastina Gel (YPG) into the conflict fold. Regime army, police and security officers were also continuing to defect in their dozens, while more senior officials were also beginning to abandon Assad on a higher level. In July alone, at least nine high-level officials announced their defections:

- Brigadier General Manaf Tlass, Republican Guard.
- Nawaf al-Fares, ambassador to Iraq and senior tribal leader from Deir ez Zour.
- Abd al-Latif al-Hariri, ambassador to the UAE.
- Khaled al-Ayoubi, chargé d'affaires at the UK embassy.
- Mohamed Hossam Hafez, consul at the Armenian embassy.
- Farouq Taha, ambassador to Belarus.
- Ikhlas al-Badawi, Aleppo Member of Parliament.
- Lamia al-Hariri, envoy to Cyprus and niece of Vice President Farouq al-Sharaa.
- Adnan Silu, former head of the Syrian chemical weapons programme.

Such defections had been compounded on 18 July by the killing of four major regime figures—the defence minister, Dawoud Rajiha; the deputy defence minister and brother-in-law to Assad, Assef Shawkat; National Security Bureau chief Hisham Ikhtiyar; and the assistant to the vice president, Hassan Turkmani—in a bomb attack inside the National Security headquarters in central Damascus's Rawda Square. To say the least, this explosion—the responsibility for which is still a matter of debate—shook things up significantly on both sides.

Amid this fast-developing conflict, a still comparatively small jihadist component was finding its feet. Jabhat al-Nusra had by now established an active presence in Syria's north (in Aleppo, Idlib and Hama), south (in Damascus and Deraa), east (in Deir ez Zour) and centre (in Homs), but had only just begun to mature from being a terrorist group limited to carrying out sporadic urban bombings to an insurgent organisation capable of conducting more sophisticated and sustained campaigns and guerrilla-type operations. It was, however, still an unpopular actor within the Syrian opposition, whose actions were perceived as damaging to the reputation and goals of the popular revolution. In fact, many Syrians at this point insisted that Jabhat al-Nusra was a creation and an agent of the regime, and that its early attacks in Damascus and Aleppo were directly facilitated by Syrian intelligence. Even the Syrian Salafist sheikh Abu Basir al-Tartusi accused Jabhat al-Nusra of working in the interests of the regime and stoking the kind of sectarian rhetoric and perceptions that the regime so hoped to pin onto the opposition.[39]

There was, in that sense, also a war of perceptions emerging in Syria, which was undoubtedly something Jabhat al-Nusra was aware of during its initial months of operation. In fact, it carried out two attacks in June and July 2012 against the Syrian state media, which had been perpetually labelling the entire Syrian opposition as 'terrorist' and part of a 'foreign conspiracy', while presenting its own security force apparatus as honourable in its increasingly brutal and uncompromising fight to subdue the revolt. The 27 June 2012 assault and bombing of the al-Ikhbariya TV headquarters in the village of Drousha outside Damascus, which killed seven, and the 19 July kidnap and 3 August execution of Syrian Arab News Agency (SANA) presenter Mohammed al-Saeed should therefore be read within that context.

Although still in an emergence phase, jihadist groups were beginning to play a more overt role in the evolving conflict in Syria. Jabhat al-Nusra was growing into a movement of potential strategic significance nationwide, and was beginning to operate in coordination with other opposition factions— mainly those with Islamist outlooks—especially in Aleppo. For example, it became prominently involved in joint operations with Kataib Ahrar al-Sham and a coalition of local Aleppo-based Islamist units known as Liwa al-Tawhid throughout August 2012, with a commander of the latter admitting 'good coordination' with Jabhat al-Nusra. Even an FSA spokesman for the Aleppo Revolutionary Council, Abu Feras, told the *Washington Post* at the time that Jabhat al-Nusra fighters who 'fight without fear or hesitation' were regarded 'as heroes' within the opposition.[40] Asked why this shift took place, trainee-dental-surgeon-turned-founding-member of Liwa Jaish al-Muslimeen Amjad Farekh stated simply: 'You are left alone dying and somebody offers you a hand—would you refuse it in order to please the ones who left you alone?'[41]

Meanwhile, as Jabhat al-Nusra's profile was rising, other jihadist groups were also starting to influence local dynamics, especially in the north. For example, after playing a lead role in its capture weeks before, Majlis Shura al-Mujahideen began aggressively exerting its influence around Bab al-Hawa in early August 2012, thereby challenging the positions of several FSA units in the area, including Kataib Farouq al-Shamal, the northern wing of Osama al-Juneidi's increasingly large nationwide Kataib al-Farouq. Inevitably, tensions rose throughout the month, and on 31 August suspected Farouq al-Shamal fighters assassinated Majlis Shura al-Mujahideen's Syrian leader Firas al-Absi (Abu Mohammed al-Shami). This single act sparked a considerable underground conflict between the two groups, which continued well into 2013 and influenced events across northern Syria.

Although more minor in strategic significance, another incident in August 2012 that contributed towards a growing perception of jihadism's ascendancy in Syria was the death of a twenty-four-year-old Chechen in Aleppo. Rustam Gelayev, the son of the noted Chechen commander of the 1990s Ruslan Gelayev, had travelled to Syria in early 2012 from Egypt, where he had been studying Arabic.[42] He ended up fighting for a small unit of Chechen fighters in Aleppo, which at the time was loosely aligned with Jabhat al-Nusra. His death was reported across international media, and, perhaps most importantly, received extensive coverage in Russia and the North Caucasus. More than any other non-Syrian nationality or race, 'Chechens' had already stood out for their emerging role in Syria's conflict in mid-2012, and indeed they had already been responsible for the formation of two significant groups, but Gelayev's death and the attention it aroused in Russia and the North Caucasus almost certainly gave a boost to Chechen recruitment to Syria's cause.

\* \* \*

The period from January to August 2012 had therefore been a formative one for the emergence and early development of a jihadist insurgency in Syria, led from the front by Jabhat al-Nusra. The steady proliferation of armed opposition groups, the arrival of finance and weaponry from abroad and the internationalisation of the crisis itself all presented opportunities for the expansion of jihadist militancy in Syria. Meanwhile, the brutal violence already being visited upon civilian populations in and of itself was a sufficient justification for such organisations and their non-Syrian components to establish a presence and an active role in the revolution. In comparison to many FSA factions, the relative independence of groups such as Jabhat al-Nusra, Kataib al-Muhajireen and Junud al-Sham from specific foreign government agendas (and their expectations) also meant they could act without externally imposed preconditions.

Their greatest source of potential, however, lay in their religiously sourced determination and the previous military and guerrilla experience of much of their senior leaderships. As the conflict in Syria was to continue to escalate in the months to come, this combination of insurgent experience and existential resolve in battle would come to define the fate of Syria's jihadist insurgency.

6

# SEPTEMBER 2012–MARCH 2013

## JABHAT AL-NUSRA RISES

With Jabhat al-Nusra now underlining its newfound role as an effective insurgent organisation in Syria, the FSA was struggling to represent a cohesive opposition structure. This, and the continued divisive impact of competing regional state provision of support to different armed factions, encouraged a process of consistent insurgent group proliferation across Syria.

From October 2012, opposition forces won a series of major strategic victories against regime forces outside Damascus and in the governorates of Idlib, Aleppo, Hasakah and Raqqa. The winter of 2012–13 set the stage for the gradual Islamisation of the northern insurgency, which itself encouraged for the first time tensions between Islamist factions and groups aligned with the FSA name.

Meanwhile, after months of allegations surrounding their role in the conflict, Iran, Hezbollah and foreign Shia militias began emerging as playing active roles in advising, training and fighting inside Syria in support of the Assad regime. A decision was made to establish a nationwide paramilitary force, known as the National Defence Force. In a Palestinian refugee camp south of Damascus, the Popular Front for the Liberation of Palestine—General Command also emerged as a pro-regime force, while the Kurdish Partiya Yekîtiya Demokrat and its armed wing began asserting control in predominantly Kurdish areas in Syria's north-east.

Through late 2012 both Syrian Islamist and foreign jihadist groups continued to increase their prominent role in insurgent operations in Syria and aligning in joint coalitions. Moreover, Syrian Islamist groups coalesced into two large fronts, the Syrian Islamic Liberation Front (SILF) and the more conservative Syrian Islamic Front (SIF). These presented a credible threat to the reputation of the exiled political opposition organisation, the National Coalition of Syrian Revolution and

Opposition Forces, or ETILAF. Jihadists and SIF increasingly began to branch out into the provision of social services and local governance, thereby establishing strong societal foundations.

By early 2013 at least 3,000 foreign fighters had joined the Syrian Jihad and several new jihadist groups had been established, some led by al-Qaeda veterans and former Guantanamo Bay detainees. Jabhat al-Nusra had consolidated its role as a serious strategic actor in Syria and had acquired solid sources of external and internal finance. The capture of Raqqa city in early March 2013 illustrated the strength that Islamists and jihadists had gained in northern Syria, but this brought with it competition and tensions with more moderate factions.

\* \* \*

Al-Qaeda has advanced beyond isolated pockets of activity in Syria and is building a network of well-organized cells ... units are spreading from city to city ... once operating as disparate, disconnected units, the al-Qaeda cells are now communicating and sometimes co-operating on missions, with a command-and-control structure evolving to match more sophisticated operations in places like Iraq and Afghanistan.[1]

This was the assessment of several unnamed US intelligence officials as quoted by the Associated Press in mid-August 2012. Indeed, by this time, 'al-Qaeda'—or, more specifically, Jabhat al-Nusra—had begun to expand into a more organised and coordinated insurgent organisation, carrying out increasingly sophisticated attacks shaped around more refined tactics, strategy and media operations. In Aleppo particularly, it had begun to integrate itself into the wider opposition dynamic, albeit initially through groups with an Islamic frame of reference. Nonetheless, late July and August marked a point of transition for Jabhat al-Nusra in Syria, whereby it was becoming more of an 'opposition' organisation both able and willing to assimilate itself into large-scale opposition offensives.

In this, the period of September 2012 to March 2013 marked Jabhat al-Nusra's comprehensive transformation into one of the most powerful insurgent organisations in Syria. By late 2012 it had become a strategically indispensable actor for the wider opposition, which generally lacked the military power alone to impose serious defeats on the regime's critical military facilities across the country. Moreover, the FSA's structural integrity as a unitary organisation with a single command structure was fast coming into question, both outside and inside Syria. Mounting stories of corruption, intra-opposition rivalries and the emerging, often bitter competition between Saudi Arabia and Qatar as the two most prominent states backing the armed insurgency were playing into the hands of jihadist factions, large and small, whose self-presented independence and internal cohesion was an attractive proposition for many desperate young Syrian men seeking to destroy their repressive regime. That jihadists were also demonstrating superior military capabilities throughout this period only added to this transformative dynamic.

Late 2012 saw the scale and strategic significance of military violence across Syria escalate considerably. While the FSA had demonstrated a localised capacity to capture territory from the regime earlier in the year, many of these victories did not prove sustainable—determinedly brutal Syrian army counter-offensives ordinarily took back lost ground. From September 2012, however, insurgent forces across northern Syria and partially in the east gained a long string of highly significant victories, which placed the regime in an existentially precarious position by early 2013. Almost without exception, all of these victories were won in part due to the frontline role of jihadists—predominantly represented by Jabhat al-Nusra—and by Syrian Salafist groups such as Kataib Ahrar al-Sham.

Early September witnessed two large suicide car bomb-led attacks by Jabhat al-Nusra. The first came on 4 September, when a Syrian fighter, 'Abu Khattab', drove a vehicle loaded with seven tons of explosives towards the Hamdan military airport near al-Bukamal in Deir ez Zour. As the bomb detonated, insurgents from Jabhat al-Nusra, several FSA units and local tribal fighters assaulted the well-defended facility from multiple axes, though the army repelled the attack later that day with the help of targeted airstrikes. Five days later another Jabhat al-Nusra suicide bomber detonated a truck loaded with explosives outside the al-Hayat hospital in Aleppo's Saad al-Ansari district, killing at least thirty people. The hospital had been transformed into a Syrian army position and several checkpoints near the facility and the nearby 7th April Stadium were raided shortly after the truck bomb was detonated. Although neither of these attacks facilitated the actual capture of significant territory, they demonstrated the capacity of groups such as Jabhat al-Nusra—with willing suicide bombers—to impose unpredictable and virtually unavoidable damage on fortified regime positions. This was a unique advantage that jihadists would come to exploit, especially in northern Syria.

While a two-week regime offensive in parts of Damascus had forced increasingly uncoordinated and poorly equipped FSA-led fighters to withdraw from the al-Hajar al-Aswad and al-Qaddam districts on 19 September, opposition positions in the suburb of Jobar were being pressed hard and reports of civilian killings spread. That same day, however, multiple insurgent units including a small contingent of Jabhat al-Nusra militants, assaulted and captured Syria's Tel Abyad border crossing, opposite the Turkish town of Sanliurfa. By now the insurgency as a whole was said to control 80 per cent of Syrian towns lying along the Turkish border,[2] which not only secured the FSA's logistical and supply channels, but crucially provided a reliable route for the ever-increasing numbers of foreign fighters arriving in Turkey determined to join the fight in Syria against the Assad regime. This loss of government control over the northern border definitively boosted the military potential of the northern insurgency, which by extension made it a region where jihadists could benefit most.

Meanwhile, the security of the Lebanese border—which had long been porous anyway—was deteriorating, with multiple reports in September of Syrian aircraft firing on suspected insurgents several kilometres inside Lebanese territory. In this case, Sunni pockets of eastern Lebanon, particularly around the towns of Arsal, Masharih al-Qaa and Jdeidah, were establishing themselves for the opposition as valuable zones for importing black-market weaponry into Syria and exporting wounded fighters to Lebanon for medical treatment. This early phase of destabilisation along parts of the Syria–Lebanon border set the stage for far greater conflict in 2013, which would see Jabhat al-Nusra use the same towns as strategic depth and later as staging grounds for an expansion of operations into Lebanon's interior.

By late September the battle for control over Aleppo, Syria's largest city, had reached a particularly high intensity. The opposition there, which now included a sizeable and powerful jihadist contingent, announced late on 27 September that at 4 p.m. it had launched a 'decisive battle' against regime positions in the city centre, the north, and in the Old City.[3] Again, this proved to be a defining moment for Jabhat al-Nusra's reputation amongst the northern FSA-led opposition. While local Aleppan members of the expanding Liwa al-Tawhid—which followed an ideology akin to the Muslim Brotherhood and enjoyed strong Qatari backing—knew the city well, it was Jabhat al-Nusra fighters and some independent 'Chechens' who gained a reputation for fighting without fear.[4]

There was a less heroic side to their tactics though, as was demonstrated in mid-September when a raid launched together with the FSA's Katibat Salman al-Farisi captured twenty soldiers near Aleppo's al-Saba'a Bahrat roundabout in the Old City. All were subsequently executed with a single shot to the head. Video of their corpses, lined neatly along a pavement, made uneasy viewing for supporters of the opposition, which had quite clearly played a role in committing a war crime alongside jihadist militants. Jabhat al-Nusra claimed responsibility for the incident on 3 October.[5]

October 2012 saw the start of what would prove to be a series of significant insurgent victories centred on large military bases and strategically placed villages and towns across Syria, particularly in the north. On 4 October a coalition of groups led by the FSA-linked Liwa Shuhada Douma seized control of an air defence base in East Ghouta outside Damascus, capturing significant quantities of weaponry and equipment. Two days later multiple insurgent groups—dominated by the FSA's Liwa Qaws al-Nasser but also including small numbers of fighters from the Islamist Suqor al-Sham, Jabhat al-Nusra and Ahrar al-Sham—captured the town of Khirbet al-Joz in the mountainous Jisr al-Shughour region of Idlib governorate. And three days after that, on 9 October, 75 kilometres south-east of Khirbet al-Joz, opposition forces captured the highly strategic town of Maraat al-Numaan, located on the Damascus–Aleppo M5 highway, cutting off the regime's principal supply line between Aleppo and Homs. It had taken only thirty-six hours to capture. To make matters worse, a concerted assault was also launched on 9 October on the connected Wadi al-Deif and Hamadiyeh military bases, not far from Maraat al-Numaan.

While FSA groups had led these three victories in Damascus and Idlib, it was a nearly entirely jihadist force that captured the al-Taana air defence base on 12 October. Located east of Aleppo on the main road to the city of Raqqa, the al-Taana base was captured by a three-group coalition comprising Jabhat al-Nusra, Kataib al-Muhajireen and Harakat al-Fajr al-Islamiyya. This marked perhaps the first significant opposition victory conducted solely by Salafist and jihadist forces.

The least extreme of the three organisations, Harakat al-Fajr al-Islamiyya had been established in Aleppo in early 2012 as a Salafist group led by several former Sednayya detainees, including Abu Hamza, who led the group's Jund al-Rahman Brigade. While a relatively small organisation in October 2012, Harakat al-Fajr al-Islamiyya had distributed its nineteen brigades across Aleppo city and Aleppo's northern, western and eastern countryside, as well as in parts of rural Idlib. Although little was ever known of its leader, Abu Abdullah al-Hakim, its senior commander, Abu Hamza, a well-built Salafist from Aleppo, gained an eminent reputation for his military leadership and strategy.

Syrian Salafist cleric Abd al-Moneim Mustafa Halima—a long-time resident of London who is better known as Abu Basir al-Tartusi—had been shown on video meeting with Harakat al-Fajr al-Islamiyya fighters in August and was subsequently rumoured to have joined the group as an ideologue. However, 'he was not affiliated to any one group, [but] he supported many', according to a senior political official in the Homs-based Liwa al-Haq, who was a close confidante of Hassan Abboud and today is the leading member of Ahrar al-Sham's external political bureau.[6]

While jihadists with an international outlook and Salafists with a Syrian focus were gaining in stature across northern Syria and in parts of the east and in Damascus, another new actor was beginning to emerge, on the other side of the fence. Allegations by opposition activists regarding the arrival of members of the Iranian military and Hezbollah militants had first begun in September 2011, but reached an intensified pitch in early 2012, with claims centring around Zabadani—where the Iranian Revolutionary Guard Corps (IRGC) was rumoured to maintain a military facility, for use in coordinating with Hezbollah in Lebanon, a 29-kilometre drive south-west—and in the Homs border town of al-Qusayr, as well as in Damascus and its reputed Shia shrine at Sayyida Zeinab. While unverified, some reports claimed that Hezbollah secretary-general Hassan Nasrallah had promised 2,000 of his 'special forces' to Assad, should 'foreign' forces infiltrate Syria, while others claimed that Hezbollah's clandestine 'Unit 901' was already active in several of Syria's battle fronts.[7]

These claims began to pick up real credence in September 2012 when the US government imposed sanctions on Hezbollah's Nasrallah for having 'overseen Hezbollah's efforts to help the Syrian regime's violent crackdown on the Syrian civilian population by providing training, advice, and extensive logistical support to the Government of Syria'. The 13 September US Department of the Treasury statement continued:

> Hezbollah has directly trained Syrian government personnel inside Syria and has facilitated the training of Syrian forces by Iran's terrorist arm, the Islamic Revolutionary Guard Corps-Qods Force (IRGC-QF). Also under Nasrallah, Hezbollah has played a substantial role in efforts to expel Syrian opposition forces from areas within Syria and coordinated its support to the Government of Syria with IRGC-QF and senior Syrian government officials. Indeed, under the direction of Nasrallah, Hezbollah since mid-2012 has escalated its support to the Government of Syria.[8]

Three days later, on 16 September, the commander of Iran's IRGC, General Mohammed Ali Jafari, announced unabashedly during a news conference that 'a number of members of the [specialist] Quds Force are present in Syria, but this does not constitute a military presence', suggesting they were acting in an 'intellectual and advisory' role.[9] This was the first official admission that Iranian security officers were in Syria, in any capacity amid the revolution. A further indication of the trajectory of this 'advisory mission' came in Jafari's subsequent claim that 'if Syria came under military attack, Iran would also give military support'. Clearly, Syria was 'under attack' already, so this differentiation appeared to be more diplomatic subtlety than practical policy distinction.

Such semantics meant little in October, when Hezbollah casualties began to hit the news. Hezbollah suffered its first confirmed casualty in Syria on 2 October. In what was subsequently described as a painstakingly planned operation, local FSA fighters killed a senior Hezbollah commander and alleged founding member of the organisation, Ali Hussein Nassif (Abu Abbas) outside the battleground town of al-Qusayr in Homs, 11 kilometres north-east of the Lebanese border. The deaths were confirmed at the time by multiple Hezbollah sources, including official spokesman Ibrahim Moussawi, although Nassif was described as acting in Syria in a non-military capacity— again, a relatively meaningless distinction for the Syrian opposition. Nassif was buried in his home town of Budai the following day, in a funeral procession attended by countless senior Hezbollah officials.[10] Adding to the evidence of Hezbollah's role in Syria, two additional funerals of Hezbollah militants were held elsewhere in Lebanon that day—one of them for thirty-five-year-old Hussein Abd al-Ghani al-Nimr—both of which were aired by the group's official television channel al-Manar.[11]

In its official claim of responsibility for killing Nassif, FSA leader Colonel Riyad al-Asad contended that his forces in Homs governorate had already killed 300 members of Hezbollah and Iranian military outfits around al-Qusayr, although this appeared to be a dramatic exaggeration at the time.

Nonetheless, a defected officer from Syria's feared air force intelligence, who spoke to *The Times* on 7 October, cited information provided to him prior to his defection in August 2012 purporting to confirm that Hezbollah was actively 'providing men and support to the Assad government and currently has about 1,500 members inside Syria'. Twenty-five busloads of these fighters, the officer claimed, had crossed the border into Syria in the summer.[12] That kind of number would make casualties an inevitability.

In a speech eight days later, amid a dramatic flurry of allegations surrounding his organisation's apparent role in Syria, Hezbollah's Nasrallah denied that his forces were 'fighting' there, but admitted that they were active in a string of twenty-three Syrian villages bordering Lebanon that were predominantly inhabited by 30,000 Lebanese Shia nationals.[13] Only a day earlier, however, thirteen Hezbollah militants in military uniforms and armed with light weapons had been captured by the FSA outside Homs. Evidently, Hezbollah had established a sizeable presence inside Syria, and whether this was largely in an advisory capacity or not, the presence of foreign armed men with distinct loyalties to Shia bodies and Syria's Alawite president was a provocation for all of the Syrian opposition, not least jihadists.

There was a simple reason why Assad had begun to turn to his closest allies, Iran and Hezbollah: his security apparatus was suffering from a dangerous shortage of manpower to meet the needs of fighting a growing nationwide insurgency. Before the revolution broke out in early 2011, the Syrian army's total deployable manpower was approximately 295,000 personnel, a considerable number of whom were Sunni, and looked upon in these conflict conditions as potentially unreliable. Loyalist units such as the Fourth, Fourteenth and Fifteenth Mechanized Divisions and the Special Forces Command had been given an unsustainably heavy role in fighting on the conflict's main frontlines since mid-2011 and they needed augmenting.[14]

Not only could Hezbollah and the IRGC—particularly the former—provide supplementary personnel for the Assad regime's offensive military operations, but their high-level of training and experience would be put to use in building a brand new paramilitary force that would play a predominantly defensive role, thereby freeing up the army to go on the offensive. Pro-regime municipalities and city districts had independently established protection militias from early on in the conflict, but the decision was made in Damascus in mid-2012 to centralise this within a 'National Defence Force' (NDF) trained mainly by the IRGC and its Quds Force.

Although not formally established until January 2013, the NDF was preliminarily active through late 2012, with IRGC officers embedded within individual units. As a strictly volunteer force, the NDF immediately gained a reputation within regime circles for its steadfast loyalty to Assad. While of clear benefit to the regime, this ultra-loyalism and the dominance of Alawite and Shia members also encouraged the NDF to become an organisation founded largely on sectarian principles. Again, the emergence of the NDF as a crucial actor in the defence of the regime—and its reputation for corruption and brutality—bolstered the jihadist presentation of the conflict in Syria as a ruthless war 'against' Sunni Islam.

Simply put, while of critical importance in sustaining the survival of the Assad regime, the increasingly clear role of Iran and Hezbollah in advising, training and militarily bolstering pro-Assad forces in late 2012 reinforced whispers that Syria's revolution and civil conflict were becoming increasingly sectarian. This was fuel to the fire for extremists on both sides. Jihadist forums on the Internet exploited this poisonous sectarian narrative on a massive level in order to recruit Sunnis from across the Middle East and from further afield to come and defend their 'brothers and sisters' in Syria—with great effect.

And likewise, networks established in the mid-to-late 2000s across Lebanon, Syria and Iraq to establish Shia militias such as Jaish al-Mahdi, Asaib Ahl al-Haq and Kataib Hezbollah that fought the US occupation in Iraq were revived to defend *their* 'brothers and sisters' against 'terrorist Sunni' militants. For Shia militias, protecting the sacred tomb of Sayyida Zeinab—grand-daughter of the Prophet Muhammad and daughter of Shia Islam's first Imam, Ali—also emerged as a particularly resonant recruitment tool, particularly considering its targeting in a car bombing on 14 June and a motorcycle-borne IED on 31 October. In particular, the job of protecting the shrine soon fell to Kataib Abu al-Fadl al-Abbas, a Shia militia group comprising fighters from Iraq, Lebanon and Syria.

Despite the understandable claims to the contrary from the Syrian opposition, Syria's conflict was gradually adopting a sectarian undertone, of which extremists on both sides were the main benefactors.

As already mentioned, one of the earliest foreign contingents to join the jihad in Syria were 'Chechens' from Russia's restive North Caucasus region. A great many of these recruits arrived via the southern Turkish town of Reyhanlı, from where a smugglers' path across the hills can bring one across the border into the Syrian village of Atmeh in Idlib. From there, a known network of *muhajireen* recruiters took new arrivals to several makeshift training camps in the hills north-east of the village.[15] It was a similar story for other foreign recruits arriving in the Turkish town of Kilis, whose journey took them south towards Azaz in northern Aleppo. After receiving two weeks of training in the use of small arms and rocket-propelled grenades (RPGs), most 'Chechen' recruits turned to Kataib al-Muhajireen, some were drawn south-west towards Junud al-Sham in northern Latakia, and others joined a series of small independent foreign fighter units in Aleppo.

The intense battle for Aleppo in mid-to-late 2012 attracted the majority of new recruits eager for battle, which seemed predominantly the case for 'Chechens' and other non-Syrians with previous militant experience. In a dispatch for *The Guardian* in late September 2012, Ghaith Abdul-Ahad reported on Omar al-Shishani's Kataib al-Muhajireen operating in Aleppo's

University district. In this one report, Ahad reported hearing the unit speaking in Chechen, Tajik, Turkish, French, Arabic and Urdu, with fighters from the North Caucasus, Saudi Arabia, Turkey, Tajikistan, Morocco, Pakistan, Jordan and Iraq—one of the latter being an AQI veteran of the 2004 battle for Fallujah. In comparison to the others, the 'Chechens' were described as 'older, taller, stronger, and wore hiking boots and combat trousers. They carried their weapons with confidence and distanced themselves from the rest, moving around in a tight-knit unit-within-a-unit.'[16] In this one story, a picture was painted of the new emerging insurgent landscape, which was gaining an increasingly international contingent containing and often led by battle-hardened 'Chechens'.

While Kataib al-Muhajireen was becoming a remarkably international faction, including within its ranks a growing portion of European Muslims and converts, it was these 'Chechens' who were assuming and consolidating their leadership of the group. As November began, 'Chechens' were involved in fighting across Aleppo, Idlib, northern Latakia, northern Hama and in western Raqqa. Their growing role, however, was arousing concern in the North Caucasus, where the Imarat Kavkaz (IK), or Caucasus Emirate—a coalition of jihadist factions in the North Caucasus—were fighting Russian and pro-Russian influence. In October the IK's website for the Republic of Dagestan had released a statement declaring it *fardh ayn* (Islamically obligatory) to fight jihad in the Caucasus[17] and in November, IK *emir* Dokka Umarov chided those who he said had betrayed his cause to:

> go out there [Syria] and say there is no Jihad in the Caucasus, that the Jihad has come to an end ... No! There is Jihad in the Caucasus and it is more serious and intense than in Syria. No one renders any assistance or support to the Jihad in the Caucasus ... Dear brothers the Mujahideen, beware of these people. I swear to Allah that for every drop of blood spilled, foreign or our own, not for the sake of Allah, we will answer fully on the Day of Judgment before Allah ... May Allah save us from these mistakes.[18]

While other parts of Umarov's statement made clear his concerns regarding 'Chechens' joining groups suspected to be receiving support from Turkey, Saudi Arabia, Egypt, the US and the UK, it was clear what the underlying message was. Too many Chechens were leaving to join the jihad in Syria, and the battle with Russia over the Caucasus was suffering as a result. Although the latest phase of the North Caucasus insurgency began only in 2009, the conflict there was by late 2012 over eighteen years old. The civil conflict and insurgency in Syria, by comparison, was only a little over a year old. Not only was it new and in a dynamic stage of growth, but Syria in itself presented a unique attraction to jihadists and potential jihadists around the world due to its prophesied role in the end of days.

This was perhaps the first exemplification of how the conflict in Syria and the growth of jihadist militancy there was having an impact upon other jihadist conflict zones around the world; with the exception of Iraq, that is, where the ISI was expanding the scale and scope of its operations at an exponential rate following the US withdrawal in 2010–11. Whether it was becoming a driver of the revolution or not, the emerging perception within the region's Sunni communities that sectarianism was beginning to determine the direction of political policy was benefiting the very ideas that the ISI had been pushing since Zarqawi's leadership of the JTWJ and then AQI in the early to mid-2000s. Indeed, significant portions of Iraq's Sunni community felt very disenfranchised and unrepresented by the central government in Baghdad, where the Shia leadership of Prime Minister Nouri al-Maliki was turning out to be increasingly restrictive and repressive of Sunni influence. By this time, the Sahwa militias in Anbar and other Sunni heartlands had essentially collapsed due to a general failure by authorities in the capital to dispatch their salaries. The ISI fed off the popular Sunni frustrations and bought off the militiamen who had previously been paid to fight against it: the pendulum was swinging in Iraq, again.

By late 2012 the Syrian regime was employing cluster munitions, helicopter gunships and fighter jets in its confrontation with the insurgent opposition and its civilian supporters. By December the Syrian army had even fired short-range unguided Scud ballistic missiles into populated areas. If that was not enough, amid international concern over detected movements of suspected Syrian chemical weapons stockpiles, activists reported an alleged chemical attack by regime forces on the FSA-controlled al-Bayadah district of Homs city on 23 December. At least six people were killed, with local medical officials reporting victims suffering symptoms of nausea, breathing difficulties and delirium.[19] This marked the regime's first alleged chemical attack of the conflict. More were to follow.

If July to September 2012 had proved to be a period when jihadists assumed a more strategically notable role in the overall conflict against the Assad regime, then November and December 2012 was when they began to underline their potential military superiority to other insurgent groups. While the umbrella of the FSA was dramatically larger in scale than any single jihadist organisation in Syria and indeed larger than of all of them combined, Jabhat al-Nusra as a single faction particularly proved in the final eight weeks of 2012 that it could swing the fate of major battles in northern Syria. Meanwhile, larger Syrian Salafist groups—such as Kataib Ahrar al-Sham, Suqor al-Sham, Harakat al-Fajr al-Islamiyya, Liwa al-Islam and the less conservative Liwa al-Tawhid were becoming more dominant altogether. Other smaller jihadist organisations established in northern Syria, such as Majlis Shura al-Mujahideen, Kataib al-Muhajireen and Junud al-Sham, as well as at least a dozen localised and independent *muhajirin* brigades in Aleppo and Idlib were all integrating themselves within their respective wider conflict theatres.

Throughout 30 October and early on 1 November, Jabhat al-Nusra and Liwa Dawud—a large sub-faction of Suqor al-Sham—launched a major assault on three regime checkpoints controlling the entrances to the town of Saraqeb in Idlib governorate. The town, Idlib's second largest, lies on the main highway between Damascus and Aleppo, and had been steadily under attack by the insurgency since late March 2012. The attacks were swift and success-ful, and by 1 November the Syrian army had withdrawn from the town alto-gether, leaving the northern road open towards the valuable Taftanaz air base 17 kilometres away.

While a very meaningful victory for the opposition as a whole, the capture of Saraqeb was tainted by the extra-judicial execution of ten soldiers captured by Jabhat al-Nusra and Liwa Dawud inside the town's main military facility. Speaking after the incident, a local activist claimed the executions were because 'there were only 10 of them, so they could not take the soldiers captive and had to kill them immediately. No trial could be held because the fighting was still going on. This is guerrilla warfare.' The same activist went on to repeat similar concerns that Syrians were expressing across much of the country:

> We have four Salafi groups who are fighting in Idlib province. The biggest group is Jabhat al-Nusra, which has members all over Syria. There is also Ansar al-Sham, the Majlis al-Shura [al-Mujahideen] group, and Suqor al-Sham. These Salafi groups are gaining support in Idlib province as they are well equipped unlike the FSA bri-gades. People also admire their bravery. They are tough fighters and when they get hold of soldiers, they kill them at once. They are getting more powerful and in the future could start forcing people to follow sharia law.[20]

Twenty-four hours later the same forces launched a concerted assault from the south on Taftanaz air base, making use of additional fighters from north of the facility. Also in November Jabhat al-Nusra was responsible for suicide bombings and car bombings in Hama, Damascus, Deraa, Deir ez Zour and

Aleppo. And while Qatar was leading the establishment of the official Syrian opposition body, the Syrian National Coalition of Syrian Revolution and Opposition Forces (ETILAF)—a body at least technically linked organisationally to the FSA—jihadists were playing lead roles in the successful capture of al-Hamdan air base and al-Mayadin artillery base in Deir ez Zour, Base 46 in Aleppo, the Marj al-Sultan helicopter base in Damascus and the strategic Tishrin hydroelectric dam in eastern Aleppo, which had doubled as a regime military base.

The scale and frequency of these victories were both a major shock to the regime and an invaluable confidence boost to participating jihadist forces, which gained significant quantities of weapons and ammunition in each victory.

The conflict's overall level of complexity also continued to rise when Jabhat al-Nusra and several FSA units in southern Damascus began launching raids and assaults into the Palestinian Yarmouk refugee camp. The camp, a sprawling 2-square-kilometre suburb of Syria's capital containing approximately 150,000 people, was run by the pro-Assad Popular Front for the Liberation of Palestine—General Command (PFLP-GC), led by Ahmed Jibril. Jibril had long maintained an alliance with the Assad family, and tensions in Yarmouk had steadily been rising since mid-2011. Increasing numbers of Yarmouk's inhabitants were expressing their support for the revolution, and thus their opposition to the PFLP-GC's stance. Through mid-2012 regime supporters claimed that Jabhat al-Nusra had begun recruitment in the camp and was using it for planning attacks elsewhere in the city. Meanwhile, the FSA was also making inroads within Yarmouk, recruiting young Palestinians to join the fight elsewhere in Damascus. From early November 2012 Jabhat al-Nusra and an emerging unit of pro-revolution Palestinians known as Liwa al-Asifa had begun armed actions against the PFLP-GC and Syrian army positions in the camp's periphery. After a steady escalation in fighting, the PFLP-GC had been expelled from the camp on 15 December, and Ahmed Jibril had fled to the pro-regime stronghold of Tartous on Syria's western coast.

Meanwhile, by late 2012 the Kurdish autonomist PYD and its armed wing, the YPG (and its female wing, the Yekîneyên Parastina Jin (YPJ)) had consolidated their hold of Kurdish-dominated areas in northern Aleppo and in the north-eastern al-Hasakah governorate. The PYD is organisationally affiliated to the widely designated terrorist organisation the Partiya Karkerên Kurdistani (PKK), and the nature of its relationship with the Assad regime was at the time highly contentious. While it had consistently expressed opposition to the repression of civilians since the outbreak of revolution in early 2011, it had also been highly critical of the opposition itself. When Syrian armed forces conducted an organised withdrawal from much of al-Hasakah in mid-July 2012 to reinforce positions in Damascus—which was facing a concerted insurgent offensive—the PYD's immediate and peaceful assumption of power raised many eyebrows. Although the PYD had agreed with the less hardline Kurdish National Council (KNC) to jointly administer Syrian Kurdish territory, the PYD and the YPG were immediately the dominant force in the area.

On 8 November, after several months of growing tensions, several small FSA factions, Jabhat al-Nusra and a smaller jihadist unit known as Ghurabaa al-Sham—named after Abu al-Qaqaa's movement in Aleppo in the 2000s—began an assault on the Syrian Kurdish border town of Ras al-Ayn in northwestern al-Hasakah. The town was still largely controlled by the Syrian army, although the PYD had established somewhat of a shadow authority since August. A week later Jabhat al-Nusra and Ghurabaa al-Sham, who were the dominant forces in the operation, had captured all army positions and forced a full regime withdrawal, leaving themselves and the YPG in place.

As part of its broader security policy, and in an attempt to prevent the jihadist offensive from expanding further into Kurdish territory, the YPG had spent the first week of fighting in Ras al-Ayn seizing control of towns situated on the main roads leading into and out of the town. Having long had its objectives for Kurdish rights and political autonomy repressed, the YPG had suddenly been provided with an opportunity, but it found itself in al-Hasakah stuck between the regime and a jihadist-heavy opposition.

On 19 November, four days after capturing Ras al-Ayn, Jabhat al-Nusra and Ghurabaa al-Sham began attacking the YPG inside the town. This was the start of a month of bitter fighting, with neither side forcing a definitive defeat upon the other. Eventually a ceasefire was agreed, and from 17 December the fighting stopped. However, the agreement had been largely negotiated between the FSA and the YPG, and both Jabhat al-Nusra and Ghurabaa al-Sham had invested less in the deal.

Although neither side subsequently met the main condition of full withdrawal from Ras al-Ayn, the ceasefire did manage to hold, and several joint Jabhat al-Nusra–YPG checkpoints were even created on the town's periphery. Nonetheless, tension remained between the jihadists and the Kurds, and the fight for Ras al-Ayn was not yet over.

With two additional elements to the conflict now introduced—the Palestinians and the Kurds—the situation in Syria had reached a new level of complexity. To add to this, the 'FSA' had virtually ceased to exist as an organisation, and in its place were hundreds of largely autonomous 'rebel' units across the country, many of which retained the FSA label but had little or no command-and-control relationship with the Turkey-based FSA leadership.

Within this labyrinthine web of insurgency and multifaceted civil conflict, jihadists were growing faster than any other portion of the opposition. But with so many actors involved and multiple intensive battlefronts now active across the country, Jabhat al-Nusra chose in November and December 2012 to begin establishing tacit localised alliances and 'military operations rooms' with other insurgent factions, including the FSA. Ordinarily, a jihadist organisation anywhere else in the world would balk at the idea of forming such pacts with 'nationalists', but Jabhat al-Nusra in particular was playing a long game, implementing the advice of theorists such as Abu Musab al-Suri and ensuring that the jihad was gradually introduced and integrated into local society.

The first such agreement was signed on 19 November, when Jabhat al-Nusra and at least thirteen other Aleppo-based factions—most with an Islamic frame of reference—rejected the establishment of the ETILAF in Doha and expressed their intent to form an Islamic state in Syria:

> We are representatives of the fighting formations in Aleppo and we declare our rejection of the conspiratorial project, the so-called national alliance ... We have unanimously agreed to urgently establish an Islamic state.[21]

Other than Jabhat al-Nusra, the signatories to the statement contained several familiar faces, including Kataib Ahrar al-Sham and Harakat al-Fajr al-Islamiyya. There was also the dominant Aleppo coalition Liwa al-Tawhid, which still identified itself as loyal to the FSA cause. Smaller Islamist units such as Liwa Halab al-Sahaba al-Islami, Liwa Dar al-Ummah and Kataib al-Islam also signed the statement, along with at least six other FSA-oriented groups. In many respects this was an indication of the ideological shift that was taking place in northern Syria, whereby groups had begun to adopt and embrace an increasingly overt Islamic foundation. However, in many cases this was primarily motivated by the failure of the 'official' Syrian opposition—exiled in Turkey—to muster up a genuinely meaningful resistance to the regime in Damascus. The horrific brutality of the fighting and the repression being meted out by regime forces also encouraged a turn towards religion.

That Kofi Annan's 'action group' of international states had met in Geneva in June 2012 and come up with a 'communiqué' that had resulted in little to nothing five months later had lent further impetus to those fighting on the ground. And while the 'FSA' was failing, jihadists were gaining the upper hand.

Nine days after the Aleppo statement—which was confusingly reversed by some signatories on 20 November, before being reinstated by others—Jabhat al-Nusra led the formation of another 'alliance' in Deir ez Zour. This one was clearly structured around unifying ten factions' military efforts in Syria's east and dedicating their efforts towards establishing governance by *sharia*. In addition to Jabhat al-Nusra, this alliance comprised smaller Islamist groups such as Katibat Jabhat *al-Da'wah* wa'l-Jihad, Katibat Jund al-Aziz, Kataib al-Ansar, Kataib al-Abbas, Liwa La Ilaha Ila Allah and Kataib al-Sa'iqa.

Such inter-insurgent unity and coordination was a trend spreading across Syria and, despite often vast ideological differences, moderate nationalist FSA groups were coming together with transnationally focused jihadists to fight 'in the same trench'. As one FSA leader explained:

> We had only one objective back then: topple the regime. That was all that mattered. As long as they [jihadists] wanted the same, then they were with us. They were brave and committed fighters and we needed that.[22]

By early December 2012 Jabhat al-Nusra had claimed responsibility for nearly 600 attacks across Syria since its first activities in November 2011,[23] with the vast majority of those having been conducted from the summer of 2012 onwards. It was clearly a fast-growing organisation with a nearly Syria-wide operational reach. Maintaining such an effort required substantial finance, and considering that Jabhat al-Nusra's mother organisation the ISI was undergoing its own strategy of recovery and re-expansion across the border in Iraq, Jabhat al-Nusra had begun seeking out additional sources of money in Syria.

Since its birth in Syria in mid-to-late 2011, Jabhat al-Nusra had sought to exploit Al-Qaeda's regional financial support networks in order to ensure that, at the very least, it remained financially viable with or without the ISI's support. In addition to the many Al-Qaeda financiers supporting its operations from the Gulf who would be designated by the US government and United Nations in subsequent months and years, Jabhat al-Nusra also began seeking a new source of funding, namely oil.

Starting in November 2012, Jabhat al-Nusra began shaping its offensive operations in the eastern oil-rich governorate of Deir ez Zour towards not only defeating the regime, but towards capturing immensely valuable oil fields. On 3 November, for example, Jabhat al-Nusra and several tribally based insurgent factions captured the large al-Ward oilfield near al-Mayadin—the first time any Syrian opposition group had seized energy assets in the conflict.[25] A month later Syria's armed opposition controlled 'three oilfields and a gas plant' in Deir ez Zour. Perhaps unsurprisingly—especially given the proximity to Iraq and its need for finance—Jabhat al-Nusra had been involved in capturing all four facilities.[26]

While Jabhat al-Nusra and other genuinely 'jihadist' organisations were now playing a frontline role in major opposition victories across northern and eastern Syria, larger and more institutionalised Syrian Salafist and Islamist groups were becoming the truly dominant players on the ground. Not only were they large in terms of manpower and well organised, these groups enjoyed reliable and significant channels of backing from supporters in the Gulf. In particular, their growth towards overshadowing the role of more moderate FSA-aligned factions was defined by their opposition to the Western world's designation of ETILAF and its affiliated Supreme Military Council (SMC) as the 'legitimate' representatives of the opposition. By late 2012 these bodies were increasingly distrusted inside Syria's opposition on the ground, due to their perceived distance and detachment from the realities of the suffering being felt inside besieged towns and cities and on the battlefield.

As such, many of these larger groups began coalescing into two official nationwide coalitions. The first, and less hardline, of the two was established in September 2012. Known as the Syrian Islamic Liberation Front (SILF), this coalition contained approximately twenty individual groups and was led by Suqor al-Sham *emir* Ahmed Eissa al-Sheikh—a former Sednayya detainee. In its founding statement the SILF framed itself as an Islamist coalition determined to establish 'a state with Islamic reference' and willing to maintain 'brotherly relations' with all groups, including the FSA. Moreover, several senior SILF leaders retained seats on the Turkey-based SMC, including Ahmed Eissa al-Sheikh, Osama al-Juneidi and 'Abd al-Qader Saleh.

At the point of its formation the SILF probably commanded a total of roughly 30,000 fighters across Syria—perhaps a third of the entire insurgency. Within its umbrella the SILF contained major names, such as Suqor al-Sham, Liwa al-Islam, Liwa al-Tawhid and Kataib al-Farouq.

If that was the first major statement of Islamist expansion, then the formation of the Syrian Islamic Front (SIF) two months later underlined the trajectory of the insurgent opposition inside Syria. On 21 December, after two or three months of drawn-out negotiations, Kataib Ahrar al-Sham announced the establishment of the SIF as a coalition of eleven predominantly Salafist factions, which included Aleppo's Harakat al-Fajr al-Islamiyya and Abu Adnan al-Zabadani's Kataib Hamza bin 'Abd al-Mutallab.

Ahrar al-Sham had earlier been involved in the formation negotiations for the SILF, but removed itself from the process in late August due to political differences. In many respects, while the SILF remained a largely military movement but with a more conservative Islamic foundation, the SIF aimed to be a social movement with a military arm, as then spokesman Talal Bazerbashi (Abd al-Rahman al-Suri) explained in the founding statement:

> It is a comprehensive Islamic front, representing Islam as a religion, a creed, a path, and a conduct ... To realize its goals, the Front relies on many different means. The military movement aims to overthrow the regime and establish security. The civil movement follows various paths—political, missionary, educational, relief, and humanitarian—within the confines of sharia rulings.[27]

This humanitarian and social side of the SIF's activities was made clear in the video announcing its formation, which included footage of the SIF's Maktab al-Ighatha (Office of Relief) paving roads, baking bread and preparing food for the poor, providing children's education, and other *da'wa* activities. Consequently, the video included clips proclaiming the role played by financial and aid donations from Turkish Islamist charity İnsan Hak ve Hürriyetleri ve İnsani Yardım Vakfı (IHH) and Qatar-based Qatar Charity (QC).[28]

Despite its conservative Salafist outlook, the SIF also maintained a marginal presence within the FSA-linked SMC. For example, the leader of Homs-based Liwa al-Haq, Abd al-Rahman Soueiss, had an SMC council seat, and even Ahrar al-Sham had attended the conferences in the Turkish city of Antalya in December 2012 that formed the SMC itself.[29]

Taken together, the formation of the SILF and SIF in late 2012 also provided an improved opportunity for Jabhat al-Nusra and other more localised jihadist factions to continue their process of integration into wider inter-factional operations against the regime. With Syrian Salafists on the rise, jihadists stood only to benefit.

It was within this context and perhaps also because of it that the US government designated Jabhat al-Nusra as an alias of AQI, and therefore as a terrorist organisation, on 11 December 2012:

> Al-Nusrah has sought to portray itself as part of the legitimate Syrian opposition while it is, in fact, an attempt by AQI to hijack the struggles of the Syrian people for its own malign purposes. AQI emir Abu Du'a [Abu Bakr al-Baghdadi] is in control of both AQI and al-Nusrah.[30]

Intriguingly, the official US designation ended with something fairly unusual—what appeared to all intents and purposes to be a statement directed to the Syrian people, rather than explicitly focused on the designation of a terrorist organisation:

> The violent, sectarian vision of al-Nusrah is at odds with the aspirations of the Syrian people, including the overwhelming majority of the Syrian opposition, who seek a free, democratic, and inclusive Syria ... Extremism and terrorist ideology have no place in a post-Asad Syria, and all responsible Syrians should speak out against al-Qa'ida and other extremist elements.[31]

It seemed at the time that the designation of Jabhat al-Nusra—while clearly an entirely legitimate act—had been timed as a last-gasp attempt to weaken an actor that was beginning to outplay and undermine those the USA wanted to succeed. US intelligence had known what Jabhat al-Nusra represented a long time earlier than December 2012, so the question remains, why did it take a year to announce the designation?

The timing may or may not have been politically influenced, but whatever the matter, the designation and the diplomatic message to the Syrian people did not have a positive impact on the ground. Three days later a dominant theme of Friday protests across the country was shaped around the slogan 'We are all Jabhat al-Nusra'.[32] Even the then president of ETILAF, Moaz al-Khatib, condemned the designation: 'The decision to consider a party fighting the regime as a terrorist party needs to be reviewed,' he told a Friends of Syria meeting in Morocco.[33] Meanwhile, even FSA officials were telling international media that Jabhat al-Nusra accounted for 7.5–9 per cent 'of the Free Syrian Army', representing an approximate 6,000–10,000 fighters nationwide, and was in the midst of 'a high rate of growth'.[34] It seemed, therefore, that Jabhat al-Nusra's military superiority and relative ideological pragmatism had seen it accepted into the broader opposition fold, at least for now.

As the winter struck hard in Syria in December 2012 and January 2013, UN secretary-general Ban Ki-moon exclaimed that the conflict had reached 'appalling heights of brutality', while Kofi Annan's replacement as UN peace envoy, Lakhdar Brahimi, warned of Syria's potential to become a 'failed state'.[35] Insurgent operations were continuing apace, with Jabhat al-Nusra, Majlis Shura al-Mujahideen and Kataib al-Muhajireen capturing the last remaining Syrian army base in western Aleppo, at Sheikh Suleiman, on 10 December. Inside Aleppo city, meanwhile, the insurgency was also on the offensive, with Liwa al-Tawhid leading the 16 December capture of the Army College, during which as many as 150 soldiers defected to the opposition. A week later, Aleppo International Airport had been encircled, and planes were ordered to cease commercial operations on 22–23 December due to a brief 'no-fly zone' imposed by Jabhat al-Nusra—bolstered by its fleet of pick-up-truck-laden anti-aircraft guns and a small inventory of man-portable air-defence systems (MANPADS) acquired by affiliated foreign fighter units such as Kataib al-Muhajireen.

Fortified by greater numbers of fighters, closer allies and an expanded budget thanks to the control and illicit sale of crudely refined oil from Deir ez Zour on a burgeoning internal black market, Jabhat al-Nusra exploited its dominant position in Aleppo to expand, but this time on a social level.

Like the Salafist group Kataib Ahrar al-Sham, Jabhat al-Nusra's ultimate aim in Syria was not only to militarily confront the *nusayri* (a derogatory term for Alawite) regime, but also to govern (i.e. control) the population and to implement *sharia* law. More than anywhere in Syria, Jabhat al-Nusra had integrated itself most successfully in Aleppo, and this was therefore the first test site for its Qism al-Ighatha, or Department of Relief.

Starting in mid-December, Jabhat al-Nusra took control of flour production and distribution in opposition-controlled districts of Aleppo city and set a fixed price for the sale of bread of 15 lira (then approximately $0.21).[36] 'In some areas, this was less than half what the bakeries had been charging earlier in the year,' said one Liwa al-Tawhid member, who explained that before Jabhat al-Nusra took control—'very forcefully, in some cases'[37]—local FSA brigades were using food as a source of income and were also given priority over short supplies, often leaving civilians to queue for several days.[38] With four grain compounds under its control and the entire distribution network under its management and protection, Jabhat al-Nusra generally ensured a more affordable and efficient provision of this staple food product to civilians during the 2012–13 winter.

Through a growing reputation for honesty and a lack of corruption, Jabhat al-Nusra gained a significant boost in Syrian recruits throughout the winter, especially in Aleppo. While these new fighters received religious and military instruction like all other potential new members before them, many were subsequently drafted into the relatively new Islamic police force established in Aleppo city in November 2012. This force was a crucial component within the al-Hay'a al-Sharia (*sharia* authority), which Jabhat al-Nusra had established with Kataib Ahrar al-Sham, Liwa al-Tawhid, Liwa al-Fatah and Harakat al-Fajr al-Islamiyya. Led by Sheikh Hassan Kirari and headquartered in an old hospital in the city's Qadi Askar district (later moved to a shopping mall in the al-Shaar district), al-Hay'a al-Sharia consisted of twelve *qadis* (or judges) who set out to implement *sharia* law across the city. However, it would come to struggle to expand into all opposition areas, with the districts of Ansari, Mashhad and Salah ad Din remaining largely under the judicial authority of the more secular-leaning Unified Judicial Council.[39]

Nevertheless, the Authority did lead to an at least perceived reduction in crime and localised corruption. As an institution, it also attracted external funding from Gulf donors, who supported the idea of *sharia* being introduced to Syria's largest city. Naturally, the Authority also gave Jabhat al-Nusra and Islamists in general a significant boost in influence across the city. This wasn't always used in an impartial manner, however, as for example when the Authority turned against Ghuraaba al-Sham and used corruption as a guise for declaring war against it as an organisation in May 2013.[40]

As 2013 began, Jabhat al-Nusra had internally consolidated itself as a 'complete' jihadist organisation. It had either cemented or was building military supremacy across its five primary provincial strongholds: in Aleppo, where it commanded approximately 2,000 fighters; in Idlib, where it commanded approximately 3,000; in Deir ez Zour, roughly 2,000; in Deraa, roughly 1,000; and in Damascus, roughly 1,000,[41] and had begun to operate on a social level, introducing *sharia*, providing humanitarian relief and offering *da'wa* (religious outreach). On an individual basis, some of these activities were complemented or assisted by other jihadist factions, and sometimes by members of Syrian Salafist groups.

Structurally, Jabhat al-Nusra was an extremely tightly controlled organisation, with an intense level of secrecy surrounding its senior leadership. It operated a pyramidal leadership command, with Jolani at the top, followed by a *majlis al-shura* (consultative council), and a series of specified councils responsible for determining and managing policies on a national level: war (*majlis al-askari*), *sharia*, fundraising, *da'wa*, media and public relations. On a provincial level, Jabhat al-Nusra structured itself to maintain one *emir* for each province of operation, with specific individuals additionally assigned to manage *sharia*, military and political (i.e. inter-group) relations. Below this provincial leadership was a series of military *emir*s, each responsible for their respective individual regions or municipalities. Throughout this pyramid structure, each level—local, regional, provincial, national—communicated and answered along a clearly delineated reporting structure.

Militarily, Jabhat al-Nusra maintained dozens of *kataib* (battalions) across the country, each commanded by a *qa'id* (leader), who was generally free to determine his unit's own operational decisions, but who took strategic orders from his provincial *emir*. More often than not each *qa'id* would retain a base, or operations room, from where he commanded and coordinated his forces on a day-to-day basis.

In terms of religious leadership, Jabhat al-Nusra also maintained a *qadi al-a'am* (grand judge), who sat on the *majlis al-shura* alongside Jolani and approximately ten other senior leaders. The *qadi al-a'am* was responsible for determining the Islamic legitimacy of Jabhat al-Nusra's existing and planned actions, as well as for managing the organisation's provincial *sharia* leaders, known as *dabet al-shari'i* (religious commissioners),[42] and the group's various internal *sharia* courts. Once the al-Hay'a al-Sharia was established in Aleppo, the *qadi al-a'am* was also responsible for ensuring its perceived religious legitimacy and the accuracy of its rulings.

Though it clearly had an interest in maximising its recruitment, Jabhat al-Nusra's system for managing this crucial aspect of its operations was strict and tightly managed. As Abu Adnan, a Jabhat al-Nusra *sharia* official in Aleppo explained in late 2012:

> We pay a great deal of attention to the individual fighter, we are concerned with quality, not quantity ... We are Syrians ... we also have foreigners who came from other countries, but that is because the wounds in the Arab lands are the same wound, and the oppression is the same oppression.[43]

Generally, in order to apply to join Jabhat al-Nusra, any potential recruit must first have obtained *tazqiyya* (a personal recommendation) from an existing member of Jabhat al-Nusra or a sufficiently respected individual affiliated to the organisation. However, it was possible for some non-Syrian nationals arriving in Syria without any insurgent group affiliation to be taken into training camps run by smaller independent *muhajirin* brigades, from which you could acquire *tazqiyya* for entry (or promotion) into the Jabhat al-Nusra recruitment process. Should one's *tazqiyya* be accepted, a new recruit generally received approximately six to eight weeks of religious and military training, with the former normally comprising a two-to-three-hour lecture every evening, after a day of physical and military instruction, which itself was apportioned according to the *al-fajr* (dawn), *al-zuhr* (midday), *al-asr* (afternoon) and *al-maghrib* (sunset) prayers, with the final *al-isha* prayer coming after the religious lecture and before sleep.[44]

Upon successfully 'graduating' from training, the final stage of a new Jabhat al-Nusra recruit's process was to pledge *bay'a* (oath of allegiance) to Jabhat al-Nusra leader Jolani. Upon doing so, the explicitly Islamic nature of this oath makes that individual unconditionally loyal to the organisation and its leadership. One particularly important consequence of the totality of this loyalty is the extent to which it reinforced the extreme level of secrecy within Jabhat al-Nusra, thereby helping to protect the internal security of the organisation from external threat.

Despite the inevitable de-escalation of conflict across Syria in the harsh winter months of January and February 2013, the insurgency as a whole maintained intense pressure on regime positions across the country. In Idlib and Aleppo in particular, the dramatic scale of gains by Islamist-led insurgent forces continued. On 11 January the SIF gained a major publicity boost when Jabhat al-Nusra and three of its component groups—Kataib Ahrar al-Sham, Harakat al-Fajr al-Islamiyya and Jama'at al-Talia al-Islamiyya—led the capture of the Taftanaz air base in Idlib. This victory represented a very significant loss of resources for the regime, which ceded between fifteen and twenty helicopters (approximately 20 per cent of total pre-war inventory) and a very large quantity of heavy weaponry, rockets and ammunition, not to mention the base itself—the largest captured by the opposition so far.

While the capture of Taftanaz was an operation carried out by the aforementioned groups, several FSA units had been involved in the assault and siege that had preceded it, including members of Suqor al-Sham and Kataib al-Farouq—both key members of the SILF and then loosely FSA-aligned. Moreover, the SMC and its then chief of staff, Selim Idriss, had been actively involved in planning operations there.[45] As such, while the fall of the base was ultimately a victory for the entire opposition, the final phases underlined the vital role played by jihadists in spearheading successful final assaults. Following Taftanaz's fall, coalitions of insurgent groups, comprising members of the SILF, SIF, FSA and Jabhat al-Nusra, began an escalated campaign of offensives targeting other regime air bases in the northern region, namely Menagh, Neirab and Kweiris, all in Aleppo. This clearly added up to a strategy of countering the regime's one remaining major military advantage—its airpower—which was not only indiscriminately killing dozens of civilians every day, but was also the biggest barrier to sustained control of open territory for the insurgency.

Within the same period, and very much linked to this now-established insurgent focus on besieging large fixed targets such as bases, Jabhat al-Nusra announced in mid-January that it had designed and begun to manufacture artillery rockets with a range of approximately 8 kilometres. Known as the Faysal-1 and Faysal-2, these relatively simple unguided rockets and their makeshift launchers could be launched from within urban or rural areas and oriented towards large targets such as military bases. Being relatively inexpensive to produce, it was rockets such as the Faysal that kept pressure on such large targets while a more expansive ground assault could be planned.

By late January Jabhat al-Nusra had fallen out, and renounced all links, with Majlis Shura al-Mujahideen after Jabhat al-Nusra had been accused of involvement in the 11 January assassination by a Tunisian jihadist in Sarmada, Idlib of Thaer Waqqas—the Kataib al-Farouq commander widely blamed for murdering Firas al-Absi on 31 August 2012.

Meanwhile, as Jabhat al-Nusra had initiated military operations in Latakia and was playing a lead role in a major offensive on Idlib city, the SIF released its seven-page political charter, in which it called for a 'civilized Islamic society in Syria, ruled by the law of God'. Unsurprisingly, 'democracy' was forbidden as a man-made concept granting man the right to rule over God's law. Nevertheless, the charter did express support for *shura* (consultation) as a method of determining wise policy and making clear that while 'Islamic sharia cannot be put to the vote ... We separate between voting to select the best among candidates, and voting on the sovereignty of sharia; the first is acceptable to us, as long as it is regulated by the sharia, but the second is of course not acceptable.'[46]

Intriguingly, the SIF charter gained the quick approval of a number of prominent Salafist ideologues, including the Jordan-based Iyad al-Qunaybi (a consistent Jabhat al-Nusra advocate) and Abu Basir al-Tartusi,[47] who was still travelling in and out of Syria, presumably via his home in London.

Meanwhile, as Croatian weaponry purchased and provided by Saudi Arabia to several core moderate FSA factions had begun to arrive in Syria, Jabhat al-Nusra launched its first major attack in the southern Quneitra governorate bordering the Israeli Golan (involving two near-simultaneous suicide car bombings) on 25 January. Both were developments of significant importance, but for different reasons and with different outcomes.

The externally provided weaponry was immediately evident to weapons specialists monitoring the conflict in Syria, with FSA fighters suddenly operating M60 recoilless guns, RPG-22s, M79 Osas and RBG-6 grenade launchers—none of which had ever been stocked by the Syrian military. The weapons themselves proved moderately valuable to the recipient groups, especially in neutralising army tanks in urban environments such as Deraa and Damascus, but the real impact at the time was in the statement the weapons' arrival in Syria made: finally, a foreign state had taken the bold step of sending potentially meaningful weaponry to the moderate opposition. With that being said, that impact was reduced six weeks later, when Kataib Ahrar al-Sham fighters were seen operating RBG-6s and M79 Osas in Hama on 1 March.[48] Two weeks after that, Jabhat al-Nusra posted images of its fighters using an M79 Osa in al-Sahweh, Deraa in mid-February and an M60 recoilless rifle in Busra al-Harir, Deraa on 2 March.[49] As subsequently became clear, the weapons had been both sold and shared between their original recipients and groups on the most Islamist end of the ideological spectrum.

Meanwhile, Jabhat al-Nusra's major assault on the headquarters of Syrian military intelligence in Quneitra on 25 January was a brazen indication of its new reach and a warning to Israel of the proximity that jihadists in Syria had now achieved. As Syria's historical frontline with Israel, the governorate of Quneitra was heavily militarised, with countless military facilities dotted across the hilly terrain overlooking the Golan, many containing some of Syria's most modern military hardware. Rumours were also widespread that Russian military intelligence maintained top-secret listening posts in Quneitra, so all in all, the region's security was a delicate matter.

By the beginning of February Kataib Ahrar al-Sham had expanded in scale yet further by announcing its *ittihad indimaji* (union or merger) with three SIF members, Harakat al-Fajr al-Islamiyya, Jama'at al-Talia al-Islamiyya and Kataib al-Iman al-Muqatila, and renaming itself Harakat Ahrar al-Sham al-Islamiyya (later, Ahrar al-Sham). Overnight this new movement, which was led by Hassan Abboud and which had long maintained particularly close relations with Jabhat al-Nusra, had become the largest insurgent group in Syria, numbering at least 15,000 fighters across the country. Its considerable size and then sustainably large sources of financial backing, mainly from private bodies in the Gulf—centred particularly in Kuwait and Qatar—meant that Jabhat al-Nusra's relationship with Ahrar al-Sham became a mutually beneficial one.

In fact, although Ahrar al-Sham appeared to have no 'official' organisational relationship with al-Qaeda, it did contain within its senior leadership a number of individuals with previous experience within al-Qaeda or its circle of associates. The most notable example was Mohammed al-Bahaiya, who was more commonly known as Abu Khaled al-Suri. Born in the early 1960s, Abu Khaled became involved in the Syrian Muslim Brotherhood-linked al-Talia al-Muqatila in the late-1970s and early 1980s, during which he became a close acquaintance of Abu Musab al-Suri. After the Hama Massacre of 1982 both men fled Syria, and by the 1990s they were involved in various jihad-related activities in Afghanistan. Though there is no evidence to suggest that Abu Khaled al-Suri was ever an official member of al-Qaeda, he appears to have at the very least played a prominent role as a facilitator in the late 1990s and early 2000s. Prominent Al-Qaeda figures have also spoken of his role in international activities with particularly high regard.

Following the March 2004 bombings in Madrid, a Spanish intelligence investigation found evidence suggesting that Abu Khaled—through his contact with Spain-based Syrian al-Qaeda official Imad Yarkas—was 'linked through personal contacts and money transfers to the terror cell' responsible for the attacks.[50] These contacts included Abu Khaled's brother-in-law, Mohammed Galeb Kalaje Zouaydi, and one of his employees, Ghasoub al-Abrash Ghalyoun.[51] Moreover, prior to the 2004 attacks, Spanish judicial officials involved in an investigation of Al-Jazeera journalist Tayseer Allouni's alleged links to al-Qaeda told the *New York Times* in December 2003 that Abu Khaled was

> an intermediary between the top Qaeda leadership in Afghanistan and elements of the network in Spain and Britain. In the late-1990s, [Abu Khaled] and his family lived for a time in Istanbul. 'He is the person who was totally trusted by many different people in the various countries and was able to coordinate and transmit orders from bin Laden'... [Abu Khaled is] also being investigated for helping to finance an unsuccessful plot in 1997 to kill the prime minister of Yemen.[52]

After the 9/11 attacks and the US-led invasion of Afghanistan nothing was heard from Abu Khaled, although Syrian Salafists and several former Sednayya detainees have claimed separately to this author that he had been held in the prison through the late 2000s after being rendered to Syria by the CIA[53]— most likely with Abu Musab al-Suri in 2005. 'Abu Khaled was released in the first few months of the revolution,' confirmed one senior member of Ahrar al-Sham's political bureau.[54] A story still only whispered about within Syria's Salafist and jihadist circles says that Abu Musab and Abu Khaled were presented with an offer from Syrian intelligence in June 2011: one of them could be released, while the other would remain indefinitely in detention in Sednayya. 'Abu Musab, may God bless him, secretly made a deal for Abu Khaled's release before he could do anything,' said one former prisoner, who rejected subsequent media claims that Abu Musab was also released.[55]

Abu Khaled immediately made his presence known within the developing Salafist circles at the time, linking up with several founding members of Ahrar al-Sham in Idlib and Hama. But he did not emerge publicly in Syria until May 2013, when al-Qaeda leader Zawahiri named him in a secret letter as his 'delegate' in Syria. He was at the time, however, a senior leader within Ahrar al-Sham and a virtual right-hand man to its leader Hassan Abboud. In fact, through this author's personal contact with Abboud from 2012 onwards, Abu Khaled appeared more of a mentor; and when questioned on Abu Khaled's links to al-Qaeda, Abboud was often terse in his response, as in December 2013: 'Abu Khaled neither is nor ever was affiliated to Al-Qaeda. He is within Ahrar as a Syrian and as a Muslim, not ever as a representative of Al-Qaeda!'[56] A month later, in January 2014, Hassan Abboud added that Abu Khaled 'was never even pre-informed of his appointment as delegate [to Zawahiri], but in reality, he never served as [Zawahiri's] delegate, even though it had been said. There was never any communication from Sheikh Zawahiri, so it came as a surprise to all of us, including Abu Khaled.'[57]

Although on a lower level, several other senior Ahrar al-Sham leaders had histories directly and indirectly linked to al-Qaeda, such as prominent military commander Eyad al-Sha'ar (Abu al-Hassan), *shari'i* Hashem al-Shaikh (Abu Jaber), senior *sharia* official Mohammed Ayman Abul-Tout (Abul Abbas al-Shami) and Bahaa Mustafa al-Jughl (Abu Hamza al-Jughl). In many respects Ahrar al-Sham appeared to represent a slight ideological moderation of al-Qaeda's stance on transnational jihad. Or to put it another way, Ahrar al-Sham appeared more akin to the very early days of al-Qaeda and of Abdullah Azzam, when the virtues of jihad were focused more on defence within a national context, while remaining a cause of relevance to Muslims worldwide. Whether there was ever an official relationship between Ahrar al-Sham and al-Qaeda is impossible to tell, but there were certainly indirect links, which in practice facilitated the continued rise in status of Jabhat al-Nusra and other smaller jihadist factions in Syria whose ideology was essentially akin to al-Qaeda's.

Nevertheless, Ahrar al-Sham remained an organisation seemingly determined to toe a line of inclusion and popularity while remaining committed to a particular Salafist conservatism. This political and ideological pragmatism was a potentially powerful strategy, as the former Guantanamo Bay detainee and director of CAGE Moazzam Begg explained, 'I learned after meeting Abu Khaled [al-Suri] ... that Ahrar had people with clout and experience in the world ... and hence were not easily dismissed by more radical elements as being too moderate.'[58]

As the winter weather slowly began to subside, February 2013 proved to be yet another month of significant insurgent victories in Syria, with jihadists continuing to play an increasingly prominent role. On the morning of 2 February a coalition of insurgents, comprising several FSA units, Liwa al-Tawhid, Ahrar al-Sham and Jabhat al-Nusra, launched an all-out offensive to capture the strategic southern suburb of Aleppo, Sheikh Said. Later that day regime forces had withdrawn west, and Sheikh Said was under opposition control, cutting off the Syrian army and NDF militiamen in western Aleppo from the strategically vital Aleppo international airport. Later that day and at the other end of Syria, Abu Adnan al-Zabadani's Kataib Hamza bin 'Abd al-Mutallab merged with two Damascus-based SIF groups—Saraya al-Maham al-Khasa and Kataib Suqor al-Islam—thereby further consolidating the potential power of the SIF.

Increasingly, major pre-planned offensives involving multiple groups were demonstrating particularly sophisticated coordination in the use of rearguard artillery fire, close-proximity tank fire and the use of ground forces moving along several axes simultaneously. With the addition of one or more jihadist suicide bombers as the 'first wave' to destroy otherwise impenetrable outer defences, these operations held a strong likelihood of success, especially in areas of northern Syria where regime forces were isolated from regular reinforcement and re-supply. These tactics had begun to emerge and were being perfected during the capture of al-Taana air base in October 2012; al-Hamdan air base, Base 46, al-Mayadin artillery base, Marj al-Sultan air base and the Tishrin dam in November 2012; Sheikh Suleiman base in December 2012; and Taftanaz air base in January 2013. But in February and early March 2013 especially, they were used with particular effect.

With a number of concerted offensives ongoing across Idlib, Jabhat al-Nusra and Ahrar al-Sham coordinated a string of three significant victories in Aleppo and Raqqa between 11 and 13 February. On the 11th Jabhat al-Nusra led a successful push—also involving FSA unit Liwa Owais al-Qarni—on the town of al-Tabqa and the nearby al-Furat dam, responsible for providing electricity to large parts of the governorates of Raqqa, al-Hasakah, Deir ez Zour and Aleppo. The following day Ahrar al-Sham led a successful assault on the al-Jarrah air base in Aleppo, capturing the entire facility and a fleet of ageing MiG fighter jets. And the day after that Jabhat al-Nusra led the capture of the strategic town of al-Shadadi in southern Hasakah, where it gained further access to valuable oilfields. All the while, Jabhat al-Nusra and Ahrar al-Sham were also managing a large offensive in Hama governorate, where pivotal regime positions and checkpoints were seized in Qalaat al-Madiq, Tel Othman, Morek, and Shalish, near the town of Kafr Nabouda.

Late February also witnessed a string of significant victories, led by Jabhat al-Nusra and Ahrar al-Sham, but which also included local FSA factions. On 22 February, for example, the FSA's Liwa al-Jafr and Jabhat al-Nusra led the capture of Syria's former nuclear facility in al-Kibar, Deir ez Zour—which had been bombed by Israel in 2007. Within the expansive desert complex, fighters discovered an apparently inoperable Scud ballistic missile, which was proudly shown off in several FSA videos later that day.

By February there were at least 3,000 foreign fighters present inside Syria fighting against the regime,[59] mostly within the ranks of jihadist organisations. As many as fifteen Tunisians alone were killed in mid-February,[60] while British foreign fighters were becoming more and more visible in jihadist propaganda coming out of northern Syria. That month the list of such groups grew with the establishment of a new jihadist organisation in Syria, Suqor al-Izz. Led by Sheikh 'Abd al-Wahed (Saqr al-Jihad), Suqor al-Izz was initially established primarily by Saudi foreign fighters who had found their way into Syria via networks that entered northern Latakia. Saqr al-Jihad was a former 'Afghan Arab,' having fought with the *mujahidin* in Afghanistan in the 1980s, and is thought to have arrived in Syria some time in late 2011. While classified US Department of Defense documents from Guantanamo Bay released by Wikileaks detail the existence of a 'Saqr al-Jihad' running al-Qaeda's al-Nibras guesthouse in Kandahar in Afghanistan,[61] it remains unclear whether this is the same individual.

Nonetheless, Saqr al-Jihad's influential network meant that he quickly attracted a number of other 'Afghan Arabs' into Suqor al-Izz's ranks, including Abd al-Malek al-Ihsai (Abu Leen), Zaid al-Bawardi (Abu Ammar al-Makki), and Abu Mohammed al-Halabi, whose jihadist histories involved fighting in Afghanistan, Bosnia, Chechnya and Iraq. Additionally, the group had within its ranks former confidantes of Osama Bin Laden, including the one-legged Adel al-Otaibi (Najmeddine Azad) and Fayez al-Mitab, who purportedly used to house Bin Laden in his residence in Saudi Arabia in the early 1990s.[62] Primarily based in northern Latakia, Suqor al-Izz remained a relatively independent unit of *muhajireen*, although it maintained an ideological affinity with Jabhat al-Nusra.

From the start, however, Suqor al-Izz established itself as active in the realms of social outreach and the provision of humanitarian relief. Presumably feeding off his pre-established sources of financial donations, Saqr al-Jihad's organisation—also at this point containing Yemenis, Indonesians and Turks—began establishing influence over the running of bakeries in rural northern Latakia, and on Fridays its fighters were known to distribute Islamic educational materials to children. Meanwhile, Jabhat al-Nusra used February to establish its second Qism al-Ighatha branch, in Idlib governorate.

In addition to being when the UK's first foreign fighter was reported killed in Syria (Ibrahim al-Mazwagi, on 2 March),[63] early March 2013 was most notable for being when the insurgency captured its first governorate capital, the city of Raqqa. Rural Raqqa had seen fairly sustained operations by insurgent factions since early February, when the largely Islamist coalition of Jabhat al-Nusra, Ahrar al-Sham and Majlis Shura al-Mujahideen captured the town of al-Tabqa and the al-Furat dam. Further north, centred around the Tel Abyad border crossing with Turkey, the insurgent picture was far more moderate, with local FSA units there—Liwa Thuwar al-Raqqa, Liwa Rayat al-Nasr, Alwiya Ahfad al-Rasoul and Farouq al-Shamal—having united within the Jabhat Tahrir Raqqa alliance. However, the bulk of the insurgent momentum against the regime in late February and early March was being directed from the west, where the Aleppo-based Islamists and jihadists were so strong.

Thus, when Ahrar al-Sham and Jabhat al-Nusra separately released videos on 2 March announcing the initiation of Operation Gharat al-Jabbar (Raid of the Almighty) to capture the city of Raqqa, they had the momentum to pose a significant threat. Early on 3 March Jabhat al-Nusra, Ahrar al-Sham, a local Salafist coalition known as Jabhat al-Wahida wa'l Tahrir al-Islamiyya (JWTI), and a small Islamic-oriented FSA faction, Liwa Muntasir Billah, launched near-simultaneous raids on fifteen Syrian army positions circling the city, all of which were successfully overrun that day. The following morning more centralised assaults were launched on the respective headquarters of the Military Intelligence and the Political Security Directorate in the centre of the city, and also on the governor's palace. By the end of the day the entire city was in insurgent hands, and the next morning the Islamist factions released a video showing Raqqa governor Hassan Jalili and Baath Party provincial secretary General Suleiman Suleiman in their hands, sitting alongside JWTI leader 'Dr Samer'.

Although of less value than cities such as Aleppo, Hama or Homs, the insurgents' capture of Raqqa was a huge symbolic victory for the opposition, especially following the sustained spate of strategic victories elsewhere in the country since September 2012. Since the first signs of civil conflict had emerged in Syria, the regime's primary focus had been on maintaining the security of the Alawite coastal heartlands in Latakia and Tartous and ensuring continued control of all primary urban centres. The loss of a provincial capital, albeit in the more isolated governorate of Raqqa, was a very real practical and psychological defeat for the regime. It was also a particularly valuable gain for Jabhat al-Nusra, which for the first time since the start of the conflict was in a position to definitively link up its established strongholds in eastern Deir ez Zour with its growing centres of power in Idlib and Aleppo, via Highway 4, running along the Euphrates River.

The final day of the assault on Raqqa—4 March—was also notable for an attack in Iraq by Jabhat al-Nusra's mother organisation, the ISI. Two days earlier, after several days of sustained battles, Syrian insurgent forces took control of half of the border town of al-Yaroubiya, including its official crossing point on the north-eastern border with Iraq. The loss of the crossing forced the withdrawal of roughly seventy Syrian army personnel into Iraqi territory, where they remained in the custody of the Iraqi army near their side of the crossing for forty-eight hours. On 3 or 4 March the Syrian soldiers were placed in several buses and driven south towards the al-Waleed crossing in the south of Anbar province, the Syrian side of which remained under Syrian army control. However, the convoy, which was under Iraqi army protection, was ambushed by ISI militants near the remote village of Akashat—over 490 kilometres south of al-Yaroubiya and 126 kilometres from their destination.

Outside Akashat, fifteen IEDs were detonated, to the left and right, and in front and behind of the convoy, trapping it within a hail of RPG, mortar and machine-gun fire. By the end of the attack forty-eight Syrian soldiers and nine Iraqi security guards were dead and the ISI had introduced itself to the Syrian conflict for the first time, though on Iraqi soil.

It turns out that the ISI's Syria-based brothers in Jabhat al-Nusra—who had been involved in the offensive on al-Yaroubiya—had tipped them off regarding the fate of the Syrian soldiers. Considering that they had withdrawn into Iraq's Ninawa province—a long-time stronghold of the ISI—it would seem highly likely that they were then placed under surveillance by the ISI prior to their departure south early on 4 March. Some kind of tip-off from within the Iraqi military or border guard then seems the most likely explanation for how the ISI was given sufficient advance notice to plant fifteen IEDs and prepare multiple firing positions for mortars and RPGs upon their arrival in Akashat later that day.

A week after the attack the ISI made it official by issuing a written statement of responsibility for 'annihilating an entire column of the *safavid* army', thereby proving the 'firm co-operation' between the Iraqi and Syrian governments.[64]

While the notoriously brutal ISI was now involving itself directly in Syrian dynamics, a long-time leader of moderate Sunni thought and public supporter of the regime, Sheikh Mohammad Said Ramadan al-Bouti, was killed, apparently in a mysterious explosion in his mosque in Damascus on 21 March.

Though initial state media reports described the explosion as having been caused by a suicide bomber hidden within a group of Islamic students in the al-Iman Mosque in the centre of Syria's capital and claiming that fifty people had been killed, a video released three weeks later onto YouTube suggested something to the contrary.

In the video, Sheikh al-Bouti was shown at a desk addressing his students, when a small explosion occurred immediately in front of him. Three seconds later, after the smoke disappeared, it was apparent that Bouti was still standing and his desk was still in place—he even found his bearings and sat up straight. However, roughly four seconds after that, a man walked in front of the camera, blocking the view to Sheikh al-Bouti, and, after the man appeared to do something to him the sheikh fell to his right, seemingly unconscious.[65] The unexplained actions of this unidentified man, and the fact that Sheikh al-Bouti was dazed but conscious before his appearance raised significant suspicions that the sheikh may have been assassinated by elements of the regime, and that the 'suicide bombing' story was a cover-up. However, no definitive evidence has ever been brought to light proving or disproving either side of the story.

Meanwhile, further north in Raqqa, another new strategic shift was taking place in late March. Specifically, intense inter-factional hostilities had broken out between Jabhat al-Nusra and Kataib al-Farouq over control of the Tel Abyad border crossing with Turkey. After capturing Raqqa city, Jabhat al-Nusra had begun expanding its influence in the governorate's northern countryside, which was controlled by the Jabhat Tahrir Raqqa coalition, itself dominated by Kataib al-Farouq—one of the largest insurgent factions in Syria and a self-professed FSA umbrella group. Tensions had been brewing between Jabhat al-Nusra and Kataib al-Farouq for some time, especially considering Farouq's continued control over border crossings at Tel Abyad and Bab al-Hawa in northern Aleppo and Jabhat al-Nusra's growing dominance in the interiors of Aleppo and Raqqa. One morning earlier in 2013, Kataib al-Farouq's leader in eastern Syria, Mohammed al-Daher (Abu Azzam) had been wounded in an attempted assassination in Tel Abyad. The attack, which involved 'several sticks of TNT wired to the ignition of a BMW vehicle Abu Azzam often [travelled] in', was immediately blamed on Jabhat al-Nusra.[66]

Several weeks later, in late March, Jabhat al-Nusra had bolstered its presence inside Tel Abyad and had begun randomly setting up makeshift checkpoints in the town and arresting Kataib al-Farouq members on a daily basis. Then, on 24 March, one such incident led to a major outbreak of fighting, during which several fighters on both sides were killed and Abu Azzam was severely injured and eventually transferred to hospital in Sanliurfa in Turkey, where he was placed under Turkish guard.[67] Though a very delicate ceasefire was agreed, this brief but deadly clash caused both sides to call up reinforcements from neighbouring towns and cities, and by 26 March the town of Tel Abyad and its surroundings were packed with militants.

In short, this episode of inter-factional fighting symbolised a natural heightening of tensions resulting from the relative rise in power and influence of jihadist forces in northern and eastern Syria, while more moderate factions such as Kataib al-Farouq were struggling to retain their territorial control and influence. The unexplained explosion inside a vehicle transporting the founder of the FSA, Colonel Riyad al-Asad, in Deir ez Zour on 25 March—which one Ahrar al-Sham political leader says was secretly traced back to Jabhat al-Nusra[68]—should almost certainly be interpreted within this emerging context.

\* \* \*

The period of September 2012 to March 2013 had been another defining phase of the Syrian conflict, marked in particular by the exponential expansion of the role that Syrian Salafist and international jihadist organisations were coming to play within it. By March 2013 the FSA had undeniably failed to constitute a single unified organisation capable of coordinating opposition operations across Syria. Hundreds of insurgent factions now existed across the country, comprising at least 75,000 armed men, at least 3,000 of whom were non-Syrians.

Meanwhile, the emergence of Iranian military and Hezbollah militant personnel fighting alongside the Syrian army and training the new loyalist NDF had brought a new international and sectarian element into play. By itself, the Syrian regime and its security apparatus were struggling against a rapidly expanding and increasingly professional insurgency, so the arrival of such foreign assistance was a move of desperation, but in the months to come it would rescue Assad from defeat.

Jabhat al-Nusra had by now become a formidable militant organisation, whose forces had played lead roles in major opposition victories across the north and east of the country and others in Damascus and in the south. Perhaps surprisingly to the outside world, it had acquired broad acceptance and admiration amongst the 'moderate' opposition. Its military superiority, relative professionalism and stance against corruption were increasingly attracting young Syrian men into its ranks and away from the traditional FSA factions that the 'Friends of Syria' were backing. As the secretary of the Union of Syrians Abroad, Mohammed Khadam, explained:

> Jabhat al-Nusra started to win the hearts and minds of the people because she was the first brigade to fight strongly and which took little for itself from the war booty. Jabhat al-Nusra showed no mercy to the regime's soldiers, but its fighters were also modest. They won all the complicated battles that the FSA could not. Its name also, it suggested Jabhat al-Nusra had no interests in establishing a state or for an involvement in politics.[69]

Concurrently, the sheer brutality of the civil conflict, the apparent emergence of chemical weapon use by the regime and the surge in sectarian rhetoric being used by most parties to the fighting on the ground meant that additional jihadist actors were manifesting themselves within the insurgent picture. While the several more established jihadist groups such as Majlis Shura al-Mujahideen and Junud al-Sham had consolidated their localised roles, others were expanding—for example, Kataib al-Muhajireen, merging with Kataib al-Khattab, Jaish Mohammed and several smaller Syrian jihadist cells to form Jaish al-Muhajireen wa'l Ansar. At the same time, altogether new jihadist groups were also forming, such as Suqor al-Izz, containing individuals with extensive histories in the international jihadist scene.

With no solution to the conflict presenting itself, and neither side looking anywhere near to definitively winning or losing on a national level, escalation looked inevitable. With foreign fighters streaming into Syria at an accelerated rate and the Iraq-based ISI now looking to nudge itself directly into play, the future looked bright—or perhaps more appropriately, dark—for Syria's jihad.

# PART III

# MAKING A SCENE

# 7

# APRIL–JUNE 2013

## THE ISLAMIC STATE JOINS THE CONFLICT

The winter of 2012–13 had underlined the truly full-scale nature of the conflict that had developed in Syria. It had also provided jihadists, especially Jabhat al-Nusra, with an invaluable opportunity to establish solid roots in communities across northern Syria, through their provision of protection and desperately needed social services.

However, while the winter had proved a season of great victories for the insurgency, the spring saw the regime and its supporting militias recover some ground. The role of Hezbollah, Iran and the newly established NDF were all crucial in gradually tipping the balance of power, especially in Syria's most strategic areas around Damascus and along the western border with Lebanon. It was Hezbollah's enhanced investment in the conflict that facilitated the regime's re-capture of the Homs town of al-Qusayr in June 2013 and which struck a deep blow to opposition morale. The primary consequence of this was a retaliatory expansion and spillover of the conflict into Lebanon, but it also sparked several global calls for Sunni mobilisation to fight Assad, Hezbollah and Iran in Syria.

Meanwhile, the most significant development during this period came in April, when the ISI announced its expansion into Syria and its intent to subsume Jabhat al-Nusra back under its command. Jabhat al-Nusra's rapid refusal to abide by this order sparked a major jihadist split, in Syria and across the world. In the short term the ISI—consequently renamed the Islamic State in Iraq and al-Sham, or ISIS— was the main benefactor, gaining a large number of Jabhat al-Nusra's foreign fighter contingent. Despite a series of letters exchanged between al-Qaeda's leader and both Jabhat al-Nusra and ISIS, the crisis remained unsolved and ISIS emerged as an operational entity in Syria in mid-May. By June ISIS had overt presences in areas of Aleppo, Raqqa and Deir ez Zour.

Amid rising opposition concern about both the true nature of their tacit ally Jabhat al-Nusra and the newly arrived ISIS, the conflict also spilled over into Turkey. On 11 May the largest terrorist attack ever to strike the country took place in the southern border town of Reyhanlı, with accusatory fingers pointed towards both ISIS and a pro-regime Alawite Marxist–Leninist militia group.

While Ahrar al-Sham assumed a frontline public role for the first time in June 2013 and identified its leader by name, Syria found itself faced by two major and competing jihadist organisations.

* * *

As April 2013 began, Syria was emerging from what had been its bloodiest month since the beginning of the revolution two years earlier. At least 6,000 people had been killed, according to those monitoring the conflict, including as many as 300 children.[1] The conflict itself had become one of all-out open warfare, with the opposition regularly employing tanks, artillery and other heavy weaponry. The capture by Jabhat al-Nusra, Ahrar al-Sham, Majlis Shura al-Mujahideen and Liwa al-Haq of huge quantities of 122-mm Grad artillery rockets, 82-mm tank shells and AT-3 Sagger anti-tank guided missiles, plus other weaponry, after the dramatic seizure of a complex of Syrian army arms depots during Operation Ibshari outside the northern Aleppo town of Khan Touman on 15 March underlined the scale of warfare then in play.[2]

Throughout the winter the opposition, increasingly led from the front by jihadist and Salafist forces, had won a string of major victories against regime positions, thereby posing for some time a genuinely existential threat to the Assad presidency, which was suffering from an increasingly debilitating shortage of loyalist manpower on the proliferating battlefields. But this trend was beginning to slow, if not reverse.

The increasingly visible presence of pro-regime militias and Iranian-backed paramilitary personnel in the early months of 2013 was beginning to herald a potential strategic rebalancing. Regime and pro-regime forces had begun to stabilise parts of Damascus and the southern governorate of Deraa, while Homs city and much of its immediate countryside, as well as the western highway to the Alawite heartlands in Tartous and Latakia were well consolidated. As such, the regime remained the dominant power across most of Syria's urban centres and had regained or consolidated its power in the country's central and western regions. 'We thought that Assad had been defeated in the winter of 2012,' said Abu Mustafa, Ahrar al-Sham's chief of external relations, 'but at that time, Iran directly interfered in the revolution in order to fight Syrians and this stopped the regime from falling.'[3]

Northern Syria, however, and particularly its rural expanses, was increasingly dominated by the opposition, and had emerged as a viable and sustainable stronghold and safe haven for jihadist militancy. While a wide array of moderate 'FSA' factions remained a critical facet of everyday life in opposition areas in the north, it was actors on the more conservative and extreme ends of the spectrum that were coming to dominate the conflict dynamics. In eastern Syria, where al-Qaeda and the ISI had years of experience and well-established contacts, Sunni tribes remained the key structure around which power was being defined, with many tribes and clans effectively representing their own security interests in cooperation with armed groups. For example, large components of the al-Oqaidat tribe in Deir ez Zour, especially those from the al-Shuheil clan, had formed relationships of interdependence with Jabhat al-Nusra, particularly surrounding the control and sale of oil. Although at times critical of Jabhat al-Nusra's ideological stance, the Sha'itat clan similarly coordinated on a local level with the group. In that sense therefore, tribes remained the key arbiters of power in the east, and those factions with pre-existing relationships with tribal leaderships and with an interest in maintaining such associations were those to benefit the most.

Notwithstanding a natural continuation of the conflict and its general escalation across Syria, the period of April to June 2013 would come to be dominated by two particularly significant developments. One caused shock waves throughout the jihadist militant community in Syria and further afield, and the other sparked a strategic shift that would come to affect the overall balance of power in Syria's civil war.

With a largely FSA-dominated force close to capturing the 49th Air Defence Battalion base in the village of Alma in Syria's southern Deraa governorate, April began with another statement of intent from the Islamist groups that had come to dominate the insurgency in Aleppo. Early on 1 April senior commanders from five groups—including Jaish al-Muhajireen wa'l Ansar, Majlis Shura al-Mujahideen and Ahrar al-Sham—announced the start of a major operation across Aleppo to besiege the city's central prison, to release all prisoners in regime custody, to secure civilian areas under regime bombardment and to re-open all access roads into Aleppo's northern districts. By the time Tajamu wa Kataib Fajr al-Islam and Liwa Suqor al-Hauran had captured the 49th Air Defence Battalion on 3 April, the Aleppo operation had won victories at the al-Kindi hospital and the northern suburb of Handarat, while significant pushes were ongoing in parts of the Old City and around the provincial branch of the Department of Agriculture.

Although its name was not on the list of the five groups that conducted the Aleppo operation, Jabhat al-Nusra was in fact actively involved on the ground. Meanwhile, elsewhere in the city, it was continuing to expand its involvement in civil management and social services. While such efforts were primarily linked to the existing al-Hay'a al-Sharia in the city, Jabhat al-Nusra was also branching out on its own initiatives, including with the establishment in early April of a local bus service in opposition-controlled districts of the city, with tickets priced at 10 lira per person and over-fifties travelling for free.[4]

With Jabhat al-Nusra thus continuing to expand in confidence and capability, and countless other Salafist and jihadist factions either consolidating their roles or emerging fresh onto the scene, al-Qaeda leader Ayman al-Zawahiri released a new message of encouragement emphasising the value of unity for their cause on 7 April:

> Let your fight be in the name of Allah and with the aim of establishing Allah's sharia as the ruling system ... Do all that you can so that your holy war yields a jihadist Islamic state ... The enemy has begun to reel and collapse.'[5]

Quite dramatically the following day, in what appeared at the time to have been a coordinated release timed to follow twenty-four hours after Zawahiri's statement, ISI leader Abu Bakr al-Baghdadi released an audio statement in which he announced and confirmed for the first time that Jabhat al-Nusra was a wing of the ISI. In his speech, released by the ISI's official media wing al-Furqan, Baghdadi described Jabhat al-Nusra's leader Abu Mohammed al-Jolani as 'one of our soldiers' and confirmed that Jolani had established Jabhat al-Nusra 'from our sons'. As such, Jabhat al-Nusra was 'an extension' of the ISI—'a part of it'—and from that point onwards he had instituted the 'cancellation of the name Islamic State of Iraq and the cancellation of the name Jabhat al-Nusra, and the joining of the two under one name: "the Islamic State of Iraq and al-Sham"'. This new and expanded organisation, Baghdadi said, would continue along 'the path that [Abu Musab al-Zarqawi] trod ... we God Willing, are following in his footsteps'.[6] As such, one could draw only one conclusion at the time: Baghdadi sought to transform his organisation into a qualitatively evolved version of the early ISI, more capable of dominating the situation and establishing a viable Islamic state. From its first day, ISIS was laying down the gauntlet.

ISIS, as it would soon become better known as—or ISIL, using 'Levant' in place of 'al-Sham'—was therefore to represent a subsumption of Jabhat al-Nusra by its 'father' organisation, the ISI. Put simply, Baghdadi appeared to be reining its increasingly self-confident and successful Syrian wing back into and under its central leadership.

Of course, the relationship between the ISI and Jabhat al-Nusra had been an issue long suspected by many analysts and governments. The US government had officially designated Jabhat al-Nusra an 'alias' of the ISI four months earlier, in December 2012. But this marked the first time that anyone from either organisation explicitly acknowledged the relationship. Not only was Baghdadi confirming that he had ordered the establishment of Jabhat al-Nusra by dispatching Jolani and others into Syria in mid-2011, he also claimed that the ISI had contributed half of its finances every month since towards Jabhat al-Nusra across the Iraqi border into Syria. The picture he painted was very much one of 'father' and 'son', or 'chairman' and 'local manager'.

Baghdadi also claimed that he had not publicly acknowledged the ISI's relationship with Jabhat al-Nusra earlier because of concerns for security and a desire for Syrians to 'get to know Jabhat al-Nusra on their own terms'. This was a strategy already well established within the al-Qaeda network around the world, when larger and better-organised affiliates covertly form new factions in new areas. Shortly after Baghdadi's statement, Aaron Zelin drew this comparison with AQAP's formation of Ansar al-Sharia in Yemen, for example.[7]

Baghdadi's statement sent shock waves throughout the Syrian revolution. Although Jabhat al-Nusra's links to al-Qaeda and the ISI had long been suspected, the suggestion that the Iraq-based ISI—which had gained a well-earned reputation for brutality and a particularly intense level of extremist thought and practice—would now begin to influence developments inside Syria was met with trepidation and fear within the opposition. Jabhat al-Nusra had seemingly been willing (at least for now) to moderate its behaviour and objectives, but the likelihood that the ISI would do the same in the form of an expanded ISIS seemed worryingly low.

But this series of dramatic statements was not yet complete. Around thirty-six hours after Baghdadi's statement announcing the incorporation of Jabhat al-Nusra into ISIS, Jolani issued an audio recording. Posted by Jabhat al-Nusra's official media wing, al-Manara al-Bayda, Jolani complained that he had not been informed of any plan by Baghdadi to announce his organisation's links to the ISI or to establish a merged ISIS structure. Although Jolani did clearly acknowledge Jabhat al-Nusra's relationship with the ISI and his experience fighting jihad with the ISI in Iraq, he refused to be subsumed into an Iraq–Syria-wide ISIS.

Addressing Baghdadi using the honorific title 'Sheikh Baghdadi, may Allah protect him', Jolani ended his statement by pledging a *bay'a* oath to al-Qaeda leader Ayman al-Zawahiri and proclaiming that 'the banner of Jabhat al-Nusra will remain' in Syria.[8] This pledge was in fact a reaffirmation of Jolani's allegiance to al-Qaeda's central leadership, which indicated at the time an element of tension between the ISI and al-Qaeda. In fact, since assuming the leadership of the ISI in 2010, Baghdadi had been known to insist that new recruits swear *bay'a* to him as *emir al-mu'minin*, or Commander of the Faithful. Historically, this title had been reserved primarily for caliphs, but Taliban leader Mullah Mohammed Omar—to whom all al-Qaeda leaders and fighters are ultimately loyal—was also known to have reserved that honour for himself.

Therefore, in April 2013 the jihadist community was faced with a serious internal conflict. The ISI, which had survived the US occupation of Iraq and was now beginning to again conduct frightening levels of violence in Iraq, had seemingly tried and failed to order its Syrian wing to merge back with the parent body. Meanwhile, the leader of that Syrian wing had publicly expressed not only his determination to lead an independent group (Jabhat al-Nusra) but to be ultimately loyal to Zawahiri in Pakistan rather than Baghdadi in Iraq.

'At the time of the announcement, I knew that the Syrian revolution had triggered a much bigger chain reaction in the geopolitical map across the Middle East. Borders were dropped down into Syria and a new age had started,' recalled Amjad Farekh, a founding member of Jaish al-Muslimeen.[9]

There is an intriguing back story to this major jihadist rupture. While Jolani may not have been forewarned of Baghdadi's intent to *announce* the merger of Jabhat al-Nusra into an expanded ISI, he *had* been aware that this was a priority on Baghdadi's immediate radar. According to multiple Syrian Salafist and jihadist sources—all requesting anonymity when discussing this subject—several months earlier, in the winter months of 2012, a secret message had been sent from Baghdadi in Iraq to Jolani in Syria insisting that Jabhat al-Nusra publish a statement announcing its historical and organisational links and ideological allegiance to the ISI. According to one source:

> Basically nobody knew widely about this at the time ... but after Da'ish [the Arabic acronym for ISIS] was formed, it was revealed and spoken about at the top levels of the mujahideen leaderships. Sheikh Baghdadi had been jealous of al-Nusra's success for a long time, but this did not become public

As it happened, the majority of Jabhat al-Nusra's *majlis al-shura* had been against the idea of announcing their links to the ISI, for fear of losing the support they had worked so hard to gain across parts of opposition-controlled Syria. Thus, Jolani turned down Baghdadi's 2012 request.

The claims made to the author by these sources—which include several former Sednayya detainees closely acquainted with the founding members of Jabhat al-Nusra as well as existing leadership figures within Ahrar al-Sham— seem to corroborate a series of allegations made by a Twitter account (@ wikibaghdady) seemingly managed by an individual with unique insight into the inner workings of the ISI. According to this author's sources, Baghdadi's deputy, Haji Bakr, had led an initial venture into northern Syria in late 2012, where he set up a secret base in northern Aleppo, either inside the town of Tel Rifaat or just to its north off the main road towards Azaz. From there, Haji Bakr exploited his history as a former officer in Iraq's air force intelligence to recruit small numbers of loyal supporters to begin laying the groundwork for an expansion of Baghdadi's Islamic State project.

Other sources have also claimed Haji Bakr was joined on this mission by ISI spokesman and long-time Syrian member Taha Sobhi Falaha (Abu Mohammed al-Adnani). In addition to Adnani's value in supporting ISI plans to establish concretely in Syria, he had been specifically tasked with a mission to carry out a major bomb attack against the Syrian political opposition in southern Turkey.[10]

In an investigative report by *Der Spiegel*'s Christoph Reuter, a similar account is provided in which Haji Bakr not only acquired loyalist recruits to prepare for a planned expansion announcement, but used them more specifi- cally to collect leveragable local-level intelligence on the inner workings of vulnerable villages and towns. Some were even placed into marriages with locally influential families so as to establish a solid and unyielding foundation in each community. Simply put, information was power, and Haji Bakr's power was collected and wielded in remarkably similar ways to those of the Saddam-era secret police and intelligence apparatus.[11]

These accounts fit one provided by @Wikibaghdady, which went as far as to claim that Haji Bakr and Baghdadi subsequently sent these 'spies in the disguise of the mujahideen ... to be close to Jolani and to monitor his move- ments'. After Jolani and Jabhat al-Nusra's *majlis al-shura* then discovered and foiled the ISI's plans to assassinate FSA leaders in Syria and to target the political opposition in Turkey, Baghdadi 'sent a strongly-worded letter and gave Jolani two choices: either execute the orders or Jabhat al-Nusra would be dissolved and replaced with the creation of a new entity'.[12]

What happened in the following months is unclear, with several differing stories shared within the Salafist and jihadist communities of northern Syria.

What does seem likely—as claimed by @wikibaghdady and corroborated to the author by several sources—is that Baghdadi and several ISI commanders then crossed from Iraq into northern Syria in February or March 2013 to launch one final push for the establishment of ISIS by way of a pre-arranged merger with Jabhat al-Nusra. 'Yes, [Baghdadi] was definitely there then, having secret meetings and making his presence known,' said one well-connected Salafist involved in the northern Syrian insurgency.

These 'secret' meetings were held with senior leaders within Jabhat al-Nusra, but also with other foreign fighter-dominated factions in Aleppo and Idlib, and with prominent Salafists involved in the revolution. Baghdadi and his deputies were not only 'making their presence known', but were preparing the broader ground for the announcement of ISIS that would come several weeks later. After these meetings, according to @wikibaghdady, it was ascertained that a noticeable portion of Jabhat al-Nusra supported the idea of establishing an Islamic state in Iraq and Syria and respected Baghdadi's leadership. This was good enough for Baghdadi.

Baghdadi and Haji Bakr were still inside Syria when the 8 April statement announcing ISIS was released. @wikibaghdady information—again confirmed to this author by multiple sources—suggested that they were residing in 'portable metal rooms'—probably a reference to shipping containers—'in a place not too far from a Syrian refugee camp'.[13] This fact, and the murky background surrounding months of pressure from the ISI to pressure Jabhat al-Nusra into submitting to its authority, reveals a relationship fraught with tension. This was at least in part due to the fact that there were portions of Jabhat al-Nusra that would have been tempted by Baghdadi's proposition. An account provided by Junud al-Sham leader Muslim al-Shishani of the immediate aftermath of the statements is consistent in this respect and serves to underline the intensive 'diplomatic' activities undertaken by Baghdadi to secure pledges of allegiance inside Syria:

> After [Jolani's 10 April] statement, Jabhat al-Nusra was divided on two fronts. Initially not many supported Abu Bakr [al-Baghdadi], but a decision on this issue from Dr Zawahiri was delayed and in that time, those who supported Abu Bakr managed to change a lot of things. Foreign fighters joined them ... and they began to visit all the foreign fighter factions. They visited me a few times, but I refused ... Back then, the largest foreign fighter group was Omar al-Shishani's and I heard that he himself hosted Abu Bakr for several days.[14]

Presumably, Jolani felt he had developed an organisation in Syria that was not only capable of surviving on its own but of thriving within the intense conflict dynamics in which it was operating—but only if it remained untainted by the divisive reputation of the ISI. As he proclaimed in his 10 April statement: 'We learnt lessons from our experience [in Iraq] concerning what is the secret of the hearts of the believers in the land of al-Sham.'[15]

Notwithstanding the tensions and potential hostility brewing under the surface both before and now after the conflicting statements by the ISI and Jabhat al-Nusra on 8 and 10 April, Syria's political and armed opposition were quick to express their concern. While all declared their total rejection of 'foreign influence' or 'foreign agendas' within the revolution, it was interesting that no group explicitly announced that it would cease cooperating with Jabhat al-Nusra. Early statements by Liwa al-Islam and the SILF stood out in this regard. Ahrar al-Sham's leader Hassan Abboud also defended the reputation of Jabhat al-Nusra, insisting that the group had only contributed positively towards the revolution and the Syrian people and as such, his group's stance would not change. This was backed up twenty-four hours later with an official Ahrar al-Sham statement announcing a successful joint assault with Jabhat al-Nusra on a Syrian army checkpoint outside Damascus.[16] However, on an official level, Jabhat al-Nusra had entered a period of media silence from which they would not emerge until June.

Meanwhile, the conflict was continuing to intensify in Idlib, where a multi-group Operations Command—led by Ahrar al-Sham, Suqor al-Sham and the Idlib Military Council—was established on 14 April to contribute towards a better coordinated offensive around the Maraat al-Numaan area. However, although such joint commands would soon become standard practice in high-intensity conflict zones across Syria, the formation of one in Idlib came too late, with regime forces breaking the months-long sieges on Wadi al-Deif and Hamadiyeh bases twenty-four hours later.[17] It seemed the era of repeated opposition victories was coming to a close.

Concurrently, a serious and highly symbolic development took place late on 20 April, when Syrian opposition fighters launched two artillery rockets into the Lebanese town and Hezbollah stronghold of Hermel and three others into the nearby village of al-Qasr. While al-Qasr and several other villages in close proximity had been subjected to mortar and rocket fire since February, this marked the first time such a sizeable municipality as Hermel had been specifically targeted. The following day another rocket struck central Hermel and five others landed in and around al-Qasr and nearby Hawsh Sayyed Ali.

Tensions had been rising on the Syria–Lebanon border for several weeks, due largely to Hezbollah's expanding role in fighting alongside and in defence of Syrian military forces. An ongoing and increasingly intense fight over the opposition-controlled town of al-Qusayr in south-western Homs, 11 kilometres from the Lebanese border, was the chief focal point of tensions. Moreover, weeks earlier on 27 February Hezbollah's Hassan Nasrallah had admitted for the first time that his fighters were actively present in a string of Syrian villages along the Lebanese border: 'no one should make any miscalculations with us,' he had said.[18]

Hezbollah's role in Syria, and particularly its key part in contributing towards an expanding regime offensive on al-Qusayr, had brought with it threats from several FSA factions and Jabhat al-Nusra to bring the conflict to Lebanon if Hezbollah continued its 'hostile' activities in Syria. The initiation of rocket attacks on urban targets in eastern Lebanon in mid-March marked the realisation of those threats. Moreover, the publication of a *fatwa* by Lebanese Salafist sheikh Ahmed al-Assir on 22 April, proclaiming that 'there is a religious duty on every Muslim who is able to do so ... to enter into Syria in order to defend its people, its mosques and religious shrines, especially in al-Qusayr and Homs', consolidated the addition of a Lebanese dynamic into Syria's civil conflict. Speaking from his Bilal bin Rabah Mosque in Abra, Sheikh Assir pointed particularly towards the the decision by 'Nasrallah and his shabiha ... to enter into [al-Qusayr] in order to massacre the oppressed' and announced that he would soon establish the Kataib al-Muqawama al-Hurra (Free Resistance Brigades) in his Lebanese home town of Sidon in order to contribute towards the defence of Syrian Sunnis. Another prominent Lebanese Sunni sheikh, Salem al-Rifai, quickly followed suit and expressed his support for Sheikh Assir's declaration.[19]

Of course, Hezbollah was one of two key regional actors militarily backing the regime in Damascus. The other was Iran, which by this time had been revealed as not only playing an active training and advisory role inside Syria, but also as hosting pro-regime militiamen in Iran for 'guerrilla combat training at a secret base'.[20] Most recipients of this training were members of and new recruits for Syria's paramilitary NDF, which by April 2013 numbered approximately 50,000 personnel and aimed to reach 100,000. According to one pro-government militiaman, a Christian named Samer who spoke to Reuters:

> It was an urban warfare course that lasted 15 days. The trainers said it's the same course Hezbollah operatives normally do ... The course teaches you important elements of guerrilla warfare, like several ways to carry a rifle and shoot, and the best methods to prepare against surprise attacks. The Iranians kept telling us that this war is not against Sunnis but for the sake of Syria. But the Alawites on the course kept saying they want to kill the Sunnis and rape their women in revenge.[21]

Naturally, this sectarian transnational dynamic provided an ideological tool ripe for exploitation by jihadists in Syria. Not only were its own forces increasingly international and representative of the global *umma*, but the enemy it was fighting was becoming more and more defined by expressions of Shia and Alawite supremacy—a perfect sectarian war, if you like. By this stage of the conflict in Syria as many as 5,500 Sunni foreign fighters had arrived from all corners of the globe to fight within the opposition, according to the International Centre for the Study of Radicalisation and Political Violence (ICSR). This included up to 600 Europeans:[22]

| Country of Origin | Estimated Foreign Fighters |
|---|---|
| Albania | 1 |
| Austria | 1 |
| Belgium | 14–85 |
| Bulgaria | 1 |
| Denmark | 3–78 |
| Finland | 13 |
| France | 30–92 |
| Germany | 3–40 |
| Ireland | 26 |
| Kosovo | 1 |
| Netherlands | 5–107 |
| Spain | 6 |
| Sweden | 5 |
| United Kingdom | 28–134 |

Note: Figures are limited to Sunni foreign fighters and based on figures officially available in open sources. Data is not universally available for all countries.

Within a week of Sheikh Assir's *fatwa* his Kataib al-Muqawama al-Hurra had been formed and new recruits had been deployed into Syria, including Assir himself, who was pictured on 30 April and 1 May armed with an AK-47 assault rifle in trenches inside Syria. At the same time, Hezbollah's Nasrallah warned the Syrian opposition that 'you won't be able to bring down Damascus and you cannot bring down the regime militarily',[23] thus warning that his forces could play a more expansive role in defending President Assad if necessary. 'Syria has real friends in the region and the world that will not let Syria fall into the hands of America, Israel, or *takfiri* groups,' Nasrallah warned.

Although Jabhat al-Nusra's senior leadership had assumed (or been forced into) public silence following its falling out with the ISI in early April and the group's media wing al-Manara al-Bayda had ceased issuing public statements, it had begun redeploying small numbers of fighters to the al-Qusayr area from Hama in the north and from the northern Damascus countryside to the south. 'As it was for many factions, defending Qusayr and fighting Hezbollah became a big priority for Nusra,' according to Abu Ahmed, a Jaish al-Islam fighter who knew some Jabhat al-Nusra members who were sent to the al-Qusayr front.

Not only would Jabhat al-Nusra begin to play an operational—but silent—role in defending al-Qusayr and its various outlying villages, it would also contribute towards mortar and Grad rocket launches into eastern Lebanon. Recruiting jihadists from around the world had already become relatively easy, but the fight for al-Qusayr and Hezbollah's role in bolstering the defence of the regime would encourage a real acceleration in foreign fighter immigration to Syria.

As tensions rose in western Homs in late April, Syria's Islamist and Salafist factions were on the offensive in the north. On 24 April Ahrar al-Sham announced a major multi-group offensive spanning northern Hama and Idlib, with the express objective of weakening regime power in the region and posing a threat to Latakia. Within twenty-four hours assaults had been launched by contributing factions on nine separate axes inside northern Latakia, and the intensity of opposition operations in Hama and Idlib had spiked notably. Ahrar al-Sham, backed by Liwa al-Haq, Suqor al-Sham, Alwiya Ahfad al-Rasoul and at least five other groups, were setting the tone for the remainder of 2013—complex coordination of large operational fronts was now necessary to pose a continued challenge to the authority of an Assad regime whose confidence was being bolstered by increased external assistance from allies in Iran, Lebanon and Iraq.

Such unity of purpose, between groups of all ideologies and backgrounds, had already been a reality for some time, but the ISI–Jabhat al-Nusra furore had generated a new level of suspicion and introspection. However, while that could potentially have encouraged divisions and paranoia between groups, a series of massacres by pro-regime paramilitaries in the western governorate of Tartous in early May served as a rallying call for unity.

Events began early on 2 May when local FSA fighters clashed with Syrian army and NDF personnel in the village of al-Bayda. Facing superior firepower, the FSA unit withdrew from the village around midday, opening up the area to locally deployed pro-regime paramilitaries and the army. For approximately three hours 'government and pro-government forces entered homes, separated men from women, rounded up the men of each neighbourhood in one spot, and executed them by shooting them at close range,' according to a Human Rights Watch report based on interviews with survivors. At least 167 people were killed in those three hours in al-Bayda, all of them 'civilian non-combatants', including at least 23 women and 14 children.[24] That same day similar clashes broke out between opposition fighters and the army in the Ras al-Nabe district of the town of Baniyas, 10 kilometres from al-Bayda. The following morning pro-regime forces stormed Ras al-Nabe, searched and looted residential buildings and, by the end of the day, as many as 188 people had been killed, including 54 children and 43 women.[25]

This was not the first recorded incidence of apparent mass killings of civilians based on their political allegiance and religious sect—both al-Bayda and the Ras al-Nabe district of Baniyas were notoriously pro-revolution areas populated almost entirely by Sunni Muslims. According to Human Rights Watch:

> The scale of killings and torching of homes and property a day after the fighting ended suggests that the government attacks may have been intended to displace a civilian population that was perceived as supportive of the opposition from an area that a government minister characterized as 'very sensitive'. Many consider it to be in the heartland of the Alawite region.

> Syria's government acknowledged that it conducted military operations in Al-Bayda and Baniyas ... Commenting on the killings ... Ali Haidar, minister of state for national reconciliation affairs, told the *Wall Street Journal* that 'mistakes' may have been made and that a government committee is investigating.[26]

Allegations of sectarian cleansing and population displacement became widespread following the massacres. In fact, statistics revealed that Tartous had been 90 per cent Alawite before the revolution, but that this had dropped to 75 per cent by July 2012 and again down to 60 per cent later that year due to the arrival of Sunnis from intense battlefronts.[27]

Taking a more nuanced line, Hassan Hassan convincingly suggested that:

> The regime probably feels that such massacres will deepen sectarian tensions and pit Sunni and Alawites against each other, thereby convincing the Alawites that they need to fight alongside the Assad regime for their survival ... the message to Sunni fighters is that the coastline is a red line. For Alawites the message is one of reassurance.[28]

It is quite likely that the killings were motivated by a whole host of factors, including those mentioned above, but also simply by the reality that brutality becomes so much more likely in conflicts fought between local communities—'intimate violence', as Stathis Kalyvas termed it in 2006.[29] Whatever the motive or cause, events in al-Bayda and Baniyas sparked mass calls for revenge within the Syrian insurgency. While countless FSA factions announced their own localised operations 'in revenge for al-Bayda and Baniyas', jihadist militants also used the events for recruitment. After all, a mobilisation to protect the Sunni community in *bilad al-Sham* was as powerful a recruiting call as any jihadist might be capable of making. As but one example, a senior Jaish al-Muhajireen wa'l Ansar leader from Azerbaijan, Abu Yahya al-Azeri, issued a formal call for all of the world's Muslims to join the jihad in Syria. Many similar invocations were made at the time, with the operational roles of Hezbollah and Iran similarly featuring as key grounds for joining the jihad.

Midway through May Turkey suffered its most deadly terrorist attack ever, when two car bombs detonated in the town of Reyhanlı, near the Syrian border, killing at least fifty-one people. The issue of responsibility for the attacks, which took place in a town heavily populated by Syrian refugees, was mysterious to say the least. While some Turkish media reported in September 2013 that ISIS had been responsible,[30] this was widely challenged by Syrian opposition members. Several Turkish nationals were detained by authorities within weeks of the attack, all of whom police claimed had links to the Assad regime.[31] This fits with the widely shared story inside Syria, which placed the blame on members of a small community of Alawites living in southern Turkey's Hatay province.

One member of this community aroused particular resentment and suspicion within opposition circles. Mihraç Ural (Ali Kayali) was born in Hatay, a provincial region that Syria has long laid a territorial claim to. As a young man Ural had joined the pro-Syrian Hatay Liberation Army, and also for a time the Marxist–Leninist revolutionary faction Türkiye Halk Kurtuluş Partisi— Cephesi (THKP-C). After being imprisoned in Adana in early 1980, Ural bribed prison authorities to grant his release, and by August of that year he had fled to Syria, where Hafez al-Assad's brother Cemil granted him Syrian citizenship. It was at this point that suspicions arose within the THKP-C and its splinter faction known as Acilciler that Ural may in fact have been an agent of Syria's intelligence service.[32]

Both prior to and during the Syrian revolution, Ural led al-Muqawama al-Souriya (the Syrian Resistance), which has occasionally been referred to as the Popular Front for the Liberation of the Sanjak of Alexandretta—referring to the name by which Hatay province was formerly known prior to its joining Turkey in the late 1930s. Headquartered in the Syrian Alawite heartland of

Latakia, Ural's al-Muqawama al-Souriya is driven by a combination of pro-Syrian sentiment and Marxist–Leninist ideology. But its involvement in driving deeply sectarian paramilitary operations in defence of Assad in north-western Syria reveals something deeper, according to Aymenn Jawad al-Tamimi:

> Beneath this image of Syrian nationalism and leftist ideology lies a more narrow sectarian emphasis on defending the Alawite and Twelver Shi'a communities. Despite the admiration shown for the atheist Che Guevara, Kayali himself cares deeply about his religious heritage and is in this respect similar to most Turkish Alawites who have generally clung to their religious traditions in contrast to the multi-faceted nature of Alawite identity in Syria ... Besides the widely circulated footage of Kayali [from early May 2013] in which he apparently calls for the necessity of cleansing Sunni areas on the coastline (most notably Baniyas), Kayali is also frequently shown ... appearing with Alawite sheikhs.[33]

Al-Muqawama al-Souriya, or at least Turkish Alawite individuals working for the same cause and with links to Syrian intelligence, are most widely blamed for the bombings in Reyhanlı. But truthfully, details are too murky for a definitive case to be made. Nonetheless, the very fact that Alawites were so widely attributed responsibility within Syrian opposition circles—and particularly within the jihadist community—only further added to the growing sectarian motivations for those fighting and considering joining the jihad in Syria.

At the same time as the Reyhanlı bombings, the first conclusive signs of ISIS operating as a distinct entity in Syria were beginning to emerge. It had been a month since Baghdadi's statement proclaiming the expansion of the ISI into Syria and, despite Jolani's refusal to subsume Jabhat al-Nusra into this expanded ISIS, it had at the time been unclear what would come from the two leaders' very public disagreement. Beginning on 14 May, several videos began to be published on YouTube claiming to show ISIS activities in Syria's Deir ez Zour, Homs and Raqqa governorates. The first grabbed attention. Shot in the city of Raqqa, which had been captured in March, the video showed three men being publicly sentenced to death and executed with single gunshots to the head in the city's central roundabout. While a video had been published in Iraq using the new ISIS name on 25 April, this marked the first evidence of ISIS operating in Syria.[34]

While this came as a shock to the world's media, preparations for ISIS's public emergence had been under way for some time—in fact, far beyond Baghdadi's arrival in northern Syria in February–March 2013. The secret meetings held in Aleppo and Idlib in March were, in a sense, confidence-building measures deemed necessary for such a dramatic announcement. But Baghdadi already had several loyalist commanders in Syria, prepared to be the initial building blocks for ISIS's birth in Syria.

One of these loyalists was Amr al-Absi, whose brother Firas had established and led Majlis Shura al-Mujahideen until his assassination in late August 2012. Amr, better known as Abu Atheer, had been a detainee in Sednayya from 2007 until his release in May 2011. Once out, he led the founding of another Salafist faction based in Homs—Katibat Usud al-Sunnah—which began establishing a presence in rural Aleppo in late 2012 after Abu Atheer assumed authority over Majlis Shura al-Mujahideen in his brother's place.

Abu Atheer himself became a roving ambassador across much of northern Syria in the early months of 2013. 'He met with loads of *muhajirin* factions back then,' according to one Islamist fighter involved in inter-group affairs in Aleppo and Idlib.[35] Abu Atheer established particularly close personal relationships with Omar al-Shishani and his Jaish al-Muhajireen wa'l Ansar jihadist group, which was becoming an increasingly powerful player in Aleppo.

It is no coincidence, therefore, that following Baghdadi's 8 April statement announcing ISIS, Abu Atheer was appointed as the ISIS *wali* (governor) in Aleppo, and shortly thereafter—after strong encouragement from Abu Atheer—Omar al-Shishani was appointed as ISIS's chief of military operations in northern Syria. Jaish al-Muhajireen wa'l Ansar, meanwhile, would remain an independent organisation for several more months, while its senior leadership fought over their respective loyalties or quests for independence.

The personal testimonies and experiences of several Salafists active in northern Syria at the time paint a portrait of Abu Atheer as an outwardly committed Islamist, but with minimal credentials as such, and a man whose loyalties were never quite consistent or necessarily trusted. 'He was a brave person,' said one Salafist who had known Abu Atheer in Homs since 2012:

> It was possible to deal with him before the announcement of the state (ISIS), but after that, it became impossible and the issue of *takfir* [excommunication from Islam] discourse became predominant. [It was a] typical product of years in jail, [which] made his rejection of other ideologies particularly harsh. [He had] very limited religious knowledge [and was] not very gifted with manners.[36]

Internal disagreements notwithstanding, it was through these kinds of personal relationships of loyalty to its cause that ISIS was born in Syria. And of course powerful individuals had their own personal followings, which provided foot-soldiers to the fledgling organisation.

The majority of ISIS's initial 'recruit base', however, came from within Jabhat al-Nusra, which effectively split into two in April and May 2013. As one Syrian Jabhat al-Nusra fighter put it, 'It was a difficult time—the Islamic State's reputation and resources and its history of fighting the Americans attracted many of our foreign brothers, especially the *khalijis* [those from the Gulf states]—many left us for their project.'[37]

By mid-May, as videos were just beginning to emerge, ISIS had thus established an active insurgent presence in Raqqa city and its surrounding countryside; in rural Aleppo and small parts of Aleppo city; and in several areas of rural Deir ez Zour. A fledgling presence in the Homs desert was also in its early stages. In almost all of these areas ISIS was operating in tandem with Jabhat al-Nusra and occasionally—such as in areas of Deir ez Zour such as al-Quriya and al-Mayadin—their names were virtually interchangeable.[38] In other areas ISIS had seemingly swallowed up entire Jabhat al-Nusra factions. This was the case in the town of Tel Abyad in northern Raqqa, for example, where clashes were renewed with Kataib al-Farouq, but this time under the guise of ISIS.

Through mid- and late May, however, Jabhat al-Nusra remained the only of the two organisations to operate openly—though totally unacknowledged by its al-Manara al-Bayda media wing—in Latakia, Damascus and Deraa. In the latter, Jabhat al-Nusra had even released two unofficial statements on 7 and 22 May detailing 'an odd-sounding laundry list of complaints and sharia rulings'.[39]

The emerging reality, in short, was that ISIS had become a new and potentially very powerful jihadist actor in the Syrian conflict and Jabhat al-Nusra had serious competition on its hands in terms of maintaining its position as the most influential of such groups in the conflict. The dust was only just beginning to settle, but there was more to this story yet to come.

Meanwhile, another storm was brewing in Homs, where the Syrian army and Hezbollah had on 19 May finally launched a widely expected offensive on al-Qusayr and a string of villages on its mountainous periphery. By this time the regime had placed a stranglehold on Homs city to the east, after a prolonged and brutal offensive against opposition fighters that had begun in February 2012. A brief insurgent counter-attack in the city in March 2013 was put down by Syrian army forces, largely thanks to an influx of Hezbollah fighters into the al-Qusayr area which had allowed for army reinforcements to be sent into the city—a principal reason for the previously mentioned start of rocket attacks on Hermel that month.

Al-Qusayr had begun to come under pressure in early May, when the Syrian army intensified its use of artillery and air strikes in the area, but 19 May marked the expansion of ground attacks. The defence of al-Qusayr was conducted by a broad variety of groups, including Kataib al-Farouq and Kataib Maghaweer al-Qusayr, but Jabhat al-Nusra also played a role. From 19 May the situation in the town became increasingly desperate and large insurgent factions across Syria began sending convoys of reinforcements. Ahrar al-Sham and Liwa al-Tawhid sent fighters from Idlib and Aleppo, while Liwa Nasr Salahaddin and Liwa al-Usra sent reinforcements from Raqqa and Deir ez Zour. Al-Qusayr in and of itself was not necessarily of existential value to the revolution, but its position overlooking the main M5 highway linking Damascus north to Homs, Hama and Aleppo, as well as its links directly into Lebanon and to the Alawite coastal heartlands north-west in Tartous and Latakia, made it of particular strategic value. But it was not only that. It was also acquiring an incredibly intense symbolic value due to the resources quite clearly being invested into its assault by Hezbollah. As such, the defence of al-Qusayr became a major priority for the revolution.

Not only did the issue of al-Qusayr arouse the attention of all involved in the revolution inside Syria, but it also triggered—for the first time on such a scale—a mass mobilisation of the region's Sunni Islamic leadership to expound the religious necessity to defend Syria's Sunni revolutionaries from attack by 'the Shia' (Hezbollah) and 'the Alawites' (the regime and its military–security apparatus).

On 22 May ten senior members of the international Muslim Scholars Association—which represents various Sunni scholars around the world—issued a statement in support of jihad against the *nusayri*s and *rafidi*s (a derogatory term referring to Shia Muslims):

> It is obligatory to support the Jihad by all means of force possible ... It is obligatory on the Mujahideen in Syria that their armies come together and unite in their discourse for an end to the siege of Qusayr and the towns, which the enemy is raiding ... On Muslims generally it is obligatory to support their brothers in what they endure, and to supply them with what they can, especially in Qusayr.[40]

A little over a week later came a similar announcement, but one that would have much more of a practical impact on legitimising the idea of travelling to Syria to join the jihad. In a speech during a rally in the Qatari capital Doha late on 31 May, prominent Muslim cleric Yusuf al-Qaradawi exclaimed:

> Every Muslim trained to fight and capable of doing that [must] make himself available ... Iran is pushing forward arms and men so why do we stand idle? The leader of the party of Satan [Hezbollah] comes to fight the Sunnis ... Now we know what the Iranians want ... They want continued massacres to kill Sunnis ...

How could 100 million Shia defeat 1.7 billion [Sunnis]? Only because [Sunni] Muslims are weak![41]

For many Muslims worldwide Qaradawi's speech in Doha would have represented sufficient sanction to travel to Syria to join in the defence of the revolution. Qaradawi—a graduate of the famous al-Azhar University in Cairo, author of over 120 books on Islam and presenter of the *al-Sharia wa'l Hayah* television show on Al-Jazeera, which was watched by as many as 60 million people around the world[42]—had both the geographical reach and ideological legitimacy to impact the flow of foreign fighters into Syria. Although impossible to measure, it seems certain that his speech did just that, not least because Saudi Arabia's Grand Mufti, 'Abd al-Aziz ibn Abdullah Al al-Sheikh, announced his support for his message one week later.[43]

By the end of May, however, the fate of al-Qusayr seemed to have already been determined. Despite the continued arrival of insurgent reinforcements, Hezbollah reportedly deployed additional forces from its specialist units— newly trained in urban warfare techniques—and personnel from Syria's ultra-loyalist Third and Fourth Mechanized Divisions arrived in the area from Damascus on 28 May. Shortly thereafter the opposition lost control of the invaluable Dabaa air base south of al-Qusayr, and the battle lines moved back to the edges of the town's north and west.[44]

The final ground assault was launched by Hezbollah personnel on 3 June. But this was preceded by a brutal bombardment of the town using artillery and a particularly valuable weapon: a 107-millimetre improvised rocket assisted munition, or IRAM. Used extensively by Iran-backed Shia militias during the US occupation of Iraq, IRAMs were used by Hezbollah in al-Qusayr to fire at and demolish entire buildings from close range—a ground-clearance tactic that refused insurgents the space for operation. A subsequent investigation of images taken of some of these IRAMs in al-Qusayr by blogger Eliot Higgins found them to have been manufactured using Iranian 107-millimetre artillery rockets, emphasizing the clearly pivotal role played in the area not only by Hezbollah but by its Iranian backer.

On the following day, 4 June, Hezbollah and Syrian army personnel moved into the centre of al-Qusayr after a negotiated insurgent withdrawal had been agreed overnight. The town was lost, and the Syrian opposition as a whole, including the jihadist components, had suffered a very significant strategic and symbolic defeat. To rub salt in their wounds, it was an outside actor (Hezbollah) that had ensured the regime's victory. Later that morning Hezbollah fighters inside Lebanon distributed sweets throughout their strongholds in the eastern

Bekaa Valley and in southern Beirut to celebrate their triumph in al-Qusayr. On the opposition side, the mood was dire. 'Qusayr was a terrible terrible defeat for the revolution. It really affected us all over Syria. Only anger and our steadfastness for the revolution and our martyrs kept us going,' as one FSA commander based in Idlib put it.[45]

Following the negotiated withdrawal, a great many insurgents crossed into Lebanon and headed towards the relative safety of the town of Arsal, which the opposition had established as a thoroughfare for logistics and the wounded—Jabhat al-Nusra would come to call the town 'the lung which the mujahideen in the Qalamoun and Syrian refugees breath from'.[46]

Many Jabhat al-Nusra militants were part of this shift into Lebanon, and as time passed after al-Qusayr's loss, the low morale and intense desire to exact revenge on Hezbollah, Iran and the Assad regime meant that Jabhat al-Nusra gained many new recruits from within the defeated FSA factions now temporarily cut off from their revolution. This in turn would allow Jabhat al-Nusra to consolidate connections it had established with Sunni militants in Lebanon's northern city of Tripoli, who had been clashing with Hezbollah supporters sporadically since 2012.

During the final days of the battle for al-Qusayr, and in the days following the withdrawal of insurgent forces from the town, the intensity of rocket attacks on eastern Lebanon from Syria spiralled. Even in late May two artillery rockets were fired into the pro-Hezbollah districts of southern Beirut, thoroughly underlining that the Syrian conflict had reached Lebanon's interior. But with the exception of fighting in Tripoli, attacks in Lebanon involving actual combat also increased. As only three examples:

– On 28 May three soldiers were killed in a raid on a checkpoint near Arsal by Syrian insurgents who then fled back into Syria.[47]
– A day after more than twelve rockets were launched in Hermel, Hezbollah militants ambushed a convoy of suspected Jabhat al-Nusra fighters near the town of Baalbek on 2 June, killing at least twelve.[48]
– On 16 June suspected Syrian insurgents ambushed a vehicle carrying members of the Shia Muslim Jaafar clan outside the town of Masharih al-Qaa, killing four people.[49]

The most significant fallout from the Syrian conflict into Lebanon in June, however, came later that month when Sunni gunmen loyal to Sheikh Ahmed al-Assir engaged in three days of heavy fighting with the Lebanese army. Eighteen soldiers, four Hezbollah militants, two civilians and as many as forty

Sunni gunmen were killed in what would later be termed the Battle of Sidon. The fighting, which lasted through 23–25 June, centred on Assir's controversial Bilal bin Rabah Mosque in Abra, and Hezbollah-linked gunmen were widely reported to have backed the Lebanese army's operation to capture or kill Assir and his famous follower Fadl Shaker, who had given up a celebrity career in singing to declare his allegiance to Assir in 2011. Assir fled his besieged mosque along with Shaker on 24 June to an unknown location.

While ISIS had by now thoroughly emerged as an active and independent militant actor in Syria, the issue surrounding whether Jabhat al-Nusra should or would merge into it remained unresolved. In fact, by early June, Jabhat al-Nusra's senior leadership and its al-Manara al-Bayda media wing had been entirely silent since 10 April. But behind closed doors, Jabhat al-Nusra and its leader Jolani had been anything but silent. While individual members of Jabhat al-Nusra's *majlis al-shura* had been engaged in extensive diplomatic initiatives on the ground to prevent further units defecting to ISIS, Jolani had sent a message to Ayman al-Zawahiri in Pakistan urging him to mediate a resolution to this dangerous dispute.

Jolani's letter—presumably sent shortly after his statement refusing to merge into ISIS—received a welcome reply when a secret letter written by Zawahiri arrived declaring that the ISIS project was cancelled and that the ISI should remain in Iraq and Jabhat al-Nusra should remain in Syria. Jolani was triumphant, and swiftly wrote a secret message to his fellow fighters. 'Indeed, we had raised the matter with Sheikh Dr Ayman al-Zawahiri—may Allah protect him—so that he might make a judgment on the matter, and verily the response has come to us.'[50]

Although Zawahiri's letter had ordered that the two groups maintain positive relations, someone within Jabhat al-Nusra clearly made the decision to rub Zawahiri's ruling in ISIS's face. Copies of both Zawahiri and Jolani's letters were subsequently leaked, revealing to the public—and, perhaps more importantly, to the international jihadist community—that Zawahiri had ruled on the side of Jabhat al-Nusra. Arab journalist Zaid Benjamin published Jolani's letter, while Al-Jazeera published the one written by Zawahiri, which is reproduced in English below:[51]

* * *

In the name of God, the Compassionate, the Merciful:

[...]

[To] the noble brother: His Excellence Sheikh Abu Bakr al-Baghdadi al-Husseini, and his brothers in the Shura of the Islamic State of Iraq, may God protect them.

[To] the noble brother: His Excellence Sheikh Abu Mohammed al-Jolani, and his brothers in the Shura of Jabhat al-Nusra li Ahl ash-Sham, may God protect them.

Salam Alaykum wa rahmat Allah wa barakaatuhu. I hope that you and those with you are well, and that God is bringing us together in what He loves and is pleased with the glory of the world and the attainment of the Hereafter. And following:

1. The people of Jihad became saddened—all of them—at the dispute that arose and appeared in the relations between our beloved brothers in the Islamic State of Iraq and Jabhat al-Nusra li Ahl ash-Sham.

2. And what happened on the part of both parties—in which we were not sought for giving orders and which we did not seek to propagate, but also we did not know about it—and the grief we heard was from media.

3. First, it is inevitable that I remind all the mujahideen and Muslims of the role of the Islamic State of Iraq in resisting the Crusader plan for making an alliance with and dividing the heart of the Muslim world, and their resistance of the aggressive Safavid–Rafidite expansionism into Iraq, al-Sham and the Arabian Peninsula.

   And it is inevitable that we praise the good deeds of our brothers in the Islamic State of Iraq and their head and amir: Sheikh Abu Bakr al-Baghdadi in extending the jihad into al-Sham with the best of men and his honouring them with financial support over adversity in which they are supported and judged. But we also have affection for our beloved people and brothers in Jabhat al-Nusra on account of the praise of Sheikh Abu Bakr al-Baghdadi and his brothers for them and their amir Abu Mohammed al-Jolani.

4. It is also inevitable that I remind all the mujahideen and Muslims of the role of our brothers in Jabhat al-Nusra li Ahl ash-Sham in their reviving of the obligation of Jihad in Sham ar-Rabat and the Jihad; and their reviving the hope of the Muslim Ummah in liberating Al-Aqsa and the establishment of the guiding Khilafah with God's permission. Likewise, [it is inevitable that I mention] their resistance to the Safavid, Rafidite, Batinite and secular enemy on the harbour of Islam in beloved Sham. And it is inevitable that we mention with appreciation their recognition of their brothers in Islamic State of Iraq for what they have brought for them as regards help, aid and assistance.

5. When the disagreement between the two excellent and interlinked groups of mujahideen was made public, I touched on the matters of the disagreement in a message from me on 1 Jumada ath-Thaniya 1434 to the two excellent Sheikhs Abu Bakr al-Baghdadi al-Husseini and Abu Mohammed al-Jolani for a freezing of the situation that existed before the disagreement for the right time to pass judgment.

6. Messages from both parties and others reached me, and based on this, I, after consultation with my brothers in Khorasan and elsewhere, and after consulting my Lord—Subhaanuhu wa Ta'aala ...—for guidance in the face of my weakness and lack of strategem, with the reason of hoping to extinguish the fire of Fitna and the disagreement between the two noble and exalted groups, I have made a decision on the matter—must'aeeban Allah—as follows:

a) Sheikh Abu Bakr al-Baghdadi was in error in his announcement of the Islamic State of Iraq and al-Sham without seeking our order, consulting us or even informing us.

b) Sheikh Abu Mohammed al-Jolani was in error of his announcement of the rejection of the Islamic State of Iraq and al-Sham and made clear his relation with al-Qaeda without seeking our order, consulting us, or even informing us.

c) The Islamic State of Iraq and al-Sham is cancelled, and work continues under the name of Islamic State of Iraq.

d) Jabhat al-Nusra is a separate entity for Jamaat Qaedat al-Jihad, following the general leadership.

e) The realm of Islamic State of Iraq is Iraq.

f) The realm of Jabhat al-Nusra li Ahl al-Sham is Syria.

g) Sheikh Abu Bakr al-Baghdadi al-Husseini is to remain emir of Islamic State of Iraq for the period of one year from the point of this ruling, after which the Shura Council of the Islamic State of Iraq is to issue a report to the general leadership for Jamaat Qaedat al-Jihad about the course of operations, with the general leadership making a decision after this on whether to continue having Sheikh Abu Bakr al-Baghdadi al-Husseini as emir or having a new emir come to power.

h) Sheikh Abu Mohammed al-Jolani is to remain emir of Jabhat al-Nusra li Ahl al-Sham for a period of one year from the point of this ruling, and after this the Shura Council of Jabhat al-Nusra li Ahl al-Sham is to issue a report to the general leadership of Jamaat Qaedat al-Jihad about the course of operations, with the general leadership making a decision after this on whether to continue having Sheikh Abu Mohammed al-Jolani as emir or having a new emir come to power.

i) Islamic State of Iraq is to provide support for Jabhat al-Nusra li Ahl al-Sham—as far as it can—for what Jabhat al-Nusra li Ahl al-Sham seeks as regards reinforcements in terms of men, arms, wealth, shelter and protection.

j) Jabhat al-Nusra li Ahl al-Sham is to provide support for Islamic State of Iraq—as far as it can—for what Islamic State of Iraq seeks as regards reinforcements in terms of men, arms, wealth, shelter and protection.

k) The two parties are to desist from any enmity in speech or deed against the other party.

l) It is obligatory on both parties and on all the mujahideen to respect the inviolability of the Muslims in their blood, support and wealth, and not one of them is to attack a Muslim or Mujahid except on the authority of a judicial ruling, with its decision making its minimum clear.

m) Every Muslim is sacrosanct to the Muslim, and so anyone who moves from one Jihad group to another is not counted as an outsider, or from one front to another, but for said person there is the sacrosanctity of the Muslim and the mujahid, even if we disapprove of his moving.

n) Anyone who becomes involved in spilling the blood of his Muslim brothers and the Mujahideen, the group will seek a firm stance against him on the basis of defending virtue and preventing vice.

o) His Excellence Sheikh Abu Khaled al-Suri is among the best known and experienced of the living mujahideen, even as we do not praise him over God, and he is appointed our representative in al-Sham on the following matters:

   (i) Judgment on any disagreement in interpretation of this ruling falls on him.

   (ii) In the event of any transgression by one of the parties against the other, he has the authority to set up a Sharia court to judge on the dispute.

p) I make it obligatory on all my brothers in Jamaat Qaedat al-Jihad, and I ask all my Muslim brothers and Mujahideen to desist from enmity in this disagreement, to refrain from provocation among the Mujahideen, and to work for the restoration of harmony, as well as unity and the unification of hearts, and the unity of ranks among the Muslims and Mujahideen.

And may they know the power and authority of these two noble groups of Mujahideen, and only speak good of them.

7. A copy of this ruling has been sent to everyone from:

a) Islamic State of Iraq

b) Jabhat al-Nusra li Ahl al-Sham

c) His Excellence Sheikh Abu Khaled al-Suri

('Verily I only desire reform to the best of my power, and I cannot give guidance except by God: in Him I trust and to Him I repent'—Qur'an 11:88).

Your brother:

Aymenn al-Zawahiri
13 Rajab 1434
Markaz al-Fajr lil-'Ilam

\* \* \*

There had been a question over the exact structural relationship between the ISI and al-Qaeda since 2006, when the ISI was formed. That year had been one of substantial change for al-Qaeda's presence in Iraq. On 15 January Abu Musab al-Zarqawi's infamous AQI announced a merger with five other Iraq-based jihadist groups: Jaish al-Taifa al-Mansoura, Saraya Ansar al-Tawhid, Saraya al-Jihad al-Islami, Saraya al-Ghurabaa and Kataib al-Ahwal. Through this merger—within which AQI was very much the dominant actor—the Majlis Shura al-Mujahideen was formed. Five months later, on 7 June, US special operations forces killed Zarqawi and his spiritual adviser Sheikh 'Abd al-Rahman following an airstrike on their position in the Iraqi city of Baqubah, leaving the recently formed Majlis Shura al-Mujahideen leaderless.

While for some jihadist groups this may have represented a killer blow, it in fact encouraged a strengthening of the organisation. Only five days later Zarqawi's successor was named as Abu Ayyub al-Masri (or Abu Hamza al-Muhajir), and four months after that, in October, Iraq's leading jihadist organisation, Majlis Shura al-Mujahideen, announced its qualitative transformation into al-Dawla al-Islamiyya fi'l Iraq (or the Islamic State in Iraq: ISI).

Up until this point, strictly speaking, the brand-new ISI was an affiliate of al-Qaeda, but when Abu Ayyub al-Masri pledged *bay'a* to the new ISI *emir* Hamid Dawoud Mohammed Khalil al-Zawi (Abu Omar al-Baghdadi) on 10 November 2006, his ultimate allegiance and that of his al-Qaeda affiliate switched to the ISI, thus technically negating (or placing on a second rung) any allegiance to al-Qaeda and its then leader, Osama Bin Laden.[52]

Such developments may appear more akin to the bureaucratic management shifts in the business world, but AQI and then the ISI were obsessively bureaucratic organisations. These small technicalities appeared to make a significant difference, even if not immediately obvious at the time. In December 2007, speaking as the then deputy leader of al-Qaeda, Ayman al-Zawahiri announced during an interview that 'there is nothing in Iraq by the name of Al-Qaeda'.[53] Former Saudi al-Qaeda commander Abdullah al-Qahtani subsequently reiterated this point in an interview with al-Arabiya.[54]

As early as 2006, al-Qaeda's central leadership was encouraging the ISI to establish an Islamic state. In June that year, for example, then deputy al-Qaeda leader Zawahiri called upon what was then Majlis Shura al-Mujahideen to 'know that the ummah has put its hopes upon you and it will be necessary for you to establish an Islamic State in Iraq, before advancing towards the occupied Jerusalem and restoring the Caliphate'.[55]

But despite this long-held encouragement, the realisation of the 2006 declaration was not well received within al-Qaeda's central leadership. It was undertaken too quickly. Writing in 2010, Adam Gadahn, a prominent American within al-Qaeda's central leadership, claimed 'the decision to declare the State (ISI) was taken without consultation from Al-Qaeda's leadership ... [which] caused a split in the mujahideen's ranks and their supporters inside and outside Iraq'.[56]

Despite this, there was clearly an extent to which al-Qaeda still saw itself as an authority 'figure' over the ISI's operations in Iraq. In 2007 and 2008, for example, ISI documents seized by coalition forces in Iraq revealed that al-Qaeda's central leadership had ordered the ISI to carry out attacks on certain targets—'against Halliburton in 2007 and the Danes in 2008 ... [and] also asked for information on the [ISI's] personnel and expenditures. When the group refused to answer corruption charges leveled by one of its former officials, al Qaeda Central summoned Masri, the group's war minister and previously the head of AQI, to the woodshed in "Khorasan" (Afghanistan or Pakistan).[57]

All of this notwithstanding, Jolani's explicit pledge of allegiance to Zawahiri had made al-Qaeda's role in this crisis impossible to ignore. And indeed, al-Qaeda was in the midst of a major crisis, which was described at the time by one Jabhat al-Nusra source, speaking to Al-Jazeera, as 'the most dangerous development in the history of global jihad'.[58] The high stakes involved here, not least in terms of salvaging the reputation and unity of the al-Qaeda network, were clear throughout Zawahiri's letter. The leader of the world's most dangerous jihadist network was attempting to strongly assert his authority. Not only would both groups revert back to their original statuses prior to April 2013, Zawahiri declared, but both Jolani and Baghdadi would be limited to twelve months as leaders of their respective organisations—their future after that to be determined by al-Qaeda's central leadership in Afghanistan and Pakistan.

Although his letter was intended to remain private and restricted to its intended audiences, Zawahiri's words were tough and to the point. There was no time for niceties. With that being said, however, a crucial determinant of al-Qaeda's more recent ability to survive, to acquire new affiliates, and to sustain operations in multiple zones of jihad was its ability to maintain positive and 'brotherly' relations between its various factions. Zawahiri's specific order that Jabhat al-Nusra and the ISI provide each other with 'support' in the form of 'reinforcements in terms of men, arms, wealth, shelter and protection' was designed very much in that light. But clearly, Zawahiri feared not only that these two groups had disagreed but that their quarrel might turn violent. Warnings regarding the sacrosanctity of Muslim life and the potential consequences for anyone found to be involved in 'spilling the blood of his Muslim brothers and the Mujahideen' presaged what was to transpire in the coming months.

Finally, the letter was also of interest for its announcement that Abu Khaled al-Suri—a senior member of Ahrar al-Sham—had purportedly been appointed as al-Qaeda's 'representative in al-Sham', with the responsibility of making judgements on disagreements over Zawahiri's ruling and for establishing *sharia* courts to rule on such disagreements when necessary. As previously discussed, there is considerable debate over whether or not Abu Khaled had been pre-warned or consulted over this apparent appointment. He undoubtedly enjoyed a substantial high-level history with the al-Qaeda organisation, but his prominent affiliation (but not a founding member) with Ahrar al-Sham—whose consistently expressed focus on Syria and not a global jihad contrasts totally with al-Qaeda's transnational outlook—raised some questions.

Whatever the truth of the matter, Abu Khaled's inclusion in Zawahiri's letter marked the first time his name had been publicly revealed as someone involved in the Syrian conflict. Prior to that, he had managed to keep his role a secret. Now out in the open, his name and his captivating history brought Ahrar al-Sham well and truly into the spotlight. Was this Syrian insurgent group, by now the most militarily powerful in Syria, linked to al-Qaeda?

Just as such questions were beginning to arise, Ahrar al-Sham's leader, who up until this point had only been known as Abu Abdullah al-Hamawi, revealed his true identity to the public for the first time. In a forty-eight-minute interview with Al-Jazeera's Arabic service, Hassan Abboud not only revealed his name, but his face. Although he ended the interview by proclaiming his intent to 'destroy by our hands the walls of the Sykes–Picot [Agreement]'—which delineated today's modern nation state borders in the Middle East—Abboud vehemently denied that Ahrar al-Sham or the Syrian Islamic Front (SIF), which it dominated, had any relationship with al-Qaeda. He did however note that 'we do a great many joint operations' with the group and 'we only see honesty in their work as well as toughness and bravery … the US designation [of Jabhat al-Nusra] will not stop us continuing to work with them.'[59]

The revelation was a big development for Ahrar al-Sham and Abboud in and of itself, but five days later Abboud suddenly appeared in Cairo, giving a keynote speech at the annual conference of the International Union of Muslim Scholars (IUMS), a coalition of scholars headed in Qatar by Yusuf al-Qaradawi. As the only Syrian insurgent figure present at the conference, Abboud clearly enjoyed some powerful backers—just travelling out of Syria to Egypt, via Turkey, was a feat by itself.

Two days later, while still in Cairo, Abboud gave a television interview on Egypt's Salafist channel, Al-Nas. Sitting alongside his then chief of external relations, Abu Mustafa, Abboud tacitly welcomed Western assistance to the revolution in Syria:

> We look at [the West's] decision to arm the opposition with suspicion … but we are happy that there will be an extra force to fight against the criminal Assad. But we want to warn our brothers not to let America interfere with what we want for our own country.[60]

While some speculated then that the close timing of Abboud's emergence and his trip to Cairo must have been strategically timed by the group, Abu Mustafa claims it was merely a coincidence: 'There was no plan at the time, it all happened so fast and the decision to travel was made late.'[61] Moreover, the political situation in Egypt was complicated at the time for Islamists—the anti-Brotherhood Tamarud movement had been established on 28 April and aimed to collect 15 million signatures supporting Mohammed Morsi's withdrawal from power by 30 June. 'There was some fear on our part,' said Abu Mustafa, 'considering the situation in Egypt at the time, but we decided to take the risk. We are a part of Syrian society and our people know us and we thought the same needed to be known to the whole world. Our case is for justice and freedom ... Our strategy was simply to present our revolution in the correct light.'[62]

Ahrar al-Sham was an unusual organisation. It walked a fine line, continuing to present itself as a Syrian Salafist insurgent faction while largely refusing to explicitly renounce the ideals of global jihad. Its ideological similarity to the ideas espoused by Abdullah Azzam during the initial months of al-Qaeda mirrored its determination to fight jihad within the Syrian national context and in order to protect Sunni people from aggression. Al-Qaeda's determination to attack the West came later in its existence, and was something that Ahrar al-Sham leaders wanted nothing to do with. 'Our struggle is against Bashar al-Assad and his allies on Syrian territory, that is all,'[63] Abboud told this author in late August 2014, only ten days before he was killed in a mysterious explosion along with over a dozen members of Ahrar al-Sham's senior leadership.

Truth be told, Ahrar al-Sham had grown into a formidable insurgent organisation with an impressively well-organised political leadership. In face-to-face meetings with senior Ahrar al-Sham officials, political deputies consistently took down minutes, and within a couple of hours of leaving follow-up questions were often sent from other leaders who had not attended. Such a concern with detail and centralised decision making—which this author has not experienced with any other Syrian insurgent faction or opposition body—probably explained its apparent acquisition of significant external backing, from Qatar and private donors across the Gulf. In June alone, with opposition success declining notably on the battlefield, Ahrar al-Sham still led the seizure of the strategically valuable town of Inkhel in Deraa governorate on 9 June and a large tank base in Hama governorate on 14 June. Its 'technical office', meanwhile, successfully hacked two pro-regime media sites and a website set up by the Assad-loyalist Syrian Electronic Army to leak documents hacked from Qatar's government.

While Ahrar al-Sham rose, the Jabhat al-Nusra–ISIS saga was not yet over. In fact, it was only just beginning. Nine days after Jolani's letter became public and six days after Al-Jazeera published Zawahiri's letter, the ISI's al-Furqan Media published an audio statement by none other than Abu Bakr al-Baghdadi himself. Issued on the same day as Jabhat al-Nusra's al-Manara al-Bayda also resumed activity, the title of Baghdadi's statement—'Remaining in Iraq and al-Sham'—left little to the imagination of what was contained within. Not only did Baghdadi insist that ISIS had indeed been established and would continue to operate in both Iraq and Syria, but he suggested that Zawahiri's letter contained 'legal and methodological' issues—an extraordinarily bold statement to make to someone of Zawahiri's standing:

> The Islamic State of Iraq and al-Sham will remain, as long as we have a vein pumping or an eye blinking. It remains and we will not compromise not give it up ... until we die.

> When it comes to the letter of Sheikh Ayman al-Zawahiri—may Allah protect him—we have many legal and methodological reservations ... After consulting with the consultative council of the Islamic State of Iraq and al-Sham ... I chose the order of Allah over the orders that contravenes Allah in the letter.[64]

Five days later, on 19 June, ISIS's chief spokesman Abu Mohammed al-Adnani issued his own audio statement, which also rejected Zawahiri's orders and criticised the al-Qaeda leader for 'jeopardizing the mujahideen's unity' and weakening the jihad.[65] ISIS's operations would continue to span both Syria and Iraq: 'one front, one leadership' and 'the borders will not separate the two', Adnani declared.[66] Criticism was also levelled at Jabhat al-Nusra and its senior leadership, which Adnani claimed was guilty of *inshiqaq* (defection)—for refusing to merge with the ISI—and were therefore dividing the *mujahideen* and encouraging insubordination.[67]

Adnani, whose birth name is Taha Sobhi Falaha, was born in 1977 in the town of Binnish in northern Syria's Idlib governorate. According to a biography written and published by prominent Bahraini ISIS *sharia* leader Turki al-Binali (Abu Hammam al-Athari) in November 2014, Adnani 'grew up with a love of mosques ... [and] memorized the Qur'an as a young man'.[68] Adnani purportedly began activities 'in jihad organisations' in 2000 and swore allegiance to Abu Musab al-Zarqawi 'in Syria with 35 others and set off to prepare for the start of fighting ... before the Americans entered Iraq and travelled to it'.[69] In the words of the US government, 'Adnani was one of the first foreign fighters to oppose Coalition forces in Iraq'.[70] Thus, Adnani was an 'instructor' at a training camp of AQI's predecessor organisation, Jama'at al-Tawhid wa'l-Jihad (JTWJ); attended the 'inauguration' of Zarqawi as AQI *emir*; became an AQI *sharia* official in Western Anbar; and was promoted to chief spokesman for the ISI and then ISIS.[71]

Adnani's words, which presented themselves even more combatively than Baghdadi's, were therefore to be taken seriously. In his position as ISIS spokesman Adnani had both the prestige and reach necessary to influence the trajectory of developments on the ground.

Firstly, it now seemed to be simply too late to reverse course—ISIS had become a concrete reality inside Syria, in part thanks to a considerable number of defections from Jabhat al-Nusra. The fact that the ISI had prepared in advance for its expansion into Syria meant that any reversal would have had to have taken place within days of the announcement. Perhaps even that would have been insufficient.

\* \* \*

Syria was now being faced with a new reality on the ground: two major jihadist groups had established themselves as prominent actors within the civil conflict. ISIS was carrying out insurgent operations against regime and pro-regime forces in several governorates, and appeared to be particularly strong already in Aleppo. For example, ISIS claimed a large suicide car bombing in the city on 17 June and was involved—in coordination with factions from the FSA, SIF, SILF and Jabhat al-Nusra—in attacks on regime positions across the city and rural countryside.

ISIS also appeared to be a growing body in Raqqa, where it had already carried out several public executions in the city and clashed heavily with the rival Kataib al-Farouq in Tel Abyad. Additional ISIS presences were confirmed in Idlib, Hama, the Homs desert and naturally also in Deir ez Zour, where several training camps—including one for children, or 'cubs', in al-Bukamal—were already in place. Deir ez Zour in particular had seen a proliferation in small jihadist factions since March 2013. One small group known as Ansar al-Sharia attracted some attention in mid-April for its involvement in a number of operations near Deir ez Zour city. But it was another group known as Harakat al-Taliban al-Islamiyya fi'l Sham that stood out the most, not least for its bellicose *takfiri* attitude and rhetoric. It took part in several joint raids on the village of Masrab in April during which civilians accused of supporting the regime were extra-judicially killed. It also released several video statements threatening to kill all non-Muslims.[72]

Not only was ISIS consolidating itself as a second major jihadist actor in Syria, but a rising tension between ISIS and Jabhat al-Nusra was also distracting Syrians and the international community from the revolution at large. Furthermore, division and hostile rhetoric between such organisations risked sparking dangerous inter-factional fighting that would draw resources away from the fight against the regime, which had already begun to reverse the course of the conflict. While the FSA and its Turkey-based SMC leadership had been willing to accommodate a comparatively pragmatic Jabhat al-Nusra, ISIS was viewed with intense suspicion within moderate insurgent circles. This too was a dangerous new dynamic.

8

# JULY–DECEMBER 2013

## RISING TENSIONS

Following on from the recapture of al-Qusayr in June, pro-regime forces launched a major assault on opposition-held districts of Homs city. In an attempt to distract from this imminent threat, northern insurgent groups rapidly carried out a number of offensives across Aleppo and Idlib. Meanwhile, further north-east, Jabhat al-Nusra and several Islamist allies were themselves distracted by intensified fighting with rival YPG Kurdish fighters in the border town of Ras al-Ayn—a development that would signify the start of a long-running hostile relationship between the two parties.

The overthrow of President Mohammed Morsi in Egypt in early July proved a valuable recruiting tool for jihadists, as the credibility of the pro-democracy exiled ETILAF opposition continued to decline inside Syria. This coincided with a discernible acceleration in the flow of foreign fighters into Syria and the establishment of several new jihadist groups in Latakia and Aleppo. Following the killing of over 1,400 people in a sarin gas attack outside Damascus in late August 2013, the flow of foreign fighters accelerated yet further.

After the threat of American-led airstrikes on Syria in retaliation for the sarin attack subsided, ISIS became increasingly self-assertive and aggressive in its behaviour, firing on protesters and killing rival insurgents in Idlib, Aleppo, Latakia and Raqqa. Despite facing resistance, ISIS expanded its control in northern and eastern Syria throughout the latter months of 2013. In other areas, however, ISIS coordinated with other insurgent factions—in Aleppo and Latakia, for example.

ISIS's divisive behaviour and the detrimental effect of its arrival in Syria on Jabhat al-Nusra meant that the principal beneficiaries in late 2013 were Syrian Islamists. Secret talks began in July–August between some of these groups regarding a potential merger and the establishment of a large coalition. Three months later the Islamic Front was formed, bringing together seven groups and their roughly 50,000 fighters. Intense controversy surrounding the value of planned Geneva II talks further encouraged Islamist unity of purpose in opposing the exiled political opposition.

Meanwhile, as spillover into Lebanon escalated in July with the first of several car bombings to strike Beirut, several concerted offensives were launched in southern Syria, and pro-regime forces intensified pressure on the insurgency in Aleppo. As 2013 drew to a close, Jabhat al-Nusra began adopting the use of Tanzim Qaedat al-Jihad before its name, as to signify its concrete allegiance to al-Qaeda, while Jaish al-Muhajireen wa'l Ansar militants began adopting the name Imarat Kavkaz, pointing to their loyalties in the North Caucasus.

Finally, escalating ISIS tensions and hostilities in northern Syria encouraged the coming together of FSA factions in a number of well-funded moderate coalitions and fronts.

* * *

As July 2013 began the conflict in Syria was reaching a level of strategic intensity not witnessed since the start of the revolution over two years earlier. Pro-regime forces were in the midst of a newly launched push on the last remaining pockets of opposition control in Homs city, focused on the districts of Khalidiyeh, al-Waar and Bab Hud. The sheer intensity of this military offensive and the potential threat of losing control of the city altogether induced the SIF and Jabhat al-Nusra—in coordination with several local FSA factions—to launch a coordinated series of major offensives targeting regime positions and transport links located on and close to Syria's principal north–south M5 highway in Idlib and northern Hama. In doing so, the insurgent forces involved hoped to draw Syrian army personnel away from Homs into multiple intense battlefronts.

To prevent having their own supply lines cut off from Aleppo, a simultaneous attack was launched on the predominantly Shia villages of Zahra and Nubl, north of Aleppo city. Since the conflict reached Aleppo in the summer of 2012, these two villages had steadily become an area of key strategic depth for the regime, particularly considering their links west to Latakia and Tartous and north to tactitly supportive Kurdish areas such as Afrin, where the PYD asserted control. This was by no means the first time that Islamist and jihadist insurgents had attacked Zahra and Nubl. More often than not, the rhetoric accompanying such attacks—which were normally limited to (indiscriminate) mortar and artillery rocket fire—tended to be harshly sectarian. However, more practically the villages were a target due to their noted strategic value to the regime in northern Syria.

Nonetheless, the selection of targets according to their sectarian make-up was becoming increasingly common for jihadists, particularly Jabhat al-Nusra and ISIS. Suicide bombings in Christian and Alawite neighbourhoods of Damascus, for example, were a monthly occurrence, at least. In July Jabhat al-Nusra detonated two suicide car bombs in the largely Alawite and fiercely pro-Assad Akrama district of Homs, killing thirty-seven people. The launching of Grad rockets—unguided systems with a maximum range of 20 kilometres—into pro-regime areas of Latakia was also increasingly common. The Assad family home town of Qardaha was a particularly favoured target in this regard.

Meanwhile, fighting was also intensifying south of Aleppo, particularly around the contested town of al-Safira 22 kilometres south-east of the city, where Ahrar al-Sham detonated a remote-controlled car bomb on 10 July. Jabhat al-Nusra and a local affiliate Ansar Khilafah also launched a successful final assault on the town of Khan al-Asal, 8 kilometres south-west of Aleppo city on 22 July, after which fifty-one soldiers were captured and extra-judicially executed on video. The town had been an especially contentious zone of battle for several months prior to its eventual capture, particularly due to an apparent chemical attack conducted there on 19 March 2013, in which at least twenty-six people died after foaming at the mouth and suffering convulsions and loss of vision.[1] Both the regime and the opposition subsequently blamed the incident on each other.

Perhaps the most significant conflict development in July, however, was the re-eruption of sustained fighting between the Kurdish YPG and a combination of Jabhat al-Nusra, ISIS, Ahrar al-Sham and Ghurabaa al-Sham. This latest bout of hostilities broke out late on 16 July, when a small group of Jabhat al-Nusra militants surrounded a mobile female YPJ unit, detaining the driver. Within an hour the YPG had deployed reinforcements into Ras al-Ayn and begun raids on key Jabhat al-Nusra positions in the town. By the morning of 17 July the YPG had rescued the YPJ driver and captured Jabhat al-Nusra's headquarters, thus effectively taking control of the town and its border crossing into neighbouring Turkey. The international nature of Jabhat al-Nusra's presence in the town was revealed several days later, when the YPG released photos of passports seized in the headquarters—from Bahrain, Qatar, Iraq, Tunisia, Egypt, the United Arab Emirates, Syria, and even the United States.[2] Fighting intensified throughout 18–20 July, as the YPG fanned out beyond Ras al-Ayn in an attempt to establish a defensive ring around the town, which was by now fully under its control. Tensions shifted 110 kilometres west to another Turkish border town, Tel Abyad. There, ISIS militants arrested several Kurdish councillors on 19 July, sparking armed clashes with the Kurdish Jabhat al-Akrad faction on 20 July that left ten people dead and Jabhat al-Nusra's local commander, 'Abu Musab', in YPG custody.

Although this would mark the beginning of a long-drawn-out period of Islamist–Kurdish conflict in northern Syria, with Ahrar al-Sham, Jabhat al-Nusra and several other factions announcing an offensive to 'cleanse' Ras al-Ayn on 24 July, the YPG and its overarching political wing the PYD was thus feeling supremely confident. Not only had it taken control of Ras al-Ayn in an efficiently quick manner, but it was also the dominant political and security actor across the remainder of Kurdish Syria—in northern regions of the Aleppo and Hasakah governorates.

On 19 July the PYD formally announced that it had written a constitution for an autonomous Syrian Kurdish region to be known as West Kurdistan. With its capital in Hasakah's Qamishli, the PYD's plan for autonomy included an intention to hold a referendum on the constitution three months later. While there had been indications that the PYD was planning such a move, it was met with universal opposition from the Syrian insurgency, the majority of which insisted on the territorial and political integrity of Syria's future, while a minority (jihadists) simply refused to acknowledge Kurdish ambitions.

While the Syrian conflict was continuing to expand and intensify internally, it was also becoming more and more inter-dependent and linked to other issues of regional and international security. For example, the overthrow of Egyptian President Mohammed Morsi on 2–3 July was met with intense frustration within the Syrian insurgency, with moderates, Islamists and jihadists all presenting Morsi's defeat as evidence that democracy and Western political systems were doomed to fail in the Middle East. On the Islamist end of the spectrum in particular, events in Egypt were perceived as definitive evidence that their ideological motivations and objectives in Syria had been justified. For ISIS, the logic was clear:

> [We] always knew that our rights can only be regained by force and that is why we have chosen the ammunition box instead of the the ballot box ... If you want to shake off injustice and create change, it can only be done by the sword. We choose to negotiate in the trenches, not in hotels. The conference lights should be turned off.[3]

With over a dozen hardline jihadist organisations playing a notable role in fighting the regime across the country, the 'opposition' in Syria was also becoming increasingly international. On 3 July senior Jaish al-Muhajireen wa'l Ansar commander Sayfullah al-Shishani issued a video address aimed at encouraging Turkish nationals to join the jihad in Syria. Like Omar al-Shishani, Sayfullah was from Georgia's Pankisi Gorge, but he had probably resided in Istanbul before entering Syria in 2012.[4] There, it seems he may have become relatively wealthy—Chechen fighters who fought under his command in Syria claim he brought $1 million in cash with him when he arrived in Syria.[5] A veteran of the Chechen conflict who had also spent a year fighting in Afghanistan, Sayfullah had opposed the arrival of ISIS in Syria from the start, which immediately introduced an element of tension into his relationship with Omar, which would result in their split in early August. At that point Sayfullah defected and established his own new and smaller faction, Jaish al-Khilafat al-Islamiyya, and Omar al-Shishani and his loyal supporters within Jaish al-Muhajireen wa'l Ansar would effectively become ISIS combatants. The specific status and allegiance of Jaish al-Muhajireen wa'l Ansar, meanwhile, would not become clear until December 2013.

Sayfullah's call to Turks was an important but symbolic one. By the summer of 2013 Turkish territory had conclusively become a key logistical hub for jihadist militants operating across the northern half of Syria. Border security was lax at best for those willing to travel overtly, while dozens of well-established smuggling networks existed for those more likely to favour covert methods of travel. Southern Turkey was full of safe houses used by jihadist recruitment networks linked to active factions inside Syria. Hatay airport was a verified way-station for arriving foreign fighters, many of whom could openly arrive dressed in military fatigues without attracting undue attention from security personnel. CNN correspondent Nick Paton Walsh described one visit to the airport in November 2013:

> As we flew in, there were two men from Mauritania, one with a limp, accompanied by a woman from Tunisia. On another flight which we saw land, two young men with large backpacks, coming from Benghazi. On another, four Libyans, also from Benghazi.
>
> Then a young, bearded man with a noticeably thick northern British accent, there to collect a friend from Leicester—the pair absolutely don't want to talk, especially when I offered them a CNN business card. Then come the Egyptians, and a Gulf Arab—he sounded Saudi—who frantically kissed and embraced the bemused driver there to pick him up.[6]

Vans and smuggler taxis would wait outside of the purview of closed-circuit television cameras to pick up the new arrivals and drive them south to the Syrian border.

Further north in Syria's interior, networks affiliated with ISIS, Jabhat al-Nusra, and several foreign fighter-dominated factions managed safe houses in Istanbul and even in Ankara, where new arrivals would stay for several days before being transported south in small groups. The journey American national and Jabhat al-Nusra suicide bomber Moner Mohammed Abusalha ('Abu Hurayrah') described from Florida to Idlib via a mosque in Istanbul 'with only $20 in my pocket'[7] provided an insight—albeit perhaps an unorthodox one—into the ease with which one could find a way to jihad in Syria.

Nevertheless, Turkey was not only proving an inviting facilitative environment for arriving foreign fighters: several hundred Turks had joined the jihad themselves by mid-2013, and dozens had died in the fighting. On 5 July a Turkish Facebook page, 'Suriye Devrimi Sehidleri' (Martyrs of the Syrian Revolution) published the details of twenty-seven Turks recently 'martyred' in Syria. These included the president of Turkish Islamic NGO Garipler Yardımlaşma ve Dayanışma Derneği, Abdurrahman Koc, who was killed fighting in Aleppo on 2 July 2013.[8]

Lebanese territory was also continuing to be targeted by Syrian insurgents determined to retaliate against Hezbollah and its supporters for defeats imposed in al-Qusayr and elsewhere. Ocasionally this targeting expanded to include the Lebanese Armed Forces (LAF), as was the case on 7 July, when a double IED attack struck an army convoy in the Bekaa Valley, wounding three. But it was two days after this that Lebanon experienced a sign of worse things to come. On 9 July fifty-three people were injured when a large car bomb detonated in the southern Beirut suburb and Hezbollah stronghold of Bir al-Abed. The attack was subsequently claimed by two different armed factions: the FSA's 313th Brigade and a previously unknown group identifying itself as Liwa Aisha al-Mo'minin. Although neither claim looked entirely reliable, it was a worrying development for Lebanese security and a quite clear example of spillover from the conflict in Syria.

Five days later Lebanese security forces detained several Syrian militants in the border town of Arsal. They had been transporting military-grade explosives, which it later turned out had been detected by the CIA, who quite remarkably informed Lebanese intelligence 'with the understanding [that the information] would be passed to Hezbollah'.[9] By the time another IED attack had taken place in eastern Lebanon—this time targeting a Hezbollah convoy in Majdal Anjar on 16 July—suspicion was falling upon Jabhat al-Nusra.

Indeed, by this time Jabhat al-Nusra's senior leadership had established contacts with former elements of Fatah al-Islam in Lebanon, most of whom resided quietly in Palestinian refugee camps in Tripoli and Sidon. Contact was also well established with the al-Qaeda-affiliated Kataib Abdullah Azzam, whose leader Majid bin Muhammed al-Majid had already spent time in Syria, hosted by Jabhat al-Nusra and the Lebanon-linked Jund al-Sham. Although Jabhat al-Nusra had not yet established an official presence in Lebanon, July marked the period when several months of preparation began to achieve results.

Beyond anything else, the most significant characteristic of July 2013 was that it marked the shift of ISIS's relationship with the broader Syrian opposition from tense to hostile. Since first emerging as an active entity in Syria in May, ISIS had been muscling itself into strategically valuable areas of opposition-controlled Syria. Towns and villages in close proximity to the Turkish and Iraqi borders appeared to be particularly attractive to it, and thus by July it had established influence, if not control, in several key northern towns such as Raqqa, Jarablus, Manbij, al-Bab, Azaz, Darat Izza and al-Dana, amongst others. Almost without exception, the arrival of ISIS influence came at the substantial cost of other more expressly Syrian insurgent factions.

On 7 July, after several weeks of increasingly overt ISIS control and the imposition of harsh Islamic behavioural laws, the people of al-Dana took to the street to protest against ISIS. The result was brutal. As many as twenty-five people were shot dead on the street, with three times that number reported wounded in local field hospitals. Later that day ISIS detained two local FSA commanders, beheaded them and placed their heads next to a dustbin in the town centre.[10]

Four days later, on 11 July, the chief of the SMC's Western Front's Finance Committee, Kamal al-Hammami (Abu Basir al-Ladkani) decided to drive to a local ISIS checkpoint in northern Latakia to try and smooth over tensions that had been building between local FSA units and Syria's new jihadists, ISIS. For several days the two sides had been taking potshots at each other after ISIS had insisted on operating independently in the area, rather than coordinating with local groups. Hammami was ambushed and shot dead by ISIS before he reached his destination.[11]

His seniority and links to the Western-backed SMC made Hammami's killing a high-profile event inside and outside Syria. But many other similar events took place in subsequent weeks. Combined with its general insistence on operating largely as an independent organisation, ISIS's visibly superior military capabilities and unsurpassed wealth, not to mention its impressive rate of growth across northern, eastern and central Syria, meant that it was perceived as a competitor by other Syrian insurgent factions.

Moreover, its increasingly gung-ho behaviour marked it as a potentially hostile competitor too.

However, ISIS was also beginning to implement a 'hearts and minds' strategy. Like Jabhat al-Nusra and Ahrar al-Sham, ISIS saw itself as an Islamic movement and, as such, civil, religious and humanitarian activities were an intrinsic part of its operating strategy. Beginning on 8 July and marking the start of the Islamic holy month of Ramadan, ISIS began holding so-called 'fun days' in parts of Aleppo where its influence was particularly strong. While free food was distributed, both children and adults were encouraged to take part in interactive games. Children were challenged to speedily eat ice creams and watermelon, and also quizzed on their knowledge of the Qur'an, with prizes presented to winners. Adult men, meanwhile, took part in games of musical chairs, arm wrestling and tugs-of-war, thus presenting quite bizarre scenes within what were urban war zones. Many of these 'days' were coordinated and led by a curiously friendly looking Tunisian known as Abu Waqqas, who even when appearing in ISIS media releases focused on military affairs always seemed to be smiling. This was the soft face of ISIS, and for some time it helped in suppressing opposition.

Such activities were nothing entirely new for Jabhat al-Nusra, which on 3 July established a media channel—Himam News Agency—entirely devoted to publicising civil and social activities. But for ISIS this seemed like a tactic consciously employed at a time when their presence in Syria seemed to be turning a corner. It is therefore probably not a coincidence that, also in July, ISIS spokesman Adnani released an audio statement in which he expressly admitted that his organisation had made mistakes:

> As for our mistakes, we do not deny them. Rather, we will continue to make mistakes as long as we are humans. God forbid that we commit mistakes deliberately. Anyone who seeks leaders and mujahideen who work without mistakes will never find them. And those who work will make mistakes, while those that sit back and watch won't make mistakes ... So how could they blame and criticize us for something that humans are compelled to do, and that they have been born with?[12]

With tensions rising between the FSA and ISIS, the main beneficiaries were those ideologically in the middle, especially Salafist groups such as Ahrar al-Sham, who were not only proving themselves successful on the battlefield but were also providing effective and widespread social services. While the FSA suffered somewhat from the distraction of ISIS and its loss of territorial influence to Islamists during this period, the consequent rise of groups with Islamist frames of reference meant that the Western-backed SMC also declined in influence on the ground. The distinction between the conservative SIF and the comparatively moderate SILF alliance, which contained several highly influential SMC members, was also becoming increasingly diminished over time. The most powerful SILF groups—Liwa al-Islam, Suqor al-Sham, Liwa al-Tawhid, Liwa Dawud—had begun meeting in secret with SIF's leading player Ahrar al-Sham in the southern Turkish town of Reyhanlı and also in northern Idlib to discuss the possibility of merging or establishing a new Islamic coalition. The extent to which ISIS was demonstrating its ideological extremism on one hand, and Jabhat al-Nusra was maintaining its comparative moderation on the other, was made starkly clear by the fact that Jabhat al-Nusra was even invited into these talks.

Early August was a very busy period for jihadists in Syria. As the month began, so too did a renewed offensive on Aleppo Central Prison, where thousands of prisoners were being held in terrible conditions. Spurred on my ISIS's spectacular assault on Abu Ghraib prison outside Iraq's capital Baghdad on 21 July—in which at least 500 prisoners were freed—ISIS, Jabhat al-Nusra, Ahrar al-Sham and Jaish al-Muhajireen wa'l Ansar all played a role in bombarding the large detention facility located just outside Aleppo city's northern boundaries. A prominent Albanian Jabhat al-Nusra commander from Skopje in Macedonia, Sami Abdullahu (Abu Khalid al-Albani) was killed on 3 August, after which the pace of operations at the prison declined.

Despite this momentary pause, a more significant operation was continuing further north in Aleppo at Menagh air base, where ISIS and Jaish al-Muhajireen wa'l Ansar had launched a final push aimed at capturing the facility after a months-long FSA-led siege. Early on 6 August, as Syria's minister of defence, Fahd al-Freij, visited his military's latest conquest in Homs's Khalidiyeh district, Menagh fell after two suicide car bombings had weakened its periphery twenty-four hours earlier. And despite some contentious debate over whether the FSA or jihadists had been responsible for the victory, the then head of Aleppo's opposition Military Council, Colonel 'Abd al-Jabbar al-Okaidi, confirmed that '[ISIS] took the lead in taking over the airport. This group [is] a reality on the ground.'[13]

The base's capture was a significant victory for the Syrian insurgency, but it was one that again underlined the strategic pre-eminence of jihadists, especially in the north. Shortly after seizing the facility and overseeing the beheading of several of the base's commanding officers, Omar al-Shishani and an Egyptian ISIS commander known as Abu Jandal al-Masri gave an interview to Al-Jazeera's Arabic service, surrounded by a contingent of fighters quite visibly from every corner of the planet. ISIS had arrived on the scene and Omar al-Shishani had won his first major victory as an ISIS military leader.

However, Shishani was just emerging from a bitter falling out with his Jaish al-Muhajireen wa'l Ansar deputy, Sayfullah al-Shishani. On 3 August Omar al-Shishani had issued a statement via the Russian-language website FiSyria announcing that Sayfullah had been engendering strife and tensions within Jaish al-Muhajireen wa'l Ansar's ranks, and had recently left the group along with his supporters. A day later Sayfullah had released his own message, denying that he had been a negative influence but admitting that he and his loyalists had left to form their own militant faction.[14] This new group would remain nameless until early September, when Sayfullah announced the establishment of the Mujahideen Kavkaz fi Sham, which he said was composed of fighters from the North Caucasus, Uzbekistan, Kyrgyzstan, Tajikistan, Kazakhstan, Azerbaijan, Russia and several other countries.[15] Five weeks after that, on 10 September, Sayfullah renamed his group Jaish al-Khilafat al-Islamiyya. Syria may well have become the centre of the global jihadist community's attention, and thus attracted an increasingly large foreign fighter contingent, but the scale and intensity of this dynamic meant that divisions and competing personalities were increasingly likely to emerge. In this case, Sayfullah and Omar's falling out was a result of two big egos clashing over the issue of ISIS and the allegiance that Jaish al-Muhajireen wa'l Ansar should have chosen.

Another significant development in early August in which jihadists played a lead role was a major multi-group coordinated offensive on regime-held territory in north-western Latakia. Beginning on 4 August, 'Operation Liberation of the Coast' involved approximately 1,500–2,000 militants from at least sixteen groups. While the offensive included several small FSA factions, the operation was designed and led by ISIS, Jabhat al-Nusra, Jaish al-Muhajireen wa'l Ansar and SIF members Ahrar al-Sham and Kataib Ansar al-Sham, as well as several smaller and newer organisations such as Harakat Sham al-Islam and Suqor al-Izz.

Within twenty-four hours of launching the offensive, the key groups involved had claimed the capture of eleven villages situated within the mountainous Jebel al-Akrad region of northern Latakia. For the first time since the beginning of the armed insurgency, fighters were within 20 kilometres of Assad's home town of Qardaha, and the situation for the regime looked dire. While initially downplayed, reports were beginning to emerge of insurgent brutality meted out on villages known for their regime support. This forced the SMC's Western Front to cease its provision of support to FSA units involved in the offensive, which, despite a visit from SMC chief of staff General Selim Idriss to the area on 11 August, precipitated a gradual decline in their involvement.

Facing such a seemingly existential threat to its heartland, the regime in Damascus called upon the paramilitary NDF and several specialist units of the army to redploy northwards via Tartous and Latakia to see off this determined offensive. By 7 August a regime counter-offensive had begun, and jihadist gains were stopped. Ten days later, after countless air and artillery strikes, pro-regime forces recaptured all positions that had been lost between 4 and 7 August.

A month later Human Rights Watch published an in-depth investigation entitled 'You can still see their blood', in which it was documented that the offensive killed about 190 civilians, including at least 67 who were 'executed or unlawfully killed ... even though they were unarmed and trying to flee'. Almost all of the alleged crimes were committed on 4 August, the first day of the offensive, and 'given that many residents remain missing, and opposition fighters buried many bodies in mass graves, the total number of dead is likely higher'.[16] The report specifically identified Jabhat al-Nusra, ISIS, Ahrar al-Sham, Jaish al-Muhajireen wa'l Ansar and Suqor al-Izz as having allegedly been involved in committing the crimes. All these groups subsequently issued statements denying that they had killed unarmed civilians, although on 25 August Jabhat al-Nusra did openly execute a prominent Alawite sheikh, Badr al-Ghazali, who had been captured by Harakat Sham al-Islam during the offensive and handed over to its custody.

Meanwhile, tensions were continuing to rise between the 'moderate' insurgent opposition and ISIS. A prominent Kuwaiti Salafist, Shafi Sultan Mohammed al-Ajmi—who would in 2014 both become Kuwait's justice minister and an American-designated Jabhat al-Nusra 'fundraiser'—released on 10 August what he claimed was leaked information regarding a plan by the then leader of Syria's political opposition, Ahmed Jarba, to establish a 6,000-man 'National Army,' which Ajmi termed a 'Sahwa' in the making. Indeed, Jarba had presented this as a future plan for the Western-backed opposition, but the project attracted no funding and did not come to fruition. Nonetheless, jihadists affiliated with ISIS were increasingly beginning to talk about suspicions that a Sahwa—a reference to the tribally based Sunni militias used by the US to fight the ISI in Iraq between 2006 and 2009—was being created in Syria to turn against the *mujahideen*.

In early August a great deal of this tension was being felt in the city of Raqqa, where ISIS appeared determined to assert its authority amid growing numbers of protests against its rule. The local Jabhat al-Nusra *emir*, Abu Sa'ad al-Hadrami, had gone to ground with his followers and refused to pledge *bay'a* to ISIS, while a contingent of Ahrar al-Sham also remained in place.

However, ISIS turned its suspicions upon a moderate FSA faction known as Alwiya Ahfad al-Rasoul. The relationship between the two groups had become increasingly strained in both Raqqa and Deir ez Zour. ISIS accused Ahfad al-Rasoul and its leader, Mahor Maher al-Noaimi, of being 'agents of the West'. After several minor skirmishes ISIS detonated four large suicide car bombs at Ahfad al-Rasoul positions in the city, including its headquarters at the main train station, on 13 August. After roughly six hours of fighting, all remaining Ahfad al-Rasoul units fled the city south to Deir ez Zour, leaving ISIS determinedly in charge in Raqqa.

During the fighting in Raqqa city, ISIS had managed to capture a senior Ahfad al-Rasoul commander, Sa'adallah Junaid, who subsequently appeared on a video giving what appeared to be a forced confession that his group oper- ated under orders given by France and Qatar.[17] Roughly three months later the leader of Ahfad al-Rasoul's Allahu Akbar Brigade, Saddam al-Jamal, defected to ISIS in Deir ez Zour after his post was captured and his brother killed. Almost certainly acting to protect himself, Jamal made similar claims to those made by Junaid:

> Originally, the Ahfad was meant to be part of the FSA, without any agenda or ambitions, and that it would be supported without any return, only to fight the Assad regime. However, we discovered later that this project has an agenda and long-term objectives. Obviously it is supported by Qatar ... we used to meet with the apostates of Qatar and Saudi Arabia and with the infidels of Western nations such as America and France in order to receive arms and ammo or cash ... many groups got trained in Jordan at the hands of the Jordanian intelligence services and Western ones. Everyone knows that when we say Jordan this means Israeli intelli- gence services. Israel is present in Jordan. All people know that.[18]

Beirut was struck by its second car bombing in two months in August, when 27 people were killed and over 200 wounded outside a Hezbollah- owned building in southern Beirut. The attack—described as the worst to hit the city in decades[19]—was claimed again by Liwa Aisha al-Mo'minin, which promised 'more' attacks:

> We send a message to our brothers in Lebanon, we ask you to stay away from all the Iranian colonies in Lebanon ... because your blood is precious to us ... But

Hassan Nasrallah is an agent of Iran and Israel and we promise him more and more [attacks].[20]

In an apparent act of revenge, unidentified militants subsequently detonated two large explosive devices outside the Sunni al-Taqwa and al-Salam Mosques in the northern Lebanese city of Tripoli on 23 August, killing 47 and wounding as many as 800 others. There was no official claim of responsibility, and despite some conspiracy theorists suggesting that it had been an inside job (in other words, carried out by Sunni militants), the message felt on the ground was clear. Even North Africa-based AQIM threatened revenge against Hezbollah: 'that vile party ... should know that it will meet retribution soon'.[21]

Meanwhile, back in Syria something far more brutal and likely to engender acts of revenge was about to take place. In the early hours of 21 August, residents of the heavily besieged East Ghouta suburbs of Damascus woke up to barrages of artillery rockets. While such bombardments were nothing particularly unusual in the area, these rockets were loaded with sarin gas—internationally recognised as a chemical weapon. There had already been several allegations regarding the apparent use of chemicals in attacks in Syria in 2013, but events on the morning of 21 August were markedly different: according to a US government statement two weeks later, 1,429 people were killed.

Heavy fighting continued in the area for forty-eight hours, which prevented a cessation of fighting necessary for UN personnel to enter the area and investigate. However, from 26 to 31 August a UN chemical weapons investigative team did manage to enter East Ghouta to collect evidence, which was used to conclude on 16 September that sarin nerve agent had been used in the attack. Multiple foreign states, including the USA, the UK and France, also concluded definitively that Syrian government forces had been responsible.[22] Indeed, as investigative journalist Eliot Higgins concluded, the two munitions used in the attack, their ranges and their trajectory suggest that only government forces based 6–8 kilometres north of the targeted areas could have launched the attack.[23] Human Rights Watch's Josh Lyons made similar conclusions in his report, using 'the debris field and impact area where the rockets struck' to calculate 'the actual trajectory of the rockets' to 'a well-known military base of the Republican Guard 104th Brigade'.[24] Adding to this analysis, the dominant group in East Ghouta, Liwa al-Islam, issued an official statement on 23 August claiming that the attack had been launched from Mount Qassioun (home to the 104th Brigade) and from the nearby Mezzeh military airport.

Within the Syrian opposition and insurgency, however, technical details were of little importance—for them, the regime was clearly responsible. Two days after the horrific attack, the leaders of the SMC's Northern, Eastern, Central and Homs Fronts threatened to resign from their posts unless the SMC proved its capacity to exact revenge and ensure that a successful investigation was conducted in East Ghouta. Jabhat al-Nusra leader Jolani issued his own statement on 25 August in which he announced that his group would carry out retaliatory attacks—Operation Volcano of Revenge—against regime and pro-regime areas under the Islamic concept of *qisas*—equating to equal retaliation, 'an eye for an eye'. One Alawite village would be attacked for every chemical-loaded rocket fired into East Ghouta, Jolani exclaimed.

ISIS and Jabhat al-Nusra consequently renewed the shelling of Zahra and Nubl in northern Aleppo, while pro-regime areas in Latakia were also rocketed. Perhaps the most significant—and immediate—acts of Jabhat al-Nusra retaliation, however, came later on 25 August, when a car bomb assassinated the governor of Hama, Dr Anas 'Abd al-Razzaq, and when the execution of Alawite sheikh Badr al-Ghazali was announced.

Although it had not been conclusively found to be a chemical weapons attack at the time, the immediate international diplomatic fallout from the East Ghouta attack was considerable. The attack had come one year and one day after President Obama had defined chemical weapons use in Syria as a 'red line' for his administration, and as such, Western states supportive of the revolution and the opposition began threatening retaliatory strikes against the Assad regime.

This immediately raised alarm bells within the jihadist community in Syria, which feared that they too would become targets of such international strikes. A prominent supporter of Fatah al-Islam, Abdullah Saker (Abu Bakr), for example, published a document entitled 'Important instructions ... before the US initiates its mission' on 27 August, in which he advised jihadists to 'change your positions, take shelter, and do not move in public'. Saker also underlined the importance of lessons learned in Mali, Iraq and Afghanistan, where the 'mujahideen [were] destroyed in a very short time' because the necessary precautions were not taken. Many other similar advisory notes were published at the time, including some that encouraged jihadists to 'provoke a torrent of misinformation about our plans and locations to confuse the enemy'.[25]

Other less extremist Islamist insurgent factions were vocal in their expressions of opposition to the prospect of international strikes in Syria. The SIF claimed on 6 September that such intervention would be undertaken only in order 'to advance the interests of the perpetrators', while ten Islamist factions in Damascus issued a statement in concert with six local sheikhs and two civil organisations claiming that strikes would constitute 'an aggression against Muslims'.

Despite such fears inside Syria, the issue of international intervention was raised in the UK Parliament, and was voted down by 285 to 272 votes on 29 August. This put President Obama under significant pressure. Since the attack he and his national security staff in the White House had been definitively threatening military action, but two days later, in a speech on the White House Rose Garden, Obama did an about-turn and announced that he too would seek Congressional approval for strikes in Syria. Although a bipartisan bill began to be drafted, it mattered little because on 14 September the US and Russia signed an agreement to bring Syrian chemical weapons stockpiles under international control and then destroyed, backed by a UN Security Council resolution.[26] Although for some in the diplomatic community this agreement had successfully stalled international military action and therefore prevented a war, it was perceived by the opposition as a betrayal of the revolution and the Syrian people. Despite their public expressions of opposition to the idea of strikes, many within Syria's Salafist community spoke privately in much the same terms as their more moderate counterparts: the West had, as far as they were concerned, revealed its true colours.

All the while the revolution continued, albeit with a substantially heightened level of anger. On 26 August Ahrar al-Sham led the capture of the town of Khanaser in southern Aleppo along with Harakat al-Fajr al-Islamiyya, Liwa al-Tawhid, Jabhat al-Nusra and seven other Islamist factions. Control of the town meant that the regime no longer had an effective supply route to its forces holding out in Aleppo city to the north, and its loss spurred on Ahrar al-Sham and its allied factions to continue pushing northwards in mid-to-late September in a new offensive—Wal Adiyat Dabha—targeting towns on Aleppo city's southern limits, including al-Safira. This would in turn spur the regime into launching a counter-offensive in October.

Another high-profile battlefront emerged around the town of Maaloula in early September. Located 50 kilometres north of Damascus but within 7.5 kilometres of Syria's principal M5 highway, Maaloula was an ancient Christian town populated primarily by Assyrians and Syriacs, many of whom still spoke Aramaic, the language of Jesus. Beginning on 4 September, a coalition formed primarily out of the FSA's Jabhat Tahrir al-Qalamoun, Jabhat al-Nusra and Ahrar al-Sham launched an assault on a checkpoint located at the only entrance to Maaloula. The attack began when a Jordanian Jabhat al-Nusra fighter, 'Abu Musab al-Zarqawi', detonated a suicide car bomb, which was followed by a ground raid. After a day of heavy fighting and a brief government counter-attack on 6–7 September, the town was effectively under insurgent control by late on 7 September. However, amid reports—which remain unsubstantiated—of indiscriminate violence being meted out to local Christian residents and places of worship, the Syrian army successfully forced out insurgent forces from Maaloula by 15 September.

Perhaps more than any other dynamic of the conflict, September 2013 was most dominated by escalated levels of inter-factional fighting between ISIS and rival factions. In particular, tensions turned to hostility between ISIS and Syria's then dominant insurgent faction Ahrar al-Sham. On 7 September a suspected ISIS suicide bomber detonated a car bomb outside Ahrar al-Sham headquarters in the Idlib town of Sarmada, and on 11 September ISIS detained and killed Ahrar al-Sham chief of relief operations, Abu Obeida al-Binnishi. The latter incident sparked Ahrar al-Sham leader Hassan Abboud to exclaim publicly on Twitter that 'they've reduced Islam to appearances and paved their own path to Hell!' Almost farcically, Abu Obeida's death was described by local sources as a huge misunderstanding that rapidly went wrong: Abu Obeida had been assisting several Turkish and Malaysian aid workers distributing assistance in Binnish, and when local ISIS fighters saw the Malaysian flag they mistook it for an American one, detained all of them and, at some point, killed Abu Obeida.

Mistaken identity or not, ISIS was beginning to act with brazen self-confidence across northern Syria. It was violently suppressing the first sign of protest in areas under its control and was forcefully defending its territorial influence against rival insurgent groups. After forcing Alwiya Ahfad al-Rasoul out of Raqqa in mid-August, ISIS turned its guns on the group in Deir ez Zour. This brought ISIS directly into combat with Jabhat al-Nusra and Ahrar al-Sham, both of which had grown close to Ahfad al-Rasoul's Deir ez Zour faction, Liwa Allahu Akbar. Significant clashes took place throughout 14–15 September, while ISIS was simultaneously threatening all-out war against FSA groups Liwa al-Nasr and Kataib al-Farouq in the northern Aleppo town of al-Bab under a campaign ISIS labelled 'Repudiation of Malignity'. ISIS's attempt to take over education practices in al-Bab provoked the ire of local FSA factions, which attempted to push back.

Fifty-five kilometres north-west of al-Bab lay the town of Azaz—a crucial thoroughfare to the Bab al-Salameh border crossing with Turkey. ISIS had been gradually expanding its influence in Azaz since July at the expense of local FSA group Asifat al-Shamal. Tensions were already high when, on

18 September, ISIS fighters detained a German doctor working in the town's field hospital on suspicion of being a spy. ISIS claimed that the man had been taking photographs near its headquarters, and so deployed reinforcements into the town and took control of Asifat al-Shamal's main base. Amid a dramatic flurry of reports coming out of the town that afternoon, ISIS killed Asifat al-Shamal's chief of media operations, Hazem al-Abidi, and took his staff prisoner.

After taking de facto control of the town by late on 18 September, ISIS agreed to enter into ceasefire negotiations led by a senior delegation from Liwa al-Tawhid, which had arrived hours earlier. The following day a deal was reached, which stipulated that both sides would exchange all prisoners within twenty-four hours and ISIS would leave Asifat al-Shamal's headquarters twenty-four hours after that. Although ISIS did release nine prisoners on 20 September, Asifat al-Shamal accused it of retaining more in its custody, including a media official, Mohammed Nour. A tit-for-tat series of accusatory statements was subsequently exchanged between the two sides, interspersed with ISIS arresting more FSA activists in the town, before several ISIS deadlines for Asifat al-Shamal to surrender expired in early October, leaving ISIS in total control of Azaz.

It was within this context that ISIS suffered its first serious casualty from inter-factional hostilities, when FSA fighters ambushed an ISIS patrol led by Osama al-Obeidi (Abu Abdullah al-Libi), ISIS's *emir* of al-Dana in Idlib, near the northern Syrian town of Hazano in Idlib governorate on 22 September. Abu Abdullah—a Libyan with a history of fighting for AQI and the ISI in Iraq—was killed.

Hostilities were also emerging between Jabhat al-Nusra and ISIS, particularly in the north-east and east of the country. In Raqqa city, Jabhat al-Nusra's *emir*, Abu Sa'ad al-Hadrami, came out of hiding to accept pledges of allegiance from Liwa Thuwar al-Raqqa and another Ahfad al-Rasoul faction, Liwa Muntasir Billah. This was a challenge too far for ISIS, which promptly located and detained Hadrami in the city on 26 September. He was never heard from again. Meanwhile, as Jabhat al-Nusra was distracted by battles with the Kurdish YPG in rural Hasakah and also around Ras al-Ayn, ISIS launched a raid on its town of al-Shadadi. Located close to al-Hasakah's provincial border with Deir ez Zour, al-Shadadi provided invaluable access to nearby oilfields, and had been captured by Jabhat al-Nusra in February. A ceasefire was eventually agreed there also.

September ended with two highly significant events that served to underline the trajectory of the insurgency as a whole, and especially the consolidation of Islamists as the pre-eminent power. On 24 September eleven of the most powerful insurgent groups in Syria—all of which maintain an Islamic frame of reference—issued a joint statement in which they totally renounced the authority and representation of the Western-backed ETILAF political opposition, otherwise known simply as 'the coalition'. The statement, issued by Liwa al-Tawhid's political chief, 'Abd al-Aziz al-Salameh, made four points:

1. The said groups invite all military and civil groups to unify within a clear Islamic frame created on an Islamic power based upon sharia arbitration and make it the sole source of legislation.
2. These groups consider that only those who suffered and sacrificed on the ground have the right to represent their faithful sons.
3. These groups consider that any outside formations, without reviewing the public opinion, cannot represent them and have their recognition. Hence, the coalition and the assumed government headed by Ahmed Tomeh do not represent them and do not have their recognition.
4. These groups and factions invite all military and civil groups to unify their word, to reject discrimination, and to prioritize the Ummah's favor over the common favor.[27]

The right of the coalition to represent insurgent factions on the ground had long been a contentious point, but after the USA had failed to follow through on its threat to strike the regime in August, and as international impetus increased for a Geneva II round of peace talks in early 2014, groups on the ground had lost their patience. Intriguingly, the list of eleven groups signing the statement began with Jabhat al-Nusra, which was not a coincidence. 'That was a statement designed to send our message to all the Western capitals,' said one then Liwa al-Islam political official.[28] The list also combined powerful members of both the SIF and SILF coalitions, all of whom were still engaged in secret unity talks. All the while, these factions were expanding. The Aleppo-based Liwa al-Tawhid was now operating in Hama; the Idlib-based Suqor al-Sham also in Hama and Qalamoun; and the powerful Damascus group Liwa al-Islam had gained pledges of allegiance in Idlib and Aleppo. Ahrar al-Sham meanwhile was running insurgent and civil operations in twelve of Syria's fourteen governorates (not al-Suwayda and Tartous).

Then, on 29 September, in a large ceremony livestreamed around the world on the Internet and held in the Damascus suburb of Douma, Liwa al-Islam announced its full merger with at least fifty other insurgent factions. From that point on, this Salafist group run by the Alloush family—Zahran as overall leader, Mohammed as political leader, and Islam as spokesman—was to be known as Jaish al-Islam (the army of Islam). It clearly enjoyed impressive levels of external funding and had by this point amassed arguably the most formidable stock of weaponry of any insurgent group in Syria. This included two 9K33 Osa (SA-8 Gecko) surface-to-air missile systems—which had already been successfully used to shoot down a Syrian military helicopter over Damascus in July—and a whole fleet of T-72, T-62 and T-54 tanks and BMP-1 armoured personnel carriers.

Thus, as September 2013 came to a close, Syria's Salafist insurgents were truly beginning to demonstrate the extent of their potential influence on the conflict. Jabhat al-Nusra, meanwhile, although numerically weakened by defections to ISIS earlier in the year, was regaining in strength thanks to continuing pledges of allegiance from smaller factions across the country. It also remained the only major jihadist organisation active in southern Syria—perhaps with the exception of the smaller Harakat al-Muthanna al-Islamiyya—where it gained headlines on 28 September by capturing Syria's customs border crossing with Jordan at al-Ramtha. ISIS, on the other hand, appeared to be going from strength to strength, continually acquiring new territorial control and influence over populations. However, every one of these ISIS gains was coming at the expense of other purely Syrian insurgent factions, and the tensions and hostilities breaking out as a result were only intensifying.

Meanwhile, the scale of the jihadist insurgency in Syria had expanded, with several new groups having established operations in the country in August and September. Most notable amongst the new arrivals was the Latakia-based Harakat Sham al-Islam, which had emerged shortly prior to its involvement in the notorious offensive in Latakia in early August. The group was founded and led by Moroccans, including two former Guantanamo Bay detainees, Mohammed al-Alami (Abu Hamza al-Maghrebi), who was killed on 5 August, and Ibrahim Benchekroune (Abu Ahmed al-Muhajir).[29]

Born in the Moroccan city of Casablanca in August 1979, Benchekroune was a veteran jihadist and a trained member of al-Qaeda. After a period of Islamic study in Pakistan in late 1999, Benchekroune made his way into Afghanistan in November 2000, where he linked up with existing Moroccan al-Qaeda cells and joined the infamous al-Farouq training camp near Kandahar, where several of the 9/11 hijackers had allegedly received training and where senior Jabhat al-Nusra military commander Abu Hamam al-Suri had been an instructor. After the US-led invasion of Afghanistan, Benchekroune fled to Pakistan via the remote and mountainous Northern Waziristan region. While driving towards the city of Lahore, Benchekroune was involved in a minor car accident, and was detained by Pakistani police at the scene and transferred into American custody. Thus began his journey to Guantanamo, where he remained until his transfer to Morocco in late 2004, where local authorities granted his release. Benchekroune's freedom did not last long however, as he was detained again in November 2005 for allegedly joining a terrorist cell, and remained in prison in Morocco until his release some time after the start of the Syrian revolution.[30]

As a group, Harakat Sham al-Islam was technically independent, although the trajectory and nature of its military operations as well as the history of its leadership strongly suggested an ideological affinity with Jabhat al-Nusra and Al-Qaeda. One jihadist who fought in Latakia also claimed that Harakat Sham al-Islam intended one day to return trained and experienced fighters to Morocco to establish an Islamic state.[31]

Another new group during this period was al-Katibat al-Khadraa, which was led primarily by fighters from Saudi Arabia and other outlying Arabian Peninsula states, such as Yemen and Oman. Primarily operational in northern Damascus and in the mountainous Qalamoun region, al-Katibat al-Khadraa was an avowedly jihadist organisation, but one with a more clearly independent stance regarding Jabhat al-Nusra and ISIS.

Additionally, Jund al-Aqsa was another jihadist faction that emerged into the open in the late summer of 2013. Primarily operational in the northern governorate of Idlib and in Hama, Jund al-Aqsa was manned by a veritably international contingent of foreign fighters. Originally founded in secret by Jabhat al-Nusra leader Jolani and one of his then deputies, Mohammed Yusuf al-Athamna ('Abd al-Aziz al-Qatari) in early 2013, the group was initially known as Saraya al-Aqsa, before being renamed Jund al-Aqsa months later in the summer. The group had been intended as strategic depth for Jabhat al-Nusra amid the impending ISI expansion into Syria, which had been detected when Adnani was spotted in northern Aleppo. Closely affiliated with Jabhat al-Nusra from the moment of its establishment, Jund al-Aqsa appeared more strictly independent by September–October 2013. Its senior leadership was said to be in close contact with renowned al-Qaeda ideologue Abu Mohammed al-Maqdisi and also Sheikh Suleiman Ulwan, and the group recruited from across the Middle East and further afield.

Thus, notwithstanding the various jihadist factions already operating across Syria—in addition to others newly created, such as Homs-based Saraya al-Sham, Aleppo-based Jaish Mohammed, Aleppo-based and primarily Uzbek Katibat al-Imam al-Bukhari and Libyan ISIS faction Katibat al-Bittar al-Libi—the insurgent environment in Syria was becoming increasingly complex and dominated by hardline actors. Numerically, groups aligning themselves with the FSA were still the largest component of the insurgency, but their comparative lack of coordination and the huge number of individual factions meant that their impact on the battlefield and overall conflict dynamics could not compete with larger and more individually capable Salafist and jihadist units. With that being said, however, the USA and its allies were becoming intensely concerned with the rise of jihadists in Syria, and in early September media reports claimed that the CIA had begun delivering arms shipments to FSA groups for the first time. There was still room for the dynamics to shift again.

As October 2013 began, Jabhat al-Nusra, Ahrar al-Sham and other ISIS rivals in northern Syria continued to push back against its aggressive expansion and behaviour. On 3 October, for example, Ahrar al-Sham released a detailed report of its investigation into ISIS's killing of its relief-operations chief Abu Obeida al-Binnishi a month earlier. In its report, Ahrar al-Sham claimed that it had held a number of meetings with ISIS commanders suspected of involvement in, or of hiding information relating to the incident, but that senior ISIS leadership figures had repeatedly delayed proceedings and avoided committing to important meetings. As such, the investigation came to no solid conclusions—except, that is, for subtly suggesting that ISIS was covering things up.

That same day, while eight invidual units of Jabhat al-Asala wa'l Tanmiyya (a moderately Islamically minded insurgent coalition with close relations in Kuwait) were pledging allegiance to Jabhat al-Nusra, a significant warning was issued to ISIS. In a joint statement, Syria's most powerful Islamist factions—Ahrar al-Sham, Liwa al-Tawhid, Jaish al-Islam, Suqor al-Sham, Liwa al-Furqan and Liwa al-Haq—demanded that ISIS withdraw all of its forces from Asifat al-Shamal facilities in Azaz and return to its original headquarters in the town—in essence, a return to the pre-18 September situation.

Despite the sheer weight behind the demand, ISIS did not budge from its dominant position in Azaz, although its belligerent behaviour did notably decline through the month of October. What ISIS did do that month, however, was to begin an English-language recruitment campaign across social media. This focus on outreach to English-speaking recruits was initially focused on a series of high-quality poster releases containing Qur'anic verses extolling the 'virtues of the mujahideen', the 'virtues of seeking martyrdom' and other similar subjects. Although not immediately apparent at the time, this represented the beginning of a highly significant ISIS operation to re-internationalise its ranks after 'Iraqising' in 2009–11.

Amid more reports of CIA assistance to the moderate Syrian insurgency in early October, this time claiming that a training programme based in Jordan had been 'ramped up',[32] Jabhat al-Nusra was on the advance in southern Syria, along with its local southern allies Ahrar al-Sham, Harakat al-Muthanna al-Islamiyya and Liwa al-Qadisiyya al-Islamiyya. In close cooperation with the FSA, these groups captured the Hajana Battalion army base on 9 October followed by the nearby Deraa al-Balad district in the south of Deraa city on 10 October. Fifteen kilometres north, but in close proximity to the Jordanian border, the town of Tafas was then captured by Ahrar al-Sham and several FSA units on 26 October. Simultaneously, throughout October Jabhat al-Nusra was intensifying its operations in Damascus in coordination with a newly formed multi-group operations room known as Jund al-Malahem, which combined Ahrar al-Sham, Liwa Shabab al-Huda, Alwiya al-Habib al-Mustafa and Katibat Issa ibn Maryam and which coordinated closely with Jaish al-Islam. With al-Qaeda leader Zawahiri stressing the importance of unity with Islamic ranks in Syria in a statement on 11 October, Jabhat al-Nusra's pragmatic maintenance of positive relations with its fellow insurgents in Syria looked in harmony with its leader's expectations at the time. Moreover, while ISIS had undoubtedly challenged Jabhat al-Nusra's position of pre-eminence in northern Syria, it remained the undisputed *jihadist* power in the south and was beginning to identify itself in public as Tanzim Qaedat al-Jihad fi Bilad al-Sham, in keeping with al-Qaeda's official identity as Tanzim Qaedat al-Jihad.

Another jihadist organisation in Syria was also beginning to adjust its identity. Members of Jaish al-Muhajireen wa'l Ansar, which by now had failed to integrate into ISIS as Omar al-Shishani had hoped, had begun identifying themselves as members of the North Caucasus-based Imarat Kavkaz (IK)—wearing T-shirts and hanging flags and posters emblazoned with the name written in English script. This affiliation, however, would not become entirely clear outside Syria until mid-February 2014, when the group began purposely releasing media content featuring the IK name.

While such jihadist groups were now reaching out or admitting their international connections increasingly overtly, more explicitly Syrian Islamists were beginning to make their political views known. In a fairly dramatic statement issued by video and text on 27 October, the leader of Suqor al-Sham and the entire SILF coalition, Abu Eissa al-Sheikh, announced on behalf of nineteen Islamic factions that they totally rejected the proposed Geneva II talks:

> We announce that the Geneva II conference is not, nor will it ever be our people's choice or our revolution's demand ... We consider it just another part of the con-

spiracy to throw our revolution off track and to abort it ... [Anyone found to attend Geneva II would have committed] treason and would have to answer for it before our courts.[33]

The message sent was highly significant as it was signed by all of the most powerful Syrian factions on the ground, including Ahrar al-Sham, Jaish al-Islam, Liwa al-Tawhid, Suqor al-Sham, Liwa Dawud, Alwiya Ahfad al-Rasoul, Liwa al-Haq, Liwa al-Furqan, al-Ittihad al-Islami Ajnad al-Sham, Liwa Mujahidi al-Sham and Kataib Nour al-Din al-Zinki, amongst others. Combined, these nineteen groups probably commanded at least 50,000 fighters across Syria. With the ETILAF set to meet two weeks later on 9 November to decide whether to attend the Geneva II talks, the message sent on 27 October was that any opposition attendance would be without the support of the most powerful insurgents on the ground. While some argued at the time that the nineteen groups were overwhelmingly situated in the northern half of Syria, a similarly powerful message had been sent from the south ten days earlier, when the FSA's Liwa Ansar al-Sunnah announced on behalf of as many as seventy other FSA factions that they renounced the authority of the ETILAF, which itself had reluctantly agreed to attend the talks in Geneva. Nevertheless, at least nine of the nineteen signatory groups on 27 October maintained operations in the southern governorates of Damascus, Deraa and Quneitra, six of which were headquartered in the south.

In November the regime piled on the pressure in Aleppo, where, after several weeks of offensive operations, the Syrian army, the NDF and Hezbollah were beginning to make inroads into opposition-held territories. A major defeat struck the opposition at the beginning of the month as the strategic town of al-Safira was lost. Testifying to the town's importance, an insurgent involved in Aleppo operations had exclaimed three weeks earlier that 'everything we have accomplished in Aleppo over the past year will vanish in two or three days if we lose Al-Safira'.[34] Its importance was equally significant on the international diplomatic level, as control of the town provided close proximity to the regime's defence factories and scientific research facilities, which were suspected to have been involved in Assad's chemical weapons programme.

Twenty-four hours after taking al-Safira, pro-regime forces also captured the nearby village of Aziziyeh, thus forcing the further withdrawal of insurgent fighters and precipitating the resignation of the opposition's Aleppo Military Council chief, General 'Abd al-Jabbar al-Okaidi, on 3 November. In a video statement accompanying his resignation, a dour-looking Okaidi condemned the international community's lack of support, which he said proved it was 'conspiring against the people and revolution'. Using similar language to that used in previous statements by insurgent factions renouncing the ETILAF (on 24 September) and Geneva II (on 27 October), Okaidi sarcastically congratulated the political opposition 'for your hotels and your political posts' and asserted that 'you hardly represent yourselves!'[35]

Things in Aleppo consequently continued to go from bad to worse, as pro-regime forces went on to capture the town of Tel Aran by 10 November; the strategic 'Base 80' located near Aleppo international airport on 11 November; the town of Tel Hassel on 15 November; and the village of al-Dwayrineh on 18 November. Moreover, and of at least equal significance, Aleppo's principal insurgent organisation, Liwa al-Tawhid, lost its founder and leader, 'Abd al-Qader Saleh, when he was mortally wounded in an airstrike that targeted an insurgent base in Aleppo on 14 November.

Such losses in Syria's largest city, where the revolution could arguably be either won or lost, posed a serious threat to both the morale and unity of the insurgency. Aleppo in particular had become the operational home to countless jihadist factions, not to mention major Salafist organisations such as Ahrar al-Sham. As such, a nationwide call was issued on 11 November by six Aleppo-based factions—Jabhat al-Nusra, Ahrar al-Sham, Liwa al-Tawhid, Kataib Nour al-Din al-Zinki, Ansar al-Mahdi and Tajamu Fastaqim Kama Umrat—for a general mobilisation of opposition forces to defend against the regime's offensive. Within twenty-four hours Ahrar al-Sham had deployed reinforcements to Aleppo from fronts in Idlib and Raqqa, and for the time being regime gains were at least slowed.

Meanwhile, ISIS was continuing its new English-language recruitment campaign and expanding its outreach in Arabic. The Islamically prophesied significance of Syria (or *bilad al-Sham*) remained a key theme used by ISIS to attract recruits from across the world, but it was also making clear its practical intention to establish an Islamic state spanning Iraq and Syria. But more emotively, ISIS was also simply expressing its apparent intent to fight the oppressive Assad regime, which had only recently killed over a thousand people in a chemical weapons attack. This protective and defensive image was one espoused by all Sunni jihadist groups in Syria, and was something made all too easy to sustain given the brutal practices of the Syrian army and its paramilitary and militant supporters.

In fact, just as ISIS was seeking to accelerate the scale and rate of its recruitment, a Turkish smuggler involved in getting foreign fighters into Syria told CNN in early November that not only had he moved 400 people across the border 'in the past few months', but the 'rate of people making the crossing had almost tripled since the chemical attacks on the Damascus suburbs in August'.[36] Clearly, there were many jihadi groups and also several less extremist Syrian insurgent factions that were recruiting or accepting foreign fighters, but ISIS's history, military prowess and impressive media presence made it a prime candidate for recruiting arriving foreigners. This was of course not to mention the fact that it had spent the last six months in Syria acquiring control of villages and towns located in close proximity to the Turkish border.

This strategic acquisition of territory continued on 21 November when ISIS boldly took effective control of the town of Atmeh in Idlib governorate, only a kilometre from the Turkish border. A well-developed foreign fighter recruitment network had operated out of Atmeh and several remote Turkish villages opposite it since at least mid-2012. While ISIS had maintained an influence in Atmeh for some time, its assault on the local headquarters of Suqor al-Sham and the detention of that group's local leader, Mustafa Waddah, and twenty-four of his men signaled that it was now taking full control. ISIS even cut down a 150-year-old tree in the town shortly afterwards, claiming that the local people had been worshipping it in place of Allah.

Events in Atmeh, as well as ISIS's beheading of Ahrar al-Sham fighter Mohammed Fares in Aleppo on 13 November in another apparent case of mistaken identity, underlined yet again to the Syrian Islamist insurgency that two threats now appeared to be confronting it in Syria: the regime and ISIS.

The highly significant establishment of the Islamic Front on 22 November should be read within this context. Coming after several months of intensive discussions between the leaders of over a dozen of Syria's most powerful insurgent factions—most of the nineteen groups that signed the anti-Geneva II statement on 27 October—the Islamic Front's formation revealed a major new actor in the conflict. Seven groups signed up to join the Front: Ahrar al-Sham, Jaish al-Islam, Suqor al-Sham, Liwa al-Tawhid, Liwa al-Haq, Kataib Ansar al-Sham and the Kurdish Islamic Front. With at least 55,000 fighters under its command and military operations ongoing in twelve of Syria's fourteen governorates, the Islamic Front was a force to be reckoned with.

Suqor al-Sham leader Abu Eissa al-Sheikh was named the leader of the Islamic Front's Shura Council, with as its deputy leader Liwa al-Tawhid's Abu Omar Hreitan. Meanwhile, Liwa al-Haq's Sheikh Abu Rateb was named general secretary; Ahrar al-Sham's Abu al-Abbas al-Shami as head of the Sharia Office; Ahrar al-Sham's Hassan Abboud as political chief; and Jaish al-Islam's Zahran Alloush as military chief. All six of these men had been pictured together in casual photographs released onto social media in the preceding

months, which had served as the initial spark for rumours that such a unification or new coalition was on the cards.

Upon its creation, the Islamic Front had big expectations for its organisational future. Soon, 'our individual names will disappear and the groups will
melt into the new merger', a member of Liwa al-Tawhid told Al-Jazeera; 'there
will be no such thing as Liwa al-Tawhid'.[37] Ideologically, it was unsurprisingly
shaped around an Islamic vision for Syria, as its formation statement expressed:

> The Islamic Front is an independent military and social force that is aimed at bring-
> ing down Assad's regime in Syria and replacing it with a just Islamic state.[38]

However, while its leaders had recently been so aggressively critical of Syria's
exiled political opposition, the Islamic Front's political bureau was established—in theory, at least—to cooperate with any body that wanted 'a revolution and not politics and foreign agendas'.[39] Nonetheless, although it did not
go as far as to contain Jabhat al-Nusra—which was invited to attend the formation negotiations—the formation of the Islamic Front was a clear protest
against the status quo. That Zahran Alloush and Abu Eissa al-Sheikh both
announced their full defection from the SMC on 5 December proved that
point clearly.

Events in Lebanon were also making an increasingly strong impression—
inside the country, in Syria and further afield. A double suicide bombing that
killed twenty-three people outside the Iranian embassy in Beirut on
19 November followed by the assassination of senior Hezbollah military commander Hassan Hawlo al-Laqqis in Beirut on 4 December underlined the fact
that the Syrian conflict had brought itself into Lebanon 'proper'. In a statement issued by its religious leader, Sheikh Sirajeddine Zureiqat, Kataib
Abdullah Azzam claimed responsibility for the Iran embassy bombing—the
first attack it was to claim in the Lebanese capital. Zureiqat warned that more
attacks would come unless Iran withdrew its forces from Syria. By natural
extension, this message was also directed to Iran's proxy, Hezbollah.

As winter began to set in in December 2013, developments relating to
ongoing tensions with ISIS drove a wedge between Syria's moderate and more
conservative Islamist insurgents. Late on 6 December, members of the FSA's
First and Second Battalions stationed at a headquarters of the Western-backed
SMC in the village of Babisqa near the Bab al-Hawa border crossing with
Turkey detected an apparent imminent attack on their position by unidentified militants, possibly members of ISIS. Within their facility in Babisqa was
a vast arms and equipment depot filled with weaponry and vehicles supplied
by the Friends of Syria and intended for the FSA. With one of his largest arms

depots under threat, SMC chief of staff Selim Idriss reportedly requested local Islamic Front fighters to urgently deploy to the facility in its defence. However, by the time a local unit of Ahrar al-Sham fighters—operating on behalf of the Islamic Front—arrived, the FSA had largely withdrawn, and the ISIS attack never materialised. Thus, Ahrar al-Sham found itself in control of the SMC headquarters. While specific details surrounding the incident do vary—with some claiming that the Islamic Front was the party that looked to attack the base—Jaish al-Islam spokesman Islam Alloush claimed that after securing the facility, Idriss 'handed us [the Islamic Front] the keys to the General Staff headquarters, while the officer in charge of the 1st Battalion gave us the keys to [his building], after it had been emptied of what was inside'.[40]

Whatever the specific details, the outcome was that the SMC had lost control of one of its most valuable facilities in Syria, and three days later Ahrar al-Sham took control of the Bab al-Hawa crossing itself. Consequently, as if to rub salt in the FSA's wounds, the UK and USA announced on 11 December that they had totally ceased their provision of non-lethal assistance to the FSA via the Bab al-Hawa crossing.

While plans for its formation dated back well beyond 6 December, the formation of the Syrian Revolutionaries Front (SRF) by the well-known nationalist Jamal Maarouf in Idlib on 9 December could have been perceived as an attempt to counterbalance the growing stature of Islamists of all kinds in northern Syria. As an avowedly moderate insurgent leader, Maarouf and his SRF retained strong and loyal links to the SMC and and its then chief supporter Saudi Arabia, which was adopting an increasingly sharp anti-extremist stance in Syria. As such, the SRF was quickly perceived by Syrian Salafists on the ground as competition and by jihadists as a potential threat. As one foreign fighter based in Idlib and Latakia claimed:

> Jamal Maarouf would do anything to get big amounts of support from the West and everyone knew this meant opposing the mujahidin. His front was merely a tool of the West.[41]

Despite the SRF's formation, the situation for the FSA looked to be going from bad to worse. While ISIS did not end up attacking Babisqa, it did forcefully take control of the town of Harem in Idlib on 9 December and Maskanah in Aleppo on 10 December. In taking the latter town, ISIS detained an Ahrar al-Sham doctor, Hussein Suleiman, whose horrifically tortured corpse would be revealed three weeks later. ISIS even went as far as to kidnap the FSA's Military Council chief in Hama governorate, Brigadier General Ahmad Berri, on 15 December.

Further south meanwhile, Jabhat al-Nusra was launching a renewed assault on the ancient town of Maaloula. Pro-regime forces elsewhere in the mountainous Qalamoun region north of Damascus had made notable several notable gains in November, including the capture of the town of Qara on 19 November and the near-total seizure of al-Nabk on 28–29 November. This second attack on Maaloula was an attempt to draw Syrian army personnel away from al-Nabk, which if taken would have allowed the regime to turn its attention to the last remaining opposition-held town on the Lebanese border, Yabroud. These were battles with high stakes for the entire opposition.

Whereas the previous attack on Maaloula in September had been initiated by a Jabhat al-Nusra suicide bomber, the offensive this time began with a covert infiltration of the town early on 30 November. By the following day, control of the town was effectively split between the regime and the opposition—which was composed of several FSA factions, al-Katibat al-Khadraa and Jabhat al-Nusra—with the centre under regime control and the outlying areas filled with insurgents. Early on the morning of 2 December, car tyres filled with timed explosives were rolled down the hill towards army positions inside the town, precipitating a successful final assault that drove the army entirely out by the end of the day.[42] During the final day of fighting, Jabhat al-Nusra took control of the town's Greek Orthodox monastery, known as Mar Thecla. While initial reporting suggested that the monastery's thirteen nuns and three maids were being held for their own safety by Jabhat al-Nusra, they were later moved to the contested town of Yabroud, where they remained in militant custody until March 2014, when they were released in an internationally mediated prison exchange with the regime.

With the fate of thirteen Christian nuns dominating the world's media, the threat jihadists in Syria were perceived to be posing to the region and the world received particularly close attention. In Syria, senior Greek Orthodox bishop Luqa al-Houry called upon Christian youth to take up arms against al-Qaeda and Sunni militancy, while Western media belatedly reported the issuing of a *fatwa* by prominent Shia Muslim cleric Grand Ayatollah Kazem al-Haeri several months earlier that legally permitted Shia men to fight in Syria's civil war against 'infidels' and in support of President Assad.[43] While such statements would only serve to further escalate a situation already spiralling out of control, the scale of jihadist militancy in Syria was indeed expanding at an exponential rate. According to the London-based International Centre for the Study of Radicalisation and Political Violence (ICSR), as many as 11,000 foreign fighters had entered Syria by mid-December 2013—double the estimate from eight months earlier:[44]

| Country of Origin | Estimated Foreign Fighters |
| --- | --- |
| Afghanistan | 12–23 |
| Albania | 9–140 |
| Algeria | 68–123 |
| Australia | 23–205 |
| Austria | 1–60 |
| Bahrain | 1 |
| Belgium | 76–296 |
| Bosnia | 18–60 |
| Bulgaria | 1 |
| Canada | 9–100 |
| Chechnya | 36–186 |
| China | 6–100 |
| Denmark | 25–84 |
| Egypt | 119–358 |
| Finland | 4–20 |
| France | 63–412 |
| Germany | 34–240 |
| Iran | 3 |
| Iraq | 59–247 |
| Ireland | 11–26 |
| Israel | 15–20 |
| Italy | 2–50 |
| Jordan | 180–2,089 |
| Kazakhstan | 14–150 |
| Kosovo | 4–150 |
| Kuwait | 54–71 |
| Kyrgyzstan | 9–30 |
| Lebanon | 65–890 |
| Libya | 336–556 |
| Luxembourg | 1 |
| Macedonia | 3–20 |
| Mauritania | 2 |
| Morocco | 77–91 |
| Netherlands | 29–152 |
| Norway | 33–40 |
| Oman | 1 |

| | |
|---|---:|
| Pakistan | 7–330 |
| Qatar | 15 |
| Russia (exc. Chechnya) | 9–423 |
| Palestine | 74–114 |
| Saudi Arabia | 386–1,016 |
| Serbia | 3 |
| Somalia | 5–68 |
| Spain | 34–95 |
| Sudan | 2–96 |
| Sweden | 39–87 |
| Switzerland | 1 |
| Tunisia | 382–970 |
| Turkey | 63–500 |
| Ukraine | 50 |
| United Arab Emirates | 14 |
| United Kingdom | 43–366 |
| United States | 17–60 |
| Yemen | 14–110 |

Note: Figures are limited to Sunni foreign fighters and based on figures officially available in open sources. Data is not universally available for all countries.

As the regime continued its offensive in the Qalamoun, aiming to definitively cut the opposition off from its support cells in eastern Lebanon, the level of hostile rhetoric within the jihadist community aimed at Iran and Hezbollah rocketed. In that context, the extent of violent spillover from Syria into Lebanon had by late 2013 become a nearly daily affair. Small numbers of mortars and artillery rockets were launched across the border towards pro-Hezbollah areas of the Bekaa, but of more significance was what was originating *inside* Lebanon.

Apart from intra-neighbourhood clashes in Lebanon's northern city of Tripoli—which had pitted armed residents of the Sunni district of Bab al-Tabbaneh and the Alawite district of Jabal Mohsen against each other since June 2011—the southern city of Sidon, the capital Beirut and countless towns in the east had witnessed incidents of violence. On 16 December two Hezbollah members were killed in a suicide car bombing that targeted a training camp run by the group near the village of Sbouba in Baalbek.[45] After several rocket attacks aimed at similar targets in the days that followed, including one claimed jointly by Jabhat al-Nusra and Kataib Abdullah Azzam, Hezbollah militants ambushed what they claimed was a group of Jabhat al-Nusra fighters in the Wadi al-Jamala area near Nahle in Baalbek on 22 December, killing thirty-two.[46]

The scale of the fatalities made this latter incident a significant event and a reminder that the Syria–Lebanon border was not only guarded on the Syrian side. However, the most significant such event came later in the month, when Lebanon's former minister of finance and ambassador to the USA, Mohamed Chatah, was killed in a car-bomb assassination in Beirut on 27 December. Chatah had been a vocal critic of Bashar al-Assad, and of Hezbollah's role in Syria and its management of an armed presence in Lebanese territory. In a statement issued after his death, former Lebanese prime minister Sa'ad al-Hariri pointed to Hezbollah as the culprits, claiming that 'those who assassinated Mohamed Chatah are the [same] ones who assassinated Rafik Hariri', another former Lebanese prime minister, who was killed by suspected Hezbollah operatives in Beirut in February 2005.

\* \* \*

Syria had seen a year of horrific violence in 2013, with a continual escalation in the regime's level of repression, ending with a catastrophically deadly chemical weapons attack outside its own capital in late August. By mid-December the regime had launched what would be a month-long campaign of continuous barrel bombing of Aleppo city, designed to displace populations and destroy the environment in which the insurgency was operating. The humanitarian situation was utterly dire, with 2.3 million Syrians having fled the country to become refugees in Lebanon, Turkey, Jordan and elsewhere, and another 6.5 million living as internally displaced persons (IDP) inside the country. In all, at least 40 per cent of the country's people had been displaced in one way or another and more than 125,000 killed. Every day an average of 3,000 Syrians were leaving their country.[47]

It was also in 2013 that jihadists definitively asserted a foothold within the conflict and upon Syrian territory. Jabhat al-Nusra continued its comparatively pragmatic strategy of cooperating tacitly with opposition groups of all stripes, despite warnings from Ayman al-Zawahiri not to ally with secularists. As the year ended, its operations spanned virtually all of Syria, and it had expanded officially into Lebanon thanks to its close relationship with Kataib Abdullah Azzam. In fact, the US government designated a Jabhat al-Nusra commander and former member of Fatah al-Islam, Osama Amin al-Shihabi, as the group's chief of Lebanon operations on 18 December 2013.[48] Kataib Abdullah Azzam, however, suffered a significant loss late in December when its leader, Majid bin Muhammed al-Majid was arrested by Lebanese authorities after being treated for kidney problems in a hospital in Beirut.[49] He subsequently died of kidney failure on 4 January 2014 whilst in custody in a Lebanese military hospital.[50]

Meanwhile, countless other foreign fighter-dominated jihadist factions were established across northern Syria throughout the year, incorporating militants from every corner of the globe, including several former Guantanamo Bay detainees and a former rapper-turned-Salafist extremist wanted in Germany, Denis Mamadou Gerhard Cuspert (Abu Talha al-Almani).

Then came ISIS, which as the year progressed revealed itself as a singly self-interested but highly capable militant actor. After winning a number of significant victories in coordination with the broader insurgent opposition in the early summer, it soon turned inwards and began operating independently, seeking its own objectives. This in turn meant that it was increasingly devoting its resources towards acquiring and consolidating control over territory already captured by the opposition, while the intensity of its fight against the Assad regime dwindled. The regime acted accordingly, seemingly providing ISIS with the necessary space to divide and weaken the opposition, sowing the seeds of discord that would reveal themselves in 2014.

As 2013 drew to a close, however, and as ISIS continued to clash with opposition factions in the towns of Kafranabel, Sarmada and Bab al-Hawa between 28 and 31 December, ISIS was engaged in a far more important offensive in Iraq. There, in the western desert province of Anbar, ISIS was exploiting a breakdown in security that had been sparked by a government-ordered attack on Sunni protest camps in the city of Ramadi and elsewhere. Considerable portions of Iraq's Sunni population had been up in arms at the perceived repressive security measures imposed by the central government in Baghdad, which was led by Shia Muslim Nouri al-Maliki. The protest camps had been formed earlier in 2013 by Sunni tribes in order to demonstrate the apparent unified opposition to the Maliki government by Iraq's western Sunni communities. However, by late 2013 they had also been infilitrated by Sunni militant groups—including ISIS and several other factions created during the US occupation by former Baathists—who sought to exploit such a ripely unstable environment for their own advantage.

Amid a newly launched Iraqi army offensive targeting ISIS in the deserts of Anbar in December, the group had launched its own offensive operations, including a complex pre-planned ambush that killed eighteen soldiers on 21 December.' That attack probably represented the last straw for Maliki, who subsequently ordered a crackdown in the final days of the month. As the tribes rose up against the central government, ISIS pounced in early January, seizing control of the city of Fallujah and, for a while, large parts of Ramadi. On the other side of the border, ISIS's chief of operations in northern Syria, Omar al-Shishani—who had split from Jaish al-Muhajireen wa'l Ansar earlier in December—had reportedly been redeployed to Deir ez Zour to help coordinate cross-border operations into Anbar and to bolster ISIS's attack on the Syrian regime's Base 137.

# 9

# JANUARY–APRIL 2014

## TURNING AGAINST THE ISLAMIC STATE

After several months of ISIS aggression and hostile acts against rival insurgent factions, 2014 began with a major offensive being launched against ISIS in northern Syria. From 4 January onwards FSA-aligned factions, Islamists, Salafists and eventually also Jabhat al-Nusra fought against ISIS's control of territory. The Islamic Front and Jabhat al-Nusra issued statements blaming the infighting on ISIS's previous behaviours and its refusal to submit to mediation and judicial investigations, to which ISIS responded with bloodcurdling threats, including declaring takfir on the FSA and exiled political opposition. Senior Ahrar al-Sham leader and al-Qaeda's appointed emissary in Syria Abu Khaled al-Suri also emerged for the first time, calling for a ceasefire.

ISIS again resisted calls from Ayman al-Zawahiri and Abdullah al-Moheisini—a popular Saudi Salafist present within the jihadist community in northern Syria—for a cessation in fighting and, despite incurring losses, began enforcing strict *Sharia* laws in Raqqa in January and February 2014. After the death of ISIS deputy leader Haji Bakr in northern Aleppo in late January, al-Qaeda's central leadership publicly disowned ISIS.

As the infighting continued and intensified, senior al-Qaeda veteran commanders began emerging in northern Syria alongside Jabhat al-Nusra. Although their identities were closely guarded secrets, their arrivals were noted on the ground. This coincided with the start of attacks in Lebanon claimed variously in the name of Jabhat al-Nusra and the al-Qaeda-linked Kataib Abdullah Azzam.

Meanwhile, as opposition forces launched offensive operations against the regime in Aleppo, Quneitra, Hama and Latakia, with the latter seeing fighters reach the Mediterranean coast for the first time, the regime initiated its own steadily successful offensive in the strategically valuable Qalamoun Mountains along the Lebanese border.

In late February 2014 ISIS began a counter-offensive against rival factions in eastern Deir ez Zour, and carried out a number of targeted attacks on key Islamist commanders and headquarters in Aleppo and Idlib. Abu Khaled al-Suri was killed in one such attack in Aleppo on 23 February. Such counter-attacks were not only military in nature, however, as ISIS also launched a scathing assault on the credibility of al-Qaeda's central leadership, claiming it had veered off the correct jihadi path.

By April the anti-ISIS offensive launched in January was a success, forcing the group to withdraw from Latakia, Hama, Idlib and western Aleppo. With Jabhat al-Nusra the last remaining major jihadist force in that north-western region, the arrival of American anti-tank weaponry—the first of its kind to appear in Syria—generated considerable attention and questions regarding whether Jabhat al-Nusra was next on the target list.

\* \* \*

With ISIS seemingly on the offensive in Iraq's Anbar province, the group's situation in Syria was set to enter a dramatic and more intensely challenging phase in January 2014.

Since emerging as an active participant in Syria's civil conflict in May 2013, ISIS had enjoyed a complex but meteoric rise to prominence. Through a combination of strategic guile, military proficiency and sheer brutality, ISIS had acquired total control of or a strong influence in at least thirty-five municipalities in Syria, and maintained military operations in as many as ten of Syria's fourteen governorates (not Tartous, Quneitra, Deraa and Suwayda). In addition to Iraq, where ISIS and its predecessor organisations had been a prominent militant faction since 2003, ISIS even claimed on 2 January 2014 to have expanded its operations into Lebanon, when it claimed responsibility for a car bombing in Beirut's southern Dahiyeh suburb. In so doing, ISIS had demonstrated the true meaning of its name, by incorporating Iraq, Syria and Lebanon into its sphere of influence.[1]

However, ISIS had clearly not achieved its extraordinary expansion across much of Syria without killing, maiming and threatening members of other insurgent organisations around it. While Jabhat al-Nusra and other jihadist groups in Syria had established themselves and consolidated their respective influences within the conflict through the management of pragmatic relations with other factions, ISIS had quickly revealed itself to be a self-serving organisation, solely seeking the attainment of its own objective—the unilateral establishment of an Islamic state—above and beyond anything else. This strategy, though successful in the immediate term, had made ISIS many enemies in Syria. The perception on the ground (quite justified until mid-2014) that the Assad regime had an interest in facilitating the rise of ISIS in Syria made this situation all the more acute.

Thus, when ISIS returned the horrifically tortured and disfigured corpse of Dr Hussein Suleiman to Ahrar al-Sham in Aleppo on 31 December 2013, it had offended once too often. Suleiman, who went by the moniker Abu Rayyan, was a physician and commander in Ahrar al-Sham who had been made responsible for the group's management of the Bab al-Hawa border crossing with Turkey since early December 2013. He had then been dispatched midway through that month to Maskanah in rural Aleppo to negotiate a solution to a dispute between Ahrar al-Sham and ISIS, but he was arrested on arrival.[2] When his body was returned two weeks later, one ear had been cut off, his teeth smashed out and the top of his head shot off.[3]

On Friday 3 January 2014 protests were planned across opposition-held areas of the country to demonstrate against ISIS's presence and its killing of Abu Rayyan. Small such protests took place in several ISIS-held villages and towns in northern Syria, including in Kafr Takharim in Idlib, where ISIS fighters opened fire and violently dispersed the dissenters. Although no casualties were reported from the incident, it quickly spread across social media, and shortly thereafter FSA fighters launched a series of seemingly coordinated attacks on ISIS positions across Aleppo and Idlib. Particularly intense fighting was reported in the towns of Marat Misrin, Azaz, Kafr Nabel and in Atareb, which ISIS had attacked the previous day. In response, ISIS factions launched raids on FSA positions in Hama and Latakia governorates and also against Liwa al-Tawhid in the Aleppo town of Deir Jamal.

In addition to Jamal Maarouf's SRF, a key instigator of the anti-ISIS attacks on 3 January had been a coalition of moderate Islamist factions known as Jaish al-Mujahideen. Established only earlier that day, Jaish al-Mujahideen was composed of eight primarily Aleppo-based groups, including Kataib Nour al-Din al-Zinki, whose leader, Sheikh Tawfiq Shahabuddin, maintained strong connections to Salafist sources in the Gulf. The Syrian Muslim Brotherhood also had a strong influence within this new anti-ISIS coalition, through the inclusion of Liwa al-Ansar, Liwa Jund al-Haramein and Liwa Amjad al-Islam within its eight constituent groups.[4] In a statement issued that day, Jaish al-Mujahideen announced that it had initiated a war of 'self-defence' against ISIS, which it accused of 'undermining stability and security in liberated areas' and said that this would continue until ISIS's 'dissolution'. Within hours, ISIS replied by warning that it would retaliate fiercely and the 'the blood of our brothers will not be shed in vain'.[5]

The Syrian conflict and insurgency was therefore witnessing the dawn of a new era—the extremists and the moderates were now at each other's throats, and the fight against the regime was temporarily demoted to second rank. But what of the insurgents in the 'ideological middle?' The Islamic Front issued an official statement on 3 January denying involvement in any offensive operations against ISIS, but ordering it to cease its aggression on the town of Atareb, where a Tunisian ISIS *emir* known as Abu Saber had been captured. Meanwhile, Islamic Front political chief and Ahrar al-Sham leader Hassan Abboud also commented that day, again denying his movement's role in fighting ISIS offensively but intriguingly suggesting that ISIS follow the example set by Jabhat al-Nusra.

Clearly, the escalating tensions between ISIS and the rest of the insurgency in Syria made such hostilities more than a likely scenario; but had the anti-ISIS attacks on 3 January been pre-planned? Speaking to this author at the time, several ISIS fighters claimed that they had experienced difficulty operating their remote radios and that their commanders reported extensive electronic interference on the afternoon that the attacks began. Moreover, could so many separate FSA factions have all launched raids against ISIS positions across multiple governorates on the same afternoon so quickly after the incident in Kafr Takharim? Considering the poor levels of coordination demonstrated by the disparate umbrella of the FSA through 2013, this seems highly unlikely.

Late 2013 had witnessed a notable coalescence of insurgent factions in Syria, particularly the establishment of Jaish al-Islam on 29 September, the Islamic Front on 22 November and the SRF on 9 December. Followed shortly thereafter by the creation of Jaish al-Mujahideen on 3 January, this unification of factions was unlikely to have been entirely a coincidence. Indeed, behind the scenes the US government had been placing considerable pressure on the two key Gulf states backing the insurgency—Qatar and Saudi Arabia—to tighten up and make their strategies of support more efficient so as to align more closely with the then objective of Washington DC. Principally, this new US-directed strategy incorporated two key concepts: firstly, the reorientation of lethal and non-lethal support to the opposition through centrally managed 'military operations centres' in Jordan and Turkey, rather than through the SMC; and secondly, the ideological and political moderation of the main insurgent actors on the ground.

While the first scheme was already well under way by late 2013, the second was a work in progress. Ahrar al-Sham and the Islamic Front remained the most dominant insurgent actors in Syria, but their ideological conservatism did not fit well with what the USA hoped for for Syria's future. Consequently, significant internal changes were initiated from the top down within the Islamic Front's principal backing state Qatar, by Emir Tamim bin Hamad al-Thani, who had assumed power from his father Hamad bin Khalifa al-Thani on 25 June 2013. Whereas three wings of the Qatari government had maintained their own largely independent Syria strategies up until this point, the Ministry of Foreign Affairs alone was granted the Syria 'file' (although external intelligence did continue its own activities).[6] Funding levels to Islamic Front factions consequently declined significantly in early 2014, precipitating a decline in operational potency within several constituent factions, including Ahrar al-Sham. Financial contributions for the opposition began to be funelled more in the direction of the US- and Saudi-backed operations room in southern Turkey, and the influence of moderates picked up.

Within this environment of insurgent unification and ideological moderation, it seems more than likely that the USA, Saudi Arabia and Qatar had a role in at the very least encouraging an anti-ISIS front in northern Syria. In a revealing piece from late January, *The Daily Telegraph*'s Ruth Sherlock claimed to reveal this:

The subsequent battle against ISIS … is being touted by local commanders as a spontaneous reaction to the spate of assassinations of comrades.

However, the Telegraph can reveal that in late December, a delegation including US and Saudi officials met in Turkey with senior rebel leaders.

According to two sources—one whose brother was at the meeting: 'They talked about the fighting with ISIS, and the Americans encouraged the commanders to attack.'

The Syrian Revolutionary Front, whose main commander, Jamal Maarouf, is allied to Saudi Arabia, and [Jaish al-Islam], a new coalition of the moderate rebels sponsored by Qatar, have continued to liaise with the CIA and Saudi and Qatari intelligence, others close to meetings said.

These groups received a boost in arms supplies. According to a source who facilitates governments' lethal and non-lethal aid to Western-friendly groups: 'Qatar sent arms first. Saudi Arabia didn't want to be out done, so one week before the attack on ISIS, they gave 80 tons of weaponry, including heavy machine guns.'

Washington did not directly give arms, he said, but backed Saudi Arabia in its funding of the groups. The United States has, however, also been giving $2 million in cash every month as an unofficial hand out, splitting that amount between western friendly rebel groups, the source added.[7]

Whatever the extent to which external orders or influence had played a part, an anti-ISIS front had been definitively opened and the coming months would be dominated by hostilities between ISIS and the remainder of the Syria-based insurgency.

Between 4 and 16 January fighting had erupted in more than sixty municipalities across the governorates of Latakia, Idlib, Aleppo, Raqqa, Hama, Homs, Hasakah and Deir ez Zour, leaving 1,069 people (including 608 anti-ISIS insurgents, 312 ISIS militants and 130 civilians) dead, according to activist reports.[8] ISIS had lost control of at least thirty municipalities and, despite heavy fighting in the city, had begun strategic moves to reinforce its position in the city of Raqqa. While Jaish al-Mujahideen and the SRF had launched the anti-ISIS operations, the Islamic Front was increasingly bearing the brunt of ISIS' counter-attack, which included at least twelve suicide car bombings at checkpoints and strategically located local headquarters, and armed raids on many more.

Given the stakes involved, the fighting in all cases was particularly intense, but reports of severe violations proliferated. ISIS was accused of multiple mass executions of prisoners in Aleppo's Qadi Askar district on 6 January; in central Raqqa on 9 January; and in Kantari outside Raqqa on 13 January. However, ISIS was not the only alleged participant in such extra-judicial killings. The SRF was accused of capturing thirty-four jihadist fighters in Idlib's Jebel al-Zawiyeh region between 4 and 6 January and of executing them and dumping their bodies down wells.[9] Most of those killed were reportedly ISIS members, but some belonged to the Jabhat al-Nusra-affiliated Jund al-Aqsa faction, including the group's Iraq-born leader, Mohammed Yusuf al-Athamna (Abu 'Abd al-Aziz al-Qatari). Athamna had been a founding member of Jabhat al-Nusra in late 2011 and was a veteran of jihad in Afghanistan—where he reportedly had been close to Abdullah Azzam, Osama bin Laden and Ayman al-Zawahiri—and in Chechnya and Iraq.[10] His corpse was discovered in a well located in the SRF headquarters in Jamal Maarouf's home town of Deir Sunbul in November 2014.

With fighting continuing between 4 and 16 January, a number of important statements were released within the Salafist and jihadist community that would come to define the trajectory of this new conflict front. On 6 January the Islamic Front released a statement proclaiming:

We fight against whoever attacks us and whoever pushes us to battle, whether they are Syrian or foreign ... In our [political] charter ... we said we are grateful and thankful to the foreigners who came to help us ... [but] we will not accept any group that claims to be a state.[11]

This was the first apparent admission by the Islamic Front that its fighters were engaging in combat against ISIS, albeit in a somewhat defensive manner. It did come after ISIS had launched assaults on facilities belonging to three of its seven factions—Liwa al-Tawhid, Suqor al-Sham and Ahrar al-Sham—in Idlib, Aleppo and Raqqa, after all.

The following day the situation escalated significantly. On 7 January Jabhat al-Nusra leader Jolani issued an audio statement in which he blamed the 'incorrect policies' of ISIS for having engendered the conditions that led to the ongoing fighting, which he also admitted his faction was involved in. Consequently, Jolani proposed an immediate ceasefire between all sides and for an Islamic court to be established to negotiate a solution to the disputes and complaints being made. 'The whole battlefield, including the foreign and local fighters, will pay the price of losing a great jihad because the regime will rebound when it was close to vanishing,' Jolani exclaimed, reminding listeners of the broader context in which this inter-factional fighting had erupted.[12]

While Jolani's statement could well have proved sufficient to de-escalate hostilities, what came only hours later ensured that the conflict would continue. Later that day ISIS spokesman Adnani released his own audio statement, entitled 'The Time to Harvest is Approaching'. In addition to commenting on the situation in Iraq, Adnani demanded that Jaish al-Mujahideen, the SRF and 'those who carry Islamic banners' repent and cease 'fighting the mujahideen and ... muhajireen who left everything and came to Syria to defend and sacrifice'. Continuing, Adnani warned those fighting ISIS in Syria to

learn from those who stood against the Mujahideen in Iraq. They are either under the ground, enslaved by the Rafidha, or on the run. You stabbed us from the back while our positions were occupied by few guards. You should have warned us if you were brave, but this is the Sahwas' way ... If you repent we promise you safety, otherwise, know that we have armies in Iraq and an army in Sham composed of hungry lions. Their drink is blood and their favorite companions are dismembered body parts. They never tasted a drink more delicious than the blood of the Sahwas. We swear to God, we will bring a thousand then a thousand then another. None of you will remain and we will make you an example.[13]

If that was not inflammatory enough, Adnani went on to declare *takfir* on the entire moderate Syrian opposition, thus declaring them legitimate targets in the eyes of ISIS:

I swear that what you are witnessing are the Sahwas. We had no doubt that they would appear but we did not expect them to appear this fast. They surprised us. Never be gentle with them. Attack the Sahwas hard and crush them hard and kill the conspiracy in its cradle ... ETILAF, the National Council, the General Staff and the Supreme Military Council represent apostasy and kufr who declared war on the State (ISIS). Therefore we regard their members as targets unless they publicly denounce it. For the soldiers of ISIS, know that we have designated awards for those who take their heads and the heads of their leaders. Kill them wherever you find them.[14]

This was a huge development for the dynamics of the conflict in Syria and there was no going back. ISIS had now declared roughly half of the insurgents in Syria to be apostates deserving of death, while the majority of the other half were also engaged in combating ISIS across the country.

Shortly after Adnani's blood-curdling statement, Bahraini pro-ISIS jihadist ideologue Abu Humam al-Athari (Turki al-Binali) issued a refutation of Jolani's peace proposal by claiming it was in fact the fault of Jolani himself—'the renegade leader'—for having defected from ISIS in April 2013.[15] For now therefore, not only had the battle-lines been drawn between ISIS and pro-FSA factions such as the SRF and Jaish al-Mujahideen, but the Islamic Front and Jabhat al-Nusra were being fully drawn into hostilities. This in turn appeared to catalyse the notable defection of several senior ISIS officials, along with their respective supporters. On 9 January, for example, ISIS's *sharia* official in Hama governorate, Ibrahim al-Masri (an Egyptian) defected to Jabhat al-Nusra along with twenty-five fighters after accusing ISIS of betraying al-Qaeda. Seven days later ISIS *sharia* official in Homs Haydar al-Qassim also defected to Jabhat al-Nusra, citing similar concerns.

As fighting continued to intensify in early January, reports emerged that senior ISIS military leader Omar al-Shishani had returned from his deployment in Deir ez Zour to lead the movement's counter-offensive operations in eastern Aleppo. Further unverified reports from Syrian activists claimed that as many as 1,300 fighters from Iraq—'ISIS special forces'—had been part of Shishani's convoy that arrived in the Aleppo town of al-Bab on 9 January.[16] With reinforcements in rural Aleppo, ISIS was gearing up for a major escalation of attacks on rival factions across northern Syria, where the Islamic Front still remained dominant. Consequently, Ahrar al-Sham's chief *sharia* official and a prominent member of the Islamic Front's Supreme Council, Abu Yazan al-Shami, issued a *fatwa* on 11 January declaring it Islamically legitimate for all Islamic fighters to fight ISIS in Syria. From that point on, the entire Islamic Front—with the partial exception of a few Ahrar al-Sham units who insisted on remaining neutral, especially in Hasakah—deployed its forces intensively to fight against ISIS. This, however, drew invaluable resources away from the fight with the regime in Aleppo, which sparked a number of Syrian army and Hezbollah advances through January.

Then, on 16 January, a matter of hours after a huge ISIS suicide car bomb struck an Islamic Front headquarters in the Idlib town of Darkush, senior Ahrar al-Sham official Abu Khaled al-Suri released his first statement in Syria in which he addressed ISIS and urged it to cease its 'incorrect practices'. Emphasising his extensive history and seniority within the upper echeclons of the jihadist community, Abu Khaled explained:

> What we hear today of crimes and incorrect practices being committed under the name of jihad and establishing the Islamic State, and being attributed to the like of the Sheikhs of Jihad such as Sheikh Osama bin Laden, may Allah have mercy on him; Sheikh Ayman al-Zawahiri, may Allah preserve him; Sheikh Abdullah Azzam, may Allah have mercy on him; Sheikh Abu Musab al-Suri, may Allah release him, and Sheikh Abu Musab al-Zarqawi, may Allah have mercy on him, who spent their life in jihad in the cause of Allah, Allah's name, is away from the correct method. So my words to you are the words of one who spent his life with those prominent men and knew them well, for they are innocent of what is being attributed to them, like the innocence of the wolf from the blood of the son of Jacob. Do not be tricked by the confusion of those who confuse ... the news of the liars.[17]

Apart from the fact that it was Abu Khaled's first public statement and his addition of the phrase 'may Allah release him' after Abu Musab al-Suri's name—which demonstrated, as previously explained, that he remained in prison in Syria—the statement did not reveal anything particularly new. However, what it served to underline was the overwhelming desire within the non-ISIS jihadist community that this dispute be resolved by 'repenting' to Allah's *sharia* and by resolving differences peacefully. This was a theme continued later that day by famed al-Qaeda ideologue Abu Qatada al-Filistini, who gave a press statement while on trial in Amman in Jordan:

> The fighting between Islamist factions should end ... Abu Bakr al-Baghdadi leader of [ISIS] ... should dissolve his group and work under Jabhat al-Nusra ... The two groups should reconcile and focus on fighting those who fight them ... You should not kidnap or kill anyone who does not carry weapons to fight you.[18]

The seemingly unified position of al-Qaeda and many of the region's most prominent jihadist ideologues—others that would soon comment included Abu Mohammed al-Maqdisi, Abu Basir al-Tartusi, Iyad al-Qunaybi and Suleiman al-Ulwan[19]—probably helped encourage a number of pledges of *bay'a* to Jabhat al-Nusra in January. During that month six insurgent factions in Damascus, six in Idlib and the already well-known Suqor al-Izz in Latakia pledged their official allegiance to Jabhat al-Nusra and to its leader Jolani. All in all, that probably added at least 2,000 fighters to Jabhat al-Nusra's ranks.

With that being said, however, by early February ISIS would also have received a number of pledges, from tribes in Aleppo and Deir ez Zour; from three units of Ahrar al-Sham and two of Jaish al-Islam; all insurgent factions in the northern town of Tel Hamis; and five small factions in Deir ez Zour.[20] Clearly, the exceptionally divisive nature of the infighting in Syria was bringing to light many actors' real allegiances, while for others it was forcing them to pick sides.

As the second half of January began, the world's focus on Syria remained upon the anti-ISIS infighting; but attention was also drawn to the fast-approaching Geneva II peace conference, due to begin in the Swiss town of Montreux on 22 January and then move to Geneva on 23 January. Opinion within the opposition community on the ground in Syria was overwhelmingly against the talks themselves, let alone whether any FSA faction should attend. Nonetheless, within the exiled political opposition the dramatic outbreak of fighting against ISIS provided an indispensable opportunity to demonstrate their anti-extremist stance. Thus amid increasing numbers of ISIS territorial withdrawals, the ETILAF political opposition announced on 18 January after a tense vote that it would indeed attend Geneva II. Facing pressure from their backers, several US-backed FSA factions did later secretly agree to send representatives to Switzerland.

Meanwhile, as it was steadily losing control of villages and towns in Idlib and western Aleppo, ISIS's much-vaunted counter-offensive began. It appeared primarily focused on retaining control of territory in close proximity to Syria's northernmost border areas with Turkey and on defending towns like al-Bab, Jarablus and Manbij that were positioned on the two main roads leading east to the city of Raqqa. Large suicide car bombings and night-time covert assassination raids were additionally used to weaken key checkpoints and to neutralise critical local headquarters belonging to groups such as Liwa al-Tawhid and Ahrar al-Sham in Aleppo. Rather than being a 'counter-offensive', the strategy was actually focused more on retaliation and strategic consolidation.

As fighting nonetheless continued, ISIS leader Abu Bakr al-Baghdadi released his first statement regarding the front that had opened up against his fighters in Syria. 'ISIS tried everything in its power to stop this war that was launched against us by some rebels ... We were forced into this war,' Baghdadi claimed, referring to the attacks that began on 3 January. In a threatening manner more akin to the tone adopted by Adnani days earlier, Baghdadi addressed those fighting ISIS:

> Repent to God for you have stabbed us in the back while our soldiers were at the front. Today you have seen our punishment and strength, and you have seen the difference between yesterday and today. Yesterday you were walking safe, sleeping assured. Today you are in constant fear and apprehension staying awake at night guarding yourselves. So here is the state extending its hand to you, so you can stop fighting it and we will stop fighting you and we can fight the Shia. And if not then know we we have soldiers that do not sleep, known to the near and far.[21]

Then, quite extraordinarily, as if totally unaware of the countless incidents of ISIS brutality and hostility meted out in the preceding months, Baghdadi addressed the Syrian people:

> As for the people in Syria: You have God, everyone trades with your blood, racing each other so that they can sit on your shoulders, or even on your corpses ... As for us we can't say anything but your blood is our blood and your destruction is our destruction. We fight in God's path and for his satisfaction and we do not fear the blame of blamers. Don't be deceived by the media for you will find us the kindest towards you and the harshest towards your enemies. God knows that we tried our best to defend Muslims and then overnight we are accused of making takfir on the Syrian population. God knows that we were the only ones that fought off criminals and overnight we turned into murderers and put our people in mass graves? God knows that thugs and thieves fled from every street/area we entered and overnight we are accused of terrifying the local population? God knows that we opened our arms towards every group and then we are accused of not recognizing any mujahid but ourselves? God knows we left our families and our homes to establish Shariah, and overnight we are accused of not turning towards Shariah?[22]

Whether genuine or not, Baghdadi's claim of ISIS's innocence was unlikely to meet receptive ears inside Syria. Nearly 1,400 people had by now lost their lives in the inter-factional fighting, including 760 anti-ISIS fighters, 426 ISIS militants and 190 civilians.[23] Moreover, ISIS's military actions barely suggested that it was actually open to compromise on the ground. In short, the subtle message Baghdadi was sending was the same as that made by his spokesman on 7 January: surrender or face the consequences.

All the while, ISIS was in the early stages of establishing its very own Islamic state in Syria. After ten days of fierce clashes between 3 and 13 January, ISIS succeeded in forcing the full withdrawal of Jabhat al-Nusra and Ahrar al-Sham from Raqqa city, leaving the city under its total control. One week later, on 19 January, ISIS's administrative authority in the city released four statements announcing the full prohibition of music being played in public; photographs of people being posted in shop windows; the sale or use of cigarettes and the popular 'shisha' water pipes; and that women must wear the full *niqab* in public and men were obligated to attend all five daily prayers at the mosque. A three-day grace period was offered for people to prepare to comply.[24]

Having heard Baghdadi's first statement on the infighting, the world was soon to hear that of the overall leader of al-Qaeda. On 23 January Ayman al-Zawahiri declared in an audio statement entitled 'An Urgent Call to Our People in the Levant' that the infighting in Syria should cease 'immediately' and for a '*sharia* committee' to be established to judge 'the various groups regarding the injustices each group claims against its jihadi sister group'.[25] Speaking against 'partisan extremism', Zawahiri's statement was primarily one calling for unity, which he said was 'more valuable for us that any organizational links'. Nonetheless, regarding the issue of *takfir*, Zawahiri was resolute:

> You know that we do not accept that the honor of a Muslim or a mujahid be touched, or his life, money, honor or dignity be attacked, or that charges of kufr or apostasy be cast on him, and we consider the jihadi organizations in al-Sham of resistance and jihad ... as our brothers, whom we don't accept to be described as apostates, infidels or heretics.[26]

Several hours after Zawahiri's statement was published by al-Qaeda's as-Sahab Media, an Islamic peace plan was announced in Syria by Abdullah bin Mohammed al-Moheisini. A popular Saudi Salafist cleric, Moheisini had been in Syria for several months and had been pictured engaging with senior members of the Islamic Front, Jabhat al-Nusra and ISIS. In announcing his 'Ummah Initiative', Moheisini called for the implementation of an immediate ceasefire and the establishment of a joint *sharia* court manned by several elected scholars from smaller jihadist factions active in the Syrian conflict (e.g. Suqor al-Izz, Jund al-Aqsa and al-Katibat al-Khadraa).[27] For the initiative to begin, Moheisini requested for all parties to the current *fitna* (discord or strife) to agree to submit to his proposition within five days—by 28 January. This included ISIS, Jabhat al-Nusra, the Islamic Front, Jaish al-Mujahideen and the SRF.

Moheisini's initiative very closely resembled the recommendations and orders made by senior al-Qaeda figures, including Zawahiri, Abu Khaled al-Suri and Abu Qatada, and, coming only hours after Zawahiri's statement, one could have speculated that the two developments were pre-planned. However, this has never been independently confirmed.

Nonetheless, Moheisini's perceived neutrality at the time, along with his broad appeal, meant his initiative promptly received positive replies. On 24 January the SRF, al-Katibat al-Khadraa, Suqor al-Izz and Jabhat al-Nusra all agreed to Moheisini's plan, while Jaish al-Muhajireen wa'l Ansar, Harakat Sham al-Islam and Jund al-Aqsa all assented on 25 January. Finally, on 26 January, the Islamic Front and Jaish al-Mujahideen confirmed their approval of the plan. This left only ISIS, which issued a statement on 27 January announcing that it rejected the initiative on the grounds that it acknowledged the legitimacy of factions who retained allegiance or links to foreign states that it deemed apostate. Unless all the organisations involved renounced their international ties and their relationships with the exiled opposition, ISIS would continue its fight.[28]

Ultimately, this should have come as no surprise, as ISIS's senior *sharia* leader Turki al-Binali had ruled only several weeks earlier that incidents of *fitna* could never be mediated by third parties as doing so would 'infringe on the right of the Muslim sovereign and his state'.[29]

If it had not seemed an intractable situation before, ISIS's rejection of Zawahiri's orders and of Moheisini's Ummah Initiative indicated that the infighting would continue for some time to come, if not indefinitely. The differences and scale of hostility were both too raw and intense to be pacified. And so, the fighting went on.

On 27 January ISIS-linked sources began admitting having suffered a significant blow: the loss of Abu Bakr al-Baghdadi's number two and chief strategist, Haji Bakr, during clashes with FSA faction Kataib wal-Wiya Shuhada Souriya in the Aleppo town of Tel Rifaat in early January. ISIS did not officially acknowledge Haji Bakr's death until 2 February, when using his moniker Abu Bakr al-Iraq, a statement explained:

We congratulate the *mujahideen* in general and in Iraq and al Sham in particular, for the martyrdom of the Mujahid Sheikh, the Commander, Abu Bakr al Iraqi [who was] knocked down by the cowardly, insidious hands in the countryside of Northern Aleppo by the criminals of the Sahwat ... [he] was one of the very first of those who joined the *mujahideen* after the Crusader invasion of Iraq [when he was appointed] to wage the war of the silencers and security work inside the cities.[30]

ISIS was not the only jihadist faction to have lost a senior member in January, however, as a senior Saudi Arabian Jabhat al-Nusra member, Abdullah Suleiman Salih al-Dhabah, was killed in a regime airstrike in Al-Bab in mid-January. Also known as Abu Ali al-Qasimi, Dhabah was number eleven on Saudi Arabia's list of forty-seven most wanted militants and was a seasoned al-Qaeda operative.[31]

Dhabah was also an alleged member of a top-secret Jabhat al-Nusra cell—which the US government would label the 'Khorasan Group' in late 2014—whose existence was at least partly devoted to continuing al-Qaeda's pursuit of spectacular attacks on the Western world. Beginning in mid-to-late 2013, a number of prominent al-Qaeda operatives had begun arriving in Syria both to bolster Jabhat al-Nusra's legitimacy in the face of ISIS's rise and to establish an al-Qaeda presence in Syria devoted to attacking the West. In addition to Dhabah, these arrivals included senior al-Qaeda official Abdul Mohsen Abdullah Ibrahim al-Sharikh, a Saudi national and third cousin of Osama Bin Laden who was also on Saudi Arabia's most wanted list. Better known as Sanafi al-Nasr, Sharikh had been a well-known online jihadist figure since at least 2005, when he was probably based in Saudi Arabia before joining al-Qaeda in Afghanistan–Pakistan in 2007. After a gradual rise up the organisation's senior ranks following the earlier US invasion of Afghanistan, US intelligence suggests that Sanafi al-Nasr moved to Iran, where for a period of time he was the 'chief of Al-Qaeda's Iran-based extremist and financial facilitation network'.[32] According to discussions this author had with both Syria-based jihadists and Western officials, Sanafi al-Nasr moved to Syria in mid-2013 and was instrumental in consolidating Jabhat al-Nusra's top-level relationship with Kataib Abdullah Azzam in Lebanon, through his close personal relationship with its then leader Majid bin Muhammed al-Majid and former leader Saleh al-Qaraawi. Sanafi al-Nasr may have been young (he was only twenty-eight when the anti-ISIS infighting began), but his jihadist credentials raised his profile substantially.

In fact, a large portion of his family had similarly extensive experience within the international jihad. Two of his six brothers—Abdulhadi Abdullah Ibrahim al-Sharikh and Abdalrazzaq Abdullah Hamid Ibrahim al-Sharikh—had been held in Guantanamo Bay before their transfer back to Saudi Arabia in September 2007, while another brother was killed fighting in Chechnya, and his father was known to senior al-Qaeda leaders.[33]

Additional members of this Khorasan Group were Saudi national Mohsen al-Fadhli—identified by the US government in 2012 as the al-Qaeda leader in Iran, with an offer of $7 million for information leading to his location[34]—and Turkish citizen Ümit Yaşar Toprak (Abu Yousuf al-Turki). The arrival of such individuals, amongst others, undoubtedly served to bolster the level of jihadist prestige that Jabhat al-Nusra could self-identify with.

Jabhat al-Nusra already included within its senior leadership figures like Abu Firas al-Suri, who fought with the Syrian Muslim Brotherhood's al-Talia al-Muqatila in 1979–80, before travelling to Jordan and then Afghanistan, where he became closely acquainted with Abdullah Azzam and Osama Bin Laden in 1983. After a period in Afghanistan training 'the mujahideen in specially prepared camps to carry out operations in India, Indonesia, Burma and Iran', a biography of Abu Firas claims that he became Bin Laden's 'envoy ... to call the people of Pakistani [*sic*] to perform jihad' and was instrumental in establishing Lashkar-e-Tayyiba and its 'political arm' Jamaat-ud-Dawa. He later moved to Yemen, and then Syria in 2013 when tensions emerged between Jabhat al-Nusra and ISIS.[35]

Another similarly experienced Jabhat al-Nusra leader was Abu Hamam al-Suri, who was a member of al-Qaeda's al-Ghurabaa and al-Farouq training camps in the late 1990s. According to Abu Hamam's biography, al-Qaeda's *majlis al-shura* appointed him *emir* of Kandahar airport and later as a training instructor in the al-Farouq camp, where he formally pledged *bay'a* to Osama Bin Laden 'by shaking hands with the Sheikh'. After the 2001 invasion of Afghanistan Abu Hamam fought alongside the famed Egyptian al-Qaeda military leader Saif al-Adl and al-Qaeda's financial chief Mustafa Ahmed Muhammad Uthman Abu al-Yazid (Saeed al-Masri). He later moved to Iraq as the 'official representative of *Tanzim Qaedat al-Jihad* from the leadership' in Afghanistan, but was arrested and deported to Syria, whose authorities promptly released him. After spending time in Lebanon in 2005, Abu Hamam was dispatched back to Afghanistan where he was eventually instructed by al-Qaeda's external operations chief 'to work inside Syria and to directly report to Al-Qaeda'. However, he was arrested in Lebanon and imprisoned until his release during the Syrian revolution, when he joined Jabhat al-Nusra.[36]

Amid the escalating infighting, Syria's broader civil conflict was continuing in January and February 2014. Throughout January Ahrar al-Sham, Jabhat al-Nusra and as many as ten local FSA insurgent factions were engaged in a concerted offensive against regime positions in the north of Hama governorate. On 1 February they won a significant victory by capturing the strategic town of Morek, which cut the regime's crucial supply line north to the Idlib-based Wadi al-Deif and Hamadiyeh military bases outside the town of Maraat al-Numaan, which had been besieged by insurgents for many months.

Further east, while pro-regime forces were on the offensive south of Aleppo city and were approaching the opposition-held Sheikh Najjar industrial zone, jihadists continued to assault and besiege the Aleppo Central Prison. A major push was launched there on 30 January and again on 6 February, when the UK's first suicide bomber in Syria, Abdul Waheed

Majid, detonated a large suicide truck bomb at the prison's outer perimeter.[37] The offensive that day was led by a coalition formed primarily by Sayfullah al-Shishani's Jaish al-Khilafat al-Islamiyya (which had by now pledged *bay'a* to Jabhat al-Nusra), Ahrar al-Sham, Jabhat al-Nusra and Junud al-Sham. Abdullah al-Moheisini was also present.

On the morning of 6 February, during the initial ground assault, Sayfullah al-Shishani was mortally wounded in what appeared to be a mortar strike. His death was later acknowledged by Jabhat al-Nusra's leader Jolani himself, who praised the contribution of his group's 'heroic knight' in the attack on the prison complex.[38] Although ultimately unsuccessful, the assault that day was the closest that the insurgency would come to capturing the prison for many months after.

Meanwhile, the insurgency was also gearing up to launch a major new offensive in Syria's southern Quneitra governorate, which borders with the Israeli-controlled Golan region. Beginning on 31 January, a broad coalition of groups, dominated numerically by FSA factions but including contingents of Jabhat al-Nusra and Ahrar al-Sham fighters, launched operations that would during the course of February capture at least fifteen regime positions and villages. Situated on its doorstep, the growing intensity of conflict in Quneitra and the role played by al-Qaeda-linked factions would ultimately drag Israel further into the wider dynamics of the conflict. Moreover, militant cells allegedly linked to Hezbollah would also conduct a number of seemingly 'false flag' attacks on Israeli territory and security forces from the area later in the year.[39]

Already an integral part of the Syrian conflict dynamic, Lebanon experienced increasing numbers of attacks in January and February 2014, including four suicide bombings claimed by the newly established 'Jabhat al-Nusra in Lebanon.' Three of these attacks targeted the Hezbollah stronghold town of Hermel in the eastern Bekaa Valley (on 16 January and on 1 and 22 February), while the other targeted Beirut's southern suburb of Haret Hreik, where Hezbollah has a significant support base (on 21 January). Meanwhile, perhaps most spectacular of all the attacks during this two-month period, Jabhat al-Nusra's ally Kataib Abdullah Azzam—both groups were simultaneously claiming repeated Grad rocket attacks on eastern Lebanese targets—carried out a double suicide car bombing outside an Iranian government cultural centre in Beirut's southern Bir Hasan district on 19 February, killing at least 6 and wounding 128. In a subsequent statement Kataib Abdullah Azzam claimed that its Saraya Hussein Bin Ali unit—the same that claimed the 19 November Iran embassy bombing—had been responsible, and stated:

We will continue ... to target Iran and its party in Lebanon (Hezbollah), in its security and political and military centres, until our demands are achieved ... First: that the Party of Iran withdraws its forces from Syria [and] second, that our prisoners are released from Lebanese prisons.[40]

While jihadists were coordinating operations in Lebanon, they were set to expand the scale of their factional fighting in Syria. On 3 February a hugely significant statement was published online from al-Qaeda's General Command. It began:

The Qaedat al-Jihad Group announces that it is in no way connected to the group called the Islamic State of Iraq and al-Sham. We were not informed of its creation. It did neither await our orders, nor were we consulted. We were not happy with this; rather, we ordered [ISIS] to stop working. Therefore, [ISIS] is not a branch of the Qaedat al-Jihad Group and there is no organizational link connecting them, and the group is not responsible for its actions.[41]

Thus, in that moment, al-Qaeda had divorced itself from ISIS altogether. While arguably a predictable development, this was nonetheless a huge event for the entire international jihadist community, as it proclaimed for the first time the total disagreement between the world's largest and most notorious jihadist organisation and one of its former affiliates that perhaps favoured itself as a potential rival. Later that day a Jabhat al-Nusra commander told Reuters that the declaration meant that his group was no longer strictly a neutral actor in the infighting plaguing Syria: 'Now we are going to war with ISIS and will finish it off once and for all.'[42]

Throughout January the majority of inter-factional fighting between ISIS and the remainder of the insurgency had seen Jabhat al-Nusra play a relatively minimised role, and an entirely defensive one at that. Quite apart from the implications resulting from al-Qaeda's disavowal of ISIS, this situation definitively changed when ISIS launched a major offensive on Jabhat al-Nusra's control of energy assets in the eastern governorate of Deir ez Zour. Largely controlled in cooperation with local tribal forces (especially members of the al-Shuheil and Sha'itat clans from the large Okaidat tribe) and FSA factions, facilities such as the Conoco gas plant and several oilfields, including one at al-Jafra, were attacked by ISIS on the morning of 2 February, leading to significant ISIS gains. Six days later, and after receiving reinforcements from Hasakah, Jabhat al-Nusra and Ahrar al-Sham initiated a counter-offensive against ISIS in Deir ez Zour, which pushed the group back and killed its provincial *emir*, Abu Dujana al-Libi.[43]

This counter-attack came twenty-four hours after Jabhat al-Nusra's leader had issued an audio statement decrying ISIS's actions earlier that month in

Deir ez Zour. After celebrating his group's previous victories in the governorate, Jolani exclaimed:

> In the midst of all these glorious epics, ISIS in Deir ez Zour shocked us by robbing some vital facilities that were under our legitimate authority in the eastern region ... to cut off supply roads for soldiers in Islam stationed inside [Deir ez Zour] city and to separate them from their strategic depth in Deir ez Zour governorate, including both the region of Conoco (gas field) and the flour mills and several other headquarters.
>
> After its liberation, everyone was surprised by the wali of ISIS in Deir ez Zour demanding his share of Conoco ... Jabhat al-Nusra decided to allocate a proportion of the output of the field to ISIS, despite the lack of their right to do so ... It is not surprising that they have stolen nearly $5 million from Jabhat al-Nusra and did not return it even until now.[44]

Not only did Jolani's statement appear to reveal the sheer scale of the wealth available from controlling these facilities in the east, but it underlined the extent to which he perceived ISIS to be a self-interested actor and a determined enemy to his cause. That Jabhat al-Nusra and its ally Ahrar al-Sham then launched a counter-attack the following day should therefore not have come as a surprise.

After two days of brutal fighting in which dozens of fighters were killed and an ISIS suicide bomber killed more than twenty people in a public market, ISIS conducted a near-total withdrawal from Deir ez Zour governorate on 10 February. For now at least, Jabhat al-Nusra and its local allies had reacquired authority in the eastern region and assumed control over the oil, gas, grain and salt resource facilities that it so heavily relied upon to financially sustain itself. However, ISIS did not leave without having the last word. In a written statement published on the Internet, ISIS's provincial authority in Deir ez Zour—known as *wilayat al-kheir*—accused Jabhat al-Nusra of 'betraying the Muslim project' and allying itself with 'deviant and corrupt parties'. In a final threat making reference to the tribal-led Sahwa awakening in Iraq, the ISIS statement exclaimed:

> It is now clear that Jabhat al-Nusra sits alongside the Sahwat and the parties trying to please the West. Only a fool would turn on someone who has been turned on before. Learn the lesson from Iraq and what the traitors and hypocrites experienced.[45]

Speaking to this author during ISIS's battles with Jabhat al-Nusra for control of Deir ez Zour, British ISIS fighter Muhammad Hamidur Rahman (Abu Uthman al-Britani)—who had been a supervisor at clothing chain Primark before leaving his home town of Portsmouth to travel to Syria—demonstrated the hostility felt within ISIS ranks for Jabhat al-Nusra:

> The group as a whole is *murtadin* (apostate), except for the few sincere ones within them. Why? They attacked us first with the likes of the FSA and for what? Oil. What most people don't understand is that Jabhat al-Nusra is mainly made up of Syrians with little or no knowledge of the religion—they are blind followers of the corrupt.[46]

Elsewhere in Syria, ISIS was continuing its retaliatory strikes on rival groups in Idlib and especially in Aleppo. On 1 February ISIS fighters assassinated senior Suqor al-Sham leader Hussein al-Dik in Hama governorate, while an ISIS suicide car bomb in Aleppo's al-Bureij district killed twenty-six people, including fifteen Liwa al-Tawhid fighters and the group's leading military commander, Adnan Bakkour. At the same time, a predominantly Chechen unit of ISIS was assaulting the Aleppo village of al-Rai, located within sight of the Turkish border. Defended by Liwa al-Tawhid and Liwa al-Fateh, the town was captured by ISIS on 3 February.

While Liwa al-Tawhid managed to prevent one double suicide attack on a local headquarters in Aleppo on 4 February by shooting both would-be bombers, another ISIS suicide car bombing struck an Islamic Front position in the Idlib town of Harem later that day. ISIS was also besieging rival positions in the 'al-Badiya' desert region in rural Homs in early February, which prompted an apparent ceasefire accord between Suqor al-Sham units and ISIS on 5 February. This latter incident proved highly controversial at the time; after the agreement became public, an official Suqor al-Sham spokesman appeared on pro-opposition television channel Orient TV and claimed that the situation was 'nebulous' as the group's senior leadership knew nothing of the agreement and would not have signed off on such an accord 'under any circumstances'. The controvsery continued throughout the day when the leader of Suqor al-Sham's *majlis al-shura*, Rashed Tuqqo, issued a formal statement admitting the following:

> I was commissioned by the Majlis al-Shura of Suqor al-Sham to negotiate a reconciliation between Suqor al-Sham and ISIS. Thanks be to Allah, The Almighty and Exalted has allowed us success and we have been able to reach a comprehensive agreement that is valid all over Syria to stop the spilling of blood and the fighting between us and our brothers in ISIS.
>
> The agreement stated the cessation of fighting [between SS and the ISIS] all over Syria; providing no assistance to any faction that fights the ISIS; and, in case of a future dispute, setting up an Islamic court that rules by Allah's Sharia with a judge

from the ISIS and a judge from SS to resolve the case. We would like to stress that our brothers in the ISIS have abided by all the clauses of the agreement we have jointly reached.[47]

While the agreement did appear to last in the Homs area for some time, Suqor al-Sham fighters were involved—albeit often in an unacknowledged capacity—in fighting against ISIS attacks in Idlib in the days that followed. After all, Suqor al-Sham leader Abu Eissa al-Sheikh remained unshakeably anti-ISIS in his public rhetoric afterwards.

After several more ISIS suicide bombings against Islamic Front positions in Markadah, Aleppo (11 February), Retyan, Aleppo (13 February) and near Bab al-Salameh (20 February), the group carried out its most dramatic attack on 23 February, killing Abu Khaled al-Suri. Although ISIS denied involvement in the attack, the killing of such a senior member of Ahrar al-Sham and an appointed chief emissary of al-Qaeda in Syria was a bold message that could only have been sent by the group. While details surrounding the incident were murky immediately following Abu Khaled's death, two particularly valuable accounts were later issued. First, Ahrar al-Sham chief *sharia* official, Abu Yazan al-Shami, released his account, based on his experience of being with Abu Khaled at the time:

> Praise be to God and peace and blessings upon the Messenger of Allah. This is the story of the martyrdom of my sheikh and my prince, the apple of my eye: Sheikh Abu Khaled al-Suri.
>
> On the morning of his death, the Sheikh arrived in Aleppo. He came to meet me in one of the movement's headquarters and began to converse about the situation in Aleppo and the necessity for attention there. During our talk, gunfire began, aimed at the building in which we were. The Sheikh rushed to take up his rifle and began firing towards the source of the gunfire with courage worthy of his heroism and concentration worthy of his struggle. I was carrying a pistol and went behind a pillar to watch the door. Then I turned and found Sheikh Abu Khaled next to me, wounded by a gunshot to his chest.
>
> At this time, a bomb was thrown. I threw myself flat but was hit. Then, an ISIS infiltrator entered. He began to comb [the area]. He closed in on me, so I opened fire on him. He turned and I fired about three shots and ran to the other side. He blew himself up with an explosive belt, as if one of the shots had hit him at close range. After the bombing, I looked for Sheikh Abu Khaled and found him; waking up, he got up from the floor and went to the sofa ... I had requested an ambulance with hand signals. Later, I went inside, where the brothers were engaged in clashes with another suicide bomber. Then, he was shot; he sat on the ground, moaning for a while. Then, he blew himself up, without anyone around him.

At that time, the brothers arrived and took up the perimeter. The Sheikh was speeding to the hospital but God desired him at His side. After this long life that he spent in the way of God, this is my testimony on what happened at the request of some of the brothers. May God accept the condolences of the umma for her deceased hero and may God take revenge on his killers, the modern-day Kharijites, and cleanse the earth of their filth.[48]

In a separate statement issued on 26 February, the Crimean deputy leader of Salahuddin al-Shishani's Jaish al-Muhajireen wa'l Ansar, a Ukrainian known as 'Abd al-Karim al-Krimsky appeared to provide an account validating that given by Abu Yazan three days earlier:

We reached the base of Ahrar al-Sham shortly after the assassination of Sheikh Abu Umeir, who was known among the Mujahideen as Abu Khaled al-Suri. It happened sometime in the afternoon. We almost arrived at the base at the same time as the event occurred. We found out everything that happened from the mujahideen of Ahrar al-Sham.

Two armed men had come to the base. They came on foot, without a car. Lots of armed mujahideen come to the base, they asked the checkpoint how to get someplace or other, or how to find this or that mujahid or amir. So that's why the Ahrar al-Sham base wasn't on the alert. They noticed that they [the armed men] spoke in a local Syrian dialect.

They came close to the building and one of them suddenly opened fire with a machine gun. Everyone who was in the yard was wounded or killed. At that moment none of the mujahideen who were in the yard of the checkpoint were carrying a machine gun, though some had handguns. Only [al-Suri] was holding an AK-SU-74. The Sheikh [al-Suri] was in the room and he opened fire in response through a window. He was mortally wounded in the chest. The second guy, under cover of the first guy's machine gun fire, chucked grenades into the building. Then, the mujahideen in the base overcame their surprise and starting to return fire.

The one who burst into the building was wounded but he was able to reach the second floor and then he blew himself up. The first one continued to fire, dashing from place to place, but he was killed with return fire.[49]

Abu Khaled's death sent shock waves across Syria and throughout the jihadist community. Despite ISIS's denials, the escalating *fitna* striking the jihad in Syria was an issue of huge concern. Ahrar al-Sham leader Hassan Abboud, who by this time had acquired a particularly positive reputation within the Syrian Salafist and jihadist fraternity, and been comparatively restrained in his comments on ISIS, granted an interview with Al-Jazeera's Arabic service in which his tone was suddenly aggressively critical of the group widely blamed for killing his mentor Abu Khaled:

There were occasional times when this organisation took part ... exceptional times, against the regime, but this was the exception rather than the rule ... rather their essential work over the past nine months was to break up a number of the mujahideen ... There's no doubt that this wrong-headed organisation, the criminal gang of [Abu Bakr] al-Baghdadi, wants to be the only one on the [battle-] field.[50]

In the days that followed the killing, additional statements were released mourning the death of Abu Khaled and indirectly blaming ISIS for being responsible. These statements included ones by Jabhat al-Nusra (on 24 February), its leader Jolani (on 24 February), senior al-Qaeda official and American national Adam Gadahn (on 29 March) and then al-Qaeda's leader Ayman al-Zawahiri (on 4 April). All celebrated the life of a man with a long history fighting jihad, with Zawahiri's statement particularly serving to underline Abu Khaled's veteran status:

I knew [Abu Khaled] since the jihad against the Russians (in the late 1980s) and I knew him to be a companion of Abu Musab al-Suri, may God release him ... he was for me and my brothers a good advisor ...

This fitna [in Syria] needs all Muslims to repel it and to form a public opinion against it and against anyone that does not accept an independent sharia court, and I stress on independent ... It is a must on every Muslim to distance himself from anyone who refuses that ...

So these extremist [ISIS] fools came and spilt forbidden blood. And it is a must on Muslims to not support those who blow up muhahideen bases and send car bombs to them and human bombs ... and whoever falls into this sin should remember he is achieving something for the enemies of Islam that they could not have achieved.[51]

Even AQAP issued a statement on 27 February demanding that parties cease the infighting. Despite this, however, the likelihood of the infighting being stopped was minuscule. As many as 3,300 people had so far been killed since 3 January,[52] making an average of 58 killed per day.

Thus, in his second statement in forty-eight hours, on 25 February, Jolani gave ISIS five days to accept a proposal for mediation or otherwise face being destroyed, 'even in Iraq'. Three days later, on 28 February, ISIS fighters were reported to have begun retreating from the towns of Azaz, Menagh, Mayer, Deir Jamal and Kafin in rural Aleppo, with a significant regrouping taking place in the strategically located towns of Jarablus and Manbij, blocking the route east to the ISIS city of Raqqa, which was fast becoming the group's de facto capital. In fact, while ISIS had begun imposing various behavioural codes upon Sunni Muslims living in Raqqa in mid-January, it took a significant step 'forward' in late February by introducing the *dhimmi* pact. As Aymenn Jawad al-Tamimi explains:

Traditionally, a 'dhimmi' in Islam is a Jew or Christian who agrees to live under the authority of an Islamic state, agreeing to pay a 'jizya' (poll tax) and enduring a number of discriminatory conditions in return for 'protection' from the state. The Qur'anic basis for this arrangement is 9:29. In practice of course, the dhimmi pact, far from being a model of historical multiculturalism ... is actually equivalent to Mafia racketeering, as failure to pay 'jizya', whose financial burdens often proved heavy historically, leads to a loss of 'protection' by the state.[53]

These 'discriminatory conditions' were exactly that and, according to the statement ISIS published in Raqqa announcing the introduction of the pact in the city, twelve rules were set to apply to the city's 'People of the Book' (Christians or Jews):

1. That they must not build in their town or the periphery a monastery, church or monk's hermitage, and must not rebuild what has fallen into disrepair.
2. That they must not show the cross or any of their scriptures in any of the roads or markets of the Muslims and they must not use any means to amplify their voices during their calls to prayer or similarly for the rest of their acts of worship.
3. That they must not make Muslims hear recital of their scriptures or the sounds of their bells, even if they strike them within their churches.
4. That they must not engage in any acts of hostility against the Islamic State, like giving housing to spies and those wanted for a reason by the Islamic State, or whosoever's brigandery is proven from among the Christians or others, they must not aid such persons in concealing or moving them or other such things. If they know of a conspiracy againt the Muslims, they must inform them about it.
5. That they must not engage in any displays of worship outside the churches.
6. That they must not stop any of the Christians from embracing Islam if he so wishes.
7. That they must respect Islam and Muslims, and not disparage their religion in any way.
8. The Christians must embrace payment of the jizya—on every adult male: its value is 4 dinars of gold ... on the Ahl al-Ghina [the wealthy], and half that value on those of middle income, and half that on the poor among them, on condition that they do not conceal anything from us regarding their state of affairs. And they are to make two payments per year.
9. They are not allowed to bear arms.
10. They are not to deal in selling pork and wine with Muslims or in their markets; and they are not to consume it [wine] publicly—that is, in any public places.
11. They should have their own tombs, as is custom.
12. That they must accept the precepts imposed by the Islamic State like modesty of dress, selling, buying and other things.[54]

ISIS was thus beginning to establish its 'Islamic state' in the city of Raqqa, the defence of which was presumably a strategic priority. It was for this reason, therefore, that Omar al-Shishani had been coordinating his forces in the eastern Aleppo towns of Jarablus and Manbij, as they sat squarely on the two main roads heading from the west to Raqqa. At the time, photographs released of Omar al-Shishani and hundreds of heavily armed ISIS fighters in this area led to speculation that a major ISIS counter-offensive was imminent. However, he was in fact coordinating a managed withdrawal of ISIS forces from the western half of northern Syria, and the movements on 28 February were simply the first preliminary stage. The much more significant withdrawal took place two weeks later, on 14 March, when all ISIS forces in Latakia, Idlib and western Aleppo withdrew entirely to Jarablus and Manbij and further to Raqqa. Meanwhile, a small contingent of ISIS militants remained in place in Homs's al-Badiya desert, in the mountainous Qalamoun region bordering Lebanon and in the East Ghouta and southern al-Hajar al-Aswad suburbs of Damascus.

All the while, the regime was continuing to place intensive pressure on the insurgency in areas of serious strategic value for its own survival. In Aleppo, a winter of sustained and brutal barrel bombing had paved the way for a concerted ground campaign targeting opposition weak spots on the city's northern and eastern periphery. Further south, the Syrian army and Hezbollah were still engaged in offensive operations in the Qalamoun, aiming to eventually defeat the last remaining pockets of the insurgency along the Lebanese border. For the Assad regime, this would serve to cut off an important channel of insurgent supplies and logistical support, while for Hezbollah it would potentially shut down a conveyor belt of car bombs and explosives that had been targeting its positions and supporters inside Lebanese territory for months on end.

The Qalamoun in particular saw a lot of action throughout March, as insurgent forces ended up conceding control of villages steadily through the month. A string of pro-regime victories began on 4 March, with the capture of the village of al-Sahel and several nearby hills. On 8 March the opposition lost control of Zara village, followed by the Rima Farms area on 11 March and the strategic town of Yabroud on 16 March. The latter had been placed under heavy artillery fire and air strikes for a month prior to the eventual Hezbollah-led 'commando raid' that led to its capture and to the death of Jabhat al-Nusra deputy *emir* in the Qalamoun, Abu Azzam al-Kuwaiti.[55]

Yabroud had been of particular strategic importance not just for its close proximity to Syria's main M5 highway and the Lebanese border, but also because it had been where Jabhat al-Nusra was holding the thirteen Orthodox

Christian nuns and three maids it had captured during their attack on Maaloula in early December 2013. The impending loss of the town had induced Jabhat al-Nusra to transfer them covertly across the Lebanese border in early March to the town of Arsal, where the Syrian insurgency was effectively in control. Although largely unknown to the world at the time, intensive final-stage negotiations were under way in early March to secure their release back into Syria as part of a large prisoner-exchange deal with the Assad regime.

According to a detailed account published in al-Monitor, a number of attempted negotiation 'tracks' had been attempted since either late December 2013 or early January 2014. Syrian pro-Assad businessman George Hasswani had played an early lead role in facilitating negotiations, and had even permitted and personally paid for Jabhat al-Nusra to house the nuns and their maids in his house in Yabroud. However, what had initially been a 'Syrian track' of negotiations began to stall, and at that point Qatari intelligence and the head of Lebanon's General Security Directorate, Major-General Abbas Ibrahim, stepped in to lead the process. After a series of delays the approaching pro-regime assault on Yabroud encouraged negotiations to intensify, and eventually it was allegedly agreed that more than 150 female detainees be released and a $16 million ransom be paid in exchange for the release of the sixteen hostages.[56] (Both Lebanon and Qatar have consistently denied any ransom was paid.) Minutes before midnight on 9 March the sixteen women were freed in a tense exchange outside Arsal[57] before being taken across the Syrian border into the town of Jdeidat Yabous. While the Syrian regime subsequently sought to play up the suffering the nuns were thought to have experienced while in Jabhat al-Nusra's custody, the lead nun, Mother Pelagia Sayaf, thanked Bashar al-Assad for working with Qatari intelligence to secure their release and claimed that they had in fact all been 'treated very well' by their captors.[58]

Meanwhile, the Syrian army and Hezbollah were still on the march in the Qalamoun, capturing the villages of Ras al-Ayn and al-Husn on 19 March, the ancient Crusader fort of Krak des Chevaliers on 20 March, and finally the villages of Flitah and Ras Maara on 29 March. The Lebanese border was thus effectively cut off, apart from the risk-laden possibility of covertly crossing the mountainous border. The leader of Syrian Lebanese jihadist faction Jund al-Sham, Khaled al-Mahmud (Abu Sulayman al-Muhajir) was also killed in the battle for Krak des Chevaliers.[59]

The fall of Yabroud in particular exposed serious underlying differences and tensions within the broader regional insurgency. According to activists on the ground at the time, a majority of the insurgent factions involved in defending Yabroud were known to be backed by Qatar, but their fellow opposition fighters who were said to enjoy Saudi backing failed to arrive to their rescue. It was only the day after Yabroud's loss that Saudi-supported factions arrived in the area and began to make some recovery gains. 'If the Saudi's guys didn't go in until now, it's clear what their game is,' said one insurgent medic speaking to the *Financial Times*.[60]

Whether true or not, the moderate portion of Syria's insurgency was suffering from a bout of serious tension and internal discord in March 2014. The SMC was experiencing a period of crisis that dated back to mid-February when it had announced the expulsion of its chief of staff, Lieutenant-General Selim Idriss, and his deputy, and their replacement with Brigadier-General 'Abd al-Ilah al-Bashir and Colonel Haitham Afeisi. Intriguingly, those pushed out were assessed at the time to be growing increasingly close to Qatar while their replacements were close allies of ETILAF president Ahmed Jarba, who himself was viewed as 'Saudi's man'. However, despite the public expulsion of Idriss, he appeared to retain the support of a majority of the SMC's General Staff members. The issue appeared largely to be that the minister of defence in the opposition's exiled, or interim, government, Assad Mustafa, opposed Idriss having any authority over insurgent logistics or operations.

After a great deal of back-and-forth and condemnatory statements from both sides through late February, Ahmed Jarba organised a series of meetings in early March that involved both '[Selim] Idriss' backers on the General Staff and [Assad] Mustafa's within the council (SMC)'.[61] Then on 6 March after a meeting at the Wyndham Hotel in Turkey's southern town of Gaziantep, Ahmed Jarba announced that an agreement had been reached whereby both Idriss and Mustafa would resign and the SMC would be expanded to appease existing complaints. However, as if to underline the crippling division existing at the time, a spokesman for Mustafa immediately issued a statement proclaiming that the 'agreement' was 'null and void' and his boss would remain in his position as defence minister. Shortly thereafter, a brawl broke out during which Jarba was punched three times.[62]

While the leadership of the FSA was facing its own internal 'battles' and the regime was enjoying some renewed confidence after victories in Aleppo and the Qalamoun, the intensity of the anti-ISIS infighting was declining somewhat in March 2014. The withdrawal of ISIS fighters from Latakia, Idlib and half of Aleppo reduced dramatically the potential for the sustained fighting witnessed in January and February. This provided both an excuse and a brief window of relative calm which a number of Salafist and jihadist factions active in those areas used to prepare for another major offensive on regime-held Latakia governorate, in what would be called Operation al-Anfal.

Beginning early on the morning of 21 March, Jabhat al-Nusra, Ahrar al-Sham, Kataib Ansar al-Sham, Junud al-Sham and Harakat Sham al-Islam launched coordinated attacks on several targets in the northern region of Latakia. Within forty-eight hours the participating forces had captured the Syrian village of Kessab, which was populated primarily by Armenians and was the last remaining regime-held border crossing with Turkey. Claims emerged at the time that Sanafi al-Nasr had been killed during the first days of the offensive, which were not officially disproved until 19 April.

In the immediate aftermath of the beginning of the offensive and the capture of Kessab, other allegations began to emerge that Turkish authorities may have actively facilitated the jihadist operation by allowing the attack to be launched from Turkish territory. Although no definitive evidence materialised to prove these claims, Turkish opposition MP Mehmet Ali Adipoğlu, who happened to be in the Turkish border area at the time, reportedly claimed to have witnessed 'dozens of Syrian-plated cars non-stop transporting terrorists and firing into the Syrian [Kessab] outpost from the military road between Gozlekciler villager and our military base at Kayapinar'.[63] Such assertions appeared to be bolstered on 23 March when the Turkish military shot down a Syrian fighter jet on a mission near Kessab. Turkish officials claimed that the jet had penetrated Turkey's airspace: 'a Syrian plane violated our airspace; our F-16s took off and hit this plane. Why? Because if you violate my airspace, our slap will be this hard,' exclaimed Turkey's prime minister, Recep Tayyip Erdoğan, shortly afterwards. Syria's Foreign Ministry subsequently countered Erdoğan's claims and blamed the incident on Turkish 'interference' in Latakia and hinting at its apparent role in the Kessab attack forty-eight hours earlier.[64]

The furore surrounding these allegations was heightened further on 27 March when leaked recordings of a conversation involving Turkey's foreign minister, under-secretary of foreign affairs, deputy chief of staff and chief of national intelligence were posted onto YouTube. Considerable attention was devoted to the apparent suggestion in the recordings that Turkey could carry out a false-flag attack purporting to be by ISIS in order to provide legitimacy for a retaliatory military assault to secure the tomb of Suleiman Shah, which was located on sovereign Turkish territory approximately 35 kilometres inside Syria. However, the discussions also covered 'weapons and ammunition problems of [insurgent] groups fighting in Syria, ammunition send to the area earlier and results achieved'.[65]

Notwithstanding allegations surrounding the role of Turkey, the capture of Kessab also sparked a significant campaign—led by the #SaveKessab hashtag—within portions of the Armenian and pro-Assad communities which claimed that the village's population and its religious sites were being violently assaulted by the jihadists who were then in control. However, no reliable or definitive evidence ever emerged to substantiate these allegations and a vast amount of imagery used in the campaign ended up being taken from horror movies and other historical conflicts elsewhere in the world. All four of the participating armed factions also vehemently denied any involvement in sectarian attacks or other such activities. The Islamic Front, for example, issued a statement on this matter on 31 March, which claimed:

> The desperate Assad regime has launched a smear campaign to portray the liberation as an act of sectarian genocide targeting the Syrian Armenian community. The Islamic Front categorically rejects this unsubstantiated accusation.

> Kessab is a city that holds military and strategic value regardless of the religious affiliation of its inhabitants ... some local residents chose to leave the city. We ensured their secure transit to areas of safety whenever it was possible ... We call upon the international community and international media organizations not to be swayed by this latest round of regime propaganda aimed at distorting the image of the Syrian revolution.

> Time and again the Assad regime, whose higher purposes are self-preservation and nothing else, is manipulating the matter of ethnic and sectarian co-existence for its own cynical interests.

> We remind the world that the Syrian revolution is based on the principals [sic] of freedom, dignity and inclusiveness ... The Islamic Front is committed to honoring the principals of this great revolution and resolved to liberating the entire coastal region.[66]

Notwithstanding such seemingly unfounded allegations, the offensive continued to make notable gains through the remainder of the month, by which time a strategic military highpoint known as Observatory or Tower 45 had been captured, along with the Qastal Maaf, Nabain and Samra areas. Insurgents were even pictured for the first time in the revolution sitting overlooking the Mediterranean Sea at Karadouran beach.[67]

In comparison with the previous multi-group offensive in Latakia, ISIS had made no contribution to Operation al-Anfal. This arguably encouraged a closer awareness of restricting activities solely to the military arena and avoiding reputationally damaging sectarian actions. Simultaneously however, the offensive itself was also buoyed by the involvement of several prominent jihadist figures, including Sanafi al-Nasr, Abdullah al-Moheisini, Saqr al-Jihad and Ibrahim Benchekroune. The key command role however, was assumed by a previously unreported but highly significant Ahrar al-Sham commander, Eyad al-Sha'ar (better known as Abu al-Hassan al-Tabuki), who had returned to Syria in 2011 after 10 years of living in exile in Ireland and before that in the Saudi city of Tabuk from the age of 10. With a sharp mind and bountiful charisma, Abu al-Hassan had developed an impressive reputation across the Syrian opposition spectrum, but he nonetheless retained a highly secretive profile. While he was settling into life in Ireland in 2002, Abu al-Hassan's brother Yasir was fighting with the mujahideen in Chechnya, from where he was dispatched as one of several militants who conducted the infamous Moscow Theatre siege in October 2002. As the only non-Russian involved and going more commonly by the *kunya* Abu Assam al-Suri, Yasir's role in the Moscow attack was barely reported at the time, but Abu al-Hassan himself revealed it on social media in March 2014, clarifying that his brother had also been active in Afghanistan.[68]

Although presenting himself as a military figure in Syria, Abu al-Hassan saw his leadership through a distinctly political lens. 'I choose my battles with the regime only when there is a political victory to be won, and only when the time is right,' he told this author in a tightly arranged secret meeting in Turkey. 'We'll only win this struggle if we think more intelligently than our enemy— it's no different to chess.'[69]

Despite the prominent individuals leading the offensive, as on previous occasions and spurred on by the death of Bashar al-Assad's cousin and senior NDF commander Hilal al-Assad in Kessab, the regime mustered the necessary resources in late March to launch a determined counter-offensive. Hilal al-Assad's replacement with prominent Syrian army officer Colonel Suheil al-Hassan, who had been commanding all military operations in Aleppo, underlined the significance that the regime lent to the need for a recovery in Latakia.[70]

As April got started, the offensive in Latakia began to face an increasingly stiff level of resistance and fight-back from pro-regime forces, and on 2 April the Syrian army escalated its assault on the valuable Observatory 45 position, killing Ibrahim Benchekroune in the process. Within twenty-four hours the army had effectively consolidated control of the position itself, while clashes continued on the surrounding hillsides and another senior Harakat Sham al-Islam leader was killed, an Egyptian known as Abu Safiya al-Masri. By this point, well over a thousand combatants had been killed since the launch of Operation al-Anfal two weeks earlier, and opposition momentum had faltered, to the advantage of the regime. By mid-May the regime had definitively regained the upper hand in northern Latakia, but Kessab would remain in jihadist hands until 15 June.

Meanwhile, after a brief period of recovery and readjustment, ISIS was gearing up for a renewed drive. With Raqqa city consolidated under its control and an effective defensive western wall established in al-Bab, Manbij and Jarablus, ISIS's strategic attention turned back east towards Deir ez Zour and across the border into Iraq and the Sunni tribal heartlands of Anbar, Salah ad Din and parts of Diyala and Ninawa provinces. In a statement issued on 3 April, ISIS spokesman Adnani sought to appeal to his organisation's roughly 10,000 fighters and their yearning for the establishment of a viable Islamic state.

> The State is becoming stronger day by day, and its attacks have not stopped since its creation. And its raids will not stop until the cross is removed, the pig is killed and jizya is installed ...
>
> I say to the Sheikhs of the tribes, history is recording and the angels are writing it down ...
>
> And to the secularists, we promised that we would come back to the areas we withdrew from and here we are. And due to Allah, we are stronger today than yesterday and our enemy is crumbling ... there is no place for you, O secularists. And it is better that you escape, saving yourself, for the Islamic State will remain—steadfast and victorious ...
>
> Know that you are fighting a failed nation ... Their hearts will be filled with fear and their weapons and equipment will be war booty. So slaughter them like sheep and kill them like flies ... So O lions of Anbar, Ninawa, Salah ad Din, Diyala, Kirkuk and Baghdad, March forward and redraw the map for you are the hope of the oppressed. The prisoners are waiting for you in Baghdad and Roumieh [a prison in Lebanon] and Aleppo and Al-Hair [in Saudi Arabia] and Abu Zabal [Cairo]. And you have an appointment in Baghdad and Damascus and Jerusalem and Mecca and Medina. Just like you have an appointment in Dabiq, Ghouta and Rome.[71]

This rousing speech was primarily aimed at ISIS's fighters in Iraq, but the apolcalyptic context contained within spoke clearly to ISIS as a transnational and counter-national state movement. The references to Baghdad, Damascus, Jerusalem, Mecca and Medina are common calls in jihadist propaganda, as is Rome. But the inclusion of Dabiq and Ghouta was a direct reference to Islamic *Hadith* that refer to both towns in Syria being the prophesied locations of battles that precede the end of the world. ISIS already had a small presence in Ghouta outside Damascus and it had been close to reaching Dabiq north of Aleppo before the initiation of the anti-ISIS front in January 2014. Clearly Adnani was preparing ISIS for something significant.

With ISIS attacks continuing to spiral across Iraq, and with the group quite clearly demonstrating its dominance in the western province of Anbar, it launched another concerted counter-attack across the border in Syria's Deir ez Zour, aiming not only to capture the extensive energy resources and territory controlled by Jabhat al-Nusra and a number of other allied insurgent factions but to link up its Iraqi and Syrian contingents once and for all.

Beginning early on 10 April, ISIS fighters travelling south from Raqqa attacked the town of al-Bukamal—11 kilometres from the Iraqi border—and the villages of Kabajeb, al-Quriya, and Taiana.[72] Although none of the attacks ultimately resulted in ISIS victories, at least eighty-six combatants were killed in a single day of fighting, with ISIS's enemies taking a considerable majority of the losses (sixty).[73] The coordinated attacks were a revealing sign of ISIS's immediate strategic priority: to focus on Syria's east and to combine its well-established and extensive influence in Iraq's Anbar with its potential to do the same in Deir ez Zour. Temporarily repelled, it would return again the following month.

In the mean time, Adnani released yet another inflammatory statement on 17 April, but this time quite extraordinarily aimed at al-Qaeda's central leadership. In an audio statement entitled 'This is not our methodology, nor will it ever be', Adnani denounced the central leadership of al-Qaeda and Ayman al-Zawahiri in particular for its perceived failure to continue the path laid out by Osama Bin Laden. Furthermore, Adnani recounted ISIS's history, making clear that upon establishing the ISI, the group was no longer organisationally an affiliate of al-Qaeda:

> Sheikh Abu Musab al-Zarqawi hastened in giving the bay'a to Sheikh Osama, may Allah have Mercy upon them both, in an effort to unite the word of the Muslims, to enrage the disbelievers and to raise the morale of the mujahideen. It was a blessed bay'a ... the dream became closer, fighting intensified, the battles heated up ... the mujahideen became steadfast and Allah granted them victory and the Majlis Shura al-Mujahideen was founded. It was only a matter of months until Allah enabled them to do so, and they then declared the Islamic State, they declared it with a high resonance and the dream became a reality ... The emir of the State and the muhajir minister may Allah have mercy on them both, announced the dissolution of Al-Qaeda in Iraq, thus ceasing to exist.

> The leaders of Al-Qaeda deviated from the right methodology, we say this as sadness overwhelms us and bitterness fills our hearts. We say it with complete regret ...

Verily Al-Qaeda today is no longer the Qaeda of Jihad and so it is not the base of jihad. The one praising it is of the lowest and the tyrants flirt with it and the deviants and the misguided attempt to woo it. It is not the base of jihad that entrenches itself among the ranks of the Sahwat and the secularists ... Verily Al-Qaeda today has ceased to the base of jihad, rather its leadership has become an axe supporting the destruction of the project of the Islamic State and the coming Caliphate. They have altered the methodology, they became suspicious, they accepted the bay'a of the dissidents, they split the ranks of the mujahideen, and they began war with the Islamic State, which was established upon the blood and skulls of the Monotheists...

They do not differentiate between the mujahideen, the Sahwat and the highway robbers. They gathered them all together and called them the Ummah ... The difference between the State and Al-Qaeda ... is a matter of crooked religion and deviated methodology ... a methodology that believes in pacifism and runs after majorities, a methodology that is shy from mentioning jihad and declaring Islamic unity, and replaces it with revolution, popularity, uprising, struggle, mass movements, propaganda.[74]

Considering the high regard in which al-Qaeda was held within the international jihadist community, Adnani's statement declaring that its senior leadership had strayed from the correct path was extraordinary. ISIS was not only fundamentally challenging the legitimacy of al-Qaeda as the leading authority within the global jihad, it was presenting itself as the rightful replacement. Thus the intra-jihadist battle had stepped up a notch and reconciliation looked all but impossible, especially in Syria, where the two parties had so openly entered into hostilities.

Within the broader context of the conflict in Syria, insurgent forces began a series of offensives across the country in support of Operation al-Anfal in Latakia. On 3 April a coalition of ten groups, including Jabhat al-Nusra, Islamic Front member Suqor al-Sham and Muslim Brotherhood-aligned Faylaq al-Sham launched the 'Echo of Anfal' offensive in Idlib, which principally aimed to cut the regime's supply line on the M5 highway between the towns of Khan Sheikhoun and Maraat al-Numaan. Additionally, the offensive aimed to reimpose a blockade on the strategic Wadi al-Deif and Hamadiyeh military facilities and to assert control in Idlib's southern countryside. Within twenty-four hours of the offensive's initiation, the villages of Babulin and al-Salhiya had been captured, thus effectively cutting the supply line as intended. A further twenty-one regime checkpoints were attacked, including Camp Khazanat, which was used as a refuelling depot for regime forces,[75] and on 8 April a major assault was launched on Khan Sheikhoun involving two huge Jabhat al-Nusra truck bombings.

Further south, another offensive—Dawn of Unity in Support of Anfal—was launched in Quneitra governorate, where a coalition predominantly composed of the moderate SRF, Jabhat Ghurabaa al-Golan and Jabhat Ansar al-Islam, along with Ahrar al-Sham and Jabhat al-Nusra aimed to capture the strategic Tel Ahmar hills, which the Syrian army used as a primary base for launching operations across the surrounding area. The hills were also invaluable artillery positions for the regime, used to target insurgent resupply convoys elsewhere in the governorate.[76] Two months previously the insurgency had succeeded in gaining control of significant swathes of Quneitra's southern countryside, and on 7 April the Tel Ahmar hills were captured, along with huge quantities of light and heavy weaponry. From that point onwards, Jabhat al-Nusra had control—or at least a strong influence—over territory 4 kilometres from Israel, and a videoed speech by the group's Quneitra *emir*, Abu al-Walid al-Shami, on Tel Ahmar shortly after its capture sent that message clearly.

While Salafists and jihadists were still playing lead roles in offensive operations like these, the stature and influence of moderate and loosely FSA-affiliated factions was discernibly increasing. The expansion of US, Saudi and Qatari-led assistance to the armed opposition in Syria through the operations centres in Jordan and Turkey was beginning to have a dynamic effect on the ground, particularly in the south and in the northern governorate of Idlib, where supplies provided across the Bab al-Hawa border crossing were bolstering the capabilities of CIA 'vetted' groups such as Liwa Forsan al-Haq, Harakat Hazm, the 13th Division and the SRF.

It was therefore fitting that it was in Idlib that the first externally supplied American weapons emerged in public in early April. In three videos published onto YouTube on 1 and 5 April, Harakat Hazm fighters were shown operating American-made anti-tank guided missile systems, known specifically as BGM-71 TOWs. Capable of firing a wire-guided anti-tank missile towards a target nearly 4 kilometres away, the missile systems were all shown being used in an operation in the town of Heesh.[77]

The appearance of such significant systems was symbolically extremely significant, as even the commonly established terms of US military sales to foreign states make it a condition that a subsequent transfer of American weaponry to a third party can only be undertaken with US government approval, often from the president himself. As such, even though these weapons may possibly have been provided by Saudi Arabia—which maintained several thousand BGM-71 TOWs in its domestic stocks—the US government would have had to have granted them permission to do so.

Militarily, the missile systems were not necessarily any more valuable to their users than several models of Soviet-era anti-tank missiles seized from the Syrian army. However, the significance was in the message that their arrival into Syria sent both to the regime—whose tanks they would target—and to jihadists, whose influence stood to decline if this was the start of a more significant support programme for the moderate insurgency.

Like the SRF and Jaish al-Mujahideen, and also the Southern Front coalition of FSA factions established on 14 February, Harakat Hazm was another relatively new FSA-linked organisation created by way of the merger of twelve small units on 25 January 2014. Divided into northern and southern divisions, led by Murshid al-Khaled (Abu al-Mutassem) and Mohammed al-Dahik (Abu Hatem) respectively, Harakat Hazm was an organisation with links to Selim Idriss—who announced the group's establishment—and loosely with the Syrian Muslim Brotherhood, which had been close to many of the twelve constituent factions' father organisation, Kataib al-Farouq.

Shortly after the first emergence of the BGM-71 TOWs in Idlib, it became clear that the weapons systems had probably been provided via the Bab al-Hawa crossing in early March, and almost certainly by Saudi Arabia with full US knowledge and support. The shipment came directly from the US-backed Military Operations Centre (MOC) in southern Turkey, and recipients had been vetted extensively by those states involved in MOC operations, particularly the CIA. The missiles themselves were initially intended for use in defence against the then ongoing regime attack on Aleppo's Sheikh Najjar industrial district, although for an unknown reason they remained in Idlib and were not used until early April.[78] Many more TOW missiles arrived in the country in the weeks and months that followed, and only into the hands of groups of so-called 'vetted' FSA groups. By September 2014, 284 TOW missiles had been filmed in use across Syria, and whereas previous externally supplied weapons systems had been rapidly proliferated to unintended recipient groups, only six had been seen in the hands of 'an organization unlikely to be a direct recipient'. That group was Ahrar al-Sham.[79] However, by early 2014, after recipeient groups had suffered separate defeats to Jabhat al-Nusra and ISIS, both jihadist groups had been filmed using TOW systems.

PART IV

CALIPHATES, EMIRATES AND DIVERGENCE

# 10

# MAY–AUGUST 2014

## DECLARING A CALIPHATE

As May began and al-Qaeda leader Ayman al-Zawahiri was blaming ISIS for sparking a 'political disaster' in Syria, the infighting continued apace, but with the most intense battles taking place in the eastern Deir ez Zour governorate. Raqqa city meanwhile, was emerging as ISIS's de facto capital.

Elsewhere in Syria, the moderate insurgency continued to display moves towards provincial and regional unity, particularly in the south, where American anti-tank weapons were appearing. In apparent reaction to the threat perceived by the moderate revival, Jabhat al-Nusra detained a leading FSA commander in Deraa, accusing him of working for foreign powers. As the two insurgent poles were increasingly defining themselves, the middle-ground Islamists published a 'Revolutionary Covenant', which presented a more mainstream outlook for Syria and its revolution.

Although this covenant sparked significant rhetorical tensions between jihadists and Syrian Islamists, including Ahrar al-Sham, cooperation on the battlefield continued. This was exemplified in two major offensives launched in Idlib in late May, during which the first American suicide bomber carried out an attack in Syria.

As June began and the world awoke to the first apparent Syria-linked attack in the Western world in Brussels, ISIS launched a major offensive across Iraq. On 10 June ISIS captured Iraq's second city, Mosul, sparking a mass Sunni armed uprising against the federal government of Nouri al-Maliki. As ISIS marched towards Baghdad, massacring hundreds of soldiers on its way, it was transferring huge quantities of captured weaponry, much of it American, into eastern Syria. This, combined with the sheer shock factor of ISIS's Iraq-based advance, induced tribes in eastern Syria to pledge allegiance to the group.

ISIS's subsequent proclamation of a caliphate, its renaming as the Islamic State (IS), and the appointment of Abu Bakr al-Baghdadi as Caliph Ibrahim shocked the world and further induced submission to ISIS in Syria's east. This was a direct challenge to the credibility of al-Qaeda, whose leaders and chief idealogues were quick to condemn the legitimacy of IS's caliphate. Nonetheless, Jabhat al-Nusra also displayed for the first time its intent to establish Islamic rule in Syria, thereby engendering concern across the remainder of the insurgency.

In the wake of IS's caliphate declaration, the group took control of Deir ez Zour and initiated a slick propaganda strategy aimed at recruiting globally. Amid a series of brutally graphic IS videos and a hardline shift within Jabhat al-Nusra's top-level leadership, moderate and Syrian Islamist insurgents announced a mass unity initiative known as Wa'tasimo.

As August began, IS launched an offensive on opposition-held areas in northern Aleppo and in Iraq; it advanced towards the Kurdish capital, Irbil, and sparked a mass exodus of Yazidi civilians onto Mount Sinjar. In response, the USA initiated an air campaign targeting IS in northern Iraq and, on 19 August, a video was released revealing the beheading of American hostage James Foley.

\* \* \*

With intra-jihadist relations at an all-time low, May continued as April had ended with a concentrated ISIS offensive targeting rival factions in Deir ez Zour. The resulting fighting, which involved both Jabhat al-Nusra and Ahrar al-Sham, was so intense and destructive that 60,000 local inhabitants of the villages of al-Busayrah, Abriha and al-Zir south-east of Deiz ez Zour's provincial capital were forced to flee their homes. While dynamics remained relatively even in early May, the balance tipped to ISIS's favour by midway through the month, with ISIS reportedly in control of large parts of eastern and western Deir ez Zour by 11 May. By that point, 10 days of inter-factional fighting in the province had killed over 230 combatants, and Reuters claimed that ISIS had been killing more Jabhat al-Nusra fighters every week than pro-Assad forces had been able to.[1]

With ISIS determinedly pushing back against losses it had incurred earlier in the year—it was doing the same in north-eastern Aleppo—the leadership-level dispute was by no means finished. On 2 May, al-Qaeda leader Zawahiri released another message in which he blamed ISIS for having introduced a 'political disaster' within the *mujahidin* in Syria, and specifically accused Baghdadi of 'sedition', the consequences of which represented 'a plate of gold' for Bashar al-Assad. Intriguingly, Zawahiri countered ISIS spokesman Adnani's claim that the ISI had ceased to be directly affiliated or loyal to al-Qaeda in 2006, by instead claiming that senior AQI official Abu Ayyub al-Masri (Abu Hamza al-Muhajir) had sent a letter to al-Qaeda's central leadership insisting that the ISI would retain AQI's loyalty and that several subsequent letters from the ISI until 2013 had indicated their allegiance to Osama Bin Laden and then himself.

Zawahiri also castigated Baghdadi's leadership and his decision to announce Jabhat al-Nusra's relationship with the ISI and al-Qaeda in April 2013, as it had previously been agreed in secret between them that this reality would remain undisclosed. Moreover, the revelation had caused 'the people of Syria [who had previously] come out in demonstrations in support of Jabhat al-Nusra' to condemn the movement and view it with suspicion.

Zawahiri's statement was then concluded with three 'orders' directed to Jolani and Jabhat al-Nusra: firstly, to cease engaging in offensive actions against ISIS; secondly, to stop accusing and slandering others; and thirdly, to accept the establishment of an independent *sharia* court to adjudicate with ISIS.[2] Forty-eight hours later Jolani issued an audio statement agreeing to abide by all three terms.

Meanwhile, after more than eighteen months of managing close coordination and healthy relations, Jabhat al-Nusra was beginning to reveal a more suspicious and assertive attitude towards those FSA factions that were most clearly being supported by the US-led MOCs in Turkey and Jordan. Already, the arrival of US-manufactured anti-tank missiles in the hands of more high-profile groups such as Harakat Hazm and the SRF had raised suspicions within the jihadist community in Syria regarding the ultimate allegiances of such groups. Moreover, the very fact that the initial launching of the anti-ISIS offensive in January had been surrounded by rumours of Western facilitation added to the fear that a group like Jabhat al-Nusra, now identified overtly as an al-Qaeda affiliate, could become the target of a counter-jihadist campaign.

On 1 May, and amid small but steady FSA-led advances in rural Deraa, the southern section of the SRF was established, bringing together more than twenty FSA factions. The video announcement featured Colonel Ahmad Na'ameh, who stated that he would be the leader of the southern SRF and would ensure that it 'corrected' the path of the revolution. For many jihadists in the south, this 'correction' was deemed to have been a not-so-subtle reference to the need to reassert the influence of the moderate FSA in the south, where groups such as Jabhat al-Nusra, Ahrar al-Sham and Harakat al-Muthanna al-Islamiyya were increasingly leading prominent operations against the regime.

However, before Jabhat al-Nusra had time to pass comment, several of the named constituent members of this new southern front of the SRF announced their refusal to be involved, amongst them Liwa Omar al-Mukhtar and Liwa Jaydor Houran.[3] Both claimed they had not even heard of this initiative, let alone signed up to join it. Consequently, the legitimacy of Colonel Na'ameh's newest faction was placed deeply into question before it had even claimed involvement in any military action.

The following day Jabhat al-Nusra issued a statement that primarily focused on discrediting Na'ameh's revolutionary credentials and describing him as an agent of foreign intelligence. Another statement released shortly thereafter announced that Na'ameh and several of his deputies were wanted by Jabhat al-Nusra's *sharia* court in Deraa. It was indeed well known that Na'ameh had become a crucial link between the MOC in Amman, Jordan and the FSA in southern Syria, particularly in terms of relaying operational information and facilitating the provision of lethal and non-lethal assistance.

By the afternoon of 3 May Na'ameh and one of his deputies, Mousa al-Ahmed from the SMC, had been captured by Jabhat al-Nusra,[4] and after three days in custody Na'ameh appeared in a video purportedly confessing to his 'crimes'. His confession, which appeared to have been carried out under duress, focused on his alleged lead role in arranging the opposition's defeat at the town of Khirbet al-Ghazaleh in May 2013. In that battle, Na'ameh had taken charge of the operation at the point at which the town appeared ready to fall. Shipments of weapons from Jordan that he was managing failed to arrive in time, thus forcing an insurgent withdrawal. In Na'ameh's 6 May 'confession' video, he claimed that his backers in Jordan had ordered him to lose the battle to avoid giving Jabhat al-Nusra a role in the victory—something that had been consistently rumoured since, including by prominent FSA commander and southern tribal figure Bashar al-Zoubi, who had earlier called for his boss's trial for mismanagement.[5]

In a chilling comment made after his confession was aired, a source within Jabhat al-Nusra claimed:

> Na'ameh confessed to everything without being tortured. For the first two days, he was well treated, then he was beaten, but it was only a light torture ... Na'ameh would give advance notice to the regime of planned attacks, he helped get rebel leaders killed.[6]

Tensions between Jabhat al-Nusra and the remainder of the Syrian insurgency were not only limited to the south, however. While the operational relationships between Jabhat al-Nusra and US-backed northern factions such as Liwa Forsan al-Haq, Harakat Hazm, the 13th Division and components of the SRF had become more distant since April, the Islamic Front's political bureau was beginning to moderate the scope of its political objectives so as to fit back within the broader opposition. The results of this evolved thinking came on 17 May, when the Islamic Front coordinated the release of a 'Revolutionary Covenant', detailing the goals and principles of their revolution. The covenant was additionally signed by al-Ittihad al-Islami Ajnad al-Sham, Jaish al-Mujahideen, Faylaq al-Sham and Alwiyat al-Furqan and was read aloud in a video statement aired on Al-Jazeera by Ahrar al-Sham leader and Islamic Front political chief Hassan Abboud:

> Revolutionary forces are fully aware of the gravity of the current situation our blessed revolution is going through, and in the pursuit of unifying efforts and joining forces within a common framework that serves the interests of the Syrian people, these forces confirm their commitment to the following:
>
> 1. The controls and limits of revolutionary work are derived from our authentic religion, avoiding fundamentalism and radicalism.
> 2. The Syrian revolution's ultimate political goal is to overthrow the current regime with all its symbols and foundations and to bring them to justice in fair trials, without acts of vengeance or retaliation.
> 3. The regime that commits terrorism against our people through regular and irregular forces, along with all the parties supporting them such as the mercenaries from Iran, Iraq, and Hezbollah, and all those who carry out aggression against our people and ex-communicate them (apostasy), such as ISIS, are military targets for the revolution. Military actions will be limited to Syrian territory.
> 4. Overthrowing the regime is a collaborative enterprise by different revolutionary forces. Based on the awareness of these forces of the regional and international dimensions of the Syria crisis, we welcome the opportunity to communicate and cooperate with regional and international parties to show solidarity with the Syrian people in a way that serves the interests of the revolution.
> 5. The preservation of Syrian territorial integrity and the prevention, by all attainable means, of any project aimed at dividing these territories is a non-negotiable revolutionary principle.
> 6. Our revolutionary forces, in their military operations, rely on Syrian elements only and believe that the military and political decisions should be entirely Syrian, rejecting any type of affiliation with foreign entities.
> 7. The Syrian people aim to establish a state of law, freedom, and justice, without any sort of pressure or dictatorship.
> 8. The Syrian revolution is a revolution based on morals and values whose objective is to obtain freedom, justice, and security for all sectors of Syrian society, with its diverse multi-ethnic and multi-sect social fabric.
> 9. The Syrian revolution is committed to the respect of human rights, which is also encouraged by our authentic religion.

10. Revolutionary forces strongly condemn the regime's targeting of civilians and recurring use of weapons of mass destruction (WMD) against the civilian population. Revolutionary forces strive to keep civilians out of the circle of violence and are firmly committed towards that end. These forces never used such weapons in the past and reiterate at the same time the absence of any WMD in their possession.

11. All that is recovered by the regime is the lawful property of the Syrian people and it will be used and administered by revolutionary forces in order to fulfill the people's demands for bringing down the regime.

Verily we call upon all other revolutionary forces on Syrian territory to sign this covenant in order to be one hand in our struggle to topple the regime.[7]

This was a highly significant development for the Islamic Front and its constituent factions, which for the first time had not included unequivocally the establishment of an Islamic state within their political objectives. Moreover, the emphasis on fighting both the regime and ISIS; the limiting of the conflict to within Syrian territory and involving only Syrian actors; the openness to relations with all international actors; and the determination to establish a future Syrian state for all sects and ethnicities was the Islamic Front's way of presenting itself to the international community as a responsible and acceptable actor. Moreover, the very fact that Hassan Abboud had been the one to read aloud the statement presented a softer and more 'nationally Syrian' image of his Ahrar al-Sham faction than had ordinarily been shown in public.

Placed within the broader context of moderates receiving increased external assistance, especially in northern Syria, and of opposition-supporting Gulf states—especially Qatar—seemingly adhering more closely to the US policy line in Syria, the publication of the Revolutionary Covenant appeared more than anything to have been an attempt to placate concerns in the West that the Islamic Front was a problem rather than part of the solution to the Syrian crisis. The fact that Ahrar al-Sham's funding levels from its most prominent backer, Qatar, had been dramatically scaled back in early 2014 may also have been a strong motivator.

Nevertheless, the Revolutionary Covenant proved to be deeply unpopular with both ISIS and Jabhat al-Nusra, both of which were quick to issue statements of condemnation. While ISIS issued a *fatwa* declaring war on the Islamic Front, it was Jabhat al-Nusra's reaction that was the most surprising, considering the close operational relationship between the two factions. In an official statement released on 21 May, Jabhat al-Nusra was highly critical of what they deemed to have been a betrayal of the Islamic principles of jihad:

[Placing regime figures into a fair trial] is contrary to what sharia has decided: in Islam, apostates deserve only the sword ... the failure to seek vengeance for the people of al-Sham is nothing other than a disappointment ... Points three, five, six, and eight all spread the spirit of civic mindedness and belonging to land and the nation ... Everyone should be aware than the Islamic State we desire is one based on religion, belief and sharia before anything else ... For us, Muslims cannot be equal to infidels...

The code says that the Syrian people aim to establish a state of justice, law, and freedom, isolated from pressures and diktats, but we believe these pressures and diktats are very obvious in the drafting of this point ... We would have very much liked to see our brethren, who signed this document, consult with us ... Everyone is aware that one of the biggest problems in arenas of jihad, about which religious scholars have warned, is the absence of consultation and the taking of decisions unilaterally.[8]

Considering that the Islamic Front had taken the lead in designing the covenant and that its political bureau was dominated by Ahrar al-Sham officials—including Abboud and his deputy Mohebedeen al-Shami—this falling out with Jabhat al-Nusra was particularly significant. Jabhat al-Nusra's then chief *sharia* official and Jolani's implicit number two, the Jordanian cleric Sami al-Oraydi, went as far as to suggest that Ahrar al-Sham and the Islamic Front were being led by monetary concerns: 'Life in mountains and caves under the rule of sharia is better than life in mansions without it, and we have the Taliban as evidence of that.'[9] In response, and in an unusual public expression of exasperation, Hassan Abboud exclaimed:

Doctor [Oraydi], instead of all this misrepresentation and one-upmanship, why don't you clarify what we did wrong? There are those who style their jihad so that they end up isolated from their Islamic nation, cut off in forests and mountains: this isn't the point of jihad.

Under pressure, Abboud was revealing a more private side of his thinking on jihad that was quite critical of the world's more established 'jihadist' organisations. In discussions with this author, for example, Abboud had been critical of the over-arching image not only of the Taliban, but also AQAP, AQIM, al-Shabaab and Boko Haram. In public, Abboud would later label Boko Haram leader Abubakar Shekau as a 'lunatic barbarian'.[10] Several weeks later, in an exclusive interview with the BBC, Abboud further laid out his moderated approach:

[ISIS militants] are the bearded version of the shabiha. ISIS does not reflect Islam in any way. Islam is a religion of peace. It is not a religion of slaughter. ISIS represents the worst image ever of Islam.

[Alawites have] been here since the 9th Century—women would drive, go to university, and wearing the hijab would be a personal choice for them...

Our idea governing model is sharia ... [but] there is a misconception in the West about sharia. It is not just a set of punishments ... sharia carries all the values of liberty and justice. We will not force it on anyone. We hope that the people would willingly call for sharia.[11]

This saga over the Revolutionary Covenant represented a significant political and ideological falling out between Jabhat al-Nusra and its long-time allies in the Islamic Front and other Islamic factions. Nonethleless, it did not appear to affect their operational relationships on the ground. Three days after the covenant's publication and nine days after 60 tonnes of explosives had been detonated under the western gate of the Wadi al-Deif military base, Jabhat al-Nusra, Suqor al-Sham and Ahrar al-Sham launched—in coordination with the SRF and Harakat Hazm—two major offensives in Idlib.

One assault was launched against the strategic Camp Khazanat checkpoint, located on the main M5 highway just south of the town of Khan Sheikhoun. Early on the morning of 25 May, two Jabhat al-Nusra suicide bombers detonated separate truck bombs at different targets, decisively weakening their defences for a ground assault that by the end of the day had captured Camp Khazanat altogether. By the following day, the last remaining checkpoint, known as al-Salam, was seized and Khan Sheikhoun came under insurgent control.

The second assault took place further north in Idlib outside the town of Ariha, where four suicide bombers detonated truck bombs in the hilly Jebel al-Arbain area with the objective of capturing two strategic regime military positions known as the al-Shami base and the Fanar Restaurant checkpoint. As with the operation on Camp Khazanat and Khan Sheikhoun, the two positions were successfully captured by the end of the day.[12] Ideological fallings out, it seemed, did not necessarily translate onto the battlefield. Jabhat al-Nusra received a huge strategic boost in Idlib after leading both victories, and its fighters drove a huge convoy—consisting of roughly twenty pick-up-truck-mounted heavy machine guns, five tanks, two armoured personnel carriers, a self-propelled radar-guided anti-aircraft 'Shilka' system and a 'Gvozdika' self-propelled howitzer—through Khan Sheikhoun on 2 June to demonstrate their newly asserted influence in the region.

Not only had the two offensives been large, simultaneous and both successful, but one of the suicide bombers had been a twenty-two-year-old American. Known in Syria as Abu Hurayrah (father of the kitten—after his fondness for cats), but born as Moner Mohammed Abusalha to a Palestinian father and an American mother in Florida, he was America's first recorded suicide bomber in the Syrian conflict. In a video testimony filmed prior to his death, Abusalha described how he had walked 5 miles from his home to the airport in Florida, before flying to Istanbul 'with only $20 in my pocket—only enough to buy a visa' in the summer of 2013. Later in the video Abusalha ripped his American passport up with his mouth before setting it on fire and concluded by saying goodbye to his parents and brother, weeping.[13] In a separate video released by al-Qaeda-linked Global Islamic Media Front, Abusalha berated Bashar al-Assad, calling him 'nothing but a donkey ... you fat pig', before snorting several times. This psychologically unstable image of Abusalha meant his threat to the USA—'we are coming for you, mark my words'—was particularly chilling, even if it did end by calling US President Obama 'you big *kuffar*'.[14]

Remarkably, in an example of the huge challenge faced by Western governments in preventing trained militants from returning home undetected and posing security threats, Abusalha had flown home to the USA for several months before returning to Syria to carry out his attack.[15]

As May drew to a close, much of Europe's attention had turned to whether or not a Syria-trained jihadist had been responsible for killing four people in a gun attack at Belgium's Jewish Museum in Brussels on 24 May. Days after the attack, a twenty-nine-year-old French national of Algerian origin, Mehdi Nemmouche, was captured in Marseille's Saint-Charles train station carrying an AK assault rifle, a pistol, a homemade ISIS flag and a video recording in which he appeared to claim responsibility for the attack. Nemmouche, subsequent investigations would reveal, had been radicalised during a period in prison, after which he travelled to Syria and fought for over a year before his return to France.[16]

With the first apparently Syria-connected terrorist attack now having taken place in the Western world, another significant contribution was yet to be made to the campaign against ISIS and Abu Bakr al-Baghdadi. On 28 May prominent Jordanian jihadist ideologue Abu Mohammed al-Maqdisi, who remained in prison in Jordan, released what was arguably the most significant anti-ISIS statement thus far, labelling it a 'deviant organization':

> To the brothers, the leaders of the Mujahideen in Khorasan, Yemen, the Islamic Maghreb, Sinai, Somalia and the Caucasus, may Allah protect them and use them to give victory to the Deen (religion) ...
>
> Perhaps you know that we have exhausted our efforts to be involved in mediation, as have other notable people, scholars, and mujahideen. [You may also know] that

we had communications with those concerned in the dispute and the infighting, and amongst them was [Abu Bakr] al-Baghdadi; I advised him privately and advised his Tanzim al-Dawla (State movement) publicly. I also responded to some of the transgressions of his official spokesman, [Abu Mohammed] al-Adnani, as much as I was able to release from prison, even though his transgressions and reckless [talk] does not deserve to be responded to, more than this ...

I also wrote to our beloved brother, the Sheikh, the Commander, the Mujahid Ayman al-Zawahiri (may Allah protect him), and I put him in the picture regarding my efforts at a reconciliation initiative or adjudicating between Tanzim al-Dawla and Jabhat al-Nusra. [I also informed him] that I would authorize some of my closest students to carry this out ...

I have also been in communication with some of those in positions of religious authority in al-Dawla, and I have documented evidence of these correspondences, which exposes their fraud, their 'beating around the bush' and their lies when dealing with the leaders of Jihad, as well as other traits, which are not fitting for Mujahideen ...

You are aware that Tanzim al-Dawla has spilled unlawful blood, and this is authenticated. [They have also] refused to comply with the [commands] of the leaders of the Mujahideen ... You are aware that the likes of these people are forcefully dominating the Muslims in Syria, voicing their ideas publicly, speaking in the name of Jihad and Mujahideen, while attiring themselves with the cloak of 'The Islamic State' and using its terminologies has sullied and will continue to sully the Jihad, the Mujahideen and the desired Islamic State ...

As a result of the words [of their leaders], their criticism and prejudice is an indication of their ill-understanding and false goals. All of this is done in order to justify their sins, their repudiation and their splitting of the ranks of the Mujahideen. These justifications prove their superficiality, shallow thinking ...

Henceforth, there is no longer a benefit to procrastinate, delay or wait. It then became incumbent upon us, and upon all of the scholars of Jihad and the leaders of Jihad all over the world to say a word of truth, join the ranks of the people of truth and make clear the group of aggressors who have refused the adjudication ...

Based on this, I announce, here, that Tanzim al-Dawla fil-Iraq wal-Sham, is a deviant organisation from the path of truth, [they are] aggressors against the Mujahideen ... They have become embroiled in the spilling of unlawful blood, the sequestration of their wealth, war booty, and [the] regions which they have liberated from the [Assad] regime. [This group] has besmirched the name of Jihad and the elite Mujahideen. [They have] turned their rifles from the chests of the apostates and those at war [with the Muslims] to the chests of the Mujahideen and the Muslims, as well as other documented deviations.

I also call upon all Mujahideen to adopt this statement [as their official stance], and publicly align with it, giving victory to the truth and its people. I also call upon the members of Tanzim al-Dawla to join the ranks of Jabhat al-Nusra, giving bay'ah to its leaders. This is our fatwa to them and what I encourage them to do and chose for them. I also call upon all Islamic Jihadi websites, and others who are concerned with the affairs of the Muslims and their Jihad, to spread this statement and give victory to it and to refrain from publishing Tanzim al-Dawla's media releases.[17]

June and July 2014 were dramatic months for ISIS, and indeed for the entire international jihadist movement. Although events began in Iraq, they directly affected the trajectory and scope of the conflict in Syria and, soon enough, the scale of developments had expanded to include Syria itself. If the ISIS–Jabhat al-Nusra split in April 2013, the anti-ISIS front in January 2014 and al-Qaeda's disavowal of ISIS in February 2014 had seemed like significant events, what was to come in the summer of 2014 was groundbreaking and would revolutionise the future of jihadist militancy around the world.

On the morning of 5 June a large convoy of ISIS militants, driving pick-up trucks and captured Iraqi army Humvees launched an assault on the city of Samarra, and quickly took control of five of its seven districts. While a bridge was deliberately destroyed by ISIS to prevent army reinforcements from entering the city quickly, an eventual military counter-attack, backed by helicopters and the specialist Golden Division, forced an ISIS withdrawal by the end of the day. In all, fourteen security force personnel were killed and forty-five other people wounded, while the army claimed to have killed forty militants.[18]

The following morning ISIS launched a similar assault on the northern city of Mosul, where it had long maintained an immense underground network of influence and was earning approximately $12 million every month through extortion.[19] It remained the only city that ISIS was consistently able to hold during the US-led surge from 2007. Fighting on 6 June spread throughout at least eight of the city's districts and included at least five ISIS suicide bombers attacking a major army arms depot. While ISIS was again forced to conduct withdrawals late that night, fighting continued in the city's west and east on 7 and 8 June, with a total of at least sixty-nine security force fatalities reported, although the real number was probably higher. On 9 June ISIS militants launched a renewed push into the city and captured a number of significant facilities, including the headquarters of the Federal Police, the city's international airport and the Provincial Council building.[20] By early on 10 June, after sporadic fighting overnight, ISIS had taken all of Mosul, Iraq's second largest city, and in so doing had captured dozens of military vehicles and hundreds upon hundreds of other weapons systems, many of them US-made. The city's main prison, Badush, was emptied of its approximately 1,500 detainees, all of whom were driven in trucks 2 kilometres into the desert and divided by sect; roughly 600 Shia men were then systematically executed in a ravine.[21]

While Mosul was in its last throes of government control, ISIS militants were launching simultaneous attacks across Iraq's Ninawa, Salah ad Din, Diyala, Kirkuk and Anbar provinces. By 10 June ISIS had continued its advance by dividing into two major columns. One travelled south-east from Mosul, advancing along Highway 80 through western Kirkuk to capture Zab, Hawija, Riyadh and Rashad and through southern Ninawa. The other headed directly south along Highway 1 into northern Salah ad Din to capture Sharqat and Suleiman Bek and then further south to Baiji and Tikrit, both of which it surrounded.

In encircling Tikrit, ISIS sparked mass panic in the nearby air academy, better known by its former name COB Speicher, where (as had occurred in Mosul) approximately 3,000 soldiers shed their military uniforms and fled on foot in fear of an impending attack. After they had fled several kilometres, ISIS armoured vehicles stopped the mass of soldiers and forced them onto trucks, which drove them to Tikrit palace. According to Human Rights Watch, as many as 770 of them were executed over the following three days—ISIS claimed to have killed 1,700.[22]

In the days that followed, ISIS continued its rampage further into government territory, capturing at least ten additional towns in Salah ad Din, as well as consolidating control over Tikrit, its second provincial capital in Iraq and third including Raqqa in Syria. From there, the route led to the city of Samarra, home to several holy Shia shrines, and then to Taji and its expansive military base and then to Baghdad.

ISIS was not alone in its Iraqi advance and in the routing of Iraqi armed forces. In fact, a large number of Sunni armed groups were contributing to this armed rebellion, including the Islamic Army in Iraq, Jaish al-Mujahideen, the 1920 Revolution Brigade, a vast confederation of tribal revolutionary councils and a coalition of Baathist organisations, most prominently Jaish Rijal al-Tariqa al-Naqshbandiyya (JRTN), which was linked to the vice chairman of Saddam Hussein's Iraqi Revolutionary Command Council, Izzat Ibrahim al-Douri. This coalition of convenience may have represented a coming together of unnatural allies, but their fight in defence of Sunni Muslims across Iraq overrode ideological differences, at least in the immediate term. In short, the cooperation was significant enough to make a difference, and so long as it did, it was likely to continue.

In addition the capture and subsequent execution of hundreds of prisoners, most of whom were Shia, ISIS also kidnapped twenty-eight Turkish truck drivers outside Mosul on 10 June and attacked the Turkish consulate in the city on 11 June, taking hostage forty-nine of its employees. In less than a week ISIS had fomented a massive armed uprising in Iraq that had quickly exposed the inherent structural weakness within the Iraqi armed forces. Not only were Sunni extremist militants now headed towards Kurdish territory in the north—the Kurdish Peshmerga assumed control over Kirkuk on 13 June after a mass Iraqi army desertion—but ISIS was getting ever closer to the capital, Baghdad, where an emergency session of Parliament on 12 June saw only 197 of 325 MPs turn up.[23]

Iraq was fast splitting along sectarian and ethnic lines, with Kurds seeking to assert their definitive authority in the north and with a vast majority of Sunnis supporting the revolution, at least for now. The Shia-led government of Nouri al-Maliki, which had long failed to acknowledge the demands of its disaffected Sunni population, was in trouble, and the solution was found in mobilising Shia fighting-age men into self-styled paramilitary forces. On 13 June, during his Friday prayers sermon, Iraq's leading Shia cleric, Grand Ayatollah Ali al-Sistani, issued a call to arms across Iraq to defend the country against 'terrorists'.[24] Although Sistani was calling upon 'citizens' to defend their country, it was clear who was the most likely receptive audience. That afternoon more than 1,000 Shia volunteers had driven north from Karbala to Taji to receive weapons training,[25] hundreds more were signing up in eastern Baghdad, and one Shia militia leader claimed to have 14,000 'volunteers' waiting in Muthanna airport to join the fight.[26] Iraqi Shia militias in Syria were reportedly dispatching fighters back to Iraq to reinforce the army[27] and the Iranian IRGC already had several hundred personnel deployed in Diyala.[28]

Another actor soon to become more involved was America. On 16 June, a day after ISIS militants captured the northern town of Tel Afar and executed 170 soldiers, President Obama notified Congress of his plan to deploy 275 military personnel into Iraq to provide support and security for American personnel at the embassy in Baghdad and a further 100 soldiers in reserve to a nearby country.[29] Though slowed, ISIS's continued advances throughout the second half of June—including the capture of the disused al-Muthanna Chemical Weapons Complex on 19 June, the Baiji oil refinery (Iraq's largest) on 21 June and the al-Qaim and al-Rutba border crossings with Syria on 21 and 22 June—added further to the sense of urgency inside Iraq, the region and the world of the need for a viable defence to be put into place.

ISIS's quite extraordinary advances across Iraq stunned many in Syria, even more than in the rest of the world. Moreover, within hours of capturing Mosul

ISIS had transferred huge quantities of captured weaponry into eastern Syria, particularly into Deir ez Zour, where Omar al-Shishani was consequently pictured posing alongside a number of American-made Humvee vehicles. Such an immediate and visible 'spillover' was a powerful source of leverage against those tribes and armed factions in Deir ez Zour who continued to hold out against ISIS dominance. Power and fear were major weapons in the ISIS toolbox, and it used them to its advantage.

On 17 June ISIS militants carried out two separate suicide bombings targeting its insurgent adversaries in Deir ez Zour—one in al-Shamatiyeh that killed a senior Jabhat al-Nusra *sharia* official and an Ahrar al-Sham commander, and another in al-Howayji that wounded a senior FSA leader. At this point ISIS controlled the town of al-Mayadin south of Deir ez Zour city, while the route south down the Euphrates river to al-Bukamal on the Iraqi border (with al-Qaim) was controlled by Jabhat al-Nusra, Ahrar al-Sham, several small FSA-linked factions and Sunni tribal militias. Securing this stretch of the Euphrates valley would effectively serve to link ISIS in Iraq to its developing capital in Raqqa via the al-Qaim–al-Bukamal crossing.

ISIS set about making this a reality on 20 June when powerful convoys were dispatched to attack and capture the towns of Mohassan, Abulil and Albu Amr along Highway 4 south of Deir ez Zour city. Five days later, after a brief period of consolidation, ISIS militants dispatched south again and launched an assault on the major Jabhat al-Nusra stronghold of al-Shuheil, 4 kilometres north of al-Mayadin. Meanwhile the majority of Jabhat al-Nusra's force in al-Bukamal, under the authority of Abu Yusuf al-Masri, pledged allegiance to ISIS, thereby inviting the group to take control. However, the town would remain effectively disputed for the time being, as demonstrated on 27 June when a suspected Jabhat al-Nusra suicide bombing targeted Abu Yusuf, wounding him. Despite resistance to ISIS's continued presence in Deir ez Zour, it was clear that the group's advance in Iraq had marginally tilted the balance of power in eastern Syria.

This cross-border influence was not only one way, however. The assault on Mosul that had begun on 6 June almost certainly to some extent involved units of ISIS militants who had earlier crossed from eastern Syria into Iraq to attack the city. Simply put, eastern Syria and Iraq represented one contiguous zone of territory for ISIS—the international border was of little relevance in terms of operational planning and strategy. The fact that ISIS militants subsequently sought to move north-west from Mosul to Tel Afar and also south towards Anbar's two crossings with Syria (near al-Rutba and at al-Qaim) underlined their intent to more definitively link their areas of operation in Syria and Iraq.

ISIS's dramatic demonstration of power in Iraq appeared to spark—or accelerate the launching of—several insurgent offensives in Syria. On the day that ISIS captured Mosul, insurgent factions in Aleppo launched a renewed push against ISIS positions in the governorate's north-east, capturing at least four villages in twenty-four hours. Further west, Ahrar al-Sham and the FSA-linked Liwa Ahrar Souriya launched the 'Echo of the Sahaba' attack on the Shia villages of Nubl and Zahra north of Aleppo city, while multi-group coalitions including Jabhat al-Nusra and Islamic Front groups initiated other offensives against regime forces on the town of Rankous in the Qalamoun and on the eastern Damascus suburbs of Jobar, Maliha and Jisreen. Moreover, a *sharia* council in Damascus's Ghouta region—composed of Jabhat al-Nusra, Ahrar al-Sham, Jaish al-Islam, al-Ittihad al-Islami Ajnad al-Sham and Faylaq al-Rahman—issued an ultimatum for ISIS to leave the area within forty-eight hours or face being pushed out by force. Amid reports of Iraqi Shia militias redploying forces from hotspots in Syria into Iraq, the fact that these targets were all struck within forty-eight hours of Mosul's fall was entirely logical.

Notwithstanding the pressure ISIS was facing in north-eastern Aleppo and around Damascus, it had consolidated control over the city of Raqqa and was in the midst of establishing it as its de facto capital. Meanwhile, its control over al-Bab, Jarablus and Manbij appeared largely secure, its presence in Homs's eastern al-Badiya desert remained in place and ISIS militants were now steadily expanding in Deir ez Zour towards the Iraqi border. This, combined with its dramatic victories in Iraq, meant that late June presented ISIS with a ripe environment for recruitment, partly from within intimidated populations in Syria and Iraq, but particularly also from within cliques of impressionable young Sunni Muslim men across the world.

While ISIS had released a series of English-language recruitment posters in October 2013, the engagement of English-speaking potential recruits had not expanded far beyond that since. However, the release on 19 June 2014 of a video entitled *There is no Life without Jihad* would mark the inception of a consequential enhancement of ISIS's recruitment strategy towards a genuinely global audience. Lasting a little over thirteen minutes and produced by ISIS's al-Hayat Media Center, this high-quality video featured three British and two Australian militants expounding on the perceived benefits of fighting jihad in Syria and Iraq for ISIS. The first speaker, who was identified as 'Abu Muthanna al-Yemeni, from Britain', who was later revealed to be twenty-year-old Nasser Muthanna from the Welsh city of Cardiff,[30] stated in a thick British accent:

We are a state implementing the sharia in Iraq and al-Sham ... We understand no borders—we have participated in battles in al-Sham and we will go to Iraq in a few days and we will fight there and come back and we will even go to Jordan and Lebanon with no problems ... the hope of this Ummah is in [Baghdadi's] neck, we hope for the khilafah (Caliphate), it's imminent ... we know it will be imminent.

Following on from Abu Muthanna's speech, another British national, identified as 'Abu Bara al-Hindi, from Britain', who was later revealed to be twenty-six-year-old Abdul Raqib Amin from Aberdeen in Scotland,[31] exclaimed:

We are all brothers and sisters ... are you willing to sacrifice the fat job you've got, the big car you've got, the family you have—are you willing to sacrifice this for the sake of Allah? Definitely if you sacrifice something for the sake of Allah, Allah will give you 700 times more than this ... All my brothers living in the West, I know how you feel when I used to live there, in your heart you feel depressed ... the cure for the depression is jihad for the sake of Allah. You feel like you have no honour ... my brothers, come to jihad and feel the honour we are feeling, the happiness we are feeling.

Launched in late May as a primarily English-language propaganda media wing, al-Hayat Media Center had emerged as a producer of slick content, and this was its most significant release to date. The sole use of British and Australian ISIS foot-soldiers and the professional quality of the filming did indeed present an image of ISIS's jihad that would have been attractive to potential recruits around the world. By this point in the conflict at least 450 British and 100 Australian nationals were thought to have travelled to Syria and Iraq, and videos like this one made the potential for those numbers to rise all the more likely. Moreover, the video's emphasis upon recruiting people not only to fight jihad but to join an 'Islamic state' in the making would prove to be a defining element of ISIS recruitment in the months to come, not least as a result of what its media apparatuses were about to announce.

On 29 June, as it continued its advance in Iraq and resisted an ultimately unsuccessful Iraqi army assault on Tikrit, and as its fighters continued to assert their influence across northern and eastern Syria, ISIS published three separate media releases within several hours of each other that would revolutionise the dynamics of international jihad.

The first of these three releases was a fifteen-minute video produced by al-Hayat Media Center and entitled *The End of Sykes–Picot*. In the video, a Chilean–Norwegian ISIS fighter identified as 'Abu Safiyya from Chile'— whose real name was later revealed to be Bastian Vasquez—provided a tour of an Iraqi borderguard post on the Syrian border recently captured by ISIS in Iraq and showed the effective lack of any border demarcating Syrian and

Iraqi territory. A police station near the border post was then shown being demolished in order to demonstrate the defeat of Iraqi government authority in the area.

The second release was a twelve-minute video produced by ISIS's al-I'tisam Media, which was entitled *Breaking of the Border* and showed US-made military vehicles captured by ISIS freely crossing the Syrian–Iraqi border. After a speech by a local ISIS commander, Abu Othman al-Libi, Abu Mohammed al-Adnani—whose face was blurred out—was shown giving a speech standing next to Omar al-Shishani, proclaiming the destruction of the Iraqi–Syrian border. Adnani was then shown using a bulldozer to forcefully break down sand berms built to demarcate Syrian and Iraqi territory.

After visually demonstrating its neutralising of sections of the Iraq–Syria border established according to the 19 May 1916 Sykes–Picot Agreement, ISIS's third and final media release of the day was by its principal media wing, al-Furqan. In a thirty-four-minute audio statement Adnani proclaimed that the time had come and the necessary conditions had been reached for ISIS to declare the establishment of a new caliphate under the leadership of Abu Bakr al-Baghdadi, who would henceforth be known simply as Caliph Ibrahim. ISIS would consequently cease to exist and would be renamed the Islamic State, and from that time onwards all Muslims were obligated to pledge *bay'a* to the caliph and his caliphate.

> The time has come for those generations that were drowning in oceans of disgrace, being nursed on the milk of humiliation, and being ruled by the vilest of all people, after their long slumber in the darkness of neglect—the time has come for them to rise. The time has come for the Ummah of Mohammed, may be peace be upon Him, to wake up from its sleep, remove the garments of dishonor, and shake off the dust of humiliation and disgrace, for the era of lamenting and moaning has gone and the dawn of honor has emerged anew. The sun of jihad has risen. The glad tidings of good are shining. Triumph looms on the horizon. The signs of victory have appeared. Here, the flag of the Islamic State, the flag of monotheism, rises and flutters. Its shade covers land from Aleppo to Diyala. Beneath it, the walls of those who claimed the rights of Allah have been demolished, their flags have fallen and their borders have been destroyed. Their soldiers are either killed, imprisoned or defeated. The Muslims are honored ... The people of heresy are humiliated. The hudud are implemented. The frontlines are defended. Crosses and graves are demolished. Prisoners are released by the edge of the sword ...

> There only remained one matter, a collective obligation that the Ummah sins by abandoning. It is a forgotten obligation. The Ummah has not tasted honor since they lost it. It is a dream that lives in the depths of every Muslim believer. It is a hope that flutters in the heart of every mujahid. It is the khilafah. It is the khilafah—the abandoned obligation of the era ...

Therefore, the majlis shura of the Islamic State studied this matter ... after the Islamic State, by Allah's grace, gained the essentials necessary for khilafah ... In light of the fact that the Islamic State has no legal constraint or excuse that can justify delaying or neglecting the establishment of the khilafah such that it would not be sinful, the Islamic State ... resolved to announce the establishment of the Islamic khilafah, the appointment of a khalifah for the Muslims, and the pledge of allegiance to the sheikh, the mujahid, the scholar who practices what he preaches, the worshipper, the leader, the warrior, the reviver, the descendent from the family of the Prophet, the slave of Allah, Ibrahim Ibn Awwad Ibn Ibrahim Ibn Ali Ibn Mohammed al-Badri al-Hashimi al-Husayni al-Qurashi ... And he has accepted the bay'a. Thus, he is the imam and khalifah for the Muslims everywhere. Accordingly, the 'Iraq and al-Sham' in the name of the Islamic State is henceforth removed from all official deliberations and communications and the official name is the Islamic State from the date of this declaration.

We clarify to the Muslims that with this declaration of the khilafah, it is incumbent upon all Muslims to pledge allegiance to the khalifah Ibrahim and support him. The legality of all emirates, groups, states, and organizations, becomes null by the expansion of the khilafah's authority and arrival of its troops in their areas.[32]

Timed to mark the start of the holy month of Ramadan, these coordinated statements and the establishment of a caliphate shook the world. Since January 2014, and in an accelerated pace since early June, ISIS had assumed de facto control over territory stretching from al-Bab in Syria's Aleppo to Suleiman Bek in Iraq's Salah ad Din, a distance of approximately 670 kilometres.[33] Within the pro-ISIS community and its own members, the establishment of the caliphate was simply the next stage in the organisation's series of advancements, and was something that should—in theory—have been welcomed throughout the Islamic world, as British ISIS fighter Abu Uthman al-Britani told this author after the proclamation and weeks before his death in Deir ez Zour:

Thank God, Allah has finally restored something that has been taken away from from the Muslims. The khilafa is the shield of the umma and now Muslims can live in an actual Islamic state, where they can live a life of honour and practise their religion to the full extent and not the watered-down version that is currently being taught in other countries. It also brings hope to the Muslims around the world who are being opressed and slaughtered.[34]

While ISIS had challenged the legitimacy of al-Qaeda already, the proclamation of a caliphate and the designation of Abu Bakr al-Baghdadi as both caliph and *emir al-mu'minin* was a direct challenge to Taliban leader Mullah Mohammed Omar, to whom the entire al-Qaeda leadership is ultimately loyal.

The scale and significance of this development, however, did not mean that it would automatically be welcomed across the jihadist community and the

Islamic world. As such, a day after a huge Islamic State (IS) military convoy paraded through Raqqa on 30 June, Baghdadi himself issued an audio statement on 1 July in which he further stressed the perceived Islamic value of his organisation's establishment of a caliphate and the idea that, if supported and consolidated, it would be the mechanism for a reassertion of Sunni Islamic honour and power in the world:

> Take up arms, take up arms, O soldiers of the Islamic State! And fight, fight!
>
> ... Indeed, the ummah of Islam is watching your jihad with eyes of hope, and indeed you have brothers in many parts of the world being inflicted with the worst kinds of torture. Their honor is being violated. Their blood is being spilled. Prisoners are moaning and crying for help. Orphans and widows are complaining of their plight. Women who have lost their children are weeping. Masājid [plural of *masjid* (mosque)] are desecrated and sanctities are violated. Muslims' rights are forcibly seized in China, India, Palestine, Somalia, the Arabian Peninsula, the Caucasus, Shām (the Levant), Egypt, Iraq, Indonesia, Afghanistan, the Philippines, Ahvaz, Iran [by the rāfidah (shia)], Pakistan, Tunisia, Libya, Algeria and Morocco, in the East and in the West.
>
> So raise your ambitions, O soldiers of the Islamic State! For your brothers all over the world are waiting for your rescue, and are anticipating your brigades ... So by Allah, we will take revenge! By Allah, we will take revenge! Even if it takes a while, we will take revenge, and every amount of harm against the ummah will be responded to with multitudes more against the perpetrator.
>
> Soon, by Allah's permission, a day will come when the Muslim will walk everywhere as a master, having honor, being revered, with his head raised high and his dignity preserved ... So let the world know that we are living today in a new era.
>
> So listen, O ummah of Islam. Listen and comprehend. Stand up and rise. For the time has come for you to free yourself from the shackles of weakness, and stand in the face of tyranny, against the treacherous rulers—the agents of the crusaders and the atheists, and the guards of the jews.
>
> ... Rulers continue striving to enslave the Muslims, pulling them away from their religion with those slogans. So either the Muslim pulls away from his religion, disbelieves in Allah, and disgracefully submits to the manmade shirk (polytheistic) laws of the east and west, living despicably and disgracefully as a follower, by repeating those slogans without will and honor, or he lives persecuted, targeted, and expelled, to end up being killed, imprisoned, or terribly tortured, on the accusation of terrorism.
>
> O Muslims everywhere, glad tidings to you and expect good. Raise your head high, for today—by Allah's grace—you have a state and khilāfah, which will return your dignity, might, rights, and leadership. It is a state where the Arab and non-Arab, the white man and black man, the easterner and westerner are all brothers. It is a

khilāfah that gathered the Caucasian, Indian, Chinese, Shāmī, Iraqi, Yemeni, Egyptian, Maghribī (North African), American, French, German, and Australian. Allah brought their hearts together, and thus, they became brothers by His grace, loving each other for the sake of Allah, standing in a single trench, defending and guarding each other, and sacrificing themselves for one another. Their blood mixed and became one, under a single flag and goal, in one pavilion, enjoying this blessing, the blessing of faithful brotherhood. If kings were to taste this blessing, they would abandon their kingdoms and fight over this grace. So all praise and thanks are due to Allah.

O Muslims everywhere, whoever is capable of performing hijrah (emigration) to the Islamic State, then let him do so, because hijrah to the land of Islam is obligatory.[35]

Despite IS's best attempts and slick propaganda media releases, however, the world's Sunni Islamic leaders were entirely condemnatory and denounced the proclamation as illegitimate. In Syria specifically, the Islamic Front, Jabhat al-Nusra and countless other Islamic factions voiced their disapproval of the declaration. Within the broader community of prominent pro-jihadist ideologues, the London-based Hani al-Sibai claimed that he nearly choked on his breakfast upon hearing the news,[36] while the famed ideologue Abu Mohammed al-Maqdisi questioned the implications of the announcement:

Will this Caliphate be a sanctuary for every oppressed one and a refuge for every Muslim? Or will this creation take up a sword against Muslims who oppose it, and with it sweep away all the emirates that came before ... and nullify all the groups that do jihad in the cause of Allah in the different battlefields before them?[37]

The Islamic Front's chief *sharia* official, Abu 'Abd al-Malek, even issued a *fatwa* announcing that whoever claimed to be caliph without having sufficiently consulted within the *ulama* 'exposes himself to be killed'—a not-so-subtle death threat to the newly proclaimed caliph.[38]

Condemnations and threats notwithstanding, IS's next major media release was another al-Furqan video in which, for the first time, Abu Bakr al-Baghdadi appeared in public and gave the Friday address at Mosul's 800-year-old Great Mosque of al-Nuri. Released on 5 July and filmed the previous day, the twenty-one-minute video showed Baghdadi dressed all in black, in an apparent reference to the Abbasid caliphs who ruled between the eighth and twelfth centuries. Before taking to the *minbar* to give his address, Baghdadi was filmed cleaning his teeth with a *miswak*—a wooden twig traditionally used by the Prophet Muhammad and made from arak wood. Not only was his first public appearance therefore full of Islamic and historical references, it was also a bold demonstration of power. Before his arrival at the mosque, local Mosul residents reported a total cessation of cellphone coverage across the city, and once in the mosque the congregation was intermixed with armed IS militants standing guard. The congregation's entire front row (which was blurred out in the video, indicating the importance of those placed there) was reportedly made up of prominent IS militants, all wearing explosive vests.[39]

Baghdadi's words were also carefully judged, beginning with a strong emphasis upon the religious importance of Ramadan (which had just begun) and the additional value of sacrifices made during its thirty days. Most importantly perhaps, he presented his position as caliph as a heavy burden and one that did not make him any 'better' than his constituents:

> I have been plagued with this great matter, plagued with this responsibility, and it is a heavy responsibility. I was placed as your caretaker, and I am not better than you. So if you found me to be right then help me, and if you found me to be wrong then advise me and make me right and obey me in what I obey Allah through you. If I disobey Him then there is no obedience to me from you. I do not promise you, as the kings and rulers promise their followers and congregation, of luxury, security, and relaxation; instead, I promise you what Allah promised His faithful worshippers.[40]

Hours later, IS's online distributors proceeded to issue the first edition of its new English-language magazine, *Dabiq*, named after the prophesied location of the final battle before end times. Slickly produced on multiple online platforms and also distributed in hard-copy format within IS territory, the magazine was a method of direct outreach to Western recruits and another element of competition with al-Qaeda, whose Yemen-based AQAP-linked affiliate Ansar al-Sharia had previously published the notorious magazine *Inspire*.

With IS's caliphate thus proclaimed and 'Caliph Ibrahim' now a public figure, the group rode a wave of confidence and momentum in eastern Syria through July. Perhaps IS had learnt its lesson from 2013—it no longer sought to conquer everything in Syria at once, but instead focused on its immediate strategic priorities. This meant directing its attention towards dominating Deir ez Zour to the extent necessary to induce tribal submission and the defeat or withdrawal of rival insurgent forces.

After the near-total capitulation of Jabhat al-Nusra in al-Bukamal on 25 June, when Abu Yusuf al-Masri had pledged allegiance to ISIS, the town finally fell totally under IS control on 2 July thanks to an influx of IS reinforcements from the Iraqi side of the border. The capture of al-Bukamal was a significant strategic victory for IS, as it gave the group total control over that section of the Iraq–Syria border. In the ten days that followed, IS would assume control of the entire governorate, with the exception of regime-controlled districts of the city and the military airport on its southern periphery. This placed IS in control of approximately 60 per cent of Syria's total potential oil production.[41]

The total collapse of anti-IS forces in Deir ez Zour appeared to have been heavily influenced by IS's immense recent demonstration of power in Iraq and by its proclamation of a caliphate. Despite the Jabhat al-Nusra-led Majlis Shura al-Mujahideen al-Sharqiyya anti-IS alliance deploying a 100-vehicle military convoy carrying as many as 1,000 fighters into al-Shuheil on 28 June, local tribes in the town pledged allegiance to IS on 3 July, along with several Islamic insurgent factions (including Jaish al-Muta al-Islami, Liwa al-Ikhlaas and Harakat al-Taliban al-Islami). The loss of al-Shuheil prompted a large-scale Jabhat al-Nusra withdrawal from the governorate to southern Syria, led by the group's eastern leader and de facto Jabhat al-Nusra deputy Abu Mariya al-Qahtani.

In the days that followed al-Shuheil's fall, IS gained a flurry of pledges of allegiance and surrenders from tribes in al-Mayadin, al-Quriya, al-Ashara, Dhiban, Swedan, al-Jazira, Sedan Shameyi and Darnej.[42] IS's assertion of dominance in Deir ez Zour had undoubtedly been facilitated by the menacing image illustrated so clearly in its Iraq offensive and in the large-scale executions it had carried out upon capturing prisoners. But the fall of Deir ez Zour and the wholesale collapse of IS's adversaries also had a great deal to do with financial inducements, as it had 'spread $2 million in the area to entice local tribes and leaders to permit their presence'.[43] Some tribes and factions continued to oppose IS's control in Deir ez Zour, most notably the Sha'itat tribe, at least 900 of whose male members were subsequently rounded up and executed in mass graves as an example of what IS would do to those who refused its authority[44] IS also established 'repentance centres' across the governorate in July to encourage a de facto surrender of male citizens, while buildings and facilities suspected to have been lived in or used by rival factions were demolished.

IS's financial clout would come to play a pre-eminent role in its continued rise in the weeks and months to come. Not only did it help the organisation to develop and implement a comparatively efficient programme of social services and governance in areas under its control, but it allowed it to offer generous salaries to new recruits, many of whom were defecting from rival factions in order to join IS. As such, this combination of enticements paved the way for what the UN Human Rights Council labelled the 'Syrian-ization' of IS in the summer of 2014,[45] which in July alone likely saw 6,300 new recruits join the group.[46]

In the aftermath of Baghdadi's proclamation of a caliphate, questions began to be raised regarding the extent to which Jabhat al-Nusra and al-Qaeda intended to one day establish expansive Islamic law in Syria. Had al-Qaeda genuinely gone 'lite', as Adnani and IS had earlier suggested? Whether this was true or not, by launching an offensive in Iraq that was incomparable in recent jihadist history, and by proclaiming the establishment of the first caliphate since 1924, IS had undoubtedly outplayed al-Qaeda on this occasion. Moreover, the worldwide attention it was receiving for its actions ensured that IS would be sure to enjoy substantial benefits in terms of external financial donations and both internal and external recruitment.

Within this new environment of ideological competition (rather than military hostility, as in previous months), a leaked recording was posted on the Internet on 11 July of Jabhat al-Nusra leader Jolani describing his organisation's plan to begin imposing *sharia* in Syria by establishing multiple Islamic emirates in the country. Speaking before a sizeable contingent of his fighters in Aleppo, including a large number of Chechens as well as Abdullah al-Moheisini, Jolani insisted that IS's declaration of the caliphate had been illegitimate but that his plan to create emirates in Idlib, Aleppo, Deraa and Ghouta would represent the rightful path:

> The time has come ... for us to establish an Islamic emirate in al-Sham, to implement the limits and punishments of Allah and his laws in every sense of the word, without compromise, complacency, equivocation, or circumvention.[47]

Clearly aware of the pressure placed on him after IS's declaration and victories in eastern Syria—which he claimed had lost his group $1.5 billion—Jolani placed a particular focus on al-Qaeda's traditional emphasis on fighting jihad in order to establish the necessary international conditions for the creation of genuine Islamic authority. As Hassan Hassan claimed at the time, Jolani 'focused on *jihad* for the sake of *jihad*, a concept that appeals to those who believe that no Islamic State or caliphate will endure within the current international order'.[48] By retaining this line, Jolani not only challenged the inherent validity of Baghdadi's caliphate, but presented an entirely different method for reaching the same goal with a more sustainable foundation and future. In other words, it represented a continuation of the ideological competition already established between the parties. With that being said, the very fact that Jolani expressed no hope or intention of one day establishing an emirate in eastern Syria served as apparent evidence of Jabhat al-Nusra's admission of total defeat to IS in Deir ez Zour.

Whoever leaked Jolani's address did so in order to demonstrate Jabhat al-Nusra did indeed intend to impose *sharia* in Syria, but that there were ideological reasons why this had not yet been attained. However, the recording sparked considerable anxiety within the moderate Syrian political opposition and insurgency, which had long maintained that Jabhat al-Nusra would remain an accepted member of the armed opposition so long as it did no interfere with the principles of the revolution and did not introduce 'foreign' interests into the conflict. This concern prompted Jabhat al-Nusra to officially deny that it had established an emirate project and that it would only consider doing so after full consultation with the Islamic scholars and *mujahideen* in Syria. This was not exactly the reassurance Syria's moderates might have hoped for, but it proved sufficient to stave off any immediate negative consequences.

In order to further dispel concerns about its intentions, Jabhat al-Nusra released a video recording of Sami al-Oraydi's Eid al-Fitr sermon—marking the end of Ramadan—on 30 July, in which he made clear that Jabhat al-Nusra did indeed intend to establish Islamic emirates, but only after a lengthy process of consulation. He did, however, also add that Jabhat al-Nusra would soon begin campaigns 'to deter corruptors' within the insurgency in Aleppo and Idlib as well as arresting hostile FSA leaders in Deraa[49]—a sign of things to come. A week later, Jabhat al-Nusra's senior commander Abu Firas al-Suri, newly named as the group's official spokesman, clarified the emirate issue further in an official video release:

> Jabhat al-Nusra did not announce an emirate in the meaning of an independent emirate, or the meaning of a state, or anything meaning close to that. We mean the emirate should be established by consulting those who have an Islamist affiliation, whether from the jihadi factions or the local leaders of the country, or the people of influence and of course, with the scholars inside and outside the country.[50]

For now, as Abu Firas explained, Jabhat al-Nusra would seek only to introduce and implement *sharia* in areas where its 'Sharia Arbitration Charter' was in place and had been signed onto by local groups in the respective area. 'In Hama alone, 14 factions signed this agreement,' Abu Firas claimed.[51]

As Jabhat al-Nusra sought both to re-bolster its jihadist credentials and placate rising fears amongst its insurgent partners in Syria, IS re-launched operations against the Assad regime in mid-July, for the first time in many months. On 16 July a large force of IS militants bombarded and then stormed the al-Shaer gas field in Homs governorate, and had the entire facility under their control by the following day. At least 270 people—soldiers, security guards and civilian employees—were killed in the attack, as many as 200 of whom were reportedly executed. In capturing the facility, not only did IS succeed in putting out of action a major source of Syrian natural gas, but the group gained at least fifteen tanks and a large amount of other valuable weaponry. The scale of the attack and fatalities, as well as the speed with which it was overrun, was a shock to regime supporters.

A week later, on 24 July, IS militants launched seemingly coordinated attacks on multiple regime-controlled military facilities and positions in the governorates of Hasakah (the 121st Regiment and the city), Aleppo (Kweiris air base), Deir ez Zour (the military airport and the city), and Raqqa (17th Division, 93rd Brigade, and Tabqa air base). Within twenty-four hours IS militants had successfully captured the 17th Division base in Raqqa, and two days after that had taken control of the 121st Regiment in Hasakah. Such significant victories were not only of value for their role in weakening the regime's position in northern Syria; more importantly, they served to bolster IS's capacity to continue expanding its military power in Syria. Within the space of ten days IS had acquired huge amounts of heavy weaponry, which could (and would) be used to reinforce its front lines elsewhere in the country and to help secure further victories, against both rival insurgents and the regime. Just from its victory at the 121st Regiment, IS captured approximately a dozen 130-mm M-46 towed field guns capable of striking targets 27 kilometres away, as well as roughly 400–500 122-mm Grad rockets, several tanks, hundreds of rocket-propelled grenades, tens of thousands of rounds of small-arms ammunition, dozens of military vehicles and trucks, assault rifles, hand grenades, and several anti-tank guided missiles.[52]

IS had barely engaged regime forces in battle since mid-2013—a fact that had led some to suggest that Assad and IS were working hand-in-hand to divide and conquer the opposition. Considering the Assad regime's well-established history of 'flirting' with jihadist militancy and attempting to exploit it for use in attaining its own policy interests, this was in many respects perfectly true, although a more accurate description would have placed both parties as acting in each other's interests, rather than strictly 'hand in hand.' In fact, elements of Syria's security apparatus almost certainly did act in such a way as to facilitate the rise of IS at the expense of the more moderate insurgent opposition. However, IS and the Assad regime were diametrical opposites, and IS militants viewed the Assad regime and Alawites in general as tantamount to the devil. As such, the likelihood that the regime and IS directly worked together is too unlikely to imagine, and therefore the fact that IS relaunched operations against the regime in July 2014 was simply an indication that it found itself in a sufficiently more confident and strategically comfortable position to do so.

As Jabhat al-Nusra and IS increasingly sought to define or redefine themselves within the context of the conflict in Syria, the role of moderate FSA-linked factions, groups with more overt Islamic frames of reference, and even other small independent jihadist factions all fell off the radar temporarily. However, their role in the broader conflict continued apace throughout July, and included most notably more concerted offensive operations in Idlib; a successful anti-ISIS offensive in Mesraba in north-east Damascus; and sustained attacks on regime influence in Deraa, Quneitra and Aleppo.

One particularly notable aspect of this period was increased discussion within Islamist insurgent circles of the further need for unifying their factions inside larger coalitions or fronts. The Islamic Front's establishment in November 2013 had been a very significant development in this regard, but with two major international jihadist organisations assuming a more public profile, the intent—at this stage more in private that in public—was to design a far broader structure to represent what were deemed to be the most representative, legitimate and capable insurgent factions from across the country. One step made in this direction, albeit a relatively small one, took place on 26 July, when all Islamic Front factions active in Aleppo agreed to fully unify their command and leadership structures under Liwa al-Tawhid's leader, 'Abd al-Aziz al-Salameh. On a more jihadist line, Jaish al-Muhajireen wa'l Ansar, al-Katibat al-Khadraa, Harakat Sham al-Islam and Harakat Fajr al-Sham al-Islamiyya all united on 25 July to form a new coalition known as Jabhat Ansar al-Din. Although expressly an independent formation, Jabhat Ansar al-Din factions did remain ultimately supportive of Jabhat al-Nusra and al-Qaeda's jihadist project.

However, by far the most significant move towards insurgent unity came in the form of the Wa'tasimo Initiative, which was announced in Idlib on 3 August as a project that would aim to unite factions within a Revolutionary Command Council (RCC). The use of the term Wa'tasimo referred back to a Qur'anic phrase meaning to 'hold fast': 'and hold fast, all of you together, to the rope of Allah and be not divided among yourselves.'[53]

In principle, the RCC was formed on 3 August, but it was expressly announced as a body that would remain open to additional members and would not elect its leadership councils and structure for at least forty-five days. As such, it represented more of an invitation to join than the immediate establishment of a working organisation:

In the name of God, Most Beneficent, Most Merciful:

Praise be to God and Prayers be on the prophet of God, his family, his companions, and those loyal to him, etc.

In compliance with God's command to 'hold fast (wa'tasimo) by the rope of God together and be not disunited', a number of scholars and students of in Syria started the 'Wa'tasimo Initiative' with the goal of uniting the factions active in Syria. Thanks be to God, a large number of the leaders of the factions and fronts spread out over several Syrian provinces met and agreed to the following:

First: To form a council to lead the revolution in Syria called the Syrian Revolutionary Command Council (Majlis Qiyadat al-Thawra al-Suriyya) to be the united body for the Syrian revolution.

Second: the Council will choose its leader and form the bureaus under him, the military and judicial bureau chief among them, within 45 days.

Third: This Council is formed with the following fronts in mind—the northern front, the eastern front, the central front, the southern front, and the western front. All factions concerned with each front shall agree on their representatives to the council. The door will remain open for other factions that wish to join the Council.

Fourth: To form a follow-up committee from among those who began this initiative.[54]

The RCC announcement was made by eighteen insurgent factions in all, including the Western-backed Harakat Hazm, the SRF, the 13th Division, the 101st Division, Liwa Forsan al-Haq and others with more Islamist foundations, such as Jaish al-Mujahideen and the Islamic Front's Liwa al-Haq, Suqor al-Sham and Jaish al-Islam. The process of expansion (attracting additional members) and proceeding towards planned elections was led by several prominent Islamists widely respected on the ground inside Syria but who were not themselves directly involved in the armed insurgency. Most prominent among these coordinators was 'Abd al-Moneim Zeineddine and the well-connected Idlibi sheikh Hassan al-Dugheim.

While unity was the overriding focus of the initiative, the underlying objective was to establish a structure that would be capable of genuinely representing the insurgency and its affiliated civil and political wings across Syria to the international community. Even amongst explicitly Western-backed factions such as the SRF and Harakat Hazm, frustration with the perceived illegitimacy of the exiled ETILAF and interim government to represent the interests of those fighting and suffering on the ground had risen to unsustainably high levels. In the months to come, this frustration would prove a sufficient and necessary motivation for a large number of additional factions to join.

As July came to an end and August began, ISIS published two notable video releases. On 28 July, in a video marking the end of Ramadan and the festival of Eid al-Fitr, ISIS released a thirty-six-minute video entitled *Upon the Prophetic Methodology*, which contained, amongst other things, the recorded executions of dozens of Iraqi soldiers in a desert pit and into a river. Released by al-Furqan, not only did the video clearly and graphically demonstrate IS military power through battle scenes from the Iraqi cities of Samarra and Ramadi, but the sheer brutality revealed in the mass executions was a manifestly threatening image informing Iraqi and Syrian armed forces of what would befall them if they were captured by IS. Such intimidation and demonstrative violence was another critical tactic employed by IS to weaken its enemies before they were attacked.

The second video was published on 2 August and was totally different. Published by the al-Hayat Media Center and entitled *Eid Greetings from the Land of the Caliphate*, this twenty-minute video was a slick production aimed solely at presenting the apparently pleasant attraction of emigrating to join the Islamic State and its caliphate. Filmed in IS's capital, Raqqa, the video began with a sermon given at a mosque during which the entire congregation pledged *bay'a* en mass to IS and 'Caliph Baghdadi'. It then separately presented eight foreign fighters from different parts of the world expounding on the perceived benefits of moving to the caliphate. The first such fighter was Abu Abdullah al-Habashi, a British national of Ethiopian descent who had been born in the UK to a Christian family, before later converting to Islam.[55] His message to viewers was distinctly clear:

> Today is a very beautiful day ... there are festivities here, everyone is out, it's a good atmosphere ... you can really feel the Eid here in the land of khilafah. I don't think there's anything better than living in the land of khilafah ... the rights and you're not living under oppression.[56]

The next featured IS fighter was identified as 'Abu Shuaib al-Somali from Finland', who was in fact Hussein Faysal Ali, the son of a former Somali presidential candidate and founder and chairman of Somalia's For Justice and Development (UCID) political party, Faysal Ali Warabi.[57] His message was equally simple:

> All I can say is that we are living with blessings here and you should come to the Islamic State ... I'm calling on all the Muslims living in the West, America, Europe, and everywhere else to come with your families to the land of khilafah.[58]

This theme of complete positivity continued throughout the video, as smiling jihadists from around the world—others shown were a Tunisian, a

Moroccan, a Belgian, a South African, a Yemeni from Indonesia and a man from the Caribbean island of Trinidad and Tobago, who was identified as 'from America'—called upon Muslims to join their holy cause. This presentation of the IS caliphate as being not only a project that all Muslims were Islamically obligated to join but one that was worthy due to the superior quality of living and personal satisfaction it gave, was a theme that continued throughout the months that followed, and with profitable results.

Meanwhile, by early August Jabhat al-Nusra's senior leadership had undergone a significant change. Having held positions of authority within Jabhat al-Nusra since its emergence in January 2012, Saudi national Abu Layth al-Tabuki (better known as Sultan al-Atawi) had been a prominent face of the organisation in eastern Syria during the battle with ISIS. Even more prominent, and a founding member of Jabhat al-Nusra, Iraqi national Abu Mariya al-Qahtani had been the organisation's chief *sharia* official and thus effectively Jolani's number two since the conflict in Syria began. He had also been based in eastern Syria, especially out of the former stronghold of al-Shuheil, and was undoubtedly Jabhat al-Nusra's most senior official in the eastern region until it was lost to IS.

The fight against IS in Deir ez Zour had been an intensely messy one, which for Jabhat al-Nusra involved close coordination with explicitly moderate FSA factions and a complicated management of relations with tribes that were widely accused of corruption, particularly surrounding money earned from the production and sale of oil. The ideological and political complications, amongst other factors, have driven a wedge between sections of Jabhat al-Nusra's senior leadership. Al-Atawi accused Abu Mariya of squandering Jabhat al-Nusra's dominance in eastern Syria and, whilst doing so, of allying with secularists. Notwithstanding the fact that the dispute—which inflated after the loss of the governorate in July—became particularly personal,[59] al-Atawi had been thrown out of Jabhat al-Nusra by early August and Abu Mariya, who had by this time relocated to Deraa, had been demoted out of his 'number two' position and replaced by Jordanian Sami al-Oraydi.

A Jordanian cleric with a Ph.D. in Islamic Studies, Oraydi was a known figure within the Levantine jihadist community prior to joining Jabhat al-Nusra. His replacement of Abu Mariya represented several things. Firstly, Oraydi was an ideological hardliner whose views on intra-insurgent dyamics differed significantly from those of Abu Mariya, who had long advocated the management of positive relations with as broad a section of the insurgency in Syria as possible. The appointment of Oraydi as chief *sharia* official coincided with a general reversion of Jabhat al-Nusra's ideological mindset to one that was inherently suspicious and hostile to moderates as potential adversaries. It would also coincide with the strengthening behind the scenes of Jabhat al-Nusra's non-Syrian senior leadership figures, many of whom had arrived from Yemen, Afghanistan–Pakistan and Saudi Arabia only in the last twelve to eighteen months. It was this top-level shift that prompted Western intelligence agencies to initiate a security alert in July 2014 over the possibility that AQAP and Jabhat al-Nusra were working together to conceal explosives more effectively within shoes and inside mobile phones.[60] Oraydi's promotion also underlined the fact that Jabhat al-Nusra's southern front in Deraa and Quneitra had proven not only its influence but also a capacity to sustain itself amid trying circumstances. After all, it was only Jabhat al-Nusra's units in Deraa that had continued to function more overtly during the organisation's wider operational silence after Baghdadi's declaration of ISIS in April 2013.

This subtle evolution at Jabhat al-Nusra's senior levels, augmented by new discussions over emirates and *sharia* implementation, meant that core Western-backed FSA factions began to view Jabhat al-Nusra with increasing suspicion. Likewise, the continued arrival of American anti-tank missiles and the influx of other assistance and finance for the payment of FSA salaries meant that Jabhat al-Nusra increasingly regarded such factions as potential future threats. In Deraa this suspicion had already emerged, while in the northern governorate of Idlib, Jabhat al-Nusra was beginning to more overtly enforce its religious rule in a unilateral fashion, prompting tensions with the SRF in particular. On 23 July, for example, Jabhat al-Nusra unilaterally took control of the Idlib town of Harem after clashing with local SRF fighters. The unexplained assassination of a senior Jabhat al-Nusra commander, Sheikh Yacoub al-Omar, near the Idlib town of Maraat al-Numaan on 1 August may have been linked to such tensions.

Within this increasingly tense environment, paranoia and mutual suspicion was rife. Islamist insurgents who were neither the 'moderate' FSA nor Jabhat al-Nusra found themselves stuck in the middle of a heated campaign of intimidation and dangerous rumour. As one European foreign fighter told this author in late July:

> Some groups are getting more and more hard core ... Jabhat al-Nusra doesn't want fighters not ready to fight IS and the FSA doesn't want Islamists. It's become a dangerous game for those of us who want to stay neutral, for each group has a reason to hit you. Even playing an IS nasheed [Islamic vocal music] in some areas is enough to get you locked up, bones broken, even killed. Kidnappings, assassinations, people working undercover—it really is crazy.[61]

Further south in the Qalamoun, Jabhat al-Nusra and IS were continuing to maintain positive relations, despite the state of full-scale war elsewhere in Syria. On 2 August, near Lebanon's border town of Arsal, Lebanese armed forces captured a Syrian IS-linked commander known as Imad Juma'a (Abu Ahmad Juma'a), whose insurgent faction Liwa Fajr al-Islam had announced its pledge of allegiance to the caliphate in July. In his twenties, Juma'a had played a role in the insurgency since its inception, having fought in his home region of Homs under the banner of the large Kataib al-Farouq. After playing a role in the battle for al-Qusayr, Liwa Fajr al-Islam fled to the Syrian border village of Qara, to Wadi Zamrani and then into Lebanon and Arsal.[62]

Juma'a's arrest prompted local IS *emir* Abu Hassan al-Filistini to order an all-out assault on Arsal, which Jabhat al-Nusra subsequently joined. By the end of the day the town was under militant control and the Lebanese army's 85th Battalion base had been stormed.[63] Fighting continued over the following five days, interspersed by several short-lived ceasefires, until finally on 7 August a truce was agreed that saw the militants withdraw and the army assume full control on 9 August. All in all, the 'Battle of Arsal' left sixty militants, nineteen soldiers and fifteen civilians dead, and at least twenty Lebanese security force personnel in militant 'custody.'[64]

In addition to concretely underlining IS's apparent presence in Lebanon—although Juma'a pledge of *bay'a* was never confirmed as having been accepted by Baghdadi—events in Arsal in early August 2014 also served to fully draw Lebanon into the now regional IS crisis. Jihadists in the Qalamoun and in the Arsal area subsequently blamed the detention of Juma'a on intelligence provided by Hezbollah, which also further emboldened the broader anti-Shia rhetoric that was already feeding violence in Syria and in parts of Lebanon. The link, therefore, began to be made increasingly confidently by jihadists between the Lebanese army, Hezbollah and Iran, all of which they viewed with the same suspicion and hostility. Including the Lebanese army in the hostilities made Lebanese stability look all the more precarious. More than anything, however, the 'Battle for Arsal' revealed the uniquely cooperative relationship between Jabhat al-Nusra and local IS-affiliated factions in the Qalamoun–eastern Lebanon region. 'I think the struggles the *mujahidin* experienced in al-Qusayr and then Yabroud and also their humiliation in fleeing to Arsal created a close bond between the groups. The *fitna* in the rest of Syria just wasn't their priority,' claimed one Islamist fighter from Homs.[65]

Just as IS-linked militants were boldly revealing to the world their capacity to operate overtly on Lebanese territory, the organisation's fighters were continuing to make significant gains in Iraq. In early August IS militants captured the northern Iraqi town of Sinjar, mainly inhabited by the Yazidi religious minority, as well as Wana and Zumar, the huge Mosul Dam and the Ain al-Zalah oilfields. Hours after capturing Sinjar, IS militants set about demolishing religious shrines; the vast majority of the town's inhabitants had fled into the nearby Sinjar mountains.[66] By 7 August IS militants had launched an attack on the Iraqi Rabia border crossing with Syria's north-eastern Hasakah governorate in a clear attempt to link their northern areas of operation in Syria. This renewed militant momentum in northern Iraq then saw IS advance into the Christian town of Qaraqosh, the towns of Makhmur, Tilkaif and al-Kwair and to a checkpoint located only thirty minutes' drive from the Kurdish capital of Irbil.

With Iraq's Kurds now also seemingly in jeopardy, and with a US-led military assistance programme now under way to bolster the capabilities of the Kurdish Peshmerga, the US government and President Obama stepped in and announced on 7 August the initiation of 'two operations in Iraq—targeted airstrikes to protect our American personnel, and a humanitarian effort to help save thousands of Iraqi civilians who are trapped on a mountain without food and water and facing almost certain death'.[67] With humanitarian airdrops being conducted over Mount Sinjar to save Yazidis besieged by IS militants, US Navy F/A-18 Hornet jet fighters launched their first air strikes against IS targets in northern Iraq on 8 August.

The immediate reaction within IS circles was of immense excitement: 'It's on ...' said several Western IS fighters on social media, while others exclaimed that retaliatory attacks on Western soil would be imminent. One apparent IS supporter based in the USA posted a photograph on Twitter appearing to show their iPhone, bearing the IS flag, being held up in front of the White House in Washington DC. Other pro-IS individuals posted advice on how to avoid being targeted by air strikes and how to manufacture home-made 'spark gap jammers' to defend against drones.

Despite its total opposition to IS's caliphate and resulting split with al-Qaeda, AQAP's chief ideologue Ibrahim al-Rubaish even issued a statement on 13 August congratulating the group on its 'victories' in Iraq 'against the puppets of the Iranians'.[68] Other sources of al-Qaeda-linked propaganda online also began to express support for IS in its battle against the 'Crusaders', and the hashtag campaign #CalamityWillBefallUS gained traction amongst both al-Qaeda and IS supporters. Despite being in an effective state of war with IS, Al-Qaeda was now demonstrating that loyalty within and between the Sunni *Umma* bore considerably more value amid external attack than without it. Thus, another AQAP statement on 15 August, written after the initiation of US air strikes in Iraq, then unequivocally stated:

> We declare our solidarity with our Muslim brothers in Iraq. We call on all Islamist groups ... to go after America as part of its plan for jihad, militarily, economically, or through the media. And we call upon every Muslim, especially anyone who can enter America, to champion his brothers by going to war against America with everything he can ... We reaffirm to our Muslim nation that we stand in one trench with our Muslim brothers in Iraq against the American Crusader and Iranian conspiracy.[69]

Within this context, IS continued its advance on regime positions in northern Syria, capturing the vast 93rd Brigade base in Raqqa on 7 August and shortly thereafter launching an expanded offensive on the regime's last remaining military facility in that province, Tabqa Air Base. The threat that IS now appeared to pose to the regime's hold over parts of northern Syria as well as the detrimental effect these losses were having within Assad's support base in Latakia and Tartous meant that the Syrian air force then considerably increased the scale of air strikes targeting IS-held territory. Whereas few if any regime air strikes ordinarily struck IS towns, at least fifty-eight targeted IS across Raqqa governorate on 16–18 August, killing dozens of people, mostly civilians.[70]

As was the case in its capture of the al-Shaer gas field, the 17th Division and the 121st Regiment in July, IS militants seized a huge amount of weaponry at the 93rd Brigade, including most notably twenty tanks and five 122-mm D-30 howitzers. For IS, such heavy weaponry was of significant value for its use in bombarding large targets from a stand-off distance, thereby weakening them for an eventual ground assault led by suicide bombers. This strategy had been successfully tried and tested across Syria—and not only by IS—but with such an expanded array of heavy weaponry at its disposal, carrying out multiple such operations would become more feasible.

One such operation where these weapons were put to use was in north-eastern Aleppo, where IS launched a new push against opposition-held villages and towns en route to the border town of Azaz. On 13 August alone, IS captured five villages on this route, including the much-prophesied Dabiq, where a major battle would purportedly take place before the end of the world. IS's father figure Abu Musab al-Zarqawi once said that Dabiq would represent his organisation's first step before conquering 'Constantinople' and 'Rome'.[71]

By 16 August IS militants had captured another five villages in north-eastern Aleppo, and the symbolic town of Marea—the birthplace of Liwa al-Tawhid and its deceased leader 'Abd al-Qader Saleh—was under constant bombardment. Should that fall, the road would have been opened to Azaz 9 kilometres away and one of the opposition's two most critically important border crossings and sources of supplies via Turkey, at Bab al-Salameh, would have been under imminent threat. In response to this seemingly existential threat, Jabhat al-Nusra dispatched reinforcements from Idlib, and the anti-IS front in Aleppo, known as Naharawan al-Sham, kicked into overdrive to defend against the impending IS advance.

On 17 August IS also captured a Japanese man named Haruna Yukawa, whose Facebook page at the time identified him as the chief executive of a private security firm and which contained photographs of him armed with an AK-47 assault rifle, seemingly visiting Peshmerga personnel in northern Iraq. Yukawa would be brutally murdered by IS some months later.

While IS on 15 August announced the establishment of a new province within its 'Islamic state'—Wilayat al-Furat, stretching across the Syria–Iraq border between al-Bukamal and al-Qaim—its presence on social media was under attack. For three days in a row, on 11, 12 and 13 August, its entire network of provincial accounts on Twitter were deleted, only to be re-established the next morning. By 14 August, however, IS appeared to have withdrawn itself entirely from Twitter, with the exception of several hundred individual member accounts. Shortly thereafter IS reappeared on a privacy-focused independent social network known as Diaspora, but by 19 August its accounts had been deleted from there as well. Clearly, the organisation's continued advances in Iraq and its involvement now in a conflict that involved kinetic US military action meant that its ability to professionally and productively operate across social media had become unacceptable.

Whether Twitter and other similar networks were removing IS accounts of their own accord or as a result of requests from US government agencies, the effect was quite dramatic. The capacity for IS to present itself as a capable militant organisation feeding off its own operational momentum disappeared, all but for the front pages the world's media continued to provide it. Over time, and after a brief period on the Russian social network site VKontakte, IS would design a workaround system, whereby automatically generated accounts on platforms like Twitter would continue to simultaneously generate official content until they were individually removed, at which point more would be created and the cycle would repeat itself.

Social media or not however, newspaper front pages and television news headlines would continue to be dominated by developments relating to IS through the second half of August. On 16 August US aircraft began launching air strikes on IS targets at and in the proximity of the Mosul Dam as part of an expanded strategy aimed not only at containing IS advances but at supporting Kurdish counter-attacks. Within forty-eight hours Iraqi and Kurdish forces had successfully recaptured the dam and President Obama celebrated what he claimed was a 'major step forward' and a sign that having 'effective partners on the ground' would reduce the risk of US 'mission creep'.[72]

In response to the loss, IS's 'media office' in Wilayat Ninawa (headquartered in Mosul) issued an English-language statement on 'Confronting the American–Kurdish Alliance', which, among other things, stated:

After the recent blessed conquests ... the slaves of secularism and agents of the Freemasons appealed to their Crusader master, the Black of Washington, to save them from the assaults of the Knights of the Khilafah, who have become very close to conquering their capital (Irbil) ...

So the dog of the Romans thrusted his airforce into a new dilemma ... and it seems this submissive fool forgot or pretended to forget the quagmire of Iraq years ago, in which tens of thousands of Crusaders were annihilated ... not to mention the material losses and financial crises that nearly wiped the United States off the map ...

And regarding the attack carried out by the Kurdish–Crusader alliance, supported by the US Air Force for the last several days ... the mujahideen of the Islamic Khilafah were able to repel them from all sides; and forced the enemy to retreat ... after the enemy suffered heavy losses in lives and equipment; and there is no truth to what has been circulated by the satellite channels of lies and deception regarding the decline of the Islamic State ... apart from some simple tactical withdrawals that were carried out by the mujahideen troops to drag the enemy into elaborate ambushes ...[73]

However much IS attempted to deny that it had lost territory, there was little doubt that US air strikes had dented the group's momentum in northern Iraq and had provided the necessary strategic depth for the Peshmerga to start a gradual push-back. While it could now boast to being involved in a large-scale war with not only 'the Shia' (Maliki, Baghdad, Iran, Hezbollah etc.) and the Kurds but also the 'Crusader West' and reap all the recruitment and reputational benefits that that brought, it also had retaliation in mind.

On 19 August IS's response came in the form of an al-Furqan Media video entitled *A Message to America*, in which American hostage and journalist James Foley was revealed alive and then shockingly, beheaded. Foley had been kidnapped in northern Syria on 22 November 2012, and his whereabouts since that moment had not been publicly revealed. The video itself began with a clip of President Obama announcing the initiation of air strikes in Iraq, tagged with the line 'Obama authorises military operations against the Islamic State effectively placing America upon a slippery slope towards a new war front against Muslims'. Foley was then introduced on camera, dressed in an orange jumpsuit purposely similar to those used at Guantanamo Bay, kneeling before an IS militant dressed in all in black with a knife in his hand. Speaking in a distinctly British accent, the militant stated clearly:

> This is James Wright Foley, an American citizen of your country. Today your air force is attacking us daily in Iraq. Your strikes have caused casualties amongst Muslims. You are no longer fighting an insurgency. We are an Islamic army, and a state that has been accepted by a large number of Muslims worldwide.

While the moment of Foley's beheading was not included in the video, his decapitated body was shown after the fact, followed by a clip revealing another American hostage, 'Steven Joel Sotloff—the life of this American citizen, Obama, depends on your next decision,' the militant proclaimed.[74]

Although the location where the video was filmed was not revealed by IS, an assessment by video and photo analyst Eliot Higgins concluded that it was recorded in the hills south of Raqqa city. In fact, as was revealed only after his death, US special operations forces had launched a covert night-time raid early on 4 July acting on intelligence suggesting that American hostages were being held in a makeshift IS prison in the village of Akrishi outside Raqqa city. The operation, which involved several dozen special forces personnel, modified Black Hawk helicopters, fixed-wing aircraft and drones, raided the prison but found nobody inside, so an attack was launched on a nearby IS training facility known as 'Camp Bin Laden', which was reportedly burned down.[75]

IS's dramatic and grisly publication of James Foley's death sparked worldwide outrage and an intensified determination to build a multinational coalition to defeat the organisation. It may have also helped spur on Qatari-led negotiations for the release of another American journalist hostage, Peter Theo Curtis, whom Jabhat al-Nusra agreed to release on 24 August in Syria's southern Golan region bordering Israel. Curtis had been held hostage by Jabhat al-Nusra for twenty-two months, and his mother, Nancy, had been personally involved in the negotiations for his release, which at one point had involved her travelling to Istanbul to meet an al-Qaeda financier. All parties involved denied that any ransom had been paid to secure his release, although ransoms ranging from $3 million to $25 million were demanded during the negotiation process.[76]

IS was not a jihadist organisation that aimed to achieve worldwide support or acceptance. Instead, its actions sought only to sow chaos, hatred and division, which itself would then foster the conditions in which it can thrive. The fact that Saudi Arabia's Grand Mufti, Sheikh 'Abd al-Aziz Al al-Sheikh, labelled it the 'number one enemy of Islam' on 19 August would have mattered little to IS. In fact, that may well have been the kind of reaction it wanted. As Moazzam Begg explained, 'they see that the more non-Muslim and apostate regimes are gathering against them, the truer their path is. Their supporters often cite the saying attributed to Ali, "if you want to recognise in which direction the most righteous among the Muslims are, then see in which directions the arrows of the *kuffar* are going"'.[77]

Such self-confidence was only further boosted with statements such as one by the US defence secretary Chuck Hagel on 21 August saying that IS was 'as sophisticated and well-funded of any group we have seen ... they are beyond just a terrorist group. They marry ideology, a sophistication of ... military prowess. They are tremendously well funded. This is beyond anything we've seen ... They are an imminent threat to every interest we have, whether it's in Iraq or anywhere else.'[78] Placing IS on such a pedestal was a golden gift to the jihadist organisation, which seeks inherently to threaten the world and spark a revolution within the Westphalian modern state structure. The fact that IS retained a considerable number of additional foreign hostages in its prisons—including Haruna Yukawa—underlined the leverage they had over the international community at this point.

Five days after IS publicised the murder of James Foley around the world, the group's militants finally overran Tabqa Air Base in rural Raqqa after using aerial drones to conduct reconnaissance on regime defensive positions. By capturing the base, IS took full control of the entire governorate of Raqqa. At least 200 soldiers were captured fleeing from the base, and in scenes similar to those recorded in Tikrit, Tel Afar and elsewhere, they were executed en masse in the desert. IS claimed to have killed 250. Moreover, like its other recent victories in northern Syria, it made away from Tabqa with a huge amount of captured weaponry, including twenty-four 57-mm AZP S-60 anti-aircraft guns, several tanks, multiple anti-tank guided missiles, a vast quantity of ammunition and twenty-three MiG-21 fighter jets, all of which appeared to be inoperational or under maintenance. The base also contained a number of radar systems for use in monitoring the surrounding airspace, including a modern Chinese CETC JY-27 'WIDE MAT' long-range system.[79]

The fall of Tabqa to IS, coming after the group's capture of four other major military facilities in northern Syria in the space of four weeks, aroused an unusual level of public expression of concern within pro-regime circles. For example, in a statement issued on his public Facebook page, Duraid al-Assad, a cousin of Bashar al-Assad, issued a demand that the ministers of defence and information resign along with the chief of staff, the air force commander 'and whoever else is responsible for the fall of Tabqa military airport'.[80] Those demands were then 'liked' by over 1,000 people in four days. It came as little surprise therefore, that the Syrian foreign minister, Walid Muallem, announced on 25 August that 'Syria is ready for cooperation and coordination at the regional and international level to fight terrorism'.[81] While this was also of course an attempt by the regime to present a reasonable anti-terrorism face to the international community amid reports of a potential expansion of US strikes into Syria, it was also an internal attempt to reassure loyalists of the regime's determination to fight terrorism in a 'legitimate' manner.

As August began to draw to a close and activists in Raqqa city began to report possible sightings of American drones in the sky, IS continued its theme of retaliation by publishing another slickly produced video, entitled *A Message in Blood to the Leaders of the American–Kurdish Alliance*, this time showing the public beheading of a Peshmerga soldier—dressed in an orange jumpsuit—in central Mosul. Fourteen other captive Peshmerga personnel are revealed as those next to be killed if President Massoud Barzani did not cease his 'alliance' with the USA and its fight against IS. Later that day IS published a video showing graphic footage of the execution of the roughly 200 soldiers captured at Tabqa air base and a statement announcing the beheading of one of the Lebanese soldiers kidnapped from Arsal in early August. The drama such releases were causing around the world was beginning to rub off abroad, including in Egypt, where jihadist group Jama'at Ansar Bayt al-Maqdis recorded the beheading of four Egyptian men it accused of spying for Israel— the video of which was posted online on 28 August. The same group would pledge *bay'a* to IS and 'Caliph Ibrahim' on 10 November.

The four-month period of May to August 2014 had been an exceptionally dramatic one in terms of what had taken place in and in close proximity to Syria. ISIS had launched a spectacular offensive in Iraq, sparked a mass rebellion in that country, and declared itself the leader of a new caliphate. After being forced out of a good deal of its territory in north-western Syria in early 2014, IS had recovered in eastern Syria, built a capital in Raqqa and imposed several major defeats on regime forces in the north. Meanwhile, Jabhat al-Nusra had undergone a number of internal changes, especially within its senior leadership, and had begun to reveal a harsher and more self-assertive level of ideological fervour than it had done previously, which generated tension with moderate FSA factions but also encouraged a broader unification intiative spanning most of Syria's 'moderate' and Islamist insurgent factions. As had been the case since the first emergence of an armed insurgency in Syria in mid-2011, the dynamics were becoming more and more complex and actors on the extreme end of the spectrum were thus continuing to reap the benefits.

Meanwhile, there would be one more significant development in Syria in the last days of August. Beginning in the early morning of 28 August, a joint force of Jabhat al-Nusra and Ahrar al-Sham fighters launched a series of assaults on Syrian army positions on Quneitra's border with the Israeli-controlled Golan. Heavy fighting ensued for several hours, but by the end of the day Jabhat al-Nusra—which was the dominant force in the operation—had effectively captured control of several border posts on the Syrian side of the 'Purple' ceasefire line and taken forty-five Fijian UN Disengagement Observer Force (UNDOF) peacekeepers hostage. After surrounding two other UNDOF positions nearby, known simply as Position 68 and 69 and manned by a total of seventy-two Filipino peacekeeping personnel, Jabhat al-Nusra offered them safe passage on condition that they surrendered their weapons.

According to an exclusive account provided by Reuters, despite an alleged order from the Indian UN force commander, General Iqbal Singh Singha, to raise a white flag and abandon their positions and weapons to Jabhat al-Nusra, the Filipino personnel turned down the offer and began a tense standoff that lasted two days. As negotiations were launched between Jabhat al-Nusra and the UN, the latter met one condition laid out by the group, that it acknowledge that the forty-five Fijians had been removed to a safe location 'for their own protection' and had thus not been 'kidnapped'. Then, on 30 August, as Jabhat al-Nusra launched an assault on Position 68 (which was manned by forty of the seventy-two Filipinos), a unit of Irish UNDOF personnel hurtled to Position 69, where they successfully rescued the remaining thirty-two. Negotiations resumed again, and Jabhat al-Nusra imposed a total blockade on Position 68, backed up by as many as 200 fighters and 20 vehicles armed with heavy machine guns. However, in the night of 30–31 August, despite seemingly being trapped, the forty Filipinos cut their way through a section of barbed wire on their position's perimeter, walked across a minefield and crossed 2.3 kilometres into Israeli territory. In a subsequent statement, the Philippines' chief of staff, General Gregorio Pio Catapang, celebrated the incident as 'the greatest escape'.[82]

Qatar subsequently exploited its uniquely influential role in hostage negotiations with Jabhat al-Nusra in early September to secure the successful release of all forty-five Fijians on 11 September. Jabhat al-Nusra had taken the step of publicly issuing its demands days earlier, which included being removed from the international list of designated terrorist organisations, the provision of humanitarian assistance to Syrians in the long-besieged Damascus suburb region of Ghouta, and compensation for three of its fighters killed in the confrontation with UNDOF. So far as could be assessed, none of these conditions were met, although ransom payments (or compensation) are rarely done in public or acknowledged.

# 11

# THE ISLAMIC STATE

The Islamic State, or IS as it had named itself by mid-2014, had come a long way since its initial inception in Jordan and Afghanistan in 1999. Beginning as a small independent group predominantly consisting of Jordanians and Palestinians, IS militants have been involved in fighting jihad in Jordan, Afghanistan, Iraq and Syria, in addition to plots and affiliated operations in several other Middle East countries. Its fifteen-year evolution into a formidable terrorist organisation capable of acting as a light infantry force and capturing, consolidating and governing large expanses of territory is not a simple story, and although this book's focus is on Syria and much of IS's history has been in Iraq, it is worth telling.

The roots of IS trace back to 1999, when its well-known founder and patriarch Ahmed Fadl al-Nazal al-Khalayleh (better known as Abu Musab al-Zarqawi) was released from detention in Jordan's al-Sawwaqa prison, where he had been serving a fifteen-year sentence for membership of a terrorist organisation known as Bayat al-Imam. This group had been founded and led by Abu Mohammed al-Maqdisi and, while in prison, Maqdisi had acted as Zarqawi's mentor.[1] However, after his release from prison, Zarqawi parted ways with Maqdisi—who was also released in 1999—and travelled to Afghanistan, where with a note of *tazqiyya* from famed London-based jihadist ideologue Abu Qatada al-Filistini, he linked up with al-Qaeda's leadership and was granted a $200,000 loan to create a terrorist training facility in the province of Herat.[2] It was there, close to Afghanistan's western border with Iran, that Zarqawi established his first camp, constructed on a patch of land personally selected for him by Taliban leader Mullah Mohammed Omar.[3]

Having established his own camp and brought with him new connections made in prison in Jordan, Zarqawi sought to train up his own new militant faction, which he initially named Jund al-Sham, but within months was renamed Jama'at al-Tawhid wa'l Jihad (JTWJ). This group's cells back in Jordan were the first to gain Zarqawi and his JTWJ international attention when their extensive plot—subsequently named the 'Millenium Plot'—to carry out attacks on Amman's Radisson Hotel and several other popular Jordanian tourist sites was foiled by Jordan's General Intelligence Directorate in December 1999.

Not only had the attacks been prevented, but the attention the plot brought to the group, and to Zarqawi specifically, forced the JTWJ underground, and little was heard of them until the US-led invasion of Afghanistan in late 2001, which followed the 9/11 attacks in the USA. Zarqawi and his band of Jordanian and Palestinian followers in Afghanistan fought the invading forces, both independently and in coordination with al-Qaeda and the Taliban in Herat and later in Kandahar. However, with their defence of Afghanistan apparently of no avail and with al-Qaeda's senior leadership fleeing to Pakistan, Zarqawi fled west into Iran in December 2001, where they were accommodated and assisted by terrorist organisation Hizb-e-Islami Gulbuddin.[4]

At some point in 2002, Zarqawi and his followers travelled through Iran and entered northern Iraq, where they set up camp in the predominantly Kurdish north and established close contacts with another jihadist organisation, Ansar al-Islam. It was these connections to a jihadist organisation operating within Iraqi Kurdish territory that US intelligence assessments in 2002 claimed could have provided a link between Saddam Hussein and al-Qaeda. In a sense, the argument was that in an attempt to leverage and control dynamics in Kurdish territories—much as the Assad family had and would continue to do in Syria—Saddam would probably have sought to establish relationships with a group such as Ansar al-Islam and, in so doing, would have had some kind of a relationship with Abu Musab al-Zarqawi and his links to al-Qaeda.

Although such a circumlocutory argument had only minimal basis in fact, Ansar al-Islam was actively fighting and launching attacks on Kurdish militias in northern Iraq in 2002, and for Saddam, placing or acquiring an intelligence contact within its senior operational structure would undoubtedly have been of value. Indeed, in an interview with the BBC in July 2002, a twenty-year veteran Iraqi intelligence officer in the custody of Kurdish forces—identified as Abu Iman al-Baghdadi—claimed that senior Ansar al-Islam leader 'Abu Wail' was working for Iraqi intelligence.[5]

Despite being an avowed Baathist and not known himself for having any particular personal devotion to Islam, Saddam Hussein exploited Islamic conservatism as a strategic counterweight to the growing influence of the Muslim Brotherhood from the early-1990s. This was a process known at the time as *Al-Hamla al-Imaniya*, or the Faith Campaign. In addition to simply allowing more conservative Islamic practice, intelligence officers were also embedded covertly within mosques and instructed both to politicise the religious discourse produced within, and to make it more hardline.[6]

The long-term consequence of this Faith Campaign—which was for a time run by senior Saddam aide and future JRTN militant leader Izzat Ibrahim al-Douri—was that many of the Saddam regime's embedded intelligence assets 'became more loyal to Salafism than to Saddam.'[7] Moreover, conservative Islamism became a glue used to tie together intra-tribal bonds in Iraq's western Sunni heartlands in Ninawa and Anbar, the removal of which would have opened intensely violent ruptures with long-lasting consequences—as would be discovered by the US and its allies years later.

Putting forward the allegations regarding Ansar al-Islam most specifically and laying the case for the invasion of Iraq, then US Secretary of State Colin Powell told the UN Security Council in February 2003:

> Baghdad has an agent in the most senior levels of the radical organization, Ansar al-Islam, that controls this corner in Iraq. In 2000, this agent offered Al-Qaeda safe haven in the region. After we swept Al-Qaeda from Afghanistan, some of its members accepted this safe haven ... Iraqi officials deny accusations of ties with Al-Qaeda ... These denials are simply not credible.[8]

Nonetheless, no evidence was ever presented in public to substantiate the allegations, which Colin Powell—still in his position as secretary of state—appeared to refute, or at least partially retract, in January 2004, ten months after Iraq had been invaded:

> I have not seen smoking gun evidence, concrete evidence about the connection [between Saddam and al-Qaeda], but I do believe the connections existed.[9]

Notwithstanding that controversy, a JTWJ training camp—in the village of Biyara in the northern province of al-Sulaimaniyah—was targeted in the initial US-led air campaign in Iraq in March 2003,[10] thereby introducing Zarqawi into a conflict that would come to define him and his still fledgling and largely untested jihadist organisation.

As an insurgency began to develop in the early months of the invasion and occupation of Iraq, JTWJ was one of the first armed organisations to demonstrate its intent. It did this most notably in August 2003 with three highly significant attacks against targets that symbolised what would be its principal targeting strategy in the months and years to come. On 7 August JTWJ militants detonated a large car bomb—the first recorded of the insurgency in Iraq—parked outside the Jordanian embassy in Baghdad, killing seventeen people and wounding more than forty. Twelve days later a JTWJ suicide bomber detonated a huge truck bomb outside the week-old offices of the UN Assistance Mission in Iraq (UNAMI), killing at least twenty people and wounding over a hundred others. The explosion had specifically targeted a section of Baghdad's Canal Hotel housing the office of the UN's Special Representative in Iraq, Sergio Viera de Mello, who was killed in the attack along with seven members of the new UN Office for the Coordination of Humanitarian Affairs (UNOCHA) information office. Zarqawi later claimed that the attack had purposely targeted de Mello in retaliation for his involvement in awarding East Timor its status as an independent state in 2002.[11] The third of JTWJ's significant August 2003 attacks took place in the southern city of Najaf on 29 August, when at least one suicide car bomb struck the Shia Imam Ali Mosque, killing ninety-five people, including the spiritual leader of the Supreme Council of the Islamic Revolution in Iraq (SCIRI), Ayatollah Mohammed Baqir al-Hakim.

As such, JTWJ had laid out clearly its strategic intent and targeting strategy from the outset. The principal focuses of its ire were Zarqawi's traditional enemy, Jordan; the international community and its supporting establishments; and Shia Muslims, which the JTWJ's extremist ideology perceived to be the greatest threat to Sunni power in Iraq and the wider Middle East. Ultimately, Zarqawi intended his fight in Syria to present the JTWJ as the defender of Sunni honour and supremacy, and to show that only by ridding Iraq of foreign occupying forces and by triggering a civil conflict dominated by sectarian hostilities could Sunnis take power again. In Zarqawi's mind, that strategic end point would be represented by the establishment of an Islamic state that would take root in Iraq and expand across the Islamic world.

From its very beginnings in Iraq, therefore, IS's predecessor organisations were deeply sectarian, and while this was indeed part of a strategic calculation relating to the domestic Sunni–Shia dynamic, it was also a result of Zarqawi's own personal hatred of the Shia faith. He went as fas as to dispatch his second wife's father—who had fought with JTWJ in Afghanistan—to carry out the 29 August bombing in Najaf,[12] and his statements and personal writings were obsessively hostile to the Shia. Most symbolically, his final public address made before he was killed by US forces on 7 June 2006 included the following diatribe:

> The Muslims will have no victory or superiority over the aggressive infidels such as the Jews and the Christians until there is a total annihilation of those under them, such as the apostate agents headed by the rafida.[13]

Six years after Zarqawi's death, the ISI's operational strategy and modus operandi was very much still dominated by sectarian anti-Shia motivations. For example, as its official spokesman, Abu Mohammed al-Adnani exclaimed in an audio statement in mid-2012 that Zarqawi's hostility to the Shia remained the most reliable and authoritative account on the issue.[14]

Through 2004–6 the JTWJ demonstrated a consistent expansion of its fight against coalition forces in Iraq, with the group having evolved from a terrorist organisation whose activities were limited mostly to large urban bombings and rural IED attacks to a more organised insurgent force that was beginning to demonstrate a capacity to influence localised dynamics and control territory, albeit often below the surface. Zarqawi himself, meanwhile, had become an internationally notorious figure for his involvement in the kidnapping and beheading of foreign hostages, including Americans—the first case being Nicholas Berg in May 2004. The use of suicide bombers by the JTWJ also increased dramatically, which only added to its reputation as a particularly brutal terrorist organisation.

Although Zarqawi had intentionally not pledged allegiance to al-Qaeda and the Taliban during his time in Afghanistan, contact was established between JTWJ and al-Qaeda's central leadership in early 2004 in order to discuss the possibility of Zarqawi's faction becoming an affiliate of al-Qaeda. After eight months of drawn-out negotiations, and despite some remaining differences in strategy and outlook between Bin Laden, Zawahiri and Zarqawi, the latter announced his pledge of *bay'a* to al-Qaeda in September 2004, and from then on the JTWJ was renamed Tanzim Qaedat al-Jihad fi Bilad al-Rafidayn, or al-Qaeda in Mesopotamia—or simply al-Qaeda in Iraq (AQI).

Although now the leader of a fully-fledged al-Qaeda affiliate engaged in a direct conflict with the USA and its coalition allies, Zarqawi's relationship with the senior leadership in Afghanistan and Pakistan was strained. The tactics and sectarian strategy embraced by the JTWJ and now AQI was in many respects at odds with the modus operandi of al-Qaeda. The particularly brutal videos of beheadings and continuous reports of mass-casualty suicide bombings in public places filled with Iraqi civilians was an issue of serious concern for al-Qaeda. From Zarqawi's point of view, Iraqi society had been corrupted, and it was a necessary evil to cleanse it through a campaign of terrifying violence. Meanwhile, on the other side of the fence, al-Qaeda's senior leadership believed in combating the rule of regional governments deemed to be 'apostate', but in doing so the infliction of civilian casualties within Muslim populations was something to be avoided whenever possible so as not to harm the image of their jihadist project. This significant difference of opinion was famously revealed in a series of letters between senior al-Qaeda leaders Ayman al-Zawhiri and Jamal Ibrahim Ashtiwi al-Misrati (Atiya 'Abd al-Rahman al-Libi) and Zarqawi in 2005. Despite broaching the subject, the issue was never definitively solved, and AQI continued its brutal reign of terror in Iraq unabashedly.

Within the continually escalating conflict in Iraq, AQI's behaviour, its relationship with al-Qaeda and its proven position as the most powerful insurgent faction in the country meant that it began to attract the support of other smaller factions. After a series of secret meetings and a closer coordination of attacks between AQI and several other groups, AQI announced on 15 January 2006 that it had merged with five jihadist groups—Saraya al-Ghurabaa, Kataib al-Ahwal, Jaish al-Taifa al-Mansoura, Saraya Ansar al-Tawhid and Saraya al-Jihad al-Islami—to form the Majlis Shura al-Mujahideen (MSM) in Iraq. United under one umbrella, the MSM would, under Zarqawi's leadership, work towards taking more definitive control of territory in Iraq's Sunni heartlands and building the path towards the establishment of an Islamic state.

However, after having attained such a qualitative evolution along his intended strategic plan in Iraq, Zarqawi was killed along with his spiritual adviser, Sheikh 'Abd al-Rahman, in a US special operations force raid in Baqubah on 7 June 2006, placing into question the future prospects of AQI's position of prominence in the Iraqi insurgent theatre. While Zarqawi's death could well have proven a debilitating blow to its future in Iraq, it appeared to accelerate a further development within the organisation.

Five days after Zarqawi's death, AQI named its new *emir* as Abu Hamza al-Muhajir (Abu Ayyub al-Masri) and in October 2006, AQI was renamed *al-Dawla al-Islamiyya fi Iraq*, or the Islamic State in Iraq (ISI). In a video announcing the establishment of the ISI, the group claimed that its dominion and intended 'state' would encompass Iraq's existing provinces of Baghdad,

Anbar, Diyala, Kirkuk, Salah ad Din, Ninawa and parts of Babil and Wasit, and that its rule 'will judge according to *sharia*, using such as an aegis for the people and to defend the religion'.[15] The ISI formation statement named its leader as Hamid Dawud Mohammed Khalil al-Zawi, better known as Abu Omar al-Baghdadi, who was given the esteemed title of *emir al-mu'minin*— normally reserved for caliphs. Four weeks later, on 10 November, AQI's new leader Abu Hamza al-Muhajir announced his pledge of *bay'a* to the ISI and Abu Omar al-Baghdadi.

Taken in isolation, this series of events, coming so soon after Zarqawi's death, appeared to underline that AQI, the MSM and now the ISI enjoyed solid foundations that were not necessarily threatened by the sudden loss of senior leadership figures. However, it also masked a serious weakness that in the months and years to come would seriously threaten the ISI's continued existence.

Immediately prior to and during the establishment of the ISI, considerable tensions and occasionally hostilities had been arising between AQI, the MSM and several smaller Sunni insurgent factions active in Iraq, including the 1920 Revolution Brigade. In Anbar, Sunni tribes were increasingly aligning themselves publicly with the government in Baghdad in an attempt to rid their areas of ISI militancy, which was beginning to demonstrate overt rule over populations by extremist Islamic principles.

In one attempt to neutralise this emerging threat prior to the ISI's establishment, the MSM under Abu Hamza al-Muhajir had followed advice from al-Qaeda's senior leadership and had begun reaching out to Sunni tribes in an attempt to co-opt them into his group's cause. One such example of this tribal outreach was the creation of the Mutayibeen Coalition in Anbar, which the MSM said had brought together three groups of *mujahideen* and six tribal forces to defend their cause.[16] One named signatory to the new coalition was Jaish al-Fatahin, which immediately following the declaration issued a statement denying that it had entered into any official relationship with al-Qaeda: 'Perhaps it happened inadvertently, but we were not made aware of [this], neither directly nor indirectly.' In response, the MSM ridiculed the complaint by suggesting that Jaish al-Fatahin's internal structure was out of touch with developments:

> It seems that that Media Wing of Jaish al-Fatahin is not aware that four out of five of the former Jaish al-Fatahin brigades have recently sworn allegiance to the Mujahideen Shura Council in Iraq under the command of brother Abu Abdullah al-Iraqi. It was agreed at the time with the commander of the brigades ... to keep the groups under the name of the Jaish al-Fatahin.[17]

This very public disagreement between what the MSM and then the ISI were keen to present as their allies was symbolic of their falling out of favour with the wider Sunni resistance and tribally led Sunni communities in western Iraq. Although the ISI had evolved qualitatively by 2006 such that it represented an independently financially viable militant organisation capable of raising $70–200 million per year,[18] it was entirely unwilling to compromise its extremist ideological fervour, and where it had attempted to control territory and govern people, it had only engendered disaffection and ultimately opposition.

By early 2007 the ISI's unilateral control of areas of Sunni western Iraq—especially in Anbar—and its unrestrained imposition of particularly extremist interpretations of *sharia* law had sparked an armed tribal fightback. Tribal Sahwa (Awakening) councils were formed to actively combat the ISI's territorial control and, operating in tandem with American and Iraqi armed forces, the Sahwa militias—with their extensive local knowledge—proved effective counter-insurgent actors.[19]

Facing a newly emboldened adversary, the ISI struggled to retain control of territory, with the notable exception of its extensive influence in the northern city of Mosul. The fact that significant portions of Iraq's Sunni community and its tribal leadership had effectively declared war on it meant that the ISI began launching retaliatory attacks on its tribal and insurgent enemies—including Kataib Thowra al-Ashrayn, the Islamic Army in Iraq, Hamas al-Iraq, Jama'at Ansar al-Sunna and Jaish al-Mujahideen—and on other minority communities deemed opposed to its jihadist project. This was most notably demonstrated on 14 August 2007, when four ISI suicide bombers detonated car bombs in several Yazidi villages in northern Iraq, killing 800 people.[20]

Notwithstanding its retaliatory attacks, including the successful assassination of Sahwa leader Sheikh 'Abd al-Sattar al-Rishawi in Ramadi on 13 September 2007, the proliferating number and increasing capabilities of the ISI's enemies meant that it quickly ceded territory and sustained considerable manpower losses. In fact, the scale of its tactical defeats meant that the USA announced the lowering of its reward for information leading to the capture or death of Abu Hamza al-Muhajir from $1 million to $100,000 in May 2008, after having already reduced it from $5 million in 2007.[21]

Since its inception in Iraq in 2003 the ISI and its predecessor organisations had become heavily influenced by the role of foreign fighters from across the Middle East and further afield. The sustained and damaging pressure placed upon the ISI from 2007 meant that a great many of these *muhajireen* fled Iraq and returned home, leaving the ISI an increasingly Iraqi organisation. A conscious shift of the organisation's senior leadership and management to the city of Mosul, however, placed a considerable amount of responsibility in the hands of a non-Iraqi, Abu Qaswarah al-Maghribi, a Moroccan–Swedish national with previous experience fighting jihad in Afghanistan. It was his death in October 2008, however, that propelled a certain Syrian, Abu Mohammed al-Jolani, into the senior ranks of ISI leadership, as he assumed the role of *wali* of Ninawa province, and thus authority over Mosul.

By mid-2009 the ISI had incurred extremely significant losses, and had been forced underground to operate again as a typical terrorist organisation rather than an insurgent force. After another six months of intelligence-led targeted raids on suspected senior ISI leaders, US-led coalition forces had successfully killed or captured thirty-four members of the ISI's forty-two-person senior leadership structure.[22]

However, rather than following through on such gains, the process of US military withdrawal from Iraq from mid-2009 to August 2010 saw security responsibility transferred to local forces, which quickly diminished the potency of the Sahwa militias. Moreover, amid a marginal uptick in ISI attacks, a sudden slowdown in salary payments to these local militiamen began a dangerous process of Sahwa attrition, which the ISI took gradual advantage of.

From late 2008 and early 2009 the ISI had begun a process of internal structural devolution, whereby it began to adopt the organisational make-up and operational behaviours of a terrorist organisation. Mosul became the chief headquarters for ISI operations, partly as a result of the group's already extensive networks in the city, but also because the Arab–Kurdish dynamic in the north was something the ISI could exploit to sustain itself. And further south the ISI sought to intensify its pressure on tribal elements still loyal to the central government. This took the dual form of intimidation and attacks coupled with a concerted attempt to recruit from within Sahwa militias by offering consistent and higher salaries than those offered by the government. Thus, by mid-2010 the ISI was offering salaries larger than the $300 per month paid by Baghdad,[23] and the Sahwa councils had dwindled into little more than local tribal self-protection militias whose loyalty could as easily be bought as sold. Increasing repression of Sunni communities and the perception this created that a Shia-led government was acting aggressively in opposition to Sunni rights was another major theme of ISI recruitment and information campaigns at the time.

Therefore, as Sunnis became increasingly disenchanted with their government and began to turn inwards within their local communities, the ISI found pockets of territory in which it could recover from the 2006–9 awakening and US troop surge. With many of its senior leaders in prison, the ISI began launching sporadic attacks on detention centres and central prisons in an attempt to rebuild and re-energise its top-level structure. And at grassroots level, the ISI accelerated its recruitment from poor and disaffected urban Sunni suburbs and in the rural desert towns in which had first been born.

Despite its Islamic state project having effectively been defeated, the ISI continued to speak and act as if it was the organisation's central objective. In 2009 and 2010 several ISI statements were released claiming that its *emir al-mu'minin*, Abu Omar al-Baghdadi, was a member of the Quraysh tribe—from which, according to Islamic tradition, the next caliph would emerge—as if to lend its cause religious legitimacy. Despite Abu Omar being killed along with AQI's leader Abu Hamza al-Muhajir on 18 April 2010, his replacement as ISI *emir* was another alleged Qurayshi, Abu Bakr al-Baghdadi.

In Abu Omar al-Baghdadi's last months the ISI began to demonstrate signs of an operational recovery, with attacks increasing in urban areas of the country, especially in Baghdad. In the second half of 2009, for example, the ISI conducted some of the largest and most deadly attacks Iraq's capital had witnessed throughout the entire war and insurgency. A total of 382 people were killed in three attacks on 19 August, 25 October and 8 December, in which government ministries were the primary targets. Simultaneously, the ISI began to demonstrate its capacity to carry out multiple bombing raids in separate cities and provinces, which would appear to indicate a recovering cross-provincial command structure.

It was only in 2011, however, that the ISI really began to appear to be on the mend. Following the withdrawal of US forces from Iraq and the consequent release of militant prisoners from US-run military prisons, several dozen of the ISI's most senior leaders found themselves back on the 'battlefield.' By mid-2014, 19 of the group's 20 identified top leadership figures had all been released in that post-US withdrawal period. In a sense, the ISI set about launching its own surge in 2011, following the conclusion of the American one started several years earlier.[24]

By exploiting political frustrations sparked by the proliferation of protest amid the Arab Spring, it expanded both the frequency and scope of its attacks, including targeting southern Shia areas of Iraq and the Kurdish north, and dispatching a senior commander into Syria to establish an insurgent wing there: Jabhat al-Nusra. Spurred on by its recovery, and by increasing complaints within Iraq's Sunni community of government abuses and suppression of Sunni political demands, the ISI began conducting coordinated attacks involving bombings in multiple provinces of the country. For example, on 15 August 2011 ISI militants carried out twenty-two bomb attacks in Baghdad and twelve other separate locations. With such capabilities on show, the ISI had moved beyond a recovery stage and was now aiming to definitively damage central government control and to destroy morale within the security apparatus.

Between 2012 and 2014 the ISI carried out a methodical process of operational expansion, based primarily on two twelve-month plans designed to create the environment necessary for it to begin assuming control over territory again. These one-year plans—Breaking the Walls, between July 2012 and July 2013; and Soldier's Harvest, between July 2013 and July 2014—aimed to achieve a number of strategic objectives, including freeing imprisoned ISI members; eroding military capabilities and reputation; collecting intelligence on local community dynamics and the armed forces; and intimidating local security force personnel and diminishing their morale. For example, ISI militants increased the number of 'close-quarters assassinations' of security force personnel by 150 per cent between mid-2013 and mid-2014,[25] which, in addition to a concerted campaign of intimidation—incorporating direct threats to army and police officers' homes and mobile phones—catastrophically weakened the resolve and commitment within Iraq's security forces to wholeheartedly combat the ISI in their local areas. Thus by June 2014 the ISI was poised to launch the advances into Mosul and further south that prompted its declaration of a caliphate at the end of July.

By September 2014, therefore, IS had gone through a fifteen-year process of evolution, through which it had survived both facing off against the US invasion of Afghanistan and the might of the US military for seven years in Iraq. Its first 'Islamic state' project had undeniably failed in Iraq in the mid-2000s, and another partial attempt in northern Syria in 2013 had prompted a similarly successful localised fightback. As such, IS's third attempt to build a viable state across Syria and Iraq in 2014 needed to incorporate significant elements of operational learning if it was to stand a chance of being anything more than a temporary project.

By this point in time, having declared its restoration of the caliphate, IS was a tightly controlled, heavily bureaucratic and surprisingly methodical terrorist organisation. And it was still that, a terrorist organisation. Despite commanding approximately 25,000–30,000 fighters at the time, and claiming to govern an expanse of territory stretching across 670 kilometres of Syria and Iraq, it remained only an unusually advanced terrorist organisation, which had evolved sufficiently to be capable of operating at times like a light infantry force on the battlefield. Moreover, it had also developed a qualitatively superior model of governance as compared to the one developed and implemented in Iraq in the mid-2000s. While still particularly extreme, its marginally moderated style of localised rule found itself more durable due to the particularly horrendous instability within which it was operating.

Internally, IS was structured like a pyramid, with Abu Bakr al-Baghdadi at the top as *emir al-mu'minin*, and under him a 'right-hand man' (formerly Haji Bakr) and two deputies—one for Syria and one for Iraq. Below that stood an eight-to-ten-man cabinet of 'ministers', a row of *wali*s (governors) and a twelve-man military council. It did not call itself a 'state' for nothing—it genuinely saw itself as one, and designed its internal structure accordingly.

Following on from Abu Bakr al-Baghdadi's assumption of power in 2010 and the rise to prominence of his right-hand man Haji Bakr, IS underwent a process of 'Iraqi-isation', whereby senior leadership positions were dealt out mainly to Iraqis, many of whom had held officer-level experience in the former Baathist regime of Saddam Hussein, and all of whom had total loyalty to Baghdadi's leadership. This process of localisation and professionalisation lent IS superior capabilities on the battlefield, but, perhaps more importantly, it encouraged a more competent formulation and conduct of medium-to-long-term strategy.

Of course, it was not enough simply to perceive oneself as a 'state' or necessarily to try to act like one. Sustainable, independent and sufficient sources of income were a crucial asset in IS's toolkit. From 2004 and 2005, IS and its predecessor organisations had consciously sought out financial self-sufficiency in order to maintain operational independence and to shield itself from international counter-terrorist financial measures. Even during its time as an official al-Qaeda affiliate, AQI was earning so much money compared to its leadership circle in Afghanistan–Pakistan that Ayman al-Zawahiri asked for a loan from Zarqawi.[26] According to a US Department of Defense database containing seized AQI–ISI documents, the organisation relied on external financial contributions for no more than 5 per cent of its income between 2005 and 2010.[27] IS's consistent focus on developing and tapping internal sources of revenue since 2010, especially in the fields of extortion and tax, as well as in oil, gas, agriculture, kidnapping for ransom and activities on the black market would tend to suggest that this figure has remained extremely low.

By the late summer of 2014, IS's total income was estimated at between $1 and $3 million per month, which made it at the time the wealthiest terrorist or insurgent organisation in the world. It needed to be, however, as its sustainability depended entirely on its capacity to pay salaries to retain its fighting force; to fund its activities in localised governance across territory under its control; to buy tribal loyalties, especially in its peripheral areas of operation; and to fund its continued military and other operations.

With regards to governance, IS had thrown down its own gauntlet by proclaiming itself a state (and, indeed, a caliphate), as the sole determinant of its success and sustainability would be its capacity to govern and placate what were already highly restless populations. As Daveed Gartenstein-Ross and Amichai Magen have succinctly put it, 'jihadists are afflicted by a fundamental dilemma: they cannot attain their goals if they don't govern, yet the record shows them repeatedly failing at governance efforts.'[28]

Without a doubt, no matter how many lessons it may have learned from the past, IS's style of governance will always be too extreme to be accepted indefinitely. Realistically, it is only the socio-political chaos and conflict that it has worked so hard to engender and exacerbate that gives it an opportunity to at least temporarily fill the governance vacuum in Sunni areas of Syria and Iraq. The lack of a better alternative in either country sets the bar rather low for a viable substitute. IS has sought to fill these gaps with limited municipal services such as policing, judiciary, free education, facilities management, local infrastructure repair and management, as well as social outreach initiatives in the form of tribal engagement, Islamic *da'wa* and recruitment into the IS structure. Public transport services are often restored where they had previously been stopped, and new services are introduced. IS has also been known to operate consumer protection offices to inspect the quality of goods sold at local markets, as well as to operate soup kitchens for the poor and to provide healthcare and vaccinations for children.[29]

Considering the instability surrounding them, and the discernible capacity of IS to provide at least rudimentary services to civilians, it is unsurprising that some of those living under IS rule in north-eastern Aleppo in August 2014 described localised IS administration as 'fast and efficient', with 'everything coordinated [and all] parts of the administration are linked, [they] share information and in general seem good at working together.'[30] Others living in Raqqa described the situation there in early September thus: 'Let us be honest, they are doing massive institutional work. It is impressive.'[31] As a result of a lack of both resources and internal expertise, IS ordinarily leaves the management and operation of local factories, food production and other similar service businesses to their original owners and employees, but lends an additional layer of oversight to ensure what they perceive to be a more egalitarian supply chain and service to the local population. In this respect, IS is known to frequently fund the subsidising of staple food products and to place caps on residential rent prices. As but one example, it financed the reduction in bread prices in Deir ez Zour in July 2014 from 200 Syrian pounds to 45, and made it mandatory for all bakeries to provide a specified sum of *zakat* (charity) to the poor.[32] IS even established a free hospital in Mosul on 9 June, a day before its total capture, and ordered the reduction of all rent prices towards a ceiling of $85 per month.[33]

Taken in isolation, much of the above may present a surprisingly positive picture of life under IS rule. However, while the jihadist organisation has indeed made some attempts to provide services, IS governance is rather like a mafia boss who hands out small carrots from his left hand while waving a sledgehammer in his right. Moreover, IS ultimately aims to build a Sunni Islamic state, and consequently non-Sunni Muslims and people of other faiths living within its territories lack the benefits enjoyed by their Sunni neighbours—as demonstrated by the localised imposition of the *dhimmi* pact on Christians and Jews and the forced expulsion of members of other faiths deemed to be apostate or idolatrous.

IS law and order is extraordinarily tough, and became increasingly so after the initiation of Western intervention in Iraq in August 2014. Strict behavioural codes are introduced from the moment IS assumes control over an area, and these are enforced by a truly medieval list of punishments, including whipping, amputation, crucifixion, stoning and being thrown off the roof of tall buildings. In short, IS relies on injecting 'the fear of God' within its communities in order to retain the stability it needs to continue expanding.

Beyond the scale and sustainability of its income and spending capacity and the quality of its governance model, the most crucial determinant of IS's long-term durability is its military momentum and capacity to continue to advance or impose defeats on its enemies. Should it be forced into a state of immobility or placed on the back foot militarily, it will quickly lose the self-fulfilling sense of confidence that brings further recruitment and inspires existing foot-soldiers to continue offensive operations. IS is founded on the simple Arabic phrase *baqiya wa tatamadad*, which literally means 'lasting and expanding'—should this phrase no longer fit the organisation it belongs to, then IS's very identity would be placed into question.

One particularly important aspect of IS's militant identity that Abu Bakr al-Baghdadi and Haji Bakr invested in from 2010 onwards, and particularly since 2013, was ensuring that the group's fighters were sufficiently vetted and more intensively trained than under previous IS leaderships. According to interviews this author conducted with IS fighters between December 2013 and August 2014, all recruits are first required to obtain *tazqiyya* from an existing IS member prior to their arrival in Syria or Iraq. After arriving, recruits are brought to pre-arranged accommodation shared with other new members. As one British IS fighter, Abu Dujana, explained in January 2014:

> I had a contact in Syria who helped me cross illegally after I was rejected at the [Turkish] border crossing. When I crossed, I drove two hours through [ISIS] territory. Everything was tranquil and beautiful and it seemed life was continuing as normal. [When I arrived], I was mainly with Syrians, but there were also Saudis, Tunisians, a handful of Brits and French.[34]

After a series of interviews on arrival, during which personal information is logged, passports copied and financial donations accepted, new recruits have to undergo several weeks of religious and military instruction. Such training is normally focused on the use of pistols, assault rifles, rocket-propelled grenades, and sometimes mortars. Fundamental military tactics are also taught, incorporating tactics for use in defensive and offensive manoeuvres. Sometimes additional training is provided on more sophisticated weapons. Upon completion, new recruits are ordinarily placed on guard and frontline (*ribat*) duty before being entrusted with more operational and offensive operations.[35]

With better-trained fighters who are forced to undergo the more mundane experiences of guarding inactive frontlines and manning the backline trenches, IS military operations additionally depend on their recruits being particularly driven by an ideological pursuit for both strategic IS success and martyrdom. This blind aggression and a total lack of a fear of death explains the reputation that IS (and other jihadist) fighters often gain for 'inhuman' bravery on the battlefield, and quite often this can be enough to push the military balance in their favour, especially when an attack is fronted by one or more sacrificial suicide bombers.

In that respect, IS militants typically carry out three different categories of military armed operations, the first being attacks such as mass-casualty urban bombings. This first operational category is primarily used by IS to target minority communities and to underline a lack of security in major urban areas—Baghdad, for example—and can generally be termed terrorist operations. In both Syria and Iraq such operations are of value for their role in inflicting major infrastructural damage and in demonstrating the group's continued reach into the heart of its enemies' principal cities. Crucially for a group like IS that seeks to sustain chaos, these bombings also tend to encourage retaliatory attacks from armed representatives of the targeted sector of society. In Iraq, IS bombings in Shia areas of the country have played a key role in prompting the re-mobilisation of Shia militias, which themselves are equally prone to carrying out acts of violence according to a sectarian targeting strategy. By encouraging a state of tit-for-tat violence, IS ensures that central governments are immediately placed at a disadvantage in de-escalating conflict dynamics, especially in traditional Middle Eastern societies where *qisas*, or the 'eye for an eye' custom is often practised. Even in unfavourable operating environments, or in a context where IS was placed on the back foot on actual open conflict frontlines, these terroristic bomb attacks would be comparatively easy to sustain.

The second category of IS operations are focused on carrying out a campaign of attritional attacks that target security force personnel and their various support structures in order to reduce their capabilities and diminish their confidence and morale. Sustaining operations in this category requires a substantial force of fighters and a constant flow of operational intelligence. For many militant and insurgent groups, these operations would remain largely limited to targeting security checkpoints, police and military patrols and small localised security facilities, but IS's methodical infiltration of urban societies in Iraq in particular meant that through 2012–14, the scope of targeting in this category was more expansive. For example, IS was well known in Sunni regions of Iraq to have acquired such significant sources of intelligence that it could target individual army and police officers in their homes, and would send others threatening messages on their personal mobile phones. This intensive campaign of intimidation was of immense value in preparing the ground for IS's rapid advances across Iraq in July and August 2014, as fear often pre-empted actual attacks and led to entire military bases (such as COB Speicher, for example) fleeing before IS militants even arrived.

The third category of IS operations is those that involve full-scale sieges and assaults on major military facilities and well-defended municipalities. In northern Syria, IS's series of victories at the al-Shaer gas field, the 17th Division, the 121st Regiment, the 93rd Brigade and then Tabqa Air Base in July and August 2014 demonstrated this clearly. Whereas the first category requires 'terrorists' and the second requires 'insurgents', this third category needs IS to deploy its militants more like members of a light infantry force operating along organised lines, on multiple axes and backed up by rearguard artillery fire, tanks and other heavy weaponry.

IS assaults within this category, however, differ in two ways from those of an orthodox infantry force in that IS launches its final ground assault with several suicide car bombings that aim to penetrate hardened defences. Secondly, the ground assaults themselves are ordinarily done at a fast pace, led first by 'technicals' (pick-up trucks loaded with heavy machine guns), tanks and armoured vehicles, and then dozens or hundreds of fighters on foot. In this respect, IS large-scale assaults bear some similarity to the traditional Bedouin *ghazwa* (raid) or the well-known military tactics of the first four Sunni caliphs—Abu Bakr, Umar, Uthman and Ali—who used 'horses and camels in lightning raids against their enemies'.[36] That these attacks are also typically carried out along multiple axes makes them something particularly hard to defend against. IS's capture of Jalula in Iraq on 11 August is a representative example in this respect, as it involved the initial use of two large suicide truck bombings, followed by twelve separate suicide bombers on foot, all of whom targeted separate checkpoints, thus opening the route for the final ground assault that took the town.[37]

From a broader perspective, and looking beyond military specifics, IS acts so as to exploit its environment in order to dominate local dynamics. Where there is a potential to tacitly cooperate with other militant factions, it will do so, but only in its specific self-interest. In a conflict theatre where it does not trust the motivations or objectives of other armed actors, it will aggressively act unilaterally, again in its own self-interest. The differing dynamics in Syria and Iraq plainly demonstrated this strategic calculus, as IS pragmatically coordinated its advances in Iraq in July and August 2014 with more moderate Islamist factions, and even with nationalist Baathists, but in Syria it emerged as an almost entirely independent actor from the time of its arrival on the scene in mid-2013. Where IS does cooperate with other actors, there are no guarantees that this will continue once it has achieved its stated objectives, and where it operates in direct opposition to other armed actors, its intrinsically hostile defence of its interests means that dynamic is unlikely to reverse unless they are forced to submit to IS dominance.

More than perhaps any other jihadist organisation in modern history, IS and its antecedents have demonstrated a remarkable durability in trying circumstances. This is the principal danger they pose: they thrive amidst chaos, they seek it out, and they have become adept at surviving under immense pressure so as to fight another day. While structurally IS will always be a terrorist organisation, it has developed a set of objectives and operational strategies that make it also much more than that. While it is indeed fundamentally driven by an extremist Islamic mindset, it is also an organisation that relates to a very specific identity—that of the disaffected who yearn for a concrete identity to protect them against the complicated and often hostile world.

IS's recovery in Iraq and subsequent dramatic expansion into Syria and into Mosul, Anbar and beyond has revealed the real threat that political instability and state collapse represents. Above all, IS would not have succeeded in the way it has had the Iraqi government of Nouri al-Maliki proven more receptive and representative of Sunni concerns and if the dictatorial regime of Bashar al-Assad had been dealt with more definitively earlier in the revolution. By taking advantage of and magnifying these failures—both local and international—IS has provided itself with environments ripe for exploitation.

As a jihadist organisation, IS also threw down the gauntlet to al-Qaeda in July and August 2014 by declaring a caliphate and demanding global pledges of allegiance. Only time would tell if its challenge would prove to be a successful one.

# 12

# SEPTEMBER–DECEMBER 2014

## STRIKES AND DIVISIONS

While in the process of building what was in effect a proto-state, IS's threat of further executions in retaliation for US-led strikes in Iraq was carried out on 2 September, when American hostage Steven Sotloff was executed. In the ten weeks that followed three more hostages were killed—two British and one more American.

Shortly after most of Ahrar al-Sham senior leadership were killed in a mysterious explosion during a secret meeting in Idlib on 9 September, Jabhat al-Nusra launched another self-declared 'anti-corruption' drive targeting moderate insurgent factions linked to the SRF in Idlib. Meanwhile, spurred on by the reality of facing its 'Crusader' enemies in Iraq's skies, IS launched a major offensive on the strategic Kurdish border town of Kobane in northern Syria. Days later, and following earlier reports of American drones flying above Raqqa, US aircraft launched air strikes against IS positions in Kobane and elsewhere in Syria's north and east. Strikes also targeted a wing of Jabhat al-Nusra allegedly involved in planning foreign terrorist operations.

After its call for lone-wolf attacks in West and amid continuing strikes against it in Iraq and Syria, IS's international pre-eminence sparked a massive increase in foreign fighter flow, reaching as many as 1,000 per month in October. Though on a smaller scale than IS, Jabhat al-Nusra was still attracting recruits, and its comparative popularity within much of the Syrian insurgency meant that strikes against it were widely condemned by Syrian opposition groups and their leaders. Consequently, Jabhat al-Nusra sought to exploit this to its advantage, by presenting the strikes as detrimental to the revolution and by portraying its role as of inherent value.

After a series of significant IS military victories against the regime that resulted in the deaths of hundreds of Syrian soldiers, the regime's support base grew frustrated. Damascus introduced strict controls on conscription and severely restricted male travel. Iran, Hezbollah, foreign Shia militias and the ultra-loyalist NDF subsequently assumed a heightened importance.

Kobane quickly became the core focus of US-led strikes against IS and, through October, weapons were dropped to YPG fighters in the city and Iraqi Peshmerga personnel were driven in via Turkey. Meanwhile, in late October Jabhat al-Nusra effectively defeated the SRF in its Idlib stronghold in Jebel al-Zawiyeh, while further Nusra 'anti-corruption' drives took place elsewhere in Syria in November.

Despite Nusra's increasingly aggressive posture, Syrian Islamists continued their cooperation with the group, and were themselves growing into dominant actors in their own right. As November came to a close, the Revolutionary Command Council was formed by seventy-two Syrian insurgent factions, many with an Islamist foundation. Aleppo's mainly Islamist armed opposition also united in late December.

As 2014 came to an end, the conflict in Syria was at an intense level nationwide. Islamists played a key role in capturing key targets in the north and south in December, while Jabhat al-Nusra began consolidating its powerful position in Idlib. IS, meanwhile, was holding out in Kobane and covertly infiltrating further into Syria's interior and south. Lastly, IS's capture of a Jordanian jet pilot in Raqqa on 24 December provided it with another source of dangerous leverage over the world's attention.

\* \* \*

With IS having declared a caliphate, and with its proto 'state' fast becoming a practical reality, international pressure was quickly building in support of countering its base in Syria. The shocking video of James Foley's execution on 19 August and the explicit threat that another American hostage would be killed if air strikes did not stop had demonstrated the extent to which US-led military intervention in Iraq had thus far failed to deter IS, but had instead provoked it to retaliation. It was well known that the majority of IS's foreign hostages were being held in Syria, and it was there that the organisation's long-term durability looked most secure—it had proven itself a militarily superior force, had consolidated control over significant portions of territory and was acting independently, without having to depend upon or worry about tacit allies, as in Iraq.

Most symbolically, IS had also established its capital in the Syrian city of Raqqa, where in early September it had begun implementing a new education curriculum in time for the start of the school year. According to its official directorate announcing the education changes, this involved the total abolition of 'music, nationalist education, social studies, history, art, sport, philosophy, social and psychology studies, and Islam–Christian religious education'.[1] In 'correcting' the style and substance of the schooling system, IS aimed to instil in children the mindsets that would make them the next generation of jihadists that would secure the future of their state.

This transmission of IS's thought was not only a 'local' phenomenon, however. Foreign recruits continued to stream into Syria at an exponential rate. According to UK intelligence officials, at least twenty British nationals were travelling into Syria to join jihadist groups every month by September 2014.[2] Pro-IS graffiti had begun to emerge in areas of Saudi Arabia, where supporters of the group were painting *baqiya wa tatamadad* on local police stations and other government-owned buildings in the middle of the night.[3]

Perhaps most significantly, IS's actions in Syria and Iraq and its proclamation of the caliphate had attracted several early pledges of *bay'a* around the world, albeit from small jihadist factions. Amongst these early proclamations were the Bangsamoro Islamic Freedom Fighters in the Philippines;[4] a splinter faction of the Filipino Abu Sayyaf Group led by Isnilon Hapilon;[5] and the Indonesia-based and imprisoned former leader of Jama'a Islamiyya, Abu Bakr al-Bashir.[6] Statements of support had also been issued by prominent AQAP-linked figure Mamoun Hatem[7] and another Pakistani Taliban splinter group, Jamaat-e-Ansar,[8] while a new Algerian militant group known as Jund al-Khilafah would emerge on 14 September and pledge allegiance to IS, before kidnapping and beheading a French man between 21 and 24 September. Meanwhile, Nigeria-based Boko Haram, Egypt-based Jama'at Ansar Bayt al-Maqdis, and several Libya-based factions including Majlis Shabab al-Islam and Ansar al-Sharia Libya were also revealing potential indications of support for IS and 'Caliph Ibrahim'.

Nonetheless, as air strikes in Iraq were beginning to bite and IS momentum was consequently slowing, the group shifted its focus back to Syria. On 2 September IS released its *Second Message to America*, a two-and-a-half minute video showing the beheading of American–Israeli journalist Steven Sotloff, the second foreign hostage to be so publicly executed in two weeks. Notably, Sotloff's killer appeared to be the same British IS militant—by now nicknamed 'Jihadi John' and later identified as Kuwait-born London resident Mohammed Emwazi[9]—who had featured in James Foley's murder. In this video, his message was again clear, depicting his actions as retaliatory consequences for coalition bombings in Iraq:

> I'm back, Obama, and I'm back because your arrogant foreign policy towards the Islamic State, because of your insistence on continuing your bombings and in

Amerli, Zumar and the Mosul Dam, despite our serious warnings ... So just as your missiles continue to strike our people, our knife will continue to strike the necks of your people.[10]

As in the previous video of 19 August, another hostage was revealed as next in line should air strikes continue to target IS. This time, the potential victim was a British national, David Cawthorne Haines. A veteran aid worker with experience in former Yugoslavia and across Africa and the Middle East, Haines had been kidnapped in Idlib in March 2013 while working for the Agency for Technical Cooperation and Development (ACTED). The failed US rescue mission in July, it was later revealed, had aimed to rescue Haines along with Foley, Sotloff and others.[11]

These barbaric murders, filmed in such a simple yet theatrically shocking manner, served to dramatically intensify the situation. Clearly, combating IS's gains in Iraq was not going to defeat the group and in the immediate term; it had sparked a type of retaliation that rendered much of the international community powerless. There was clearly no interest in abiding by IS's demands to cease strikes in Iraq, and as such, the lives of David Haines and any other foreign hostages in IS custody were in real peril. They were caught up in a battle of wills between an apocalyptic jihadist organisation convinced the end of the world was coming and a coalition of international states that sought at the very least to contain the growing jihadist threat emanating from Iraq and Syria.

Syria however, posed a far more complex challenge when compared to Iraq, not least due to the role of Iran. Within the Iraqi context, Iran had also intervened in defence of the central government in Baghdad and in opposition to the IS-led jihadist advance. In so doing, Iran was generally acting in order to achieve the same results as the USA; but in Syria it was decisively working for the Assad regime's survival while the USA and its allies hoped for its demise. Consequently, any US intervention in Syria risked drawing the ire of Tehran, whose potential to play spoiler had been well demonstrated during the occupation of Iraq and whose continuation in multi-lateral talks on its nuclear programme was dependent only on its continued willingness to engage.

Despite the complications of launching air-based intervention in Syria, the decision was made in Washington that action needed to be taken. Beginning in early September, anti-IS activists began reporting, photographing and filming what determinedly appeared to be American MQ-1 Predator drones flying above Raqqa. A less verifiable claim had been made by an IS militant in the Aleppo town of al-Bab on 31 August, though he shared no visual evidence to back up his claim. Nonetheless, it appeared that preparations were probably being made for an expansion of US strikes into Syria.

Meanwhile, the intensifying situation and likelihood that strikes would reach Syrian territory, not to mention IS's increasingly brutal behaviour inside Syria—where public floggings, crucifixions and beheadings were becoming a near-daily affair—meant that reports of IS defections were beginning to emerge. Even the Syrian military, which had largely left IS to expand and fester in Syria's north and east, had begun to fight back. In thirty-six hours of air strikes on 6 and 7 September, for example, the Syrian military pummelled the city of Raqqa and areas of Deir ez Zour. However, IS had begun to go underground amid threats of US strikes and the Syrian air force's 'dumb' (unguided) bombs had a terrible habit of indiscriminately killing civilians. One strike hit a bakery in Raqqa on 6 September and killed forty-one civilians, while another strike in Deir ez Zour killed nineteen civilians in a market. Anti-IS protests, although very small, were beginning to re-emerge, and in Deir ez Zour a small covert anti-IS faction known as the White Shroud and led by a man known as 'Abu Aboud' had begun carrying out hit-and-run and assassination attacks around the town of al-Bukamal.[12]

Perhaps most notably during this period of rising pressure, one British IS fighter claiming to speak on behalf of a group of thirty told the ICSR in London in early September that they hoped to return home and enrol in deradicalisation programmes in order to avoid prison:

> We came to fight the regime and instead we are involved in gang warfare. It's not what we came for but if we go back, we will go to jail ... Right now, we are being forced to fight—what option do we have?[13]

IS media nonetheless continued to present an image of dominance and brutal power. On 7 September a lengthy video was released showing the group's final assault on Tabqa Air Base in which IS fighters were shown firing automatic weapons at hundreds of Syrian soldiers fleeing the base over open territory. At the end of the video several hundred of these soldiers were shown being marched through the Raqqa desert to a clearing, where they were all shot dead at point-blank range.

It was within this environment that President Obama gave a thirteen-minute speech at the White House on 10 September in which he announced for the first time that US policy would be to target IS militants 'wherever they are', including 'in Syria, as well as in Iraq'.[14] In addition to including Syrian targets within its scope, Obama also announced that strikes would broaden to seek out IS's 'leadership, logistical and operational capability' and would aim to 'deny it sanctuary and resources to plan, prepare and execute attacks'. A further deployment of 475 American military advisers would additionally be sent to Iraq, thereby bringing to 1,600 the number of US military personnel in the country. As well as announcing the newly expanded scale and scope of American intervention against IS, Obama was particularly assertive in his description of the group's depravity:

> Now let's make two things clear: ISIL is not 'Islamic'. No religion condones the killing of innocents, and the vast majority of ISIL's victims have been Muslims. And ISIL is certainly not a state ... It is recognized by no government, nor the people it subjugates. ISIL is a terrorist organization, pure and simple.
>
> ... These terrorists are unique in their brutality. They execute captured prisoners. They kill children. They enslave, rape, and force women into marriage. They threatened a religious minority with genocide...
>
> If left unchecked, these terrorists could pose a growing threat beyond [the Middle East]—including to the United States ... Our objective is clear: we will degrade and ultimately destroy ISIL through a comprehensive and sustained counter-terrorism strategy.[15]

The following day Obama's secretary of state, John Kerry, convened talks in the Saudi city of Jeddah bringing together the region's Arab states and Turkey to discuss the growing multinational campaign against IS. The talks were a remarkable success, and by their end Kerry had won the support of ten Arab states—Egypt, Iraq, Jordan, Lebanon, Kuwait, Bahrain, Oman, Qatar, Saudi Arabia and the UAE—for a coalition to fight the jihadist group across Iraq and Syria. 'The participating states agreed to do their share in the comprehensive fight against ISIL, including ... as appropriate, joining in the many aspects of a coordinated military campaign against ISIL,' Kerry announced after the talks.[16]

This growing international coalition may have laid down the gauntlet for IS—which began evacuating its facilities across Syria—but it also aroused significant concerns within Syria's moderate opposition circles. While the ETILAF announced that it would support the USA and its allies carrying out anti-IS operations in Syria, statements were issued demanding that this be done in concert with FSA factions on the ground and with an expanded 'train and equip' programme to bolster their capabilities. The Syrian Muslim Brotherhood, meanwhile, which was an integral part of the melting-pot that was the Syrian opposition, proclaimed its opposition to any international strikes in Syria 'unless the first bullet is directed at Assad's head'.[17] Unsurprisingly, Iran and Russia expressed opposition to unilateral military actions being conducted in Syria, while Syrian minister Ali Haidar insisted that 'any action of any type without the approval of the Syrian government is an aggression against Syria'.[18]

Within this intensifying international dynamic, the conflict in Syria was continuing unabated. In Hama, Jabhat al-Nusra, Jund al-Aqsa and several other Islamic Front and FSA factions were engaged in multiple offensive operations, including in Halfaya and Mahrada north-west of the city and around Hama military airport, to the city's south-west. Fighters involved in the operations claimed that Jabhat al-Nusra leader Jolani was personally leading the operations around Mahrada and had given a rousing speech on 2 September before four major checkpoints were captured.

Further south, the regime was continuing its siege of opposition-controlled districts on Damascus's outskirts, including Jobar, where at least forty air strikes were carried out on 2–3 September in apparent retaliation for a 'tunnel bomb'—a tunnel filled with explosives and detonated under a strategic target—that Jaish al-Islam had used to destroy a building used for housing pro-regime militiamen on 1 September.

Following on from the UNDOF hostage crisis and also heightening tensions between the Syrian and Israeli armed forces, insurgents launched yet another offensive in Quneitra on 4 September, aiming to secure control of more territory in the countryside outside the town of Quneitra. Jabhat al-Nusra, Harakat al-Muthanna al-Islamiyya, and a coalition of FSA factions aligned with the Southern Front and SRF comprised the major players involved. Within twenty-four hours the village of Mashara and the Majduliya hospital had been captured, the latter having been a significant army position in the area. By 9 September the 90th Brigade base had also been captured, along with at least four other villages. Ultimately, this left the insurgency in control of approximately 70 per cent of Quneitra governorate.

In Aleppo, the threat of a continued IS advance west and north from its stronghold towns of al-Bab, Manbij and Jarablus encouraged the formation of a highly unusual alliance between the Kurdish YPG, six FSA factions and the Islamic Front's Liwa al-Tawhid. Announced formally on 10 September, the Burkan al-Furat (Euphrates Volcano coalition) aimed to fight back against IS in Aleppo and also in rural Raqqa. Considering the widespread distrust of the YPG within opposition circles in Aleppo, the formation of such an alliance underlined the significance of the threat the various factions deemed to be posed by IS.

On 9 September Ahrar al-Sham was dealt a potentially crippling blow, when a large portion of its senior leadership was killed in an explosion in Idlib. That day a major meeting was convened involving a majority of Ahrar al-Sham's leaders to dicuss the organisation's political positioning. After initially excluding itself from the grouping of eighteen factions that announced the establishment of the RCC and the Wa'tasimo Initiative on 3 August, Ahrar al-Sham had signed onto the project on 21 August. In addition to its publication of the controversial Revolutionary Covenant on 17 May, Ahrar al-Sham was steadily undergoing a significant process of political moderation, whereby its political bureau—led by Ahrar al-Sham leader Hassan Abboud, with Mohebedeen al-Shami as his deputy—were implementing moves aimed at better integrating with broader multi-group structures 'on the ground'.

The meeting was held in the basement of a former agricultural research centre in the village of Ram Hamdan and, some time after beginning, an explosion shook the building, filling the basement with thick smoke. Disoriented and unable to escape, at least twenty-four senior Ahrar al-Sham figures died—not of injuries sustained in the explosion but of smoke inhalation and suffocation. Images of their bodies subsequently revealed no obvious injuries, apart from being covered in soot. Included within the list of those killed was Hassan Abboud and his deputy Mohebedeen al-Shami, Ahrar al-Sham *sharia* chief Abu 'Abd al-Malik, deputy *sharia* chief Abu Yazan al-Shami, and several leading military commanders, including Abu Talha al-Makhzumi, Abu Ayman Ram Hamdan and Abu Hamza. The incident sent shock waves throughout Syria, with questions being raised as to what had been responsible for the explosion. Some reports claimed that a suicide bomber had been behind it, while others attributed the deaths to a chemical attack. The official Ahrar al-Sham and Islamic Front line at the time, however, was that the building had been struck by a car bomb. As time passed, rumours would also spread that a foreign power—either Iran or the USA—may have been responsible, as both had an interest in destroying what still was Syria's most powerful insurgent group. By mid-2015, hardline elements within Jabhat al-Nusra—or Al-Qaeda—had also become suspects, as they opposed Ahrar al-Sham's considered political moderation.

A key question also raised as the dust settled was what impact this would have upon what remained of Ahrar al-Sham. The next morning the organisation appointed its new leader, Hashem al-Sheikh (Abu Jaber), his deputy, Mohannad al-Misri (Abu Yahya al-Ghab) and a new military chief, Abu Saleh Tahan. Both figures were given terms of 12 months within their new leadership roles, to be renewed or ended a year later. Abu Jaber had a history in militancy, having acted as a facilitator for AQI during the US occupation of Iraq, while during the revolution he had been Ahrar al-Sham's leader in Maskanah in Aleppo, where he had confronted IS earlier in the year. When this author expressed concern regarding the possibility that Ahrar al-Sham could reverse its phase of moderation, three of its remaining senior leaders contacted him separately to insist that this would not be the case. Clearly, the issue of where Ahrar al-Sham stood politically was an important one for the group's remaining leaders.

In fact, following the death of so much of its leadership, a significant internal discussion was initiated behind the scenes focused around a comment Abu Yazan al-Shami had made only two weeks earlier. Following a terse statement made by Jordan-based jihadist ideologue Iyad al-Qunaybi in which he condemned Islamic movements willing to cooperate with more 'moderate' Syrian rebel factions, Abu Yazan posted an online comment indirectly critiquing Qunaybi's stance and more intriguingly, distancing himself from the ideas of Salafi-jihadism:

> When people like you—may God bless you—and like [Abu Mohammed] al-Maqdisi in his last publications echo the culture of takhwin (accusations of treason), whisper campaigns and casting aspersions on any faction that isn't Salafi-jihadist with obtuse, airy turns of phrase, then [Jabhat] al-Nusra is pushed towards becoming a movement of societal rejection... We care for the Syrian battlefield, because it is our country and our revolution. (Of course, I assume our dear brother [Abdullah] al-Moheiseni would say this is 'Sykes-Picot' ☺). So know, by brothers from all factions—from [Harakat] Hazm to [Jabhat] al-Nusra—yes, I was Salafi-jihadist, and I was imprisoned in the [Assad] regime's jails for it. Today, I ask for God's forgiveness and repent to Him, and I apologize to our people for involving them in Quixotic battles of which they have no need.[19]

Attention soon turned back to IS, however, as a new video was published on 13 September—*A Message to the Allies of America*—in which British hostage David Haines was beheaded. Featuring again, 'Jihadi John' addressed the prime minister: 'This British man has to pay the price for your promise, [David] Cameron, to arm the Peshmerga against the Islamic State.' Another UK national and aid worker, Alan Henning, was subsequently identified as the next victim should the UK not cease its activities in combating IS.

Intriguingly, both Jabhat al-Nusra and pro-al-Qaeda jihadist ideologue Abu Qatada had made efforts to secure Alan Henning's release, with a Jabhat al-Nusra commander entering into negotiations with IS shortly after his kidnap in December 2013[20] and Abu Qatada writing IS's senior leadership a letter requesting his release shortly thereafter.[21] Following David Haines's killing, both Abu Qatada and Abu Mohammed al-Maqdisi issued statements of condemnation. While standing trial in Amman, Abu Qatada denounced 'the killing and slaughtering of the journalists' and described IS as 'a bubble that will soon burst'.[22] Maqdisi wrote an official retort online in which he said that those who 'enter Muslim lands to engage in charitable activities are not spies and should be treated as *musta'minun*, or people who request and are given *aman*, an assurance of protection'.[23]

All the while, another British hostage in IS captivity was being prepared for use in another disturbing propaganda design. On 18 September British war photographer John Cantlie—who was kidnapped (for a second time) with James Foley in November 2012—appeared in an IS video entitled *Lend me your Ears*, in which he spoke to the camera while sitting at a table in front of a black background. In an indication of IS's intent to use Cantlie for a different kind of propaganda purpose, Cantlie explained that 'in the next programmes, I'm going to show you the truth ...' and ended by saying, 'Join me for the next few programmes and I think you may be surprised at what you learn.' But Cantlie's grim situation was also laid bare:

> Now I know what you're thinking. You're thinking, 'he's only doing this because he's a prisoner. He's got a gun to his head and he's being forced to do this, right?' Well, it's true. I am a prisoner. That I cannot deny. But seeing as I've been abandoned by my government and my fate now lies in the hands of the Islamic State, I have nothing to lose.[24]

As IS continued to to underline its hostility to the Western world and to escalate its use of foreign hostages as weapons of war, Jabhat al-Nusra was beginning to more definitively assert its unilateral authority in Idlib. Beginning on 14 September, it began moving into the villages of Sahl al-Ruj and Hafsarjah north-west of Idlib city in what it claimed was an 'anti-corruption drive' targeting factions linked to Jamal Maarouf's SRF. By the following day the towns were effectively under Jabhat al-Nusra control and broader clashes had broken out in the region between it and the SRF. However, mediation launched locally by the Islamic Front succeeded on 18 September in establishing a ceasefire and a *sharia* court to adjudicate between the two sides.

As the fighting had been raging on 16 September, an unusually precise Syrian air strike targeted Maarouf in his Idlib home town and headquarters in Deir Sunbul—he was wounded and his deputy killed. That same day, another precise air strike killed the leader of Liwa al-Ayman al-Billah, a sub-unit of Harakat Hazm, in the Homs town of Talbiseh.[25] These strikes, which would clearly have been carried out by the regime based on strong intelligence of the targeted individuals' whereabouts, were probably conducted by one of only four Syrian MiG-29 fighter jets that had recently been upgraded to the SM standard by Russia's manufacturer of MiG jets, RAC MiG, which had opened a new office in Damascus's Mezzeh district. Consequently, these upgraded jets were now capable of operating with far more sophisticated air-to-ground weapons systems, including the Kh-29T/TE (AS-14 Kedge) and KAB-500KR guided missiles.[26] The same jets were most likely used in similar strikes against seven FSA headquarters in southern Syria in mid-October.[27] Weakening the moderate insurgency and therefore facilitating the rise to prominence of Islamists had been a consistent and key element of the regime's strategy, and this appeared to be the key motivator in this case.

In apparent retaliation for Burkan al-Furat's first operations, which saw the YPG target units of IS fighters in Kurdish territory east of Jarablus, IS launched an offensive towards the Kurdish town of Kobane (known in Arabic as Ayn al-Arab) on the Turkish border on 16 September. Within twenty-four hours the strategic bridge across the Euphrates river leading to Kobane had been captured, and by 19 September a large force of IS militants, tanks and artillery had advanced into sixty villages in the area around the town. This lightning advance, led primarily by an IS battalion—Liwa al-Aqsa—closely linked to Omar al-Shishani and heavily manned by militants from the North Caucasus, had taken the YPG and its 'rebel' allies by surprise, pushing much of their forces into Kobane itself. Concerned for the fate of the town's Kurdish population within the context of Kurdish–IS war across the border in Iraq, YPG spokesman Redur Xelil pleaded: 'The international community has to take action. If not, there will be a new genocide, but this time in Kobane.'[28] He was referring to the IS assault on Yazidis in Sinjar, where reports of mass killings and the enslavement and rape of women had been rife.

As IS forces continued to advance towards Kobane town and had begun artillery bombardment of it from positions 15 kilometres away, IS spokesman Adnani issued a chilling message, excerpts of which follow:

> O soldiers of the Islamic State, what a great thing you have achieved by Allah! ... Who are you O soldiers of the Islamic State? From where have you come? What is your secret? Why is it that the hearts of the East and West are dislocated by their fear of you? Why is it that the chest muscles of America and its allies shiver out of fear of you? Where are your warplanes? Where are your battleships? Where are your missiles? Where are your weapons of mass destruction? Why is it that the world has united against you? Why have the nations of disbelief entrenched together against you? What threat do you pose to the distant place of Australia for it to send its legions towards you? What does Canada have anything to do with you?

> ... O soldiers of the Islamic State, be ready for the final campaign of the crusaders. Yes, by Allah's will, it will be the final one.

... O America, O allies of America, and O crusaders, know that the matter is more dangerous than you have imagined and greater than you have envisioned ... You fight a people who can never be defeated. They either gain victory or are killed.

... O crusaders, you have realized the threat of the Islamic State, but you have not become aware of the cure, and you will not discover the cure because there is no cure. If you fight it, it becomes stronger and tougher. If you leave it alone, it grows and expands. If Obama has promised you with defeating the Islamic State, then Bush has also lied before him.

... And so we promise you by Allah's permission that this campaign will be your final campaign. It will be broken and defeated, just as all your previous campaigns were broken and defeated, except that this time we will raid you thereafter, and you will never raid us. We will conquer your Rome, break your crosses, and enslave your women, by the permission of Allah, the Exalted.

... And O Obama, O mule of the jews. You are vile. You are vile. You are vile. And you will be disappointed, Obama. Is this all you were capable of doing in this campaign of yours? Is this how far America has reached of incapacity and weakness? Are America and all its allies from amongst the crusaders and atheists unable to come down to the ground? Have you not realized—O crusaders—that proxy wars have not availed you nor will they ever avail you? Have you not realized, O mule of the jews, that the battle cannot be decided from the air at all? Or do you think that you are smarter than Bush, your obeyed fool, when he brought the armies of the cross and placed them under the fire of the mujahidin on the ground? No, you are more foolish than him.

... O Americans, and O Europeans, the Islamic State did not initiate a war against you, as your governments and media try to make you believe. It is you who started the transgression against us, and thus you deserve blame and you will pay a great price. You will pay the price when your economies collapse. You will pay the price when your sons are sent to wage war against us and they return to you as disabled amputees, or inside coffins, or mentally ill. You will pay the price as you are afraid of travelling to any land. Rather you will pay the price as you walk on your streets, turning right and left, fearing the Muslims.

... America and its allies rose in order to save the world from the 'terrorism and barbarity of the Islamic State' as they allege. They rallied the entire global media, driving it with false arguments to delude the masses and lead them to believe that the Islamic State was the root of evil and the source of corruption, and that it was the one killing and displacing the people ... To the extent that Kerry, the uncircumcised old geezer, suddenly became an Islamic jurist, issuing a verdict to the people that the Islamic State was distorting Islam, that what it was doing was against Islamic teachings, and that the Islamic State was an enemy of Islam. And to the extent that Obama, the mule of the jews, suddenly became a sheikh, mufti (Islamic scholar that issues verdicts), and an Islamic preacher, warning the people and preaching in defense of Islam, claiming that the Islamic State has nothing to do with Islam.

... So O muwahhid, do not let this battle pass you by wherever you may be. You must strike the soldiers, patrons, and troops of the tawāghīt. Strike their police, security, and intelligence members, as well as their treacherous agents. Destroy their beds. Embitter their lives for them and busy them with themselves. If you can kill a disbelieving American or European—especially the spiteful and filthy French—or an Australian, or a Canadian, or any other disbeliever from the disbelievers waging war, including the citizens of the countries that entered into a coalition against the Islamic State, then rely upon Allah, and kill him in any manner or way however it may be. Do not ask for anyone's advice and do not seek anyone's verdict. Kill the disbeliever whether he is civilian or military, for they have the same ruling. Both of them are disbelievers.

... If you are not able to find an IED or a bullet, then single out the disbelieving American, Frenchman, or any of their allies. Smash his head with a rock, or slaughter him with a knife, or run him over with your car, or throw him down from a high place, or choke him, or poison him. Do not lack. Do not be contemptible ... If you are unable to do so, then burn his home, car, or business. Or destroy his crops... If you are unable to do so, then spit in his face.[29]

With the now very real threat of IS-inspired 'lone-wolf' attacks on the front pages of newspapers across Europe, America, Canada and elsewhere, and with IS now in control of roughly 100 villages outside Kobane, the USA launched its first air strikes in Syria early on 22 September. The initial round of strikes, which also involved aircraft from Bahrain, Jordan, Saudi Arabia, Qatar and the UAE, targeted fourteen IS positions in Raqqa, Deir ez Zour and Hasakah. A separate set of eight strikes also targeted members of Jabhat al-Nusra in Aleppo and Idlib that US intelligence claimed were plotting an imminent attack against US and Western targets. A total of at least 120 militants were killed.

That strikes targeted IS was entirely predictable, but it was the inclusion of strikes against Jabhat al-Nusra that aroused particular additional attention. US officials described the targeted militants allegedly plotting attacks as members of the 'Khorasan Group', which included the earlier mentioned Mohsen al-Fadhli, Abu Yousuf al-Turki and Sanafi al-Nasr. Although a name invented by US intelligence, the 'Khorasan Group' may have represented a secretive cell within Jabhat al-Nusra known simply as the 'Wolves', which some Salafist insurgents would speak about privately when pushed. The strikes on the 'Khorasan Group' reportedly killed Abu Yousuf al-Turki, and also targeted the Kuwaiti Mohsen al-Fadhli and a twenty-four-year-old French convert and expert bomb-maker, David Drugeon, both of whom 'almost certainly survived'.[30] Intriguingly, some reports citing European intelligence officers claimed in October that Drugeon had been an agent of France's foreign intelligence agency, the Directorate-General for External Security (DGSE) before defecting to al-Qaeda,[31] although this was also denied.[32]

As the USA continued to carry out strikes on IS positions in Syria in the days that followed, its State Department formally designated both Jaish al-Muhajireen wa'l Ansar and Harakat Sham al-Islam as terrorist organisations, while the Treasury Department placed Omar al-Shishani under financial sanction as a designated terrorist.

Meanwhile, the very apparent lack of any action against the Assad regime brought a considerable flurry of condemnations from the insurgent opposition. The fact that seven women and three children were killed in one of the first strikes—by a cruise missile—in Idlib did not help,[33] and neither did the targeting of Jabhat al-Nusra, which remained a widely popular actor seen as a still integral component of the revolution and insurgency.

While the Islamic Front was quick to voice its criticism, with its Homs-based Liwa al-Haq talking of 'a war against Muslims', this anger and frustration was not merely an issue for Islamists. Within seventy-two hours of the strikes beginning, at least ten insurgent factions openly backed by the USA had issued official denunciations. Harakat Hazm labelled the strikes as 'an attack against our national sovereignty'; the 13th Division said they were 'aimed at weakening the revolution'; and the SMC claimed that they 'only benefit the regime'. As an indication of the tension the strikes aroused, an urgent meeting was called in Istanbul between US-backed FSA groups and their US counterparts in which the Americans complained that 'friends don't speak against friends', to which the reply was, 'true friendship means coordination'[34]—a reference to the fact that no US-backed groups were either warned of the impending strikes or called upon to help coordinate them. 'There was absolutely no coordination,' as one FSA spokesman put it.[35] 'We saw it on TV like everybody else,' said Harakat Hazm leader Hamza al-Shamali, 'We were shocked, we're supposed to be allies.'[36] A week after the strikes began, the leader of the US-backed 13th Division, Ahmed al-Saoud, complained of there being 'popular anger towards us' due to his group's close relationship with the West.[37]

On the first Friday after the strikes (26 September), many of the weekly protests held by opposition activists across the country were dedicated to expressing support for Jabhat al-Nusra. Like IS, the group had by that point gone mostly underground and its individual fighters had largely ceased operating on social media. However, Jabhat al-Nusra's official spokesman, Abu Firas al-Suri, issued a veiled warning to the coalition states participating in a statement published on 27 September:

We are in a long war. This war will not end in months nor years. This war could last for decades ... It's not a war against Jabhat al-Nusra, it's a war against Islam ... [Coalition] countries have done a despicable act that will put them on the list of those targeted by jihadist forces all over the world.[38]

A day later Jabhat al-Nusra leader Jolani issued a long and complex statement, in which he not only predictably condemned the strikes but disseminated what amounted to a call for support and defections to his cause, excerpts from which follow:

America, since the outbreak of the demonstrations in Syria ... strove in all clarity to destroy the work of jihad through numerous means, beginning by placing Jabhat al-Nusra on the terror list, even before Jabhat al-Nusra announced its association with Tanzim Qaedat al-Jihad, then through their attempts to use political leaders through the so-called coalition to rule over the people of al-Sham.

... [The West's] retreat after the wars in Afghanistan and Iraq was a lesson full of lessons ... but it seems to us that America and its allies have a lack of comprehension ... Perhaps they might regain consciousness before they are destroyed, for they stand on the brink of a volcano that is soon to erupt.

... Oh people of America and Europe, what shall you reap from your war against Muslims and mujahideen, besides more tragedies and sorrows on your country and your children ... Beware of your leaders fooling you to believe that soldiers will not be put on the ground, but will strike from afar, and your children will be safe from the blows of the mujahideen. But this is what will transfer the battle to the heart of your lands, the Muslims will not stand as an audience does, watching your bombing and killing of their children in their lands, while you are safe in your lands. The taxes of war will not be paid by your leaders alone, but it is you who will pay the bulk of them, so you have to save yourselves from this war and stand against the decision of your rulers.

... You were informed several times by Sheikh Osama [Bin Laden] that the only solution to avoid war with the mujahideen is by lifting your hands from their areas completely and stop your support and protection of the Jews, and to desist from plundering the wealth of the Muslims ... If you do that, I think you will be safe from the mujahideen and Muslims, if you stick to your own matters...

Our people in Al-Sham ... the strikes that are targeting us by the crusader alliance will seek to weaken the lines of our ribat and our operations against the nusayris ... Oh people of al-Sham, take a stand in this matter, and be firm against those who have allied with the worshippers of the cross from amongst our fellow citizens...

We promise that Jabhat al-Nusra will continue with whatever strength it possesses, stationed on all fronts fighting the enemies of Allah of the Nusayri regime and its allies...

Oh soldiers of Jabhat al-Nusra, be kind to the people of al-Sham, do not burden them with more than they can bear, attend to their service and lower your wings for them.[39]

IS's capture of five major military facilities from the regime in July and August and the hundreds of fatalities that were so brutally and graphically incurred engendered a level of frustration within pro-regime circles that had not been seen for many months. With forced civilian enlistment levels also rising within regime-controlled areas of the country, especially in the coastal heartlands of Latakia and Tartous, the cost of sustaining a defence against a determined insurgency was increasing.

When a car bomb exploded outside a primary school in the Alawite Akrama district of Homs city on 1 October, dozens of children were wounded, and by the time a second suicide bomber had struck minutes later, fifty-three people were dead, forty-six of them children, most under the age of twelve.[40] The utterly shocking nature of the attack—for which there was never a claim of responsibility—sparked immediate anger within the neighbourhood. The following day local Alawites organised a mass protest and, in scenes bizarrely similar to those seen in early anti-government demonstrations in 2011, locals chanted, 'The people want the fall of the governor'—even using the same intonation used by protesters three years earlier.[41] Ten days later the people's demands were indirectly met when Damascus announced the sacking of Homs's Military Intelligence chief, Brigadier Abdul Karim al-Salloum, and Security Committee head, Major-General Ahmed Jamil.[42]

Another incident in which the regime targeted its own military leaders took place in October in reaction to the loss of a joint Syrian–Russian signals intelligence and electronic warfare facility to the FSA and Jabhat al-Nusra near Tel al-Hara in Deraa. Operated primarily by the radio electronic wing of Russia's special operations Main Intelligence Directorate (GRU), the base had been equipped with high-tech listening equipment probably used to 'record and decrypt radio communications from every rebel group in Syria'[43] and to monitor developments in Syria's traditional enemy Israel, making it of huge strategic importance in the overall conflict and Damascus's broader geopolitical position. Its capture on 5 October, however, sparked rumours that Syrian military insiders had played a role in facilitaing the facility's fall. As many as 56 regime officers were arrested and executed in the days and weeks following the defeat at Tel al-Hara.[44]

As it later turned out, there had been an internal betrayal, from one of the most senior regime commanders in southern Syria. General Mahmoud Abu Araj, the commander-in-chief of Syria's 121st Mechanized Brigade, had been communicating with opposition sources for several weeks prior to the assault on Tel al-Hara. In the days leading up to the operation, 'Abu Araj smuggled out detailed plans of defensive positions, force strength, military orders, code words, and information about Iranian military reinforcements from his headquarters in the town of Kanakar.' He even 'went so far as to deploy his troops in ways that made it easier for the rebels to defeat them... [and] to evade capture... Abu Araj and the rebels he was working with staged a fake ambush when he was travelling near Sanamayn, 18km east of Tel al-Hara.'[45]

Following the facility's fall on 5 October, Abu Araj began a slow process of covert transfer south towards the Jordanian border, which he finally crossed ten days later on 15 October. Despite his rather heroic role in securing the victory and ensuring his safe defection, Abu Araj died a month later of a terminal heart defect.

As October continued, several small protests took place in the city of Tartous, where citizens demonstrated against the scale of the regime's enlistment and conscription of local men into the armed forces and the NDF. By this point all men born between 1973 and 1991 were liable to be conscripted into the army or reserve forces[46] beyond the normal eighteen-month compulsory service. Moreover, on 31 October Damascus instituted a law whereby anyone found to be refusing enlistment would receive a five-year prison sentence.[47] Such harsh central government policies strongly suggested that the security forces were suffering from a serious manpower shortage, the consequences of which only local populations would feel.

One significant consequence of this was the dramatic rise in the influence of Iranian military personnel and foreign Shia militias, including Hezbollah, in the military strategies of the Syrian regime. This by extension exacerbated the jihadist view of the transnational nature of the conflict in Syria as one between and in support of faiths—a conflict pitting the Sunni community against its Shia and Alawite enemies, in short.

One conflict theatre where Hezbollah and other foreign militias were playing a key role was Aleppo. Almost as if to emphasise the fact that the US-led coalition was leaving the Syrian regime alone, the Syrian army launched a significant offensive in Aleppo in early October, focused in particular on opposition control in the north-east of the city. Sometimes within only 10 or 20 kilometres of US strikes, Syrian army artillery, air strikes and barrel bombings intensified significantly as opposition control of the Handarat district of the city came under pressure. In an apparent attempt to divert some of the regime's attention away from Handarat and the north-east, Ahrar al-Sham and Jabhat al-Nusra launched an offensive of their own south of Aleppo, aiming towards the town of al-Safira and its defence factories, which were thought to be a principal manufacturer of barrel bombs that had been so immensely destructive in Aleppo city over the previous twelve months. Within twenty-four hours they had successfully captured five villages and they offensive had done its job—the threat to Handarat had been neutralised.

Despite being targeted by US strikes and despite the arrival of 1,500 Kurdish fighters in Kobane from Turkey on 28 September, IS militants had advanced into the town's outer periphery by the night of 1 October. Attacking primarily from the south and east, IS militants found themselves on 5 October in a state of all-out battle, fighting street-to-street battles with YPG militiamen and facing targeted American air strikes on their static firing positions. By 6 October, IS had taken control of a majority of the strategic Mishtenur Hill, situated on the town's south-eastern corner, and raised its black flag for all to see, including journalists watching from the Turkish side of the border only 2 kilometres away. After a further four days of fighting, which at times was so intense that it included hand-to-hand combat, IS had pushed into the town centre and captured the YPG's headquarters, and had approximately 40 per cent of the town under its control.[48] With the situation looking desperate and IS militants still advancing, the USA carried out fifty-three airstrikes in the area between 13 and 17 October, but still IS advanced, using multiple suicide bombers in an attempt to overwhelm YPG defensive positions.

In a noticeable shift, and in an attempt to re-energise the Kurdish forces, US military transport aircraft airdropped 24 tonnes of weapons and 10 tonnes of medical supplies to YPG-controlled territory on 19 October. Two 'bundles' of weapons separately fell into the hands of IS militants, one of which was filmed, showing several crates of new hand grenades and rocket-propelled grenades, while the other was reportedly targeted in an air strike shortly thereafter.[49] Preparations were also under way to send a contingent of Kurdish Peshmerga personnel into Kobane via Turkey—the first eighty arrived in the town on 29 October.

After multiple IS raids and assaults aiming to take control of Kobane's crossing with Turkey were repelled, IS's al-I'tisam Media published a five-and-a-half-minute propaganda video entitled *Inside Ayn al-Islam*. Showing British hostage John Cantlie 'reporting' from inside the town—which IS refers to as Ayn al-Islam, instead of its traditional Arabic name Ayn al-Arab—the video first showed footage filmed by an IS-controlled drone flying over Kobane, followed by an account delivered by Cantlie claiming that IS militants were in control of the town's 'southern and eastern sectors' and that 'there are no YPG, PKK or Peshmerga in sight'. He did admit, however, that 'air strikes did prevent some groups of *mujahideen* from using their tanks and heavy armour as they'd have liked, so they entering the city and using light weapons instead, going house to house'.[50] The video, probably filmed roughly a week before its release on 27 October, was clearly a propaganda ploy seeking to dispel the serious losses that IS was taking in its persistent attempt to capture the town.

Earlier in the month, on 3 October, IS had released a video showing the beheading of British hostage Alan Henning. Entitled *Another Message to America and its Allies*, the video began with Henning giving a pre-prepared IS statement: 'Because of our parliament's decision to attack the Islamic State, I as a member of the British public, will now pay the price for that decision.' As in previous videos, 'Jihadi John' featured front and centre and, in a reference to the UK Parliament's decision on 26 September to approve air strikes against IS in Iraq, he asserted: 'The blood of David Haines was on your hands, Cameron ... Alan Henning will also be slaughtered, but his blood is on the hands of the British parliament.'[51] American aid worker Peter Edward Kassig was then identified as IS's next potential victim.

Having now so brutally executed four foreign hostages—two American and two British—and with another American next in line, IS had placed Western governments in a corner. Moreover, the group's mass displacement of Yazidis in northern Iraq and widespread allegations of war crimes relating to their 'sexually-motivated campaign' against Yazidi women and girls[52] was continuing to flood the media. While there had been some doubt regarding the extent of this 'campaign', with several sources inside IS-controlled territory denying claims of 'slave markets' having been established for selling Yazidi women, the group itself acknowledged in its fourth edition of *Dabiq* magazine on 12 October that it perceived Yazidis as *mushrik* (polytheists) and this open for enslavement, including as concubines. Excerpts follow:

> ... Upon further research, it was determined that this group (Yazidis) is one that existed since the pre-Islamic jahiliyya (period of ignorance) ... the apparent origin of the [Yazidi] religion is found in the Magianism of ancient Persia, but reinterpreted with elements of Sabianis, Judaism and Christianity, and ultimately expressed in the heretical vocabulary of extreme Sufism.

> ... Accordingly, the Islamic State dealt with this group (Yazidis) as the majority of fuqaha (experts in Islamic jurisprudence) have indicated how mushikrin should be dealt with. Unlike the Jews and Christians, there was no room for jizyah payment. Also, their women could be enslaved unlike female apostates who the majority of fuqaha say cannot be enslaved and can only be given an ultimatum to repent or face the sword. After capture, the Yazidi women and children were then divided according to the sharia amongst the fighters of the Islamic State who participated in the

Sinjar operations, after one fifth of the slaves were transferred to the Islamic State's authority to be divided as khums (an Islamic tax on Muslim armies).

... This large-scale enslavement of mushrik families is probably the first since the abandonment of this sharia law. The only other known case—albeit much smaller—is that of the enslavement of Christian women and children in the Philippines and Nigeria by mujahideen there.

... The enslaved Yazidi families are now sold by Islamic State soldiers as the mushikrin were sold by the Companions [of the Prophet Muhammad].

... It is interesting to note that slavery has been mentioned as one of the signs of the Hour as well as one of the causes behind al-Malhamah al-Kubra (the 'Great Battle' preceeding the end of the world).

... Before Shaytan (the Devil) reveals his doubts to the weak-minded and weak hearted, one should remember that enslaving the families of the kuffar and taking their women as concubines is a firmly established aspect of the sharia.[53]

This shocking revelation, which was laid out so clearly within the pages of one of IS's premium products, underlined not only the truly apocalyptic nature of IS's guiding ideology but the extent to which civilians within its targets were in danger. The fate of Kobane, for example, gained an even higher level of urgency, while the proximity of IS militants to the Ismaili town of al-Salamiyah in Hama governorate also became an issue of potential concern.

As hard as it was to comprehend, IS's extreme brutality and utterly uncompromising attitude to its adversaries and non-Muslims at large did succeed in attracting recruits. The publication of gruesome beheadings, mass executions and suicide bombings, for example, aroused particularly intense levels of excitement—almost a frenzy—within IS's online support community, some of whom were known to have later travelled to join the group's fight in Syria and Iraq. On 14 October Pakistani Taliban spokesman Shahidullah Shahid announced his pledge of *bay'a* to IS and 'Caliph Ibrahim', along with five other of the group's operational commanders, Saeed Khan, Daulat Khan, Fateh Gul Zaman, Mufti Hassan and Khalid Mansour.[54] They were all subsequently dismissed from the Pakistani Taliban, which, like al-Qaeda, retained loyalty to Taliban leader Mullah Mohammed Omar.

A week later, after his release from an SRF prison where he was accused of maintaining links to IS, Jaish al-Muhajireen wa'l Ansar's Saudi *sharia* official Abu Azzam al-Najdi defected to IS along with approximately forty or fifty of his fighters. Najdi had previously been a major facilitator for jihadist militancy fundraising in Syria, and Abdullah al-Moheisini had recommended in April 2014 that potential foreign fighter recruits touch base with Najdi before arriving in Syria.[55] His personal account explaining why he chose to defect read like an IS propaganda statement, but did contain elements of frustration that other Salafists in 'opposition'-controlled Syria frequently spoke about at the time:

I've been asked a lot about my reason for leaving [Jaish al-Muhajireen wal Ansar] and pledging allegiance to the Islamic State.

I would say, frankly, that no one has a successful plan to implement God's law except the Islamic State. It has established Islamic courts and implemented the hudud in its territory. Meanwhile, if we go and look at the other side, we find not only sincere battalions but also—on the same land—criminal battalions and apostate battalions supported by the military councils that call openly for the establishment of a democratic state. Then we fight on the fronts while they work behind us to carry out their projects and plots ... Yes, there are those who work [at that], but they'll never succeed—although only God knows—because of their division and fragmentation. Even the courts that have been established have seen what they've seen because of nepotism and what have you ...

You might say that the [Islamic] State has made mistakes. I say that they themselves admit these mistakes, and they work to rectify them and hold accountable the responsible party. They've established Islamic courts and implemented the hudud so you see nothing here but the rule of Islamic law. Stores close at prayer time, women are modest in the markets, nobody sells cigarettes or anything else.

I say this is not the time for division with the Islamic state. The nations of disbelief have gathered against us, so we must come to [the Islamic State's] aid. This is not the time for the division of 'groups'. Rather, it is the time for solidarity and union.[56]

The growing tensions developing between Western-backed insurgent factions and jihadists such as Jabhat al-Nusra and Jaish al-Muhajireen wa'l Ansar—especially in Idlib and partially also in parts of Aleppo—was a principal theme behind localised defections to IS in this period. Another such incident took place on 17 October when Rashid Taku, a former senior commander in Jaish al-Sham—a short-lived coalition of Salafist factions established in February 2014 to be neutral in the anti-ISIS infighting—defected, along with a number of loyalist fighters from Idlib. Many other such defections took place throughout the second half of 2014, although most remained unreported. 'It was a serious issue for groups, especially in the north—we all knew Da'ish's money and its image was attracting our fighters. All we could do was keep a close watch and educate them on the illegitimacy of Da'ish's project,' was how one Salafist commander in the Islamic Front put it at the time.[57]

By late October 2014 IS's image and its perseverance against external attack meant it was receiving as many as 1,000 foreign fighter recruits every month into Syria.[58] Notwithstanding this remarkable rate of jihadist influx into Syria,

Adnani's call for IS supporters around the world to carry out lone attacks also appeared to be having an effect; on 20 October a twenty-five-year-old Canadian convert to Islam, Martin Couture-Rouleau, drove into two soldiers in the Canadian capital, Ottawa, wounding both of them, one mortally. Subsequent investigations found that Couture-Rouleau—who had used the names Ahmed Rouleau and Abu Ibrahim al-Canadi—had been influenced to support the IS cause by online propaganda materials.[59] Although purportedly unrelated to Couture-Rouleau's attack or to IS, a second attack took place in Ottawa on 22 October, when another Muslim convert, thirty-two-year-old Michael Zehaf-Bibeau launched a series of gun attacks outside and within the Canadian Parliament, killing one soldier.

Only days earlier, British security officials had described ongoing counter-terrorism operations in the country as being at an 'exceptionally high' rate, and that 218 arrests had been made in the UK since January 2014 and dozens of 'vulnerable' people were enrolled in deradicalisation programmes.[60] Similarly, Germany's domestic intelligence service the BfV warned on 28 October that the security situation in the country regarding 'ultra-conservative Salafism' was 'critical' and that 225 suspects were being monitored across the country in 2014, compared to only eighty or ninety in previous years.[61]

Clearly, the continuing conflict in Syria, its facilitating effect upon the rise of jihadist militancy there and in IS's expansion in Iraq and Syria was spilling over into the rest of the world. The initiation of external military intervention, albeit only by air and not involving ground troops, had also had a clear escalatory impact on the attraction and bellicosity of homegrown extremism, with implications at home and abroad.

Meanwhile, conflict in Syria was indeed continuing. Facing a continued manpower shortage and reliance on paramilitary forces whose offensive capabilities did not match their use as instruments of defence, the Syrian regime was still expanding its use of inordinately indiscriminate barrel bombs. Since the winter of 2013–14 Aleppo city had borne the brunt of this horrifically savage tactic, but their use had spread across the country. Amid continuing US airstrikes, the regime managed a dramatic increase in its use of airpower, carrying out 769 air strikes (including barrel bombings) in the ten-day period of 20–30 October, killing at least 221 civilians, a third of whom were children.[62]

Amid this unforgiving bombardment, the regime remained in control of Damascus and the route north along the strategic north–south M5 highway through Homs, west into the coastal strongholds in Latakia and Tartous and north into Aleppo. So long as it maintained control of this, the regime was safe—excluding the possibility of an internal coup or externally determined regime change. The regime did not have total control of the M5, however, as a coalition of FSA, Islamic Front and Jabhat al-Nusra had captured the northern Hama town of Morek, which was directly on the highway, in February. Control of Morek blocked the regime's M5 supply line from Hama city into Idlib and forced regime supply deliveries to be conducted by air or by taking diversionary routes west or east, which risked ambush. A major regime offensive in the area in mid-October succeeded in recapturing the town, inflicting a significant strategic defeat upon the opposition and particularly the Islamic Front, which had been the last force in its defence on 23 October.

The loss of Morek appeared to give rise to an unusual and termporarily successful Jabhat al-Nusra assault on Idlib city to the north, which aimed to re-cut regime supply lines from the south into the city itself. Lasting only a day, the offensive involved four suicide car bombings early in the morning, which targeted army checkpoints on the city's southern outskirts and then ground assaults on a hill overlooking the city, known as Tel al-Mastouma, and the city's southern districts. Although short-lived, the attack on Idlib was the first of this scale since 2012 and served as a reminder of the potential for insurgents—and particularly groups such as Jabhat al-Nusra, as well as Jund al-Aqsa, which played a role—to attack the regime in its urban centres. It was also a warm up for a bigger and better planned offensive several months down the line, in 2015.

Elsewhere in Idlib, meanwhile, the tensions between Western-backed factions and Jabhat al-Nusra finally boiled over on 26 October. While Jabhat al-Nusra's attention was focused on the launching of the Idlib city offensive, which it accused the SRF of refusing to contribute towards, their bases south of the city in the mountainous Jebel al-Zawiyeh area came unexpectedly under attack by factions within the SRF. The village of al-Bara was where the hostilities began, reportedly because an SRF unit there pledged allegiance to Ahrar al-Sham, drawing an aggressive response from other SRF units in the area, which attempted to arrest them. Shortly thereafter, Harakat Hazm fighters began setting up checkpoints throughout the area to prevent Jabhat al-Nusra or its allied forces—including Ahrar al-Sham, Suqor al-Sham and Jund al-Aqsa—from coming to its assistance. This brought Harakat Hazm into the conflict, and by the end of 29 October Jabhat al-Nusra had captured the SRF's strongold in Deir Sunbul and Harakat Hazm's principal headquarters in Khan al-Subl, forcing Jamal Maarouf to flee north to the Turkish border town of Reyhanlı.

By the time a ceasefire was agreed on 1 November, Jabhat al-Nusra had effectively imposed a total defeat upon both the SRF and Harakat Hazm—two of the most prominent US-backed organisations in Syria—and assumed control of the Jebel al-Zawiyeh region. Moreover, to rub salt in the wound, many Harakat Hazm fighters had defected to Jabhat al-Nusra during the final battles and brought along with them stocks of US-provided weaponry, including the highly prized, though symbolic BGM-71 TOW anti-tank missiles.

Although still subject to a ceasefire, Jamal Maarouf issued a video statement in which he defiantly claimed that the SRF would continue its 'war' against Jabhat al-Nusra in Idlib. Despite the bravado, however, Maarouf had fled his base, leaving many of his fighters behind.[63] Jabhat al-Nusra had established itself by force as the dominant power in the region and proceeded to capture several more villages in the preceding days, including several within sight of the Bab al-Hawa border crossing with Turkey. Although accounts from the ground back up the 26 October story from al-Bara as being the spark that lit the fire, Jabhat al-Nusra had had the SRF in its sights for several months, having accused it of corruption, war profiteering and a betrayal of the revolution by allying with the USA. Similar tensions based around allegations of corruption were developing elsewhere in Syria, including in Damascus where the locally dominant Jaish al-Islam was confronting two local groups, Jaish al-Ababil and Jaish al-Ummah. Car bombs targeted senior commanders of both groups on 17 and 19 October, respectively.

Nonetheless, with regard to Jabhat al-Nusra's emerging hostility to groups in Idlib, a great deal was motivated by the consolidation of the West versus jihadist dynamic. Idlib was a major stronghold of Western-backed insurgent groups, and was also a key recipient of Western-financed civil councils and administration. That Jabhat al-Nusra sought to assert its influence most overtly there before anywhere else in Syria was entirely predictable. That it was beginning to do the same in Deraa in the south was equally logical. Speaking after the Idlib clashes, a local activist in Idlib described the shifting balance of power and perceptions in the region following on from the initiation of US-led strikes in Syria:

> When American airstrikes targeted Jabhat al-Nusra, people felt solidarity with them, because Nusra are fighting the regime and the strikes are helping the regime ... Now people think that whoever in the Free Syrian Army gets support from the USA is an agent of the regime.[64]

On 4 November Jabhat al-Nusra's leader issued a forty-minute audio statement in the form of an interview in which he laid out a number of his group's principal strategic positions within the new dynamics. Jolani expressly threatened Hezbollah with a number of purportedly imminent attacks 'so that it understands the danger of standing as an ally to Assad' and laid out clearly that he perceived Western-backed factions as explicitly hostile to the 'mujahideen'. Excerpts follow:

> Some factions have started sending a multitude of people for training and arming. Supplies of arms and ammunition enter every day, to support these factions, so that they may be the hands of the Americans and the West in the lands of Syria ... [The West] will arm and train them to eliminate Jabhat al-Nusra and [IS], which is the stated goal. But of course they will also target all of the Islamic factions as well, or all factions that do not submit to Western policy that will be imposed on the region. So this will be carried out in all liberated territories.

> ... As for other areas where armed groups are present but the regime have the upperhand, such as Damascus, Homs, Hama, Latakia, Tartus and Qalamoun—the regime will try to regain control of these areas. And exploit the weakness that is caused in the liberated territories, where jihadis are prominent. Then after that, if things sucessfully proceed as such, they will announce a stop or the end of the war, which will be similar [to] the Dayton Agreement that occurred in Bosnia. They will think about creating the same agreement in Syria and end the war. They will then combine the governments—the Regime and the Interim Government—and the Regime will effectively have sovereignty because by their assumption, it is more capable and more competent in controlling the country, having had experience administrating it for more than forty years, especially because of the weak and repeated failures to establish an interim government.

> ... Our brothers in Qalamoun are hiding a lot of suprises up their sleeves, and the true battle in Lebanon has not yet begun, and the coming [battles] by the Permission of Allah will be more disastrous and bitter for Hezbollah. Perhaps Hassan Nasrallah will bite his fingers out of regret for what he has done to the Sunnis in Syria in the coming days, Inshallah.

> ... Jamal Maarouf transgressed against our people there, in the cities of al-Bara and Kansafarah, he has a large number of thieves and highway robbers [amongst him]. They transgressed against our people there, as well as against our men in Jabhat al-Nusra, and has tasted a share of his enmity toward us after repeated attacks of this man and his group on our people in Idlib, and against Jabhat al-Nusra and some other factions, of course, the fighting as rumored, was not only between Jabhat al-Nusra and the Syrian Revolutionaries Front, but there were two brigades of Suqor al-Sham and two brigades of Ahrar al-Shaam and Jund al-Aqsa and also ordinary people from Jebel al-Zawiyah present as well. Which shows that it was like a revolution by the people against the leader of this gang. These factions saw repeated transgressions from this gang against our people in Idlib, and we took a decision that Syrian Revolutionaries Front (SRF) should be anulled, specifically in the northern regions, because most of the trasngressions were carried out by them in

these regions. They changed from being a faction opposing the regime into a gang transgressing against this one and that one. Removing them became necessary. We do not deny that there are among the SRF in the north, some factions, affiliates, brigades and battalions that are desirous to fight the Regime and do not abandon their fronts against the Regime. And they are of course not included, nor held accountable for crimes commmited by Jamal Maarouf and those with him.

I add to this that most of the factions in the north, have been asking us to prohibit the presence of Jamal Maarouf and his gang. This request was not from those who are hostile towards him ( Jamal Maarouf) but from his allies. In fact even from some of the factions that issued statements of denouncement and condemnation [of fighting] and who called for reconciliation, and for the matter to be taken to an Islamic Court and so on. This was in the media, but on the ground, were demanding that we end its existence and continue in this campaign to end it fully.

... At any time, if Jamal Maarouf or others openly repents and cuts all ties with outside [forces], ties that work with the Americans or Saudi Intelligence or any Intelligence affiliated to other countries, and repents openly and returns to his family and people, he then would be a brother to us, who we will defend, and will defend us, who we shall seek assistance from, and he shall seek assistance from us in truth and goodness.

Before the dispute between us and [IS], approximately 70% of the leaders of Jabhat al-Nusra were muhajireen. Then after the dispute the ratio diminished to 40% of the leaders being from the Muhajireen. As for the soldiers, they make up approximately 30% to 35% of the entire number of Jabhat al-Nusra. This is a normal ratio for a jihadi group in such circumstances. We are always striving to receive muhajireen and we invite them to come forth to the Land of al-Sham.[65]

In setting out his official positions on the implications of Western support to moderate insurgent factions; to his group's planned retaliation against Hezbollah; and to the reasons behind the recent Idlib infighting, Jolani was revealing a more assertive posture than had been seen for some time. The predictable threats to Hezbollah notwithstanding, he was presenting Jabhat al-Nusra's role in Syria as its name was originally intended—a 'front of support' for the Syrian revolution that was purportedly answerable to the people's demands. In depicting Jabhat al-Nusra's recent actions in Idlib as a popular move that many had hoped for, and in linking this to a presentation of coalition strikes in Syria as being damaging to the revolution, Jolani was directly appealing for popular acceptance and support. Admittedly, it was true that many insurgent factions spoke poorly of Maarouf behind his back—this author has experienced that on many occasions—but it was also explicitly clear that Jabhat al-Nusra's 'anti-corruption' drive in Idlib was motivated more by a desire to dominate an area of crucial value to the Western-supported opposition.

Nonetheless, Jabhat al-Nusra remained to all intents and purposes, and despite its increasingly assertive and self-interested behaviour, an insurgent organisation that a majority of Syrians refused to turn against—so long as it continued to play a valuable role in fighting the regime. 'Nusra has never acted to damage the revolution,' said one FSA leader with close links to the US-led MOC in southern Turkey, 'and the people see it as an honourable organisation—why would I think to turn against it when that's the case?'[66] With that being said, while moderates continued to express support for Jabhat al-Nusra—perhaps out of fear as much as respect—insurgent factions on the more Islamist end of the spectrum were shifting their views in private. 'You know something? Nusra has begun to move in the wrong direction recently', said a senior Ahrar al-Sham official to this author in October, 'and we're watching things closely. Until now, nothing has changed in our relationship, but we are careful.'[67]

Clearly, Jabhat al-Nusra's behavioural shift was ruffling some feathers and not everyone was happy. The takeover of Jebel al-Zawiyeh was a serious defeat for Western strategy in northern Syria, especially as the moderate insurgency in neighbouring Aleppo was in a desperate situation facing off against advances by both IS and the regime. Nonetheless, US strikes—presumably based on human intelligence gleaned from sources on the ground—continued to target members of the 'Khorasan Group' in Idlib and Aleppo on 5, 13, and 19 November. Most notably, one of the strikes on 5 November targeted a house belonging to an Ahrar al-Sham commander, who sources confirmed to this author had been hosting a prominent al-Qaeda leader that night in his home. Subsequent news reports and an Ahrar al-Sham statement claimed only that the strike had targeted a base in Babsiqa near the Bab al-Hawa crossing. That strike caused outrage within much of the opposition community, with one SMC official telling this author hours later, 'It shows what the Americans really want in Syria—to destroy the revolution, it is simple.'[68]

Within the broader conflict, Jabhat al-Nusra was continuing to play a notable role in operations across the country, but particularly so in Aleppo, Idlib, Hama, Damascus and Deraa–Quneitra. In the latter southern governorates Jabhat al-Nusra was engaged in simultaneous assaults on the towns of Sheikh Miskin and Nawa in early November. Taking advantage of depleted army resources in the south, the joint FSA–Jabhat al-Nusra offensive succeeded in capturing Nawa on 9 November, along with several small military facilities, including a tank base. By the following day, the 112th Brigade base situated between Nawa and Sheikh Miskin had also been captured and half of Sheikh Miskin was in opposition hands. Amid consistently heavy fighting, the situation then remained fairly static until late November, when regime reinforcements from Homs—composed of both regular army and Hezbollah personnel—managed to carry off a noticeable counter-attack that temporarily placed Jabhat al-Nusra and the FSA on the back foot.

Further north, Jabhat al-Nusra, Jaish al-Islam, Ahrar al-Sham and several local FSA units launched another offensive towards al-Safira and the defence factories in southern Aleppo in late November, capturing at least seven villages in quick succession on 20 November. On the other side of Aleppo city, Jabhat al-Nusra and Jaish al-Mujahideen escalated their bombardment and siege of the Shia towns of Nubl and Zahra on 22 November, and for the first time advanced into Zahra's outer limits, capturing a number of buildings overlooking the town itself. The apparent threat posed to one of the Syrian army's most important staging grounds for Aleppo operations prompted a concerted volley of artillery and air strikes against opposition areas elsewhere in Aleppo, but, undaunted, the Islamic Front launched its own simultaneous offensive in Aleppo city's north-east, targeting regime forces in the Handarat and Breij Hill area. Although the battle lines rarely moved significantly, the fight for Aleppo was draining considerable resources on both sides.

Another zone of significant Jabhat al-Nusra operations in November was in the Qalamoun, where insurgent factions had been steadily recovering from their string of strategic defeats earlier in the summer. One complicating factor in the area was the presence of IS. Although for a long time the relationship between Jabhat al-Nusra and IS had been cooperative in the Qalamoun, this was beginning to change. IS's senior leaders in the area were reportedly becoming increasingly assertive of their perceived right to dominate decision making, and rumours were widespread that IS was seeking to expand its caliphate into the region. Within this context, Jabhat al-Nusra and the Islamic Front worked to consolidate their relations with local FSA factions, the result being the establishment of a joint Qalamoun command on 25 November that notably excluded IS altogether. Not only was IS ignored, but the command's founding statement had as one of its objectives 'to fight the khawarij of this age'—a historical Islamic reference to Muslims who developed particularly extremist beliefs.[69]

In keeping with Jolani's 4 November threat of attacks against Hezbollah, Jabhat al-Nusra's militants in the Qalamoun launched a planned attack on the group's defensive positions in the village of Flitah on 24 November, killing as many as fifteen Hezbollah fighters. The following day, in what appeared to be a related attack, Jabhat al-Nusra and allied FSA factions attacked Hezbollah and NDF checkpoints outside Yabroud, capturing at least five. Without coordinating with IS, insurgent forces in the Qalamoun seemed more capable of launching effective operations, at least for the moment.

With regards to IS specifically, the group had noticeably slowed the intensity and reduced the scope of its offensive operations in northern and eastern Syria since the initiation of US strikes in late September. It nonetheless continued to exert control over as much as a third of Syrian territory; and further inside Syria, IS militants continued to attack regime positions in eastern Homs, capturing the al-Shaer gas field for a second time on 30 October and then the linked al-Hayyan Gas Company facility on 1 November. A simultaneous attack was launched on Syria's largest and most strategically valuable air base—'T4'—but this was repelled on 2 November by an elite desert force known as Suqor al-Sahara (the Desert Falcons). The following day, however, IS's advance in the area continued as its militants captured the al-Jahar gas field along with a quantity of military vehicles and weapons.[70] Tit-for-tat advances continued between both sides throughout November, ending in the regime's eventual recapture of all gas facilities on 1 December, although many had been damaged or destroyed in the fighting.

From a broader perspective, IS and its caliphate continued to receive pledges of *bay'a* through November, most notably from Egyptian group Jama'at Ansar Bayt al-Maqdis on 9 November. Four days after this became known, Abu Bakr al-Baghdadi issued a significant statement in which he acknowledged recent pledges of allegiance to his leadership, specifically accepting those from Algeria (Jund al-Khilafah), Saudi Arabia, Yemen, Libya (Majlis Shura Shabab al-Islam) and Egypt (Jama'at Ansar Bayt al-Maqdis). His failure to mention ones given in Pakistan, the Philippines and Indonesia suggested that they had (yet) been accepted into the IS fold. In a later issue of *Dabiq* magazine, IS explained that this was because pledges of bay'a were not accepted until the prospective group had established effective modes of communication and command-and-control with IS's central leadership and until a suitable affiliate leader had been selected. Nonetheless, from this point onwards, Baghdadi announced that IS's had established *wilayat* (states) in all these areas, thus including Wilayat al-Haramein (Saudi Arabia), Wilayat al-Yemen (Yemen) and Wilayat al-Sina'a (Sinai, Egypt).[71] In addition to announcing his organisation's first official expansion outside Syria and Iraq, Baghdadi warned that 'volcanoes of jihad' would soon erupt across the world, and he specifically called upon his supporters in Saudi Arabia to launch attacks on the country's ruling royal family.[72]

The expansion of IS into five countries across the region was a highly significant development, and lent credence to threats issued by the group and its senior leadership against targets across the Middle East. It was also Baghdadi's first credible statement of competition with al-Qaeda since his declaration of the caliphate, as IS could now viably claim to be an international organisation—despite the small nature of any publicly stated or visible IS presence in Saudi Arabia and Yemen. It also carried a lot more weight a week later when gunmen in the Saudi capital, Riyadh, carried out a drive-by shooting, targeting a Danish man, Thomas Hopner. Hopner survived the attack, and on 2 December a video uploaded by the pro-IS al-Batar Media Foundation identified the assailants as 'Supporters of the Islamic State in Bilad al-Haramein'.

The attack in Riyadh was followed by further incidents: a Canadian man was stabbed by an unidentified assailant in a shopping mall in Saudi Arabia's eastern city of Dhahran on 30 November, and an American female teacher was killed in a knife attack in a mall in the UAE's emirate of Abu Dhabi on 1 December. Although no links were publicly acknowledged between IS and the latter two attacks, and a woman was arrested for carrying out the killing in Abu Dhabi, the incidents came within a context of heightening tension in the region regarding the threat posed by pro-IS 'lone wolves'.

The battle for Kobane continued unabated throughout November, with YPG fighters now reinforced by both Peshmerga personnel and a small contingent of FSA insurgents. At the same time, further west in Aleppo a decision had been made by the region's various jihadist factions that Jaish al-Muhajireen wa'l Ansar leader Salahuddin al-Shishani would travel to IS's capital, Raqqa, with a proposal to cease the infighting between their organisations. The meeting that resulted, which almost certainly involved IS's northern leader, Omar al-Shishani, was a dramatic failure, according to an account provided by Jaish al-Muhajireen wa'l Ansar's website Akhbar al-Sham. 'In response to the proposal to end the war with the mujahideen of the Islamic jamaats, such as Jabhat al-Nusra, Ahrar al-Sham and others, the leadership of IS announced that they would not end the war because the emirs of all these factions are hypocrites and infidels.'[73]

With an end to the infighting a seeming impossibility, IS published a video appearing to reveal the beheading of British hostage Peter Kassig and the decapitation of twenty-two Syrian soldiers. The sixteen-minute video entitled *Although the Disbelievers Dislike It* began with an account of IS's history since 2003, before introducing a particularly brutal scene showing in full detail the beheading of twenty-two Syrian soldiers by twenty-two IS fighters, almost all of whom were foreign—probably including militants from Britain, Belgium, France, Chechnya, Kazakhstan, Philippines and Switzerland, amongst others. Each led individually by his executioner, the victims were marched in single file past a box of knives from which each militant picked one en route to the spot where the beheadings took place. 'Jihadi John' appeared once again in this sequence, standing in the middle, stating:

> To Obama, the dog of Rome, today we are slaughtering the soldiers of Bashar and tomorrow we will be slaughtering your soldiers. And with Allah's permission, we will break this final and last Crusade, and the Islamic State will soon, like your puppet David Cameron said, will begin to slaughter your people on your streets.[74]

After this horrifically graphic sequence, the video transferred to a scene appearing to show Kassig's decapitated head at the feet of 'Jihadi John,' which the video claimed was filmed in the Aleppo town of Dabiq. This video was different to previous ones showing the murder of Western hostages. Kassig was not shown alive beforehand, but instead only his severed head was shown. Some imagery analysts subsequently claimed that 'Jihadi John' may have been superimposed over a backdrop of Dabiq and that a body double may in fact have been involved during certain scenes.[75] In addition to the absence of his body on camera—which jihadists would typically use to prove the nature of the execution—an investigation by the Quilliam Foundation and the Terrorism Research and Analysis Consortium (TRAC) revealed that the brief images of Kassig's head show what appear to be a gunshot wound above his left eye, and a prominent British surgeon claimed he also could not 'visualize successful decapitation in the manner that they present in this one photo'. Another surgeon concurred, concluding that 'this was a post facto attempt at creating a beheading event when [Kassig] was likely already deceased'.[76] Taken together, this would tend to suggest that Kassig may have been shot some time prior to the execution video being shown, possibly while resisting his captors.

Kidnapped en route to Deir ez Zour in October 2013, Kassig had shared an IS cell with John Cantlie and a French journalist, Nicolas Henin (who was released in April 2014), and during his incarceration had converted to Islam, taking the name 'Abd al-Rahman Kassig.' His kidnap by IS, his time in their custody and the fact that he was threatened with execution despite his conversion to Islam had generated considerable tensions within the jihadist community. One prominent Jabhat al-Nusra commander who had served in Deir ez Zour, Abu Omar al-Okaidi, had commented in late October that Kassig had allegedly 'performed a successful surgical operation on me while under bombardment' and had also removed shrapnel from the head of another

Jabhat al-Nusra commander in the area... he treated most of those wounded in al-Huwaiqa and al-Rashidiya' in Deir ez Zour.[77]

During the controversy over his detention, well-known American lawyer Stanley Cohen, whose previous clients had included members of Hamas and Osama Bin Laden's son-in-law Suleiman Abu Ghaith, had initiated a major effort to secure Kassig's release that involved influential al-Qaeda-linked individuals in Kuwait and Abu Mohammed al-Maqdisi and Abu Qatada in Jordan. The process involved Maqdisi engaging with senior IS *sharia* official and one of his former students Turki al-Binali—initially through their wives—in an attempt to persuade IS to release Kassig. However, after making some discernible progress, and despite an assurance from Jordanian intelligence that Maqdisi's efforts would not be interrupted, he was arrested in Amman on 27 October, effectively destroying any hopes of further progress, let alone success.[78]

As November was drawing to a close Jabhat al-Nusra continued its 'anti-corruption' drive, raiding and capturing bases belonging to FSA factions. On 28 November alone, Jabhat al-Nusra stormed the headquarters of Liwa Khalid bin al-Walid in the town of al-Rastan (its leader was executed by Jabhat al-Nusra on 19 December); the US-backed Alwiyat al-Ansar near Maraat al-Numaan; and the US-backed Jabhat Haq al-Muqatila in Hama.

Within this challenging context, the extraordinarily ambitious Wa'tasimo Initiative announced in the southern Turkish city of Gaziantep on 29 November that it had successfully coordinated the establishment of the RCC from seventy-two insurgent factions. In addition to all seven of the Islamic Front's constituent groups, including Ahrar al-Sham, the RCC's signatories also included factions from the Islamist 'middle ground' such as Kataib Nour al-Din al-Zinki and Jaish al-Mujahideen as well as most US-backed factions, including the SRF, Harakat Hazm, Suqor al-Ghab, the 13th and 101st Divisions and Liwa Forsan al-Haq.

That the RCC was established at all, especially within such a divisive environment on the ground, represented a spectacular success for the initiative, but tensions remained nonetheless. Immediately following the announcement, complaints arose from the moderate camp, with accusations that the RCC was overly Islamist. Despite this, however, the dissenting factions remained within the structure. After all, it represented the first time that such a broad section of the insurgency had come together under one organisational roof to establish a structure composed of actors definitively involved in action 'on the ground'. The lack of a unified opposition political-military structure with a genuine on-the-ground credibility had been a long complaint across all corners of the opposition inside Syria, so the RCC's potential value seemed to overpowered any claims of Islamist imbalance.

The RCC was a complex organism, headed by a president—Qais al-Sheikh, a judge from Deir ez Zour who was for a short time the opposition interim government's minister of justice. In addition to a deputy president (Ahmad al-Ragheb) and secretary-general (Naji al-Nahar), the RCC was composed of a 17-member Executive Council headed by Sobhi al-Rifai; a 73-member and geographically divided General Command; a 219-member General Commission; and offices for political, military and civil affairs. Notably, the Military Office was headed by defected Lieutenant-General Mohammed al-Haj Ali, a well-known opposition figure with close contacts in Qatar, who notably had attempted to establish an opposition national army in September 2012. The Political Office, meanwhile, was headed by Mohammed Alloush, the political chief of Jaish al-Islam and a cousin of its leader, Zahran Alloush. Lastly, the Civil Office was headed by a pediatriatician from Latakia who ran a field hospital in the province's northern mountains.

Considering both the structural complexity and the broad spread of factions involved, the RCC represented not only a significant accomplishment but also a huge challenge ahead. Despite its position on the most conservative end of the Syrian insurgent spectrum, Ahrar al-Sham had acquired a number of notable positions within the RCC, including two of seventeen seats on the Executive Council. The Islamic Front secured at least another two seats—one each for Liwa al-Haq and Jaish al-Islam. The RCC's Political Charter, which had been published in October, was indeed clear on its intent to work 'from the rulings of the true Islamic religion' using the consultative *shura* 'as the basis of the enterprise', but it also explicitly stated its desire to create 'a civilized life for [Syria's] diverse social fabric, in which all its [ethnic and religious] components enjoy freedom and justice'. It even stated that the RCC would adopt the 'independence flag' that the FSA had used since its establishment in July 2011—and not, therefore, one containing Islamic iconography.[79]

In a reflection of the pressure on Islamic groups resulting from their prominent role, one of those four Ahrar al-Sham-Islamic Front seat members told this author shortly after his appointment was leaked that 'this is massive responsibility and challenge. I just hope it was all worth it.'[80] However, for moderates, the RCC was less of a risk and, despite ideological concerns, the potential seemed to outweigh the immediate negatives. 'We will face very big challenges in the next weeks and months to make this work, but it's a great move forward for the revolution,' one FSA commander who enjoyed solid backing from the USA, told this author the day after the RCC's formation.[81]

From the start, a principal objective within the RCC was in the area of judicial administration. During the extensive negotiations leading to its formation the RCC had formed a working group composed on one side of Islamic Front (primarily Ahrar al-Sham) *sharia* officials and on the other a team of defected civil judges and lawyers to investigate the feasibility of adopting the Unified Arab Code as the official source of legal authority across opposition-controlled Syria. RCC President Qais al-Sheikh had already played a prominent role in pushing the code into civil-led opposition courts across northern and central Syria,[82] but the behind-the-scenes work on the subject was a significant indication of the RCC's objectives. Although fundamentally based on the *sharia*, the Unified Arab Code is codified—a concept that truly conservative Islamists reject altogether. However, an indirectly linked study of the code by the pro-Islamic Front Hayat al-Sham al-Islamiyya in August 2014 came to positive conclusions as to its value and potential.

Another principal objective of the RCC was to establish Mohammed al-Haj Ali's pet project, a national army. According to the RCC's announced plans, each signatory group would be expected to contribute a minimum of 100 fighters with their weapons in order to create a 7,000-man force. This almost certainly represented the biggest logistical challenge for such a new organisation. As such, the RCC's first military action, conducted under the aegis of its 'Central Front', did not take place until 20 February 2015, when Wa'tasimo chief coordinator and respected Islamic figure 'Abd al-Moneim Zeineddine led the launching of nearly twenty Grad rockets from truck-bearing multiple rocket launchers in northern Latakia. Interestingly, footage from the attack revealed flags of both the FSA and the Islamic Front, on separate launchers, seemingly demonstrating the coordination of multiple factions.

As December began, so too did the winter, which every year forced a reduction in the intensity of fighting on the ground. The battle for Kobane nonetheless continued unabated as Kurds fought jihadists street by street, interspersed by periodic IS car bombings and targeted US airstrikes. IS had undoubtedly lost the momentum they had enjoyed in the early weeks of its assault on the town, but it maintained a solid presence in parts of its southern and north-western areas. Despite losing hundreds of fighters, IS appeared determined to demonstrate its resolve by the sheer number of personnel it could sacrifice in order to do so. By this time, US-led strikes in Syria had become heavily focused on the battle in Kobane, with 127 of 152 strikes—or 84 per cent—conducted in Syria in December targeting IS in and around Kobane.[83]

Having reduced its overt military operations across much of the rest of northern and eastern Syria—with the exception of a ten-day assault on Deir ez Zour military airport from 3 to 12 December—IS set about pursuing a policy of covert expansion and acquisition of influence further in Syria's interior. Its affiliated units in the Qalamoun were being steadily drawn into the core IS fold, with previously discussed implications for the dynamics in that area. IS units in southern Damascus were also becoming more open about their presence, and had begun carrying out *da'wa* activities in al-Hajar al-Aswad. Despite its expulsion from Damascus's East Ghouta suburbs earlier in the year, locals also began to report the arrival of alleged IS sleeper cells in November and December.

Perhaps the most notable example of IS efforts to expand during this period came further south, in Deraa. Since the mysterious assassination of Ahmed Kassab Masalmeh—a jihadist veteran and former associate of Osama Bin Laden who had arrived in Syria in 2012—outside Deraa city on 11 November, rumours had proliferated that several local FSA units may have secretly pledged *bay'a* to IS and were laying the necessary roots for its official arrival to southern Syria. Within this context, Jabhat al-Nusra and its local ally Harakat al-Muthanna al-Islamiyya had begun to more overtly assert themselves in Deraa.

While allegations had been thrown at small groups like Saraya al-Jihad, Liwa Tawhid al-Janub and several other similar factions, the tensions erupted into conflict with regard to a larger group, Liwa Shuhada Yarmouk. Senior Jabhat al-Nusra commanders Abu Mariya al-Qahtani, Abu Hassan al-Kuwaiti and Abu Osama al-Adni—all of whom had earlier fled from the group's defeat to IS in Deir ez Zour—had publicly accused the group and its leader of having entered into a relationship with IS in early December 2014.

With tensions mounting and several reports of kidnapping and attempted assassinations, Liwa Shuhada Yarmouk fighters arrested three Jabhat al-Nusra militants and one of their wives and their children in the south-western town of Jamla on 14 December, accusing them of being part of a hit squad planning to target Yarmouk members. Within hours heavy fighting had erupted between the two groups in Jamla, Saham al-Jolan and around the town of Tasil, where Jabhat al-Nusra militants stormed Liwa Shuhada Yarmouk's headquarters. Activist reports from on the ground claimed that Harakat al-Muthanna al-Islamiyya and even local units of the moderate southern SRF had joined in the fighting against Liwa Shuhada Yarmouk, suggesting that this was a broader campaign.

With concerns rising that the conflict would soon spiral out of control, Harakat al-Muthanna al-Islamiyya stepped aside from the hostilities and issued a statement demanding that both sides release prisoners and accept a proposal of *sharia* adjudication, which had been presented by a multi-group court earlier on 15 December. A truce was subsequently announced later that day, although that did not prevent further sporadic clashes breaking out between the two sides in western Deraa in the days that followed. Abu Mariya al-Qahtani was wounded during one of those clashes on 19 December, and the attention that received forced yet more resources to be placed into negotiating a more permanent ceasefire agreement. Finally, on 26 December, several Liwa Shuhada Yarmouk leaders surrendered themselves to the *sharia* court and hostilities were ended.

Other inter-factional fighting continued elsewhere in Syria, with Jabhat al-Nusra continuing to expand its control and influence in Idlib. Unexplained assassination attempts targeting prominent Western-backed commanders were multiplying, with a Suqor al-Ghab leader killed in Hama and a Harakat Hazm leader wounded in Aleppo, both on 12 December. Meanwhile, Jaish al-Islam's dominance of the Damascus insurgency, especially in the Douma suburb in the north-east, was continuing to produce tensions with smaller factions such as Jaish al-Ummah, which had been accused of corrupt practices. Within this context, a Jaish al-Islam commander was killed in a car bomb attack on his base in al-Dumayr, 40 kilometres north-east of Damascus on 10 December, for example.

Insurgents were also continuing to combat IS, especially in Aleppo's north-eastern countryside and also in Deir ez Zour, where covert cells—many linked to the secretive 'White Shroud'—were carrying out increasingly frequent targeted attacks against IS commanders and checkpoints. For example, on 18 December alone, a car bomb struck an IS base in al-Mayadin and an IED targeted IS fighters in al-Bukamal. While incidents of defections to IS also continued—with 60 Jabhat al-Nusra militants joining from Idlib at the start of the month and roughly 400 Faylaq al-Sham fighters joining the group from Homs on 13 December—other rival insurgent factions were (as in Deraa) acting to pre-emptively prevent others, as occurred on 23 December when Jabhat al-Nusra stormed the headquarters of Liwa Uqab al-Islam in Hama after their pledge to IS.

Despite the winter weather Jabhat al-Nusra led two major victories in Syria in December. The first took place on 7 December, when two Jabhat al-Nusra car bombs—including one that utilised a South African 'Mamba' mine-resistant armoured personnel carrier that had been seized from UNDOF peacekeepers in late August—preceded an assault with Ahrar al-Sham and several FSA factions on the town of Sheikh Miskin in Deraa. The operation was ultimately successful and secured insurgent forces control of the Deraa–Damascus Route 5 road that runs alongside the principal M5 highway.

The second, and arguably more strategically significant, victory took place a week later, when, despite ongoing tensions in Idlib, approximately 3,000 members of Jabhat al-Nusra, Ahrar al-Sham and Jund al-Aqsa launched a major assault on the Wadi al-Deif and Hamadiyeh military bases near Maraat al-Numaan. Preparations for the operation had been made for ten days prior to the assault, with Ahrar al-Sham fighters arriving from Hama and Aleppo to reinforce those already in Idlib. Abdullah al-Moheisini had also travelled to Maraat al-Numaan to take part himself, and was filmed operating a field artillery system firing on Wadi al-Deif during the attack. Seven large checkpoints were captured during the first day's operations, at which point Jabhat al-Nusra concentrated its forces the following morning on an assault on Wadi al-Deif while Ahrar al-Sham and a small contingent of Jund al-Aqsa militants attacked Hamadiyeh. By midday regime forces had withdrawn, and both bases were under Islamist control. Having been under attack by opposition forces since October 2012, the taking of both Wadi al-Deif and Hamadiyeh was a huge victory for the opposition, but the total dominance of Islamists in their eventual capture underlined the new balance of power in Idlib, and indeed further afield. To stress this yet further, Jabhat al-Nusra filmed itself using an American BGM-71 TOW anti-tank missile that Harakat Hazm fighters had ceded control of during the infighting in late August. 'By God, this is a proud day for the revolution,' the leader of one US-backed Idlib-based group proclaimed to this author upon receiving news of the bases' capture. At the same time, and having heard his compatriot's comment, a senior Ahrar al-Sham official reminded the author, 'Don't forget, the *mujahideen* won these bases.'

Meanwhile, the excruciating battle for Aleppo was raging on, with regime forces closing in and totally encircling the city, placing opposition forces and remaining civilians inside the pro-revolution eastern districts under siege. In this respect, combat over the strategically invaluable Hanadarat district in the city's north-eastern periphery escalated considerably in December, placing the opposition's very existence in danger. Despite this, or perhaps precisely because of it, a proposal made by UN and Arab League envoy to Syria, Staffan de Mistura, to 'freeze' conflict and the use of air strikes and heavy bombardment in Aleppo had been unqualifiedly dismissed by Aleppo's insurgent factions. The fact that de Mistura had visited Damascus and met with Bashar al-Assad in early September[84]—the man responsible for flattening large parts of Aleppo in barrel-bomb attacks that had killed thousands since the start of conflict there—but had failed to meet with any Aleppo insurgent leaders until two months later, in December,[85] quite frankly destroyed any hopes of acquiring opposition support from the outset.

Nevertheless, despite the awful situation in Aleppo, the hoped-for solution to the pressure being placed upon the city's insurgency came on 25 December when, after several months of drawn-out negotiations that were launched on the sidelines of the Wa'tasimo Initiative talks, five of Aleppo's most powerful insurgent groups united under al-Jabhat al-Shamiyya. Composed of the Islamic Front (in Aleppo, this meant mainly Liwa al-Tawhid and Ahrar al-Sham), Kataib Nour al-Din al-Zinki, Jaish al-Mujahideen, Tajamu Fastaqim Kama Umrat, and Jabhat al-Asala wa'l Tanmiyya. Although not involved in the new front directly, both Jabhat al-Nusra and Jaish al-Muhajireen wa'l Ansar were expressly supportive of its formation. And in a sign of Ahrar al-Sham's continued high profile, its local military commander, Abu Amr, was appointed as the front's overall military leader. As a former Sednayya detainee whose brother was a senior spokesman in Syria's other dominant insurgent faction, Jaish al-Islam, Abu Amr's appointment was one that would ensure al-Jabhat al-Shamiyya friends in the right places. With that being said, and in a move similar to that made by the RCC, the front's logo used the traditional revolutionary flag as its basis; and indeed, it received a congratulatory message from Wa'tasimo chief coordinator 'Abd al-Moneim Zeineddine.[86]

With IS still under pressure from US-led coalition strikes, it gained a significant gift in late December when Jordanian F-16 pilot Muath al-Kasasbeh's jet crashed into a lake near Raqqa. Kasasbeh had managed to eject from his aircraft in time to survive, but, still strapped into his seat, he was taken prisoner by jubilant IS militants. The official US military account at the time claimed that Kasasbeh's jet had experienced a technical malfunction, but in a subsequent 'interview' IS released in its sixth edition of *Dabiq* magazine on 29 December, Kasasbeh allegedly said:

> We entered the region of Raqqa to sweep the area, then the striker jets entered to begin their attack. My plane was struck by a heat-seaking missile. I heard and felt its hit. The other Jordanian pilot in the mission ... contacted me from a participating jet and told me that I was struck and that fire was coming out of the rear nozzle of my engine. I checked the system display and it indicated that the engine was

damaged and burning. The plane began to deviate from its normal flight path, so I ejected. I landed in the Furat River by parachute and the seat caught on the ground, keeping me fixed, until I was captured by soldiers of the Islamic State.[87]

Pro-IS sources online were quick to publish photographs showing Kasasbeh being pulled out of the water, and additional photographs of him were published in his extended interview in *Dabiq*.

With the apparent collapse of the UN's plan to de-escalate the conflict, major jihadist-led victories in Syria's south and north, rising inter-factional tensions and hostilities prompting the decline of Western-supported moderates, and IS not budging from its territory and now in possession of a Jordanian jet pilot, another year of conflict ended in Syria. Far from their being any discernible solution to the war, it seemed that dynamics were only just beginning to settle after the anti-ISIS fighting, IS's declaration of a caliphate and US-led intervention. The next phase of the conflict—one in which jihadists would most likely rise to prominence amid continued moderate divisions and failure—was just beginning.

# 13

## JANUARY–JUNE 2015

### TIPPING THE SCALES

Despite receiving a much-needed boost at the end of 2014 with the capture of Jordanian pilot Muath al-Kasasbeh, IS's central battle for Kobane appeared increasingly desperate as 2015 began. The death of one of its most prominent *sharia* officials, Saudi national Othman al-Nazeh, along with his brother Khaled, in a US airstrike in the predominantly Kurdish town on 2 January[1] was symbolic of the downward trajectory of IS's three-month assault on the town. In receiving substantial assistance—in the form of manpower, logistics and weaponry—from Iraqi Kurdish Peshmerga and the US-led anti-IS coalition, the Kurdish YPG had proven itself a capable and reliable partner in the expanding fight against IS.

Despite coming under increasingly intense pressure and having lost approximately 75 per cent of the town by mid-January, IS nonetheless continued throwing personnel into the battle. For many observers its almost illogical determination to continue fighting a losing battle underlined the movement's apocalyptic worldview. While it was made only minimally public at the time, US anti-IS coalition officials spoke privately in early 2015 of some air strikes killing as many as 75–100 IS militants at a time in the Kobane area. Moreover, further east from the town, closer to Raqqa city, small and makeshift training camps were being used to rapidly train newly arrived foreign fighters and to prepare them for deployment to the Kobane front. Throughout January these camps and their students were repeatedly bombarded by American air-to-surface missiles—only to re-activate the following day for another several dozen new recruits, who would be obliterated twenty-four hours later in another air strike.[2] Clearly, IS's recruitment capacity had not been diminished, but the value of sacrificing so much manpower, impending apocalypse or not, seemed increasingly difficult to comprehend.

It was all but inevitable, therefore, that by the end of January 2015 IS had been comprehensively defeated and forced to withdraw from Kobane. Despite at least two IS suicide bombings in the town on 15 and 16 January, several days of concerted coordination between YPG fighters and coalition aircraft surrounding the strategically pivotal Mishtenur Hill between 15 and 19 January resulted in an IS retreat from the hill and the YPG's symbolic raising of their yellow-and-red flag at its summit on 19 January. From that point on, IS's supply lines in Kobane were severed both from the south-west (in towns such as Manbij and al-Bab) and from the south-east (in Raqqa). The tide had thus definitively turned, and eight days later IS's last remaining positions in small pockets of Kobane's eastern and southern periphery had been overrun and the YPG had declared victory.

Meanwhile, and further south-east, IS was beginning to face a new and more hidden threat in its relative safe haven of Deir ez Zour, bordering Iraq. There, an increasingly organised anti-IS resistance force appeared to be emerging out of the shadows.

On Tuesday 6 January IS's deputy chief of *hisba*—an Islamic police force committed to 'commanding right and forbidding wrong'—was found dead in the town of al-Mayadin, beheaded by unknown assailants who had left a note saying 'This is evil, you Sheikh'. The victim, an Egyptian known as Abu Zayd al-Masri, had been a well-known figure in the area known to have publicly 'declared war' on the use of tobacco, narcotics and alcohol. That his decapitated head contained an unlit cigarette left in the mouth was a telling sign of how such strict behavioural restrictions threatened to undermine IS's existentially important control of territory. Later that day another two IS militants were attacked separately in al-Mayadin: one was run over by a car and the other struck with a metal object by an assailant on a motorcycle.[3]

The following day three more IS militants were kidnapped, and forty-eight hours later three more were killed while in a vehicle near an IS office in the village of al-Bulil.[4] In the days that followed, IS military commanders deployed security units onto the streets of al-Mayadin, al-Bulil and many other towns searching for men suspected of involvement in the attacks. Several Internet cafes were raided and their equipment confiscated, after purported claims of responsibility had appeared online in the name of a shadowy group known as al-Kafn al-Abyad, or the White Shroud—an anti-IS organisation that had first emerged in parts of Deir ez Zour in September 2014. Purportedly composed of three rebel factions whose forces had been defeated by IS in mid-2014 (Liwa al-Qadisiyya al-Islamiyya, Jabhat al-Asala wa'l Tanmiyya and Liwa al-Mujahid Omar al-Mukhtar), the White Shroud had thus far emerged as the only seemingly organised anti-IS force in Syria, with active cells in key urban areas such as al-Bukamal, al-Mayadin and even Deir ez Zour city.[5]

In the days that followed, several more attacks on IS personnel and facilities were reported across the governorate. In response, dozens of men were arrested by IS and interrogated. One man was publicly beheaded in al-Mayadin's town centre and his corpse crucified and placed on display for three days. At least sixteen more men were publicly executed through mid-January on charges of carrying out attacks on IS assets in coordination with the regime.[6] Little mention was made of the attacks having been linked to the opposition.

IS was not the only armed group in Syria engaged in conflict with other rival factions in early 2015, however. After several months of tensions, during which members of both groups had been taking pot shots at each other and setting up checkpoints aimed at reducing the other's freedom of movement in the besieged Damascus suburb of Douma, Jaish al-Islam and Jaish al-Ummah finally came to blows in January. After a number of sporadic clashes on 2 and 3 January, Jaish al-Islam leader Zahran Alloush announced assertively on 4 January the launching of an operation he termed 'Cleansing the Country of the Filth of Corruption'. The principal and specified target of this 'cleansing' was Jaish al-Ummah. The group had been blamed for its involvement in racketeering, drug dealing and other mafia-like behaviour for many months, and although Jaish al-Islam's inevitable defeat of the group several days later was largely welcomed by Douma's residents, the unforgivingly aggressive solution adopted by Alloush raised questions as to Jaish al-Islam's willingness to 'overstep' the authority of local judicial bodies created to solve such issues.[7]

Although Jaish al-Ummah had only been established in Douma in September 2014, its downfall marked a sad end to a rebel movement that could have come to symbolise some of the very earliest images of the revolution. Its leader, Abu Ali Khabiya, for example, had been an early defector and was the first FSA leader to march into Damascus's central al-Midan district during the rebel offensive in July 2012. But despite containing such revolutionary figureheads, the group's presence in Douma had focused more on financial objectives, with the group famously having imposed taxes on all food entering Douma through its only available crossing.[8] More generally, citizens accused the group of behaviours not too different from those of the pro-regime *shabiha* militias across the country.

Two months after defeating the SRF in Idlib, Jabhat al-Nusra was emerging as an increasingly self-assertive jihadist movement in northern Syria, whose leaders appeared month by month to be pushing a more typically al-Qaeda-like extremist line. International intelligence bodies continued to claim that Jabhat al-Nusra-linked 'Khorasan Group' militants were planning attacks on the West from inside Syria.[9] With its deputy leadership now headquartered in the south and led by hardline Jordanian Sami al-Oraydi, the frequency of extremist action increased. For example, Jabhat al-Nusra militants demolished a thirteenth-century tomb of famed Islamic scholar Imam Nawawi in the Deraa town of Nawa near Jordan on 7 January.[10] And a week later, a woman accused of adultery was publicly executed in Idlib.[11] Such acts had previously been remarkably rare.

At the same time, Jabhat al-Nusra had also set its sights on small rival factions, many of which it accused of corruption as a pretext for turning on them. Days after fighters affiliated with its hardline *dar al-qada'a* judicial system raided and shut down 'Free Police' stations in Aleppo's Hreitan, Anadan and Kafr Hamra on 6 January, Jabhat al-Nusra conducted a series of coordinated arrest campaigns against members of several small FSA units within the Tajamu Tahrir Homs coalition in Homs governorate. It also entered into a series of tit-for-tat escalatory incidents with the most prominent US-backed rebel group in the north, Harakat Hazm. As the first publicly acknowledged recipient of American BGM-71 TOW anti-tank guided missiles in April 2014, and being composed primarily of several former sub-factions from within the early Saudi-backed early 'super group' Kataib al-Farouq,[12] Harakat Hazm had come to represent the public face of a US–Saudi initiative aimed at bolstering moderate FSA influence within an increasingly Islamist north. While a series of clashes between Jabhat al-Nusra and Harakat Hazm, and also with the Aleppo coalition al-Jabhat al-Shamiyya, in Aleppo in late January quickly petered out, such incidents were a harbinger of more conflict to come. Most surprisingly, Jabhat al-Nusra even clashed repeatedly with Ahrar al-Sham fighters in Idlib, reportedly over a dispute regarding 'spoils' gained during the anti-SRF fighting in late 2014.

Although inter-factional tensions were undoubtedly rising across parts of Syria, adding yet further complexity to an already complicated conflict, there were also positive and forward-looking moves made more broadly within the armed opposition. Organisationally, portions of the Western-backed FSA in southern Syria continued to coalesce within well-structured and internationally supported formations, such as Jaish al-Awal (the First Army), established on 1 January. Led principally by its three component group leaders, Colonel Sabr Safer, Major Abdulatif al-Hourani and Major Abu Osama al-Jolani,[13] the First Army announced its formation within a context of the broader Southern Front presenting itself as the most reliable partner of the West in ensuring liberal values for Syria's future.

Interestingly, within a climate of increasing scepticism and cynicism regarding international UN-led efforts to de-escalate the conflict and open up pathways towards peace, it was the Southern Front that released a 'Political Programme for Post-Assad Syria' in early January. While a majority of other armed groups in Syria—from truly 'moderate' FSA factions to Ahrar al-Sham—had intensified their own internal discussions regarding what a negotiated political solution for Syria would look like and how to practically reach such an eventuality, the Southern Front's early and public thinking on the subject stood out for its apparent maturity. This was despite, or perhaps precisely because of, widespread allegations that the Southern Front's close relations with the multinational Military Operations Centre (MOC) in Amman meant that its political and military activities and strategy were at least partly directed from abroad.

A great deal of thinking on the subject of politics and negotiated solutions was at the time primarily limited to the confines of Track II initiatives, such as those then run by the Brookings Institution (then from September 2015, by The Shaikh Group) and the Center for Humanitarian Dialogue (HD Center). The exiled opposition ETILAF was of course still centrally focused on this issue, but its dire state of relations with the armed opposition effectively rendered its activities and involvement in international initiatives on the subject meaningless.

However, this would gradually change through 2015 following the early January election of forty-nine-year-old Damascene doctor Khaled Khoja to the post of ETILAF president. Although international media declared Khoja at the time to be refreshingly independent of foreign backing—from the regional influences of Saudi, Qatar and Turkey—he was in fact particularly close to political power players in Ankara. Throughout his first presidential term, Khoja exploited Turkey's extensive relations with armed opposition groups, and embarked on a quiet but effective process of engagement with armed opposition leaderships, reaching as hardline as Ahrar al-Sham. By the time of his re-election in August 2015, delegations of armed group leaders were visiting ETILAF's headquarters near Istanbul's Ataturk International Airport on a weekly basis.

Notwithstanding the world's almost obsessive attitude towards IS and the continued prominence of Jabhat al-Nusra, many other jihadist groups were continuing to play a prominent role in determining localised conflict dynamics across Syria. From the Jabhat Ansar al-Din coalition and Junud al-Sham in Aleppo and Latakia; to Jund al-Aqsa and the Turkistan Islamic Party (TIP) in Idlib and Hama; and to Harakat al-Muthanna al-Islamiyya in Deraa and Quneitra, jihadists had definitively established themselves as key players in the Syrian conflict and within its broader anti-government insurgency.

Intriguingly, new jihadist factions also continued to establish themselves in the country, especially in the more favourable environments prevalent in the north. In January 2015 one new such group was al-Katibat al-Tawhid wa'l Jihad. Primarily composed of Uzbeks and militarily active in Aleppo, Idlib and the Qalamoun mountains north of Damascus, al-Katibat al-Tawhid wa'l Jihad had formerly been a loosely aligned wing of Jabhat al-Nusra, before splintering and becoming independent in late 2014.

This had been emerging as an increasingly common strategy employed by Jabhat al-Nusra to expand its tacit levels of influence across multiple battle theatres. As early as Jund al-Aqsa in January 2013, well-structured jihadist units had been splitting off from Jabhat al-Nusra to act—on paper—as independent groups; but in reality these were powerful Jabhat al-Nusra affiliates whom the mother group could one day call upon to act as strategic depth within particularly valuable battles. In a sense, it was a way for al-Qaeda to ensure that it had fingers in many pies at once. When it chose to invest particularly intensively in one, it would always have an established 'ally' in place to team up with.

January 2015 also marked the month in which the world's attention briefly switched to France, following a series of attacks against targets in Paris, beginning with the offices of satirical magazine *Charlie Hebdo*. While that attack and others linked to it were carried out by the AQAP-linked brothers Chérif and Saïd Kouachi, three other attacks—against a jogger, a policewoman and a Jewish supermarket—were seemingly conducted in coordination with the Kouachis, but by a pro-IS jihadist, Amedy Coulibaly. In the days following his death during the attack on the kosher Hypercacher supermarket in Paris's eastern Porte de Vincennes, Coulibaly's Algerian–French wife, Hayat Boumeddiene, fled to Turkey and joined IS in Raqqa.

Having already demonstrated its capacity to induce international security instability through videoed beheadings of foreign hostages in Syria, IS's call in

September 2014 for its supporters to carry out attacks on its behalf in the West now also seemed to be having an effect. Moreover, IS was continuing to expand internationally, transforming itself into a transnational jihadist movement capable of genuinely competing with al-Qaeda for global pre-eminence.

However, IS's losses in Kobane and parts of Iraq, compounded by intensifying Syrian regime air strikes on IS territories—including one that killed sixty-five people near the Kurdish–Arab city of Qamishli on 20 January—were undermining the sense of momentum the group so desperately needed to sustain in order to justify its image of God-given righteousness. As such, IS sought to again expand its manipulation of international dynamics by revealing to the world that it was holding two Japanese hostages.

In a video released on 20 January and entitled *A Message to the Government and the People of Japan*, the now notorious British IS militant Mohammed Emwazi stood clad all in black bearing a military knife and presented Haruna Yukawa and Kenji Goto. 'To the prime minister of Japan, although you are 8,500 kilometres from the Islamic State, you willingly volunteered to take part in this crusade,' Emwazi proclaimed. 'You have proudly donated $100 million to kill our women and children, to destroy the homes of the Muslims.' Therefore, he said, saving the lives of Yukawa and Goto would cost $100 million each.[14]

By pointing to Japanese involvement in 'this crusade', IS appeared to be referring to an announcement made three days earlier in Cairo by Japan's prime minister, Shinzo Abe, in which he declared that his country would pledge $200 million in non-military assistance to countries involved in the anti-IS coalition.[15] Ignoring the inherent pacifist foundations of Japan's politico-military and constitutional structures, a deadline of seventy-two hours was given by IS, before, it said, the hostages would be killed.

Yukawa, who was described in reporting at the time as a troubled man who had recently declared bankruptcy, lost his wife to lung cancer and spent a month homeless in a Tokyo park, had sought to become a military contractor, and had travelled to the region in the spring of 2014. With the advisory backing of Japanese nationalist Nobuo Kimoto, Yukawa established a company called Private Military Co. and travelled to northern Syria in April. Yukawa had quickly sought out Goto, a known Japanese war correspondent, for help getting to Iraq, where he wanted to experience more professionally how to work and survive in a war zone. After a brief stint in northern Iraq, where Yukawa embedded with Kurdish Peshmerga personnel—photos of which he subsequently posted onto his Facebook profile—he travelled back to Syria in

July, spending most of his time in Aleppo. A month later Yukawa was captured by IS during a battle with rebels north of Aleppo city. Video of his capture was quickly posted onto YouTube by a foreign IS militant.[16] Nothing was then heard of him until his appearance alongside Goto and Emwazi in January the following year.

As a war correspondent, Goto was familiar with operating in conflict zones, but in comments given to Reuters in August 2014 he made clear his perception that Yukawa lacked the necessary experience to be in Iraq or Syria. 'He was hapless and didn't know what he was doing. He needed someone with experience with him.' Therefore, after Yukawa fell into IS hands, and despite Goto's wife having given birth to their second child only weeks earlier, he flew from Japan to Turkey and slipped into Aleppo on October 25, seeking somehow to rescue Yukawa. He was then not seen or heard from again until appearing in the haunting January video.[17]

Whilst setting up a crisis response unit in Jordan's capital, Amman, the Japanese government remained firm, insisting that it would not submit to terrorism. Three days after first appearing on video, however, Yukawa was beheaded by IS and footage of his body was displayed in a new video released online the following day. In that video Goto declared that IS was no longer demanding a financial ransom in exchange for his life, but now wanted an Iraqi female jihadist released from prison in Jordan within twenty-four hours.

The woman, Sajida al-Rishawi, had been arrested by authorities in Amman on 9 November 2005, after her explosives belt failed to detonate during an attack conducted on behalf of AQI. Alongside her husband, Ali Hussein Ali al-Shammari, Rishawi had stormed a wedding party in the city's Radisson Hotel. Later sentenced to death for her involvement in the attack, which killed sixty people,[18] Rishawi was in the midst of a long-drawn-out appeal when Goto announced on video that her release had been demanded by IS. IS's appeal for Rishawi was telling, not least due to the organisation's continued sense of connection and loyalty to its earlier predecessors, founded and led by Abu Musab al-Zarqawi: Rishawi was rumoured to be the sister of one of Abu Musab al-Zarqawi's closest aides.[19]

Despite the deadline passing by without incident, Goto appeared in yet another IS media release on 29 January, announcing a further new shift in demands from IS. This time only in audio form, Goto was heard announcing:

> I am Kenji Goto. This is a voice message I've been told to send to you. If Saijda al-Rishawi is not ready for exchange for my life at the Turkish border by Thursday sunset 29th of January Mosul time, the Jordanian pilot Muath al-Kasasbeh will be killed immediately.[20]

There is a murky but important background to these shifting demands and the sudden emergence of Rishawi and Kasasbeh as key to the fate of IS's Japanese hostages. While in prison in Jordan, pre-eminent al-Qaeda ideologue Abu Mohammed al-Maqdisi had heard about IS's capture of a Jordanian pilot when the detention facility's imam had issued a facility-wide prayer for him. According to subsequent interviews with Maqdisi, he then sought out permission from Jordanian authorities to enter into negotiations with IS, which was grudgingly granted.[21]

In early January 2015 Maqdisi first penned a letter directly to Abu Bakr al-Baghdadi in which he made a direct reference to Kasasbeh's value in securing the Islamically important release of a Muslim sister: Rishawi. As Maqdisi claimed in the letter—written in the Muslim month of Rabi al-Awwal 1436 (equating to 23 December 2014–21 January 2015)—Zarqawi had sought Rishawi's release prior to his death in 2006, but nobody had yet succeeded.[22] It was now time to try again.

Near-simultaneously, Maqdisi also reached out to contacts within IS's senior leadership in northern Syria via the smartphone application Telegram Messenger. The platform had become increasingly popular amongst the Islamist militant community in Syria, Iraq and Jordan as it was equipped with settings that allow for encrypted messages or those that 'self-destruct' shortly after being read by the recipient. It was in these messages, many of which Maqdisi sent to IS's top *sharia* official and his former student, Turki al-Binali, that the Jordanian ideologue presented the idea of swapping Rishawi for Kasasbeh. For an avowed supporter of al-Qaeda, the fate of a Japanese war correspondent was unfortunately of little interest to Maqdisi.

However, while Maqdisi's desire to have Rishawi released from prison in Jordan seemed to be a reflection of his genuine concern for a *mujahida*, IS was playing a multiple double-cross. Unknown to many, but tweeted by anti-IS activist Abu Ibrahim al-Raqqawi on 8 January 2015, Kasasbeh was in fact already dead, having been burned alive in a cage in early January:

> A group of #ISIS members in #Raqqa are talking among them enthusiastically about the execution of Jordanian pilot, Maath al-Kassassbeh, who was burned to death by #ISIS.[23]

Unbeknownst to Maqdisi, the key to saving Rishawi was therefore already dead. Having detected potential indications that Kasasbeh had in fact been killed, Jordanian intelligence instructed Maqdisi to seek video evidence containing time-verifiable information that their pilot was still alive. In response, by late January, IS sent Maqdisi a password-protected electronic file, which they claimed contained the necessary proof of life. However, Maqdisi was not sent the password. Then followed several days of difficult negotiations, during which Maqdisi and his aides, including 'jihadi doctor' and al-Qaeda-linked figure Dr Munif Samara, became increasingly distrustful of the IS figures on the other end of the phone.[24]

Operating on a lower level, and more focused on the fate of Goto, a separate track of contact was also ongoing between a Japanese pro-jihadist figure, Hassan Ko Nakata, and a Chechen IS commander known as Omar Gharaba. Nakata had already travelled to Syria in September 2014 in an attempt to personally negotiate the release of Yukawa, but in January 2015 he was working occasionally in indirect cooperation with Japanese intelligence. However, Japanese authorities refused to formally enter into negotiations and little progress was made.[25]

With all of this continuing, IS released a further video on 31 January in which Goto's decapitated corpse was graphically revealed. Again appearing as IS's public face of foreign hostage beheadings, Emwazi addressed Prime Minister Abe and triumphantly declared:

> Because of your reckless decision to take part in an unwinnable war, this knife will not only slaughter Kenji [Goto], but will also carry on and cause carnage wherever your people are found. So let the nightmare for Japan begin.[26]

Although no mention of Kasasbeh or Rishawi was made in the video, Jordan announced the following morning that it was still determined to secure an exchange of Rishawi for Kasasbeh. 'We are still prepared to hand over the convict Sajida al-Rishawi in return for the return of our son and hero,' Jordanian government spokesman Mohammed al-Momani announced to international media on 1 February.[27] However, authorities in Amman appeared to be clinging to a last shred of hope by this point. In later media reporting, Jordanian officials claimed that Kasasbeh's death had in fact been suspected internally as early as 3 January, while British authorities had by that time also concluded that the pilot's probable death had taken place between 5 and 8 January.[28]

Two days later IS's deceit was revealed—first in private to Maqdisi, when he was finally sent the password to open the electronic file. To his horror, the password spelled: 'Maqdisi the pimp, the sole of the tyrant's shoe, son of the English whore.'[29] Moreover, upon opening the file, his computer screen revealed the gruesome death of Kasasbeh, as petrol was poured over his body and he was burned alive in a metal cage. Later that day IS posted the video onto the Internet, and its thirst for horror and graphically barbaric violence was underlined for all to see. The next day Jordan retaliated by hanging Rishawi and another jihadist on death row, Ziyad Khalaf al-Karbouli.[30]

As with the execution of British hostage Alan Henning, Maqdisi's attempts to negotiate with IS revealed again the stark ideological differences between it and al-Qaeda. In a subsequent interview with Jordanian TV channel Al-Ru'ya, Maqdisi condemned IS's understanding of jihad as being limited—and indeed devoted solely—to 'slaughter and killing'. The killing of any person 'by fire', he said, was explicitly prohibited by the Prophet Muhammad.[31] By and large, this latter declaration was agreed upon by Islamic figures within both the conventional theological circles, but also within the Salafist and pro-al-Qaeda communities. Notorious Jordanian Salafist Mohammed al-Shalabi (Abu Sayyaf) claimed at the time that the killing

> weakens the popularity of Islamic State, because we look at Islam as a religion of mercy and tolerance. Even in the heat of battle, a prisoner of war is given good treatment ... Even if the Islamic State says Muaz bombed and burned and killed us and we punished him the same way he did to us, we say OK, but why film the video in this shocking way?![32]

For itself, IS's internal theological authority claimed that burning Kasasbeh alive was justified as reciprocating the effect of air strikes he would have been involved in conducting over IS territories:

> The Hanafis and Shafis have permitted it, considering the saying of the Prophet: 'Fire is only to be administered as punishment by God' as an affirmation of humility. Al-Muhallab said: 'This is not an absolute prohibition, but rather on the path to humility.'

> Al-Hafez ibn Hajar said: 'What points to the permissibility of burning is the deeds of the Companions and the Prophet put out the eyes of the Uraynians with heated iron ... while Khalid bin al-Walid burnt people of those who apostasised.'

> And some of the Ahl al-Ilm have been of the opinion that burning with fire was prohibited originally, but then on retaliation it is permitted.[33]

In the days that followed Kasasbeh's gruesome killing, the Jordanian military reacted to mass public outpourings of protest and anger at IS by launching a spate of intensified air strikes against IS positions. 'Our punishment and revenge will be as huge as the loss of the Jordanians,' declared Jordanian army spokesman Mamdouh al-Ameri on 4 February,[34] as Jordanian F-16s fired missiles at IS targets in northern Syria. While Jordanian fury was meted out on IS territory, the loss of an anti-IS coalition pilot had the reverse effect upon the UAE, which temporarily ceased all air strikes against IS. IS also claimed several days later, though without any substantive evidence, that it had been a Jordanian air strike that killed American hostage and aid worker Kayla Jean Mueller.[35]

Elsewhere in Syria, the broader opposition–regime conflict was entering an entirely new stage. While the intensity of fighting was set to continue unabated, the capacity for the regime and its allies to sustain heavily invested efforts in every corner of the country was gradually declining. By February 2015 regime strategists had almost certainly come to this realisation, but it was not to translate into a discernible strategic shift on the broader battlefield until one final spring offensive could be launched. After all, throughout the winter, pro-regime militias—a great many of which were backed by Iran, with some others organisationally linked to Shia militia movements in Iraq—had been receiving planeloads of new recruits from Afghanistan, Pakistan, Iran, Yemen, Lebanon and elsewhere.[36]

Through the winter and into February 2015, the Syrian Arab Air Force continued to demonstrate that it remained the regime's most potent weapon and means of suppressing its people and the revolutionaries living within them. Opposition-controlled areas of Aleppo city had already been pounded by barrel bombs, but continued to be targeted nonetheless. Meanwhile, areas of rural Homs, Deraa city and its outlying areas and the besieged East Ghouta suburbs outside Damascus all suffered a similarly miserable fate. In the first ten days of February, for example, Syrian air strikes and barrel bombs killed at least 250 people in East Ghouta. As those bombs were falling, the Syrian Observatory for Human Rights reported that it had recorded at least 210,000 fatalities in the conflict since March 2011, with the number probably at least 85,000 higher.[37]

The situation in East Ghouta was already terrible. 'That winter was the worst,' said Abu Rami, an activist living in Irbin. 'Our people were so tired from war, from the barrels and from being so hungry every day. And it was winter, so we were cold too.'[38] Perhaps resulting from the sheer pressure felt within these besieged areas, the first months of 2015 saw a series of separate inter-factional conflicts erupt between rival Islamist factions in East Ghouta. Notwithstanding Jaish al-Islam's war on Jaish al-Ummah in January, Jabhat al-Nusra and al-Ittihad al-Islami Ajnad al-Sham entered into a brief fray in early February after a number of the latter's commanders and religious leaders were mysteriously assassinated in Irbin.[39] Days after that, Faylaq al-Rahman initiated a campaign of attacks on suspected IS cells in Saqba and Hamouriya,[40] while March saw periodic protests erupt against both Jaish al-Islam and Jabhat al-Nusra, often resulting in localised clashes.

Fortunately for the opposition in general, none of these tensions sparked anything more significant, but it certainly served to underline how Syria's prolonged conflict was producing big and powerful armed factions willing and able to fight each other, even amid the ongoing state of all-out war with the regime.

Meanwhile, the regime in Damascus continued to be courted by UN special envoy Staffan de Mistura, who visited the capital on 11 February and announced that he saw Assad as 'part of the solution' to Syria's conflict.[41] While de Mistura's staff were quick to clarify that his comments were linked more to 'short-term efforts to de-escalate violence' rather than to long-term objectives of ending the conflict altogether, the damage had been done.[42] In a split second, the envoy's already bad reputation among the armed opposition was destroyed. There would be no coming back from that comment, whether it was intentional or misunderstood. The fact that he had just visited Damascus, where by that time as many as 350 people, including 120 children, had been killed by airstrikes and barrel bombs since the beginning of the month, made his misjudged remarks all the more galling.[43]

Five days after his comments were published the RCC Executive Council met in the southern Turkish town of Reyhanlı and agreed to issue a statement condemning the 'biased' UN special envoy and declaring:

> The Council along with all of its [seventy-two] factions has decided to reject meeting the UN mediator due to his dishonest position towards the revolution and of the Syrian people.[44]

In a remarkably blasé response, a spokeswoman for de Mistura replied to the media with the following comment:

> We are aware of the referred-to statement and continue to follow with interest and concern the reactions coming out from the different groups and entities.[45]

Two weeks later, amid continued talk of the UN special envoy's 'Aleppo ceasefire' initiative, all the main factions of Aleppo met alongside ETILAF president Khaled Khoja in the southern Turkish town of Kilis and announced that they too refused any further engagement with the UN. In a speech issued by the then political leader of al-Jabhat al-Shamiyya, Zakaria Malahfji, the newly formed 'Aleppo Revolutionary Commission' declared:

> We refuse to meet with Mr Staffan de Mistura if it is not on the basis of a comprehensive solution to Syria's drama through the exit of Bashar al-Assad and his chief of staff, and the prosecution of war criminals ... Syria and its people are indivisible. The blood of our brothers in Deraa, in Ghouta, in Homs, and in other provinces is no less important than our blood in Aleppo.[46]

Perhaps spurred on by de Mistura's comments, the opposition's replies and the UN's clear and continued determination to get Assad and his underlings on board with any potential peace or ceasefire initiative, the regime launched two major military operations in February. First, approximately 5,000 Hezbollah and other Shia militiamen, backed by specialist units of the Syrian army and Republican Guard, initiated a concerted offensive against opposition positions in southern Syria, focused principally on a triangle of territory between south-west Damascus, Deraa city and the small western governorate of Quneitra. For the regime, this was pivotally important territory that secured the primary south–north route from Jordan to Damascus as well as Hezbollah's logistical and supply routes from Damascus to Lebanon and key minority areas in southern Damascus.

The regime, Iran and Hezbollah had spent weeks preparing for the offensive, principally by deploying large numbers of additional forces into forward-operating bases in northern Deraa, Quneitra and Suwayda. Some of this provided additional cover for an allegedly secret Iranian-backed Hezbollah unit designed to operate covertly within Quneitra in order to target Israel. This unit was purportedly led by Jihad Mugniyeh, the son of Hezbollah's notorious military leader Imad Mugniyeh. Jihad was killed in an Israeli air strike in Quneitra on 18 January alongside his unit 'mentor', IRGC commander General Mohammed Ali Allah-Dadi.[47] Several other Iranian and Lebanese Hezbollah commanders were amongst those killed in the targeted strike, which was carried out by an Israeli helicopter gunship. Ten days later two Israeli soldiers were killed in an IED attack on the Quneitra–Israeli Golan border, in what was clear Hezbollah retaliation.[48]

Within the first forty-eight hours of the southern offensive's launch, pro-regime forces successfully captured a number of important target towns, including Deir al-Adas, Deir Maker and Denaji. Pro-regime forces also had the strategic town of Sheikh Miskin on their list of immediate objectives, after much of the town and its neighbouring 82nd Brigade base had been captured by opposition fighters in late January. Shortly thereafter, and as Syria's minister of defence paid a triumphant visit to the frontline, reported live by Hezbollah's al-Manar TV station, Abu Osama al-Jolani of the recently formed First Army was quoted referring to the defence of positions under assault as a 'battle [that] could be lengthy' and where 'guerrilla warfare' was the only strategy available for the opposition.[49] For a time, therefore, the regime appeared to have the advantage.

However, rough winter weather and poor visibility meant that the air force went for several days without being able to carry out air strikes in support of its forces on the ground between 11 and 15 January. Without air cover, and as the opposition recomposed its forces, the regime's 'battle for the south' slowed in both progress and intensity. Casualties mounted during this brief period of intense stalemate, with at least ninety-three combatant fatalities reported in four days in Deraa alone.[50]

From a broader perspective, the regime's southern offensive in February was also pivotally important in terms of what its strategic design symbolised. Reports from the ground at the time underlined that Iran and Hezbollah had assumed the lead command role and that their forces were the ones fighting the most pivotal battles, with Syria's armed forces left largely to play support roles. The increasing prominence of Iran in determining the regime's warfare strategy and ground operations through late 2014 and now into early 2015 was not an entirely popular development within pro-Assad circles—especially when this still failed to ensure successful results on the battlefield, whether against IS or the opposition as a whole. Intriguingly therefore, ten Syrian army officers were reported executed by their commanders after being accused of coordinating or cooperating with the opposition.[51]

A month later two of Assad's most powerful intelligence chiefs were fired due to an apparent physical falling out over this new Iran–Assad regime dynamic. According to reports, General Rostom Ghazali, the head of Syria's Political Intelligence branch and a native of Deraa governorate, had complained bitterly about being left out of the offensive in the south and being replaced by Iranian and Lebanese commanders. In response, General Rafiq Shahadeh, the head of Syria's Military Intelligence, expressly blocked Ghazali's attempts to get involved, and at some point the two reportedly engaged in a 'violent disagreement' after which Ghazali was hospitalised.[52] Subsequent reports of Ghazali's death in late April added further to suspicions of intra-regime tensions, although some countered this and suggested that smuggling had been the cause of Ghazali's falling out with Shahadeh.[53]

Amid such apparent divisions in the south, the regime's focus shifted northwards later in February, as it launched another offensive on Aleppo, this time seemingly with the objective of decisively defeating the opposition's last remaining hold over parts of the city's north and north-east. As in the south, however, it was pro-regime militiamen who took the lead in the offensive, but this time many of them were Asian recruits with minimal training. 'They were crazy, sometimes as brave as those who fight in [Jabhat] al-Nusra, but they didn't know what they were doing. Honestly, they were a confusing enemy to fight,' commented one Islamist fighter based at the time in the village of Bashkoy.[54]

Also as in the southern offensive, pro-regime forces made early gains against comparatively unprepared opposition fighters. Bashkoy and at least three other villages were taken on the first morning (17 February), for example. However, within twenty-four hours a rapidly formed coalition of moderate FSA units, Ahrar al-Sham and hardline jihadist Jaish al-Muhajireen wa'l Ansar and Jabhat al-Nusra militants imposed several significant counter-attack defeats on the inexperienced 'crazy' militiamen facing them on the other side. By the close of 18 February at least seventy pro-regime militiamen and eighty opposition fighters had been killed[55] in what on-the-ground reports described as especially intense fighting, often 'hand-to-hand'.

The rapid reversal of regime fortunes in Aleppo was again indicative of how stretched the Syrian military and its militia partners were becoming. Increasingly strict army drafting regulations and an expansion of militia recruitment to include older and younger men, as well as foreigners from further afield, simply did not appear sufficient to secure the kind of offensive military potential that President Assad had been able to wield in 2013 and early 2014. By April 2015 the regime had gone as far as setting up checkpoints within pro-regime villages, towns and city districts in order to check cars and buses for young men dodging the draft. Security guards were also placed at university gates to check the records of both students and male teachers.[56]

Within this environment, Iran remained a resolute financial and military supporter, and the arrival and initiation into active operations of ten newly overhauled Iranian Sukhoi-22 fighter bombers in early March 2015 signified the latest provision of advanced weaponry from Iran to the Assad regime. The Su-22s were put to immediate use in quelling a re-emerging and increasingly confident, if still relatively localised, grouping of rebels in Homs, centred around the town of Talbiseh.[57]

Perhaps the most direct beneficiary of regime weakening on its peripheries was IS. Having borne the brunt of six months of air strikes in Iraq and Syria by February 2015, the group had not lost vast amounts of territory, but its indefatigable push for Kobane through the winter had seen it lose hundreds of men—possibly several thousand. Although neither Syrian opposition nor Syrian regime forces had demonstrated any particularly intensive resolve to drive IS out of the core of its territorial 'state,' the Kurdish YPG—despite its structural links to the PKK, a designated terrorist organisation—had emerged as a determined and capable (with US air support) anti-IS actor.

After more comprehensively sealing the town of Kobane in early February, the YPG's more north-eastern contingents set about launching a major offensive against IS positions in Hasakah governorate. Beginning in force on 21 February and benefiting from invaluable assistance lent by American fighter jets and MQ-1 Predator drones, the YPG advanced on IS's key bastion in the town of Tel Hamis near the Iraqi border. Its situation north-east of the governorate capital and south-west of another key IS stronghold in the oil town of al-Shadadi meant that taking Tel Hamis would result in serious damage to IS's reach into Syria's north-eastern corner and its access to unofficial border crossings into northern Iraq and towns such as Sinjar and Tel Afar. Kurdish Peshmerga also played a key support role in the early days of the offensive, firing long-range artillery across the Syria–Iraq border and into small farming villages that IS controlled around Tel Hamis.

Within five days of concerted and coordinated assaults from multiple axes, the YPG took Tel Hamis and forced an IS withdrawal southward. Unfortunately, as so often had been the case during the Syrian conflict, it was other minority communities that suffered the consequences of the combatants' wars and interests. The area around Tel Hamis and another key town, Tel Tamr, was home to a sizeable Syriac Christian population. Tel Tamr was controlled and administered jointly by the YPG and the Syriac Military Council, a militia movement comprising mainly male members of north-east Hasakah's Syriac Christian community. The Syriac Military Council had played a role in anti-jihadist operations in parts of Hasakah since as early as December 2013, but was only drawn into this YPG offensive when IS launched a retaliatory attack on Tel Tamr and kidnapped as many as 250 Christian civilians.[58]

Just as IS was taking pickaxes to dozens of priceless statues and sculptures from as far back as the seventh century BC in a museum in Mosul[59] (and later bulldozers to the ancient city of Hatra),[60] it was also venting its wrath against ancient Christian communities. Although seventeen men and two women were released on 1 March, four days after IS's loss of Tel Hamis, the remaining 'more than 200' Assyrians continued to languish in IS custody well into the summer of 2015.[61]

While suffering consistent losses to the YPG in the north-east, ISs attention shifted southwards into the deserts of central Homs and south-eastern Hama in March. After receiving pledges of *bay'a* from further jihadist cells in Yemen and also from Boko Haram in Nigeria, and killing at least forty-five Kurds at a Nowrūz (new year) celebration in Qamishli, IS began a methodical two-pronged advance westwards into Syria's interior.

On one axis, IS militants attacked the village of Sheikh Hilal, where it massacred as many as seventy people, variously described as both civilians and members of the paramilitary NDF.[62] At first glance, the attack on Sheikh Hilal appeared to indicate further IS determination to target small minority communities for shock effect. Only 12 kilometres west from Sheikh Hilal, on an easy drive along 'Road 42', lay al-Sa'n, the first in a string of Ismaili villages and towns leading to al-Salamiyah, where the founding father of the Ismaili sect, Ismail bin Jaafar, is buried.[63] Some Western diplomats maintained privately at the time that an all-out IS assault on al-Salamiyah could have had the same mobilising effect in terms of inducing a resolute international intervention as IS's attack on Sinjar Mountain in Iraq in August 2014.[64]

On the other, perhaps more strategically important, axis, IS militants began launching pincer raids on areas in Homs's desert, around the town of al-Sukhna and further south-west outside the town of Palmyra (also known as Tadmur), famed for its ancient ruins. A major assault was launched on Tadmur airport and on a series of regime-run gas facilities on the approach to al-Furqlus. Although al-Sukhna had been captured by Jabhat al-Nusra, Jaish al-Islam and several small FSA units in October 2013, it had been quickly recaptured by regime forces at the time. Critically placed on the M20 highway, control of al-Sukhna guaranteed that the regime's supply lines between Damascus and Deir ez Zour remained open. The town was also a key bastion of Syria's notorious specialist force, Suqor al-Sahara,[65] which had been IS's primary adversary in the vast expanse of Homs's desert, designated by IS as its Wilayat al-Badiyya.

Although no major IS gains were made in the early stages of this westward offensive, it was a new dynamic that would gradually escalate in scale and significance in the weeks and months to come.

Jabhat al-Nusra also had new advances on its mind in February and March 2015. After so comprehensively defeating the SRF in Idlib, it was fast emerging as a dominant actor in Syria's north-west governorate. Although its publicly declared policy was to cooperate with all 'non-corrupt' opposition forces who credibly dedicated themselves to fighting the regime, it had begun to assert its authority in an increasingly independent and aggressive fashion. Occasionally, this brought it into actual violent clashes with rival groups, such as the FSA's 7th Brigade in the mountains of Jebel al-Zawiyeh in mid-February. But more often, it simply meant that many other groups in the region were beginning to view their long-time jihadist ally through a slightly more suspicious lens. Despite that, Jabhat al-Nusra's almost unrivalled capabilities on the battlefield ensured that it was still seen as an invaluable military partner while the Assad regime remained in place.

Consequently, turning against Jabhat al-Nusra was an immensely risky business—one that had rarely if ever brought with it any benefit. Having periodically come to blows with Jabhat al-Nusra ever since siding with the SRF in Idlib in late October 2014, Harakat Hazm's newly focused Aleppo forces were again operating in close proximity to al-Qaeda. During its defeat alongside the SRF, a great many Harakat Hazm fighters had defected to Jabhat al-Nusra and Ahrar al-Sham, leaving the group a fraction of its size when formed in January 2014.

Thus, it came as somewhat of a surprise to many in late November when Harakat Hazm—numbering roughly 400–500 fighters, mostly deployed in Aleppo—began stirring up trouble with Jabhat al-Nusra. Although it was minimally reported at the time, Harakat Hazm had begun setting up make-shift checkpoints on the main roads between western Aleppo and Idlib, periodically arresting Jabhat al-Nusra fighters and stalling the group's supply lines. 'Really, Hazm was causing too many problems for all of us, not only Nusra,' said one FSA-linked leader from Aleppo. 'It was strange really, nobody understood why they became a big problem, but they were troublemakers and we all wanted them gone by the end.'[66]

After Harakat Hazm arrested five Jabhat al-Nusra members and executed several more, including prominent commander Abu Eissa al-Tabqa, Jabhat al-Nusra released an official statement on 25 February declaring war on the group. 'From the date of this announcement's publication, [we] consider what has been called "Harakat Hazm" in all its components, a direct target,' the communiqué declared.[67] Jabhat al-Nusra quickly launched a number of fierce assaults on Harakat Hazm's primary bases, including the Syrian army's old 46th Regiment base west of Aleppo, killing at least thirty fighters.[68] Thanks both to its apparently mischievous behaviour and Jabhat al-Nusra's fearful reputation, nobody came to Harakat Hazm's aid and, by early on 1 March, the group announced its full dissolution. While its leadership fled across the border into the Turkish towns of Gaziantep and Reyhanlı, some of its fighters chose to join the Aleppo coalition al-Jabhat al-Shamiyya.[69]

'It was a sad time for the revolution in Aleppo. We represent Syria's most modern and cosmopolitan city and the fight here has been so difficult for such a long time. Despite Hazm's mistakes, nobody I knew wanted to see us turning against each other and betraying the revolution, even for a short time,' said another Aleppo-based FSA commander. 'Really, these conflicts between factions are a dangerous development. I fear for the future, because people hold grudges. Things like this will not just be forgotten.'[70]

Whatever the potential future implications, the brief but highly significant bout of infighting in Aleppo yet again underlined Jabhat al-Nusra's capacity to determine its own fate and to defeat those who stood in its way. In capturing Harakat Hazm's headquarters in the 46th Regiment base, al-Qaeda had now got its hands on American-made and supplied BGM-71 TOW anti-tank guided missiles, some of which were proudly showed off as *ghanima* (booty) from the battles.[71] As with the defeat of the SRF, there was a terrible irony to such consequences of Harakat Hazm's defeat.

However, not all was necessarily playing to Jabhat al-Nusra's advantage. The group was simultaneously facing a series of low-level demonstrations against its presence in opposition-controlled areas of southern Damascus. Far more significant was the death of Jabhat al-Nusra's military leader, Abu Hamam al-Suri, in Idlib. Although the exact circumstances surrounding his death remain unclear—with conflicting accounts saying he was killed in a US air strike, a Syrian air strike, and a Syrian 'military operation', on 5 March, 6 March or in late February—his death marked a major blow to al-Qaeda's top-level leadership in Syria. As a long-time al-Qaeda veteran who graduated second out of the al-Farouq training camp in Afghanistan, behind one of the 9/11 hijackers,[72] Abu Hamam was a prominent jihadist with extensive connections into al-Qaeda's senior military leadership. He was also a Syrian, whose public face as a key Jabhat al-Nusra leader had served to sustain the group's claim that it was Syrian above all other transnational considerations.

Meanwhile, despite continuing to receive invaluable financial, political and military support from Iran and Russia, pro-regime forces appeared by March increasingly vulnerable in areas comparatively peripheral to Assad's most critical strategic interests. Even Aleppo city, which in mid-to-late 2014 had looked to some like a candidate for total regime victory, saw the near-total demolition of the headquarters of the city's branch of Air Force Intelligence on 3 March, after jihadists detonated an extensive 'tunnel bomb', killing dozens of personnel.[73]

Most stark of all, however, were signs in mid-March that pro-regime forces were initiating preliminary moves towards slimming down their force levels in Idlib city. Key regime-held transport routes out of the city and into key country-side bastions—such as the predominantly Shia villages of al-Fuah and Kafraya; east towards the Abu al-Dhuhour air base; and south towards al-Mastouma and al-Qarmeed, leading towards the al-Ghab Plain and northern Hama—were all substantially beefed up in the middle of the month. A proportion of tanks and armoured vehicles deployed in Idlib city were also gradually redeployed into these valuable areas in a sign of things to come. Idlib was set to see the most significant and sustained series of opposition victories since at least 2013.

Before the real drama was to begin, Ahrar al-Sham announced its full merger with fellow Islamic Front member, Idlib-based Suqor al-Sham, on 22 March. Although the latter group had dwindled in size over the past year—thanks in large part to the outbreak of conflict with IS—it remained a key actor in Idlib, and its leader, Abu Eissa al-Sheikh, was a well-regarded revolutionary, respected not only for his consistent dedication to the revolution but for his considerable familial losses suffered during the conflict. The merger announcement was made by Ahrar al-Sham leader Hashem al-Sheikh, who clarified that Ahrar al-Sham would retain its name and Abu Eissa would become its deputy political leader.

While this further strengthened Ahrar al-Sham's hand in Idlib, potentially as a subtle counter-balance to Jabhat al-Nusra's growing assertiveness in the region, it also served to underline the consistent success of Ahrar al-Sham's strategy of acquiring new factions through a 'mergers and acquisitions' policy. Since its very first days as Kataib Ahrar al-Sham in late 2011 and 2012, the group had steadily expanded through a development of constructive relationships with other factions. By early 2015 it was undoubtedly the single largest and most powerfully influential armed opposition group in Syria, excluding IS.

The merger was also a final preparatory step for the formation of a new grand coalition in Idlib. Established two days later on 24 March while Jabhat al-Nusra, Harakat al-Muthanna al-Islamiyya and Ahrar al-Sham joined with the Southern Front in capturing the town of Busra al-Sham in Deraa, the Jaish al-Fateh military operations room was presented as an Idlib-based alliance of seven armed groups—Jabhat al-Nusra, Jund al-Aqsa, Ahrar al-Sham, Faylaq al-Sham, Ajnad al-Sham, Liwa al-Haq and Jaish al-Sunnah—whose principal and immediate objective was to take control of Idlib city. Addressing their 'families' in the city, the operations room's founding statement declared:

> We are on the outskirts of this almighty city of Idlib. We have not betrayed you and we have not forgotten how the regime oppresses you ... [and] your screams calling for the fall of the regime, and we promise that our minds will not be at ease and we will not rest until we uproot the oppressor and replace him with merciful and just Islamic rule.[74]

Answering a call for regime forces to defect to Jaish al-Fateh through a time-limited amnesty and before it was too late, at least forty-five soldiers and five officers reportedly switched sides later that day.[75]

After an intense bombardment of Idlib city and known regime positions through the day on 24 March, several initial specialist ground forces were sent in during the night. Led by three suicide bombers—two from Jund al-Aqsa,

Abu Omar al-Kuwaiti and Karar al-Najdi, and one unidentified militant from Jabhat al-Nusra—these early assaults saw the city limits penetrated and several regime checkpoints captured. By the morning of 25 March the battle front-lines had become clear, with Jabhat al-Nusra largely running operations on the city's north, while Ahrar al-Sham and Jund al-Aqsa split the south and east, with the western front encompassing the remaining forces of Jaish al-Fateh.

Having already slimmed down its forces in the city, the regime proved incapable of defending against such an all-out and multi-pronged assault on Idlib, and by early on 28 March the entire city was under Jaish al-Fateh control. This was only the second governorate capital to be captured from the regime since the start of the revolution, the only other being IS's de facto capital, Raqqa. Its capture also meant that supply lines north to the Shia militia and pro-regime strongholds in al-Fuah and Kafraya were now cut off, while key regime positions south of the city—such as Ariha and Jisr al-Shughour—now lay open to attack.

Although Jaish al-Fateh represented a broad spread of Islamically minded opposition factions—from core jihadists in Jund al-Aqsa and Jabhat al-Nusra, to Syrian Salafists in Ahrar al-Sham, through to the Muslim Brotherhood-aligned Faylaq al-Sham and the even more moderate FSA faction Jaish al-Sunnah—the image of Idlib's capture was one carried out by *shalwar kameez*-wearing men with long beards. Indeed, the two numerically dominant factions involved were Ahrar al-Sham and Jabhat al-Nusra, while several smaller jihadist groups had also played a limited role, such as the TIP and Katibat al-Tawhid wa'l Jihad. Aware of this, Jaish al-Fateh was quick to announce that their plans for the newly liberated Idlib city were civil focused. Ahrar al-Sham leader Hashem al-Sheikh issued a formal written statement stressing the importance of 'presenting a spotless image of Islam's engagement with and management of the affairs of the people'.

> To our people in the free Idlib, here are your sons who have expended their spirits and spilled blood in order to lift from you the injustice of this criminal regime. Spread the good news, by the will of God. They who put their leaders before their soldiers did not come to build for themselves a following or an emirate. So aid your brothers and share in their jihad by running the city, and carry out their affairs as a way to account for the share due to Allah.[76]

Two days later Jabhat al-Nusra leader Jolani also chimed in, seeking to present the capture of Idlib as a victory for the Syrian people, but one that would nonetheless see Islamic law established as a perceived means for justice and stability:

We congratulate the ummah for the great victory achieved at the hands of her sons, the mujahideen, in the honorable city of Idlib. Likewise, we congratulate the mujahideen for their great unification [within Jaish al-Fateh] ... We value and appreciate all who participated. Militarily, from among the commanders and soldiers, administrators, reporters, medical centers and factory workers ...

And we salute the actions of our family in the city of Idlib ... We promise them that they will not see from their sons except the best manners and good social relations, and they will be delighted by Allah's permission with the justice of Allah's Sharia. That which protects their religion, their blood, their sanctities and their wealth. That which protects their honor and dignity ... That which watches over their security and establishes consultation [al-Shura] and strives for the rights of the poor, and establishes justice within them.

The mission of preserving what has been gained through victory is much harder than achieving victory ... As such, we in Jabhat al-Nusra confirm it is not our goal to rule or monopolize the city with the exclusion of others ... for truly, consultation [al-Shura] is the best system ... We point to the importance of preserving the positions and public services ... Additionally, those employed in the public service sector such as health services, electricity, water, bakeries, communications and cleaning services should be called upon to return to their positions and to continue their work...

A supervisory committee should be formed by the different groups to assess the condition of those workers and carry out their requirements in helping them conduct their duties to the best of their ability, and to take them to account should they fall short in that.

We stress the importance of establishing a Sharia court as quickly as possible, to judge between the people to solve any disagreements between them. It is upon all civilians to raise their complaints and mistreatments to the court even if these are rights from decades before, because rights do not fade with the passing of time.[77]

Notwithstanding the debate and concerns regarding Idlib's future governance system, reality struck home fast in the city when the regime's reaction to defeat was to pummel it with barrel bombs and airstrikes. The city's central square, in which stands an old clock-tower, was all but destroyed within forty-eight hours of its capture, for example. As with many other areas across Syria, such indiscriminate regime bombardment induced a great many civilians to flee, thereby removing the professional civil administrators that Jaish al-Fateh required to continue their work in running the city. Whether Jabhat al-Nusra, Jund al-Aqsa and Ahrar al-Sham wanted genuine civil governance or not, it wouldn't work if all capable people had chosen to become internally displaced instead.

Beyond the straightforward facts surrounding Idlib's capture, there is an important backstory, which demonstrates more clearly the intra-opposition and intra-Islamist dynamics in the governorate, which had been fast becoming al-Qaeda's favoured stomping ground.

The victory in Idlib demonstrated a level of inter-factional coordination that had arguably not been seen before in Syria. The capture of a governorate capital in the space of four days was remarkable by any standards, but it was also the result of at least eight months of broader grand strategic planning, aiming ultimately for the capture of the entire governorate. The attack on Idlib city had been planned since the winter of 2014, having been explicitly—but secretly—linked to the long-planned offensive on the Wadi al-Deif and al-Hamadiyeh bases in mid-December 2014.[78]

Moreover, beginning in November 2014, Ahrar al-Sham in particular had begun receiving considerably increased levels of logistical and military support from Turkey and, to some extent, also from Qatar. With US and allied attention firmly fixed on IS and seemingly ignoring the fate of the revolution in Syria, Turkey appeared to make the decision then that it held the responsibility of imposing a more direct threat upon the Assad regime's hold over northern Syria. In addition to money to cover salaries, Ahrar al-Sham and several other groups, including Faylaq al-Sham, took delivery of increased volumes of 122-mm Grad rockets, tank shells, the necessary materials for constructing home-made artillery rockets and mortars, as well as AK-series assault rifles, anti-tank recoilless rifles and small-arms ammunition.[79] Much of this was stockpiled away, and some proved invaluable in securing the victories at Wadi al-Deif and al-Hamadiyeh in December.

Within this environment of intensified Turkish involvement and support, Ahrar al-Sham initiated discussions in December 2014 with other Idlib-based factions on the subject of unifying within a single coalition or operations room. Some US-backed factions, such as Liwa Forsan al-Haq and Liwa Suqor al-Jebel—both of which received military training in Qatar—could not or would not join a body containing Jabhat al-Nusra, but suggested at the time that they would nonetheless support any operations that such a body could eventually lead. It was no coincidence, therefore, that both these groups ended up playing a crucially important role in supporting Jaish al-Fateh's subsequent offensives through April and May, particularly by utilising their US-made anti-tank missiles.

The initial objective was that after attacking and capturing Wadi al-Deif and al-Hamadiyeh, an all-out assault would be launched on Idlib city. After that, so the theory went, the regime's principal military and logistical lifelines in Ariha, Jisr al-Shughour, al-Mastouma, al-Qarmeed and elsewhere would follow. Playing out this long-term strategy would leave the regime critically weak in Idlib, and its heartlands in Latakia and its key lines of defence in Hama would be vulnerable to attack. It was a bold idea by all standards, but with additional Turkish support and an increasingly clear need to encourage further unity across Syrian factions to prevent Jabhat al-Nusra dominance, there appeared to be broad support for it at the time.[80]

While the fight against the regime was far and away the primary focus of all Syrians involved, constructively balancing Jabhat al-Nusra's growing strength was also on people's minds at the time. Although not made public, Ahrar al-Sham's top-level political and overall leadership had become concerned at the increasingly prominent use of the 'al-Qaeda' name by Jabhat al-Nusra when referring to their activities. Speaking to this author throughout the winter of 2014–15, these senior Ahrar al-Sham officials described their concerns regarding Jabhat al-Nusra, that it was beginning to 'walk down the wrong path',[81] resulting in 'values that contradict those we started within the revolution'.[82] Ahrar al-Sham leader Hashem al-Sheikh went as far as to declare this concern subtly in public, during an interview with Al-Jazeera Arabic in April 2015, in which he declared that Jabhat al-Nusra's affiliation with al-Qaeda was a danger to the Syrian people.[83]

Notwithstanding such concerns, Ahrar al-Sham had long been and still was undoubtedly Jabhat al-Nusra's most valuable enabler in Syria. Its consistently strong coordination with the group on the battlefield and its early cooperation with multi-group *sharia* judicial bodies across the country ensured that Jabhat al-Nusra found itself an integrated revolutionary actor early on in the conflict. Nevertheless, while there were certainly no signs that Ahrar al-Sham would be turning against Jabhat al-Nusra militarily any time soon, there was a definite awareness within the group's top levels that its long-time ally could become increasingly difficult to manage, so a delicate counter-balancing was needed. Jaish al-Fateh appeared to be a constructive attempt at just that policy.

As April 2015 began, therefore, the conflict in Syria had entered a new stage in which the regime's manpower and other limitations were beginning to emerge more clearly. For right or wrong, the Jaish al-Fateh concept being demonstrated in Idlib had rapidly proved its value by producing an extremely effective military adversary to regime control in Idlib. Moreover, regional geo-political dynamics were also changing. With Turkey already asserting a much-expanded role in determining the trajectory of the conflict in northern Syria, and particularly in Idlib, the opposition's capture of the Nassib border crossing with Jordan on 1 April similarly suggested that Amman had chosen to roll its dice definitively in favour of the rebels. Up to that point, this last remaining commercial crossing with Jordan had been a no-go zone for opposition forces, after the Amman-based MOC had insisted it remain tacitly under regime control.

The eruption of conflict in Yemen in late March 2015—between Houthis and forces loyal to former president Ali Abdullah Saleh on one side, and southern separatist militias and forces loyal to 'Abd Rabbuh Mansour Hadi on the other—had also sparked a Saudi-led military intervention in the region. Saudi's air operations utilised intelligence and logistical support provided by the USA and involved personnel from eight other Arab states. Such a rapid regional mobilisation was a source of frustration for Syrians four years into a civil conflict, but it also revealed an environment in which Riyadh—with a new and more interventionist leadership now in place following the death of King Abdullah in January 2015—was more willing to get its hands dirty in pursuit of its interests. Behind the scenes, the first major consequence of this new Saudi approach was a gradual rapprochement between Riyadh and both Qatar and Turkey, with all three states coming more closely together in terms of Syria policy than had been the case since the start of the revolution in 2011.

Consequently, despite frustration that such strikes had never been launched to rescue them from their oppression in Syria, rebel groups from a variety of different political and ideological backgrounds began publicly expressing their support for the Saudi intervention in Yemen—seen as part of a broader struggle against Iran-led Shia expansionism in the region.

Amid this regional coming together, Jaish al-Islam leader Zahran Alloush suddenly appeared in Istanbul, having spent the better part of four years in Damascus leading his forces in battle against the regime.[84] Alloush had smuggled himself into Jordan first, from where he flew to the Turkish city and appeared in early photographs meeting with Syrian Islamic figures Sheikh Osama al-Rifai (president of the Syrian Islamic Council) and Sheikh Mohammed Karim Rajeh (chairman of the Syrian Association of Islamic Scholars). Alongside Zahran was his cousin and political chief, Mohammed Alloush, a stocky middle-aged man with a sharp, quick thinking and assertive political mind.

Jaish al-Islam maintained close connections in Saudi Arabia, perhaps thanks to the fact that Zahran's father and famed Salafist cleric, Sheikh Abdullah Mohammed Alloush, was a long-time resident of the country. The arrival of one of the revolution's most famous and notorious faces into a Turkish city was indicative of the new geo-political situation. Moreover, the relatively new Turkish-backed ETILAF president, Khaled Khoja, had also paid a secret visit to Saudi Arabia at the beginning of April.[85]

That Alloush later held extensive joint meetings with the senior leadership of Ahrar al-Sham in Istanbul (including Hashem al-Sheikh, Abu Mohammed al-Sadeq and Abu Eissa al-Sheikh) on 1 May was arguably even more significant, as both groups sought to de-escalate their competitive relationship. Previously, the rivalry between these two 'mega groups' had effectively split the Islamic Front in two, with its various other factions agreeing to merge into one or the other, leaving only Jaish al-Islam and Ahrar al-Sham at the end. For Turkey, ensuring that these two groups transitioned into a more constructive and productive partnership would have seemed a sure way of boosting the revolution's potential in Syria.

The changing geo-political landscape, combined with Jaish al-Fateh's victory in Idlib, undoubtedly injected a much-needed dose of adrenaline into the armed opposition in March and April 2015, but it also complicated things in other areas. The major Aleppo coalition, al-Jabhat al-Shamiyya, for example, had proven itself to be an excellent idea in theory, but the differing outlooks and regional relationships of its constituent groups meant that in practice it remained more of a name than a single body. Due to the intensity of the battle in Aleppo city against the regime and north of the city against IS, al-Jabhat al-Shamiyya had sought from its early days to establish single unified sources of funding and support, but the divergent interests of its individual factions meant that this proved practically impossible. Much to the disappointment of those in Aleppo, the coalition quietly announced its dissolution on April 19.[86]

Meanwhile, seemingly largely unaware of such broader developments, IS exploited the improving spring weather to launch a variety of new offensive operations across Syria that would seek to shake up existing dynamics.

On 1 April, for example, IS militants based in southern Damascus's al-Hajar al-Aswad district crossed north into the Palestinian Yarmouk refugee camp, allegedly assisted by a number of sympathetic Jabhat al-Nusra members angry at recent arrests of their members by Palestinians seeking the assassin of a local Hamas official, Yahya al-Hourani.[87] While much of the camp had fallen under IS control within twenty-four hours, the group was briefly forced to withdraw, before re-entering en masse on 4 March. There then followed several days of particularly intense urban fighting between the jihadists and local residents and members of the Palestinian semi-opposition group Aknaf Bayt al-Maqdis. By 6 March the true complexity of Yarmouk revealed itself when pro-regime elements from the PFLP, the PFLP-GC, Fatah al-Intifada and the

Palestine Liberation Army (PLA) all entered the camp and launched a separate regime-backed offensive against IS. It eventually petered out, however, with IS still in control of a majority of Yarmouk by 8 April.

Four days later, after collecting forces and weapons from neighbouring districts, Jaish al-Islam launched its own concerted counter-offensive against IS, targeting the group primarily in its relative stronghold in al-Hajar al-Aswad. That attempt also largely failed to dislodge IS from its positions of control, with the group subsequently expanding the battle east into the opposition-controlled Barzeh and al-Qaboun neighbourhoods. IS remained in control of much of Yarmouk in the following weeks and months, with pro-regime forces still seeking to expel the group from the camp in July 2015.

In addition to its deadly escapades in Yarmouk, which caused only further misery in an already dire area, IS also escalated the pace of its operations in the Qalamoun mountains bordering Lebanon, fighting the regime, Hezbollah and occasionally also turning its guns on the opposition. Although this latter dynamic had been a reality for some time, patience was wearing thin, and on 4 April Jaish al-Islam, Ahrar al-Sham and several other FSA-affiliated factions announced their initiation of anti-IS operations in the region. As with other areas across the country, IS's absolute enmity towards all but its own forced a reduction in opposition forces' capacity to fight the regime, thereby freeing up pro-Assad personnel, including those within Hezbollah, who were in the midst of planning a long-awaited spring offensive in the Qalamoun mountains.

Similarly, IS also sought to continue its guerrilla-type operations in northern Aleppo, targeting Jabhat al-Nusra, Ahrar al-Sham and other local rebel forces on their frontline positions opposite IS territory. Beginning on 6 April with a double suicide car bomb and ground attack on joint Jabhat al-Nusra and Liwa al-Tawhid positions around the strategic town of Marea and near Hwar Kilis, IS gradually escalated the scale and frequency of such attacks into May and June, finally inducing the USA to carry out its first air strike in support of opposition forces north of Aleppo on 6 June.

Also through late April and into early May, IS sought to redress dynamics in southern Syria. Based in the town of al-Qahtaniya in Quneitra governorate, the recently formed pro-IS faction Jaish al-Jihad launched a series of surprise attacks on the FSA-linked Liwa Ahrar Nawa on 27 April, sparking several days of fighting that ended up drawing in Jabhat al-Nusra and Ahrar al-Sham, both of which came to the FSA's defence. That battle ended in defeat for Jaish al-Jihad—itself composed primarily of pro-IS Jabhat al-Nusra defectors—by the end of the first week of May. However, that would not be the last time that pro-IS factions in southern Syria sparked inter-factional fighting in 2015.

Further eastwards, IS also launched a series of night-time lightning raids into Suwayda governorate in mid- and late April, attacking the Khalkhalakh air base and several small Druze villages. Lessons learned from those attacks encouraged Druze communities in Syria's south-east to begin forming their own self-defence militias throughout the spring. Key mobilising Druze figures such as Sheikh Yousuf Jerbo and Sheikh Hamud al-Hanawi and Syrian army Brigadier-General Nayef al-Aqil proved effective coordinators of new militias such as the Dir al-Watan, which tied their survival both to their Druze and pro-Assad national identities.[88]

Beyond seeking to stir further complexity into an already messy conflict, IS also used April and May to expand actual control of territory in Syria. Initially, it launched a series of renewed attacks against regime forces in Deir ez Zour city, capturing at least three neighbourhoods in the north as well as Saqer Island on the Euphrates River, all between 6 and 15 May. A renewed focus on Deir ez Zour was almost certainly sparked by the redeployment of notorious Syrian Brigadier-General Issam Zahraddine—the commander of the specialist 104th Republican Guard Brigade—from Deir ez Zour to East Ghouta outside Damascus.[89] Up until then, Zahraddine's leadership of the eastern front against IS had arguably been the key barrier preventing it from taking the city altogether.

Further west meanwhile, along the Deir ez Zour–Homs M20 highway, IS launched a final all-out one-day assault on al-Sukhna in Homs, capturing it on 13 May. During the final phase of the attack, IS anti-tank units who were occupying several points of high ground overlooking the town's principal checkpoints launched guided missiles nearly simultaneously, destroying several regime T-72 tanks and opening the way for IS's *inghimasi* 'special forces' to initiate a final ground push. At this point, remaining Syrian military and NDF personnel began fleeing en masse from their positions along one single escape route. In a final unforgiving act of brutality, additional contingents of IS militants overlooking the route opened fire with small arms and heavy weapons, killing dozens of fleeing soldiers—all filmed on video from several different angles.[90]

On the same day, IS also launched a major assault on the well-known town of Palmyra, site of a significant Syrian military presence and the famous 2,000-year-old ruins designated as a UNESCO World Heritage Site. Separate attacks were carried out that day, on 13 May, on the town's northern al-Amari-yah district, on its military airport to the east and on a large complex of arms depots to the north-west. The valuable T3 gas pumping stations located east of Palmyra were also attacked. One week later, on 20 May, the entire town had fallen into IS hands, sparking international fear that its invaluable ruins would be destroyed. Although this was ignored at the time, the group followed up its victory in Palmyra by launching multiple simultaneous assaults on several regime-controlled gas facilities in the surrounding desert, rapidly cutting 45 per cent of the entire country's gas and electricity production capacity.[91]

IS had little immediate interest in demolishing the ruins at this point, as the vast majority of them did not qualify as objects of 'idol worship' the way other objects and areas in Iraq had. Moreover, the group's capture of the town had by itself attracted sufficient worldwide attention to preclude the need for provocative acts of historical destruction. Moreover, Palmyra's capture came only three days after IS had also conquered the western Iraqi city of Ramadi following months of battles with police and army personnel. The group's final assault on that city reportedly involved thirty suicide car bombs, ten of which each had an explosive yield similar to that used in the Oklahoma City bombing of April 1995.[92]

Despite suffering consistent losses to the Kurdish YPG in north-eastern Syria and elsewhere in Iraq, as well as being the target of an intelligence-led US Special Operations raid that killed senior Tunisian commander Abu Sayyaf east of Deir ez Zour city, IS reminded the world in May 2015 that it remained a potent military force capable of winning significant and damaging victories against its adversaries. It also showed off its recruitment of Gulmorod Halimov, who until 23 April had been the head of the Tajik Interior Ministry's special forces unit OMON,[93] and published a video showing off its medical facilities in Raqqa, the style of which seemed intentionally modelled on the British National Health Service.[94] And to counter reports from *Guardian* journalist Martin Chulov that its leader Abu Bakr al-Baghdadi had been incapacitated in an airstrike,[95] IS released an audio message given by its leader on 14 May. In it, Baghdadi referred explicitly to recent events in Yemen and the Saudi-led intervention there, as well as recent IS offensives in Iraq and Syria. He also issued a further call for global recruitment to the IS cause, insisting that 'there is no excuse for any Muslim not to migrate to the Islamic State'.[96]

While IS was back on the offensive, so too was Jabhat al-Nusra, thanks to the continued advances of Jaish al-Fateh in Idlib. Following on from the capture of Idlib city at the end of March and initially repelled attempts to take al-Mastouma in early April, approximately 12,000 Jaish al-Fateh forces regrouped and launched three simultaneous offensives on 22 April, on Jisr al-Shughour, on al-Mastouma and the nearby al-Qarmeed checkpoint, and on the Sahl al-Ghab region crossing Idlib and northern Hama. Within three days

Jaish al-Fateh had taken near-complete control of the town of Jisr al-Shughour, with the exception of the 'National Hospital', to which remaining regime security forces had fled and barricaded themselves in. That offensive had been led by Eyad al-Sha'ar (Abu al-Hassan), the Afghan veteran Ahrar al-Sham commander, whose family had lived in Jisr al-Shughour until they fled during regime–Islamist tensions in the late 1970s and set up home in Saudi Arabia and later Ireland. Twenty-four hours later, on 26 April, the Qarmeed military checkpoint fell to Jaish al-Fateh, after a huge suicide truck bomb detonated by a Jabhat al-Nusra militant from the Maldives obliterated its outer defences.

In all three operations, Jaish al-Fateh forces were backed up from the rear by US-backed FSA factions such as Liwa Forsan al-Haq, the 1st Coastal Division, Liwa Suqor al-Jebel and others. A considerable number of US-made and US-provided anti-tank guided missiles were expended to ensure that Jaish al-Fateh's ground forces were able to win territorial gains. Previously, the provision of US weaponry to 'vetted' groups had been made conditional on the recipients not using those weapons in direct cooperation with jihadist groups such as Jabhat al-Nusra. Under such conditions, all those 'vetted' groups active in northern Hama and throughout Idlib would have been contravening their agreements with the USA. However, following on from Jaish al-Fateh's victory in Idlib, FSA groups in the region had been instructed by their backers based in Turkey to increase their cooperation with the Islamist-led advances, according to multiple FSA leaders involved.[97]

With fighting in the Sahl al-Ghab region continuing apace throughout late April and into early May, Jaish al-Fateh forces again regrouped following their victories and prepared for a renewed push on al-Mastouma, Ariha and Jisr al-Shughour's National Hospital. By the middle of May a final assault was ordered on al-Mastouma, and on 19 May it fell to Jaish al-Fateh. Within its storage buildings were not only crates full of weapons, but boxes piled high with UN humanitarian assistance packages intended for civilians but stolen by the Syrian army.[98] Three days later the National Hospital in Jisr al-Shughour was captured after several further jihadist suicide bombings, and on 28 May the strategic town of Ariha also fell, revealing stores full of World Food Progamme (WFP) aid packages.[99] In the space of a month, Jaish al-Fateh had effectively imposed a near-total strategic defeat upon the regime in Idlib. Its only remaining areas of control in the governorate by the end of May were the Shia villages of al-Fuah and Kafraya and the minimally active Abu Dhuhour air base.

Jaish al-Fateh was clearly demonstrating the value of close multi-group cooperation in the battle against the regime, but the enabling role this had for bolstering Jabhat al-Nusra went largely ignored for a time. Moreover, the scale of the coalition's operations was also increasingly drawing in smaller but just as hardline jihadist factions. Junud al-Sham, the TIP and al-Katibat al-Tawhid wa'l Jihad all gained considerably in stature through their prominent involvement in each of Jaish al-Fateh's main victories in May. Having then captured territory, these groups were consequently afforded a role in their future governance and control, in accordance with the Islamic tradition of sharing the bounties of victory.

Nevertheless, the victories by themselves bolstered opposition confidence across the country, encouraging the formation of new Jaish al-Fateh coalitions in Aleppo (26 April), the Qalamoun (4 May) and southern Syria (20 June). Within this environment of renewed self-belief and confidence in the revolution's capacity to win an outright military victory, the opposition continued its tough stance towards UN special envoy de Mistura's initiative for peace in Syria. Following on from previous statements in February and early March, the UN continued to issue invitations to rebel groups—from vetted FSA factions to Ahrar al-Sham and Jaish al-Islam—to attend ongoing 'consultations' in Geneva. Bolstered by confidence gleaned from events on the ground, but also angered by de Mistura's continued insistence to speak to armed groups separately when the desire had been to do so jointly, the RCC convened a secret meeting of roughly fifty factions in Turkey on 10 May. During the meeting, the factions' senior leaders agreed to again refuse to cooperate with the UN initiative, issuing a statement signed by thirty-seven factions, including Ahrar al-Sham:

> While we confirm our genuine will in dealing with the international community and its organizations trying to achieve a just solution to the Syrian situation ... We require a great deal of precision and transparency where every effort or attempt is made to find a solution for Syria. Without basing it on a clear and solvable foundation, there will not be true acceptance.

> Your [De Mistura's] stands and statements, especially with regards to your declaration that Bashar al-Assad is part of the solution in Syria show a clear stumble in your manner of dealing with Syrian affairs. You have a clear impression of your indifference to the atrocities committed by the regime in Syria, such as the Douma massacre committed by the regime while you were being hosted, at a distance not far from your place of residence in Damascus. You voiced no objection or condemnation to the regime's massacre. You showed no compassion towards the victims ...

> We were careful to deliberate your invitation and to discuss its contents. We decided to decline your invitation because we believe that our participation in these discussions will not be a constructive step in elaborating a real solution to the situation in Syria for the following reasons:

1. Your invitation lacks any fundamentals or clear instruments capable of reaching realistic outcomes ...
2. The deliberate undermining of rebel factions and rebel action groups, while on the one hand inviting the regime, its representatives and various groups affiliated with him...
4. The invitation of Iran to these deliberations ...[100]

Intriguingly, and in an explicit sign of how Turkey had become a dominant influence behind determining northern opposition dynamics at this stage of 2015, when it was sent to this author separately by two rebel signatories, the English version of this RCC statement signed by thirty-seven of the most powerful armed groups across Syria appeared to have been distributed from an e-mail address within the Turkish Ministry of Foreign Affairs.

Opposition victories and increased rebel confidence also induced a renewed sense of panic within regime circles and fear in pro-regime communities. After the loss of Jisr al-Shughour, and in a relatively rare public appearance, Bashar al-Assad gave a speech on 6 May marking Syria Martyrs' Day in which he acknowledged recent losses, but insisted they came within a broader context:

> Today, we are fighting a war, not a battle. War is not one battle, but a series of many battles ... We are not talking about tens or hundreds but thousands of battles and ... it is the nature of battles for there to be advances and retreats, victories and losses, ups and downs ...

> [Beware of] a spirit of frustration or despair at a loss here or there. In battles ... anything can change except for faith in the fighter and the fighter's faith in victory. So when there are setbacks, we must do our duty as a society and give the army morale and not wait for it to give us morale.[101]

With the Syrian armed forces already stretched thin, having lost at least 80,000 personnel since 2011,[102] and with foreign Shia militias still streaming into Damascus, often via Beirut or Baghdad, Hezbollah was playing an increasingly important role in regime defence and offence. In the pro-regime Alawite heartland of Latakia, it had for the first time begun establishing official party offices in the first half of 2015, with one located in the expensive Baghdad Street area of the city, opposite the provincial police headquarters. Hezbollah even took over a Sunni mosque and converted it into a Shia religious seminary. According to local reports, both of these facilities were being used by May 2015 as Syrian Hezbollah recruitment centres. Speaking to NOW Lebanon media, one source purportedly close to the Syrian army's Desert Falcons claimed that from those two offices Hezbollah was willing to cover 'all the expenses and procedures to facilitate' the recruitment and training of Syrian Shia and Alawite men willing to fight for the party.[103]

Meanwhile, Hezbollah's forces—most likely operating in close coordination with Iran's IRGC and Quds Force—including the specialist Unit 313, had been planning a final offensive in the Qalamoun to finally rid the Lebanese border of all armed opposition activities. Several months of reconnaissance operations had been conducted, making use of the group's newly constructed airstrip in the Bekaa Valley, which it used to launch Iranian-made surveillance drones, such as Iranian Ababil-3s and possibly also the more advanced Shahed-129.[104] This much-awaited Qalamoun offensive finally got under way at the beginning of May, but faced stiff resistance from the start, particularly due to the 29 April formation of Jaish al-Fateh fi Qalamoun, which brought together Jabhat al-Nusra, Ahrar al-Sham and several FSA-affiliated units within the Jaish al-Qalamoun and 'Cling to the Rope of God Gathering' movements.[105]

However, further trouble with IS in early May forced the newly established Jaish al-Fateh fi Qalamoun to formally declare war on the jihadist group, again distracting opposition forces from the battle against the regime. Consequently, as the month continued, Hezbollah and other pro-regime forces made consistent gains in the mountains, capturing a number of pivotally important positions and peaks, including Talat Moussa, Fleita, Talat al-Harf and Dahr al-Hawa, all within the offensive's first two weeks.

Elsewhere in Syria, the regime offensive in the south continued apace throughout April and May, with particularly intense battles being fought over the town of Busra al-Harir. Both Jabhat al-Nusra and Ahrar al-Sham were brought into the area in late April to reinforce defensive lines amid heavy regime attack.[106] The armed opposition in Homs—which was in early May primarily restricted to a 50-kilometre stretch of territory north of Homs city centred around the towns of Talbiseh, al-Rastan, al-Houleh and al-Ghanto—also began to more effectively coalesce into a united force, launching a joint offensive aiming to break the regime's northern Homs supply lines. The operation involved Jabhat al-Nusra, Ahrar al-Sham, a new coalition of groups known as Jaish al-Tawhid and at least four other FSA-affiliated factions.[107]

Despite its continued, or perhaps improved, integration within opposition revolutionary dynamics in the form of Jaish al-Fateh coalitions across the country, Jabhat al-Nusra's al-Qaeda jihadist credentials made themselves clear again through April and May, with the reported deaths of two prominent al-Qaeda veterans. Firstly, on 16 April, the former deputy to Mohsen al-Fadhli, al-Qaeda's Iran chief and then 'Khorasan Group' leader, was killed in Idlib. A Saudi national subject to a $5 million reward, Adel al-Harbi, was thought to have been playing an active role within Jaish al-Fateh's Idlib operations at the time of his death. However, his extensive connections within al-Qaeda's highest operational levels made his broader involvement in more suspect transnational activities likely.

The second significant death took place on 25 May, when it was reported that former Algerian army officer and al-Qaeda weapons and explosives expert Said Arif had been killed in a US airstrike, also in Idlib. Arif was wanted in connection with his alleged involvement in a plot to bomb a Christmas market in the French city of Strasbourg in December 2000, and had been convicted and sentenced for his role in the 'Chechen Network' involved in plotting to blow up the Eiffel Tower in 2003. He escaped house arrest in France in October 2013,[108] and initially joined Jabhat al-Nusra before switching to Jund al-Aqsa and becoming its military chief.

Arif's death and his identification by Idlib-based jihadists as Jund al-Aqsa's military leader revealed and underlined the extensive structural connections between Jabhat al-Nusra and Jund al-Aqsa. The latter's founding leader, Mohammed Yousuf al-Athamna (Abu Abdelaziz al-Qatari) had been a commander in Jabhat al-Nusra when Jolani ordered him to establish a new jihadist faction, Saraya al-Aqsa, in early 2013 in order to protect al-Qaeda's project in Syria against the feared scheming of Baghdadi and the ISI. While his group was later renamed Jund al-Aqsa, Athamna was killed by ISIS in January 2014 while attempting to mediate a peaceful solution to the intra-factional fighting that had broken out earlier that month, but which Jund al-Aqsa had refused to be involved in. Ever since Athamna's death, Jund al-Aqsa's senior leadership has remained solidly loyal to the al-Qaeda and Jabhat al-Nusra cause, but its lower ranks are widely suspected to have been infiltrated by those with pro-IS sentiments.

As May drew to a close, Jolani himself granted two face-to-face interviews—though with his face covered—to Al-Jazeera's Arabic service and its correspondent Ahmed Mansour, who himself appeared overly keen to present a positive image of the al-Qaeda affiliate. In the first hour-long interview, televised on 27 May, Jolani revealed that al-Qaeda leader Ayman al-Zawahiri had instructed Jabhat al-Nusra to cease using Syria as a base for planning attacks against 'the West or Europe, so as not to muddy the war'. Jolani however insisted that despite the fact that 'our mission in Syria is [ensuring] the downfall of the regime, its symbols and its allies, like Hezbollah', if his group continued to be targeted by the USA 'all options are open—anyone has the right to self-defence'.[109]

This instruction from Zawahiri actually came within a broader set of directives, contained within a secret letter sent to Jolani in early 2015. In the document Zawahiri had made clear a new and more comprehensive vision for Jabhat al-Nusra in Syria. According to two well-connected Syrian Islamists with links into Jabhat al-Nusra's Shura Council, the letter instructed Jolani to better integrate his movement within the Syrian revolution and its people; to coordinate more closely with all Islamic groups on the ground; to contribute towards the establishment of a Syria-wide *sharia* judicial court system; to use strategic areas of the country to build a sustainable al-Qaeda power base; and finally to cease any activities linked to attacking the West.[110]

Jolani subsequently disseminated Zawahiri's instructions, but he was doing so after a period in which Jabhat al-Nusra had been more overtly asserting its authority and more extremist attitudes. By ordering a re-moderation of his organisation's behaviour, Jolani was banking on the authority that both his and Zawahiri's names counted for in Syria. By and large, a majority of Jabhat al-Nusra abided by the instructions, but perhaps the most controversial of Zawahiri's orders—the cessation of Western attack plotting—struck a nerve amongst some of those operating covertly within the 'Khorasan Group'. While many of these transnationally focused jihadists desisted from their external operations and agreed to integrate into Jabhat al-Nusra's more conventional force structure, there were some individuals who refused to do so. These jihadists subsequently became somewhat isolated from broader dynamics in Idlib and Aleppo, and continued to attract US air strikes, potentially including Said Arif in May 20.[111]

Another interesting aspect of Jolani's first interview was his comments regarding minority, non-Sunni communities in Syria. The essence of his message was that Jabhat al-Nusra 'only fights those who fight us', and that with regard to Alawites, for example, 'if [they] leave their religion and leave Bashar al-Assad, we will protect them'. Christians meanwhile could live in peace under a future non-conflict state of Jabhat al-Nusra rule, but would be required to pay the *jizya* tax in exchange for their 'protection'. So in short, Jolani presented an image that was for many less extreme than the positions taken by IS, but it was nonetheless a vision that few Syrians shared or wanted for their country. 'That first interview was important for us,' said one Islamist commander based in Khan Sheikhoun in Idlib. 'Jolani was trying to show a harmless discourse, but even then it was clear what Nusra's future intentions were. I'm a Syrian Muslim and I'm happy to fight alongside Nusra for the time being because the regime remains our focus, but that was not an image of Syria's future I want at all.'[112]

Jolani's second hour-long interview, which aired on 3 June, focused more on Jabhat al-Nusra's state of relations with IS. 'There is no solution between us and them in the meantime, or in the foreseeable future. We hope they repent to God and return to their senses ... if not, then there is nothing but fighting between us,' Jolani declared. While evading direct questions relating to the then finished internal debate within Jabhat al-Nusra regarding its relationship with al-Qaeda—'this topic was given much more than its real size,'[113] he said—Jolani made clear repeatedly that his source of authority remained Ayman al-Zawahiri. There was no indication whatsoever that Jolani considered, let alone favoured, the option of splitting from al-Qaeda.

Jolani also placed a significant focus on what he saw as Jabhat al-Nusra's existential state of war, not only with the Assad regime, but almost more importantly with Iran and Hezbollah. While this was a clearly consistent al-Qaeda and Jabhat al-Nusra position, Jolani was quite likely seeking to counter complaints within the broader international jihadist community that his group was failing to more resolutely confront Hezbollah inside Lebanon, while IS was determinedly seeking to link up its minimal forces in the Qalamoun with its extending supply lines from Deir ez Zour up to Palmyra and beyond.

This continued competitive dynamic with IS, in which Jabhat al-Nusra needed to consistently demonstrate not only success on the battlefield but also prove its jihadist credibility, saw Jolani present his Syria-based group as but the latest stage in a long list of Islamic jihadist movements. Jolani called this Jabhat al-Nusra's 'inherited jihad', having seen it previously 'renewed' by al-Qaeda and extended into 'Iraq, Yemen, Somalia, Mali, Algeria' and now the Levant.

> We have people whose hair had gone gray in the mountains of Afghanistan and elsewhere ... They had been involved in the war against the [Assad] regime in the Levant in the 1980s ... [and] went to Afghanistan and were involved in the war against the Russians, then the war between the factions there and the Taliban government, and then the American war, before returning to the Levant to fight the [Assad] regime.[114]

Jolani subsequently went on to describe the influences of historical extremist scholars, such as Sayyid Qutb and Hassan al-Banna in Egypt, but criticised the later 'deviation' of the Muslim Brotherhood. This placing of Jabhat al-Nusra within a broader and more ideologically extensive historical jihadist context was a consistent theme for Jabhat al-Nusra throughout the summer of 2015, and was in fact the subject of a slickly produced forty-three-minute documentary entitled *Heirs of Glory* released in late June.

As Jolani spoke to Al-Jazeera, presumably seeking to present what he saw as a more accurate picture of what Jabhat al-Nusra stood for, IS continued to seek advances across different parts of Syria. As June began, IS launched another offensive on the regime-held southern half of Hasakah city (the north was controlled by the YPG). The attack was carried out along three distinct axes, including a sustained bombardment of the Kawkab military base to the city's east. At least two large suicide truck bombs were used at the start, as IS militants sought to penetrate the city's outer defences. Within three days at least fifty regime soldiers had been killed, including twenty who were beheaded,[115] but an intense spate of regime air strikes and personnel reinforcements ensured that the offensive was at least temporarily repelled by June 8.

Meanwhile, IS also continued its westward offensive past Palmyra and its surrounding gas fields and other energy-related facilities, to attack and briefly capture the strategically vital town of Hassia, located on Syria's primary north–south M5 highway. This demonstration of IS's reach sparked panic within pro-regime circles. With the key strategic town of al-Qusayr roughly 20 kilometres away and the Lebanese border even closer, an IS offensive force in Hassia was a powerful statement of intent. Lebanon was almost certainly on IS's horizon—both literally and strategically—as was its intent to cut Damascus off from Homs and the coast. That represented an existentially threatening scenario for Assad.

Further north, IS militants based in towns such as Manbij, al-Bab and Dabiq continued to cause serious trouble to the broad grouping of opposition forces sitting along the 'Marea line' north of Aleppo. In early June IS militants again launched a concerted push towards Marea, and also the village of Souran, 7 kilometres to the north. This again brought Jabhat al-Nusra and Ahrar al-Sham squarely into battle with IS. For the first time, IS took control of a majority of Souran by 2 June. As its forces advanced, rebels furiously protested as they witnessed Syrian air force jets carry out repeated strikes on their positions outside Souran and Marea. Remarkably, the US embassy in Syria, temporarily based in Beirut in Lebanon, tweeted out an accusatory statement, accusing the Assad regime of complicity in assisting IS's offensive north of Aleppo:

> Reports indicate that the regime is making airstrikes in support of #ISIL's advance on #Aleppo, aiding extremists against Syrian population.

> We have long seen that the #Asad regime avoids #ISIL lines, in complete contradiction to the regime's claims to be fighting ISIL. #Syria

> With these latest reports, #Asad is not only avoiding #ISIL lines, but actively seeking to bolster their position. #Syria

At the same time, however, rebels complained that US-led coalition jets had refused to carry out air strikes in their defence against IS assault. 'We are desperate! Da'ish is advancing and we don't have nearly enough supplies to defend forever. I myself have sent coordinates of Da'ish positions to the Americans, but they did not even reply,' said Zakaria Malahfji, the political chief of Tajamu Fastaqim Kama Umirta and former political head of the recently dissolved al-Jabhat al-Shamiyya Aleppo coalition.[116]

As Jabhat al-Nusra, Ahrar al-Sham and a variety of other groups urgently diverted fighters from other Aleppo and Idlib fronts to Marea and Souran, regime artillery and air strikes continued to target their transport routes and gathering points. 'It was never this blatant,' commented an FSA Thuwar al-Sham spokesman at the time.[117] One US air strike, for the first time ever, did appear to target a unit of IS militants near Souran on 6 June, but no more coalition support came. Gradually, IS slowed its advance north of Aleppo, but the threat had not passed forever.

IS's operations on both Hasakah city and north of Aleppo appeared to have been launched as attempted distractions or diversionary attacks amid the threat faced from its chief nemesis, the Kurdish YPG, which had continued exerting pressure on IS's hold of territory west of the Syria–Turkey border town of Ras al-Ayn. Since 6 May the YPG had led an offensive operation—Operation Martyr Rubar Qamishlo—beginning in northern Hasakah around Ras al-Ayn and directed southwards and to the west. In its initial stages the YPG had received assistance from the Syriac Military Council.

The intended objective for the YPG and its US coalition partners was to capture IS's critically important border town of Tel Abyad, where the group continued to receive new recruits from around the world, as well as other financial and logistical supplies. From 27 May to 1 June this YPG-led ground offensive—incorporating several small FSA factions within the 'Volcano Operations Room'—took control of more than twenty-four villages, and the speed of their advances continued through to the middle of June.

By 10 June, in fact, peripheral parts of the battle had reached Tel Abyad itself, and with fighting in the area increasingly intense and destructive, particularly around the town of Suluk, thousands of civilians began pouring over the border into Turkey. By 13 June at least 13,000 people had fled the area as refugees, with Turkish soldiers reportedly using force to prevent further flows across the border.[118] Two days later an all-out YPG and FSA assault captured Tel Abyad in its entirety, completing a quite remarkable advance since early in the year. Notwithstanding the thin splattering of Arab FSA fighters involved, the YPG now effectively controlled 400 kilometres of contiguous territory along the Turkish border[119]—a fact not lost on Ankara, which viewed the YPG with intense suspicion due to its PKK links.

In fact, those fears were almost certainly the primary factor behind a subsequent Turkish-encouraged opposition campaign that accused the YPG of 'ethnically cleansing' Arab parts of northern Raqqa. 'Da'ish attacks and kills those it captures. PYD and PKK seize certain regions and force people living there to migrate,' claimed Turkish foreign minister Mevlüt Çavuşoğlu on 16 June.[120] Perhaps unsurprisingly, thirteen of the most powerful armed opposition groups in northern Syria (including Ahrar al-Sham, Jaish al-Islam, Ajnad al-Sham and Faylaq al-Sham), all of whom retain strong links to Turkey, issued a joint statement on 15 June, explicitly accusing the Kurds of 'ethnic cleansing' against Arab Sunnis in western Hasakah and northern Raqqa as part of a 'PKK terrorist scheme'. Shortly thereafter, the Turkey-based ETILAF political opposition dispatched a 'fact-finding mission' to the Turkish side of the Tel Abyad border, but the PYD/YPG prevented their entry three times in a row, prompting more accusations of Kurdish hostile intentions to Arabs. By late August these accusations had lessened in public, but tensions remained as high as ever.

Kurdish–Arab tensions notwithstanding, spurred on by its victory in Tel Abyad, the YPG and its band of FSA allies continued their offensive, pushing southwards towards IS's capital, Raqqa. A week after capturing Tel Abyad, a further major defeat was forced upon IS, as it lost both its base in the Syrian army's former 93rd Brigade facility and the nearby town of Ain Issa. Riding a wave of success, Pentagon spokesmen began referring to IS militants as having 'cracked' under pressure. Undoubtedly, IS had incurred serious strategic and territorial losses through late May and June, but, following on from accusations surrounding its intentions in more explicitly Arab-majority areas of Raqqa governorate, the YPG quickly qualified its objectives by stating that the IS capital 'is not on our agenda'.[121]

Compounding IS's losses in northern Raqqa, the USA also carried out a number of specifically targeted air strikes against high-value IS leaders in June. Senior Tunisian commander Tariq al-Harzi—wanted by the US government for his alleged role in coordinating recruitment from Libya and facilitating a transfer of $2 million in donations from an individual in Qatar—was killed in a drone strike in al-Shadadi on 16 June. Only a day earlier, Tariq's brother Ali— wanted by the US government for his alleged involvement in the September 2012 attack on the US consulate in Benghazi in Libya—was killed in another drone strike near Mosul in Iraq.[122] Such intelligence-led strikes, possibly result-ing from information gleaned during the 16 May raid on Abu Sayyaf's com-pound in Deir ez Zour, continued into July, with the reported deaths of senior Uzbek, Syrian and Iraqi IS leaders in Raqqa and north-east Syria.

Faced with this intensified pressure, IS banned much of WiFi Internet availability in Raqqa and proceeded to demonstrate its consistent strategy of using escalatory tactics to distract from its losses. The first step in this respect was the distribution of yet another professionally produced video, this time revealing in high definition and from multiple angles its victims being killed in a sadistic fashion. Released on 23 June, the video showed several men killed by being locked in a car and targeted by an RPG at close range; others were locked in a metal cage surrounded by waterproof cameras and drowned in a clear-water pool; and yet more men were executed after explosive cords were tied around their necks in a row and detonated. Gruesome barely seemed a sufficient descriptor.

Forty-eight hours later IS launched seemingly coordinated assaults on Kobane and Hasakah city, clearly seeking to divert YPG resources away from Ain Issa and any potential further advances towards Raqqa. Early on 24 June roughly forty IS militants—mostly Kurds dressed variously in FSA and YPG uniforms—stormed Kobane, detonating a suicide car bomb near the Turkish border and attacking YPG checkpoints throughout the town. That same morning two IS suicide truck bombs and four IS suicide bombers on foot detonated themselves outside YPG and Syrian army positions in Hasakah, sparking a major ground assault on the southern half of the city. Further west, a smaller contingent of IS militants set off from Raqqa and attacked Ain Issa, seeking to recapture the town taken from them only days earlier.

By 28 June IS had massacred at least 220 civilians in Kobane in an attack driven by revenge for the group's loss in the town earlier in the year.[123] Attempting to play down the attack and the fact that IS had demonstrated an ability to infiltrate the site of the US-led coalition's biggest and most high-profile victory against IS in Syria, the US military labelled the attack on Kobane a 'limited incursion'.[124] Such misjudged comments aside, IS success-fully recaptured Ain Issa and temporarily recaptured an eastern portion of Tel Abyad on 30 June, while managing to sustain the offensive in Hasakah city into early July, displacing as many as 120,000 people in the process.[125]

Elsewhere in Syria, the attention given to the south by both moderate FSA elements and Islamists and jihadists was steadily increasing. After his extended visit to Turkey, Jaish al-Islam leader Zahran Alloush flew south to Amman in early June, where he held extensive meetings with representatives of the FSA's Southern Front, as well as with the multinational MOC.[126] Beyond dynamics relating to IS, the Syrian conflict and those involved in it found themselves in June within a new and shifting environment. Jaish al-Fateh had dealt a near-total defeat to the regime in Idlib, while the regime's hold on the Homs–Lebanon gap seemed at its most tenuous for two years. Hezbollah and Iran had considerably intensified their frontline involvement in key operations, sparking internal regime discontent and divisions. Meanwhile, new leadership in Saudi Arabia had seen that country embark on a fresh conflict in Yemen, while tying its strategic relations more closely with Turkey and Qatar with regard to Syria. ETILAF president Khaled Khoja was also strengthening his own relations with all sides of the Syrian armed opposition, whilst announcing plans to dissolve the Supreme Military Council.

The key topic of discussion in Amman during Zahran Alloush's brief visit, however, was the long-planned and much-awaited southern offensive, which was nearing activation. Ever since 2013 the opposition and its various external supporters had spoken of the potential for a major FSA-led advance from Deraa up to southern Damascus, but, with the exception of various half-baked attempts, little had ever developed in the way of a genuine threat to the regime.

A preliminary stage of the plan was initiated on 9 June, when a huge attack was launched by the Southern Front—with Zahran Alloush playing a behind-the-scenes command role—on one of the regime's most important military positions in southern Syria, the base of the 52nd Brigade. In a lightning assault backed up by artillery and tank fire, the entire base fell into FSA hands in the space of six hours. Suddenly, the regime's key logistical link between Deraa and its loyalist communities in Suwayda had fallen, and for the opposition, the south now lay open for attack. The following morning the FSA's First Army marched east into Suwayda and attacked the expansive al-Thaala air base. Soon joined by Ahrar al-Sham, and allegedly also by Jabhat al-Nusra, the attack on the air base gained international attention, as fears grew over the fate of the area's minority Druze population.

While opposition forces in the south had issued no specific threat to the Druze minority, concerns had arisen following an incident further north in Idlib, where Jabhat al-Nusra militants had killed at least twenty Druze men, women and children in a purported property dispute. In the days and weeks preceding the killings, Druze leaders in the small village of Qalb Loze had been increasingly fearful of Jabhat al-Nusra's aggressive behaviour. One Druze sheikh had appealed to other Idlib social figures in early June for help:

They've been coming to our homes and they want to remove our sons, our boys between 10 and 14 years old, and put them in a training camp for two months. We don't know what they're going to teach them, and they're threatening us. They want to take away our weapons.[127]

The deadly incident in Qalb Loze had developed during building work that a Tunisian Jabhat al-Nusra commander had undertaken on several empty houses seized by the group during Jaish al-Fateh's advances. When representatives of a local family disputed Jabhat al-Nusra's right to build a separating wall in one building, an argument ensued, which quickly turned violent, as one Druze civilian described soon after:

Jabhat al-Nusra tried to arrest members of the family that objected. Some Nusra fighters readied their rifles and others moved to put the family into a car. One Nusra member put his rifle aside so he could push one of them in more easily.

The brother of the man being pushed tried to take that rifle from the ground. A second Nusra fighter shot him, and at that instant the fighter who had dropped his gun moved towards it so the brother of the detainee wouldn't take it. The Nusra bullets hit two people, the fighter who was going for his gun and the Druze brother who tried to take it.

After their comrade was killed, Nusra called for backup over their walkie-talkies and opened fire on passersby and nearby houses, killing 23 innocent people ... If not for the mediation of rebels in Kafr Takharim, God only knows what would have happened.[128]

Despite Jolani's claims in his Al-Jazeera interview, the killings in Qalb Loze sparked panic within minority communities across Syria, particularly amongst the country's relatively small Druze population, which for so long had managed to remain largely uninvolved in the conflict. Intriguingly, the mediation described at the end of the passage above was led by Ahrar al-Sham, which also issued a formal statement condemning the killings, alongside other Islamist groups such as Ajnad al-Sham.

Nonetheless, the damage had been done. Despite attempts by Lebanon-based Druze leader Walid Jumblatt to reassure his Syrian compatriots of Jabhat al-Nusra's perceived better intentions—by describing what happened in Qalb Loze as 'an isolated incident'[129]—almost overnight and facing a concerted rebel offensive involving Jabhat al-Nusra in Suwayda, Syria's Druze in the south turned definitively to the regime for protection. Druze spiritual leader Sheikh Abu Khaled Shaaban issued a number of public statements calling on men to rush to join the NDF and other 'popular committee' militias to defend al-Thaala air base and any other targets of the rebel offensive in

Suwayda. Consequently, and thanks in large part to Druze reinforcements, the attack on al-Thaala was repelled by 12–13 June.

After a short-lived and unsuccessful FSA-led offensive aimed at completing opposition control of Quneitra governorate, Ahrar al-Sham and Jabhat al-Nusra led the establishment of a new Jaish al-Fateh coalition for southern Syria on 20 June. Including seven other smaller groups within its ranks, some of which fell loosely under the FSA umbrella, the southern Jaish al-Fateh had an ambiguous relationship with the FSA's Southern Front from the start. While the Southern Front had been entirely aware of the several weeks of talks that preceded the new Jaish al-Fateh coalition's formation, it had retained a distance. And despite a number of statements and suggestions that the Southern Front would cease all cooperation with Jabhat al-Nusra, no evidence emerged to substantiate such claims.

In fact, when the Southern Front announced the start of its much-anticipated 'Southern Storm' offensive on Deraa city on 24 June, both Ahrar al-Sham and Jabhat al-Nusra actively cooperated with its forces, though quietly and in the background. The principal goal of Southern Storm was to capture Deraa city and force a regime withdrawal to the town of Izra'a, located roughly a third of the way north towards Damascus.[130] After civilians were given twenty-four hours to evacuate the city, the military operations began on 25 June, with quick gains made in the city's north.

Unfortunately for the opposition, however, the Southern Storm offensive proved as disappointing as previous attempts. Massive regime bombardment and air strikes quickly stalled the rebel momentum gained on the first day. By early July there was discernibly little movement on the frontlines, and accusations had begun to fly around within the Southern Front as to why they had failed quite so quickly. They had not given up though, and, following a brief investigation, which highlighted issues relating to the leaking of information by media activists that revealed operational plans and rebel positions to the regime, it was agreed that a second offensive would be planned; that one, Operation Righteous Storm, began on 23 July.

In short, as the Syrian revolution entered its fifth summer, the battle against the Assad regime was still very much on. Now more than ever, developments both inside and outside the country appeared to be encouraging an intensification of the pressure on the Assad regime's survival. However, while the opposition was celebrating repeated victories in Idlib, it was still suffering elsewhere. A military victory still seemed a very long way away, as the leaderships of all major Syrian groups were admitting privately.[131] As such, the armed opposition as a whole began focusing more on issues of politics and engaging with the subject of what a negotiated political solution—in the form of an immediate transition in Syria—might look like.

The key instigator of this discussion was the RCC and the president of its Executive Council, Sobhi al-Rifai. Crucially, the RCC had by and large managed to retain the entire breadth of Syria's armed opposition spectrum, including Ahrar al-Sham, within its structure since its formation in late 2014. Several leading Ahrar al-Sham officials maintained positions on the nineteen-member Executive Council, including Ahrar al-Sham's chief of foreign political relations, Labib al-Nahhas (Abu Ezzeddine al-Ansari). Zahran Alloush's cousin Mohammed was also the RCC's political chief. By also containing all the US vetted groups, the RCC quite clearly had chosen not to discriminate by ideology. Of course, however, Jabhat al-Nusra and its many like-minded jihadist factions were not included.

Within an environment in which armed groups were intensifying their engagement in internationally backed Track II processes, and key European states were expanding the scale and breadth of their contact with armed groups (including Ahrar al-Sham), the RCC held a large meeting in the southern Turkish city of Reyhanlı on 10–11 June, during which all seventy-two RCC member factions, plus influential opposition civil society and religious figures, gathered to discuss the political foundations of the revolution, and what a political solution to the conflict might look like. It subsequently published three documents: (1) a final statement outlining the process of the two-day meeting and its general outcomes; (2) a 'Vision Agreed Upon by Conference Members Regarding a Political Solution in Syria'; and (3) the RCC's '16 Points'. The latter two documents were particularly interesting as windows into the revolution's thinking, especially considering that they incorporated those groups such as Ahrar al-Sham that still remained intensely close to Jabhat al-Nusra on broader conflict levels.

In the 'Vision' document, the RCC meeting laid out twelve 'political steps ... that must be followed for Syria to transition back to being a member of the family of nations, within the international community':

1. Continuing the battle against the regime until the fall of its head, key pillars, and leading figures; expelling of all militias and forces brought in to save the regime from falling, such as Hezbollah, and all other mercenaries, all of whom have committed war crimes against the Syrian people.
2. Militant factions will provide for national security, put an end to chaos and the spread of weapons, and prevent internal fighting; they will also protect public

and property and assist institutions of civil society in easing normal life for the Syrian people.

3. The factions, along with revolutionary and national powers, call for a general national conference that represents those factions and revolutionary powers, along with all segments of Syrian society that participated in liberating the nation, while also incorporating all specialists and experts for all specializations.

4. The general national conference will elect a transitional governing body with full legislative and executive powers, with its powers limited to one year or two (at the utmost).

5. The national conference will elect a specialist body of legal scholars, experts, and other desired specialists with the announcement that the 1950 constitution will be used until a new constitution is prepared and voted upon.

6. Freedom of the press and media will be secured, along with freedom to form political parties; preparation will take place for elections of the final phase, and all measures will be taken to hold these elections.

7. Rebuilding and restricting military and security institutions on a national basis, with each institutions' members barred from party affiliation.

8. Work to return refugees and internally displaced persons to their towns, cities and homes, and providing all necessary services for their safety, health, and decent life.

9. Reformulating the independent judiciary, building on the principle of separation of powers, and forming special courts to try members of the regime who have committed crimes against the Syrian people.

10. Issue a general pardon on verdicts past against politicians under different pretexts, and freeing them.

11. With regards to the points of the Geneva 1 Communique, the text and points that refer to the division of power in the transitional period are considered texts and points that have been abrogated by the war crimes and crimes against humanity committed by the regime, for which it has been condemned. No regime that has committed these crimes, with condemnations from the nations of the world as well as rights groups, humanitarian organizations and international organizations, can share in ruling the people against which it has committed these crimes. Therefore, Bashar has no right to be a party to the transitional period.

12. The Syrian woman has participated in the revolution in an important role, whether as wife to a martyr or mother of a revolutionary, and the Syrian woman is therefore counted as the match (note: duplicate, indistinguishable twin—i.e. equal in every way but not literally the equal) of man, and this guarantees her active role in the process of building to come.[132]

Considering the sheer breadth of Syrians represented in the RCC meeting in Reyhanlı, the '16 Points' document was also particularly revealing, especially with regards to points insisting on no single group being 'entitled to claim sole representation of the Syrian people' and the total rejection of any potential 'partition' or threat to the 'unity and territorial integrity of Syria'.

As June 2015 came to a close, a new chapter in the Syrian conflict and in the Syrian Jihad appeared to be opening. Despite facing continued, and in fact increasing, numbers of US-led coalition air strikes in Syria and suffering serious losses to Kurds in the north-east, IS was still a formidable military force whose militants were beginning to bear down on key regime positions in the centre of the country and towards the Lebanese border. However, the loss of Tel Abyad had made a serious dent in the group's ability to recruit foreign fighters on the large scale it had previously enjoyed.

Therefore, the summer of 2015 would probably prove crucial in determining IS's future capacity to demonstrate further military momentum and follow through on its threat to expand further into southern Syria and to penetrate the Lebanese border. Early reports of IS sleeper cells beginning to awaken in late June in western Aleppo and throughout Idlib appeared to herald an attempt by the group to destabilise opposition areas in the hope of weakening its adversaries and recapturing invaluable territory with crossings into Turkey.

Meanwhile, IS's key jihadist competitor in Syria was reaping the benefits of its top-down phase of 're-moderation' earlier in 2015 that had ensured its integration into perhaps the most successful multi-group coalition of the revolution, Jaish al-Fateh. In playing such a key role in the conquering of almost an entire governorate in the space of two-and-a-half months alongside not just other Syrian Islamists but also US-backed 'vetted' FSA factions, Jabhat al-Nusra had again played its cards right and underlined to others that it should be seen as far more valuable as a partner of the revolution than as an enemy. Despite growing awareness within all Syrian revolutionary circles that Jabhat al-Nusra was also beginning to present itself more overtly as 'al-Qaeda,' the revolution and its fight against the regime simply remained too important a priority.

Jabhat al-Nusra's relative success notwithstanding, the group was also experiencing a not unsubstantial level of internal strife, as a pragmatist wing, led primarily by Saleh al-Hamawi and Abu Mariya al-Qahtani, were becoming increasingly vocal critics of overly assertive Jabhat al-Nusra behaviour. While Jolani had thus far succeeded in maintaining his delicate balancing act of incorporating this pragmatist wing within an organisation whose veteran al-Qaeda figures were becoming more and more prominent, and which still relied on an at least 60 per cent Syrian contingent of fighters, it was becoming more and more difficult to sustain. Although Jolani claimed that Western attack plotting had ceased within Jabhat al-Nusra, some 'Khorasan Group' members remained isolated from his broader command structure, and continued US air strikes on Jabhat al-Nusra positions suggested that some level of suspicious activity or plotting was continuing.

As Jabhat al-Nusra was struggling to define its exact identity, its long-time ally and enabler Ahrar al-Sham was also entering a phase of redefining how much of an Islamic movement it could be whilst retaining such strong logistical and operational connections with a country such as Turkey and espousing a political vision that would fit within the broader revolution and thus ensure its future prominence. Turkey's intensified engagement with the armed opposition and Qatar's re-entry into positive relations with Saudi Arabia appeared to encourage Ahrar al-Sham to slightly modify its stance inside Syria, and, more overtly, to begin presenting itself as a political and not just a military actor. The latter half of the summer would represent a period in which that thinking matured.

Notwithstanding such internal deliberations, it had become starkly clear by late June that Ahrar al-Sham had consolidated its status as the most influential armed group in Syria, capable of determining military dynamics across much of the country. Most recently, it had been the primary instigator behind the Jaish al-Fateh concept, which had not only demonstrated remarkable success in Idlib, but was also then replicated in several further key battle theatres with the regime.

With that being said, the role of bodies such as Jaish al-Fateh and the capacity of a group such as Ahrar al-Sham to bring in factions on the most extreme end of the spectrum ensured that jihadist actors of various stripes became integrated within local conflict dynamics, especially in northern Syria. Although they remained outside Jaish al-Fateh, transnational jihadist organisations affiliated on various levels with al-Qaeda—including the TIP, Katibat al-Tawhid wa'l Jihad, Junud al-Sham, Jaish al-Muhajireen wa'l Ansar and Jama'at Ansar al-Islam—had all become integral players in battles that were defining the entire Syrian conflict. Not only that, but their role in securing victories on the ground meant that they were also afforded a share of the responsibility in defending and often governing 'liberated' territories.

In a phase of the Syrian revolution where alliances, coalitions and large operations rooms were becoming the established method of coordinating major battles, the integration of dangerous international jihadists was becoming a hard-and-fast reality. Moreover, and especially in the case of Idlib, the fact that these groups had been part of such a dramatic series of successes meant that the bonds formed in securing such victories would be extremely difficult to break.

Although the shifting geo-political and internal revolutionary political dynamics may have been transforming the Syrian conflict in favour of groups that spoke on a more 'national' basis, the 'Syrian Jihad' was exploiting its military value to ensure it was not left behind.

14

# THE SYRIAN JIHAD

The Syrian conflict experienced a number of profound developments in July and August 2015 that, when combined, had the potential to fundamentally alter the dynamics not only of the war itself, but the status of jihadist movements within it. While some of these shifts were driven by jihadist actors, many also incorporated broader and new political and geo-political dimensions. By September 2015 actors on all sides appeared to be grappling to position themselves within what was quickly emerging as a new phase in the conflict. As had been the case in previous years, jihadists were again centre stage in attempting to manipulate changing dynamics for their own benefit.

By the time October began and Russian aircraft had initiated strikes against opposition forces in theaters surrounding the Assad regime's coastal heartlands, jihadists in Syria no longer had to work to maneuver themselves into a strategically favorable position. Despite proclaiming its mission as one aimed at neutralizing IS and 'terrorism,' a great many Russian strikes targeted FSA factions, many of which received support from the US as so-called 'vetted' groups. Moscow's strategy was thus more accurately described as one aimed at buttressing an ailing regime in Damascus. Consequently, its ill-defined fight against 'terrorism' was set to become a self-fulfilling prophecy, as Syria's genuinely moderate opposition began coordinating more closely with Al-Qaeda and other similar jihadist factions than had been the case for some time. Rather than fighting jihadist militancy, Russia's military intervention was fueling it like never before.

For its part, IS had spent July and August escalating the intensity and scale of its offensive operations, targeting opposition-held areas north of Aleppo city throughout the late summer months, principally against the towns of Marea and Souran and on their routes west towards Tel Rifaat and Azaz. From early July IS militants utilised multiple suicide truck bombs and heavy artillery to launch a number of concerted offensives in this westward direction, along what was then popularly being called the 'Marea line'. In threatening to capture Souran and Marea, IS was demonstrating a much-feared potential to cut opposition supply lines via the Syria–Turkey border crossing at Bab al-Salameh, which could have had existential consequences for all opposition forces in Aleppo city and its surrounding countryside.

The 'Marea line' was a series of defensive positions manned by Jabhat al-Nusra, Ahrar al-Sham and a number of mainstream Islamist and FSA rebel factions. The latter groups had long complained of a debilitating lack of support from the Turkey-based multinational Joint Operations Center (Müşterek Operasyon Merkezi'ne; MOM), as well as the remarkable failure of US-led anti-IS coalition forces to conduct air strikes in their defence, amid IS advances.

Within this challenging context, a brief attempt by Islamist opposition groups to launch a new offensive against regime positions in Aleppo city under a new coalition named Ansar al-Sharia in early July was quickly overshadowed by a major near-simultaneous IS push towards Azaz. Yet again, and whether true or not, it appeared to many observers that there was a regime–IS relationship of mutual defence, whereby one consistently came to the rescue of the other around Aleppo. Whatever the truth, IS continued its gradual intensification of offensive manoeuvres north of Aleppo throughout July and August, for a time capturing Souran, and even appearing to use chemical artillery shells, possibly containing mustard gas, on two occasions.[1]

It was another IS-linked event on the Syria–Turkey border, however, that was to comprehensively transform dynamics in northern Syria. On 20 July a twenty-year-old Turkish Kurd, Şeyh Abdulrahman Alagoz, calmly walked towards a demonstration being held jointly by the youth wing of Turkey's Marxist–Leninist Ezilenlerin Sosyalist Partisi (ESP) and the Sosyalist Gençlik Dernekleri Federasyonunun (SGDF) in Turkey's southern border town of Suruç. These youth activists had gathered at Suruç's Amara Cultural Centre in preparation for crossing into Syria to help with reconstruction projects in Kobane, just 10 kilometres across the border. With little warning, and standing amongst the crowd, Alagoz detonated his explosives vest, killing thirty-three people and leaving over a hundred others wounded.[2]

After identifying the bomber, Turkish authorities claimed that Alagoz had travelled to Syria approximately six months earlier, where he had linked up with IS militants. His mother confirmed only that he had travelled 'abroad' six months before the attack.[3] With the Suruç bombing coming amid heightening rhetoric from Ankara regarding the need to more comprehensively deal with cross-border threats from Syria—principally the Kurds, but also IS—the mass death toll provided Turkey with a means to begin to justify a more overtly interventionist posture. It also provided Turkey sceptics, including the country's considerable Kurdish population, to claim that a conspiracy was afoot, tacitly blaming the Turkish government for having masterminded the bombing so as to create a justification for military intervention in northern Syria against the YPG and in northern Iraq against the PKK.

Three days after the attack in Suruç, five IS militants opened fire with an RPG and machine guns targeting a unit of Turkish soldiers near Kilis, killing one and wounding two. Later that day, and with tension on its border with Syria rapidly increasing, Turkey announced that it had finally agreed to give the USA military access to Incirlik air base for its anti-IS air operations.[4] Two weeks later, six US air force F-16 jets, several MQ-1 Predator drones and 300 air force personnel had been deployed to the base in preparation for activating anti-IS operations from Turkey.[5] The first drone strike from Incirlik took place on 4 August, while F-16s began operations on 12 August.[6]

Perhaps even more significant was Turkey's initiation of its own air operations against IS in northern Syria and also the PKK in northern Iraq from 24 July. There had been signs that Turkey was preparing to more overtly intervene in northern Syria since the spring, when government statements began expressing an unwillingness to accept growing threats along its southern border. By late June opposition leaders such as Kemal Kılıçdaroğlu of the Cumhuriyet Halk Partisi (CHP) were speaking of 'the drums of war ... being beaten for vested interests'.[7]

By introducing itself as an active military adversary of IS, and by re-activating hostilities with the PKK after a two-year ceasefire, Turkey sought to establish what its government officials called a 'de facto safe zone' in northern Aleppo. In practice, this meant an area of territory roughly 110 kilometres wide in which neither IS nor the Kurdish YPG would be permitted access.[8]

In short, Turkey was indeed concerned by IS's intensified threat to opposition control in northern Aleppo, but it also vehemently opposed any further expansion of the YPG's territorial expansion westwards beyond northern Raqqa and into its pocket of influence around Afrin in the north-western Aleppo countryside. Doing so would have effectively established a de facto semi-autonomous Kurdish state in northern Syria. While Turkey's actions were therefore influenced primarily by its own national and regional security interests, the implications for Syria's conflict were potentially profound.

Turkey's stated objective of creating a 'safe zone,' which appeared to draw at least partly on US plans to establish an 'IS-free zone' in northern Aleppo, necessitated a close operational coordination with armed groups on the ground. Consequently, Turkish intelligence convened several meetings of Aleppo-based groups—including Ahrar al-Sham and the al-Jabhat al-Shamiyya coalition—on 27 and 28 July to ascertain a willingness to cooperate with such a mission, for which Ankara received unanimous support. This was far from surprising, considering the intensely close relations already established between Turkey's foreign intelligence branch, the Millî İstihbarat Teşkilatı (MIT), and the vast majority of Syrian armed factions active across northern Syria.

Jabhat al-Nusra and its other jihadist allies active in northern Aleppo were not included in these meetings or other broader Turkish-backed plans. As such, several members of Jabhat al-Nusra's *majlis al-shura* convened a meeting with Ahrar al-Sham, al-Jabhat al-Shamiyya and several other FSA factions on 4 August in which the group derided attendees for their 'submission to a nationalist project', which it perceived as 'serving only Turkish interests'.[9] One Jabhat al-Nusra official even went as far as to threaten a resumption of Western attack planning if Turkey's plans continued and if they revealed any anti-al-Qaeda objectives.[10] Despite taking such a forceful position, Jabhat al-Nusra was unable to influence its long-time battlefield partners, including Ahrar al-Sham, to budge. The following day the Istanbul-based Syrian Islamic Council—led by Sheikh Osama al-Rifai and close to many mainstream Islamic rebel factions—published a *fatwa* declaring all cooperation with Turkey permissible.[11]

Facing such wholesale strategic isolation, Jabhat al-Nusra withdrew its forces from northern Aleppo's border areas with Turkey on 6 August and confirmed on 9 August:

> ... our withdrawal from our positions against the khawarij [IS] in the northern countryside of Aleppo. This is because:

> We in Jabhat al-Nusra do not hold the opinion that it is allowed to enter this alliance according to Sharia. Not in terms of joining its ranks, nor in terms of seeking its help and not even coordinating with it. The decision of the actual battle was not a strategic choice originating from free will of the fighting groups, but its actual aim is Turkish national security.[12]

To rub salt in Jabhat al-Nusra's wounds, its most consistent ally and enabler in Syria, Ahrar al-Sham, then proceeded to issue a statement on 11 August in which it expressed its admiration of Turkey as 'the most important ally of the Syrian revolution'. Consequently, Ahrar al-Sham's political office declared:

We believe that the announcement of Turkey's intention to establish a safe zone in the north of Syria is a matter that serves the interests of the Syrian people. The safe zone will have positive repercussions on the humanitarian, political and military levels, the benefits of which will be felt by both countries. The safe zone is also a necessary measure to bolster Turkey's national security and to stop in its tracks terrorist or secessionist plans by Daesh and the PKK.

We take this opportunity to stress the unbreakable bond and the common destiny of the Syrian and Turkish peoples and underscore the need for strategic ties with Turkey to become the cornerstone for a common approach to tackling current and future challenges.[13]

By coming out so openly in praise of Turkey and so clearly in opposition to Jabhat al-Nusra's more strictly Islamist assessments, Ahrar al-Sham's political office was demonstrating, perhaps for the first time, a vast political–strategic policy divergence with the al-Qaeda affiliate that it had so long been linked with.

While this new dynamic with Jabhat al-Nusra was developing, Ahrar al-Sham found itself entering a new phase of political positioning. Driven by senior political office leaders who sought to moderate Ahrar al-Sham's image—including Abu Abdulrahman al-Suri, Abu Azzam al-Ansari, Talal Bazerbashi, Labib al-Nahhas and Abu Mustafa—Ahrar al-Sham launched an unprecedented attempted outreach to the West in July.

After four months of internal discussions that had brought together the group's senior political, military and religious leaderships, a new 'discourse' was designed in which it was agreed that Ahrar al-Sham would begin presenting itself as an integral part of the revolutionary landscape and an actor with strictly no international objectives or links with al-Qaeda. Top-level meetings were held in northern Syria, southern Turkey and in Istanbul to design the specific language behind this revised image. Traditionally hardline leadership figures such as Eyad al-Sha'ar (Abu al-Hassan)—an Irish resident and veteran of the Afghan jihad whose brother Yasir was killed undertaking the Moscow theatre siege in 2002[14]—and military chief Abu Saleh Tahan were involved throughout.[15]

The first step in the public activation of this process was the publication of an editorial in *The Washington Post* on 10 July. Penned by Labib al-Nahhas (or Abu Ezzeddine al-Ansari), Ahrar al-Sham's chief of foreign political relations, the article was entitled 'The deadly consequences of mislabeling Syria's revolutionaries' and was a sharp critique of the Obama administration's approach to the Syrian crisis:

As has become obvious, the Obama administration's response to the Syrian conflict is an abject failure. No clear strategy has been determined; the administration's 'red lines' have not been honored. Short-term, stopgap measures informed by the Iraq and Afghanistan experiences, along with the noise generated by a media fixated on the Islamic State, have taken priority over achievable, long-term goals. The result: a death toll commonly estimated at between 200,000 and 300,000 people (though it's certainly higher), more than 11 million displaced and numerous cities in ruins.

Nowhere is this failure clearer than in the consequence of the misguided way that Syrian revolutionaries are labeled as either 'moderate' or 'extremist'.

... The group to which I belong, Ahrar al-Sham, is one example. Our name means 'Free Men of Syria'. We consider ourselves a mainstream Sunni Islamic group that is led by Syrians and fights for Syrians. We are fighting for justice for the Syrian people. Yet we have been falsely accused of having organizational links to al-Qaeda and of espousing al-Qaeda's ideology.

Nothing could be further from the truth. We believe that Syria needs a national unifying project that cannot be controlled or delivered by a single party or group and should not be bound to a single ideology. We believe in striking a balance that respects the legitimate aspirations of the majority as well as protects minority communities and enables them to play a real and positive role in Syria's future. We believe in a moderate future for Syria that preserves the state and institutes reforms that benefit all Syrians.

... Despite a disappointing lack of genuine engagement from the international community, we remain committed to dialogue. The issues that need to be discussed are how to end Assad's reign, how to defeat the Islamic State and how to ensure that a stable and representative government in Damascus puts Syria on the path to peace, reconciliation and economic recovery while avoiding the disintegration of the state. It is not too late for the United States to change course. Kerry's 'third option' exists—but only if Washington is willing to open its eyes and see it.[16]

Eleven days later, after former US ambassador and envoy to Syria Robert Ford published an article encouraging American dialogue with Ahrar al-Sham,[17] Nahhas published a second editorial in the British newspaper *The Daily Telegraph*. Specifically addressing a British audience, Nahhas condemned former Labour Party leader Ed Miliband for his successful blocking of Prime Minister David Cameron's attempt to launch military strikes against the Assad regime after the August 2013 sarin gas attack, and linked that political decision to the rise of IS in Syria:

Almost two years ago, the House of Commons met to decide whether to take military action against Bashar al-Assad. Few people would have predicted that the vote by MPs, taken a week after the Syrian dictator attacked opposition-controlled suburbs of Damascus with chemical weapons, would set off a chain reaction in the region and beyond, the cost of which we are only beginning to fathom. Keen to exorcise the ghost of Tony Blair and score political points, the Labour leader Ed Miliband marshalled just enough votes to defeat the Government motion. President Obama quickly developed cold feet about punitive strikes and the rest, as they say, is history.

And what a history it has been. Four million Syrian refugees, eight million internally displaced, and three hundred thousand civilians dead, the vast majority at the hands of Assad's murderous conventional war machine, tells only part of the story. The aftershock of that vote was felt further afield, as far as Moscow in fact, where President Vladimir Putin felt he could capitalise on the West's lack of resolve to pursue his expansionist policy in Ukraine.

In Raqqa too people were taking notice. The so-called Islamic State, then only a pale shadow of what it is today, capitalised on the West's failure to rein-in Assad to advance their propaganda narrative: the West is in cahoots with Assad and his Shi'ite Iranian backers in a conspiracy to defeat and humiliate Sunni Arabs in the region. Good luck trying to explain the inside politics of the Westminster village to the angry and traumatised residents of those Damascus suburbs.

Between the West's inaction, Assad's megalomania, Iran's imperialist ambitions, Russia's Cold War revenge fantasy and Isil's cruelty and madness lay the majority of Syrians whose sole aims in revolution was freedom, dignity and a better quality of life. We in Ahrar Al-Sham and other Armed Revolutionary Groups (ARGs) fight for those Syrians. We raised arms because we had no other choice—either we unconditionally surrender or we fight for the freedom of our people from Assad, Iran and Isil. We choose the latter.

The spirit of those early uprising days still lives on, but we realise that the longer the war goes on, the less there will be of Syria to save. Ahrar Al-Sham wants to see the end to Assad's reign, Isil comprehensively defeated and a stable and representative government in Damascus formed that puts Syria on the path to peace, reconciliation and economic recovery. We would like to see a political system that respects the identity and legitimate political aspirations of Syria's majority while protecting minority communities and enabling them to play a real and positive role in the country's future. We want to see Syria's unity and territorial integrity preserved and an end to the presence of foreign militias on Syrian soil.

We realise that that our vision cannot be achieved by military means alone. There will need to be a political process in place and we know that that means making tough decisions ...

Ahrar Al-Sham, as a mainstream Sunni Islamist group deeply rooted in the revolutionary landscape, is forging that alternative. But those expecting a 'perfect' Sunni alternative according to Western liberal standard are sure to be disappointed. As we should all know by now, political systems and models of government cannot be imported into the Middle East and expected to flourish where historical experiences, political cultures and social structures are so radically different. There needs to be a major role for religion and local custom in any political arrangement that emerges out of the debris of conflict, and it should be one that corresponds with the prevailing beliefs of the majority of Syrians.[18]

The publication of these two editorials was not just the first public airing of this new Ahrar al-Sham political 'discourse', but they also represented the rise to pre-eminence of two brothers among the group's newest and most influential political decision makers. The origin of this new political leadership lay in Ahrar al-Sham's merger with Homs-based Liwa al-Haq in December 2014. Following that merger, Liwa al-Haq's overall leader, Sheikh Abu Rateb, was appointed Ahrar al-Sham's leader in Homs, while the group's two political leaders were integrated into Ahrar al-Sham's political office.

These two men were Labib al-Nahhas and his brother, Abu Azzam. After losing both parents in a car crash in Syria, Labib and Abu Azzam moved to Spain, where they were brought up by relatives and soon acquired Spanish citizenship. By the time protests began erupting in Syria in early 2011, Labib had spent time in America's West Coast and had moved to London and acquired British residency. A devout Muslim who spoke fluent Arabic, Spanish and English with an American tinge, Labib represented the kind of internationally experienced leadership material that a group such as Ahrar al-Sham had long sought. In fact, Labib had been a close confidant of Ahrar al-Sham's founding leader Hassan Abboud since late 2011, often sitting privately with him and discussing the revolution in a mixture of Arabic and English (Abboud had been an English teacher). By early 2015 Labib was appointed Ahrar al-Sham's foreign political chief, while Abu Azzam found himself a senior political official and a leading member of Ahrar al-Sham's *majlis al-shura*.[19]

Although Ahrar al-Sham's bold new political 'discourse' succeeded in attracting a great deal of attention in the West, and sparked renewed internal deliberations in the White House and State Department regarding whether to begin talking to the group, there were some within Ahrar al-Sham who opposed the outreach, or at least had second thoughts once it was a public reality. Abu Mohammed al-Sadeq, a Kurd from Afrin and the group's *sharia* chief, was one prominent detractor, while military leader and known hardliner Abu Saleh Tahan was also thought to distrust the political office's new line of thinking, despite having been involved in its early design.[20]

This induced a particularly intense and consequential internal debate within Ahrar al-Sham over how to resolve the imminent expiration of Hashem al-Sheikh's 12-month term as leader in mid-September. Beginning in mid-July, the entire Ahrar al-Sham movement entered into a period of introspection during which Hashem al-Sheikh announced secretly that he had no intention of continuing as leader and that new 'fresh blood' should be raised. Through a process of internal deliberation across the group's various fronts and departments, several potential candidates were selected for a final vote within Ahrar al-Sham's *majlis al-shura*. These included Labib al-Nahhas' brother Abu Azzam, the group's political chief Abu Abdulrahman al-Shami, a military commander based in Latakia, Abu Ali al-Sahel, and Hashem al-Sheikh's deputy, Mohannad al-Misri.

On 12 September, a day after the vote had been taken within the 12-person *majlis al-shura*, Ahrar al-Sham announced its new leader was Mohannad al-Misri, who was better known as Abu Yahya al-Ghab and Abu Yahya al-Hamawi. Born in 1981 in the town of Qalaat al-Madiq in Syria's Sahl al-Ghab region, Mohannad had trained as a civil engineer after graduating from Latakia's Tishreen University. In August 2007, he was arrested by Syrian intelligence authorities and held in Damascus' notorious Sednayya Prison, where he first became acquainted with Ahrar al-Sham's future founding leader, Hassan Abboud and his close confidante Abu Talha al-Makhzoumi (also known as Abu Talha al-Ghab). After his release from prison in a government amnesty issued during the first days of the revolution in March 2011, Mohanned had travelled back home to Qalaat al-Madiq, where he helped found one of Kataib Ahrar al-Sham's very first units, Sarayat Osama bin Zayd.[21]

As the months and years passed, Mohannad steadily rose in prominence within Ahrar al-Sham, acquiring an impressive reputation for his capabilities in security and military organisational planning. His close relationship with Hassan Abboud and other leading Ahrar al-Sham figures had served to ensure his stature within the movement was higher than his relative youth might otherwise have afforded. Thus, his election as leader in September 2015 represented an intriguing choice in which the group had not necessarily chosen their most moderate option in line with the new discourse, but someone that represented a 'safe option' capable of maintaining internal cohesion amid challenging times.

Ahrar al-Sham's editorials also aroused some derision and condemnation from Jabhat al-Nusra figures present in Syria, and also from leading Al-Qaeda ideologue Abu Qatada al-Filistini, who penned a strong online critique in which he exclaimed:

> Is the West really waiting for what Labib al-Nahhas from Ahrar [al-Sham] is saying? The answer is no. The discourse is a failure. It will not achieve the objectives of Ahrar

al-Sham's leadership, but it will make them hostile to the surrounding Islamic environment, especially the jihadist current... This [article] is evidence that the group is weak in its thinking... Perhaps some of the leaders of this policy accepted bribes in this respect. What I suspect is that some malicious people embroiled them in this unhelpful mess and sought to market this discourse...they have connived in the night to scheme up an ugly future. Which is to say that the group is ready to fight the whole jihadi movement in exchange for the acceptance of its credentials.[22]

Despite the intense debate it engendered within the broader Salafi and Salafi-jihadi communities, it was hard to ignore Ahrar al-Sham's political office's intensified diplomatic role. Through July, August and September, Labib and other Ahrar al-Sham political officials led Turkish-facilitated negotiations with Iran over the fate of the besieged towns of Zabadani (north-west of Damascus) and al-Fuah and Kafraya (north of Idlib). While several ceasefires were agreed—on 12, 14 and 27 August—fighting continued throughout much of the period, with Ahrar al-Sham, Jabhat al-Nusra and others holding out in Zabadani and pro-regime militia forces defending al-Fuah and Kafraya from Jaish al-Fateh's assaults. Finally, a more solid six month truce agreement was signed in late-September between Iran and Hezbollah on one side, and Ahrar al-Sham and Idlib's Jaish al-Fateh on the other. The UN and Turkey had acted as mediators and reportedly as guarantors of the agreement, which stipulated amongst other things that 10,000 civilians would be evacuated from Al-Fuah and Kafraya in Idlib in exchange for the withdrawal of all armed fighters from Zabadani, along with their weapons.[23] Considering the breadth of actors involved, the ceasefire was a considerable development.

In addition to the fact that Ahrar al-Sham had risen to represent the entire Syrian opposition in multilateral negotiations, the role of Iran and the total absence of Assad regime involvement in the talks was also particularly noteworthy. Iran had been assuming more and more of a command and leadership role in Syria's most strategically important battles for some time, but the exclusion of Damascus from negotiating over Syrian territory underlined Tehran's broader assumption of control.

With Iran's role in the Syrian conflict continuing to increase and Ahrar al-Sham's military dominance transforming into political leadership backed by an increasingly assertive Turkey, IS continued throughout late July and August to seek to offset its losses in north-east Syria and in parts of Iraq by advancing into Syria's interior and south.

Following its capture of Palmyra earlier in the summer, IS militants continued their westward advance towards the Lebanese border, capturing the largely Christian village of al-Qarayatain and several surrounding villages on

5 August. Ten days later IS militants had demolished al-Qarayatain's 1,500-year-old Mar Elian monastery[24] and advanced as far as temporarily seizing the Jousiyeh border crossing with Lebanon south-west of the town of al-Qusayr late on 16 August.[25] That remarkable advance was eventually repelled by Hezbollah, but served as a dramatic indication of IS's expanding reach and a clear intent to definitively penetrate core regime territory in western Homs and to pose a direct threat to Lebanese territorial integrity.

Meanwhile, IS also continued to stir trouble in southern Damascus—expanding as far as the al-Qadam and al-Asali districts in late August and early September[26]—while the tacitly pro-IS linked faction Liwa Shuhada Yarmouk continued to operate as a hostile adversary to opposition forces in the southern governorate of Deraa.

In an apparent further attempt to distract from its struggles further north, IS also began taking advantage of its control of UNESCO World Heritage Sites in Palmyra. Having already demolished two small Palmyra sites in June and publicly executed twenty-five regime soldiers in the Roman amphitheatre in July, IS beheaded eighty-two-year-old former Syrian antiquities chief Khaled al-Asaad and strung up his body publicly in the centre of town in mid-August.[27] The following week the 2,000-year-old Temple of Baalshamin was demolished[28] and, days later, so too was the most prized site in Palmyra, the Temple of Bel.[29]

If its advances in northern Aleppo and central Syria, as well as its targeting of Christian communities and demolishing of internationally protected historical sites was not enough, IS also began using chemical weapons in August. Following first reports of its use of mustard gas against Kurdish Peshmerga personnel in northern Iraq in mid-August,[30] the group was accused of using similar chemicals contained within artillery shells against Syrian opposition forces near Marea through late August and into September. After being shown photographic evidence from one such attack, in which a man's back was pictured covered in large bulbous yellow blisters, British chemical weapons expert Hamish de Bretton Gordon was quoted in the media stating that 'the injury photos look straight out of a textbook.'[31] And indeed they did. Doctors and other rescue personnel in northern Aleppo subsequently took to wearing gas masks, protective gloves and occasionally full chemical suits when treating victims of IS bombardments in the area.

Commenting on his personal blog soon after these attacks, a well-known Dutch IS militant known only as 'Yilmaz' appeared to admit that his group was using chemical weapons:

The regime uses chemical warfare on a regular basis these days, and nobody bats an eye—yet when IS captures it from them and uses it against them, it's all of a sudden a huge problem?

Fight them the way they fight you.[32]

Notwithstanding the fact that IS's apparent chemical attacks targeted the opposition, not the regime, and although IS itself never admitted the attacks, the final trick seemingly played out of the group's book from July onwards was a continuous serious of targeted suicide bombings and assassinations—some successful and some foiled—against prominent Islamist figures throughout Idlib, Aleppo and Hama. Beginning in early July with a large suicide bombing in the Salem Mosque in the Idlib town of Ariha that killed at least twenty-five Jabhat al-Nusra militants, the attacks also targeted members of Ahrar al-Sham and Faylaq al-Sham. Most notably, former Sednayya detainee and senior Ahrar al-Sham leader Abu Abdulrahman al-Salqini was killed in Salqin in Idlib on 14 July and Faylaq al-Sham founding member Sheikh Mazen al-Qasum was killed in Saraqeb in Idlib on 24 July. Word on the ground immediately turned to blaming IS 'sleeper cells' hiding within Jund al-Aqsa, but little evidence emerged to substantiate this. Nonetheless, jihadist militants of one allegiance or another were very clearly demonstrating their capacity to effectively target key pillars of northern Syria's Islamist community, and IS was seen by most as the principal instigator.

Amid the continued dominance of jihadists and their Islamist allies in northern Syria, the US 'train and equip' mission finally turned into a reality in mid-July—albeit a small reality, which soon turned into a disaster. Led by the very capable chief commander of US Special Operations in the Middle East, Major-General Michael Nagata, the 'train and equip' mission had been hobbled from its early days, when it took nearly six months for Nagata's office to receive its first funds.[33] Then came issues in recruiting Syrians for the mission and pushing them through the restrictive 'vetting' process, which required among other things that men swear an oath to fight only IS and not regime forces—an expectation that for most rebels was virtually inconceivable due to the regime's vastly higher killing rate of ordinary Syrians.

Nonetheless, despite early numerical difficulties, the intention within US Central Command (CENTCOM) was to begin integrating trained recruits into existing larger vetted factions active in northern Aleppo so as to individually bolster multiple units' capabilities on the frontline against IS. Their gradual deployment was also intended to steadily erode the pre-eminent role of the Kurdish YPG in fighting IS, which had become a source of increasing ethnic Arab–Kurd frustration, and sometimes hostility, within Syria's moderate opposition circles. Perhaps most valuably, a majority of fighters would have received the necessary training to call in US-led coalition air strikes. Therefore, when the first batch of fifty-four trained and equipped fighters entered northern Aleppo on 14 July, there was great deal of anticipation for what effect they might have upon existing anti-IS operations.

Arriving in such a small group, one would have thought the fifty-four men would have made an effort to cross quietly into Syria. However, the team of American-trained fighters—equipped with brand-new American 120-mm mortars, M240 machine guns mounted on new Toyota pick-up trucks and Mk14 Enhanced Battle Rifles—presented their convoy for photographs immediately after crossing the Syrian border. Within hours their arrival was common news on social media.

The following morning some of the fifty-four, led by Colonel Nadim Hassan, were confronted by a Jabhat al-Nusra patrol near Azaz and warned to stay away from the group's areas of operation.[34] Two weeks later Hassan and his deputy, Farhan Jassem, were kidnapped by Jabhat al-Nusra after leaving a meeting with other rebel leaders in Azaz, sparking panic. The following day, on 31 July, Jabhat al-Nusra claimed responsibility for capturing Hassan and Jassem, and proceeded to launch an overnight assault on their base near Azaz. That attack targeted the headquarters of Division 30, a relatively new FSA faction established as a recruitment pool for the train and equip mission. Five Division 30 fighters were killed, eighteen wounded and another twenty captured during the attack, which was eventually repulsed thanks to a concerted series of US air strikes that targeted Jabhat al-Nusra's advancing forces.

In the days that followed, Division 30 members reportedly fled the Azaz area towards Kurdish-controlled Afrin, into the north-western refugee camp in Atmeh and across the border into southern Turkey. Very quickly—almost overnight—the $500 million train and equip mission had been virtually destroyed. Its credibility had certainly suffered a huge dent. Despite the US air strikes, and subsequent indications from American officials that President Obama had signed off on a policy to defend the train and equip troops from attack by any party (including the regime),[35] Division 30 released a statement on 4 August purportedly declaring that it had renounced its links to the US-led coalition and would not fight Jabhat al-Nusra. Two days later Syrian sources said much of Division 30 had gone into hiding.[36]

Fast-forward six weeks and a second batch of 71 trained and equipped fighters were deployed into northern Aleppo and as with the first group, major debilitating issues arose. Almost as soon as the 71 arrived in country, one of their commanders handed over half of their US-provided pick-up trucks and 25 per cent of their ammunition to Jabhat al-Nusra in return for their safety. Reports quickly emerged on social media that Al-Qaeda had been given American military supplies, but CENTCOM repeatedly asserted with '100 per cent' certainty that the accusations were false until three days later, it was forced to admit the truth.[37]

If US policy in Syria was not experiencing enough of a credibility challenge in early August, its targeted air strike on a weapons depot in Atmeh in Idlib governorate dealt a near-mortal blow to America's reputation. Late on 11 August six missiles struck several buildings belonging to a group known as Jaish al-Ummah, which had been used to manufacture and store homemade mortars and artillery shells for use in Jaish al-Fateh operations elsewhere in Idlib.

Originally founded in Homs, Jaish al-Ummah was an FSA-affiliated faction which fled north following opposition defeats in Homs in late 2013. While the presence of jihadists in the surrounding area cannot necessarily be discounted, the airstrikes were understandably perceived by Syrians as having targeted an entirely legitimate and moderate revolutionary actor. Moreover, the strikes killed eighteen people, including five young sisters aged between four and ten, and a three-person family of internally displaced persons.[38] Social media were immediately awash with images of the dead girls and several other wounded children, as well as emotional video interviews conducted by famed activist Hadi al-Abdullah with the girls' grandfather and mother. In a subsequent interview former ambassador Robert Ford tellingly declared: 'The Americans need to get a strategy and then they need to get the tactics right.'[39]

Yet again, jihadists had been presented with an invaluable gift by their Western adversaries. Such horrific civilian losses, pictured for all to see, were bad enough, but CENTCOM's extraordinarily confused denial and then confirmation of a strike in the area due to 'multiple spellings of Atme'[40] sparked consternation and fury within broader opposition circles. 'When we saw that, we honestly lost all faith in America,' said one Idlib-based commander. 'When they can't even get spellings right in Syria, how can we trust them in other things?'[41]

Such catastrophic misjudgements aside, US airpower was put to more effective use elsewhere in August, with the targeted killing of deputy IS leader Fadl Ahmed Abdullah al-Hiyali (better known as Haji Mutaz or Abu Muslim al-Turkmani) in a drone strike near Mosul on 18 August.[42] Six days later, another such strike killed British 'IS hacker' Junaid Hussain, who had been responsible for breaking into CENTCOM's social media accounts in 2014, and had been accused of involvement in influencing several foreign IS-related plots in 2015.[43]

Both deaths dealt severe blows to specific aspects of IS's top-level command and operational structures, and revealed the strong likelihood that US intelligence had acquired one or multiple assets capable of penetrating the highest levels of the IS jihadist movement. While the strategic consequences of such losses would take a long time to become clear, the slow and methodical process of building intelligence and operationalising leads into a kinetic military campaign was gradually becoming clear in the US-led strategy against IS.

Elsewhere in Syria, the regime–opposition conflict continued apace. Pro-regime forces were increasingly demonstrating a strategic focus upon securing so-called 'useful Syria'—meaning Damascus, the route north through the Qalamoun and Homs, and then west into the coastal areas of Tartous and Latakia. Hezbollah's supply lines from Damascus to Beirut, through towns such as Zabadani, were also of clear value. Fearing the potential loss of territory in Hama and the resulting threat that would pose to its crucial stranglehold over Homs, pro-regime forces ploughed considerable resources into defending areas of Sahl al-Ghab from advancing Jaish al-Fateh forces. Additional resources were also deployed into northern Latakia, where Jabhat al-Nusra and Ahrar al-Sham had begun launching unpredictable raids and probing attacks into the Jebel al-Turkman Mountains. Both of these areas experienced increasingly frequent reports of sightings of Iranian personnel and equipment, including drones, as well as the first—though at the time unconfirmed—appearances of Russian-speaking soldiers, newly delivered Russian armoured vehicles, drones and even new MiG and Sukhoi fighter jets.[44]

With manpower issues continuing to plague its capacity to retake territory, the regime remained principally reliant on airpower to suppress opposition forces. The Damascus suburb of Douma, still home to Jaish al-Islam and several other Islamist factions such as Ajnad al-Sham and Faylaq al-Rahman, bore the brunt of this largely indiscriminate regime tactic in August, with at least 117 people killed and 530 wounded in a public market in Douma on 16 August and a further 55 people killed a week later in the same area.[45] As on previous occasions, including the sarin gas attack of August 2013, the regime carried out the first of those attacks—quickly labelled within opposition circles as the Douma Massacre—during a visit to the country by a senior international official, this time UN aid chief Stephen O'Brien, who was quite clearly powerless to do much more than declare: 'I am horrified by the total disrespect for civilian life in this conflict.'[46]

* * *

Amid such brutality, and a state of still intractable and highly complex conflict, Syria had long consolidated its status as an immensely fertile breeding ground for jihadist militancy. By August 2015 at least 240,000 people had been recorded killed in Syria, at least 111,000 of whom were civilians, including nearly 12,000 children. A further 2 million people had received injuries of varying levels of severity, and over half of the entire pre-war population was internally displaced or had become refugees.[47] The knock-on effect of this huge population displacement was only then beginning to make itself clear to European populations hundreds and thousands of miles away, as refugees began streaming into Europe in August and September 2015, catalysing a renewed policy focus on 'how to solve Syria.'

Due to the inherent complexity resulting from the sheer number of different external actors involved in fighting or supporting proxies to fight on their behalf in Syria, the revolution had transformed into a seemingly intractable civil conflict. Iran and Russia had consistently proven resolute backers of the Assad regime, not necessarily out of any particular loyalty to Bashar himself, but more out of a recognition that his rule ensured the security of their strategic interests. Following on from the historic Iran 'nuclear deal', there was no sign that Tehran would have been willing to consider a political solution—or at least one also acceptable to stake-holders on the opposite side. Amid intensified diplomatic activities between Russia and both Saudi Arabia and the USA, Moscow had also only expanded its military assistance to the Assad regime and by October, had begun its own military operations in support of the regime. Whether or not this had represented Iranian and Russian positioning in advance of any grand political deal or was more simply an embodiment of both countries' refusal to consider any alternative to the status quo remained to be seen.

Although a change in Saudi Arabia's leadership brought with it a more assertive geo-political strategy, Riyadh's bandwidth did not appear sufficient to deal comprehensively with Syria while it remained preoccupied with its war in Yemen. Moreover, despite clear signs of a rapprochement between Riyadh and Doha, a single unified regional pro-revolution policy appeared far from reality. As long as countries such as Saudi Arabia, Qatar, Turkey and Jordan continued to act independently of each other, and often in different directions and with different partners, the Syrian opposition looked set to struggle to reach its real potential, whether militarily or politically. So long as that continued to be the case, a political solution was likely to remain a long way away, and jihadists would undoubtedly continue to reap the benefits. With a Russian military intervention underway by October, that latter reality looked concretely secured.

The current Western focus on countering terrorism in Syria is both understandable and ill conceived. IS's dramatic advances in Iraq and its proclamation of a caliphate in mid-2014 grasped the attention of what had been otherwise preoccupied capitals in the West. While IS posed an immediate threat to regional security at that point, the underlying factors behind the group's recovery and expansion went largely ignored. Political failure and instability combined with dangerous social fissures and rising perceptions of sectarianism had contributed towards the establishment of socio-political conditions in which extremists can thrive. Although nowhere symbolised that reality better than Syria, combating terrorism remained the only policy priority in Washington, London, Paris and elsewhere, while one of IS's most valuable recruitment mechanisms and a more challenging problem to fix remained securely in place: the Assad regime. In a sense, IS had become a convenient obsession.

Terrorism has indeed become a colossal issue in Syria. The total number of Sunni jihadist militants in the country may well be considerably higher than 50,000—taking into account IS, al-Qaeda and all other independent factions. While IS is already actively encouraging lone-wolf attacks in the West and seeking to destabilise Turkey, al-Qaeda's principal strategic objective remains the targeting of Western assets around the world. Therefore, existing efforts to counter jihadist safe havens in Syria must undoubtedly continue, but within a more comprehensive strategic vision that encompasses a realisation that unstable and repressive government only drives factors such as conflict, resentment and extremism that jihadists exploit.

Within Syria, a country long known for its liberal attitude towards the Islamic faith and towards being a harmonious multi-sect society, sustained conflict, death, displacement and suffering generated an environment in which groups such as Jabhat al-Nusra could find willing acceptance. As Moazzam Begg said, 'Syrians were not really "jihad-minded", but they were Muslims, who like most people in times of great hardship, turn to God.'[48]

From a more regional and international perspective, the development and perpetuation of conflict in Syria, a country loaded with Islamic prophecy relating to the end of the world, would always have presented a major attraction to the world's jihadist community. The extensive jihadist networks developed in Syria during the early 2000s and the history of its brutal repression of the Muslim Brotherhood added further to its jihadist potential. It was therefore far from surprising that at least 25,000 foreign Sunni fighters had travelled to Syria to fight jihad, including as many as 6,000 from Europe.[49] This made the Syrian Jihad one of unprecedented scale, even surpassing the mass migration of *mujahideen* to Afghanistan in the 1980s. Not only was the scale unparalleled, but the scope was similarly significant, with more than twenty transnationally minded jihadist factions having established themselves in Syria since 2011.

Syria was also fast becoming the central focal point of global jihadism's ideological and structural evolution. The world now faced an international security reality that contained not just one major international jihadist movement—al-Qaeda—but two, with the rise of the Islamic State. The intense competitive and often hostile dynamic between these two global jihadist actors had emerged from and been defined within Syrian territory.

Moreover, it is also important to note that Syria has assumed critical importance as a major zone of Shia jihadism, with some studies having suggested that the numbers of Shia foreign fighters may even outweigh their Sunni counterparts.[50] As one of the very few experts assessing the phenomenon of Shia militancy in Syria, Phillip Smyth estimated that '12,000–15,000 such fighters have rotated through Syria' during the four-year conflict.[51] This has produced a mutually reinforcing dynamic, whereby each side's expansion encourages the other to grow yet further. With no viable path thus far established towards a potential political solution and with a Russian military intervention further muddying the waters and serving as fuel on an already thriving jihadist fire, the Syrian Jihad looks set to continue its upward trajectory.

The terrorist threat thus emanating from Syria had, through 2014 and 2015, drawn in increasing levels of international intervention, and both political and military interference. A horrifically brutal and incredibly complex civil conflict had therefore become a key determinant of international stability. Increasingly large and uncontrollable flows of Syrian refugees into Europe throughout the summer of 2015 was but one of many unintended consequences of a war spinning out of control. The haunting nature of Syria's conflict, however, meant that even such humanitarian crises brought with them the possible—though by then undemonstrated—threat of jihadist militants exploiting mass refugee flows to infiltrate target countries in the West.

After years of concerted counter-terrorism pressure and drone strikes targeting its central leadership in Afghanistan, Pakistan and Yemen, al-Qaeda has increasingly come to represent a collective of like-minded jihadist factions loosely held together by a sense of Islamic loyalty to the tradition of al-Qaeda Central. Ayman al-Zawahiri has failed to live up to the image of global leadership developed by his predecessor, Osama Bin Laden. Individual al-Qaeda affiliates, particularly AQAP in Yemen and Jabhat al-Nusra in Syria, have come to represent the key sources of hope for the movement's continued relevance worldwide.

IS meanwhile has emerged as a genuinely viable, if not potentially superior, competitor to al-Qaeda. Since its declaration of a caliphate in mid-2014, IS has demonstrated a surprisingly effective capacity for international expansion through its acquisition of *wilayat*. By September 2015 IS had grown to the extent that it claimed to manage nineteen *wilayat* in Syria and Iraq and a further fifteen around the world—in Libya, Saudi Arabia, Yemen, Algeria, Egypt, Afghanistan–Pakistan, Nigeria and Russia's North Caucasus. A majority of the 25,000 foreign Sunni jihadist fighters who had travelled into Syria since 2011 had done so in order to join IS and, despite the group's loss of territory along the Turkey–Syria border through 2015, the flows continued. Clearly, IS's unrivalled levels of brutality, its thirst for continuous worldwide attention and its demonstrated capacity to sustain momentum as a transnational movement made it a jihadist force to be reckoned with.

Emanating from Syria and Iraq, this new global dynamic of intra-jihadist competition has produced two contrasting models of international jihad. The al-Qaeda 'model' has now come to represent something focused on developing and implementing a patient long-term strategy of integrating *mujahidin* into localised conflicts and embedding them within tribal or communal dynamics. In so doing, individual al-Qaeda affiliates seek to root themselves into revolutions and rebellions containing a broader popular character, thereby ensuring that their role within unstable societies becomes more durable. Over time, having established themselves concretely within such dynamics, al-Qaeda affiliates will have established what Zawahiri has termed 'safe bases', from which the broader movement's international objective of attacking the West can eventually be planned and implemented.

IS, meanwhile, has demonstrated itself to be an entirely different kind of strategic actor, focused on attaining rapid and dramatic results. Notwithstanding its deserved reputation for brutality, mass killing, slavery, rape and other criminal tactics, it has also demonstrated an impressive capacity for implementing well-planned long-term campaigns aimed at destabilising a local area, incorporating sustained intimidation tactics and targeted attacks on key nodes of local power; followed by light-infantry-style all-out military assaults aimed at assuming total control over expansive territory. IS's ability to act simultaneously or in sequence as terrorist cells, insurgent factions and light infantry units against the same enemy has afforded it an invaluable advantage over its conventional army adversaries in Syria and Iraq.

Ultimately, IS is a counter-state movement that explicitly aims to destroy nation-state boundaries and to expand, and thus legitimise, its self-proclaimed caliphate and Islamic state project. Al-Qaeda, on the other hand, appears to have learned the lessons of the past and developed a strategy that allows it to protect itself against traditional counter-terrorist strategies. The rapidity with which US-led coalition airstrikes against Jabhat al-Nusra were perceived as anti-revolutionary acts by a broad cohort of opposition Syrians was testament to the medium-term success of that social integration strategy.

The hostile competition between al-Qaeda and IS in Syria has potentially huge international ramifications, with both movements now competing to carry out or influence the carrying out of terrorist attacks on Western soil. The attacks that took place in France in February 2015 underlined that new dynamic, with the Kouachi brothers being linked to AQAP and Amedy Coulibaly and his partner Hayat Boumeddiene having at the very least a stated allegiance to IS. That Coulibaly claimed to have coordinated the attacks with the Kouachi brothers[52] and the fact that one of the brothers sent a text message to Coulibaly an hour before the attack on the *Charlie Hebdo* offices on 7 January[53] further underlined the threat.

The dramatic and headline-grabbing nature of IS has placed jihadist militancy at the top of today's global agenda. However, in so doing, this has distracted attention from the very root causes of the conflict in Syria that IS and other jihadists so deeply depend upon to survive. The intractability of the conflict is not solely a result of its inherent complexity, but also the failure of the world's major countries to more definitively decide to end it, whether through military or political means, or a combination of the two. Death by chemical weapons, barrel bombs, torture, starvation or drowning on Europe's shores—all are exploited by jihadists as evidence of Western indifference to Muslim suffering. This sense of victimhood has long been a core facet of jihadist recruitment and localised legitimacy, and it is something IS has played upon to great effect.

In addition to making jihadist militancy and terrorism a key focus of international attention, IS's dramatic emergence as a major international security threat has also internationalised intra-jihadist competition. This has arguably resulted in a considerable escalation in the threat posed to Western security both directly by terrorist organisations and also by so-called self-starter or lone-wolf violent extremists. Whereas the Western world faced a Sunni jihadist terrorism threat solely from al-Qaeda in 2010–11, the competition now between two major transnational jihadist organisations to demonstrate their credibility by directing or encouraging attacks in Europe, the USA and elsewhere has produced a dynamic of continuous and mutually reinforcing escalation.

At the end of the day, however, IS has developed a supremely powerful ideological idea that aims to appeal to a mass audience of Sunni Muslims. It does indeed include a strong element of apocalyptic thought within its world-view, but it principally fights for *the* Islamic state—for Sunni Islam and for the right of Sunnis to salvage the pride and honour felt during the previous eras of the caliphate. IS does not recruit based on its intent to spark the end of the world, but instead it presents an image of Sunni power and self-worth, which within political societies divided by issues of sect—as in Iraq and Syria—can be an attractive prospect. Its military power, slick image and relative wealth also provide for some the hope of real practical potential, and so long as it can sustain an image of operational continuity—not necessarily momentum—it will reap the benefits of what it purports to offer. This will prove particularly true if the group continues to encourage and inspire terrorist attacks in the Western world. Speaking shortly before his death in early 2014, British IS fighter Abu Uthman warned this author of this likelihood should the world intervene against his fellow jihadists:

> When they send their troops from around the world to fight my brothers, then don't be surprised when they retaliate back in their lands. If someone slaps you across the face for hours, would you just stand there and let it happen? No, then why should it be any different for Muslims? Enough of the *umma* is united to ensure that you will eventually feel the consequences of your government's aggressive actions.[54]

The emergence, consolidation and growth of jihadist militancy in Syria has been as much about the failure of moderates and their external supporters as it is been about jihadist success. When protests erupted in Syria in the spring of 2011 and the regime's security apparatus mobilised to carry out its local and then broader crackdowns, it should have been obvious to the world where things were going. Bashar al-Assad and his close inner circle had proved their opposition to genuine political reform throughout the preceding years while underlining their willingness to risk dealing with and attempting to manipulate jihadist militants to suit their policy agendas. Moreover, the failure of domestic socio-economic policy since the early 2000s had created a vast urban sub-class, much of which embodied the kind of social, religious and political disaffection that extremists can feed upon so easily.

In the international diplomatic arena, the failure to more fully get behind the revolution and its fledgling Free Syrian Army in mid-to-late 2011 allowed a deeply damaging dynamic to develop—that of competing and often mutually exclusive strategies of opposition support from Turkey, Saudi Arabia and Qatar. Remarkably quickly, rival FSA factions with separate funding sources and operational allegiances and priorities found themselves fighting the same war, but under the auspices of rival powers with separate interests. The subsequent failures of both the exiled political and on-the-ground insurgent opposition to better synthesise their efforts to overthrow the Assad regime provided the space within which jihadists could emerge and claim a stake in the conflict. Moreover, the consistent failure of initiatives aimed at uniting the moderate insurgency inside Syria encouraged the proliferation of factions such that by the late-2015, as many as 1,500 operationally distinct insurgent groups were operating across Syria. Within such immensely complex circumstances, and with so many factions competing for external financial support, incidences of insurgent and opposition corruption and double-dealing increased—which again benefited jihadists, who ordinarily presented an image of non-corruption.

Furthermore, as the conflict continued, casualties mounted and the Assad regime escalated the use of weaponry at its disposal, from troops, to tanks, to helicopters, to fighter jets, to Scud missiles, and finally to chemical weapons. The consistent failure of the international community to stand by its values of protecting civilians against repression through the global principle of 'Responsibility to Protect' and enforcing international law with respect to war crimes and use of prohibited weapons continued to lend legitimacy to the world-view espoused by Sunni jihadist militants.

Throughout four years of closely engaging with foot-soldiers and leaders from across the Syrian insurgency, it became clear to this author that those on the more moderate end of the spectrum were increasingly adopting a political perspective of the conflict and its relation to broader international dynamics that was more widely shared by jihadists. In effect, these views can be summed up as follows: either the world is immorally unconcerned about the suffering of Sunni Muslims or it actively seeks to covertly assist or indirectly facilitate the suppression of Sunni Islam and its adherents across the world.

For many Syrians, the very fact that the world was standing by as dozens of its citizens were maimed and killed every day by a regime whose military was pushing metal barrels filled with explosives and home-made shrapnel from helicopters to free fall and explode in civilian neighbourhoods was enough to buy into the idea that a group such as Jabhat al-Nusra had their backs. For other similarly disaffected young men determined to fight back, against both the regime and the 'system', the wealthy and powerful IS could be an equally attractive proposition.

More broadly, the relative failure of moderates and the rise of jihadists within the conflict in Syria has seen diverse groups of Syrian Islamists become the mainstream revolutionary actors, capable of defining the trajectory of the insurgency and determining the viability of any potential solution to the crisis. When combined with indications that jihadists such as Jabhat al-Nusra may be emerging as increasingly self-assertive actors unwilling to cooperate with state-backed opposition projects like that planned by Turkey in mid-2015, and with the increasingly overt and active political nature of Syria's Islamist insurgent groups since late 2014, it appears all but inevitable that Syria's Islamists will have to be acknowledged as necessary partners in any future peace and political process. Having established themselves as powerful detractors of the exiled political opposition, along with the trust it had placed in the 'Friends of Syria' to support the revolution through to victory, these groups' staunch political positions had by and large proved accurate by late 2014. Although primarily visible only behind the scenes, the main consequence of this vindication was that core FSA groups had begun to adopt many of the same political positions as their Syrian Islamist compatriots. Moreover, by mid-2015, even the exiled ETILAF political opposition had begun to engineer much of their political positioning to better fit the 'standards' and stances adopted by the armed opposition.

Generally, this 'reintegration' of the more conservative end of the Syrian insurgent spectrum into the broader mix was also a result of the fact that jihadists such as Jabhat al-Nusra who had long presented themselves as relative pragmatists were now revealing their true transnationally minded colours. Speaking with this author, Ahrar al-Sham's external relations chief, Abu Mustafa, demonstrated this new and more unified and collaborative approach adopted by Salafists by denying that the FSA had failed and describing it as something much broader than typically understood from outside:

> The Free Army battalions and factions are all Syrian rebels. Although we have not
> yet attained a central leadership and in spite of the intermittent and geographically

distinct difficulties of the war, as well as the brutal actions of the regime and its supporters, the Free Army has continued to coordinate across all of its parts and it is fighting back. It has not failed yet.[55]

This, coming from such a senior Ahrar al-Sham official, was highly significant messaging for how Salafists now viewed themselves within the broader insurgent and opposition dynamic. Moreover, when Ahrar al-Sham's then leader Hashem al-Sheikh told Al-Jazeera during an extended interview on 17 April that Jabhat al-Nusra's links to al-Qaeda endangered Syria's people, a clear delineation was emerging. By mid-2015 Jabhat al-Nusra's long-time ally Ahrar al-Sham appeared to be definitively grappling with its capacity to moderate politically while clearly having assumed a dominant role as the most powerful armed opposition group in Syria.

With that being said, it remains undeniably true that for the opposition as a whole to continue to put up an effective fight against regime and pro-regime forces, jihadists remain an indispensable force. Jabhat al-Nusra's more or less consistent focus on limiting the extent of its extremist behaviour and behavioural expectations across Syria, combined with its particular effectiveness on the battlefield and willingness to cooperate with a broad spread of opposition groups, has placed it in an ideal position to continue to exploit the ongoing conflict. Although Jabhat al-Nusra has appeared to act in a gradually more self-assertive manner through 2015, it still appears unlikely that it will be discernibly isolated by the rest of the insurgency, at least so long as the Assad regime stays in place. After four years of merciless conflict, ideological differences and politico-ideological objectives are more likely than not to be put aside in favour of continuing a fight with a better chance of success. Moreover, Jabhat al-Nusra has had four years to build a broader supporting environment in northern Syria, which is now composed of a number of other al-Qaeda-aligned militant groups which provide it with invaluable strategic depth and a set of 'on-demand' local allies.

Moreover, Russia's intervention has now provided Jabhat al-Nusra with an invaluable opportunity to continue to sell itself as an invaluable supporter of the revolutionary cause.

So despite the increasingly complex nature of the various intra-insurgent and intra-jihadist dynamics in Syria, jihadists of all kinds look set to play a prominent role in Syria's future for some time to come. If the world has learned one thing from jihadist organisations over the past fifteen years, it is that they are not easily defeated, by either the near or the far enemy. Moreover, the longer the conflict in Syria lasts, and the longer jihadists such as IS manage to retain control over territory sufficient to claim the existence of an 'Islamic state', the more foreign fighters will continue to stream into the country, further bolstering the long-term potential and threat posed by jihadists. No matter how many label IS's state project illegitimate, it will always be attractive to some, as Moazzam Begg warned this author:

> The Muslim world has been yearning for the return of its 'shield' and central representative authority for over eighty years ... Now that someone has finally declared it—no matter who—as long as he has the muscle to defend it, implements what they believe to be sharia (to the letter), terrifies his enemies, implements Islamic social, economic and educational codes, brings security to the people and defends them against enemy forces, then that's enough.[56]

Those involved in the Syrian Jihad have had four years to build their foundations and establish themselves concretely within the country. From Afghanistan, to Somalia, to Nigeria and to Iraq, jihadists have consistently survived and persevered. We should expect no different from those involved in the Syrian Jihad.

# NOTES

PREFACE

1. 'About 6,000 Europeans are reportedly fighting with jihadist groups in Syria', AFP, 13 April 2015.

INTRODUCTION

1. Richard Kerbaj, 'Twice as many UK jihadists as police thought, officials say', *The Sunday Times*, 19 April 2015.
2. Mariam Karouny, 'Insight—Syria's Nusra Front may leave Qaeda to form new entity', Reuters, 4 March 2015; 'al-Nusra Front denies plans to break away from al-Qaeda', *Middle East Eye*, 9 March 2015; 'Sheikh Abu Mariya al-Qahtani speaking on the subject of breaking the ties between Jabhat al-Nusra and al-Qaeda', published on JustPaste.it on 21 April 2015.

1. BREAKING DOWN THE BARRIERS: PROTEST

1. Hugh MacLeod, 'Syria: how it all began', Global Post, 23 April 2011.
2. 'Syria: prisoners of conscience in Damascus Central Prison declare hunger strike', In Defence of Marxism, 9 March 2011. The original letter (no longer available) was published by the Syrian Observatory for Human Rights.
3. 'Jailed Kurds on Syria hunger strike: rights group', AFP, 10 March 2011.
4. Human Rights Watch, 'Syria: the silenced Kurds', October 1996.
5. Author interview with Amjad Farekh, January 2015.
6. Hugh MacLeod, 'Inside Deraa', Al-Jazeera, 19 April 2011.
7. Author interview with Amjad Farekh, January 2015.
8. Phil Sands, Justin Vela and Suha Maayeh, 'Blood ties: the shadowy member of the Assad clan who ignited the Syrian conflict', *The National*, 20 March 2014.

## 2. UNDERLYING INSTABILITY

1. 'Statement by 99 Syrian Intellectuals', *al-Hayat*, 27 September 2000.

2. Andrew Tabler, 'Squaring the circle?' *Syria Today*, June 2006.

3. All figures released by the United Nations Conference on Trade and Development's (UNCTAD) World Investment Report in October 2007.

4. Majid Rafizadeh, 'In Syria, follow the money to find the roots of the revolt', *The Daily Beast*, 8 April 2013.

5. According to data collected by the World Bank.

6. *Baseline Water Sector Report*, GTZ Modernization of the Syrian Water Sector, Support to Sector Planning and Coordination, State Planning Commission, 2009.

7. Francesca de Chatel, 'The role of drought and climate change in the Syrian Uprising: untangling the triggers of the revolution', *Middle Eastern Studies* 50, 4 (2014).

8. D. Haidar and Francesca de Chatel, 'Leaving the land', *Syria Today*, May 2009.

9. United Nations Human Rights Council (UNHCR), *Report of the Special Rapporteur on the Right to Food on his Mission to Syria, Addendum*, 27 January 2011.

10. Ibid.

11. United Nations Office for the Coordination of Humanitarian Affairs, *Syria Drought Response Plan 2009*, 2009.

12. Patrick Seale, *Asad: The Struggle for the Middle East* (Berkeley: University of California Press, 1990), pp. 92–3.

13. Robin Bidwell, *Dictionary of Modern Arab History* (Abingdon: Kegan Paul International, 1998), p. 289.

14. Thomas Pierret, *Religion and State in Syria: The Sunni Ulama under the Ba'th* (New York: Cambridge University Press, 2013), p. 69.

15. Annabelle Bottcher, *Syrische Religionspolitik unter Assad* (Freiburg im Breisgau: Arnold-Bergstrasser-Institut, 1998), pp. 117–19.

16. Line Khatib, *Islamic Revivalism in Syria: The Rise and Fall of Ba'thist Secularism* (Abingdon: Routledge, 2011), p. 154.

17. Pierret, *Religion and State in Syria*, p. 78.

18. Mohammed Said Ramadan al-Bouti, 'Hakadha nashaat al-qawamiyya' [This is how nationalism was born], *Hadarat al-Islam* 3, 6 (1963).

19. Andreas Christmann, 'Islamic scholar and religious leader: a portrait of Muhammad Sa'id Ramadan al-Buti', *Islam and Christian–Muslim Relations* 9, 2 (1998), p. 163.

20. Joseph Holliday, 'The Assad Regime: From Counterinsurgency to Civil War', *Middle East Security Report* 8 (Washington, DC: Institute for the Study of War, 2013), p. 27.

## 3. SYRIA'S FLIRTATION WITH JIHADISM

1. Ghaith Abdul-Ahad, 'Outside Iraq but deep in the fight', *Washington Post*, 8 June 2005.
2. Author interview with former Aleppo-based police official, September 2015.
3. Ibid.
4. Ibid.
5. 'Syrian Intelligence Chief Attends CT Dialogue with S/CT Benjamin, 24 February 2010', Wikileaks.
6. Abdul-Ahad, 'Outside Iraq but deep in the fight'.
7. Juliette Terzieff, 'Syrians told to prepare for fight with US/Iraq war is just the beginning, leaders say', Chronicle Foreign Service, 31 March 2003.
8. Ziad K. Abdelnour, "Syria's Proxy Forces in Iraq," *Middle East Intelligence Bulletin*, Vol. 5, No. 4, April 2003.
9. Abdul-Ahad, 'Outside Iraq but deep in the fight'.
10. Ian Black and Chris McGreal, 'Conflict will create 100 Bin Ladens, warns Egyptian president', *The Guardian*, 1 April 2003.
11. Ziad K. Abdelnour, 'Syria's proxy forces in Iraq', *Middle East Intelligence Bulletin*, 5, 4 (April 2003).
12. 'Arab neigbours queue for ticket to martyrdom', *Sydney Morning Herald*, 1 April 2003.
13. Abdelnour, 'Syria's proxy forces in Iraq'.
14. 'Syria gives passports to suicide bombers', *The Times*, 1 April 2003.
15. Mitch Frank, 'Help from an unlikely ally', *TIME Magazine*, 23 June 2002.
16. William Maclean, 'al-Qaeda ideologue in Syrian detention—lawyers', Reuters, 10 June 2009.
17. Sebastian Rotella, 'Italian police link Syria to al Qaeda extremists/Nation served as way station for terror recruits, probe finds', *Los Angeles Times*, 16 April 2003.
18. 'Bombers, bank accounts, and bleedout: al-Qa'ida's road in and out of Iraq', Combating Terrorism Center at West Point, 22 July 2008.
19. James Denselow, 'Iraq's Ho Chi Minh Trail: the Syrian–Iraqi border since 2003', *CTC Sentinel*, 15 May 2008.
20. US Department of the Treasury, 'Treasury designates members of Abu Ghadiyah's network facilitates flow of terrorists, weapons, and money from Syria to al Qaida in Iraq', 28 February 2008.
21. Martin Chulov, 'ISIS: the inside story', *The Guardian*, 11 December 2014.
22. Abdul-Ahad, 'Outside Iraq but deep in the fight'.
23. Denselow, 'Iraq's Ho Chi Minh Trail'.
24. 'Bombers, bank accounts, and bleedout'.
25. Statement by the director of national intelligence, John D. Negroponte, to the Senate Select Committee on Intelligence, 2 February 2006.

26. 'US must talk to Syria on Mideast peace—Syrian minister', Kuwait News Agency (KUNA), 4 September 2006.

27. Philippe Bolopian and Mouna Naim, 'Des jihadistes viseraient 36 personnalités antisyriennes au Liban', *Le Monde*, 7 December 2006.

28. Peter Neumann, 'Suspects into collaborators', *London Review of Books*, 28 March 2014.

29. Michael R. Gordon and Wesley S. Morgan, 'The general's gambit', *Foreign Policy*, 1 October 2012.

30. Gordon and Morgan, 'The general's gambit'.

31. Bill Roggio, 'al Qaeda in Iraq operative killed near Syrian border sheds light on foreign influence', Long War Journal, 3 October 2007.

32. Andrew McGregor, 'Controversial Syrian preacher Abu al-Qaqa gunned down in Aleppo', Jamestown Foundation, 16 October 2007.

33. 'Radical Syrian cleric "shot dead"', BBC News, 29 September 2007.

34. 'Death of a cleric', NOW, 5 October 2007.

35. For example, Abdulrahman al-Rashed, 'The killing of Abu al Qaqaa', *Asharq al-Awsat*, 3 October 2007.

36. Muhanad Mohammed, 'Iraq al Qaeda militant says Syria trained him', Reuters, 30 August 2009.

37. Gordon and Morgan, 'The general's gambit'.

38. Ibid.

39. Ibid.

40. Neumann, 'Suspects into collaborators'.

41. Abdul-Ahad, 'Outside Iraq but deep in the fight'.

42. Ibid.

43. Ibid.

44. Lieutenant Colonel Joel Rayburn, 'Blowback—Iraq comes to Syria', Hoover Institution, 23 February 2012.

## 4. MARCH–DECEMBER 2011: JABHAT AL-NUSRA FORMS

1. Katherine Marsh, 'Syrian regime launches crackdown by shooting 15 activists dead', *The Guardian*, 24 March 2011; 'Zwanzig Demonstranten bei syrischer Stadt Daraa getötet', *Neue Zürcher Zeitung*, 25 March 2011; 'Syria unrest: troops kill 10 protesters in Deraa', BBC News, 24 March 2011.

2. Author interview with Amjad Farekh, January 2015.

3. Author interview with Abu Mustafa, January 2015.

4. 'Gunfire in locked-down Syrian city', Al Jazeera, 19 April 2011.

5. Khaled Yacoub Owais, 'Muslim Brotherhood endorses Syria protests', Reuters, 29 April 2011.

6. 'Syria: Defectors Describe Orders to Shoot Unarmed Protesters', *Human Rights Watch*, 9 July 2011.

7. Rania Abouzeid, 'The jihad next door', Politico, 23 June 2014.

8. Aron Lund, *Syria's Salafi insurgents: the rise of the Syrian Islamic Front*, UI Occasional Paper no. 17 (Stockholm: Swedish Institute for International Affairs, March 2013), p. 38.

9. Author interview with Mohammed Khadam, January 2015.

10. Bassem Mroue, 'Key al-Qaida militant reportedly killed in Syria', Associated Press, 27 January 2014.

11. Abouzeid, 'The jihad next door'.

12. Aron Lund, 'As Rifts Open Up in Syria's al-Qaeda Franchise, Secrets Spill Out', *Syria in Crisis*, 10 August 2015.

13. 'Abu Mohammed al-Jolani, a medical student from an Idlibi family, born in Deir ez Zour,' *Akhbar al-Souriyeen*, 11 July 2015.

14. Abouzeid, 'The jihad next door'.

15. Author interview with Abu Abdullah, November 2014.

16. Noman Benotman and Roisin Blake, 'Jabhat al-Nusra: A Strategic Briefing', Quilliam Foundation, 8 January 2013.

17. Information collected from interviews with Syrian Salafists within Jabhat al-Nusra and linked to the group, 2014–2015.

18. Full video available: 'al-Manārah al-Bayḍā' Foundation for Media Production presents: "Declaration of the Support Front (Jabhat al-Nuṣrah): For the People of Syria from the Mujāhidīn of Syria in the Fields of Jihād"', Jihadology, 24 January 2011.

19. Meir Amit Intelligence and Terrorism Information Center, 'The al-Nusra Front', 23 September 2013, p. 19.

20. Ibid.

21. Victoria Nuland, 'Terrorist designations of the al-Nusrah Front as an alias for al-Qa'ida in Iraq', United States Department of State, 11 December 2012.

22. Aaron Zelin, 'Syria's new jihadis: meet the terrorist group that's ruining the revolution', *Foreign Policy*, 22 May 2012.

## 5. JANUARY–AUGUST 2012: JABHAT AL-NUSRA EMERGES

1. Interview with General Martin Dempsey, Fareed Zakaria GPS, CNN, aired 19 February 2012.

2. Author interview with Moazzam Begg, February 2015.

3. Jean-Pierre Filiu, *Apocalypse in Islam* (Berkeley and Los Angeles: University of California Press, 2012), pp. 187–188.

4. Hassan Hassan, 'A jihadist blueprint for hearts and minds is gaining traction in Syria', *The National*, 4 March 2014.

5. 'What's in the names of terrorist groups (1): Jabhat al-Nusrah li-Ahl al-Sham min Mujahidi al-Sham fi Sahat al-Jihad', Mr Orange's War Tracker, 14 May 2013.

6. Rukmini Callimachi, 'In Timbuktu, al-Qaida left behind a manifesto', Associated Press, 14 February 2013.

7. Hassan Hassan, 'Jihadis grow more dangerous as they conquer hearts in Syria', *The National*, 6 March 2013.

8. From a compilation of reports, approximately fifteen of twenty-six fatalities on 6 January 2012 and four of twenty-eight fatalities on 10 February 2012 were civilian. No specific breakdown of casualties was provided for the 23 December 2011 attacks, although reports claimed that 'most' of the forty deaths were civilian.

9. Author interview with Moazzam Begg, February 2015.

10. Kelly McEvers, 'Syrian army drives rebels from embattled city', NPR, 1 March 2012.

11. Author interview with former FSA fighter from Homs (anonymous), January 2015.

12. Dominic Evans, 'Annan to meet Assad, seeking end to Syria violence', Reuters, 9 March 2012.

13. International Crisis Group, 'Syria's phase of radicalisation', Middle East Briefing no. 33, 10 April 2012, p. 4.

14. *Karam al Zeitoun* Tumblr Page, managed by Syrian activist 'syrianfreedomls'.

15. '15,000 elite Iranian special-ops "head" to Syria', Russia Today, 10 February 2012.

16. 'Syrian rebels say they hold seven Iranians hostage', Reuters, 27 January 2012.

17. Aaron Zelin, 'Jihadists in Syria can be found on the Internet', al-Monitor, 18 October 2012.

18. 'Syrian rebels get arms from abroad—source', Reuters, 24 February 2012.

19. Elizabeth Dickinson, 'Playing with fire: why private gulf financing for Syria's extremist rebels risks igniting sectarian conflict at home', Brookings Institution, Saban Center Analysis Paper no. 16, December 2013.

20. US Department of the Teasury, 'Treasury designates twelve foreign terrorist fighter facilitators', 24 September 2014.

21. Jason Burke, 'al-Qaida leader Zawahiri urges Muslim support for Syrian uprising', *The Guardian*, 12 February 2012.

22. 'Fatah al-Islam militants killed in Syria', *Daily Star*, 24 April 2012.

23. International Crisis Group, 'Syria's phase of radicalisation', p. 1.

24. Meir Amit Intelligence and Terrorism Information Center, 'The al-Nusra Front'.

25. Elizabeth O'Bagy, 'Jihad in Syria', Institute for the Study of War, Middle East Security Report 6, September 2012, p. 36.

26. Author calculations.

27. O'Bagy, 'Jihad in Syria', p. 30.

28. Bill Roggio, 'Abdullah Azzam Brigades names leader, advises against attacks in Syria's cities', Long War Journal, 27 June 2012.

29. 'Army: top al-Qaeda chief in country left for Syria', *Daily Star*, 17 May 2012.

30. Alan Cullison, 'Meet the rebel commander in Syria that Assad, Russia and the US all fear', *Wall Street Journal*, 19 November 2013; Nina Akhmeteli, 'The Georgian roots of ISIS commander Omar al-Shishani', BBC, 9 July 2014; US Department of the Teasury, 'Treasury designates twelve foreign terrorist fighter facilitators'.

31. Joanna Paraszczuk, 'Syria: who is Muslim Abu Walid Shishani? Part one', From Chechnya to Syria, 26 March 2014.

32. Ruth Sherlock, 'Leading Libyan Islamist met Free Syrian Army opposition group', *The Telegraph*, 27 November 2011.

33. Mary Fitzgerald, 'The Syrian rebels' Libyan weapon'.

34. Ibid.

35. Author calculations.

36. Author interview with a founding member of Kataib Ahrar al-Sham, who requested anonymity.

37. Josh Rogin and Eli Lake, 'Foley abduction linked to British jihadi kidnapping ring', *The Daily Beast*, 20 August 2014.

38. Mike Giglio, 'Syrian rebel leader Mustafa al-Sheikh says victory against Assad not in sight', *The Daily Beast*, 26 July 2012.

39. Two statements released on Tartusi's 'Islamic opposition to the Syrian regime' Facebook page on 27 January and 27 February 2012—no longer available online.

40. Liz Sly and Justin Vela, 'In Syria, group suspected of al-Qaeda links gaining prominence in war to topple Assad', *Washington Post*, 19 August 2012.

41. Author interview with Amjad Farekh, January 2015.

42. Murad Batal al-Shishani, 'Chechens fighting in Syria complicate a complex conflict', *The National*, 3 May 2013.

## 6. SEPTEMBER 2012–MARCH 2013: JABHAT AL-NUSRA RISES

1. Bradley Klapper and Kimberley Dozier, 'al-Qaeda building well-organized network in Syria: US intelligence officials', Associated Press, 10 August 2012.

2. 'Most of Syria's land is outside regime control, says rebel colonel', AFP, 23 September 2012.

3. Martin Chulov, 'Syrian rebels in "decisive battle for Aleppo" as regime hits back in capital', *The Guardian*, 28 September 2012.

4. Author interview with Liwa al-Tawhid commander, December 2014.

5. 'Jihadist group claims execution of 20 Syria soldiers', AFP, 3 October 2012.

6. Author interview with senior Ahrar al-Sham political official, January 2015.

7. Nicholas A. Heras, 'What is Hezbollah's role in the Syrian crisis?' *Terrorism Monitor* 10, 20 (2 November 2012), Jamestown Foundation.

8. US Department of the Treasury, 'Treasury designates Hizballah leadership', 13 September 2012.

9. Marcus George, 'Iran's Revolutionary Guards commander says its troops in Syria', Reuters, 16 September 2012.

10. Elizabeth A. Kennedy, 'Official: Hezbollah fighters killed in Syria', Associated Press, 2 October 2012.

11. 'FSA claims responsibility for killing of Hezbollah commander', *The Daily Star*, 3 October 2012.

12. 'The Times: Assad backed by 1,500 Hezbollah fighters', Naharnet, 7 October 2012.

13. Dana Khraiche, 'Nasrallah denies Hezbollah members fighting with Syrian regime', *The Daily Star*, 11 October 2012.

14. Charles Lister, 'Dynamic stalemate: surveying Syria's military landscape', Brookings Doha Center, 19 May 2014.

15. Author interview with former Jabhat al-Nusra fighter, January 2014.

16. Ghaith Abdul-Ahad, 'Syria: the foreign fighters joining the war against Bashar al-Assad', *The Guardian*, 23 September 2012.

17. Mark Youngman, 'The North Caucasus insurgency's Syrian balancing act', Jihadology, 7 September 2013.

18. 'VIDEO: Address of the Emir of Caucasus Emirate, Dokku Abu Usman, to Syria's Mujahideen', Kavkaz Center, 13 November 2012.

19. Jack Khoury, 'Syrian rebels claim Assad regime used chemical weapons', *Ha'aretz*, 24 December 2012.

20. Julian Borger and Matthew Weaver, 'West backs Qatari plan to unify Syrian opposition', *The Guardian*, 2 November 2012.

21. 'Syrian Islamists reject Western-backed opposition', Associated Press, 19 November 2012.

22. Author interview with FSA leader, December 2014.

23. Nuland, 'Terrorist designations of the al-Nusrah Front'.

24. As alleged by the US Department of the Treasury and the US Department of State in a series of designations in 2014.

25. 'Syria rebels "capture oilfield" in Deir Ezzour', BBC News, 4 November 2012.

26. Author interview with two Sunni tribal leaders from Deir ez Zour, December 2014 and January 2015.

27. Lund, *Syria's Salafi insurgents*, p. 15.

28. Aaron Zelin, 'The Syrian Islamic Front's order of battle', *Al-Wasat*, 22 January 2013.

29. Elizabeth O'Bagy, 'The Free Syrian Army', Institute for the Study of War, March 2013, p. 40.

30. Nuland, 'Terrorist designations of the al-Nusrah Front'.

31. Ibid.

32. 'Syrians march in support of Jabhat al-Nusra militants', France 24, 16 December 2012.

33. Samia Nakhoul and Khaled Yacoub Oweis, 'Syrian opposition urges review of al-Nusra blacklisting', Reuters, 12 December 2012.

34. David Ignatius, 'al-Qaeda affiliate playing larger role in Syria rebellion', *Washington Post*, 30 November 2012.

35. Ruth Sherlock, 'Inside Jabhat al-Nusra—the most extreme wing of Syria's struggle', *The Telegraph*, 2 December 2012.

36. Rania Abouzeid, 'Interview with official of Jabhat al-Nusra, Syria's Islamist militia group', *TIME*, 25 December 2012.

37. Author interview with Liwa al-Tawhid fighter, December 2014.

38. Kelly McEvers, 'Jihadi fighters win hearts and minds by easing Syria's bread crisis', NPR, 16 January 2013.

39. 'Aleppo's Sharia authority: tyranny in the guise of religion', *al-Akhbar*, 31 December 2013.

40. Thomas Pierret, 'Implementing "Sharia" in Syria's liberated provinces', Foundation for Law, Justice, and Society, 7 August 2013.

41. A combination of author's calculations and Ignatius, 'al-Qaeda affiliate playing larger role in Syria rebellion'.

42. 'Jabhat al-Nusra: a strategic briefing', Quilliam Foundation, 8 January 2013.

43. Abouzeid, 'Syria's Islamist militia group'.

44. As described by several Jabhat al-Nusra fighters interviewed by the author throughout 2013–14.

45. O'Bagy, 'The Free Syrian Army', p. 25.

46. Syrian Islamic Front answer, as provided on AskFM on 19 January 2013.

47. Aaron Zelin, 'The Syrian Islamic Front: a new extremist force', Washington Institute for Near East Policy, 4 February 2013.

48. 'Video shows non-FSA jihadists Ahrar al-Sham using Croatian weapons', Brown Moses Blog, 1 March 2013.

49. 'Evidence of Jabhat al-Nusra with Croatian weapons', Brown Moses Blog, 23 March 2013.

50. Aron Lund, 'Who and what was Abu Khalid al-Suri? Part I', Carnegie Endowment for International Peace, 24 February 2014.

51. Thomas Joscelyn, 'Syrian rebel leader was bin Laden's courier, now Zawahiri's representative', Long War Journal, 17 December 2013.

52. Desmond Butler, 'Spanish Judge Harbors Bias, Says Reporter in Terror Case', *The New York Times*, 14 December 2003.

53. Author interview with two former Sednayya detainees and a prominent Salafist active in the insurgency, December 2014 and January 2015.

54. Author interview with senior Ahrar al-Sham political official, January 2015.

55. Author interview with a Syrian Salafist and former Sednayya prisoner, January 2015.

56. Author dialogue with Hassan Abboud, December 2013.

57. Author dialogue with Hassan Abboud, January 2014.

58. Author interview with Moazzam Begg, February 2015.

59. Author calculations.

60. Author's tweet, citing Aaron Zelin: 'RT: @azelin There have been about 10–15

Tunisians announced dead in Syria fighting with Jabhat al-Nusra in only past few days', Twitter, 21 February 2013.

61. For example: JTF-GTMO-CDR MEMORANDUM FOR Commander, United States Southern Command, 3511 NW 91st Avenue, Miami, FL 33172, SUBJECT: Recommendation for Continued Detention Under DoD Control (CD) for Guantanamo Detainee, ISN US9YM-000178DP (S), 13 January 2008; and: JTF-GTMO-CDR MEMORANDUM FOR Commander, United States Southern Command, 3511 NW 91st Avenue, Miami, FL 33172, SUBJECT: Recommendation for Continued Detention Under DoD Control (CD) for Guantanamo Detainee, ISN US9SA-000154DP (S), 31 March 2007.

62. Abdullah Suleiman Ali, 'Saudi jihadists flow into Syria', al-Monitor, 8 December 2013.

63. Richard Kerbaj and Malik al-Abdeh, 'Dead at 21: Britain's veteran jihadist', *The Sunday Times*, 3 March 2013.

64. 'Al-Qaeda in Iraq claims deadly attack on Syrian troops', BBC News, 11 March 2013.

65. Jim Muir, 'Syria "death video" of Sheikh al-Bouti poses questions', BBC News, 9 April 2013.

66. Rania Abouzeid, 'In Syria, the rebels have begun to fight among themselves', *TIME*, 26 March 2013.

67. Ibid.

68. Author interview with senior Ahrar al-Sham leader, January 2015.

69. Author interview with Mohammed Khadam, January 2015.

## 7. APRIL–JUNE 2013: THE ISLAMIC STATE JOINS THE CONFLICT

1. 'March was bloodiest month in Syria war: rights group', Reuters, 1 April 2013.

2. Charles Lister, 'A militant Islamist/jihadi nexus is emerging in northern and eastern Syria: some thoughts on an increasingly cooperative militant alliance', TwitLonger, 22 March 2013.

3. Author interview with Abu Mustafa, January 2015.

4. Jenan Moussa tweet: 'Jabhat Al Nusra solved transport problem in Aleppo. They started bus service for 10 Liras per person. Ppl over 50 rise bus for free,' Twitter, 7 April 2013.

5. 'Qaeda chief urges Syria rebels to seek Islamic state', AFP, 7 April 2013.

6. Abu Bakr al-Baghdadi, *Wa Bashshir al-Mu'minin*, al-Furqan Media, 9 April 2013.

7. Aaron Zelin, 'al-Qaeda announces an Islamic state in Syria', Washington Institute for Near East Policy, 9 April 2013.

8. Abu Mohammed al-Jolani, *Kalima sawtiyya lil Fatih Abu Mohammed al-Jolani*, al-Manara al-Bayda, 10 April 2013.

9. Author interview with Amjad Farekh, January 2015.

10. Aron Lund, 'As Rifts Open Up in Syria's al-Qaeda Franchise, Secrets Spill Out,' *Syria in Crisis*, 10 August 2015.

11. Christoph Reuter, 'The terror strategist: secret files reveal the structure of Islamic State', *Der Spiegel*, 18 April 2015.

12. Matthew Barber, 'New ISIS leaks reveal particulars of al-Qaida strategy', *Syria Comment*, 12 January 2014.

13. Barber, 'New ISIS leaks reveal particulars of al-Qaida strategy'.

14. Video statement by Junud al-Sham leader Muslim al-Shishani, 4 July 2014.

15. Aymenn Jawad al-Tamimi, 'The Islamic State of Iraq and al-Sham', *MERIA*, 11 December 2013.

16. Author's tweet: '1st claimed example of continued Jabhat al-Nusra-Ahrar al-Sham cooperation: SIF just claimed joint attack on checkpt in Rif Dimashq—Syria', Twitter, 13 April 2013.

17. Jonathan Dupree, 'Syria update: regime breaks siege of Wadi al-Deif', Institute for the Study of War, 18 April 2013.

18. Babak Dehghanpisheh, 'Hezbollah, Syrian opposition clashes intensify, raise fears in Lebanon', *Washington Post*, 2 March 2013.

19. 'Assir calls for jihad in Syria', NOW Lebanon and AFP, 22 April 2013.

20. 'Insight—Syrian government guerrilla fighters being sent to Iran for training', Reuters, 4 April 2013.

21. Ibid.

22. Aaron Zelin, 'European foreign fighters in Syria', International Centre for the Study of Radicalisation and Political Violence, 8 April 2013.

23. Anne Barnard and Hania Mourtada, 'Leader of Hezbollah warns it is ready to come to Syria's aid', *New York Times*, 30 April 2013.

24. Human Rights Watch, '"No one's left": summary executions by Syrian forces in al-Bayda and Baniyas', September 2013.

25. Ibid.

26. Ibid.

27. Elizabeth O'Bagy, 'Syria update: Assad targets Sunni along Syria's coast', Institute for the Study of War, 10 May 2013.

28. Hassan Hassan, 'Lessons from a massacre that Assad looks to exploit', *The National*, 8 May 2013.

29. Stathis Kalyvas, *The Logic of Violence in Civil War* (New York: Cambridge University Press, 2006), pp. 333–36.

30. 'ISIL threatens Erdogan with suicide bombings in Ankara, Istanbul', *Today's Zaman*, 30 September 2013.

31. 'Turkey charges prime suspect in car bombings, report says', al-Arabiya, 21 May 2013.

32. 'Mihrac Ural, a man with a long history of terrorism', *Today's Zaman*, 14 May 2013.

33. Aymenn Jawad al-Tamimi, 'A case study of "The Syrian Resistance", a pro-Assad militia force', *Syria Comment*, 22 September 2013.

34. Pieter van Ostaeyen, 'The ar-Raqqa executions—confirmation of the Islamic State in Iraq and as-Sham', pietervanostaeyen Blog, 15 May 2013.

35. Author interview with an Islamist fighter, December 2014.

36. Author interview with Salafist from Homs, February 2015.

37. Author interview with a Syrian Jabhat al-Nusra fighter, February 2015.

38. Aymenn Jawad al-Tamimi, 'Jabhat al-Nusra and the Islamic State of Iraq and ash-Sham: Deir ez Zour and the wider east of Syria', Musings of an Iraqi Brasenostril on Jihad, Jihadology, 27 June 2013.

39. Aron Lund, 'Is Jabhat al-Nosra breaking apart?' *Syria Comment*, 22 May 2013.

40. Aymenn Jawad al-Tamimi, 'Syria: jihad and the battle for Qusayr', Aymenn Jawad al-Tamimi's Blog, 27 May 2013.

41. 'Top cleric Qaradawi calls for jihad against Hezbollah, Assad in Syria', al-Arabiya, 2 June 2013; 'Top Muslim cleric al-Qaradawi urges Sunnis to join Syria war', AFP, 1 June 2013.

42. Alexander Smoltczyk, 'Islam's spiritual "Dear Abby": the voice of Egypt's Muslim Brotherhood', *Der Spiegel*, 15 February 2011.

43. 'Saudi Grand Mufti praises Qaradawi's stance on Hezbollah', al-Arabiya, 6 June 2013.

44. Elizabeth O'Bagy, 'The fall of al-Qusayr', Institute for the Study of War, 6 June 2013.

45. Author interview with Idlib-based FSA commander, November 2014.

46. 'Excuse us ... our people in Lebanon', al-Manara al-Bayda, 7 August 2014.

47. 'Three Lebanese soldiers killed by gunmen—military source', Reuters, 28 May 2013.

48. Rakan al-Fakih, 'Hezbollah slays dozen Syrian rebels in Lebanon ambush', *Daily Star*, 2 June 2013.

49. '4 dead, including 2 from Jaafar clan, as car comes under fire in Arsal outskirts', Naharnet, 16 June 2013.

50. Aymenn Jawad al-Tamimi, 'Sheikh Jowlani of Jabhat al-Nusra Announces Abrogation of Islamic State of Iraq and ash-Sham', 6 June 2013.

51. English translation courtesy of Aymenn Jawad al-Tamimi, 'Sheikh Aymenn al-Zawahiri annuls Islamic State of Iraq and ash-Sham', Aymenn Jawad al-Tamimi Blog, 9 June 2013.

52. Charles Lister, 'Profiling the Islamic State', Brookings Doha Center, 1 December 2014.

53. Will McCants, 'State of confusion: ISIS' strategy and how to counter it', *Foreign Affairs*, 10 September 2014.

54. Romain Caillet, 'The Islamic State: leaving al-Qaeda behind', Syria in Crisis, Carnegie Endowment for International Peace, 27 December 2013.

55. Ayman al-Zawahiri, *Ritha shahid al-ummah wal amir al-istishhadiyain Abu Musab al-Zarqawi*, al-Sahab Media, June 2006.

56. Adam Gadahn, *Bayan bi-sha'an alaaqat Jamaat Qaedat al-Jihad bil Jamaat al-Dawla al-Islamiya fil Iraq wal Sham*, al-Fajr Media Center, late 2010.

57. Ibid.

58. Basma Atassi, 'Qaeda chief arbitrates Syria's "jihad crisis"', Al-Jazeera, 9 June 2013.

59. Charles Lister and Aaron Zelin, 'The crowning of the Syrian Islamic Front', *Foreign Policy*, 24 June 2013.

60. Ibid.

61. Author interview with Abu Mustafa, February 2015.

62. Ibid.

63. Author interview with Hassan Abboud, 28 August 2014.

64. Abu Bakr al-Baghdadi, *Baqiya fil Iraq wal Sham*, al-Furqan Media, 15 June 2013.

65. 'Jihad and Terrorism Threat Monitor (JTTM) weekend summary', *MEMRI*, 22 June 2013.

66. Abu Mohammed al-Adnani, *Fadharhum wa ma Yaftarun*, al-Furqan Media, 19 June 2013.

67. JTTM Weekend Summary, 22 June 2013; Tamimi, 'The Islamic State of Iraq and ash-Sham'.

68. Turki al-Binali, *al-Lafz al-Sani fi Tarjamat al-Adnani*, 26 May 2014. A translated English version was also published: 'A biography of IS spokesman Abu Muhammad al-Adnani as-Shami', pietervanostaeyen Blog, 2 November 2014.

69. Ibid.

70. US Department of State, 'Terrorist designation of Abu Mohammed al-Adnani', 18 August 2014.

71. 'A biography of IS spokesman Abu Muhammad al-Adnani as-Shami'.

72. Author's tweet: 'New grp in Syria: Harakat Taliban al-Islami threatens attacks vs non-Muslims & to behead Assad supporters', Twitter, 21 April 2013.

8. JULY–DECEMBER 2013: RISING TENSIONS

1. United Nations, 'United Nations mission to investigate allegations of the use of chemical weapons in the Syrian Arab Republic', 13 December 2014.

2. Author's tweet: 'So far passports from Bahrain, Qatar, Iraq, Tunisia, Egypt, US, UAE & Syria IDs seized in Jabhat al-Nusra HQ in Ras al-Ayn, al-Hasakah', Twitter, 22 July 2013.

3. Erika Solomon, 'Syria's Islamists disenchanted with democracy after Mursi's fall', Reuters, 7 July 2013.

4. 'North Caucasus caucus'; 'Turkish fighters in Syria, online and off', Jihadology, 20 August 2013.

5. Joanna Paraszczuk, 'Sayfullah Shishani "fought in Chechnya, Afghanistan"', *From Chechnya to Syria (Blog)*, 20 June 2014.

6.  Nick Paton Walsh, 'The secret jihadi smuggling route through Turkey', CNN, 5 November 2013.
7.  Mike Giglio, 'One man's journey to become the first American suicide bomber in Syria', BuzzFeed News, 7 August 2014.
8.  'North Caucasus Caucus'; 'Turkish fighters in Syria, online and off'.
9.  Mitchell Prothero, 'CIA tips off Hezbollah about bombing plot', McClatchy DC, 17 July 2014.
10. Nour Malas, 'Syria killings open rift in anti-Assad ranks', *Wall Street Journal*, 12 July 2013.
11. Valerie Szybala, 'al-Qaeda shows its true colors in Syria', Institute for the Study of War, 1 August 2013.
12. Aaron Zelin, 'al-Qaeda in Syria: a closer look at ISIS (Part I)', Washington Institute for Near East Policy, 10 September 2013.
13. Michael Weiss, 'Col. Oqaidi on al-Qaeda, UN inspectors and Kurdish militias', NOW Lebanon, 18 August 2013.
14. Irina Razafimbahiny, 'An in-depth look at Chechen fighters in Syria—Part I: Sayfullah al-Shishani and his circle', MEMRI, 6 December 2013.
15. Ibid.
16. Human Rights Watch, 'You can still see their blood', 11 October 2013.
17. '"Confession" of conspiracy', Syria Direct, 13 August 2013.
18. 'Senior member of the SMC defects to ISIS and details foreign involvement in the opposition', Brown Moses Blog, 2 December 2013.
19. Zeina Karam, 'Car bomb kills 14 in Beirut suburb', Associated Press, 15 August 2013.
20. Laila Bassam, 'Car bomb kills 20 in Hezbollah's Beirut stronghold', Reuters, 15 August 2013.
21. 'Al Qaeda blames Hezbollah for Lebanon bombings', Reuters, 24 August 2013.
22. Louis Charbonneau and Michelle Nichols, 'UN confirms sarin used in Syria attack; US, UK, France blame Assad', Reuters, 16 September 2013.
23. Eliot Higgins, 'Finding the exact location of an alleged chemical munition, and what it could mean', Brown Moses Blog, 26 August 2013; Eliot Higgins, 'Who was responsible for the August 21st attack?' Brown Moses Blog, 16 September 2013.
24. Josh Lyons, 'Dispatches: mapping the sarin flight path', Human Rights Watch, 17 September 2013.
25. Charles Lister, 'New fears for Syria's jihadists', *Foreign Policy*, 29 August 2013.
26. Anne Gearan and Scott Wilson, 'US, Russia reach agreement on seizure of Syrian chemical weapons stockpile', Washington Post, 14 September 2013.
27. Pieter van Ostaeyen, 'Syria—a new Islamic Union or an informal alliance?', pieter-vanostaeyen Blog, 28 September 2013.
28. Author interview with Jaish al-Islam political official, January 2014.

29. Aymenn Jawad al-Tamimi, 'Moroccan Guantanamo detainees fighting in Syria's civil war', Jihadology, 18 September 2013.
30. Cedric Labrousse, 'Abu Ahmad al-Maghrebi (Ibrahim Bencheqroun), jihad veteran killed in Syria', *The Arab Chronicle*, 2 April 2014.
31. Aymenn Jawad al-Tamimi, 'Muhajireen battalions in Syria', Jihadology, 13 December 2013.
32. Greg Miller, 'CIA ramping up covert training program for moderate Syrian rebels', *Washington Post*, 2 October 2013.
33. '19 Syria rebel groups reject Geneva talks', AFP, 27 October 2013.
34. Sam Dagher, 'Battles rage around Syria chemical weapons sites', *Wall Street Journal*, 11 October 2013.
35. Marlin Dick, 'Leading FSA commander quits, lashes out at lack of support', *Daily Star*, 4 November 2013.
36. Paton Walsh, 'The secret jihadi smuggling route'.
37. Basma Atassi, 'Major Syrian rebel groups join forces', Al-Jazeera, 22 November 2013.
38. Ibid.
39. Ibid.
40. Aron Lund, 'Showdown at Bab al-Hawa', Carnegie Endowment for International Peace, 12 December 2013.
41. Author interview with a foreign fighter, November 2014.
42. 'Syrian rebels roll exploding tires into Maaloula army outposts', AFP, 2 December 2013.
43. Qassim Abdul-Zahra, 'Shiite cleric issues fatwa in support of fighting in Syria war: Grand Ayatollah Kazim al-Haeri supports Assad', Associated Press, 19 December 2013.
44. Aaron Zelin, 'Up to 11,000 foreign fighters in Syria; steep rise among Western Europeans', International Centre for the Study of Radicalisation and Political Violence, 17 December 2013.
45. Rakan al-Fakih, 'Two Hezbollah members dead after Baalbek bomb', *Daily Star*, 19 December 2013.
46. 'Hezbollah ambush kills 32 Islamist fighters in E. Lebanon', *Daily Star*, 23 December 2013.
47. 'Syrian refugee crisis map', *Washington Post*, 16 December 2014.
48. US Department of State, 'Terrorist designation of Fatah al-Islam associate Usamah Amin al-Shihabi', 18 December 2013.
49. Ali Hashem, 'al-Qaeda-affiliated emir arrested in Lebanon', al-Monitor, 1 January 2014.
50. 'Jihadist militant leader in Lebanon Majid al-Majid dies in custody', BBC News, 4 January 2014.

## 9. JANUARY–APRIL 2014: TURNING AGAINST THE ISLAMIC STATE

1. Charles Lister, 'Syria's new rebel front', *Foreign Policy*, 8 January 2014.
2. Marlin Dick, 'ISIS condemned for brutal murder of fellow jihadist', *Daily Star*, 3 January 2014.
3. Joshua Landis, 'The battle between ISIS and Syria's rebel militias', Syria Comment, 4 January 2014.
4. Aron Lund, 'The mujahideen army of Aleppo', Carnegie Endowment for International Peace, 8 April 2014.
5. Dominic Evans, 'Syrian rebels launch fierce offensive against al Qaeda fighters', Reuters, 4 January 2014.
6. Author's discussions with officials in Qatar, January–March 2014.
7. Ruth Sherlock, 'US secretly backs rebels to fight al-Qaeda in Syria', *The Telegraph*, 21 January 2014.
8. 'More than 1,000 killed in Syria rebel infighting: activist group', Associated Press, 16 January 2014.
9. Marlin Dick, 'Body of jihadist leader found in Idlib', *Daily Star*, 11 November 2014.
10. Syrian Observatory for Human Rights, '10 months after his disappearance, founder and leader of Jund al-Aqsa found killed in a well', 10 November 2014.
11. 'Islamic Front issues strong warning to ISIS', *Daily Star*, 6 January 2014.
12. Ben Hubbard and Anne Barnard, 'Qaeda group leader in Syria suggests Islamic court to end rebel infighting', *New York Times*, 7 January 2014.
13. 'Iraq update 2014 #5: "The Time to Harvest is Coming"—ISIS statement', Institute for the Study of War, 8 January 2014.
14. Ibid.
15. Cole Bunzel, 'The Islamic state of disunity: jihadism divided', Jihadica, 20 January 2014.
16. 'Lex Runderkamp: 1300 ISIS soldaten onderweg naar Aleppo', NOS, 5 January 2014.
17. Thomas Joscelyn, 'Alleged message from Zawahiri's Syrian representative posted online', Long War Journal, 17 January 2014.
18. 'Radical cleric urges Islamists to end Syria infighting', AFP, 16 January 2014.
19. Aaron Zelin, 'Inside baseball on Syrian rebel infighting', War on the Rocks, 7 February 2014.
20. Ibid.
21. 'Translation of the new audio message by Abu Bakr al-Baghdadi', pietervanostaeyen Blog, 19 January 2014.
22. Ibid.
23. 'Nearly 1,400 dead since Syria rebel–jihadist clashes began', AFP, 23 January 2014.
24. Stephen Kalin, 'al Qaeda offshoot imposes strict Islamic rules in north Syria', Reuters, 20 January 2014.

25. 'Ayman al-Zawahiri calls upon jihadi groups in Syria to stop infighting', Flashpoint Partners, 23 January 2014.

26. Ibid.

27. Abdullah al-Moheisini, *Mubadarat al-ummah*, Tawhed, 25 January 2014. www. tawhed.ws

28. Ibid.

29. Turki al-Binali, *Khatt al-midad fil radd ala al-duktor Iyad*, December 2013.

30. Bill Roggio, 'ISIS confirms death of senior leader in Syria', Long War Journal, 5 February 2014.

31. 'Wanted Saudi al Qaeda militant killed in Syria—SITE', Reuters, 24 January 2014.

32. US Department of the Treasury, 'Treasury designates additional supporters of the al-Nusrah Front and al-Qaida', 22 August 2014.

33. Thomas Joscelyn, 'Head of al Qaeda "Victory Committee" in Syria', Long War Journal, 6 March 2014.

34. US Department of State, 'Rewards for justice—al-Qaeda reward offers', 18 October 2012.

35. 'Silsalah al-shahada: chain of testimonies. Shaykh Abu Firas al-Suri', al-Baseera Media Productions, 21 March 2014.

36. 'Silsalah al-shahada: chain of testimonies. Sheykh Farouq Abu Hamam al-Suri', al-Baseera Media Productions, 27 March 2014.

37. 'UK suicide bomber in Syria named as Abdul Waheed Majid', BBC News, 12 February 2014.

38. Bill Roggio, 'al Nusrah Front praises Chechen commander killed in Aleppo', Long War Journal, 10 February 2014.

39. Nicholas Blanford, 'Behind Israeli strikes on Syria, a simmering battle with Hezbollah', *Christian Science Monitor*, 19 March 2014.

40. 'Iranian cultural office targeted in Lebanon', Al-Jazeera, 19 February 2014.

41. *Bayan bi-shan alaqat Jamaat Qaedat al-Jihad bi-Jamaat al-Dawla al-Islamiya fil Iraq wal Sham*, 3 February 2014.

42. Oliver Holmes, 'al Qaeda breaks link with Syrian militant group ISIL', Reuters, 3 February 2014.

43. 'Activists say top ISIS commander killed in Syria', al-Arabiya, 8 February 2014.

44. Abu Mohammed al-Jolani, 'The forewarned is forearmed', al-Manara al-Bayda, 7 February 2014.

45. Untitled statement released on JustPaste.it on 10 February.

46. Author interview with Abu Uthman al-Britani, February 2014.

47. Daniel Abdullah, 'The ISIS–Suqour al-Sham truce: is it real and can it last?' Syria Comment, 6 February 2014.

48. Sheikh Abu Yazan al-Shami, 'The story of martyrdom: Sheikh Abu Khaled al-Suri', 23 February 2014.

49. Joanna Paraszczuk, 'Syria: how "al Qa'eda mediator" al-Suri died—a jihadist's account', EA Worldview, 26 February 2014.

50. Hassan Abboud interview with Al-Jazeera, 23 February 2014.

51. Ayman al-Zawahiri statement marking the death of Abu Khaled al-Suri, 4 April 2014.

52. '3,300 people killed in Syria rebel infighting this year', Reuters, 26 February 2013.

53. Aymenn Jawad al-Tamimi, 'The Islamic State of Iraq and ash-Sham's dhimmi pact for the Christians of Raqqa province', Syria Comment, 26 February 2014.

54. Ibid.

55. 'Assad troops say Yabroud "possibly the most difficult" fight', AFP, 17 March 2014.

56. 'How the Maaloula nuns were freed', al-Monitor, 11 March 2014.

57. Hussein Dakroub, 'Kidnapped nuns' harrowing ordeal ends', *Daily Star*, 10 March 2014.

58. Anne Barnard and Hwaida Saad, 'Nuns released by Syrians after three-month ordeal', *New York Times*, 9 March 2014.

59. 'Syrian army seizes famed Krak des Chevaliers fort in border push', Naharnet, 20 March 2014.

60. Erika Solomon, 'Betrayal and disarray behind Syrian rebel rout in Yabroud', *Financial Times*, 21 March 2014.

61. Aron Lund, 'The Free Syrian Armies: failed reconciliation', Carnegie Endowment for International Peace, 26 March 2014.

62. Susannah George, 'Throwing windmills at the Wyndham', *Foreign Policy*, 20 March 2014.

63. Fehim Tastekin, 'Fall of Kassab will be costly for Turkey', al-Monitor, 31 March 2014.

64. 'Turkey shoots down Syrian fighter jet', Al-Jazeera, 24 March 2014.

65. Tastekin, 'Fall of Kassab will be costly for Turkey'.

66. 'Statement 11: Statement from the Islamic Front on the liberation of the city of Kessab', Islamic Front Political Office, 31 March 2014.

67. Isabel Nassief and Charlie Caris, 'Rebels reopen the Latakia front', Institute for the Study of War, 9 April 2014.

68. 'Were foreigners involved in the Nord-Ost hostage crisis?' *North Caucasus Caucus (Blog)*, 30 August 2015.

69. Author interview with Abu al-Hassan, March 2015.

70. Ibid.

71. Abu Mohammed al-Adnani, 'And he will grant them the authority to practice their religion, that which he has chosen for them', 3 April 2014.

72. Aymenn Jawad al-Tamimi and Cedric Labrousse, 'The fighting in Abu Kamal (Albukamal): background and analysis', *Brown Moses* (Blog), 12 April 2014.

73. '"86 dead" as Syria's al-Qaeda allies repel jihadists', AFP, 11 April 2014.

74. Abu Mohammed al-Adnani, 'This is not our methodology, nor will it ever be', al-Furqan Media, 17 April 2014.

75. Nate Petrocine, 'Rebel operations in Idlib province during the spring of 2014', Institute for the Study of War, 31 July 2014.

76. 'Activist: "Quneitra's revolutionaries have met the call of Latakia"', Syria Direct, 10 April 2014.

77. Charles Lister, 'American anti-tank weapons appear in Syrian rebel hands', Huffington Post, 6 April 2014.

78. Ibid.

79. 'Syria: Countrywide Conflict Report #4,' Carter Center, 11 September 2014, p. 24.

10. MAY–AUGUST 2014: DECLARING A CALIPHATE

1. Oliver Holmes, 'al Qaeda's Iraqi offshoot gains ground in Syria amid rebel infighting', Reuters, 12 May 2014.

2. Ayman al-Zawahiri, 'A testimony to preserve the blood of the mujahideen in al-Sham', as-Sahab Media, 2 May 2014.

3. 'Dara'a, what happened, why now: the formation of the Southern Syrian Revolutionary Front', TahrirSy, 6 May 2014.

4. Ibid.

5. Phil Sands and Suha Maayeh, 'Syrian rebel colonel "confesses" to foreign hand in rout', The National, 8 May 2014.

6. Ibid.

7. The Revolutionary Covenant, released by the Islamic Front on 17 May 2014.

8. 'Nusra rejects Islamist militia's code of honor', Daily Star, 21 May 2014.

9. Sam Heller, 'Islam's lawyers in arms', Foreign Policy, 6 June 2014.

10. Hassan Abboud tweet: 'It's very odd how Shekau insists to look as a lunatic barbarian using Islamic terminology to intentionally associate such an image to Islam', Twitter, 25 August 2014.

11. 'Defiant Syrian rebels offer stark choice', BBC News, 3 June 2014.

12. Petrocine, 'Rebel operations in Idlib province'.

13. Michael S. Schmidt and Mark Mazzetti, 'Suicide bomber from US came home before attack', New York Times, 30 July 2014.

14. Video testimony of Moner Mohammed Abusalha released by the Global Islamic Media Front on 29 July 2014.

15. Schmidt and Mazzetti, 'Suicide bomber from US came home'.

16. 'Brussels Jewish Museum killings: suspect "admitted attack"', BBC News, 1 June 2014.

17. Sheikh Abu Mohammed al-Maqdisi, 'A call to the ummah and mujahideen', 28 May 2014.

18. Joel Wing, 'Islamic State of Iraq and the Levant storm Samarra in Salahuddin', Musings on Iraq, 6 June 2014.

19. Deputy Assistant Secretary Brett McGurk, Statement for the Record, Senate Foreign Relations Committee Hearing: Iraq at a Crossroads: Options for US Policy, 24 July 2014.

20. Joel Wing, 'Islamic State of Iraq launches battle of Ninewa in Mosul', Musings on Iraq, 10 June 2014.

21. Human Rights Watch, 'Iraq: ISIS executed hundreds of prison inmates', 30 October 2014.

22. Tim Arango, 'Escaping death in northern Iraq', *New York Times*, 3 September 2014.

23. 'More than half of Iraqi legislators skip Parliament session', AFP, 12 June 2014.

24. 'Sistani calls on Iraqi civilians to fight ISIS', AFP, 13 June 2014.

25. 'Iraq cleric issues call to arms against ISIL', Al-Jazeera, 14 June 2014.

26. Alissa J. Rubin and Rod Nordland, 'Seeing their gains at risk, Shiites flock to join militias', *New York Times*, 13 June 2014.

27. Nicholas Blanford, 'ISIS' Iraq offensive could trigger Hezbollah to fill gap left in Syria', *Daily Star*, 16 June 2014.

28. Fatih Karimi and Laura Smith-Spark, 'ISIS militants still pressing forward in Iraq', CNN, 14 June 2014.

29. Julia Pace, 'Obama: 275 US forces deploying to Iraq', Associated Press, 16 June 2014.

30. Tom Whitehead, 'Iraq crisis: British student identified as recruiting ISIS jihadists', *The Telegraph*, 20 June 2014.

31. 'ISIS member from Scotland "killed" in Iraq', Sky News, 16 July 2014.

32. Abu Mohammed al-Adnani, 'This is the promise of Allah', al-Furqan Media, 29 June 2014.

33. Charles Lister, 'ISIS: what will the militant group do next?' BBC News, 27 June 2014.

34. Author interview with Abu Uthman al-Britani, July 2014.

35. Abu Bakr al-Baghdadi, 'A message to the mujahidin and the Muslim ummah in the month of Ramadan', al-Hayat Media Center, 1 July 2014.

36. Thomas Hegghammer, 'Calculated caliphate', Lawfare, 6 July 2014.

37. Suleiman al-Khalidi, 'Jihadist thinker says Islamic caliphate will cause Islamist infighting', Reuters, 2 July 2014.

38. Video statement published by the Islamic Front, 4 July 2014.

39. Mitchell Prothero, 'Islamic State releases video of Baghdadi in Mosul in new assertion of authority', McClatchy DC, 6 July 2014.

40. 'Abu Bakr al-Baghdadi appears in video, delivers sermon in Mosul', SITE Monitoring Service, 5 July 2014.

41. Ma'ad Fayad, 'ISIS in control of 60 percent of Syrian oil: sources', *Ashraq al-Awsat*, 11 July 2014.

42. Jennifer Cafarella, 'ISIS advances in Deir ez-Zour', Institute for the Study of War, 5 July 2014.

43. Josh Rogin, 'US ignored warnings before ISIS takeover of a key city', *The Daily Beast*, 10 July 2014.

44. 'Mass grave of 230 tribespeople found in Syria's Deir Ezzour: monitoring group', *al-Akbar*, 18 December 2014.

45. Michelle Nichols, 'UN rights inquiry says more Syrians joining Islamic State', Reuters, 25 July 2014.

46. 'ISIS recruits at record pace in Syria: Observatory', *Daily Star*, 20 August 2014.

47. Thomas Joscelyn, 'al Nusrah Front spokesman explains differences with Islamic State in video appearance', Long War Journal, 13 August 2014.

48. Hassan Hassan, 'al Nusra declares an "Islamic emirate", but is it significant?' *The National*, 15 July 2014.

49. Ahmed Abazid, 'Analysis: Nusra Front and the new phase', Zaman al-Wsl, 10 August 2014.

50. Joscelyn, 'al Nusrah Front spokesman explains differences'.

51. Ibid.

52. Charles Lister, 'Not just Iraq: the Islamic State is also on the march in Syria', The Huffington Post, 7 August 2014.

53. Aron Lund, 'The Revolutionary Command Council: rebel unity in Syria?' Carnegie Endowment for International Peace, 1 December 2014.

54. 'Translation: the formation of the Syrian Revolutionary Command Council', Goha's Nail Blog, 3 August 2014.

55. Vikram Dodd, 'British jihadi reportedly killed in Syria fighting for ISIS', *The Guardian*, 21 November 2014.

56. *Eid Greetings from the Land of the Caliphate*, al-Hayat Media Center, 2 August 2014.

57. 'Faisal Ali Warabi: that's my son in jihadist video', Hiiraan Online, 6 August 2014.

58. *Eid Greetings from the Land of the Caliphate*.

59. Sam Heller, 'Recriminations on social media shed light on Jabhat al-Nusrah's inner workings', Jihadology, 4 November 2014.

60. Mark Hosenball, 'Phones, shoes to face scrutiny as airport security tightened: US', Reuters, 3 July 2014.

61. Author interview with a European foreign fighter in Idlib, July 2014.

62. Venetia Rainey, 'Who is Imad Ahmad Jomaa?' *Daily Star*, 4 August 2014.

63. Radwan Mortada, 'The Islamic State expands into Lebanon', *al-Akhbar*, 4 August 2014.

64. 'Kahwagi: army will do utmost to free hostages', *Daily Star*, 12 August 2014.

65. Author interview with an Islamist fighter from Homs, January 2015.

66. Matthew Barber, 'IS routs Peshmerga, takes control of Sinjar mountains, jeopardizes Yazidi homeland', Syria Comment, 3 August 2014.

67. Office of the Press Secretary, the White House, 'Statement by the president', 7 August 2014.

68. Mohammed Ghobari, 'Yemeni Qaeda leader hails Islamic State's gains in Iraq', Reuters, 13 August 2014.

69. 'Yemen's AQAP calls on Islamists to target America after Iraq air strikes', Reuters, 15 August 2014.

70. 'Syrian government air strikes target Islamic State in Raqqa', Reuters, 17 August 2014; 'Syrian forces hit Islamic State in Raqqa, destroy water plant', Reuters, 18 August 2014.

71. Charles Lister, 'As ISIS closes in, is it game over for Syria's opposition in Aleppo?' CNN, 15 August 2014.

72. Spencer Ackerman, '"Recapture" of Mosul Dam from ISIS a major step forward, says Obama', *The Guardian*, 19 August 2014.

73. 'Statement on the raids of confronting the American–Kurdish alliance', Wilayat Nainawa, Media Office, 17 August 2014.

74. Alexander Dziadosz and Michael Georgy, 'Islamic State video purports to show beheading of US journalist', Reuters, 20 August 2014.

75. Oliver Holmes and Jason Szep, 'US hostage rescuers dropped from night sky, Syria activist says', Reuters, 22 August 2014; Spencer Ackerman, 'James Foley: US reveals failed special forces mission within Syria', *The Guardian*, 21 August 2014.

76. Rukmini Callimachi, 'Peter Theo Curtis, released by al Qaeda's Syrian branch, flies home to his family', *New York Times*, 26 August 2014.

77. Author interview with Moazzam Begg, February 2015.

78. Missy Ryan, 'Islamic State threat "beyond anything we've seen"—Pentagon', Reuters, 22 August 2014.

79. 'The Islamic State resets balance with spoils of Tabqa airbase', Oryx Blog, 25 August 2014.

80. Mariam Karouny, 'Islamist gains in Syria alarm some Assad allies', Reuters, 29 August 2014.

81. 'Syria willing to cooperate with US, UK to see air strikes against Islamic State terrorists, foreign minister says', AFP, 25 August 2014.

82. Louis Charbonneau and Manuel Mogato, 'How UN troops defied orders, opened fire and escaped Syrian rebels', Reuters, 12 September 2014.

## 11. THE ISLAMIC STATE

1. Joas Wagemakers, 'Abu Muhammad al-Maqdisi: a counter-terrorism asset?' Combating Terrorism Center, 15 May 2008.

2. 'Tracking al Qaeda in Iraq's Zarqawi: interview with ex-CIA analyst Nada Bakos', Musings on Iraq, 30 June 2014.

3. Bruce Riedel, *The Search for al Qaeda: Its Leadership, Ideology, and Future* (Washington, DC: Brookings Institution Press, 2010), p. 94.

4. Saif al-Adel, 'My experience with Abu Musab al-Zarqawi', *Minbar al-Tawhid wal Jihad*.

5. Jim Muir, 'Iraqi Kurds fear Islamic militant group', BBC News, 24 July 2002.

6. Kyle Orton, 'Saddam's Former Loyalists Are Leading ISIS—as True Believers,' *National Review*, 20 July 2015.

7. Joel Rayburn, *Iraq after America: Strongmen, Sectarians, Resistance* (Hoover International Press, 2014), p.102.

8. 'US Secretary of State Colin Powell addresses the UN Security Council', the White House, 5 February 2003.

9. 'No proof links Iraq, al-Qaida, Powell says', NBC News, 8 January 2004.

10. Dr Nimrod Raphaeli, 'The Sheikh of the Slaughterers: Abu Mus'ab al-Zarqawi and the al-Qaeda connection', Middle East Media Research Institute, 1 July 2005.

11. Christopher Hitchens, 'Why Ask Why?' Slate, 3 October 2005.

12. Zaki Chehab, *Inside the Resistance: Reporting from Iraq's Danger Zone* (New York: Nation Books, 2006), p. 47.

13. Nibras Kazimi, 'Zarqawi's anti-Shia legacy: original or borrowed?' Hudson Institute, 1 November 2006.

14. Abu Mohammed al-Adnani, 'al-Iraq ya ahl al-Sunnah', al-Furqan Media, 24 February 2012.

15. Bill Roggio, 'The rump Islamic emirate of Iraq', Long War Journal, 16 October 2006.

16. Bill Roggio, 'al-Qaeda's grand coalition in Anbar', Long War Journal, 12 October 2006.

17. Evan Kohlmann, 'Controversy grows over supposed unity of Iraqi mujahideen as al-Qaida announces founding of Sunni Islamic state', Counterterrorism Blog, 20 October 2006.

18. Matthew Levitt, 'Declaring an Islamic state, running a criminal enterprise', The Hill, 7 July 2014.

19. Lister, 'Profiling the Islamic State'.

20. 'Yazidis in Iraq: a tough time', *The Economist*, 13 November 2013.

21. Mike Mount, 'Reward for wanted terrorist drops', CNN, 13 May 2008.

22. Thom Shanker, 'Qaeda leaders in Iraq neutralized, US says', *New York Times*, 4 June 2010.

23. Timothy Williams and Duraid Adnan, 'Sunnis in Iraq allied with US rejoin rebels', *New York Times*, 16 October 2010.

24. 'Behind The Revival Of The Islamic State in Iraq, Interview With Naval War College Prof Craig Whiteside', *Musings on Iraq (Blog)*, 22 June 2015.

25. Michael Knights, 'ISIL's political–military power in Iraq', CTC Sentinel, 27 August 2014.

26. Susan B. Glasser and Walter Pincus, 'Seized letter outlines al Qaeda goals in Iraq', *Washington Post*, 12 October 2005.

27. Hannah Allam, 'Records show how Iraqi extremists withstood US anti-terror efforts', McClatchy DC, 23 June 2014.

28. Daveed Gartenstein-Ross and Amichai Magen, 'The jihadist governance dilemma', The Monkey Cage, 18 July 2014.

29. Lister, 'Profiling the Islamic state'.

30. Goha's Nail, 'Manbij and the Islamic State's public administration', Jihadology, 22 August 2014.

31. Mariam Karouny, 'In northeast Syria, Islamic State builds a government', Reuters, 4 September 2014.

32. Hassan Hassan, 'Islamic State in Syria, back with a vengeance', Sada, 14 July 2014.

33. Jenna Lefler, 'Life under ISIS in Mosul', Institute for the Study of War, 29 July 2014.

34. Lister, 'Profiling the Islamic state'.

35. Ibid.

36. Diana Darke, 'How ISIS misuses early Islamic history to justify its actions', DianaDarke (Blog), 23 August 2014.

37. Knights, 'ISIL's political–military power in Iraq'.

## 12. SEPTEMBER–DECEMBER 2014: STRIKES AND DIVISIONS

1. Aymenn Jawad al-Tamimi, 'The Islamic State's educational regulations in Raqqa province', Aymenn Jawad al-Tamimi's Blog, 28 August 2014.

2. UK intelligence officials cited in the Sunday Times on 31 August 2014.

3. Abigail Hauslohner, 'Jihadist expansion in Iraq puts Persian Gulf states in a tight spot', Washington Post, 13 June 2014.

4. 'BIFF, Abu Sayyaf pledge allegiance to Islamic State jihadists', GMA Network, 16 August 2014.

5. Ibid.

6. 'Jailed Indonesian terrorist Abu Bakar Bashir has been funding ISIS: anti-terrorism chief', Straits Times, 15 July 2014.

7. Fakhri al-Arashi, 'Senior Al-Qaeda Leader Calls For Followers To Support ISIS', National Yemen, 5 July 2014.

8. Ihsanullah Tipu Mehsud and Declan Walsh, 'Hardline splinter group, galvanized by ISIS, emerges from Pakistani Taliban', New York Times, 26 August 2014.

9. 'IS militant "Jihadi John" named as Mohammed Emwazi from London', BBC News, 26 February 2015.

10. A Second Message to America, al-Furqan Media, 2 September 2014.

11. Meg Warner, 'UK prime minister vows to fight ISIS as terrorists threaten to execute Briton: "We won't be cowed by these barbaric killers"', New York Daily News, 3 September 2014.

12. Marlin Dick, '"White Shrouds" mobilize against ISIS in Syria', Daily Star, 4 August 2014.

13. Lewis Smith, 'British jihadists becoming disillusioned with fighting rival rebels and want to come home', The Independent, 5 September 2014.

14. Steve Holland and Roberta Rampton, 'Obama orders US airstrikes in Syria against Islamic State', Reuters, 11 September 2014.

15. 'Obama's speech to Americans on defeating Islamic State', Reuters, 11 September 2014.

16. Jason Szep, 'US wins Arab support for Syria/Iraq military campaign', Reuters, 11 September 2014.

17. Hassan Hassan, 'Confronting the Islamic State', Carnegie Endowment for International Peace, 11 September 2014.

18. 'Syria warns against foreign intervention after Obama's speech', Reuters, 11 September 2014.

19. Sam Heller, 'Ahrar al-Sham's Abu Yazan: "It's our country and our revolution,"' *Abu al-Jamajem* (Blog), 5 September 2014.

20. Tom Harper, 'Alan Henning: al-Qaeda appealed to ISIS to release British aid worker following kidnap', *The Independent*, 15 September 2014.

21. Joas Wagemakers, 'IS' beheadings of Western hostages: jihadi ideologues speak out', Jihadica, 22 September 2014.

22. Mahmoud Sharaan, 'Jordan confronts ISIS domestically and abroad', *al-Akhbar*, 25 September 2014.

23. Wagemakers, 'IS' beheadings of Western hostages'.

24. 'Islamic State releases video it says shows British journalist John Cantlie', Reuters, 19 September 2014.

25. Osama Bin Zaid and Dan Wilkofsky, 'Moderate rebel leaders being picked off in "new phase" of battle', Syria Direct, 17 September 2014.

26. Stijn Mitzer, 'Russia helps keep Syria's MiG-29s flying', *IHS Jane's Defence Weekly*, 11 June 2014.

27. Suha Maayeh and Phil Sands, 'From dumb bombs to precision weapons, Assad regime ramps up airstrikes on rebels', *The National*, 27 October 2014.

28. 'Syrian Kurds warn of mounting crisis as ISIS advances, takes more villages', Fox News, 19 September 2014.

29. Abu Mohammed al-Adnani, *Inn'a Rabaka la bil mirsad*, al-Furqan Media, 21 September 2014.

30. Paul Cruickshank, 'French bomb-maker with Khorasan radicalized over "several years"', CNN, 1 November 2014.

31. Mitchell Prothero, 'Sources: US air strikes in Syria targeted French agent who defected to al-Qaeda', McClatchy DC, 5 October 2014.

32. Daveed Gartenstein-Ross, 'Was David Drugeon a French intelligence agent?' War on the Rocks, 4 November 2014.

33. Chris Woods, 'Pentagon in denial about civilian casualties of US airstrikes in Iraq and Syria', *Foreign Policy*, 3 December 2014.

34. Siobhan Gorman and Maria Abu-Habib, 'Syria airstrikes roil rebel alliances', *Wall Street Journal*, 27 September 2014.

35. Tom Perry, 'US-led air strikes pose problem for Assad's moderate foes', Reuters, 30 September 2014.

36. Clarissa Ward, 'Fighting ISIS: US counting on moderate rebel force', CBS News, 30 September 2014.

37. Perry, 'US-led air strikes pose problem for Assad's moderate foes'.

38. 'Syrian al Qaeda offshoot vows retaliation against US-led air strikes', Reuters, 27 September 2014.

39. Abu Mohammed al-Jolani, 'For the people of integrity, sacrifice is easy', al-Manara al-Bayda, 28 September 2014.

40. '53 killed in Homs explosions, 46 of them children', Syrian Observatory for Human Rights, 2 October 2014.

41. Anne Barnard and Mohammad Ghannam, 'Protests erupt in Homs over bombings that killed dozens of Syrian schoolchildren', *New York Times*, 2 October 2014.

42. 'ISIS, Assad forces face off in Deir Ezzour', *Asharq al-Awsat*, 15 October 2014.

43. 'Captured Russian spy facility reveals the extent of Russian aid to the Assad regime', Oryx Blog, 6 October 2014.

44. Phil Sands and Suha Maya, 'Exclusive: The Spy who fooled the Assad regime,' *The National*, 20 March 2015.

45. Ibid.

46. 'Syria update: October 17–October 29, 2014', Institute for the Study of War.

47. Christopher Kozak, 'The Assad regime under stress: conscription and protest among Alawite and minority populations in Syria', Institute for the Study of War, 15 December 2014.

48. 'Islamic State fighters capture Kurd HQ in Syria's Kobane: monitor', AFP, 10 October 2014.

49. 'ISIL fighters show off weapons likely seized from US airdrop', Al-Jazeera America, 22 October 2014.

50. *Inside Ayn al-Islam*, al-I'tisam Media, 27 October 2014.

51. Matt Spetalnick and Sylvia Westall, 'Islamic State beheads British hostage Henning in new video', Reuters, 4 October 2014.

52. Matthew Barber, 'If the US wanted to, it could help free thousands of enslaved Yazidi women in a single day', Syria Comment, 16 September 2014.

53. *Dabiq* magazine, issue 4, al-Hayat Media Center, 12 October 2014.

54. '6 top Pak Taliban commanders announce allegiance to ISIS', PTI, 14 October 2014.

55. Sam Heller, 'Abu Azzam al-Najdi: "'No one has a successful plan to implement God's law except the Islamic State'", Abu al-Jamajem Blog, 22 October 2014.

56. Ibid.

57. Author interview with a Salafist commander in the Islamic Front, September 2014.

58. Greg Miller, 'Airstrikes against Islamic State do not seem to have affected flow of fighters to Syria', *Washington Post*, 31 October 2014.

59. Allan Woods, 'How Martin Couture-Rouleau became an aspiring Islamic State fighter', *The Star*, 26 October 2014.

60. Michael Holden, 'Britain warns of "exceptionally high" level of anti-terrorism activity', Reuters, 17 October 2014.

61. Alexandra Hudson and Sabine Siebold, 'Germany warns security situation "critical" due to radical Islam', Reuters, 28 October 2014.

62. 'Syrian air strikes kill over 200 civilians in 10 days: monitor', Reuters, 30 October 2014.

63. Mariam Karouny, 'al Qaeda group seizes bastion of Western-backed rebels in Syria's Idlib region', Reuters, 1 November 2014.

64. Liz Sly, 'US-backed Syria rebels routed by fighters linked to al-Qaeda', *Washington Post*, 2 November 2014.

65. 'English translation of the interview with Jabhat al-Nusra leader Abu Muhammad al-Julani', pietervanostaeyen Blog, 11 November 2014.

66. Author interview with an FSA leader, October 2014.

67. Author interview with a senior Harakat Ahrar al-Sham al-Islamiyya official, October 2014.

68. Author interview with SMC official, November 2014.

69. Abdallah Suleiman Ali, 'IS imminent threat in Deraa', al-Monitor, 3 December 2014.

70. 'Islamic State says seizes second gas field in Syria', Reuters, 3 November 2014.

71. Abu Bakr al-Baghdadi, *Wa'law kariha la kafirun*, al-Furqan Media, 13 November 2014.

72. 'Islamic State leader urges attacks in Saudi Arabia—speech', Reuters, 13 November 2014.

73. Joanna Paraszczuk, 'Did IS refuse truce with Syrian Islamist factions?' Radio Free Europe Radio Liberty, 13 November 2014.

74. *Although the Disbelievers Dislike it*, al-Furqan Media, 16 November 2014.

75. Colin Freeman, 'Peter Kassig "killed by gunshot before he was decapitated"', *The Telegraph*, 14 December 2014.

76. 'Detailed analysis of Islamic State propaganda video: *Although the Disbelievers Dislike it*', Quilliam Foundation and the Terrorism Research and Analysis Consortium (TRAC), 21 January 2015.

77. Tweets by Abu Omar al-Okaidi (@aL3kade2) on 20 October 2014.

78. Shiv Malik, Ali Younes, Spencer Ackerman and Mustafa Khalili, 'The race to save Peter Kassig', The Guardian, 18 December 2014.

79. Maxwell Martin, 'Charter of the Revolutionary Command Council', Wilayat Nowhere Blog, 8 December 2014.

80. Author interview with Islamic Front official and RCC Executive Council member, November 2014.

81. Author interview with FSA commander, November 2014.

82. Maxwell Martin, '"The Unified Arab Code—a study and assessment" by the Islamic Sham Organization', Wilayat Nowhere Blog, 5 December 2014.

83. US Department of Defense, 'Operation Inherent Resolve: targeted operations against ISIL terrorists'.

84. 'President al-Assad: Syria is ready to provide cooperation to make de Mistura's mission a success', Syrian Arab News Agency, 12 September 2014.

85. 'Report: UN envoy to meet Syrian rebels in Turkey', Today's Zaman, 8 December 2014.

86. Aron Lund, 'The Levant Front: can Aleppo's rebels unite?' Carnegie Endowment for International Peace, 26 December 2014.

87. Dabiq magazine, issue 6, al-Hayat Media Center, 30 December 2014.

## 13. JANUARY–JUNE 2015: TIPPING THE SCALES

1. 'Saudi IS cleric killed in northern Syria', Associated Press, 3 January 2015.

2. Author interviews with senior and operations-level Anti-ISIL Coalition personnel, February–April 2015.

3. 'Islamic State "police" official beheaded—Syria monitor', Reuters, 6 January 2015.

4. 'Islamic State attacked for third time in eastern Syria—reports', Reuters, 10 January 2015.

5. Aymenn Jawad al-Tamimi, 'The White Shroud: a Syrian resistance movement to the Islamic State', Syria Comment, 22 October 2014.

6. Suleiman al-Khalidi, 'Islamic State beheads militiaman as opposition attacks mount', Reuters, 15 January 2015.

7. Ammar Hamou, Dan Wilkofsky and Kristen Gillespie, 'Questions of "overstepping" judiciary as Jaish al-Islam claims Douma victory', Syria Direct, 9 January 2015.

8. Ibid.

9. Cassell Bryan-Low, 'UK MI5 chief Andrew Parker warns of threat of al Qaeda attack in West', *Wall Street Journal*, 8 January 2015.

10. Tom Perry, 'Extremists destroy 13th century Muslim tomb in Syria', Reuters, 8 January 2015.

11. 'Nusra Front executes Syrian woman accused of adultery', *al-Akhbar*, 14 January 2015.

12. Charles Lister, 'American anti-tank weapons appear in Syrian hands', Huffington Post, 6 April 2014.

13. 'Birth of the First Army', Syrian Rebellion Observatory, 1 January 2015.

14. *A Message to the Government and the People of Japan*, al-Furqan Media, 19 January 2015.

15. 'Japan PM Shinzo Abe pledges $2.5bn in Middle East aid', BBC News, 17 January 2015.

16. 'From homeless in Japan to hostage in Syria: how Haruna Yukawa ended up in a warzone', Reuters, 27 August 2014.

17. Antoni Slodkowski, 'Japanese reporter's bid to save friend led to IS abduction', Reuters, 21 January 2015; Shuan Sim, 'ISIS beheads Haruna Yukawa: why the Japanese hostages were in Syria', *International Business Times*, 24 January 2015.

18. 'Sajida Rishawi resurfaces as bargaining chip 10 years after Amman bombings', *Jordan Times*, 28 January 2015.

19. Ray Sanchez, 'Who was Sajida al-Rishawi? And why did ISIS care about her?' CNN, 4 February 2015.

20. Suleiman al-Khalidi and Linda Sieg, 'Islamic State purportedly sets new deadline for hostage swap', Reuters, 29 January 2015.

21. Author interview with prominent Syrian Salafist leader, March 2015.

22. Joas Wagemakers, 'Maqdisi in the middle: an inside account of the secret negotiations to free a Jordanian pilot', Jihadica, 11 February 2015.

23. Abu Ibrahim al-Raqqawi, Twitter, 8 January 2015.

24. Shiv Malik, Ali Younes, Spencer Ackerman and Mustafa Khalili, 'How ISIS crippled al-Qaida', *The Guardian*, 10 June 2015.

25. Antoni Slodkowski, 'Radical scholar provided Japan with channel to IS at hostage crisis peak', Reuters, 9 February 2015.

26. Sylvia Westall and William Mallard, 'Islamic State says beheads Japanese hostage Goto', Reuters, 1 February 2015.

27. 'Jordan still ready for swap with Islamic State to free pilot', Reuters, 1 February 2015.

28. Shane Harris, 'ISIS snuff films' sleight of hand', *Daily Beast*, 4 February 2015.

29. Malik et al., 'How ISIS crippled al-Qaida'.

30. 'Jordan executes Sajida al-Rishawi after pilot murder', al-Arabiya, 4 February 2015.

31. Wagemakers, 'Maqdisi in the middle'.

32. Sami Aboudi and Suleiman al-Khalidi, 'Clerics denounce burning alive of pilot as un-Islamic', Reuters, 4 February 2015.

33. Aymenn Jawad al-Tamimi, 'Islamic State justification for burning alive the Jordanian pilot: translation and analysis', 4 February 2015.

34. 'Jordan executes 2 prisoners after ISIS killing of pilot', Associated Press, 4 February 2015.

35. 'Islamic State says female US hostage killed in Syria', Reuters, 6 February 2015.

36. Christoph Reuter, 'Syria's mercenaries: the Afghans fighting Assad's war', Spiegel Online, 11 May 2015.

37. 'Syria death toll now exceeds 210,000, rights group says', Reuters, 7 February 2015.

38. Author interview with Abu Rami, April 2015.

39. 'Ajnad al-Sham accuses Nusra of killing commander in Ghouta', Zaman al-Wasl, 6 February 2015.

40. Chris Kozak, 'Syria situation report: January 27–February 2, 2015', Institute for the Study of War, 4 February 2015.

41. 'Bashar al-Assad "part of the solution" in Syria, says UN envoy', AFP, 14 February 2015.

42. Anne Barnard, 'UN envoy says Assad is crucial to defusing conflict in Syria', *New York Times*, 13 February 2015.

43. Ibid.

44. 'Revolutionary Command Council criticizes de Mistura', *The Syrian Observer*, 19 February 2015.

45. Ibid.

46. Rita Daou, 'Syria rebels reject envoy plan to freeze Aleppo fighting', AFP, 1 March 2015.

47. David Daoud, 'Jihad Mughniyeh assassination halted Hezbollah, Iran attempt to establish terror infrastructure on Syria border', *The Algemeiner*, 1 April 2015.

48. Phillip Smyth, 'Israel is the new front in the Syrian war', *Foreign Policy*, 28 January 2015.

49. Tom Perry, 'Syrian rebel leader vows guerrilla war in south against Hezbollah, govt', Reuters, 12 February 2015.

50. 'Scores dead in intensified fighting in southern Syria: monitor', Reuters, 15 February 2015.

51. Ibid.

52. 'Syria's Assad fires two spy chiefs: security source', AFP, 20 March 2015.

53. Aron Lund, 'The death of Rustum Ghazaleh', Carnegie Endowment for International Peace, 30 April 2015.

54. Author interview with Islamist fighter from Aleppo, March 2015.

55. 'Fighting rages in Aleppo as UN sees "hope" for peace', Al-Jazeera, 18 February 2015.

56. Maya Gebeilly, 'Pro-regime Syrians support army but dodge draft', AFP, 19 April 2015.

57. 'Oryx', 'Iranian fighter-bombers operating in Syria', Bellingcat, 16 March 2015.

58. Sam Dagher, 'Syrian Kurds repel Islamic State weekend attack on Christian villages', *Wall Street Journal*, 8 March 2015.

59. Isabel Coles and Seif Hameed, 'With sledgehammer, Islamic State smashes Iraqi history', Reuters, 26 February 2015.

60. Kareem Shaheen, 'ISIS video confirms destruction at UNESCO world heritage site in Hatra', *The Guardian*, 5 April 2015.

61. 'Islamic State releases 19 Christians, more than 200 still captive: monitor', Reuters, 1 March 2015.

62. Oliver Holmes and Mariam Karouny, 'Islamic State moves west to attack Syrian army in Homs: monitor', Reuters, 24 March 2015.

63. Kareem Shaheen, 'ISIS launches assault on pro-Assad forces in western Syria', *The Guardian*, 25 March 2015.

64. Author interviews with Western diplomats, September 2014–February 2015.

65. 'The Islamic State's spring offensive: al-Sukhna', Oryx Blog, 23 May 2015.

66. Author interview with Aleppo-based FSA leader, March 2015.

67. Dan Wilkofsky, Mohammed al-Haj Ali and Muatasem Jamal, 'Jabhat al-Nusra declares war on Harakat Hazm', Syria Direct, 26 February 2015.

68. 'al-Nusra kills 30 fighters in Hazm and gains control in the western countryside of Aleppo', Syrian Observatory for Human Rights, 28 February 2015.

69. 'Syria's Hazzm rebel group dissolves itself after losses, joins Shamiyah Front', *Ya Libnan*, 1 March 2015.

70. Author interview with Aleppo-based FSA commander, March 2015.

71. Umberto Bacchi, 'Syria: al-Qaeda Nusra Front shows off huge cache of US weapons seized from moderate Harakat Hazm rebels', *International Business Times*, 4 March 2015.

72. Thomas Joscelyn, 'al Qaeda veteran reportedly targeted in Syria', Long War Journal, 6 March 2015.

73. 'Syria conflict: blast hits Aleppo intelligence HQ', BBC News, 4 March 2015.

74. Malak Chabkoun, 'Avoiding chaos post-liberation of Idlib city', Al-Jazeera Center for Studies, 30 March 2015.

75. 'As rebels close in, Idlib regime company defects to opposition', Syria Direct, 25 March 2015.

76. Hashem al-Sheikh, 'A Congratulatory statement for the liberation of Idlib province', Ahrar al-Sham, 29 March 2015.

77. Abu Mohammed al-Jolani, 'A victory from Allah, and near conquest', al-Manara al-Bayda, 1 April 2015.

78. Charles Lister, 'Why Assad is losing', *Foreign Policy*, 5 May 2015.

79. Author interviews with Ahrar al-Sham, Faylaq al-Sham and other Islamist figures based in Idlib and Aleppo, March–April 2015.

80. Ibid.

81. Charles Lister, 'Are Syrian Islamists moving to counterbalance al-Qaeda? Will it Last?' Markaz, 23 March 2015.

82. Author interview with senior Ahrar al-Sham leader, December 2014.

83. 'Ahrar al-Sham leader criticizes al-Nusra's link to al-Qaeda and attacks Da'ish', All4Syria, 19 April 2015.

84. 'Top Damascus rebel in Turkey amid regional moves', NOW Lebanon, 20 April 2015.

85. Ibid.

86. 'Key Islamist group Shamiya Front dissolves itself: source', Zaman al-Wasl, 17 April 2015.

87. Zeina Karam, 'Suffering rises in Yarmouk after ISIS takeover', Associated Press, 10 April 2015.

88. Aymenn Jawad al-Tamimi, 'The new Druze militia factions of Suwayda province', Syria Comment, 8 August 2015.

89. Christopher Kozak, 'New ISIS offensives in the Syrian civil war', Institute for the Study of War, 15 May 2015.

90. 'Oryx,' 'The Islamic State's spring offensive: al-Sukhna', Oryx Blog, 23 May 2015.

91. Yezid Sayigh, 'The war over Syria's gas fields', Syria in Crisis (Carnegie), 8 June 2015.

92. Justin Fishel, 'Fall of Ramadi: 30 car bombs, 10 as big as Oklahoma City blast, US official says', ABC News, 20 May 2015.

93. Andrew Roth, 'Police commander from Tajikistan appears in ISIS video', *New York Times*, 29 May 2015.

94. 'Islamic State NHS-style hospital video posted', BBC News, 24 April 2015.

95. Martin Chulov and Kareem Shaheen, 'ISIS leader Abu Bakr al-Baghdadi "seriously wounded in air strike"', *The Guardian*, 21 April 2015.

96. Mitchell Prothero, 'New Islamic State audio ends talk that leader Baghdadi is incapacitated', McClatchy DC, 14 May 2015.

97. Lister, 'Why Assad is losing'.

98. 'Humanitarian aid supplies once again found to be used to sustain Assad's war effort', National Coalition of Syrian Revolution and Opposition Forces, Press Release, 22 May 2015.

99. Gilad Shiloach, 'Syrian army accused of hoarding UN food for starving civilians', Vocativ, 29 May 2015.

100. RCC statement 'To the UN special envoy Staffan de Mistura', 12 May 2015.

101. 'Syria's Assad says losing battles does not mean war is lost', AFP, 7 May 2015.

102. Gebeilly, 'Pro-regime Syrians support army but dodge draft'.

103. 'Hezbollah boosts presence in Latakia', NOW Lebanon, 7 May 2015.

104. Nicholas Blanford, 'Hizbullah airstrip revealed', *IHS Jane's Defence Weekly*, 23 April 2015.

105. 'Rebels move against Hezbollah in Qalamoun', NOW Lebanon, 4 May 2015.

106. 'Rebels put up fierce resistance in Daraa town', NOW Lebanon, 21 April 2015.

107. 'Rebels start Homs offensive', NOW Lebanon, 6 May 2015.

108. US Department of State, 'Terrorist designation of Said Arif', 18 August 2014.

109. 'Syria not a launching pad for attacks on West says al-Nusra chief in TV interview', *The Guardian*, 28 May 2015.

110. Charles Lister, 'An internal struggle: al Qaeda's Syrian affiliate is grappling with its identity', Huffington Post, 31 May 2015.

111. Ibid.

112. Author interview with Islamist commander, based in Khan Sheikhoun, Idlib, June 2015.

113. Thomas Joscelyn, 'The al Nusrah Front's "inherited jihad"', Long War Journal, 5 June 2015.

114. Ibid.

115. Institute for the Study of War, 'Syria situation report: May 27–June 2, 2015', June 2015.

116. Author interview with Zakaria Malahfji, 4 June 2015.

117. Anne Barnard, 'Assad's forces may be aiding new ISIS surge', *New York Times*, 2 June 2015.

118. Tom Perry, 'Syrian Kurds push deeper into Islamic State stronghold', Reuters, 13 June 2015.

119. Suleiman al-Khalidi and Umit Bektas, 'Syrian Kurds claim capture of border town from Islamic State', Reuters, 15 June 2015.

120. Humeyra Pamuk and Umit Bektas, 'Turkey sees signs of "ethnic cleansing" by Kurdish fighters in Syria', Reuters, 16 June 2015.

121. Tom Perry and Laila Bassam, 'Syria Kurds seize town from Islamic State near its "capital"', Reuters, 23 June 2015.

122. Missy Ryan, 'US drone strike kills a senior Islamic State militant in Syria', *Washington Post*, 2 July 2015.

123. Tom Perry, 'Syrian Kurds thwart big Islamic State attack on border town', Reuters, 1 July 2015.

124. David Alexander, 'Islamic State seen as potent force a year after caliphate declaration: Pentagon', Reuters, 29 June 2015.

125. Sylvia Westall, 'Kurds secure Syria's Kobani as Islamic State targets northeast', Reuters, 28 June 2015.

126. Author interviews with Jaish al-Islam and other Syrian Islamist officials, July 2015.

127. Nour Samaha, 'Trapped between Assad, Israel and al-Qaeda', *Foreign Policy*, 22 June 2015.

128. 'Nusra emir to Idlib Druze: give me 1,000 rifles', Syria Direct, 11 June 2015.

129. Samaha, 'Trapped Between Assad, Israel and al-Qaeda'.

130. Jennifer Cafarella, 'Rebels launch new offensive in southern Syria', Institute for the Study of War, 2 July 2015.

131. Author interviews with Syrian armed opposition leaders, July–August 2015.

132. Revolutionary Command Council '16 Points' document, June 2015.

## 14. THE SYRIAN JIHAD

1. See for example: 'ISIL suspected of using mustard gas in Syria's Aleppo', Al-Jazeera, 24 August 2015; 'Activists accuse Daesh of using mustard gas in Syria', al-Bawaba, 2 September 2015.

2. '22-year-old becomes 33rd activist to die in Suruc bombing', *Hurriyet Daily News*,

14 August 2015; 'Suruc massacre: "Turkish student" was suicide bomber', BBC News, 22 July 2015.

3. 'Suruç katliamında 'Adıyamanlı genç' iddiası', Radikal, 21 July 2015.

4. Kareem Shaheen and Constanze Letsch, 'Turkey to let anti-ISIS coalition use air-base after soldier's death', *The Guardian*, 23 July 2015.

5. 'US sends six jets, 300 personnel to Turkey base in Islamic State fight', Reuters, 9 August 2015; Corey Dickstein, 'Armed drone flown out of Incirlik air base in Turkey strikes Islamic State', Stars and Stripes, 5 August 2015.

6. 'US warplanes launch first air strikes against ISIS targets in Syria', AFP, 12 August 2015.

7. Tulay Karadeniz and Daren Butler, 'Turkey says any Syria measures not act of war but to preserve border security', Reuters, 30 June 2015.

8. Karen DeYoung and Liz Sly, 'US–Turkey deal aims to create de facto "safe zone" in northwest Syria', *Washington Post*, 26 July 2015.

9. Author interview with meeting attendee, August 2015.

10. Author interview with three Aleppo-based Islamist officials, September 2015.

11. Fatwa issued by the Syrian Islamic Council's Fatwa Committee by text on 4 August 2015: http://www.islamsyria.com/portal/consult/show/870.

12. 'Statement on the latest events in Aleppo's northern countryside', al-Manara al-Bayda, 9 August 2015.

13. 'Statement regarding the safe zone in northern Syria', Ahrar al-Sham Political Office, 11 August 2015.

14. 'Were foreigners involved in the Nord-Ost hostage crisis?' NorthCaucasusCaucus Blog, 30 August 2015.

15. Author interviews with senior Ahrar al-Sham leaders, June–August 2015.

16. Labib al-Nahhas, 'The deadly consequences of mislabeling Syria's revolutionaries', *Washington Post*, 10 July 2015.

17. Robert S. Ford and Ali El Yassir, 'Yes, talk with Syria's Ahrar al-Sham', Middle East Institute, 15 July 2015.

18. Labib al-Nahhas, 'I'm a Syrian and I fight ISIL every day: it will take more than bombs from the West to defeat this menace', *Daily Telegraph*, 21 July 2015.

19. Author interviews with leading Syrian Islamists, January–September 2015.

20. Author interview with Ahrar al-Sham leaders and Syrian Islamist sheikhs, August–September 2015.

21. Aron Lund, 'Abu Yahia al-Hamawi, Ahrar al-Sham's New Leader', *Syria Comment*, 12 September 2015.

22. Abu Qatada al-Filistini online comment, posted on *Justpaste.it* on 21 July 2015.

23. 'Hezbollah announces truce covering three Syrian towns', *Al-Jazeera*, 26 September 2015.

24. 'Islamic State in Syria demolishes ancient Mar Elian monastery', BBC News, 21 August 2015.

25. 'ISIS attacks Hezbollah near north Lebanon border', NOW Lebanon, 19 August 2015.

26. 'Street battles rage as ISIL inches deeper into Damascus', Al-Jazeera, 1 September 2015.

27. Kareem Shaheen and Ian Black, 'Beheaded Syrian scholar refused to lead ISIS to hidden Palmyra antiquities', *The Guardian*, 19 August 2015.

28. Jethro Mullen, 'ISIS reported to have blown up ancient temple in Palmyra', CNN, 25 August 2015.

29. 'Syria's Palmyra Temple of Bel "severely damaged" by IS', BBC News, 31 August 2015.

30. Barbara Starr, Jim Sciutto and Elise Labott, 'US investigating "credible" reports IS used chemical weapons', CNN, 14 August 2015.

31. Louisa Loveluck, 'Islamic State accused of using mustard gas in the battle around Aleppo in Syria', *Daily Telegraph*, 23 August 2015.

32. Post by 'Chechclear' on Tumblr, 31 August 2015: http://chechclear.tumblr.com/post/128053574499/how-is-it-acceptable-to-use-chemical-weapons-and#notes

33. Author interview with senior Train and Equip official, June 2015.

34. Author interview with Western diplomatic officials and Aleppo-based opposition sources, July–August 2015.

35. Geoff Dyer, 'Obama authorizes air strikes in Syria', *Financial Times*, 3 August 2015.

36. Author interview with Syrian opposition sources in Aleppo, 5–6 August 2015.

37. Nancy A. Youssef, 'Pentagon Admits: U.S. Gear in Qaeda's Hands', *The Daily Beast*, 25 September 2015. Michael Weiss, 'Syrian Defector from U.S.-trained Force Found With U.S. Hardware', *The Daily Beast*, 24 September 2015.

38. Michael Weiss, 'Did the US just kill 5 kids in Syria?' *Daily Beast*, 12 August 2015.

39. Ibid.

40. As revealed in e-mails exchanged between CENTCOM's Combined Joint Task Force—Operation Inherent Resolve (CJTF-OIR) and Turkish journalist Ragip Soylu, 12 August 2015.

41. Author interview with Idlib-based rebel commander, August 2015.

42. Helene Cooper and Rukmini Callimachi, 'Airstrike kills a deputy to ISIS leader, US says', *New York Times*, 21 August 2015.

43. Kimiko de Freytas-Tamura, 'Junaid Hussain, ISIS recruiter, reported killed in airstrike', *New York Times*, 27 August 2015.

44. See for example: 'New evidence proves Russian military directly engaging in Syrian Civil War', Oryx Blog, 29 August 2015; Michael Weiss, 'Russia puts boots on the ground in Syria', *Daily Beast*, 1 September 2015; Alex Fishman, 'Russian jets in Syrian skies', YNet News, 31 August 2015.

45. 'At least 52 killed in Douma as Assad sustains fierce aerial campaign', Zaman al-Wasl, 24 August 2015.

46. 'UN aid chief slams "horrifying" disregard of civilian life in Syria', Al-Jazeera America, 17 August 2015.

47. 'More than 330,000 people die while about 13,000,000 wounded and displaced since the beginning of Syrian revolution', Syrian Observatory for Human Rights, 6 August 2015.

48. Author interview with Moazzam Begg, February 2015.

49. 'About 6,000 Europeans are reportedly fighting with jihadist groups in Syria', AFP, 13 April 2015.

50. William Booth, 'Israeli study of foreign fighters in Syria suggests Shiites may out-number Sunnis', *Washington Post*, 2 January 2014.

51. Author's interview with Phillip Smyth, February 2015.

52. Jamie Dettmer, 'In video, Coulibaly says he coordinated with Hebdo shooters', *Daily Beast*, 11 January 2015.

53. Jason Hanna and Margot Haddad, 'Report: Cherif Kouachi texted Coulibaly an hour before Paris attacks began', CNN, 17 February 2014.

54. Author interview with Abu Uthman al-Britani, February 2014.

55. Author interview with Abu Mustafa, January 2015.

56. Author interview with Moazzam Begg, February 2015.

# BIBLIOGRAPHY

'4 dead, including 2 from Jaafar clan, as car comes under fire in Arsal outskirts', *Naharnet*, 16 June 2013.

'6 top Pak Taliban commanders announce allegiance to ISIS', PTI, 14 October 2014.

'19 Syria rebel groups reject Geneva talks', AFP, 27 October 2013.

'22-year-old becomes 33rd activist to die in Suruc bombing', *Hurriyet Daily News*, 14 August 2015.

'53 killed in Homs explosions, 46 of them children', Syrian Observatory for Human Rights, 2 October 2014.

'"86 dead" as Syria's al-Qaeda allies repel jihadists', AFP, 11 April 2014.

'3,300 people killed in Syria rebel infighting this year', Reuters, 26 February 2013.

'15,000 elite Iranian special-ops "head" to Syria', Russia Today, 10 February 2012.

Abazid, Ahmed, 'Analysis: Nusra Front and the new phase', Zaman al-Wsl, 10 August 2014.

Abdelnour, Ziad K., 'Syria's proxy forces in Iraq', *Middle East Intelligence Bulletin*, 5, 4 (April 2003).

Abdul-Ahad, Ghaith, 'Outside Iraq but deep in the fight', *Washington Post*, 8 June 2005.

———, 'Syria: the foreign fighters joining the war against Bashar al-Assad', *The Guardian*, 23 September 2012.

Abdullah, Daniel, 'The ISIS–Suqour al-Sham truce: is it real and can it last?' Syria Comment, 6 February 2014.

Abdul-Zahra, Qassim, 'Shiite cleric issues fatwa in support of fighting in Syria war: Grand Ayatollah Kazim al-Haeri supports Assad', Associated Press, 19 December 2013.

Aboudi, Sami and Suleiman al-Khalidi, 'Clerics denounce burning alive of pilot as un-Islamic', Reuters, 4 February 2015.

'About 6,000 Europeans are reportedly fighting with jihadist groups in Syria', AFP, 13 April 2015.

Abouzeid, Rania, 'Interview with official of Jabhat al-Nusra, Syria's Islamist militia group', *TIME*, 25 December 2012.

——, 'The jihad next door', Politico, 23 June 2014.

——, 'In Syria, the rebels have begun to fight among themselves', *TIME*, 26 March 2013.

'Abu Bakr al-Baghdadi appears in video, delivers sermon in Mosul', SITE Monitoring Service, 5 July 2014.

Ackerman, Spencer, 'James Foley: US reveals failed special forces mission within Syria', *The Guardian*, 21 August 2014.

——, '"Recapture" of Mosul Dam from ISIS a major step forward, says Obama', *The Guardian*, 19 August 2014.

'Activist: "Quneitra's revolutionaries have met the call of Latakia"', Syria Direct, 10 April 2014.

'Activists accuse Daesh of using mustard gas in Syria', al-Bawaba, 2 September 2015.

'Activists say top ISIS commander killed in Syria', al-Arabiya, 8 February 2014.

al-Adnani, Abu Mohammed, 'This is not our methodology, nor will it ever be', al-Furqan Media, 17 April 2014.

'Ahrar al-Sham leader criticizes al-Nusra's link to al-Qaeda and attacks Da'ish', All4Syria, 19 April 2015.

'Ajnad al-Sham accuses Nusra of killing commander in Ghouta', Zaman al-Wasl, 6 February 2015.

Akhmeteli, Nina, 'The Georgian roots of ISIS commander Omar al-Shishani', BBC, 9 July 2014.

Alexander, David, 'Islamic State seen as potent force a year after caliphate declaration: Pentagon', Reuters, 29 June 2015.

Ali, Abdallah Suleiman, 'IS imminent threat in Deraa', al-Monitor, 3 December 2014.

——, 'Saudi jihadists flow into Syria', al-Monitor, 8 December 2013.

Allam, Hannah, 'Records show how Iraqi extremists withstood US anti-terror efforts', McClatchy DC, 23 June 2014.

'Arab neigbours queue for ticket to martyrdom', *Sydney Morning Herald*, 1 April 2003.

Arango, Tim, 'Escaping death in northern Iraq', *New York Times*, 3 September 2014.

'Army: top al-Qaeda chief in country left for Syria', *Daily Star*, 17 May 2012.

'As rebels close in, Idlib regime company defects to opposition', Syria Direct, 25 March 2015.

'Assad troops say Yabroud "possibly the most difficult" fight', AFP, 17 March 2014.

Atassi, Basma, 'Major Syrian rebel groups join forces', Al-Jazeera, 22 November 2013.

——, 'Qaeda chief arbitrates Syria's "jihad crisis"', Al-Jazeera, 9 June 2013.

'At least 52 killed in Douma as Assad sustains fierce aerial campaign', Zaman al-Wasl, 24 August 201.

'Ayman al-Zawahiri calls upon jihadi groups in Syria to stop infighting', Flashpoint Partners, 23 January 2014.

# BIBLIOGRAPHY

Bacchi, Umberto, 'Syria: al-Qaeda Nusra Front shows off huge cache of US weapons seized from moderate Harakat Hazm rebels', *International Business Times*, 4 March 2015.

Barber, Matthew, 'If the US wanted to, it could help free thousands of enslaved Yazidi women in a single day', Syria Comment, 16 September 2014.

——, 'IS routs Peshmerga, takes control of Sinjar mountains, jeopardizes Yazidi homeland', Syria Comment, 3 August 2014.

——, 'New ISIS leaks reveal particulars of al-Qaida strategy', *Syria Comment*, 12 January 2014.

Barnard, Anne, 'Assad's forces may be aiding new ISIS surge', *New York Times*, 2 June 2015.

——, 'UN envoy says Assad is crucial to defusing conflict in Syria', *New York Times*, 13 February 2015.

Barnard, Anne and Mohammad Ghannam, 'Protests erupt in Homs over bombings that killed dozens of Syrian schoolchildren', *New York Times*, 2 October 2014.

Barnard, Anne and Hania Mourtada, 'Leader of Hezbollah warns it is ready to come to Syria's aid', *New York Times*, 30 April 2013.

Barnard, Anne and Hwaida Saad, 'Nuns released by Syrians after three-month ordeal', *New York Times*, 9 March 2014.

'Bashar al-Assad "part of the solution" in Syria, says UN envoy', AFP, 14 February 2015.

Bassam, Laila, 'Car bomb kills 20 in Hezbollah's Beirut stronghold', Reuters, 15 August 2013.

Batal al-Shishani, Murad, 'Chechens fighting in Syria complicate a complex conflict', *The National*, 3 May 2013.

Benotman, Noman and Roisin Blake, 'Jabhat al-Nusra: A Strategic Briefing', Quilliam Foundation, 8 January 2013.

Bidwell, Robin, *Dictionary of Modern Arab History*. Abingdon: Kegan Paul International, 1998.

'BIFF, Abu Sayyaf pledge allegiance to Islamic State jihadists', GMA Network, 16 August 2014.

Bin Zaid, Osama and Dan Wilkofsky, 'Moderate rebel leaders being picked off in "new phase" of battle', Syria Direct, 17 September 2014.

'Birth of the First Army', Syrian Rebellion Observatory, 1 January 2015.

Black, Ian and Chris McGreal, 'Conflict will create 100 Bin Ladens, warns Egyptian president', *The Guardian*, 1 April 2003.

Blanford, Nicholas, 'Behind Israeli strikes on Syria, a simmering battle with Hezbollah', *Christian Science Monitor*, 19 March 2014.

——, 'Hizbullah airstrip revealed', *IHS Jane's Defence Weekly*, 23 April 2015.

——, 'ISIS' Iraq offensive could trigger Hezbollah to fill gap left in Syria', *Daily Star*, 16 June 2014.

Bolopian, Philippe and Mouna Naim, 'Des jihadistes viseraient 36 personnalités antisyriennes au Liban', *Le Monde*, 7 December 2006.

'Bombers, bank accounts, and bleedout: al-Qa'ida's road in and out of Iraq', Combating Terrorism Center at West Point, 22 July 2008.

Booth, William, 'Israeli study of foreign fighters in Syria suggests Shiites may outnumber Sunnis', *Washington Post*, 2 January 2014.

Borger, Julian and Matthew Weaver, 'West backs Qatari plan to unify Syrian opposition', *The Guardian*, 2 November 2012.

Bottcher, Annabelle, *Syrische Religionspolitik unter Assad*. Freiburg im Breisgau: Arnold-Bergstrasser-Institut, 1998.

al-Bouti, Mohammed Said Ramadan, 'Hakadha nashaat al-qawamiyya' [This is how nationalism was born], *Hadarat al-Islam* 3, 6 (1963).

'The brigadier-general "Mahmud Abo Arraj" has escaped from the regime army', Syrian Observatory for Human Rights, 24 October 2014.

'Brussels Jewish Museum killings: suspect "admitted attack"', BBC News, 1 June 2014.

Bryan-Low, Cassell, 'UK MI5 chief Andrew Parker warns of threat of al Qaeda attack in West', *Wall Street Journal*, 8 January 2015.

Bunzel, Cole, 'The Islamic state of disunity: jihadism divided', Jihadica, 20 January 2014.

Burke, Jason, 'al-Qaida leader Zawahiri urges Muslim support for Syrian uprising', *The Guardian*, 12 February 2012.

Cafarella, Jennifer, 'ISIS advances in Deir ez-Zour', Institute for the Study of War, 5 July 2014.

————, 'Rebels launch new offensive in southern Syria', Institute for the Study of War, 2 July 2015.

Caillet, Romain, 'The Islamic State: leaving al-Qaeda behind', Syria in Crisis, Carnegie Endowment for International Peace, 27 December 2013.

Callimachi, Rukmini, 'Peter Theo Curtis, released by al Qaeda's Syrian branch, flies home to his family', *New York Times*, 26 August 2014.

————, 'In Timbuktu, al-Qaida left behind a manifesto', Associated Press, 14 February 2013.

'Captured Russian spy facility reveals the extent of Russian aid to the Assad regime', Oryx Blog, 6 October 2014.

Chabkoun, Malak, 'Avoiding chaos post-liberation of Idlib city', Al-Jazeera Center for Studies, 30 March 2015.

Charbonneau, Louis and Manuel Mogato, 'How UN troops defied orders, opened fire and escaped Syrian rebels', Reuters, 12 September 2014.

Charbonneau, Louis and Michelle Nichols, 'UN confirms sarin used in Syria attack; US, UK, France blame Assad', Reuters, 16 September 2013.

de Chatel, Francesca, 'The role of drought and climate change in the Syrian Uprising: untangling the triggers of the revolution', *Middle Eastern Studies* 50, 4 (2014).

Chehab, Zaki, *Inside the Resistance: Reporting from Iraq's Danger Zone* (New York: Nation Books, 2006).

Christmann, Andreas, 'Islamic scholar and religious leader: a portrait of Muhammad Sa'id Ramadan al-Buti', *Islam and Christian–Muslim Relations* 9, 2 (1998).

Chulov, Martin, 'ISIS: the inside story', *The Guardian*, 11 December 2014.

——, 'Syrian rebels in "decisive battle for Aleppo" as regime hits back in capital', *The Guardian*, 28 September 2012.

Chulov, Martin and Kareem Shaheen, 'ISIS leader Abu Bakr al-Baghdadi "seriously wounded in air strike"', *The Guardian*, 21 April 2015.

Coles, Isabel and Seif Hameed, 'With sledgehammer, Islamic State smashes Iraqi history', Reuters, 26 February 2015.

'"Confession" of conspiracy', Syria Direct, 13 August 2013.

Cooper, Helene and Rukmini Callimachi, 'Airstrike kills a deputy to ISIS leader, US says', *New York Times*, 21 August 2015.

Cruickshank, Paul, 'French bomb-maker with Khorasan radicalized over "several years"', CNN, 1 November 2014.

Cullison, Alan, 'Meet the rebel commander in Syria that Assad, Russia and the US all fear', *Wall Street Journal*, 19 November 2013.

Dagher, Sam, 'Battles rage around Syria chemical weapons sites', *Wall Street Journal*, 11 October 2013.

——, 'Syrian Kurds repel Islamic State weekend attack on Christian villages', *Wall Street Journal*, 8 March 2015.

Dakroub, Hussein, 'Kidnapped nuns' harrowing ordeal ends', *Daily Star*, 10 March 2014.

Daou, Rita, 'Syria rebels reject envoy plan to freeze Aleppo fighting', AFP, 1 March 2015.

Daoud, David, 'Jihad Mughniyeh assassination halted Hezbollah, Iran attempt to establish terror infrastructure on Syria border', *The Algemeiner*, 1 April 2015.

'Dara'a, what happened, why now: the formation of the Southern Syrian Revolutionary Front', *TahrirSy*, 6 May 2014.

Darke, Diana, 'How ISIS misuses early Islamic history to justify its actions', *DianaDarke* (Blog) 23 August 2014.

'Death of a cleric', *NOW*, 5 October 2007.

'Defiant Syrian rebels offer stark choice', BBC News, 3 June 2014.

de Freytas-Tamura, Kimiko, 'Junaid Hussain, ISIS recruiter, reported killed in airstrike', *New York Times*, 27 August 2015.

Dehghanpisheh, Babak, 'Hezbollah, Syrian opposition clashes intensify, raise fears in Lebanon', *Washington Post*, 2 March 2013.

Denselow, James, 'Iraq's Ho Chi Minh Trail: the Syrian–Iraqi border since 2003', *CTC Sentinel*, 15 May 2008.

'Detailed analysis of Islamic State propaganda video: *Although the Disbelievers Dislike it'*, Quilliam Foundation and the Terrorism Research and Analysis Consortium (TRAC), 21 January 2015.

Dettmer, Jamie, 'In video, Coulibaly says he coordinated with Hebdo shooters', *Daily Beast*, 11 January 2015.

DeYoung, Karen and Liz Sly, 'US–Turkey deal aims to create de facto "safe zone" in northwest Syria', *Washington Post*, 26 July 2015.

Dick, Marlin, 'Body of jihadist leader found in Idlib', *Daily Star*, 11 November 2014.

———, 'ISIS condemned for brutal murder of fellow jihadist', *Daily Star*, 3 January 2014.

———, 'Leading FSA commander quits, lashes out at lack of support', *Daily Star*, 4 November 2013.

———, '"White Shrouds" mobilize against ISIS in Syria', *Daily Star*, 4 August 2014.

Dickinson, Elizabeth, 'Playing with fire: why private gulf financing for Syria's extremist rebels risks igniting sectarian conflict at home', Brookings Institution, Saban Center Analysis Paper no. 16, December 2013.

Dickstein, Corey, 'Armed drone flown out of Incirlik air base in Turkey strikes Islamic State', Stars and Stripes, 5 August 2015.

Dodd, Vikram, 'British jihadi reportedly killed in Syria fighting for ISIS', *The Guardian*, 21 November 2014.

Dupree, Jonathan, 'Syria update: regime breaks siege of Wadi al-Deif', Institute for the Study of War, 18 April 2013.

Dyer, Geoff, 'Obama authorizes air strikes in Syria', *Financial Times*, 3 August 2015.

Dziadosz, Alexander and Michael Georgy, 'Islamic State video purports to show beheading of US journalist', Reuters, 20 August 2014.

'English translation of the interview with Jabhat al-Nusra leader Abu Muhammad al-Julani', pietervanostaeyen Blog, 11 November 2014.

Evans, Dominic, 'Annan to meet Assad, seeking end to Syria violence', Reuters, 9 March 2012.

———, 'Syrian rebels launch fierce offensive against al Qaeda fighters', Reuters, 4 January 2014.

'Evidence of Jabhat al-Nusra with Croatian weapons', Brown Moses Blog, 23 March 2013.

'Faisal Ali Warabi: that's my son in jihadist video', Hiiraan Online, 6 August 2014.

al-Fakih, Rakan, 'Hezbollah slays dozen Syrian rebels in Lebanon ambush', *Daily Star*, 2 June 2013.

———, 'Two Hezbollah members dead after Baalbek bomb', *Daily Star*, 19 December 2013.

'Fatah al-Islam militants killed in Syria', *Daily Star*, 24 April 2012.

Fayad, Ma'ad, 'ISIS in control of 60 percent of Syrian oil: sources', *Ashraq al-Awsat*, 11 July 2014.

'Fighting rages in Aleppo as UN sees "hope" for peace', Al-Jazeera, 18 February 2015.

Filiu, Jean-Pierre, *Apocalypse in Islam*. Berkeley and Los Angeles: University of California Press, 2012.

Fishel, Justin, 'Fall of Ramadi: 30 car bombs, 10 as big as Oklahoma City blast, US official says', ABC News, 20 May 2015.

Fishman, Alex, 'Russian jets in Syrian skies', YNet News, 31 August 2015.

Fitzgerald, Mary, 'The Syrian rebels' Libyan weapon', *Foreign Policy*, 9 August 2012.

Ford, Robert S. and Ali El Yassir, 'Yes, talk with Syria's Ahrar al-Sham', Middle East Institute, 15 July 2015.

Frank, Mitch, 'Help from an unlikely ally', *TIME Magazine*, 23 June 2002.

Freeman, Colin, 'Peter Kassig "killed by gunshot before he was decapitated"', *The Telegraph*, 14 December 2014.

'From homeless in Japan to hostage in Syria: how Haruna Yukawa ended up in a war-zone', Reuters, 27 August 2014.

'FSA claims responsibility for killing of Hezbollah commander', *The Daily Star*, 3 October 2012.

Gadahn, Adam, *Bayan bi-sha'an alaaqat Jamaat Qaedat al-Jihad bil Jamaat al-Dawla al-Islamiya fil Iraq wal Sham*, al-Fajr Media Center, late 2010.

Gartenstein-Ross, Daveed, 'Was David Drugeon a French intelligence agent?' War on the Rocks, 4 November 2014.

Gartenstein-Ross, Daveed and Amichai Magen, 'The jihadist governance dilemma', The Monkey Cage, 18 July 2014.

Gearan, Anne and Scott Wilson, 'US, Russia reach agreement on seizure of Syrian chemical weapons stockpile', *Washington Post*, 14 September 2013.

Gebeilly, Maya, 'Pro-regime Syrians support army but dodge draft', AFP, 19 April 2015.

George, Marcus, 'Iran's Revolutionary Guards commander says its troops in Syria', Reuters, 16 September 2012.

George, Susannah, 'Throwing windmills at the Wyndham', *Foreign Policy*, 20 March 2014.

Ghobari, Mohammed, 'Yemeni Qaeda leader hails Islamic State's gains in Iraq', Reuters, 13 August 2014.

Giglio, Mike, 'One man's journey to become the first American suicide bomber in Syria', BuzzFeed News, 7 August 2014.

———, 'Syrian rebel leader Mustafa al-Sheikh says victory against Assad not in sight', *The Daily Beast*, 26 July 2012.

Glasser, Susan B. and Walter Pincus, 'Seized letter outlines al Qaeda goals in Iraq', *Washington Post*, 12 October 2005.

Goha's Nail, 'Manbij and the Islamic State's public administration', Jihadology, 22 August 2014.

Gordon, Michael R. and Wesley S. Morgan, 'The general's gambit', *Foreign Policy*, 1 October 2012.

Gorman, Siobhan and Maria Abu-Habib, 'Syria airstrikes roil rebel alliances', *Wall Street Journal*, 27 September 2014.

'Gunfire in locked-down Syrian city', Al Jazeera, 19 April 2011.

Haidar, D. and Francesca de Chatel, 'Leaving the land', *Syria Today*, May 2009.

Hamou, Ammar, Dan Wilkofsky and Kristen Gillespie, 'Questions of "overstepping" judiciary as Jaish al-Islam claims Douma victory', Syria Direct, 9 January 2015.

Hanna, Jason and Margot Haddad, 'Report: Cherif Kouachi texted Coulibaly an hour before Paris attacks began', CNN, 17 February 2014.

Harper, Tom, 'Alan Henning: al-Qaeda appealed to ISIS to release British aid worker following kidnap', *The Independent*, 15 September 2014.

Harris, Shane, 'ISIS snuff films' sleight of hand', *Daily Beast*, 4 February 2015.

Hashem, Ali, 'al-Qaeda-affiliated emir arrested in Lebanon', al-Monitor, 1 January 2014.

Hassan, Hassan, 'Confronting the Islamic State', Carnegie Endowment for International Peace, 11 September 2014.

———, 'Islamic State in Syria, back with a vengeance', Sada, 14 July 2014.

———, 'Jihadis grow more dangerous as they conquer hearts in Syria', *The National*, 6 March 2013.

———, 'A jihadist blueprint for hearts and minds is gaining traction in Syria', *The National*, 4 March 2014.

———, 'Lessons from a massacre that Assad looks to exploit', *The National*, 8 May 2013.

———, 'al Nusra declares an "Islamic emirate", but is it significant?' *The National*, 15 July 2014.

Hauslohner, Abigail, 'Jihadist expansion in Iraq puts Persian Gulf states in a tight spot', *Washington Post*, 13 June 2014.

Hegghammer, Thomas, 'Calculated caliphate', Lawfare, 6 July 2014.

Heller, Sam, 'Abu Azzam al-Najdi: "No one has a successful plan to implement God's law except the Islamic State"', Abu al-Jamajem Blog, 22 October 2014.

———, 'Islam's lawyers in arms', *Foreign Policy*, 6 June 2014.

———, 'Recriminations on social media shed light on Jabhat al-Nusrah's inner workings', Jihadology, 4 November 2014.

Heras, Nicholas A., 'What is Hezbollah's role in the Syrian crisis?' *Terrorism Monitor* 10, 20 (2 November 2012), Jamestown Foundation.

'Hezbollah ambush kills 32 Islamist fighters in E. Lebanon', *Daily Star*, 23 December 2013.

'Hezbollah boosts presence in Latakia', NOW Lebanon, 7 May 2015.

Higgins, Eliot, 'Finding the exact location of an alleged chemical munition, and what it could mean', Brown Moses Blog, 26 August 2013.

———, 'Who was responsible for the August 21st attack?' Brown Moses Blog, 16 September 2013.

Hitchens, Christopher, 'Why Ask Why?' Slate, 3 October 2005.

Holden, Michael, 'Britain warns of "exceptionally high" level of anti-terrorism activity', Reuters, 17 October 2014.

Holland, Steve and Roberta Rampton, 'Obama orders US airstrikes in Syria against Islamic State', Reuters, 11 September 2014.

Holliday, Joseph, 'The Assad Regime: From Counterinsurgency to Civil War', *Middle East Security Report* 8. Washington, DC: Institute for the Study of War, 2013.

Holmes, Oliver, 'al Qaeda breaks link with Syrian militant group ISIL', Reuters, 3 February 2014.

——, 'al Qaeda's Iraqi offshoot gains ground in Syria amid rebel infighting', Reuters, 12 May 2014.

Holmes, Oliver and Mariam Karouny, 'Islamic State moves west to attack Syrian army in Homs: monitor', Reuters, 24 March 2015.

Holmes, Oliver and Jason Szep, 'US hostage rescuers dropped from night sky, Syria activist says', Reuters, 22 August 2014.

Hosenball, Mark, 'Phones, shoes to face scrutiny as airport security tightened: US', Reuters, 3 July 2014.

'How the Maaloula nuns were freed', *al-Monitor*, 11 March 2014.

Hubbard, Ben and Anne Barnard, 'Qaeda group leader in Syria suggests Islamic court to end rebel infighting', *New York Times*, 7 January 2014.

Hudson, Alexandra and Sabine Siebold, 'Germany warns security situation "critical" due to radical Islam', Reuters, 28 October 2014.

'Humanitarian aid supplies once again found to be used to sustain Assad's war effort', National Coalition of Syrian Revolution and Opposition Forces, Press Release, 22 May 2015.

Human Rights Watch, 'Iraq: ISIS executed hundreds of prison inmates', 30 October 2014.

——, '"No one's left": summary executions by Syrian forces in al-Bayda and Baniyas', September 2013.

——, 'Syria: the silenced Kurds', October 1996.

——, 'Syria: defectors describe orders to shoot unarmed protesters', *Human Rights Watch*, 9 July 2011.

——, 'You can still see their blood', 11 October 2013.

Ignatius, David, 'al-Qaeda affiliate playing larger role in Syria rebellion', *Washington Post*, 30 November 2012.

Institute for the Study of War, 'Syria situation report: May 27–June 2, 2015', June 2015.

International Crisis Group, 'Syria's phase of radicalisation', Middle East Briefing no. 33, 10 April 2012, p. 4.

'Iraq cleric issues call to arms against ISIL', Al-Jazeera, 14 June 2014.

'Iraq update 2014 #5: "The Time to Harvest is Coming"—ISIS statement', Institute for the Study of War, 8 January 2014.

'ISIL fighters show off weapons likely seized from US airdrop', Al-Jazeera America, 22 October 2014.

'ISIL suspected of using mustard gas in Syria's Aleppo', Al-Jazeera, 24 August 2015.

'ISIL threatens Erdogan with suicide bombings in Ankara, Istanbul', *Today's Zaman*, 30 September 2013.

'ISIS, Assad forces face off in Deir Ezzour', *Asharq al-Awsat*, 15 October 2014.

'ISIS attacks Hezbollah near north Lebanon border', NOW Lebanon, 19 August 2015.

'ISIS member from Scotland "killed" in Iraq', Sky News, 16 July 2014.

'ISIS recruits at record pace in Syria: Observatory', *Daily Star*, 20 August 2014.

'Islamic Front issues strong warning to ISIS', *Daily Star*, 6 January 2014.

'Islamic State attacked for third time in eastern Syria—reports', Reuters, 10 January 2015.

'Islamic State fighters capture Kurd HQ in Syria's Kobane: monitor', AFP, 10 October 2014.

'Islamic State leader urges attacks in Saudi Arabia—speech', Reuters, 13 November 2014.

'Islamic State NHS-style hospital video posted', BBC News, 24 April 2015.

'Islamic State "police" official beheaded—Syria monitor', Reuters, 6 January 2015.

'Islamic State releases 19 Christians, more than 200 still captive: monitor', Reuters, 1 March 2015.

'Islamic State releases video it says shows British journalist John Cantlie', Reuters, 19 September 2014.

'The Islamic State resets balance with spoils of Tabqa airbase', Oryx Blog, 25 August 2014.

'Islamic State says female US hostage killed in Syria', Reuters, 6 February 2015.

'Islamic State says seizes second gas field in Syria', Reuters, 3 November 2014.

'The Islamic State's spring offensive: al-Sukhna', Oryx Blog, 23 May 2015.

'Islamic State in Syria demolishes ancient Mar Elian monastery', BBC News, 21 August 2015.

'IS militant "Jihadi John" named as Mohammed Emwazi from London', BBC News, 26 February 2015.

'Jailed Indonesian terrorist Abu Bakar Bashir has been funding ISIS: anti-terrorism chief', *Straits Times*, 15 July 2014.

'Jailed Kurds on Syria hunger strike: rights group', AFP, 10 March 2011.

'Japan PM Shinzo Abe pledges $2.5bn in Middle East aid', BBC News, 17 January 2015.

'Jihadist group claims execution of 20 Syria soldiers', AFP, 3 October 2012.

'Jihadist militant leader in Lebanon Majid al-Majid dies in custody', BBC News, 4 January 2014.

'Jihad and Terrorism Threat Monitor (JTTM) weekend summary', *MEMRI*, 22 June 2013.

al-Jolani, Abu Mohammed, 'The forewarned is forearmed', al-Manara al-Bayda, 7 February 2014.

'Jordan executes 2 prisoners after ISIS killing of pilot', Associated Press, 4 February 2015.

'Jordan executes Sajida al-Rishawi after pilot murder', al-Arabiya, 4 February 2015.

'Jordan still ready for swap with Islamic State to free pilot', Reuters, 1 February 2015.

Joscelyn, Thomas, 'Alleged message from Zawahiri's Syrian representative posted online', Long War Journal, 17 January 2014.

———, 'Head of al Qaeda "Victory Committee" in Syria', Long War Journal, 6 March 2014.

———, 'al Nusrah Front spokesman explains differences with Islamic State in video appearance', Long War Journal, 13 August 2014.

———, 'The al Nusrah Front's "inherited jihad"', Long War Journal, 5 June 2015.

———, 'al Qaeda veteran reportedly targeted in Syria', Long War Journal, 6 March 2015.

———, 'Syrian rebel leader was bin Laden's courier, now Zawahiri's representative', Long War Journal, 17 December 2013.

'Kahwagi: army will do utmost to free hostages', *Daily Star*, 12 August 2014.

Kalin, Stephen, 'al Qaeda offshoot imposes strict Islamic rules in north Syria', Reuters, 20 January 2014.

Kalyvas, Stathis, *The Logic of Violence in Civil War*. New York: Cambridge University Press, 2006.

Karadeniz, Tulay and Daren Butler, 'Turkey says any Syria measures not act of war but to preserve border security', Reuters, 30 June 2015.

Karam, Zeina, 'Car bomb kills 14 in Beirut suburb', Associated Press, 15 August 2013.

———, 'Suffering rises in Yarmouk after ISIS takeover', Associated Press, 10 April 2015.

Karam, Zeina and Qassim Abdul-Zahra, 'al Qaeda's Nusra Front leader stays in Syria's shadows', *The National*, 4 November 2013.

Karimi, Fatih and Laura Smith-Spark, 'ISIS militants still pressing forward in Iraq', CNN, 14 June 2014.

Karouny, Mariam, 'Insight—Syria's Nusra Front may leave Qaeda to form new entity', Reuters, 4 March 2015.

———, 'Islamist gains in Syria alarm some Assad allies', Reuters, 29 August 2014.

———, 'In northeast Syria, Islamic State builds a government', Reuters, 4 September 2014.

———, 'al Qaeda group seizes bastion of Western-backed rebels in Syria's Idlib region', Reuters, 1 November 2014.

Kazimi, Nibras, 'Zarqawi's anti-Shia legacy: original or borrowed?' Hudson Institute, 1 November 2006.

Kennedy, Elizabeth A., 'Official: Hezbollah fighters killed in Syria', Associated Press, 2 October 2012.

Kerbaj, Richard, 'Twice as many UK jihadists as police thought, officials say', *The Sunday Times*, 19 April 2015.

Kerbaj, Richard and Malik al-Abdeh, 'Dead at 21: Britain's veteran jihadist', *The Sunday Times*, 3 March 2013.

'Key Islamist group Shamiya Front dissolves itself: source', Zaman al-Wasl, 17 April 2015.

al-Khalidi, Suleiman, 'Islamic State beheads militiaman as opposition attacks mount', Reuters, 15 January 2015.

———, 'Jihadist thinker says Islamic caliphate will cause Islamist infighting', Reuters, 2 July 2014.

al-Khalidi, Suleiman and Umit Bektas, 'Syrian Kurds claim capture of border town from Islamic State', Reuters, 15 June 2015.

al-Khalidi, Suleiman and Linda Sieg, 'Islamic State purportedly sets new deadline for hostage swap', Reuters, 29 January 2015.

Khatib, Line, *Islamic Revivalism in Syria: The Rise and Fall of Ba'thist Secularism*. Abingdon: Routledge, 2011.

Khoury, Jack, 'Syrian rebels claim Assad regime used chemical weapons', *Ha'aretz*, 24 December 2012.

Khraiche, Dana, 'Nasrallah denies Hezbollah members fighting with Syrian regime', *The Daily Star*, 11 October 2012.

Klapper, Bradley and Kimberley Dozier, 'al-Qaeda building well-organized network in Syria: US intelligence officials', Associated Press, 10 August 2012.

Knights, Michael, 'ISIL's political–military power in Iraq', CTC Sentinel, 27 August 2014.

Kohlmann, Evan, 'Controversy grows over supposed unity of Iraqi mujahideen as al-Qaida announces founding of Sunni Islamic state', Counterterrorism Blog, 20 October 2006.

Kozak, Christopher, 'The Assad regime under stress: conscription and protest among Alawite and minority populations in Syria', Institute for the Study of War, 15 December 2014.

Kozak, Christopher, 'New ISIS offensives in the Syrian civil war', Institute for the Study of War, 15 May 2015.

Kozak, Chris, 'Syria situation report: January 27–February 2, 2015', Institute for the Study of War, 4 February 2015.

Labrousse, Cedric, 'Abu Ahmad al-Maghrebi (Ibrahim Bencheqroun), jihad veteran killed in Syria', *The Arab Chronicle*, 2 April 2014.

Landis, Joshua, 'The battle between ISIS and Syria's rebel militias', Syria Comment, 4 January 2014.

Lefler, Jenna, 'Life under ISIS in Mosul', Institute for the Study of War, 29 July 2014.

Levitt, Matthew, 'Declaring an Islamic state, running a criminal enterprise', The Hill, 7 July 2014.

'Lex Runderkamp: 1300 ISIS soldaten onderweg naar Aleppo', NOS, 5 January 2014.

Lister, Charles, 'American anti-tank weapons appear in Syrian rebel hands', Huffington Post, 6 April 2014.

Lister, Charles, 'Are Syrian Islamists moving to counterbalance al-Qaeda? Will it Last?' Markaz, 23 March 2015.

——, 'As ISIS closes in, is it game over for Syria's opposition in Aleppo?' CNN, 15 August 2014.

——, 'Dynamic stalemate: surveying Syria's military landscape', Brookings Doha Center, 19 May 2014.

——, 'An internal struggle: al Qaeda's Syrian affiliate is grappling with its identity', Huffington Post, 31 May 2015.

——, 'ISIS: what will the militant group do next?' BBC News, 27 June 2014.

——, 'A militant Islamist/jihadi nexus is emerging in northern and eastern Syria: some thoughts on an increasingly cooperative militant alliance', TwitLonger, 22 March 2013.

——, 'Not just Iraq: the Islamic State is also on the march in Syria', Huffington Post, 7 August 2014.

——, 'Profiling the Islamic State', Brookings Doha Center, 1 December 2014.

——, 'Syria's new rebel front', Foreign Policy, 8 January 2014.

——, 'Why Assad is losing', Foreign Policy, 5 May 2015.

Lister, Charles and Aaron Zelin, 'The crowning of the Syrian Islamic Front', Foreign Policy, 24 June 2013.

Loveluck, Louisa, 'Islamic State accused of using mustard gas in the battle around Aleppo in Syria', Daily Telegraph, 23 August 2015.

Lund, Aron, 'The death of Rustum Ghazaleh', Carnegie Endowment for International Peace, 30 April 2015.

——, 'Is Jabhat al-Nosra breaking apart?' Syria Comment, 22 May 2013.

——, 'The Free Syrian Armies: failed reconciliation', Carnegie Endowment for International Peace, 26 March 2014.

——, 'The Levant Front: can Aleppo's rebels unite?' Carnegie Endowment for International Peace, 26 December 2014.

——, 'The mujahideen army of Aleppo', Carnegie Endowment for International Peace, 8 April 201.

——, 'The Revolutionary Command Council: rebel unity in Syria?' Carnegie Endowment for International Peace, 1 December 2014.

——, 'Showdown at Bab al-Hawa', Carnegie Endowment for International Peace, 12 December 2013.

——, Syria's Salafi insurgents: the rise of the Syrian Islamic Front, UI Occasional Paper no. 17. Stockholm: Swedish Institute for International Affairs, March 2013.

——, 'Who and what was Abu Khalid al-Suri? Part I', Carnegie Endowment for International Peace, 24 February 2014.

Lyons, Josh, 'Dispatches: mapping the sarin flight path', Human Rights Watch, 17 September 2013.

Maayeh, Suha and Phil Sands, 'From dumb bombs to precision weapons, Assad regime ramps up airstrikes on rebels', *The National*, 27 October 2014.

Maclean, William, 'al-Qaeda ideologue in Syrian detention—lawyers', Reuters, 10 June 2009.

MacLeod, Hugh, 'Inside Deraa', Al-Jazeera, 19 April 2011.

MacLeod, Hugh, 'Syria: how it all began', Global Post, 23 April 2011.

Malas, Nour, 'Syria killings open rift in anti-Assad ranks', *Wall Street Journal*, 12 July 2013.

Malik, Shiv, Ali Younes, Spencer Ackerman and Mustafa Khalili, 'How ISIS crippled al-Qaida', *The Guardian*, 10 June 2015.

——, Ali Younes, Spencer Ackerman and Mustafa Khalili, 'The race to save Peter Kassig', *The Guardian*, 18 December 2014.

'al-Manārah al-Bayḍā' Foundation for Media Production presents: "Declaration of the Support Front (Jabhat al-Nuṣrah): For the People of Syria from the Mujāhidīn of Syria in the Fields of Jihād"', 24 January 2011, Jihadology.net.

Marsh, Katherine, 'Syrian regime launches crackdown by shooting 15 activists dead', *The Guardian*, 24 March 2011.

Martin, Maxwell, 'Charter of the Revolutionary Command Council', Wilayat Nowhere Blog, 8 December 2014.

——, '"The Unified Arab Code—a study and assessment" by the Islamic Sham Organization', Wilayat Nowhere Blog, 5 December 2014.

'Mass grave of 230 tribespeople found in Syria's Deir Ezzour: monitoring group', *al-Akbar*, 18 December 2014.

McCants, Will, 'State of confusion: ISIS' strategy and how to counter it', *Foreign Affairs*, 10 September 2014.

McEvers, Kelly, 'Jihadi fighters win hearts and minds by easing Syria's bread crisis', NPR, 16 January 2013McEvers, Kelly, 'Syrian army drives rebels from embattled city', NPR, 1 March 2012.

McGregor, Andrew, 'Controversial Syrian preacher Abu al-Qaqa gunned down in Aleppo', Jamestown Foundation, 16 October 2007.

Mehsud, Ihsanullah Tipu and Declan Walsh, 'Hardline splinter group, galvanized by ISIS, emerges from Pakistani Taliban', *New York Times*, 26 August 2014.

Meir Amit Intelligence and Terrorism Information Center, 'The al-Nusra Front', 23 September 2013.

'Mihrac Ural, a man with a long history of terrorism', *Today's Zaman*, 14 May 2013.

Miller, Greg, 'Airstrikes against Islamic State do not seem to have affected flow of fighters to Syria', *Washington Post*, 31 October 2014.

———, 'CIA ramping up covert training program for moderate Syrian rebels', *Washington Post*, 2 October 2013.

Mitzer, Stijn, 'Russia helps keep Syria's MiG-29s flying', *IHS Jane's Defence Weekly*, 11 June 2014.

Mohammed, Muhanad, 'Iraq al Qaeda militant says Syria trained him', Reuters, 30 August 2009.

al-Moheisini, Abdullah, *Mubadarat al-ummah*, Tawhed, 25 January 2014.

'More than 1,000 killed in Syria rebel infighting: activist group', Associated Press, 16 January 2014.

'More than 330,000 people die while about 13,000,000 wounded and displaced since the beginning of Syrian revolution', Syrian Observatory for Human Rights, 6 August 2015.

'More than half of Iraqi legislators skip Parliament session', AFP, 12 June 2014.

Mortada, Radwan, 'The Islamic State expands into Lebanon', *al-Akhbar*, 4 August 2014.

'Most of Syria's land is outside regime control, says rebel colonel', AFP, 23 September 2012.

Mount, Mike, 'Reward for wanted terrorist drops', CNN, 13 May 2008.

Mroue, Bassem, 'Key al-Qaida militant reportedly killed in Syria', Associated Press, 27 January 2014.

Muir, Jim, 'Iraqi Kurds fear Islamic militant group', BBC News, 24 July 2002.

———, 'Syria "death video" of Sheikh al-Bouti poses questions', BBC News, 9 April 2013.

Mullen, Jethro, 'ISIS reported to have blown up ancient temple in Palmyra', CNN, 25 August 2015.

al-Nahhas, Labib, 'The deadly consequences of mislabeling Syria's revolutionaries', *Washington Post*, 10 July 2015.

———, 'I'm a Syrian and I fight ISIL every day: it will take more than bombs from the West to defeat this menace', *Daily Telegraph*, 21 July 2015.

Nakhoul, Samia and Khaled Yacoub Oweis, 'Syrian opposition urges review of al-Nusra blacklisting', Reuters, 12 December 2012.

Nassief, Isabel and Charlie Caris, 'Rebels reopen the Latakia front', Institute for the Study of War, 9 April 2014.

'Nearly 1,400 dead since Syria rebel–jihadist clashes began', AFP, 23 January 2014.

Neumann, Peter, 'Suspects into collaborators', *London Review of Books*, 28 March 2014.

'New evidence proves Russian military directly engaging in Syrian Civil War', Oryx Blog, 29 August 2015.

Nichols, Michelle, 'UN rights inquiry says more Syrians joining Islamic State', Reuters, 25 July 2014.

'No proof links Iraq, al-Qaida, Powell says', NBC News, 8 January 2004.

Nuland, Victoria, 'Terrorist designations of the al-Nusrah Front as an alias for al-Qa'ida in Iraq', United States Department of State, 11 December 2012.

'Nusra emir to Idlib Druze: give me 1,000 rifles', Syria Direct, 11 June 2015.

'al-Nusra Front denies plans to break away from al-Qaeda', *Middle East Eye*, 9 March 2015.

'Nusra Front executes Syrian woman accused of adultery', *al-Akhbar*, 14 January 2015.

'al-Nusra kills 30 fighters in Hazm and gains control in the western countryside of Aleppo', Syrian Observatory for Human Rights, 28 February 2015.

'Nusra rejects Islamist militia's code of honor', *Daily Star*, 21 May 2014.

O'Bagy, Elizabeth, 'The fall of al-Qusayr', Institute for the Study of War, 6 June 2013.

———, 'The Free Syrian Army', Institute for the Study of War, March 2013.

———, 'Jihad in Syria', Institute for the Study of War, Middle East Security Report 6, September 2012.

———, 'Syria update: Assad targets Sunni along Syria's coast', Institute for the Study of War, 10 May 2013.

'Obama's speech to Americans on defeating Islamic State', Reuters, 11 September 2014.

'Oryx', 'Iranian fighter-bombers operating in Syria', Bellingcat, 16 March 2015.

'Oryx', 'The Islamic State's spring offensive: al-Sukhna', Oryx Blog, 23 May 2015.

Owais, Khaled Yacoub, 'Muslim Brotherhood endorses Syria protests', Reuters, 29 April 2011.

Pace, Julia, 'Obama: 275 US forces deploying to Iraq', Associated Press, 16 June 2014.

Pamuk, Humeyra and Umit Bektas, 'Turkey sees signs of "ethnic cleansing" by Kurdish fighters in Syria', Reuters, 16 June 2015.

Paraszczuk, Joanna, 'Did IS refuse truce with Syrian Islamist factions?' Radio Free Europe Radio Liberty, 13 November 2014.

O'Bagy, Elizabeth, 'Syria: how "al Qa'eda mediator" al-Suri died—a jihadist's account', EA Worldview, 26 February 2014.

Paton Walsh, Nick, 'The secret jihadi smuggling route through Turkey', CNN, 5 November 2013.

Perry, Tom, 'Extremists destroy 13th century Muslim tomb in Syria', Reuters, 8 January 2015.

———, 'Syrian Kurds push deeper into Islamic State stronghold', Reuters, 13 June 2015.

———, 'Syrian Kurds thwart big Islamic State attack on border town', Reuters, 1 July 2015.

———, 'Syrian rebel leader vows guerrilla war in south against Hezbollah, govt', Reuters, 12 February 2015.

———, 'US-led air strikes pose problem for Assad's moderate foes', Reuters, 30 September 2014.

Perry, Tom and Laila Bassam, 'Syria Kurds seize town from Islamic State near its "capital"', Reuters, 23 June 2015.

Petrocine, Nate, 'Rebel operations in Idlib province during the spring of 2014', Institute for the Study of War, 31 July 2014.

Pierret, Thomas, 'Implementing "Sharia" in Syria's liberated provinces', Foundation for Law, Justice, and Society, 7 August 2013.

———, *Religion and State in Syria: The Sunni Ulama under the Ba'th*. New York: Cambridge University Press, 2013.

'President al-Assad: Syria is ready to provide cooperation to make de Mistura's mission a success', Syrian Arab News Agency, 12 September 2014.

Prothero, Mitchell, 'CIA tips off Hezbollah about bombing plot', McClatchy DC, 17 July 2014.

———, 'Islamic State releases video of Baghdadi in Mosul in new assertion of authority', McClatchy DC, 6 July 2014.

———, 'New Islamic State audio ends talk that leader Baghdadi is incapacitated', McClatchy DC, 14 May 2015.

———, 'Sources: US air strikes in Syria targeted French agent who defected to al-Qaeda', McClatchy DC, 5 October 2014.

'Al Qaeda blames Hezbollah for Lebanon bombings', Reuters, 24 August 2013.

'Al-Qaeda in Iraq claims deadly attack on Syrian troops', BBC News, 11 March 2013.

'Radical Syrian cleric "shot dead"', BBC News, 29 September 2007.

'Radical cleric urges Islamists to end Syria infighting', AFP, 16 January 2014.

Rafizadeh, Majid, 'In Syria, follow the money to find the roots of the revolt', *The Daily Beast*, 8 April 2013.

Rainey, Venetia, 'Who is Imad Ahmad Jomaa?' *Daily Star*, 4 August 2014.

Raphaeli, Nimrod, 'The Sheikh of the Slaughterers: Abu Mus'ab al-Zarqawi and the al-Qaeda connection', Middle East Media Research Institute, 1 July 2005.

al-Rashed, Abdulrahman, 'The killing of Abu al Qaqaa', *Asharq al-Awsat*, 3 October 2007.

Razafimbahiny, Irina, 'An in-depth look at Chechen fighters in Syria—Part I: Sayfullah al-Shishani and his circle', MEMRI, 6 December 2013.

'Rebels move against Hezbollah in Qalamoun', NOW Lebanon, 4 May 2015.

'Rebels put up fierce resistance in Daraa town', NOW Lebanon, 21 April 2015.

'Rebels start Homs offensive', NOW Lebanon, 6 May 2015.

'Report: UN envoy to meet Syrian rebels in Turkey', Today's Zaman, 8 December 2014.

Reuter, Christoph, 'Syria's mercenaries: the Afghans fighting Assad's war', Spiegel Online, 11 May 2015.

———, 'The terror strategist: secret files reveal the structure of Islamic State', *Der Spiegel*, 18 April 2015.

'Revolutionary Command Council criticizes de Mistura', *The Syrian Observer*, 19 February 2015.

Riedel, Bruce, *The Search for al Qaeda: Its Leadership, Ideology, and Future* (Washington, DC: Brookings Institution Press, 2010).

Roggio, Bill, 'Abdullah Azzam Brigades names leader, advises against attacks in Syria's cities', Long War Journal, 27 June 2012.

———, 'ISIS confirms death of senior leader in Syria', Long War Journal, 5 February 2014.

———, 'al Nusrah Front praises Chechen commander killed in Aleppo', Long War Journal, 10 February 2014.

———, 'al Qaeda in Iraq operative killed near Syrian border sheds light on foreign influence', Long War Journal, 3 October 2007.

———, 'al-Qaeda's grand coalition in Anbar', Long War Journal, 12 October 2006.

———, 'The rump Islamic emirate of Iraq', Long War Journal, 16 October 2006.

Rogin, Josh, 'US ignored warnings before ISIS takeover of a key city', The Daily Beast, 10 July 2014.

Rogin, Josh and Eli Lake, 'Foley abduction linked to British jihadi kidnapping ring', The Daily Beast, 20 August 2014.

Rotella, Sebastian, 'Italian police link Syria to al Qaeda extremists/Nation served as way station for terror recruits, probe finds', Los Angeles Times, 16 April 2003.

Roth, Andrew, 'Police commander from Tajikistan appears in ISIS video', New York Times, 29 May 2015.

Rubin, Alissa J. and Rod Nordland, 'Seeing their gains at risk, Shiites flock to join militias', New York Times, 13 June 2014.

Ryan, Missy, 'Islamic State threat "beyond anything we've seen"—Pentagon', Reuters, 22 August 2014.

———, 'US drone strike kills a senior Islamic State militant in Syria', Washington Post, 2 July 2015.

'Sajida Rishawi resurfaces as bargaining chip 10 years after Amman bombings', Jordan Times, 28 January 2015.

Samaha, Nour, 'Trapped between Assad, Israel and al-Qaeda', Foreign Policy, 22 June 2015.

Sanchez, Ray, 'Who was Sajida al-Rishawi? And why did ISIS care about her?' CNN, 4 February 2015.

Sands, Phil and Suha Maayeh, 'Syrian rebel colonel "confesses" to foreign hand in rout', The National, 8 May 2014.

Sands, Phil, Justin Vela and Suha Maayeh, 'Blood ties: the shadowy member of the Assad clan who ignited the Syrian conflict', The National, 20 March 2014.

'Saudi Grand Mufti praises Qaradawi's stance on Hezbollah', al-Arabiya, 6 June 2013.

'Saudi IS cleric killed in northern Syria', Associated Press, 3 January 2015.

Sayigh, Yezid, 'The war over Syria's gas fields', Syria in Crisis (Carnegie), 8 June 2015.

Schmidt, Michael S. and Mark Mazzetti, 'Suicide bomber from US came home before attack', New York Times, 30 July 2014.

'Scores dead in intensified fighting in southern Syria: monitor', Reuters, 15 February 2015.

Seale, Patrick, *Asad: The Struggle for the Middle East*. Berkeley: University of California Press, 1990.

'Senior member of the SMC defects to ISIS and details foreign involvement in the opposition', Brown Moses Blog, 2 December 2013.

Shaheen, Kareem, 'ISIS launches assault on pro-Assad forces in western Syria', *The Guardian*, 25 March 2015.

———, 'ISIS video confirms destruction at UNESCO world heritage site in Hatra', *The Guardian*, 5 April 2015.

Shaheen, Kareem and Ian Black, 'Beheaded Syrian scholar refused to lead ISIS to hidden Palmyra antiquities', *The Guardian*, 19 August 2015.

Shaheed, Kareem and Constanze Letsch, 'Turkey to let anti-ISIS coalition use airbase after soldier's death', *The Guardian*, 23 July 2015.

Shanker, Thom, 'Qaeda leaders in Iraq neutralized, US says', *New York Times*, 4 June 2010.

Sharaan, Mahmoud, 'Jordan confronts ISIS domestically and abroad', *al-Akhbar*, 25 September 2014.

'Sheikh Abu Mariya al-Qahtani speaking on the subject of breaking the ties between Jabhat al-Nusra and al-Qaeda', published on JustPaste.it on 21 April 2015.

Sherlock, Ruth, 'Inside Jabhat al-Nusra—the most extreme wing of Syria's struggle', *The Telegraph*, 2 December 2012.

———, 'Leading Libyan Islamist met Free Syrian Army opposition group', *The Telegraph*, 27 November 2011.

———, 'US secretly backs rebels to fight al-Qaeda in Syria', *The Telegraph*, 21 January 2014.

Shiloach, Gilad, 'Syrian army accused of hoarding UN food for starving civilians', Vocativ, 29 May 2015.

'Silsalah al-shahada: chain of testimonies. Shaykh Abu Firas al-Suri', al-Baseera Media Productions, 21 March 2014.

'Silsalah al-shahada: chain of testimonies. Sheykh Farouq Abu Hamam al-Suri', al-Baseera Media Productions, 27 March 2014.

Sim, Shuan, 'ISIS beheads Haruna Yukawa: why the Japanese hostages were in Syria', *International Business Times*, 24 January 2015.

'Sistani calls on Iraqi civilians to fight ISIS', AFP, 13 June 2014.

Slodkowski, Antoni, 'Japanese reporter's bid to save friend led to IS abduction', Reuters, 21 January 2015.

Slodkowski, Antoni, 'Radical scholar provided Japan with channel to IS at hostage crisis peak', Reuters, 9 February 2015.

Sly, Liz, 'US-backed Syria rebels routed by fighters linked to al-Qaeda', *Washington Post*, 2 November 2014.

Sly, Liz and Justin Vela, 'In Syria, group suspected of al-Qaeda links gaining prominence in war to topple Assad', *Washington Post*, 19 August 2012.

Smith, Lewis, 'British jihadists becoming disillusioned with fighting rival rebels and want to come home', *The Independent*, 5 September 2014.

Smyth, Phillip, 'Israel is the new front in the Syrian war', *Foreign Policy*, 28 January 2015.

Solomon, Erika, 'Betrayal and disarray behind Syrian rebel rout in Yabroud', *Financial Times*, 21 March 2014.

———, 'Syria's Islamists disenchanted with democracy after Mursi's fall', Reuters, 7 July 2013.

Smoltczyk, Alexander, 'Islam's spiritual "Dear Abby": the voice of Egypt's Muslim Brotherhood', *Der Spiegel*, 15 February 2011.

Spetalnick, Matt and Sylvia Westall, 'Islamic State beheads British hostage Henning in new video', Reuters, 4 October 2014.

Starr, Barbara, Jim Sciutto and Elise Labott, 'US investigating "credible" reports IS used chemical weapons', CNN, 14 August 2015.

'Statement by 99 Syrian Intellectuals', *al-Hayat*, 27 September 2000.

State Planning Commission, *Baseline Water Sector Report*, GTZ Modernization of the Syrian Water Sector, Support to Sector Planning and Coordination, 2009.

'Street battles rage as ISIL inches deeper into Damascus', Al-Jazeera, 1 September 2015.

'Suruç katliamında 'Adıyamanlı genç' iddiası', Radikal, 21 July 2015.

'Suruc massacre: "Turkish student" was suicide bomber', BBC News, 22 July 2015.

'Syria: Countrywide Conflict Report #4', Carter Center, 11 September 2014.

'Syria: prisoners of conscience in Damascus Central Prison declare hunger strike', In Defence of Marxism, 9 March 2011.

'Syria conflict: blast hits Aleppo intelligence HQ', BBC News, 4 March 2015.

'Syria death toll now exceeds 210,000, rights group says', Reuters, 7 February 2015.

'Syria gives passports to suicide bombers', *The Times*, 1 April 2003.

'Syria not a launching pad for attacks on West says al-Nusra chief in TV interview', *The Guardian*, 28 May 2015.

'Syrian air strikes kill over 200 civilians in 10 days: monitor', Reuters, 30 October 2014.

'Syrian army seizes famed Krak des Chevaliers fort in border push', Naharnet, 20 March 2014.

'Syrian forces hit Islamic State in Raqqa, destroy water plant', Reuters, 18 August 2014.

'Syrian government air strikes target Islamic State in Raqqa', Reuters, 17 August 2014.

'Syrian Islamists reject Western-backed opposition', Associated Press, 19 November 2012.

'Syrian Kurds warn of mounting crisis as ISIS advances, takes more villages', Fox News, 19 September 2014.

Syrian Observatory for Human Rights, '10 months after his disappearance, founder and leader of Jund al-Aqsa found killed in a well', 10 November 2014.

'Syrian al Qaeda offshoot vows retaliation against US-led air strikes', Reuters, 27 September 2014.

'Syrian rebels get arms from abroad—source', Reuters, 24 February 2012.

'Syrian rebels roll exploding tires into Maaloula army outposts', AFP, 2 December 2013.

'Syrian rebels say they hold seven Iranians hostage', Reuters, 27 January 2012.

'Syrian refugee crisis map', *Washington Post*, 16 December 2014.

'Syrians march in support of Jabhat al-Nusra militants', France 24, 16 December 2012.

'Syria's Assad fires two spy chiefs: security source', AFP, 20 March 2015.

'Syria's Assad says losing battles does not mean war is lost', AFP, 7 May 2015.

'Syria's Hazzm rebel group dissolves itself after losses, joins Shamiyah Front', *Ya Libnan*, 1 March 2015.

'Syria's Palmyra Temple of Bel "severely damaged" by IS', BBC News, 31 August 2015.

'Syria unrest: troops kill 10 protesters in Deraa', BBC News, 24 March 2011.

'Syria warns against foreign intervention after Obama's speech', Reuters, 11 September 2014.

'Syria willing to cooperate with US, UK to see air strikes against Islamic State terrorists, foreign minister says', AFP, 25 August 2014.

Szep, Jason, 'US wins Arab support for Syria/Iraq military campaign', Reuters, 11 September 2014.

Szybala, Valerie, 'al-Qaeda shows its true colors in Syria', Institute for the Study of War, 1 August 2013.

Tabler, Andrew, 'Squaring the circle?' *Syria Today*, June 2006.

al-Tamimi, Aymenn Jawad, 'The Islamic State of Iraq and ash-Sham's dhimmi pact for the Christians of Raqqa province', Syria Comment, 26 February 2014.

———, 'The Islamic State's educational regulations in Raqqa province', Aymenn Jawad al-Tamimi's Blog, 28 August 2014.

———, 'Islamic State justification for burning alive the Jordanian pilot: translation and analysis', 4 February 2015.

———, 'Jabhat al-Nusra and the Islamic State of Iraq and ash-Sham: Deir ez Zour and the wider east of Syria', Musings of an Iraqi Brasenostril on Jihad, Jihadology, 27 June 2013.

———, 'Moroccan Guantanamo detainees fighting in Syria's civil war', Jihadology, 18 September 2013.

———, 'Muhajireen battalions in Syria', Jihadology, 13 December 2013.

———, 'The new Druze militia factions of Suwayda province', Syria Comment, 8 August 2015.

———, 'Sheikh Aymenn al-Zawahiri annuls Islamic State of Iraq and ash-Sham', Aymenn Jawad al-Tamimi Blog, 9 June 2013.

———, 'Syria: jihad and the battle for Qusayr', Aymenn Jawad al-Tamimi's Blog, 27 May 2013.

———, 'The White Shroud: a Syrian resistance movement to the Islamic State', Syria Comment, 22 October 2014.

al-Tamimi, Aymenn Jawad and Cedric Labrousse, 'The fighting in Abu Kamal (Albukamal): background and analysis', *Brown Moses* (Blog), 12 April 2014.

Tastekin, Fehim, 'Fall of Kassab will be costly for Turkey', *al-Monitor*, 31 March 2014.

'The Times: Assad backed by 1,500 Hezbollah fighters', *Naharnet*, 7 October 2012.

'Three Lebanese soldiers killed by gunmen—military source', Reuters, 28 May 2013.

'Top cleric Qaradawi calls for jihad against Hezbollah, Assad in Syria', al-Arabiya, 2 June 2013.

'Top Damascus rebel in Turkey amid regional moves', NOW Lebanon, 20 April 2015.

'Top Muslim cleric al-Qaradawi urges Sunnis to join Syria war', AFP, 1 June 2013.

'Tracking al Qaeda in Iraq's Zarqawi: interview with ex-CIA analyst Nada Bakos', Musings on Iraq, 30 June 2014.

'Translation: the formation of the Syrian Revolutionary Command Council', Goha's Nail Blog, 3 August 2014.

'Translation of the new audio message by Abu Bakr al-Baghdadi', pietervanostaeyen Blog, 19 January 2014.

'Turkey charges prime suspect in car bombings, report says', al-Arabiya, 21 May 2013.

'Turkey shoots down Syrian fighter jet', Al-Jazeera, 24 March 2014.

Turki al-Binali, *Khatt al-midad fil radd ala al-duktor Iyad*, December 2013.

'UK suicide bomber in Syria named as Abdul Waheed Majid', BBC News, 12 February 2014.

'UN aid chief slams "horrifying" disregard of civilian life in Syria', Al-Jazeera America, 17 August 2015.

United Nations Human Rights Council (UNHCR), *Report of the Special Rapporteur on the Right to Food on his Mission to Syria, Addendum*, 27 January 2011.

United Nations Office for the Coordination of Humanitarian Affairs, *Syria Drought Response Plan 2009*, 2009.

US Department of Defense, 'Operation Inherent Resolve: targeted operations against ISIL terrorists'.

US Department of State, 'Rewards for justice—al-Qaeda reward offers', 18 October 2012.

———, 'Terrorist designation of Abu Mohammed al-Adnani', 18 August 2014.

———, 'Terrorist designation of Fatah al-Islam associate Usamah Amin al-Shihabi', 18 December 2013.

US Department of State, 'Terrorist designation of Said Arif', 18 August 2014.

US Department of the Treasury, 'Treasury designates additional supporters of the al-Nusrah Front and al-Qaida', 22 August 2014.

———, 'Treasury designates Hizballah leadership', 13 September 2012.

US Department of State, 'Treasury designates members of Abu Ghadiyah's network facilitates flow of terrorists, weapons, and money from Syria to al Qaida in Iraq', 28 February 2008.

US Department of the Teasury, 'Treasury designates twelve foreign terrorist fighter facilitators', 24 September 2014.

'US must talk to Syria on Mideast peace—Syrian minister', Kuwait News Agency (KUNA), 4 September 2006.

'US sends six jets, 300 personnel to Turkey base in Islamic State fight', Reuters, 9 August 2015.

'US warplanes launch first air strikes against ISIS targets in Syria', AFP, 12 August 2015.

van Ostaeyen, Pieter, 'The ar-Raqqa executions—confirmation of the Islamic State in Iraq and as-Sham', pietervanostaeyen Blog, 15 May 2013.

van Ostaeyen, 'Syria—a new Islamic Union or an informal alliance?', pietervanostaeyen Blog, 28 September 2013.

'Video shows non-FSA jihadists Ahrar al-Sham using Croatian weapons', Brown Moses Blog, 1 March 2013.

Wagemakers, Joas, 'Abu Muhammad al-Maqdisi: a counter-terrorism asset?' Combating Terrorism Center, 15 May 2008.

———, 'IS' beheadings of Western hostages: jihadi ideologues speak out', Jihadica, 22 September 2014.

———, 'Maqdisi in the middle: an inside account of the secret negotiations to free a Jordanian pilot', Jihadica, 11 February 2015.

'Wanted Saudi al Qaeda militant killed in Syria—SITE', Reuters, 24 January 2014.

Ward, Clarissa, 'Fighting ISIS: US counting on moderate rebel force', CBS News, 30 September 2014.

Warner, Meg, 'UK prime minister vows to fight ISIS as terrorists threaten to execute Briton: "We won't be cowed by these barbaric killers"', New York Daily News, 3 September 2014.

Weiss, Michael, 'Col. Oqaidi on al-Qaeda, UN inspectors and Kurdish militias', NOW Lebanon, 18 August 2013.

———, 'Did the US just kill 5 kids in Syria?' Daily Beast, 12August 2015.

———, 'Russia puts boots on the ground in Syria', Daily Beast, 1 September 2015.

'Were foreigners involved in the Nord-Ost hostage crisis?' NorthCaucasusCaucus Blog, 30 August 2015.

Westall, Sylvia, 'Kurds secure Syria's Kobani as Islamic State targets northeast', Reuters, 28 June 2015.

Westall, Sylvia and William Mallard, 'Islamic State says beheads Japanese hostage Goto', Reuters, 1 February 2015.

Whitehead, Tom, 'Iraq crisis: British student identified as recruiting ISIS jihadists', The Telegraph, 20 June 2014.

Wilkofsky, Dan, Mohammed al-Haj Ali and Muatasem Jamal, 'Jabhat al-Nusra declares war on Harakat Hazm', Syria Direct, 26 February 2015.

Williams, Timothy and Duraid Adnan, 'Sunnis in Iraq allied with US rejoin rebels', New York Times, 16 October 2010.

Wing, Joel, 'Islamic State of Iraq launches battle of Ninewa in Mosul', Musings on Iraq, 10 June 2014.

———, 'Islamic State of Iraq and the Levant storm Samarra in Salahuddin', Musings on Iraq, 6 June 2014.

Woods, Allan, 'How Martin Couture-Rouleau became an aspiring Islamic State fighter', The Star, 26 October 2014.

Woods, Chris, 'Pentagon in denial about civilian casualties of US airstrikes in Iraq and Syria', Foreign Policy, 3 December 2014.

'Yazidis in Iraq: a tough time', The Economist, 13 November 2013.

'Yemen's AQAP calls on Islamists to target America after Iraq air strikes', Reuters, 15 August 2014.

Youngman, Mark, 'The North Caucasus insurgency's Syrian balancing act', Jihadology, 7 September 2013.

al-Zawahiri, Ayman, Ritha shahid al-ummah wal amir al-istishhadiyain Abu Musab al-Zarqawi, al-Sahab Media, June 2006.

Zelin, Aaron, 'European foreign fighters in Syria', International Centre for the Study of Radicalisation and Political Violence, 8 April 2013.

———, 'Inside baseball on Syrian rebel infighting', War on the Rocks, 7 February 2014.

———, 'Jihadists in Syria can be found on the Internet', al-Monitor, 18 October 2012.

———, 'al-Qaeda in Syria: a closer look at ISIS (Part I)', Washington Institute for Near East Policy, 10 September 2013.

———, 'The Syrian Islamic Front: a new extremist force', Washington Institute for Near East Policy, 4 February 2013.

———, 'The Syrian Islamic Front's order of battle', Al-Wasat, 22 January 2013.

———, 'Syria's new jihadis: meet the terrorist group that's ruining the revolution', Foreign Policy, 22 May 2012.

———, 'Up to 11,000 foreign fighters in Syria; steep rise among Western Europeans', International Centre for the Study of Radicalisation and Political Violence, 17 December 2013.

'Zwanzig Demonstranten bei syrischer Stadt Daraa getötet', Neue Zürcher Zeitung, 25 March 2011.

# INDEX

INDEX